Society

ALSO BY ELY CHINOY

Automobile Workers and the American Dream
Sociological Perspective
A RANDOM HOUSE STUDY IN SOCIOLOGY

Society

AN INTRODUCTION TO SOCIOLOGY

SECOND EDITION

Ely Chinoy

SMITH COLLEGE

Foreword by Charles H. Page

RANDOM HOUSE
New York

ACKNOWLEDGMENTS

To The American Historical
Association and to Professor Eric Lampard
for permission to reprint from Eric
Lampard, INDUSTRIAL REVOLUTION (1957);
and to Appleton-Century-Crofts, Division of
Meredith Publishing Company, for
permission to reprint from Ralph Linton,
THE STUDY OF MAN (Copyright 1936
D. Appleton-Century Co. Inc.).

PHOTO CREDITS:
Marilyn Silverstone from Magnum,
The Bettmann Archive, Sybil Shelton from Monkmeyer,
NORAD Photo, Charles Harbutt from Magnum

To Helen, Michael, and Claire

Foreword

There is no more exacting undertaking for sociologists than producing a general textbook of high standard. The paucity of such volumes suggests the difficulty of the task; and the continuing viability of a tiny number of excellent general works, which man the shelves side by side with numerous more youthful (and often more popular) but less sturdy volumes, suggests the infrequency of its accomplishment. What then are the principal merits of a good introductory study in this many-sided field?

To attempt to answer this question is as dangerous perhaps as to specify the virtues of a good spouse. In both cases durability may be desirable, but it alone makes neither a fine mate nor a first-rate book. And in each case, not only are individual needs and tastes an important matter, but also, speaking sociologically, group-anchored patterns of preference abound. Yet, as to the *textbook*, I shall risk some generalizations.

A good general textbook, first, requires an informed and judicious *selection* from sociology's mounting and frequently disparate materials. Clearly, an author cannot "cover the field": He must choose, from a wide assortment, a particular battery of conceptual working tools, certain specific theories, and a limited amount of substantive information. At its worst, this selection is based on an evaluation of what is currently most marketable—the textbook joins the grand parade of "pop-ular culture." At its best, the choice of concepts, theories, and findings reflects a wide knowledge of sociology's persistent problems, accomplishments, and limitations; dedication to its potentialities; and consistent use of a single theoretical orientation together with an appreciation of alternative approaches. In a good textbook things hang together, but the synthesis, like society itself, is partial. Effective selection thus demands informed, meticulous, and mature stock taking.

Second, a good general textbook promotes the *dual educational function* of sociology. It must be of course an effective introduction to the discipline itself—bringing out clearly the distinctive nature and principal features of sociological analysis and demonstrating how this mode of analysis helps substantially to reveal the major contours of social structure and social change. If the book performs this function ably it will be as well a stimulating and informative instrument of general education. For all readers—including the large majority of students who do not continue in the field—the textbook, to be sure, should enhance objective understanding of a changing social world, but it should also help the individual to relate *himself* to that world, to evaluate it, to make choices. Like the superior teacher, an outstanding textbook can be a guide to both knowledge and wisdom.

These high goals cannot be gained in

any large measure if the guidance is obscured by murky or prolix writing. Therefore a third requirement for a good textbook is *lucidity*. I do not refer to a breezy "style" or to routine interpolation of gay anecdote, nor am I suggesting that textbook authors should seek to rival the master essayists—sociologists have other fish to fry. But painstaking formulation and clarity of exposition, as I have argued elsewhere, are an important part of scholarly craftsmanship. In the case of the introductory textbook, these qualities should merge with precise and consistent employment of technical terminology, on the one hand, and, on the other, sensitivity to conventional use of language. Sociological writing is prose of one sort or another—it should not be a barrier to communication.

Finally, a good textbook should be written for a literate and presumably educated readership: It should show *respect* for both student and teacher. Every point need not be hammered home relentlessly, nor need every passing reference be explicated for the benefit of the uninformed. If a textbook is to avoid being a dull tome, if it is to spur curiosity, it must not attempt encyclopedic dimensions, and it must leave some room "between the lines." A general work should not become for the student a symbol of something he "has had"; it should be both an introduction to and an invitation to revisit an exciting intellectual enterprise.

These proposed requirements of the meritorious introductory textbook are large demands. They suggest that the author of such a work must be, at once, a devoted and critical student of his field, a wise and experienced scholar-teacher, and a concerned member of the human community. That they are realistic goals, however, is amply reaffirmed by Ely Chinoy's *Society*.

Princeton, New Jersey, 1960

This revision of Ely Chinoy's *Society* retains what I believe to be important characteristics of an outstanding general introduction to sociology, as they are sketched above. This is not always the case wth revisions, for sometimes they are marred by conspicuous signs of patchwork in a hasty effort to "keep up with the field"—and with the market. Certainly Professor Chinoy has brought *Society* abreast of the current sociological enterprise (insofar as possible during these boom years of the discipline), exploiting effectively numerous recent studies in such specialized sociological fields as science, education, military organization, and "modernization." But he has done much more: Both the format and the substance of the introductory chapters have been substantially revised with a view to the needs of student readers; these chapters and others are marked by even greater conceptual consistency than in the original edition; theoretical and interpretive modifications and innovations have been made in the light of the changing scene in sociology and in the larger social order. With this new *Society*, Ely Chinoy again has demonstrated by deed that a "text" can be a fine *book*.

CHARLES H. PAGE
Santa Cruz, California, 1966

Preface

This book seeks to communicate to the reader the high intellectual adventure to be found in exploring the contours of society. It is an exploration that leads into both the esoteric and the mundane, that moves from difficult heights of abstraction to concrete levels of description. It requires of the adventurer the ability or willingness to look for the subtle and profound in the commonplace. It leads into the most sensitive areas of human life—faith, religion, family life, politics. It demands the antiseptic quality of the surgeon and the sensitivity that enables one to enter into the full range of feeling and sentiment inherent in social life.

The specific objectives of this book are, first, to present the principal concepts that define the sociological perspective; second, to explain and illustrate the nature of sociological analysis; third, to provide a comprehensive picture of society by examining the major institutions and forms of social organization contained within it; and fourth, to suggest the dimensions of important theoretical problems of persisting relevance—for example, the relations between individual and society, the social conditions that encourage conformity or stimulate deviant behavior, and the causes and consequences of such master trends as bureaucratization, the growth of cities, and the progress of science.

In pursuing these objectives, even on an elementary level, one must necessarily cope with fundamental questions of sociology. Answers to many of these questions now command substantial agreement, although there remain—as there always must—important theoretical differences. An introduction to sociology, therefore, is necessarily a form of stock taking, an effort to state briefly much of the central body of sociological thought. Such a statement inevitably reflects in some measure the particular views of the author, but it is hoped that this book will provide an analysis of the principles of sociology from which the reader can derive an objective and systematic understanding of both the discipline and the realities of social life that it seeks to comprehend.

No sooner does an author see his work in print than he is likely to recognize its deficiencies. For the author of a text, this perception is facilitated by the criticisms and suggestions that are freely and unstintingly offered by colleagues and students. A second edition provides the opportunity to take the work once more in hand and to seek to remedy its inadequacies, as well as to bring it up-to-date.

The chief additions here are a fuller treatment of socialization, explicit consideration of the problems of social change, and a discussion of educational institutions. The treatment of various other topics—bureaucracy, economic institutions, the Negro in America, for example—has been expanded to include both recent data and problems not touched upon in the first edition. References have been up-dated, material that has been superseded by better or more recent research findings has been replaced, the suggested readings have been revised and enlarged to include significant work published since this book first appeared, and an effort has been made to clarify those points that readers found puzzling or ambiguous.

Anyone who tries to present the basic ideas of a discipline and to illustrate and document them with the fruits of research is inevitably indebted to all those scholars upon whose contributions he has drawn. This indebtedness is acknowledged in the text in the usual fashion. In addition, there are several people to whom I have special obligations.

The general perspectives that inform the book have been markedly influenced by several of my teachers, to whom acknowledgment is gratefully made: to the late Jay Rumney, who introduced me to the study of sociology as a rational, humane discipline; to Robert S. Lynd, for his insistence upon the moral commitment of the social scientist and upon the need to keep sight of the real men and women whose lives are only partially encompassed in the abstractions of sociology; and to Robert K. Merton, not only for his substantive contributions, but also

for communicating the nature and excitement of sociological analysis.

My greatest debt is to Charles H. Page, friend, colleague, and editor. I have drawn freely upon his wide learning, and his scholarly judgment and editorial aid have contributed materially to whatever virtues this book may possess.

I have learned much from my colleagues at Smith College, with whom I have participated in a cooperative effort to introduce students to sociology, and from the many students whose questions and interests have directed my attention toward important problems. For their critical comments on the first edition and their suggestions for revision I am indebted to Irving Louis Horowitz, Charles Hubbel, Douglas Rennie, Mildred Weil, and especially to Peter I. Rose. I am also grateful to those others—colleagues and students—who corrected my errors, offered specific suggestions, and encouraged me by their interest.

My wife, Helen Krich Chinoy, not only put up with the difficulties attendant upon the initial effort and the second endeavor while pursuing her own scholarly work, but also contributed significantly through her critical judgment and editorial skill.

ELY CHINOY
Northampton, Massachusetts, 1967

Contents

9   Racial and Ethnic Groups

10   Bureaucracy

11   Communities: Ecology and Urbanization

PART THREE: SOCIAL INSTITUTIONS

12   Technology and Economic Institutions

PART FIVE: SOCIAL ORDER, DEVIANCE, AND CHANGE

PART SIX: CONCLUSION

List of Tables

List of Figures

PART ONE

The sociological perspective

1
Science and Sociology

Sociology as science

Sociology seeks to apply to the study of man and society the methods of science. It rests upon the assumption common to all the social sciences that the scientific method can make a significant contribution to our understanding of man's character, actions, and institutions and to the solution of those practical problems that men face in their collective experience.

The explicitly scientific approach to the study of social life emerged in the nineteenth century. The word "sociology" itself was coined by a French philosopher, Auguste Comte, who offered an elaborate prospectus for the scientific study of society in a series of volumes published between 1830 and 1842. By the end of the nineteenth century a small array of still significant sociological classics had been produced. In the United States, where sociology sank its deepest roots, the American Sociological Society had been established, the *American Journal of Sociology* had begun publication, and sociology was being taught in several major universities.

Despite these beginnings, however, sociology is essentially a twentieth-century discipline. Many of its ideas and most of its reliable data have been accumulated only since 1900. Like other sciences its

progress has accelerated as the number of sociologists and the resources available for research have increased. Resistance to the scientific study of society has gradually waned (although it has not yet totally disappeared[1]), but many decades were required before sociology gained full acceptance as a legitimate academic field. Indeed, it was only in the 1950s and 1960s that some major universities and colleges (Johns Hopkins in the United States and Oxford and Cambridge in England, for example) finally incorporated sociology into their curricula. When the National Science Foundation was set up in the United States after World War II to support scientific inquiry, sociology was initially excluded but within a few years managed to establish its claim to funds for research. In recent years sociological concepts have gained wide currency among scholars in other fields—history, political science, economics, literary criticism—and among practitioners in law, medicine, education, social work, and business. Sociological findings and interpretations have elicited widespread interest from nonacademic audiences. And these trends have been evident not only in the United States and Europe, where sociology was born, but also in many other nations in Africa, Asia, and Latin America, whatever their political or religious character.[2]

Reflection about the nature of man and society, even the recording of careful observations, is of course neither new nor confined to social scientists. Plato's *Dialogues* contain keen and still accurate comments on men's motives and behavior, as do Machiavelli's *The Prince* and Montesquieu's *The Spirit of Laws*. Where can one find a more perceptive discussion of crime and the criminal than in Dostoyevsky's *Crime and Punishment* or a more suggestive exploration of men's concern with social position than in the novels of Jane Austen?

Sociologists should not ignore these sources of insight and understanding or disregard the plays of Shakespeare, the essays of Montaigne, the work of novelists, playwrights, literary critics, philosophers, and theologians. But social science cannot be satisfied with literary insight or philosophic reflection. The tested and verified conclusions toward which the social scientist strives differ markedly from the speculations of philosophers and theologians, the commentaries of reflective observers of the human scene, and the impressions of creative writers. These observations and interpretations are frequently acute and penetrating, but they are also sometimes wrong, or no more than partially true, and they are usually unsupported by systematic or reliable evidence. Samuel Johnson's comment that "Patriotism is the last refuge of a scoundrel" and his remark that "Almost all absurdity of conduct arises from the imitation of those we cannot resemble" are the shrewd judgments of a wise and witty man; yet not all patriots are scoundrels, nor does striving to be what one is not always lead to absurd conduct. At the risk of losing the bite and impact of such neat

aphorisms or the aesthetic appeal of great poetry or a wonderfully wrought novel or short story, the sociologist asks for the evidence, tries to identify the conditions under which specific assertions hold true, and recognizes that all conclusions about human behavior are necessarily tentative, including his own.

What are the prerequisites for the scientific study of man and society and what are its essential characteristics? The term *science* has been given many meanings. Historically it once signified any branch of knowledge or study. In the Middle Ages the "seven liberal sciences" were the *Trivium* (grammar, logic, and rhetoric) and the *Quadrivium* (arithmetic, music, geometry, and astronomy). In modern times science has come to be used chiefly in two distinct though related ways. It has been defined as any body of knowledge based upon reliable observations and organized into a system of general propositions or laws. It has also been taken to mean the methods by which systematic and accurate knowledge about the "real" world is acquired, as opposed to the intuition, speculation, and more or less casual, though often penetrating, observations of literature, philosophy, or theology. Intuition and speculation need not—should not—be excluded from scientific inquiry, but they must become part of a process in which insight and hunches are subject to careful, systematic testing and conclusions rest solely upon the authority of logic and fact.

The propositions that make up any body of scientific knowledge are generalizations; they refer not to individual events or entities, but to classes or types of phenomena. The concern of the botanist is not a particular tree or flower, that of the chemist not the specific reaction in a test tube. The physicist is not interested in a single atomic explosion, nor the sociologist in an isolated action or an individual family. Science is concerned with the repetitive pattern, the shared attribute or characteristic, those things that events or elements or trees or persons have in common. All science rests upon the assumption, so clearly explored and delineated by Alfred North Whitehead, that there is an "order of nature" which man can discover.[3] Indeed, were there no such assumption, were there no such order (although here we are making a philosophical assumption), there could be no science. The introduction of this assumption into the study of man and society was essential for the development of social science.

Science, both as knowledge and as method, incorporates two essential elements—the rational and empirical. As substantive knowledge, science is made up of logically related propositions that must also be supported by empirical evidence. As method, it emphasizes reliable and objective observation and logical analysis. Neither of these elements alone constitutes science. Were any internally consistent logical system to be considered a science, then John Calvin's *Institutes of the Christian Religion* and St. Thomas Aquinas' *Summa Theologica* might claim scientific standing. Alternatively, were any organized body of facts and observations to be described as science, then, as Ralph Ross has pointed out, cookbooks, Sears Roebuck catalogues, and telephone directories would also have to be included.[4]

Scientific generalizations must be subjected, directly or indirectly, to empirical tests. Much of the recorded "social thought" of the past contains theories that seek to incorporate the available knowledge concerning man and society into logical schemes. But no matter how logical or reasonable the generalizations

that these theories contain, they have no scientific standing unless they are confirmed by reliable evidence. Frequently they are supported only by isolated examples and casual observation.

Facts alone, however, cannot speak for themselves. Only when they are related to one another, or to general ideas, can they be incorporated into a body of scientific knowledge. The fact that an electric bulb gives off light gains scientific relevance only when linked with other facts concerning both electricity and the filament in the bulb. That the number and proportion of college students in the United States have increased markedly in recent years gains sociological meaning only when this growth is related to the state of the economy, the values of the society, and to other features of contemporary American life.

The objectivity of science

The chief characteristic of both scientific analysis and observation is objectivity. The validity of any conclusion and the reliability of any observation are—or should be—independent of the values and beliefs of the scientist. Two plus two equals four, whether calculated by a Communist, a Catholic, a Moslem, or an African witch doctor. Women in the United States, as in most countries, live longer than men, a conclusion that both men and women should reach on the basis of the available data. The scientist tries to follow his data and the logic of his analysis wherever they may lead. Ideally, he keeps his philosophical views, political allegiances, religious beliefs, social preferences, and personal feelings from in any way influencing his results. He must avoid those biases that, in the words of

Francis Bacon, a seventeenth-century advocate of an empirical approach to the study of nature, "so beset men's minds that truth can hardly find an entrance." (Bacon identified four kinds of biases, or *Idols,* as he called them: Idols of the Tribe, the limitations stemming from man's natural defects of understanding; of the Cave, the false notions an individual acquires from "education, habit and accident"; of the Marketplace, the confusions introduced by the nature of language; and of the Theater, ideas derived from philosophical systems and reasoning.[5])

Objectivity is likely to be far more difficult to achieve in all the social sciences than in the natural sciences, for men inevitably bring to their study of themselves and their society a body of ideas that may affect their observations and bias their conclusions. As psychologists have clearly demonstrated, men often see what they are prepared—or what they wish—to see. The facts to which they pay attention, or, more precisely, the phenomena in the world around them that they report as facts, are largely determined by the things they have learned, the beliefs to which they subscribe, the values they hold. Because men acquire, necessarily, a great number of ideas and opinions as they grow into adult members of a society, sociologists bring to their inquiries a set of preconceptions that they must eliminate or control in order to prevent biased observations or distorted interpretations of their findings.

No one can function as a member of society without some knowledge of how men behave, of the motives that drive them, of the prevailing customs and conventions. Indeed, such knowledge provides the substantial measure of predictability that enables men to live together without endless strife and difficulty. Consider merely how uncertain and confusing one's daily life would be if it were impossible to predict how students and teachers, bus drivers and store clerks, bank tellers and policemen, fathers and fiancées were going to act.

Such "common sense" knowledge, however, can inhibit scientific inquiry, for it sometimes leads men to make questionable assumptions about human behavior, to interpret their findings in conformity with their opinions rather than with either facts or logic, or even to decry the very necessity for sociological study. The tendency to regard as natural what is widespread or conventional in one's own society, the view (called "ethnocentrism" by sociologists and anthropologists) that one's own group is the measure of man everywhere, constitutes a major obstacle to scientific objectivity. When peoples of the West were engaged in the relatively free and unfettered economic competition of nineteenth-century capitalism, it seemed only natural to economists that "the propensity to truck, barter and exchange" was an inherent element in human nature. Comparative evidence from many societies, however, runs counter to this assumption; the form and extent of economic exchange and the values placed upon it vary widely in different parts of the world. The alternative to projecting one's own standards, beliefs, and values upon others may, however, be the equally unwarranted conclusion that strange or foreign customs can only be unhuman and those who practice these customs are therefore actually less than human.

Because sociology frequently deals with the things with which men are familiar, and about which they do possess some "common sense" knowledge, it has sometimes been labeled a science of the obvious, whose major activity consists in carefully documenting in elaborate detail, with tables of painstakingly gained statistics, what men already know. Clearly this criticism has no merit when one studies the unfamiliar, whether foreign or domestic. But it is a criticism most pointedly and frequently made when sociologists study things close to home—family life, reading habits, community organization, political practices.

The pursuit of reliable knowledge in a field where everyone is likely to feel that he already knows the answers inevitably exposes the sociologist to criticisms from many directions. As Robert K. Merton has pointed out:

Should . . . systematic inquiry only confirm what has been widely assumed . . . [the sociologist] will of course be charged with "laboring the obvious." He becomes tagged as a bore, telling only what everybody knows. Should investigation find that widely held social beliefs are untrue . . . he is a heretic, questioning value-laden verities. If he ventures to examine socially implausible ideas that turn out to be untrue, he is a fool, wasting effort on a line of inquiry not worth pursuing in the first place. And finally, if he should turn up some implausible truths, he must be prepared to find himself regarded as a charlatan, claiming as knowledge what is patently false. Instances of each of these alternatives have occurred in the history of many sciences, but they would seem especially apt to occur in a discipline, such as sociology, that deals with matters about which men have firm opinions presumably grounded in their own experience.[6]

Sociologists, it is true, are occasionally so immersed in their endeavors that perspective is lost and any collection of information that is systematically assembled and leads to a generalization seems portentous, even when it only indicates that what we have always believed is true. But since "common sense" knowledge is frequently flawed by inaccuracy and limited in its scope, particularly in a large and complex society, the sociologist's

error lies not in testing conventional opinion but in reporting as a significant finding, frequently in pedantic, abstract language, what men already "know" to be true.

The extent of error in the taken-for-granted knowledge of Americans was clearly indicated by research conducted during World War II by the Army's Research Branch.[7] Such widely accepted notions as the following turned out to be false: that educated men were more likely to suffer psychological breakdown in military service than those with less education; that southern soldiers were better equipped to survive the rigors of tropical climate than northerners; that Negroes were less ambitious for promotion than Whites; that men from rural backgrounds took army hardships better than city-reared soldiers. "That a belief is common . . . ," the American anthropologist Alfred L. Kroeber has observed, "is as likely to stamp it as a common superstition as a common truth."[8] Error, moreover, is frequently coupled with ignorance. How accurate a picture of the life of the poor and almost poor do those who live in comfortable middle-class suburbs possess? Do citizens on farms and in small towns, clerks in five-and-ten-cent stores, and workers in factories have a reliable view of the operations of centralized government? How much do college professors know about the world of business, or businessmen of the values and life of college professors? Yet each person believes that he knows, in some fashion and to some extent, how his society operates; indeed, as we have already pointed out, he must know something if he is to function effectively within it.

In seeking for the objectivity and reliability of science, one must not only exclude mere opinions as to facts and the relations that obtain among them, but one must also avoid the judgments and evaluations that may color men's thinking about themselves and their society. When Aristotle discussed the nature of civil society he not only offered explanations for what he saw, he also indicated, explicitly and implicitly, his own preferences. From the many social, or sociological, theories which have been developed in the course of human history, men have usually deduced or defended their own preferences in the organization of human society. As the eighteenth-century writer Bernard de Mandeville observed: "One of the greatest Reasons why so few People understand themselves, is that most Writers are always teaching Men what they should be, and hardly ever trouble their heads about what they really are." [9]

The distinction between careful description and analysis on the one hand and evaluation on the other, however, is not always clear, and the latter is frequently substituted for the former. It is perhaps easier to deprecate juvenile delinquency or a high divorce rate than to explain their existence; it is simpler to make political speeches lauding America as a land of opportunity than to try to assess how much opportunity exists, for whom it exists, and whether it is increasing or decreasing. The task of the sociologist, however, is not to judge, but to explain, not to argue for some given or desired state of affairs, but to examine the workings of society and the consequences which flow from alternative ways of doing things. "A moral judgment," Robert M. MacIver has said, "no matter how much we may agree with it, cannot be a substitute for the proper study of causes." [10]

It is no easy task for men to put aside their values and preconceptions, to see with the wise and innocent eyes of the boy who shouted: "But the Emperor has no clothes!" Men who expect women to be soft and emotional and find that most of the women they know do exhibit these qualities may not readily accept the possibility that these are not inherent feminine traits but may be the product of a particular kind of experience and education. Southerners who acquire, as they grow up, the belief in innate Negro inferiority find it difficult to accept the findings of modern research into racial differences. Those who believe that lack of ambition is a moral failing are reluctant to accept the view that it may result from lack of opportunity and encouragement.

Objectivity in sociology is difficult to achieve, but not impossible. The social changes that have made sociology both possible and desirable have also made it easier for men to become objective about the social life around them. Few nations now live in a state of stagnant isolation in which new ideas or challenges to accepted ways are rare or infrequent. Even totalitarian states find it difficult to choke off entirely the flow of communication from outside their boundaries. Men everywhere are now often, or even constantly, exposed to different values and customs that may lead them to look more dispassionately at their own. This is especially true if these new values command serious, even if critical, attention, though under some conditions the responses they engender inhibit rather than foster detachment and objectivity. When alien ways of life offer a strong challenge to established institutions and interests, men may refuse to examine their own practices and beliefs and will, instead, reject or deny the findings of those whose professional business it is to study the workings of society.

Scientific objectivity about man and society requires some understanding of one's own preferences and beliefs and can be substantially facilitated by the body of ideas—the concepts and theories—that one uses in making observations and in interpreting the data one collects. Objectivity, therefore, may be generated by sociological study itself. Familiarity with sociological data and systematic training in the nature and methods of sociological inquiry potentially make it possible both to control one's biases by becoming aware of them and to bypass one's preconceptions by approaching social phenomena from a different angle of vision. As we examine the structure and functioning of other societies we may achieve a clearer perspective about our own. As we analyze our society we may perhaps see ourselves more clearly in relation to the world in which we live.

Science and concepts: the problem of jargon

We have thus far not defined sociology, other than to identify it as a scientific study of man and society. But this statement tells us what sociology is about, not what it is or how it differs from anthropology, psychology, economics, political science, and history, all of which also study man and society. To offer a definition at this point in order to isolate the essential ingredients in sociology and to distinguish it from the other social sciences would be of little value. We might define sociology as the study of human groups, of social relationships, of social institutions, or, perhaps more elaborately, as "the science which attempts to develop an analytical theory of social action systems in so far as these systems can be understood in terms of the property of common-value integration." [11] But we should understand these definitions only after we had explored the meaning of the

key terms or concepts, that is, the meaning of "groups," "social relationships," "social institutions," and "social action systems" and "common-value integration." In so doing we should also necessarily introduce still other terms whose meaning we should then have to define.

The first step toward the understanding of sociology, as of any scientific discipline, is the mastery of its basic concepts. We referred earlier to "the things in the world around them that men report as facts." What men see, we noted, depends upon what they expect to see, what they look for. Their expectations are defined by the categories, or concepts, with which they think. Ideas, after all, are the tools with which we organize and interpret what we see and hear and do.

The concepts of sociology, then, provide the intellectual instruments with which the sociologist works. They define the phenomena to be studied, and they differentiate sociology from the other social sciences, each of which has its own body of concepts. They focus attention upon those selected aspects of reality with which we shall be concerned, and they provide the terms in which problems are posed and answered.

In Part One we shall examine the basic concepts of sociology and explore some of its fundamental problems. Those concepts we present here, however, do not exhaust the conceptual arsenal used by the sociologist. As we deal with the several areas and forms of social life—the family, religion, social stratification, power and authority, large-scale organization, and so on—it will be necessary to supplement the broad categories which provide the framework for sociological inquiry with more limited and more specific concepts.

In devoting a large part of this book to an exposition of concepts and the definition of key terms, we expose ourselves to a frequently made charge that we are merely creating and manipulating a distinctive jargon which adds little to human understanding. We may be taxed with using familiar terms in unfamiliar ways, with offering what seem to be esoteric labels for otherwise familiar phenomena; in sum, with creating an unusual and unnecessary terminology. In part, of course, this criticism is another reflection of the "common sense" approach to the understanding of man and society. Yet this is a criticism that must be examined before we proceed.

First, it is important to observe that this complaint is rarely leveled with the same critical animus against the "natural" sciences, whose learned journals are almost completely impenetrable to the nonprofessional. It is clearly not the existence of a distinctive vocabulary that provokes criticism, but the nature of the field and its relationship to human life.

Since sociology deals with many of the ordinary features of social life, to the layman there appears to be little need for distinctive terminology or for careful definition of terms he himself frequently uses. As we have noted, any member of a society knows something about its workings. Everyone can provide a plausible and reasonable explanation for many of the actions of people with whom he associates, or of whom he hears. Both behavior and the reasons for it can be described in everyday language, as can the organization of groups with which each man is familiar or in which he participates. When the student of human behavior applies special terms to commonplace actions and substitutes for common-sense explanations statements that include in many instances unfamiliar and high-sounding words, the sensibilities of the outsider are offended. When common-sense explanations are not available,

many persons are likely to deny the possibility of any explanation, scientific or otherwise. "Free will" or "the uniqueness of the individual" or some other phrase is called upon to justify this denial of the possibility of understanding and explanation.

Second, the fruits of scientific social research are not yet so rich or so widely known that its peculiar terminology will be accepted just as that of the natural sciences has been accepted. Of course, its practical application is not the sole test of the value of social science; its contribution to knowledge and understanding is in itself justification for its existence. Nevertheless, it is probably true that only when the social scientist can demonstrate that he can successfully contribute directly to the welfare of his society will the public accept without question or criticism his freedom to speak in his own private language to the professionals in his field.

To the extent that sociology creates a language for professional use, it will probably be necessary to develop simultaneously a corps of popularizers similar to those who present the findings of natural science to the public in terms that the intelligent layman can understand. Such a corps of popularizers appears to be already in the making. Although popular writers need possess no professional qualifications and therefore differ widely in their ability to present adequately the findings of serious scholars, they will inevitably have considerable influence—for good or for ill—upon the public image and repute of sociology. Some sociologists may, of course, perform a dual role—as researcher and as popularizer. But to insist that every sociologist must confine himself to language that can be understood by any intelligent person is probably to impose an insuperable handicap upon the development of social science.

Third, there is also a perhaps understandable suspicion of the man who tries to study others as objectively as the lepidopterist studies butterflies or the ichthyologist studies fish. Since knowledge can be power, men are sometimes distrustful of those who know too much and can talk about human beings and their behavior in a language that cannot readily be understood. Those who lack power are fearful of a potential new wielder of influence or control. Those who already occupy important positions or possess vested interests in society are likely to be hostile to men who may either directly or indirectly offer a challenge to their privileges and perquisites by analyzing the nature of their power. Since men are usually deeply committed to their own ways of life, looking upon them not only as natural and inevitable but also as morally right, they tend to offer staunch resistance to any questioning or analysis that seeks to explain their ways of life in scientific terms, for such an explanation seems to question both their inevitability and their moral propriety.

Yet the criticism of sociological jargon is sometimes warranted. There are undoubtedly a good many instances in which sociologists have been guilty of the overuse or unnecessary use of special terminology (a sin we shall try to avoid). We may attribute excessive jargon to the enthusiasm of fresh practitioners in the field or of those caught up in the excitement generated in what is, after all, a relatively new and rapidly growing field. In part, too, jargon is a result of efforts of a young discipline to mark out its area of study and to achieve academic respectability.

Despite its abuses, however, we cannot do away with distinctive, sharply defined terminology. The usual ambiguities of everyday language can be avoided only by insisting upon the precise use of words. When new ideas emerge it is frequently necessary to find new terms with which to identify them.

The nature of concepts

Before we can examine the basic sociological concepts it is necessary to define more clearly the nature of concepts and to explain and illustrate why they are so important. Put most simply, a concept is a general term that refers to all members of a particular class of objects, events, persons, relationships, processes, ideas. Everyone frequently uses concepts. Like the much-cited hero of Molière's *Le Bourgeois Gentilhomme* who found that he had been speaking prose only after he had been doing so for forty years, we have all used concepts ever since we learned to talk. Learning to use language and to think entails the growth of an ability to employ general rather than specific terms and ideas, to think of "toys" rather than of a particular toy, of "boys" rather than of the boy next door, of "water" rather than of a particular thirst-quenching drink. As the distinguished French sociologist Émile Durkheim pointed out: "The system of concepts with which we think in everyday life is that expressed by the vocabulary of our mother tongue; for every word translates a concept." [12]

If our ordinary conversation constantly utilizes concepts, what are the differences between them and the concepts of science? The latter are both more precisely defined and more abstract or general in their application. In daily conversation the meaning of the words we use is taken for granted; we assume that others know what we are saying. For most purposes this assumption is safe enough, even though many words have more than one meaning. The appropriate meaning is indicated in each case by the specific context, verbal or social, in which the term is used. If we talk about our "family," for example, we may be referring to our parents, brothers, and sisters (what the sociologists call the "nuclear family"), or to all our kinfolk; the meaning will normally be made clear by the conversation in which the word appears.

Many commonly used terms have no precise meaning, nor can they be understood from the contexts in which they do appear. If we try to set up precise and generally acceptable definitions of communism, subversion, liberalism, loyalty, or freedom, or of such nonpolitical terms as friendship, success, and ambition, we will quickly see that for these words there is no simple meaning upon which most people agree. As students of semantics have frequently pointed out, many words, particularly the "big ones," are often used more for their emotional value than for any concrete meaning they may have. Like the fisherman's "big ones," they often elude capture, and their meaning is as reliable as the fisherman's tale. But our language serves not only to communicate ideas, but also, by the overtones of many words, to indicate feelings and attitudes and even on occasion to suggest possible courses of action. (There are some semanticists who argue that the source of many of the social and political problems we face lies in the confusions created by a nonscientific language, or, in Bacon's terms, by the Idols of the Marketplace. It is unlikely, however, that eliminating semantic confusion would eliminate our problems, for there exist in society real conflicts of interest and concrete difficulties engendered by existing institutions.)

Since science requires rigorous logical analysis as well as careful objective observation, the meaning of the terms which it uses must be as clear and precise as possible, independent of different contexts and free from ambiguities and complex overtones. Unlike those disciplines which have escaped from the liabilities of the language of everyday discourse by utilizing a mathematical terminology or by coining new words whenever necessary, sociology has on the whole developed a vocabulary based upon terms current in popular usage. Such common words as *culture, group, role, status, power, authority, function, race,* and *bureaucracy* have become important sociological concepts. Their definition requires the analysis of the things to which they refer—in semantic terminology, their *referents.* (In philosophical terminology, the definitions of sociological concepts must be real and not nominal definitions, that is, they must identify the central elements in the phenomenon being analyzed rather than being merely an "agreement or resolution concerning the use of verbal symbols." [13])

The concepts of sociology, like those of any science, refer to types or classes of events, persons, and relationships—for example, to revolutions or doctors, to cooperation or conflict. Much, if not most, of our everyday conversation, on the other hand, deals with specific individuals, occasions, situations, and material things. We talk of our family, our jobs, our relationship with a member of the opposite sex. We spend little time considering in general terms the nature of the family, of jobs, or of dating. The task of sociology, as of all sciences, is to analyze classes of phenomena, not individual cases. The sociologist will be concerned with divorce in a particular family or with a revolution at a particular time and place in order to throw light on the nature of divorce or of revolutions as types of social phenomena. In the long run—and this is a major contribution of sociology—the deeper our understanding of divorce or revolution or other social phenomena in general, the greater is apt to be our understanding of specific instances.

Concepts are derived or created by *abstracting* selected aspects or features of phenomena from the total complexity of reality. Despite its formidable label—abstraction—this process is not a purely esoteric exercise, for it is frequently, if unwittingly, pursued by most of us. As Cohen and Nagel point out:

> All thinking proceeds by noting certain distinguishable features in things, symbolizing such selected features by appropriate counters, and then reasoning upon such abstracted features by means of the symbols. In dealing intellectually with some concrete, specific situation, we do not pay attention to all the infinitely complex relations which it has, or to all of its qualities. On the contrary, we neglect almost all of the qualities and relations which a thing has, and note only those features which enable us to view that thing as an instance or example of indefinitely repeatable patterns or types of situations. Thus our knowledge of things involves abstraction from the infinitely complex and perhaps unique properties which situations have.[14]

Although concepts are sometimes called "constructs," thus emphasizing the fact that they are creations of human thought and not necessarily inherent in the nature of social reality, it is important to be aware of the fact that they are not simply arbitrary products of inquiring and imaginative minds. They may refer to purely hypothetical processes or entities which cannot be directly observed or experienced, such as atoms in physics, the ego in psychology, or institutions in sociology. Yet even these highly abstract concepts emerge from some kind of obser-

vation of experience; they represent efforts to impose some kind of intellectual order upon the flux and diversity of life. Because concepts stem from the interplay of imagination and observation we shall try to suggest, as we introduce and make use of the categories of sociology, the nature of the observations from which they derive.

The uses of concepts

Concepts, then, lead us to look for patterns or regularities or uniformities in the world around us. We are seeking for that feature or aspect of a particular family which is similar to the features of other families, for the attributes shared by men as members of a group, or for the forms of organization which characterize collective activities. We are not concerned with the idiosyncratic, or the peculiar, which intrigues the creative writer or frequently the historian, but with those repetitive patterns which eventually can be distinguished as we observe the behavior of men and women in society.

To seek for patterns or regularities is not, as sometimes charged, to deny uniqueness or individuality. Any process of generalization ignores those characteristics that distinguish one individual from another, whether it be an individual person, volcano, or atomic explosion. In ignoring the unique qualities of any of these single entities, it may appear that science denies their existence. This is simply not true. Nor is there a necessary conflict between an interest in the unique and a concern with repetitive features of life or nature. They constitute alternative ways of paying attention to the world around us, each with its own distinctive values, and each contributing something to the other.

Sociology's interest in the "group" has sometimes been contrasted with psychology's emphasis upon the "individual," as if only the former dealt with recurrent aspects of human life. In this case the antithesis between the general and the particular does not apply; both disciplines are concerned with patterns or regularities —sociology with those to be found in the relations of individuals and groups to one another and in the structure and functioning of groups, psychology with those uniformities to be discovered in the structure and functioning of individual personalities. (We shall have more to say of the difference—and relations—between these two disciplines in Chapter 4.)

In defining the concepts of sociology then, we are setting forth the nature and limits of the sociological perspective. Our concepts focus attention upon those selected aspects of reality with which we shall be concerned. In effect, they also distinguish sociology from the other social sciences, each of which, because of its own perspective, sees different aspects of the same social phenomena. We can perhaps illustrate this point very simply. Eating a slice of buttered toast for breakfast can be analyzed in terms of the nutritive value of the food consumed, the eating habits of individuals, the economics of the bread, dairy, and home appliance industries, conventional or customary dietary patterns, or even as a possible source of social friction because the wife does not make the toast dark enough to suit her husband's taste. The key words in each case—"nutritive value," "individual habits," "economics of industries," "conventional or customary patterns," and "social friction"—are drawn from different disciplines: nutrition, psychology, economics, and sociology. The student in each field will use his own categories and will usually disregard the possibility that the same event might also be looked at from other points of view. (There is often, of course, some overlapping in the perspectives of the several social sciences, and concepts in one discipline are often used—and sometimes misused—by workers in another.)

By focusing attention upon selected aspects of reality, concepts in effect tell us what to look at. But they also tell as what to look *for* when we approach specific empirical questions. For example, if we wished to explain the existence of delinquent gangs of teen-agers, our general concepts would guide our search for factors that might be relevant. As sociologists we would collect data to see whether delinquent gangs drew their members from all *social classes*, all *ethnic groups*, and all types of *communities*, or whether delinquency was equally frequent in all the various kinds of *social groups*. We would try to see what *cultural values* were involved in this form of *deviant behavior* and would explore the distinctive features of the teen-ager's *roles* in whatever groups the gangs were drawn from. We would examine the *social relationships* within the gang and its relations to other groups and *institutions*.[15] The italicized terms illustrate the concepts with which the sociologist operates. He need not know much about delinquent gangs when he starts; he assumes on the basis of much evidence and past experience that these general concepts probably will lead him to the specific factors relevant to the problem.

The use of abstract concepts makes possible the derivation of generalizations relevant to a wide range of observations, Deviant behavior, for example, refers not only to delinquency, but also to political corruption, cheating on examinations, philandering, and any other activities which run counter to accepted social standards. Similarly the term *bureaucracy* has been defined so that it includes elements of social structure found not only in government, but in banks, insurance companies, factories, labor unions, universities, veterans' associations, and other large organizations. Analysis of the range of phenomena included in these general categories will obviously yield broader generalizations than would be obtainable if each form of deviant behavior or of bureaucratic organization were considered separately. Since the goal of science is a body of theory covering the widest possible range of phenomena, from which inferences may then be drawn about specific cases, some sociological concepts will tend, as the science grows, toward a constantly higher level of abstracton.

So significant a part of sociology are its concepts that the history of the discipline is in part a history of conceptual elaboration and refinement. Many concepts have been suggested for organizing and analyzing social phenomena. Some have come into general use whereas others have gained currency for a time, only to be displaced by more precise or more refined categories of observation and analysis. There is usually little question of the truth or falsity of a concept, although it is possible for one to be wrong. To say that men are quadrupedal mammals is obviously false since we know what men look like and how they get about. Or to say that a family consists only of the mother and her children runs counter to our accumulated observations of family life. But in most cases where alternative concepts are available the choice usully depends upon which one is more useful in accounting for the facts being scrutinized.

Considerable difference of opinion still exists among sociologists about which concepts should be used and how they should be defined. For example, Talcott Parsons, one of the major contemporary theorists, has formulated a set of categories for analyzing social systems and social action that he identifies as the "pattern variables," but many other writers make little use of his ideas. Some sociologists emphasize *ecological* concepts, those having to do with the relationship between the community and the habitat (the biological and physical environment), but others pay little attention to these categories. In addition to such conceptual differences there is also some degree of terminological disorder; we will find, for instance, that the terms society, culture, institution, social structure, and status are used to refer to various kinds of sociological phenomena and, conversely, that the same phenomenon is on occasion given different labels.

Disagreement and inconsistency, while frequently inconvenient and confusing, are not unique to sociology; they exist, although in varying degrees, in every field. In each discipline there is continuing testing and refinement of the many alternative concepts that scholars offer for use in the competitive market of ideas. The extent of conceptual differences in sociology is in part a product of its rapid development. Many still valuable works written in the past, even the relatively recent past, use concepts that have since been refined or replaced by more precise terms. As the volume and tempo of research increase, the inadequacies of present concepts become more readily apparent, and new categories are frequently required to deal with fresh data and new distinctions. Although there has been an increasing consensus within sociology, we cannot look forward to an end of the process of conceptual analysis and clarification, for this process is an inherent and persisting feature of any scientific discipline.

These facts require that the presentation of concepts in the following chapters include not only the definitions to be used in this book but also, in certain instances, a review of alternative usages. Any definition is in part arbitrary; the essential requirement is consistency of usage. Consistency, however, is sometimes confined only to a particular context; the same term may apply to different, though usually related, aspects of socal life. Culture, for example, may refer to the whole way of life of a society or, more narrowly, to that segment of a way of life that encompasses values, knowledge, beliefs, and symbols. Which meaning is intended will usually emerge from the context, or it will be made explicit. (For a full discussion of culture, see Chapter 2.)

Science and theory

Concepts alone do not constitute a discipline; they merely provide the building blocks with which a science, as a body of substantive knowledge, is constructed. In approaching the analysis of specific problems more is required than the awareness of potentially relevant variables furnished by a conceptual apparatus. Nor is the end result of scientific inquiry merely the categorizing and classification of social phenomena, however important and necessary these steps may be. The goal of science is the building of theory, a body of logically interrelated propositions that assert determinate relations among the phenomena being studied.

The nature of sociological theory can be illustrated in the following example:

(1) Men tend to behave according to the expectations of others.

(2) If men change their associates

they are likely, therefore, to acquire the attitudes and behavior of those with whom they have recently established social relationships.

(3a) It might therefore be expected that if northerners with little bias toward Negroes move to the Deep South they will in time acquire southern racial attitudes and conform to southern racial customs, since their new associates will expect such attitudes and actions. (John Dollard, a northern sociologist and social psychologist who studied a southern community, has commented: "The development of attitudes appropriate to a changed reality is nicely illustrated by the behavior of white outsiders who come into Southerntown and become permanent residents. They soon take over, it is said, the attitudes proper to their caste and class toward the Negro. My own observation tends to bear out this statement." [16] The "changed reality," of course, includes the differing expectations of those permanent residents with whom the newcomer necessarily associates.)

(3b) The rate and extent of this change, however, will depend upon whether they associate chiefly with southerners or with other migrant northerners.

(4a) Similarly, southerners with prevailing southern attitudes toward Negroes are likely to change their racial attitudes and behavior if they move to the North.

(4b) But, again, the rate and extent of change will depend upon whether they associate chiefly with other migrants like themselves, with northerners who share their views, or with northerners with little bias toward the Negro.[17]

There is interesting experimental evidence for the broad generalizations of which propositions 3a, 3b, 4a, and 4b are specific examples, namely, that men's attitudes and judgments tend to conform to those of the group of which they are a part, but that dissident views can be sustained if they are shared by others, even if only a minority. In an experiment by Solomon Asch, each person in a group was asked to compare the length of a particular line with one of three other lines of different lengths. All but one of the group were primed to give incorrect answers. The unknowing subjects tended to change their judgments to conform to those of the others, despite the fact that objectively the latter were wrong. But when two unknowing subjects were in the group, they apparently sustained one another, for they refused to change their judgments to conform to the erroneous answer of the others.[18]

All of the propositions in this example of sociological theory suffer from overgeneralization, for they ignore important variables and fail to specify the conditions under which they would hold true, or might require modification. For example, the intensity with which men hold to their opinions will affect their responsiveness to the expectations of others and therefore their susceptibility to change. It is probable that southerners are more deeply committed to their attitudes toward Negroes than are white northerners; the latter would therefore be more prone to change their opinions and behavior under changing circumstances than would southerners. Further, people are more likely to take into account the opinions of those about whose judgments they are concerned—for whatever reasons: love, respect, fear, or expediency—than the expectations of persons about whose opinions they do not care.

Despite such limitations, these propositions can serve to demonstrate the nature of theory and the elements of which it is composed, and its uses and value as well. The extent to which concepts are utilized should be obvious; expectations of others, customary associates, migrants, northerners, southerners, rate of change, attitudes, and customs are all general categories, each of which includes numerous specific items. Without them description and analysis would be impossible. But the theoretical significance of these concepts lies in the relationships which can be established among the variables they represent.

The six propositions are all logically related; the pairs, 3a and 3b, and 4a and 4b, can be derived logically from the initial, more general statements. This logical development is possible because some of the concepts are inclusive of others; migrants, for example, include both northerners and southerners who move, and the concept of the "expectations of others" obviously has very wide reference. The six propositions clearly vary in their scope and generality; the first two are extremely broad, the following two pairs much more limited in their applicability. If the latter had been elaborated they would have led to the formulation of empirical generalizations, that is, of propositions that summarize "observed uniformities of relationships between two or more variables."[19] In this case the generalizations would be of the following order:

More northerners who move to the South and acquire southern friends change their attitudes toward Negroes than do migrant northerners who associate chiefly with others of a similar background. (This assumes that their attitudes are originally similar and not "anti-Negro.")

Fewer southerners who move to Detroit, where they are very numerous, change their attitudes toward Negroes than do southerners who move to a city where such migrants are few in number.

We can represent the first of these propositions in the following tabular form:

	Those whose attitudes change	Those whose attitudes do not change	Total
Migrants from the North who associate with native southerners	$A(\%)$	$B(\%)$	$X(100\%)$
Migrants from the North who associate with other migrants	$C(\%)$	$D(\%)$	$Y(100\%)$

If the presumed relationship betwen social relationships and change of attitude obtains for northern migrants, then A should be a larger proportion of X than C is of Y; conversely, B should be a smaller proportion of X than D is of Y; or, to use hypothetical figures, 70 per cent of migrants who associate with natives might change their attitudes toward Negroes, compared with, say, 35 per cent of those who associate chiefly with one another. Whether this difference is significant in any given research would depend upon the number of persons who were studied, and how they were selected. The value of this schematic formulation lies in its statement of the kind of statistical data needed in order to ascertain the validity of empirical generalizations. Empirical propositions of this sort, which merely assert that two things occur together, constitute both the evidence for general theoretical propositions and the facts to be explained by theory.

Sociology contains a great many empirical generalizations, and research continues to add to their number. Rural families are usually larger than urban families. Divorce occurs less frequently among men and women with college education than among those with less education. Poor people spend proportionately more of their income for food than do wealthy people. Delinquent gangs are more commonly found in slum areas of cities than in middle- or upper-class areas. More women migrate from farms to cities than men. And so on. The task of sociology is to account for empirical generalizations such as these and to incorporate them into a system of general propositions, or theory.

The value of theory stems from its inclusiveness and generality. As soon as some action or event or situation can be conceptualized and placed into a category whose relationship to other variables is known, it becomes possible to draw useful inferences. What applies to southern or northern migrants may hold for farmers who move to the city, for urbanites who move to the suburbs, and for successful men who move from New York City's lower east side to the upper east side. (This by-passes, of course, the possibility that migration may occur after attitudes and behavior have changed rather than before; migration itself may result from antecedent changes in the persons who move. In any empirical study it would be essential to know the attitudes and practices existing before men moved in order to be able to assess both the changes that occur afterward and the reasons for such changes.) Theory is then both economical and informative, since statements can be made about an individual case or about an empirical generalization without necessarily investigating it in great detail. Each of these inferences, of course, must usually be tested in research, for it is possible that other relevant circumstances may affect the relationships between the variables.

By identifying the conditions under which events are likely to occur, theory makes possible prediction and perhaps some measure of control. Such predictions, it should be remembered, are not forecasts. They do not assert that something will in fact happen, but only that *if* certain conditions exist it is likely to happen. The birth rate will probably rise, for example, if the age of marriage goes down, or if the proportion of women in the child-bearing ages who are married goes up. One could only forecast a rise in the birth rate if one knew that the age of marriage was declining or that the proportion of married women among those in the 15-to-45-year-old group was rising.

It is necessary to emphasize the practical value of theory, for abstract and generalized knowledge about social life and human behavior is often contrasted invidiously with the "practical" approach of the man of affairs; the presumed sterility of "ivory-tower thinking" is set against the apparent productivity of the activities of the businessman, the practical politician, the organizer and executive; the knowledge-oriented researches of the social scientist are looked upon as of little value when compared with the action-oriented efforts of the social worker or town planner or social reformer. At a time when the fruitfulness of abstract scientific theory is so eloquently illustrated in each nuclear explosion and orbiting earth satellite, it seems hardly necessary to reiterate the fact that scientific theory can, in the long run, be eminently practical, far more so, indeed, than presumably time-tested practices and common sense. And yet when one deals with theories of man and society it is necessary to repeat this important lesson. So contained are most men in their immediate social context and so committed to the prevailing common-sense in-terpretations of behavior and events that abstract generalizations are not readily accepted.

It is sometimes said in criticism of theory that it narrows or limits what men see, for it confines their vision to those variables incorporated in the theory and therefore prevents them from seeking other and frequently important facts. Obviously this claim is true: In paying attention to some aspects of reality we necessarily disregard or ignore others. This is not a fatal criticism, however, for science is inherently self-correcting. No theory is ever final, and as new and unexplained facts appear it becomes necessary to revise what was heretofore accepted. Further, sociology is not an exclusive road to understanding. Nor does it deny the validity or desirability of other roads, scientific or otherwise. Sociology is one road among others, although in our modern, complex society it can be one of great significance and value.

The value of sociology

Sociology, both as tested theory and as a body of reliable facts, possesses a double value: It can add to man's understanding of himself and his society, and it can contribute to solutions of problems he faces in achieving and maintaining the kind of society in which he hopes to live. We have already referred to the limitations of common-sense knowledge. In a rapidly changing world, such knowledge inevitably becomes unreliable, both as a source of understanding and as a guide to action. Traditional explanations that may once have been reasonably accurate no longer apply as circumstances change. The increasing complexity of modern society creates problems for which there are no ready-made answers. In this situation sociology constitutes a useful, even essential, source of reliable knowledge for both the individual and society.

The relevance of sociology to many of the problems faced by society and its constituent parts hardly needs elaboration. Surely, reliable facts are more useful than heresay or untested generalizations, and a systematic understanding of cause and effect, of the relations among facts, is a better guide to action than the uncertain results of trial and error or the unreliable precepts handed down by tradition. And yet the lesson presented long ago by Herbert Spencer in a much-cited passage needs continually to be repeated:

You see that this wrought-iron plate is not quite flat: it sticks up a little here towards the left—"cockles," as we say. How shall we flatten it? Obviously, you reply, by hitting down on the part that is prominent. Well, here is a hammer, and I give the plate a blow as you advise. Harder, you say. Still no effect. Another stroke? Well, there is one, and another, and another. The prominence remains, you see: the evil is as great as ever—greater, indeed. But this is not all. Look at the warp which the plate has got near the opposite edge. Where it was flat before it is now curved. A pretty bungle we have made of it. Instead of curing the original defect, we have produced a second. Had we asked an artisan practiced in "planishing," as it is called, he would have told us that no good was to be done, but only mischief, by hitting down on the projecting part. He would have taught us how to give variously-directed and specially-adjusted blows with a hammer elsewhere: so attacking the evil not by direct but by indirect actions. The required process is

less simple than you thought. Even a sheet of metal is not to be successfully dealt with after those common-sense methods in which you have so much confidence. What, then, shall we say about a society? "Do you think I am easier to be played on than a pipe?" asks Hamlet. Is humanity more readily straightened than an iron plate? [20]

In its origins sociology was frequently considered to be an instrument for dealing with social "evils." Increasingly it now seems to be providing an approach and point of view useful in interpreting and understanding the complex and difficult world in which we live. Despite frequent criticisms of sociology—its jargon, methods, and ideas—critics, novelists, historians, and others are making widespread use of its perspectives and findings.

The hopes and aspirations of any discipline almost inevitably outrun its achievements. Humanity, even with a fully developed social science as its instrument, is not likely to "straighten" itself, and sociology is as yet an exceedingly imperfect tool. But "the sociological imagination," to use C. Wright Mills' hopeful phrase,

is a quality of mind that seems most dramatically to promise an understanding of the intimate realities of ourselves in connection with larger social realities. It is not merely one quality of mind among the contemporary range of cultural sensibilities—it is *the* quality whose wider and more adroit use offers the promise that all such sensibilities—and in fact, human reason itself—will come to play a greater role in human affairs.[21]

Notes

[1] See, for example, Russell Kirk, "Is Social Science Scientific?" *The New York Times Magazine,* June 25, 1961, pp. 11 ff. For a rejoinder, see Robert K. Merton, "The Canons of the Anti-Sociologist," *The New York Times Magazine,* July 16, 1961, pp. 14 ff. Both articles are reprinted in Milton L. Barron (ed.), *Contemporary Sociology* (New York: Dodd, Mead, 1964), pp. 29–35, 35–40.

[2] For a discussion of the spread of interest in sociology in other countries, see

Edward Shils, "The Calling of Sociology," in Talcott Parsons *et al.* (eds.), *Theories of Society*, II (New York: Free Press, 1961), 1405–9.

[3] Alfred N. Whitehead, *Science and the Modern World* (Cambridge, Eng.: Cambridge University Press, 1946), Ch. 1.

[4] Ralph G. Ross, *Symbols and Civilization* (New York: Harcourt, 1962), p. 1.

[5] For an early but still useful discussion of the biases that get in the way of objective sociological inquiry, see Herbert Spencer, *The Study of Sociology*, originally published in 1873 and republished in many editions.

[6] Robert K. Merton, "Notes on Problem-Finding in Sociology," in Robert K. Merton, Leonard Broom, and Leonard S. Cottrell, Jr. (eds.), *Sociology Today* (New York: Basic Books, 1959), pp. xv–xvi *n.*

[7] See Paul F. Lazarsfeld, *"The American Soldier:* An Expository Review," *Public Opinion Quarterly*, XIII (Fall, 1949), 377–404.

[8] Alfred L. Kroeber, *The Nature of Culture* (Chicago: University of Chicago Press, 1952), p. 27.

[9] Bernard de Mandeville, *The Fable of the Bees* (London: 1723), p. 25.

[10] Robert M. MacIver, *Social Causation* (Boston: Ginn, 1942), p. 148.

[11] Talcott Parsons, *The Structure of Social Action* (New York: McGraw-Hill, 1937), p. 768.

[12] Émile Durkheim, *The Elementary Forms of the Religious Life*, trans. by J. W. Swain (New York: Free Press, 1947), p. 433.

[13] Morris R. Cohen and Ernest Nagel, *An Introduction to Logic and the Scientific Method,* (New York: Harcourt, 1934), pp. 224–31. For an excellent discussion of definitions in sociology, see Robert Bierstedt, "Nominal and Real Definitions in Sociological Theory," in Llewellyn Gross (ed.), *Symposium on Sociological Theory* (Evanston: Row, Peterson, 1959), pp. 121–44.

[14] *Ibid.*, p. 371.

[15] For sophisticated sociological analyses of delinquent gangs, see Albert K. Cohen, *Delinquent Boys* (New York: Free Press, 1955); and Richard A. Cloward and Lloyd E. Ohlin, *Delinquency and Opportunity* (New York: Free Press, 1960).

[16] John Dollard, *Caste and Class in a Southern Town* (Garden City: Doubleday Anchor Books, 1957), p. 17. Dollard also notes the relevance of this tendency for research: "Undoubtedly many researchers who have gone South . . . have been seduced by the hospitality of the middle- and upper-class southern white people, have formed agreeable ties with them, and have thereupon been pulled into the southern mode of perception of the racial problem" (p. 37).

[17] For an analysis of the racial attitudes of some southerners who move north, see Lewis M. Killian, "The Effects of Southern White Workers on Race Relations in Northern Plants," *American Sociological Review*, XVII (June, 1952), 327–31.

[18] See Solomon Asch, "Effects of Group Pressure upon the Modification and Distortion of Judgments," in Eleanor E. Maccoby, Theodore M. Newcomb, and Eugene L. Hartley (eds.), *Readings in Social Psychology* (3rd ed.; New York: Holt, 1958), pp. 174–83.

[19] Robert K. Merton, *Social Theory and Social Structure* (rev. ed.; New York: Free Press, 1957), p. 95.

[20] Herbert Spencer, *The Study of Sociology* (10th ed.; London: Routledge, 1882), pp. 270–1. In 1936 Karl Mannheim, one of the leading and most influential sociologists, wrote: "For it is surely a striking commentary on the age in which we live, that whilst should any one try to repair his car without knowing the first thing about its machinery he would by common consent be dubbed a fool, yet no such derision is displayed toward those who, possessing no clear knowledge of cause and effect, believe that hitches in the mechanism of society can be set right by emotional resentments or irrational movements against social forces." "The Place of Sociology" in *The Social Sciences: Their Relations in*

Theory and Teaching (London: LePlay, 1936), p. 164.

[21] C. Wright Mills, *The Sociological Imagination* (New York: Oxford, 1959), p. 15. For a useful discussion of the contribu-

tion of sociology to a general education, see Robert Bierstedt, "Sociology and General Education," in Charles H. Page (ed.), *Sociology and Contemporary Education* (New York: Random House, 1964), pp. 40–55.

Suggestions for further reading

BIERSTEDT, ROBERT. "Nominal and Real Definitions in Sociological Theory," in Llewellyn Gross (ed.), *Symposium on Sociological Theory*. Evanston: Row, Peterson, 1959, pp. 121–44.
An enlightening discussion of definitions in sociology that clears up a considerable amount of theoretical confusion and controversy. Written with a felicity of style characteristic of this distinguished sociologist.

MILLS, C. WRIGHT. *The Sociological Imagination*. New York: Oxford, 1959, Ch. 1, "The Promise."
An important statement on the cultural role of social science in the modern world.

PAGE, CHARLES H. (ed.). *Sociology and Contemporary Education*. New York: Random House, 1964.
A collection of essays on the intellectual and cultural contributions of sociology.

PARSONS, TALCOTT. "Some Problems Confronting Sociology as a Profession," *American Sociological Review*, XXIV (August, 1959), 547–59.
A recent statement by a leading sociologist on the present status of sociology as a profession and on its uses and prospects.

ROSS, RALPH. *Symbols and Civilization.* New York: Harcourt, 1962.
An excellent brief discussion of the nature of science, its methods, and its applicability to the study of society.

SPENCER, HERBERT. *The Study of Sociology.* First published in 1873 and republished in many editions.
A still useful analysis of the sources of bias in sociological inquiry.

THOMLINSON, RALPH. *Sociological Concepts and Research.* New York: Random House, 1965.
A brief and useful "survey of how modern sociologists go about their daily chores."

2

Society and culture

Patterned behavior and collective life

Sociology begins with two basic facts: The behavior of human beings shows regular and recurrent patterns, and human beings are social animals and not isolated creatures.

The fundamental events of birth, death, and marriage, the private details of bathing, eating, and love-making, the public occurrences of vote-getting and producing or selling goods, and the myriad other activities in which men engage usually follow recognizable patterns. We often lose sight of the repetitive nature of most social action, however, for when we observe those persons around us we are more likely to notice their idiosyncrasies and personal quirks than their similarities. But if we compare ourselves with Frenchmen or Japanese or Trobriand Islanders we find ourselves saying: We do it this way; they do it that way. Charles Horton Cooley, one of America's first important sociologists, once observed: "Is it not the case that the nearer a thing is to our habit of thought the more clearly we see the individual . . . ? The principle is much the same as that which makes all [Chinese] look pretty much alike to us: we see the type because it is so different from what we are used to, but only one who lives within it can fully perceive the differences among individuals." [1]

In studying ourselves as we might study the Chinese or any other society different from our own, we abstract the recurrent features of behavior from the unique. When men respond to a personal introduction with a standardized phrase— "How do you do?"—the intonation, the tone, the volume may vary, but the verbal formulation remains the same. Some people shake hands energetically, with a strong grasp, while others have a limp and flabby handshake; these personal differences have significance in the social interchange which takes place, but they do not deny the existence of the patterned form of behavior which recurs when people meet.

The repeated aspects of human action are the basis for any social science. Without ascertainable patterns there could be no science, for generalization would be impossible. Sociology is distinguished from economics, political science, and psychology by the particular patterns it studies and how it looks at them. Those features of behavior upon which sociology focuses its attention are derived from the second basic fact upon which the discipline rests—the social character of human life.

"Man," wrote Aristotle more than two thousand years ago, "is naturally a political animal [in modern terms the word usually translated as *political* might more appropriately be translated as *social*] and . . . whosoever is naturally and not artificially unfit for society must be either inferior or superior to men." Adam Ferguson, an eighteenth-century Scottish moral philosopher, once observed in terms which are still appropriate: "Both the earliest and the latest accounts collected from every quarter of the earth, represent mankind as assembled in troops and companies; . . . [a fact which] must be admitted as the foundation of all our reasoning relative to man."[2] There are records of human beings who somehow manage to survive with little care or without normal association with other humans, but such cases of "feral man," as they are called, and of abused and rejected children show few of the characteristics normally attributed to man.[3]

In attempting to account for the apparent regularities of human action and the facts of collective life, socioloists have developed two concepts, *society* and *culture*, which may be considered basic to sociological investigation. Each of these terms has a long history. *Society* derives initially from attempts made during the sixteenth and seventeenth centuries to differentiate the state from the totality of social organization, although systematic analysis of the nature of society came only with the emergence of sociology. The term *culture* gained initial currency in Germany in the eighteenth century, was first used in anthropology by Edward Tylor, an English scholar, in 1871, and has come to be widely used in sociological discourse only in the twentieth century.[4] Both terms have been variously employed, and there is as yet no complete consensus as to their meaning. Despite this variation—or perhaps because of it—they can serve to define and suggest in a general fashion the nature and limits of the subject matter of sociology. It

should be noted, however, that the phenomena to which culture and society refer do not exist independently of one another. Although we can distinguish between them analytically, human society cannot exist without culture, and culture exists only within society.

Society

Despite its importance there is no clear-cut agreement as to the meaning of *society*, even among social scientists or, more particularly, sociologists, some of whom have labeled their discipline the "science of society." "In the long history of the literature dealing with the life of human beings in groups," Gladys Bryson has commented, "perhaps no word offers less precision in usage than the word 'society.' "[5] We cannot therefore suggest a definition to which all, or perhaps even most, sociologists would give assent. Nor is there anything to be gained by adding another to the already imposing array of alternatives. Instead we can best carry forward our analysis by exploring the various meanings which have been given to the term and by examining briefly the uses to which they are put. As we pointed out earlier, conceptual differences often mean that people are looking at, or at least emphasizing, different aspects of the same phenomenon.

In its most general usage, society refers merely to the basic fact of human association. For example, the term has been employed "in the widest sense to include every kind and degree of relationship entered into by men, whether these relations be organized or unorganized, direct or indirect, conscious or unconscious, cooperative or antagonistic. It includes the whole tissue of human relations and is without a boundary or assignable limits.

Of amorphous structure itself, it gives rise to numerous, specific, overlapping and interconnected societies, but is not exhausted by them." [6] This conception of society, which seems on occasion to encompass all of humanity, or mankind at large, serves chiefly to focus our attention upon a broad range of phenomena central to the analysis of human behavior, namely the varied and multiform relationships into which men necessarily enter in the course of group life.

The concept of *social relationship* is based upon the fact that human behavior is oriented in innumerable ways to other persons. Not only do men live together and share common opinions, values, beliefs, and customs, they also continually interact, responding to one another and shaping their behavior in relation to the behavior and expectations of others. The lover's effort to please the object of his affections, the politician's attempts to win the support of the electorate, the soldier's obedience to the orders of his commanding officer—these constitute familiar examples of behavior oriented to the expectations, desires, and wishes, whether real or imagined, of others. Action may be modeled on that of someone else; the child imitates his father, the teen-ager apes her favorite movie star. Behavior may be calculated to elicit responses from others, as in the child's effort to gain parental approval, or the actor's attempt to move his audience. It may be based on expectations as to how others will behave—for example, the boxer's feint before delivering a blow or the doctor's technique in reporting his diagnosis to a patient.

Interaction, however, is not one-sided, as these illustrations may suggest. The electorate responds in some fashion to the politician's actions, and he may then alter his methods or persist in his strategy,

with further consequences in the attitudes and behavior of voters. The officer's behavior will be affected by the manner in which his men obey his orders. Courtship is not merely a case of hunter and hunted; to change the metaphor, two can and do play the game as well as one. Interaction, as the word itself suggests, is not a momentary occurrence, not a single response to a single stimulus; it is a persisting process of action and reaction.

A social relationship may be said to exist when individuals or groups possess reciprocal expectations concerning the other's behavior so that they tend to act in relatively patterned ways. To phrase the point differently, a social relationship consists of a pattern of human interaction. Parents and children respond to each other in more or less regular ways, based upon mutual expectations. The patterned interactions of student and teacher, policeman and automobile driver, salesman and buyer, worker and employer, doctor and patient, constitute social relationships of various kinds. From one point of view, then, society is the "web of social relationships."

Society, as the "whole tissue" or "whole complex scheme" of social relationships, can be distinguished from those specific societies in which men group themselves. The emphasis in some definitions of a society, however, is frequently upon the persons rather than upon the structure of relationships. Georg Simmel, one of the founders of modern sociology, considered a society to be "a number of individuals connected by interaction," [7] while the anthropologist Ralph Linton identified a society as "any group of people who have lived and worked together long enough to get themselves organized and to think of themselves as a social unit with well-defined limits." [8] This view of a society, although of value in directing attention to the network of relationships which hold together specific aggregations of people, is too general to be very useful. As thus defined, society could include any of the multiplicity of groups found among men. It could refer to "Society," members of the upper class whose doings are reported in newspaper "society pages." It could encompass organizations of many kinds: the Society of Friends, the Society for the Advancement of Management, the American Ethnological Society, as well as the endless array of clubs, lodges, fraternities, criminal groups, and professional organizations. It could include families, kinship groups, and clusters of friends. Although some writers do use "society" to refer to any kind of group, this term usually denotes a special kind of social unit.

Society, then, is that group within which men can live a total common life, rather than an organization limited to some specific purpose or purposes. From this point of view a society consists not only of individuals related to one another, but also of interconnected and overlapping groups. Thus, American society comprises 195 million or more individuals (in 1965) tied together in a complex network of relations, of approximately 48 million families (increasing by about .5 million families per year), of the multiplicity of urban and rural communities, religious denominations and sects, political parties, races and ethnic groups, social and economic classes, unions, business and veterans organizations, and the infinite variety of other voluntary organizations into which the population is divided. On the other hand, a simple society such as that of the Andaman Islands west of Burma consisted before the arrival of Europeans of a small population organized primarily into tribes, local groups, and families. The society of India incudes the various religious groups, the innumerable castes and the "outcastes," the different races, the many tribes, the economic and political aggregates and organizations, and so on.

In any society smaller groups may be found within larger and individuals simultaneously belong to various groups. Ethnic groups and social classes give rise to voluntary associations, cliques and factions emerge in political parties and other groups, families belong to country clubs and churches and engage in neighborly activities. Each person may participate in a family, a peer group, a business enterprise, or a union or professional organization. A society, then, can be analyzed in terms of its constituent groups and their relations to one another.

Culture

Each society possesses a way of life or, in our terminology, a *culture*, that defines appropriate or required modes of thinking, acting, and feeling. Culture, as thus used in sociological inquiry, has a much-wider meaning than it is usually given. In conventional discourse, it refers to the "higher" things in life—painting, music, sculpture, philosophy; the adjective *cultured* stands close to cultivated or refined. In sociology culture refers to the totality of what is learned by individuals as members of society. Tylor's old (1871) but still widely cited definition indicates its scope: "Culture is that complex whole which includes knowledge, belief, art, morals, law, custom, and any other capabilities acquired by man as a member of society." The technique of brushing one's teeth, the Ten Commandments, the rules of baseball or cricket or hop scotch, the procedures for choosing a president or prime minister or members of the Supreme Soviet are as much a part of culture as the latest volume of avant-garde poetry, Beethoven's Ninth Symphony, or the *Analects* of Confucius.

Regularities of behavior do not in themselves constitute culture. They occur in large part because men possess culture, because they have common standards of good and bad, right and wrong, appropriate and inappropriate, and possess similar attitudes and share a fund of knowledge about the environment—social, biological, and physical—in which they live. Culture, George Murdock has noted, is to a large extent "ideational": it refers to the standards, beliefs, and attitudes in terms of which people act.

Recognition of the ubiquity and significance of culture, Ralph Linton has pointed out, is "one of the most important scientific developments of modern times." He continues:

It has been said that the last thing which a dweller in the deep sea would be likely to discover would be water. He would become conscious of its existence only if some accident brought him to the surface and introduced him to air. Man, throughout most of his history, has been only vaguely conscious of the existence of culture and has owed even this consciousness to contrasts between the customs of his own society and those of some other with which he happened to be brought into contact. The ability to see the culture of one's own society as a whole, to evaluate its patterns and appreciate their implications, calls for a degree of objectivity which is rarely if ever achieved.[9]

Because our culture is so much a part of us we take it for granted, frequently assuming that it is a normal, inevitable, and inherent characteristic of all mankind. (The implications of this assumption, known as "ethnocentrism," for the study of society and culture were discussed in Chapter 1.) Anthropologists have often reported that when they ask members of small preliterate groups why they act in some particular fashion they receive an answer which amounts to "That's just the way it's done" or "It's customary." "When Captain Cook asked the chiefs of Tahiti why they ate apart and alone, they simply replied, 'Because it is right.' "[10] Habituated to their own way of life, men frequently can conceive of no other. Among Americans, the expression "It's just human nature" is a characteristic explanation for many actions—competing for fame and power, profit-seeking, marrying for love or for money. Yet this "explanation," which by seemingly explaining everything explains nothing, is itself a manifestation of the ethnocentrism of Americans.

The importance of culture lies in the fact that it provides the knowledge and the techniques that enable man to survive, both physically and socially, and to master and control, insofar as it is possible, the world around him. Man seems to possess few if any instinctive skills and no instinctive knowledge which might enable him to sustain himself, either singly or in groups. The salmon's return from the sea to spawn and die in fresh water, the annual migration of birds from one part of the world to another, the nest-building of the mud wasp, and the complex living patterns of ants and bees are all inherited forms of behavior which seem to appear automatically at the appropriate times. They are not learned from parents or from other members of the species. Man, on the other hand, survives by virtue of what he learns.

Man is not, however, the only animal that learns to act instead of responding automatically to stimuli. Dogs can be taught a good deal and can learn from experience, as can horses and cats, monkeys and apes, and rats and white mice. But by virtue of his greater brain power and his capacity for language, man can learn more and therefore possesses greater flexibility of action than other animals. He can transmit a great deal of what he learns to others, including his young, and he can in part control the world around him—even to the point of transforming much of it. Man is the only animal to possess culture; indeed, this is one of the crucial distinctions between man and other animals.

Of central importance in the definition of culture is the fact that it is both *learned* and *shared*. Men, we have said, do not inherit their habits and beliefs, their skills and knowledge; they acquire them during the course of their lives. What they learn comes from the groups into which they are born and in which they live. The habits acquired by an infant are likely to be patterned on those of its family and of other persons close at hand. (Not all habits reflect customs or culture, however, for some are merely personal idiosyncrasies.) In an endless number of ways—via explicit instruction, the application of punishment and the offering of rewards, identification with elders and imitation of their behavior— each generation learns from its predecessors. Behavior which is universal, though not learned, or is peculiar to the individual, is not part of culture. (Both unlearned behavior, such as reflexes, and personal idiosyncrasies may, however, be influenced or modified by culture. Indeed, except for biological peculiarities, individual aberrations are defined by their relationship to, or deviation from, cultural patterns.)

The learned and shared character of culture has led to its occasional identification as the "superorganic" or as man's "social heritage." The former term, used by Herbert Spencer, emphasizes the relative independence of culture from the realm of biology (of which we shall say

more in Chapter 3) and its distinctive quality as a product of social life. "Social heritage" calls attention to culture's historical character and therefore to the possibilities of growth and change; it suggests the need for analyzing and understanding its temporal dimensions of which we shall have more to say later. (See Chapters 5 and 20.)

The components of culture

Culture is clearly so inclusive a concept that its principal components should be identified, labeled, analyzed, and related to one another. These components can be grouped roughly in three large categories: institutions, the rules or norms which govern behavior; ideas, that is, knowledge and belief of all varieties—moral, theological, philosophical, scientific, technological, historical, sociological, and so on; and the material products or artifacts which men produce and use in the course of their collective lives.

INSTITUTIONS   We shall define institutions as "*normative* patterns which define what are felt to be . . . proper, legitimate, or expected modes of action or of social relationship." [11] Such norms or rules pervade all areas of social life: how one eats and what one eats, how one dresses, decorates oneself, responds to others, how one looks after children or the aged, and how one behaves in the presence of members of the opposite sex. Not all behavior conforms to rules, either explicit or implicit, but most actions of any individual reflect the presence of some accepted standards of behavior which he has learned from others and which in some measure he shares with them.

The concept of institution, like that of

culture, has been variously defined, and the definition given above, which we shall use, represents only one of several alternatives. Because the other uses of the term appear frequently in sociological literature, it is necessary to detour briefly in order to note these other meanings, even though we shall try to be consistent in our own usage. Earlier definitions, which have been steadily refined or clarified, included not only normative patterns, but also what we shall identify later as groups and as social organization. We still find occasionally in sociological literature (and frequently in everyday discourse) an organization of individuals referred to as an institution: Harvard College, for example, or the Republican Party. This usage coincides with the early definition by William Graham Sumner: "An institution consists of a concept (idea, notion, doctrine, interest) and a structure. The structure is a framework, or apparatus, or perhaps only a number of functionaries set to cooperate in prescribed ways at a certain conjuncture. The structure holds the concept and furnishes instrumentalities for bringing it into the world of facts and action in a way to serve the interests of men in society." [12] Both the norms *and* the group are included in this definition of an institution. There is an increasing measure of agreement that the term should be used only to refer to patterns of approved or sanctioned behavior, and that other terms should be used to denote the organizational aspects of such behavior and the group of persons involved.

Instead of limiting *institution* to specific social norms or rules—the Ten Commandments, laws against murder or burglary, business practices, or conventions governing daily social intercourse—some writers view an institution as a set of interrelated norms, a "normative system" centered around some type of human ac-

tivity or some major problem of man in society such as providing subsistence and shelter (property, building techniques, "free enterprise"), caring for children (parenthood, the family), or maintaining order and harmony (the state). [13]

Whether one chooses this encompassing definition or the more limited one used in this volume is largely a semantic problem; there is no inherent correctness in either, and both refer to aspects of social life that are important and require analysis. The definition adopted here provides a generic concept for the variety of norms that govern social behavior: folkway, *mos* (the plural form, mores, is conventionally used), custom, convention, fashion, etiquette, law. The definition of *institution* as a "normative system" emphasizes the fact that the multiplicity of rules which govern the actions of men in society are tied together in a more or less organized fashion. There are, however, various ways of identifying (conceptualizing) these systems of norms—as clusters of rules that indicate how persons in particular positions in society, doctors or parents, for example, should act; as bodies of norms that organize the relations of people to one another in social groups; or in terms of their contribution to the performance of socially necessary or important tasks such as educating children or cultivating the soil. We shall necessarily examine all of these types of systems of institutions in this book.

One basic distinction among institutions is that between *folkways* and *mores*, concepts first employed by the pioneer American sociologist William Graham Sumner. A folkway is merely the conventional practice, accepted as appropriate but not insisted upon. The person who does not follow the rule may be looked upon as eccentric or merely as a staunch individualist who refuses to be bound by convention. The occasional man who objects to the irrationality of men's clothing, for example, and refuses under any circumstances to wear a tie is ignoring one of our folkways.

Mores are those norms, or institutions, which are morally strongly sanctioned. Conformity is enforced in various ways, and failure to conform elicits moral disapproval and frequently positive action. Examples are readily available: thou shalt not kill, thou shalt not steal, thou shalt love thy father and mother. Mores are looked upon as essential to the well-being of the group.

The line between folkways and mores is not always easy to draw. Clearly there is a kind of continuum, ranging from those conventions or customs that are loosely observed to those which are most insistently enforced. The rules governing modesty in dress or the consumption of wine and whiskey, for example, may be difficult to categorize. They elicit some moral disapproval if ignored or violated, but clearly do not carry the same moral sanction as adultery, theft, or murder. Moreover, there are wide differences in the attitudes of various social groups toward these rules.

Despite the absence of a sharp dividing line between them, the concepts of folkways and mores possess considerable heuristic value. They focus attention upon significant dimensions or aspects of social norms, the moral sanction attached to them, and the extent to which they are considered to be essential to social well-being.

A second dimension of institutions emerges from the contrast between *customs* and *laws*. The former comprise "long-established usage," those practices that have gradually become accepted as appropriate modes of behavior: the rou-

tines of work or leisure, the conventions of warfare, the rituals of religious observance, the etiquette governing social relationships. Customs are sanctioned by tradition and sustained by the pressures of group opinion. Laws, on the other hand, are rules enacted by those who exercise political power and they are enforced through the machinery of the state. They may or may not have the sanction of tradition. They are characteristic of complex societies with well-developed political systems; in those simple societies without distinctive political institutions and recognized sources of political authority law appears, if at all, only in embryonic form. In such simple societies behavior is regulated chiefly by custom, new rules are likely to emerge gradually rather than by formal enactment, and enforcement is not assigned to specific persons operating through a recognized governmental machinery.

The distinction between customs and laws cuts across folkways and mores. Some customs have the moral sanctions characteristic of the mores, while others are more or less casually accepted conventions. Similarly, some laws are supported by strong moral sentiments—thou shalt not kill—while others may virtually lack any moral support, except for whatever attitudes and sentiments sustain conformity with the law in general. Many laws regulating business practice fall into this latter category.

The line between custom and law, like that between folkways and mores, is not always easily drawn, particularly in simpler societies, in which the political structure from which law emerges and through which it is enforced is only partially developed. Even in more complex societies, like our own, the relations between law and custom are frequently complex and distinctions between them difficult to draw. Some customary rules may be embodied in law, Sunday blue laws, for example, whose legal character has sometimes persisted after the customs which gave rise to legislative enactment have changed. Conversely, politically enacted rules may eventually gain an extra-legal, traditional sanction, a process which is clearly apparent in the history of American attitudes toward and sentiments about the Constitution. In addition, laws frequently acquire a barnaclelike accretion of customary practice which is as strongly enforced as though it were written into the law; witness the complex array of conventions and traditional practices governing the actions of Congress.

The concepts of custom and law do not encompass all forms of social norms. There are many institutions that do not seem to fit into either category, despite their apparent inclusiveness. The operating procedures of corporations and the rules of voluntary organizations such as the League of Women Voters, the National Association of Manufacturers, and the American Medical Association are, with a few exceptions, neither sanctioned by tradition nor enforced by the state.

Despite these difficulties the conceptual distinction between law and custom does call attention to important differences in the origins of institutions and in the methods by which they are enforced. There are *crescive* institutions, to use another term drawn from Sumner, which, like Topsy, just grow, and those that are enacted and formally born at a given time. Clearly a different explanation will be required for the origin of a crescive than for an enacted institution, although the latter includes both laws and those formal rules promulgated by officials of nonpolitical organizations. The methods of enforcement may be largely informal, confined to the demands of tradition and

the more or less subtly—or obviously—expressed opinions of others, or may be limited to the formal machinery of government, or may, to varying degrees, combine both mechanisms.

These categories for the analysis of institutions do not exhaust the complexity or variety of social norms, or their various aspects or dimensions. For the rules which govern behavior include the transitory standards of fad and fashion, the symbolic rituals of religious and patriotic observance, and the ceremonies which mark significant occasions. They include further the rules of scientific procedure sanctioned neither by tradition nor by legislative enactment, but only by the rationally based consensus of scientists, and the empirically tested methods of rational economic enterprise. (All of these rational norms may, of course, contain traditional or customary elements.) We need not explore these several types of institutions here; they will concern us at appropriate points in subsequent chapters.

Institutions, we have said, account, in their many forms, for much of the regularity of behavior that we observe; it is because men possess these learned and shared standards that their actions seem to be alike, or at least similar. This statement, however, may suggest a degree of conformity that typically does not exist. Norms vary in the degree of conformity that they require, depending in some measure upon the nature of the approved or interdicted behavior. One cannot be just a little bit of a murderer. On the other hand, the amount of time which college students may be expected, or required, to devote to their studies may vary widely. The rules of dress, etiquette, and speech may be couched in such general terms that some variety will be expected within the limits set by the culture. In many cases, that is to say, the norms prescribe a range of behavior or set the limits beyond which it would be inappropriate or wrong to stray.

Even when the institution is precisely defined, the actual behavior of men and women is likely to vary around the norm from virtual nonconformity to elaborate overconformity. In many colleges and universities, for example, students are expected to devote two hours to study for each hour spent in class, or about thirty hours each week for a student carrying fifteen hours of class work. It is probably safe to say that most students do not meet this requirement; the actual time spent may vary from none to forty or fifty or even sixty hours per week, with an average probably somewhat less than thirty. Any analysis of institutions and behavior and the relations obtaining between them must therefore take into account the fact that both the definition of social norms and the description of actual conduct often refer to a range of behavior around some central tendency.

It is, of course, obvious that many institutions are often ignored in practice, that men break the Ten Commandments, do not give their seats to women in public conveyances, and doctor their income-tax returns. They defy the sex mores, disregard conventions governing work and play, and ignore the requirements of fashion. Indeed, the starting place for much sociological inquiry has been the effort to account for socially deviant activities—crime, delinquency, divorce, suicide—rather than for conventional behavior.

The fact that men do ignore or violate social norms indicates that conformity too cannot be taken for granted and must also be explained. When one accounts for patterned behavior by reference to cultural definitions of proper or expected behavior, one has taken only the first step in sociological analysis. Institutions are not self-enforcing, and it is necessary to discover why men conform to social rules, as well as ascertaining how institutions arise and what circumstances account for their persistence and for the changes that take place in them. In part, of course, men conform to social norms because they are taught to do so; they learn the customs and conventions of their culture as they are brought up and educated. (See the discussion of *socialization*, Chapter 4.) In part, they conform because of sanctions, pressures, and controls, which are institutionalized and built into the structure of society. (See the discussion of social control, Chapter 18.)

IDEAS: BELIEFS, KNOWLEDGE, AND VALUES
The second major component of culture, *ideas*, encompasses a varied and complex array of social phenomena. It includes the beliefs men hold about themselves and the social, biological, and physical world in which they live, and about their relations to one another, to society and nature, and to such other beings and forces as they may discover, accept, or conjure up. It embraces the whole vast body of ideas by which men account for their observation and experience—folklore, legend, proverbs, theology, science, philosophy, practical know-how—and which they take into account or rely upon in choosing alternative lines of action. It encompasses the forms in which men express their feelings about themselves and others and their responses, emotional and aesthetic, to the world around them.

In addition to cognitive and expressive ideas, men also learn and share the values by which they live, the standards and ideals by which they define their goals, select a course of action, and judge themselves and others: success, rationality, honor, courage, patriotism, loyalty, efficiency. These values are not specific rules for action but general precepts to which men give their allegiance and about which they are likely to have strong feelings. They represent as well the shared attitudes of approval and disapproval, the judgments of good or bad, desirable or undesirable, toward specific persons, things, situations, and events.

The term *value*, however, is sometimes used for the *objects* or *situations* which are defined as good, proper, desirable, worthwhile: for money, wives, jewelry, success, power, fame, rather than for shared sentiments or judgments. Values then acquire their character by virtue of men's judgments but are distinguished from them. It is this distinction that Robert M. MacIver emphasizes in differentiating between attitudes and interests, between the *"subjective* reactions, states of consciousness within the individual human being, with relation to *objects"* and the objects themselves.[14] Values, as things to which men assign desirability or importance, may then be beliefs or institutions, as well as the third general component of culture, material objects. The views men express as to the nature of God, or of man or society itself, may be subscribed to so intensely that they become objects of value; men may possess as strong an interest in their belief in God or their commitment to some scientific doctrine as they do in money or power. "For a vested interest in understanding," John K. Galbraith writes, "is more preciously guarded than any other treasure." [15] Similarly, institutions acquire value in men's eyes, and certainly many of the material objects created by men become the locus of approval or disapproval, desire or envy.

That men should evaluate their property, their laws and customs, ideas, and even themselves and others is perhaps in-evitable as they make the choices inherent in social life. Viewing the same phenomenon from different conceptual perspectives—as instruments of production, rules governing behavior, or beliefs orienting man to nature and society, on the one hand, and as objects of value on the other—is not necessarily a source of confusion; it is rather a means for widening our vision and increasing our understanding.

The ideas men share—cognitive, expressive, and evaluative—consist of a body of symbols through which they can communicate with one another. Communication is a fundamental social process, for it is only through the exchange of ideas that organized social life is possible. What distinguishes man from other creatures is the development of a symbolic language that goes beyond crude signs or signals which can convey only limited information or serve as direct stimuli to action. While other animals communicate through gestures and a relatively simple assortment of sounds, only man has evolved a language which can express abstract ideas and the complexities of emotional or aesthetic response. As the philosopher Ernst Cassirer has pointed out, what transformed Helen Keller from a blind deaf-mute capable only of very limited participation in social life into a fully human being was the flash of insight that words stood for things, that "everything has a name." [16] Symbolic language is both a basic constituent of culture and that which makes its elaboration and cumulation possible.

Some writers would confine the term *culture* only to the body of ideas, the symbols that men share and through which they exchange meaningful communication, thus distinguishing it from the system or structure of social relationships. This definition can be very useful and appears to be gaining substantial currency among sociologists. It enables one to distinguish between symbolic systems—language, beliefs, knowledge, and expressive forms—and their interrelations in contrast to the organized pattern of interaction among individuals and groups.[17]

MATERIAL CULTURE   The third major component of culture is perhaps the easiest to define. It consists of those material things that men create and use, ranging from the primitive instruments of prehistoric man to the most advanced machinery of modern man. It includes the stone ax and the electronic computer, the outrigger canoe of the Polynesians and the luxury liner, the teepee of the Indians and the skyscraper of the modern city.

To identify these material objects as elements of culture without reference to their nonmaterial concomitants, however, can easily be misleading. When we refer to such objects we are apt to take for granted their uses, their value, and the requisite practical or theoretical know-how. Yet machines or tools obviously are hardly useful unless their owners possess the knowledge and skill needed to operate or apply them. The same objects may be put to many alternative uses. Rings, for example, may be worn on one's fingers, arms, or legs, or may be put through one's lips, nose, or ears; all these uses may be found among the peoples of the world. The Quonset huts so familiar to World War II veterans as barracks or office quarters have been subsequently used as homes, garages, storage buildings, barns, factories, and roadside hot-dog stands. In William Morris's Utopian novel, *News from Nowhere,* the Houses of Parliament are reduced to storage houses for dung.

With different uses, of course, go dif-

ferent evaluations and meanings. Paintings may be treasured and displayed or hidden in the attic, seen as great artistic achievements or the scribblings of eccentrics. Automobiles may be visible symbols of social standing or merely practical utilities which provide transportation. Two crossed pieces of wood may be a religious symbol or fuel to be burned in order to keep warm. The division between ideas—knowledge, values, traditional beliefs—and material culture, though often useful, is therefore in a sense quite arbitrary, for to describe cultural artifacts fully it is necessary to know their uses, the attitudes assigned to them, and the body of knowledge and skills needed to produce them.

The organization of culture

It has been necessary, in this description of the components of culture, to refer several times to the complex relationships which exist among the several elements that make up the whole, between institutions and values, for example, or between values and artifacts. These relationships constitute one significant focus of sociological analysis. This analysis may remain at the level of culture in general, or, more frequently, it can be directed toward *a* culture, the cluster or system of institutions, values, beliefs, and objects possessed by a particular group of people. Thus we may consider separately American culture, the culture of India, of the Trobriand Islanders of the Western Pacific, and of the many separate tribes, peoples, and nations of the world. It is only by comparing these specific cultures that we may eventually enlarge our understanding of culture in general.

The components of any particular culture are not randomly assorted, but form a more or less coherent whole. Institutions such as marriage, for example, must be seen in relation to the values that men and women pursue in family life, norms governing the division of labor, and the general values concerning the place of men and women and the rights of individuals. The structure of the culture—its organizing principles and the relations among the parts—is therefore relevant to an understanding of any specific cultural pattern.

The components of any culture, as well as the culture as a whole, can be thought of as consisting of more or less independent systems, each with its own structure or organization. There is in the mores, Sumner pointed out, "a strain toward consistency," and a similar tendency is to be found throughout the culture and within its components—institutions, values, expressive symbols, bodies of knowledge, technological systems. There is nothing automatic about these tendencies; they emerge because men characteristically try to reduce the tension or conflict generated by contradictory or competing demands or ideas, and to maintain some order in their relations with one another.

Role and status

By establishing rules that govern behavior and values by which men judge their own actions and those of others, culture also defines the pattern of social interaction that binds men together in an organized social life. Of central importance in analyzing social interaction are the concepts of *role* and *status*. These concepts provide a link between the analysis of *society* and of *culture*, and are of considerable value in establishing the relationships between the individual and his culture and society. (We shall have more to say of this problem in Chapter 4.)

The concepts of role and status derive from certain basic observations about the nature of institutions. As one considers the variety of social norms or standards of behavior it is apparent that relatively few of them apply universally to all people. Some apply only to limited groups, others only to one person. Some apply in one context in which an individual happens to be; others apply in different contexts. We find these points illustrated by one of our basic and presumably universal mores: thou shalt not kill. The person who commits murder is guilty of the most serious crime in the whole criminal calendar. If caught he may be subject to the extreme penalty, or at least to the maximum possible penalty. But this rule does not apply to certain people under specified circumstances. The policeman in pursuit of his duty, the public executioner carrying out the edict of a legally constituted court, the soldier in battle, even on occasion the husband betrayed—these may kill another person or persons without being subject to criticism or sanction. Nor do we define such killings as murder; our verbal distinctions reveal our social values. The central fact in these illustrations is that the rule does not apply to people who occupy certain *positions* in society. The terms used in our illustrations—policeman, public executioner, soldier, husband—refer to such positions, or, in sociological terms, *statuses*. Each of these statuses carries with it a set of rules or norms which prescribe how the person who occupies it should or should not behave under particular circumstances. That cluster of norms we call a *role*. Status and role are thus two sides of a single coin. Status is a socially identified position; role is the pattern of behavior expected or required of persons who occupy a particular status.

The concept of role is, of course, not new, as illustrated by Shakespeare's oft-quoted lines:

All the world's a stage,
And all the men and women merely players:
They have their exits and their entrances;
And one man in his time plays many parts,
His acts being seven ages.

These ages, or, to use our modern and less poetic vocabulary, roles, included the infant, schoolboy, lover, soldier, "justice," "pantaloon," and lastly "second childishness."

The long ancestry of the idea of social role does not necessarily mean, however, that the concept has been systematically used in the past. One will frequently find that some concept can be traced back to Biblical or classical sources, or to the writings of philosophers or poets or novelists. Our earlier citations of Aristotle and of Adam Ferguson give evidence that many basic ideas have been available for a very long time, a fact that has sometimes given rise to the argument that sociology frequently offers nothing more than familiar knowledge in a new package. What is new about the concept of role, or of many other modern concepts which embody older ideas, is the attempt to organize knowledge systematically, to test ideas against an accumulation of evidence, and to further knowledge by pushing beyond the original perceptions. The atomic theory of matter, it has been pointed out, probably was first formulated by Democritus, but the ancient Greeks possessed no science of physics which enabled them to split the atom. That men play "many parts" is familiar, but the systematic analysis of the relations among them, the processes by which they are acquired and learned, the

"strains" that may exist among the roles one plays, and the relationships between roles and personality provide fresh insight into behavior. Science consists not merely of acute and penetrating observations (as the social sciences are sometimes viewed) but of orderly and cumulative development of knowledge. It entails the integration of findings so that they do not remain the random perceptions of wise men, sometimes erroneous and sometimes only partly true, but become firmly established scientific lore available to all.

Nonetheless we can use Shakespeare's theatrical image to develop and explain the concepts of role and status. The theatrical role performed by "players" exists independently of the individuals, who must learn their lines and acquire the appropriate gestures and manners. Social roles are also learned as men and women acquire the culture of their group, although roles may become so much a part of the individual personality that they are played without awareness of their social character. (It is interesting to note that professional actors have long argued about the extent to which they must "live" their parts in order to perform them well.[18]) Roles are not people; they are the parts played on the social stage, and they can be analyzed separately just as the drama can be considered apart from the performance and the performers.

The elements of a social role are both obvious and subtle. We know, for example, what a teacher is supposed to do in his professional role: to transmit to his students some kind of information or skill, and to follow more or less acceptable and understood methods of doing so. But in some communities a teacher also has been expected to avoid tobacco and liquor, and female teachers are not expected to wear slacks in public. In a study of the sex roles of college women it was reported that many of them "played dumb," belittled their intellectual achievements, and submitted to male leadership and authority when on dates because they felt that this was what men expected of them.[19] In an investigation of local union leadership in the United Automobile Workers it was discovered that union officers were expected to give no evidence of personal ambition. "The worst that can be said of a union leader is that he is an 'opportunist,' or that he is 'ambitious.' "[20]

As these illustrations suggest, many features of a social role are only implicit. As social actors men become aware of some of the rules which govern their behavior only when others disregard them or when the question of ignoring or violating them comes up. An important task of sociology is to discover not only the obvious and explicit norms which define and regulate men's actions but also those which usually remain hidden beneath the surface.

Men can be said to play or perform social roles; they fill or occupy statuses. Status is a kind of social identification tag which places people in relation to others and which also always implies some kind of role. Each man occupies many statuses and plays many roles. A man is a husband or bachelor or widower, a business executive or factory worker or professional, a Catholic or Protestant or Jew. He is a community leader or an ordinary citizen, baseball fan, an avid fisherman, an amateur photographer. Each of these identifications constitutes a status and carries with it expectations of behavior, however precisely or vaguely defined, however rigidly or loosely enforced.

How a person behaves, therefore, depends in large part upon the particular position in which he finds himself—or in which he would like to be—and the role expectations that go with it. For example, a teacher is expected to disregard the sex of his students in assigning or evaluating their academic work. (The occasional teacher-student marriage indicates that sometimes the teacher has failed to ignore the sex of at least one of his students or, more likely, that teacher and student have encountered one another outside the classroom where they could disregard their academic roles and behave as male and female—although these are also socially defined roles and not merely biologically shaped patterns of behavior.) The tightfisted businessmen who is very generous in his contributions to charity and the hard-boiled racketeer who treats his wife, children, and aged mother with love and affection are not necessarily illustrative of hypocrisy or split personality, nor is the Indian warrior who carefully protected his loved ones by joyfully removing the scalps of his enemies. They are all behaving at different times in ways appropriate to the particular status they happen to be occupying and the role they are playing. When a man refuses to raise the wages of his employees or sets out ruthlessly to take business away from his competitor, perhaps even to drive him out of business, he is acting as a businessman; in responding to an appeal from some charity he is behaving as a respected and influential member of the local community. The racketeer may shed his "business" role when he crosses his threshold in the evening.

The importance of social roles lies not only in the extent to which they regulate behavior, but also in the fact that they enable men to predict the actions of others and therefore to fashion their own actions accordingly. Social relationships therefore exist between or among the roles played by members of a society. These

Ascribed status imposes its own demands. Here the heir to several million dollars learns appropriate social skills at a formal dancing class.

relationships are not only indirectly defined by values which provide general standards of behavior—courtesy, respect, obedience—but also by specific institutional prescriptions which indicate how occupants of defined statuses are expected to behave toward one another. Judges are not supposed to give preference to a litigant in a court on the basis of his age, sex, religion, wealth, or color (unless such preference is legally defined). Children are expected to follow their parents' rules as to when they go to bed, whether or not they can go out to play, and what they should eat for dinner. Men should tip their hats to women, walk on the outside of the sidewalk when accompanying women, and rise when a woman enters the room.

As our illustrations may suggest, roles and statuses are built upon various kinds of foundations. Certain biological facts provide the basis for differentiating some roles and statuses. In every society dif-

ferent roles are built upon the facts of age and sex. We distinguish, for example, infant, child, adolescent, adults of different varieties—young adults, the middle-aged, the old. In every society men and women occupy distinct positions and are expected to behave differently, even to vary in character and personality, although societies differ widely in their definitions of sexual roles. Other biological features are sometimes, though not universally, seized upon as the basis for distinct statuses and roles. In Western society, as Talcott Parsons has shown in some detail, the ill person occupies a definite position which permits, encourages, and even requires certain kinds of behavior.[21]

But most roles and statuses emerge from the process of collective living itself. There is always some economic division of labor which entails the differentiation of positions and duties. As men deal with problems of maintaining order and harmony in society there develop distinct political roles and statuses: congressman, M.P., commissar, mayor, party chairman, precinct captain, judge. Religious practices and beliefs provide other grounds for social differentiation: priest, monk, nun, bishop, minister, deacon, rabbi. As societies grow larger and more complex, new positions and new expectations of behavior emerge: movie star, astronaut, probation officer, nursery school teacher, computer programmer, propagandist, atomic physicist, go-fors (errand boys for theatrical producers and directors), beatniks, *tummlers* (social directors in Catskill Mountain resorts—"a versatile *jongleur*, who performed frenetically around the clock and twice as fast on rainy days to keep restive guests from checking out"[22]), and countless others.

Among the many statuses men may come to occupy, we may distinguish those which are *ascribed* and those which are *achieved*. An ascribed status derives from attributes over which a person has no control—age, sex, or color, for example—or from membership in a group to which he is assigned by others—family, religion, nationality. On the basis of an ascribed status he is expected to acquire and perform certain roles. An achieved status is entered upon by some direct or positive action: One must get married in order to become a husband or wife, secure a majority of votes cast to become a Congressman, or graduate from medical school in order to become a doctor. Ascription limits access to status positions: A man cannot become a woman, a Boston Irishman cannot become a Lowell or Cabot, an Indian untouchable can never

be a member of the Brahmin caste. Insofar as the number of persons who can fill a particular status is restricted—only a limited number of students are admitted to medical school, only one person at a time can be President, not everyone can rise to the top in industry—potential occupants must compete, demonstrating in some fashion their abilities to perform the relevant role.

One of the more significant aspects of a status is the value placed upon it, the respect or prestige it carries in the eyes of others. Each position—and its correlative role—is ranked by members of a society as superior or inferior. Doctors in the United States, to take an obvious example, have a higher social standing than pharmacists, and toolmakers rank higher than farm laborers. In many societies

Differences between male and female roles are based only in part upon biological differences; what is deemed appropriate for each sex is to a large degree a cultural matter. BELOW: *This woman is a locomotive engineer in the Soviet Union, where women do many jobs that are usually left to men in the United States and Western Europe.* RIGHT: *In some parts of the world, it is not unusual for men to stand by while women perform tasks thought to be too heavy or difficult for them elsewhere. Indian women are pulling a large roller to crush stones for a road, under the eyes of a group of idling men.*

warriors have been more highly esteemed than merchants or artisans. Thus Herodotus, the ancient Greek historian, observed: "The Thracians, the Scyths, the Persians, the Lydians, and almost all other barbarians, hold the citizens who practice trades, and their children, in less repute than the rest, while they esteem as noble those who are aloof from handicrafts, and especially honour such as are given wholly to war." In classical China, on the other hand, warriors were ranked below scholars.

Status is used frequently to refer only to the ranking of a social position or role, or of the occupants of such roles, and one major aspect of any society is the hierarchy of roles and of persons, which constitutes one aspect of its organization or structure. (We shall examine the hierarchical ranking of statuses and roles and of persons in some detail in Chapter 8, where we deal with social stratification.) This rank order is sociologically important because it contributes to the ordering of social interaction and the structure of social relationships and provides motivation for various kinds of social behavior; the by now familiar term "status-seeking" refers to behavior designed to enhance one's social standing or lead to the acquisition of a more prestigious social position.

Groups, categories, and statistical aggregates

The complex array of roles and statuses that define the behavior of individuals and their relations with one another constitutes what sociologists call *social organization* or *social structure*. The term *social structure* is used occasionally to refer to any patterned regularity of behavior or interaction. This latter use emphasizes the element of pattern in the term "structure," but we shall stress the element of relationship among parts implicit in the word.

Social organization, however, also contains a variety of interconnected and often overlapping groups or collectivities, each with its own particular structure of roles and statuses. In everyday conversation, *group* is usually applied indiscriminately to many different collections of people. A handful of mountaineers operating an illicit still in the Kentucky hills, members of a ladies' club, a teen-age gang in Harlem or the Bronx, a Boy Scout troop, the 60,000 or so workers at the Ford River Rouge plant, the more than a million members of the United Automobile Workers, and the employees of U.S. Steel are all likely to be called "groups." So are the President's Cabinet, the some 100,000 people who each year attend the Army–Navy football game, and the mob of irate southerners who surrounded Little Rock High School when Negro students first tried to enter its doors in September, 1957. Each nation is frequently identified as a group, as are the innumerable families, clans, moieties, and tribes found among primitive peoples. Members of the Catholic Church, Jews, government employees, a movie audience, beatniks, the rich and the poor, those earning from $4,000 to $5,000 a year, members of the Democratic or Republican Party, the Communist Party of the Soviet Union, professors, electricians, bankers, men, women, fans of some popular singer or movie actress, readers of comic books or of sociology texts—each of these is likely to be labeled in ordinary conversation as a group. Within some of these "groups" there may be still others: The Catholic Church is divided into parishes and dioceses, into a number of religious orders such as the Dominicans, Franciscans, and Jesuits; it contains such distinct entities as the college of Cardinals and the Curia Romana (the papal administration). Within the government bureaucracy are the innumerable offices, bureaus, agencies, departments, and interdepartmental committees, as well as informal cliques and sets of friends. Political parties have their national and state committees, precinct organizations, and factions; labor unions have locals, departments, and executive committees.

This legion of groups is obviously so diversified that it would be difficult, if not impossible, to characterize them in general terms. A family, with its relatively limited numbers, its recognized roles and statuses, and its sense of corporate identity clearly differs in important ways from the Catholic Church, with its elaborate hierarchical organization and its millions of members who share a set of beliefs and values and follow the same religious practices; from electricians or bankers who possess the same status but have little if any awareness of a collective identity; and from admirers of a popular singer who are grouped together simply because they share a single attribute. Sociologists therefore face the task of distinguishing types of human collectivities and establishing a precise language for their analysis.

As a first step in performing this task we may distinguish among social groups, social categories, and statistical aggregates.

A social group consists of a number of persons whose relationships are based upon a set of interrelated roles and statuses. They interact with one another in a more or less standardized fashion determined largely by the norms and values they accept. They are united or held together by a sense of common identity or a similarity of interests which enables them to differentiate members from nonmembers. The social group then is identified by three attributes: patterned interaction, shared or similar beliefs and values, and, to use Franklin H. Giddings' phrase, consciousness of kind.

In defining a social group in this way we have narrowed the meaning conventionally assigned to it, limiting its reference and making it somewhat more precise. A family, according to this definition, is a group, as is a labor union, a social club, a number of friends who see one another occasionally, and the students of a college or university. Men, women, owners of television sets, adolescents, hoboes, and readers of *True Story* magazine are not social groups.

These collections of people who do not possess the attributes of a group can be separated in turn into two distinct divisions. One, which we may call a *social category*, consists of persons who have a similar status and therefore in this respect perform the same social role—for instance, men, electricians, adolescents, bankers, or hoboes. The second, which we call a *statistical aggregate*, is made up of persons who possess a similar social attribute by virtue of which they can logically be thought of together—the readers of comic books and readers of *Harper's Magazine*, addicts of rock and roll and admirers of Brigitte Bardot, baseball fans, jazz devotees, and persons who commit suicide.

Although sociologists are chiefly concerned with social groups and categories, statistical aggregates are also, inevitably, important subjects for analysis. Often we wish to explain why people fall into particular aggregates, or to account for the differences between them. Why do some people read *Harper's Magazine* while others read *True Story?* Why do some Englishmen read the pontifical London *Times* while others read the tabloid *Daily Express?* Who are the readers of detective stories, the admirers of rock and roll, the people who commit suicide, and those who become drug addicts? In answering these questions, structural facts—that is, some information about the groups to which men belong and the statuses they occupy—will usually be necessary. Protestants commit suicide more often than Catholics, readers of *Harper's* are more likely to be professionals than readers of *True Story*, adolescents are more likely to prefer rock and roll than are adults. These facts provide the beginning of explanations which require some further knowledge of the nature of the groups people come from and of the roles they play.

Statistical aggregates are also important because they sometimes point to significant aspects of social structure or provide the basis for the emergence of social groups. A common interest in baseball, for example, or in modern jazz or antiques may be one of the ties that bind a group of friends together. Respect for physical prowess may be the basis upon which teen-age gangs select their leaders. An income of more than $10,000 per year may enable its recipients to achieve positions of high reputability in the community. In some cases, persons with similar attributes coalesce into groups: Fans of a popular singer become a mob trying to tear the shirt off his back or, more quietly, join fan clubs; rabid racists establish Citizens' Councils, or ride out in white sheets to terrorize Negroes; admirers of George Bernard Shaw establish Shavian societies.

Social categories share with statistical aggregates potentialities for the emergence of full-fledged groups. Because of

this fact Morris Ginsberg has lumped together as *quasi-groups*

such entities as social classes, which, without being groups, are a recruiting field for groups, and whose members have certain characteristic modes of behavior in common; and other incipient groups such as collections of individuals interested in the same pursuits or favouring the same policy, for example, employers of labour who have not yet formed any association in the defense of their interests, or individuals interested in particular sports, or in social reform, who yet possess no definite organization.[23]

By virtue of their common physical attributes, Negroes, for example, can be classified as a statistical aggregate. To the extent that they are assigned a particular status in society they become a social category. Because of the difficulties stemming from their position they have tended to become "race conscious," to form voluntary organizations devoted to improving their circumstances. They seek to eliminate discrimination and the constraints imposed upon them because they are Negroes and to achieve the status their individual abilities warrant, so that their racial attributes would be reduced merely to attributes characteristic of a statistical aggregate.

One task of the sociologist is to specify the conditions under which the transformation from category or aggregate to group takes place. What forces, for example, lead a social class to become conscious of its existence and problems and to act as a more or less cohesive whole? When do workers form unions, employers an employers' association, or consumers a league for the protection of their interests? Why do movie fans join clubs and professional men join civic associations and professional societies?

The concepts of group, category, and statistical aggregate are sometimes difficult to apply to specific collections of people. Although many human aggregations are readily subsumed under one or another of these concepts, others are ambiguous in character and defy ready classification. From one point of view American physicians are merely a social category, from another they constitute a highly organized and powerful association. Many members of a social class have little sense of a collective identity, but others may be strongly "class-conscious" and seek to develop class-based organizations. Advocates of a proposed reform may be in process of establishing a new political group, and members of an emerging profession may be hesitantly feeling their way toward formation of a professional society.

These concepts, then, serve chiefly as heuristic devices, that is, they suggest questions and direct inquiry. Discussion in general terms of groups, social categories, and statistical aggregates takes us but a short step in the direction of systematic analysis. Merely determining that a particular collection of people is one or the other provides only a minimal beginning for systematic study; after this determination has been made one must proceed to account for the existence of a statistical aggregate, or explore the nature of a particular category and its significance for society, or analyze the structure and functions of a social group.

The definition of a social group is also essentially of heuristic value: It calls attention to significant variables which must be examined. Interaction, values, solidarity, the defining characteristics of social groups, are, after all, variable; they do not possess a fixed "value," if we may borrow mathematical terminology. There may be more or less interaction among persons who stand to one another in diverse kinds of relationships. Members of

a group may subscribe to only one norm or belief or many, or may hold to their ideas with differing degrees of intensity. Members may be strongly or weakly identified with each other; the group, that is, may be more or less solidary. Each of these variables must then be examined and its relationship to others determined.

Types of social groups

The distinction between social groups, social categories, and statistical aggregates, we have said, is only a first step toward the ordering and classification of human collectivities. The enormous variety of social groups, a variety that we clearly recognize in our everyday vocabularly with such terms as *crowd, audience, public, clique, gang, club, fraternity, association,* has led to many attempts to establish a taxonomy of groups similar to that used in biology to classify plants and animals. Theoretically, any such classification must rest upon an explicit principle (the *fundamentum divisionis*) that should have a significant relationship to other facts of social life; to divide men into those with red hair and those without, for example, may make logical or aesthetic sense, but it is not likely to lead to any sociological understanding. Many criteria have been used in the classification of social groups, both those which we have already identified as the variables that define the group and other group attributes such as size, duration, function, and location. Unfortunately, none of these all-encompassing efforts has been very helpful in analysis and research. Sociologists therefore continue to employ categories based upon diverse criteria to describe and analyze various kinds of groups. Although these categories do not meet the criteria of a logical taxonomy—they are not mutually exclusive nor do they encompass all the groups with which we are familiar—they identify the more important kinds of social groups.

Perhaps the central problem in the analysis of groups is the nature of the relations existing among their members. One fundamental distinction is between those groups characterized by close and intimate relations, the *primary group,* and those that lack such relations. The primary group includes the play group, friends, family, in some cases the neighborhood, and even on occasion an entire, necessarily small, society. Relations within a primary group tend to be personal, permissive of spontaneity, and typically (although not necessarily) long-lasting; they are based upon diffuse, generalized mutual expectations rather than upon narrowly defined and precise obligations. Members of a family are expected to love one another, while workers in an office associate with one another only in ways required by their jobs—unless they become friendly, that is, develop a *primary* relationship. The members of a primary group are held together by the intrinsic value of the relations themselves rather than by a commitment to an explicit organizational goal.

The family, although clearly a primary group, occupies a special category. Unlike more spontaneous and informally based groups, its existence is institutionally sanctioned. Although based to some degree on biological facts of sex and age, its structure is defined by law and tradition. Everyone belongs to a family and familial roles are more or less the same for all family groups within a society or a culturally distinct segment within it. We shall explore the nature, origins, and functions of primary groups other than

the family in Chapter 6 and of the family and related institutions and structures in Chapter 7.

Primary groups and relations are often found within larger "secondary" groups such as trade unions, business corporations, governmental agencies, political parties, schools and universities, farmers' cooperatives, and fraternal societies. Many of these groups are *associations,* made up of individuals who come together to seek some similar or common goal or goals, or in advocacy of a like or common interest. As our illustrations suggest, the range of goals or interests around which associations may be organized is extremely large. Moreover, many associations do not confine themselves to a single aim; veterans' organizations, for example, typically lobby for veterans' legislation, encourage their version of patriotism and patriotic values, and provide social centers for their members.

Associations often possess a *formal* or *bureaucratic* organization, a type of social structure we shall examine in detail in Chapter 10. Since such groups are established for the pursuit of specific interests, members come together in limited contexts and for limited purposes. In contrast with the primary group, relations tend to be formal and impersonal, clearly formulated rules govern much of the behavior of members, and possibilities of spontaneity are limited. Roles tend to be segmental, that is, limited in their requirements to the official or formal tasks performed as members of the group, rather than inclusive. A familiar example of formal organization can be seen in the modern office, with its allocation of duties to secretaries, typists, clerks, office manager, receptionist, telephone operator, and others, with clear lines of authority and responsibility, and with the entire functioning of the office governed by a more or less explicit set of rules and regulations, frequently set down in some kind of rule book.

In addition to these two types of organization—the primary group and the formal association—there are other significant kinds of social groupings that must be included in any analysis of the structure of society. *Ethnic groups* are made up of persons who share a common cultural tradition which unites them in a single social entity. From one point of view, any society, with its distinctive culture, constitutes an ethnic group. But within many of the politically unified societies of the modern world some groups are set off to some degree by their practices, beliefs, religion, or language—and in some cases by distinctive physical characteristics as well. In the United States there are the Irish, Italians, Japanese, Chinese, Mexicans, French-Canadians, Jews, Greeks, Indians, and so on. In Belgium there are the Walloons and the Flemish; in Switzerland the German-, French-, Italian-, and Romansh-speaking groups; in the Union of South Africa the Afrikaaners, English, Jews, Cape Colored, and the Blacks (the latter divided into many distinct tribes); in the Soviet Union the Great Russians, Ukrainians, Latvians, Lithuanians, Jews, Uzbeks, Georgians, and several dozen more.

Membership in an ethnic group is ascribed; individuals derive their ethnic status from the family into which they are born and acquire its cultural attributes as they grow up. Sharing a cultural tradition that in some measure marks them off, members of an ethnic group are likely to associate more frequently among themselves than with outsiders and to share a common identity that in turn affects their relations to one another and to others. The clarity with which an ethnic group can be distinguished, the degree to which

its members hang together, and the extent of their loyalty to the group of course vary widely. Moreover, the internal structure of the group is significantly affected by its position in the larger society, that is, its relations to other groups.

Ethnic differences are frequently closely tied to *social classes*, groups that are arranged in some order of superiority or inferiority in society. Although sometimes ill-defined, social classes play an important part in any society. As we shall see in Chapter 8, there are many definitions of social classes still current in contemporary sociology; in fact there is probably less agreement on this than on almost any other major concept. Classes are sometimes identified as groups, sometimes as social categories; in fact they may be either. Some students identify classes by economic position, others by social standing or rank in the community, still others by political power. We need not deal here with the complex problems raised by these diverse approaches; all of these structural divisions are important in the life of a society, and they are typically closely related to one another.

Members of a class share a common position—economic, social, or political—that may be ascribed or achieved. A person acquires his class position initially from his family; indeed, families rather than individuals constitute the units of social class. Even in the United States, where the ideology of "equal opportunity" dominates and status is presumably based chiefly upon achievement, there are obvious advantages in being the son of a rich and well-known man rather than of a poor one. Other societies— India, for example—give much less room for achievement and rely much more heavily upon ascription to place people in the social order.

A common class position is likely to

carry with it similar values, beliefs, and ways of acting—although there may well be differences in behavior and attitude between persons born into a class and those who move into it by their own efforts—or lack of effort. These common characteristics may lead to a corporate awareness or class consciousness that binds members into a social unit and propels leaders to collective action. One problem for sociologists, as we noted earlier, is to identify the conditions under which the shift from a social category to a group occurs and to assess the consequences.

Primary groups, associations, ethnic groups, and social classes are obviously not mutually exclusive and their complex interrelationships constitute a central problem in the analysis of social organization. The ubiquitous primary group is found within associations, ethnic groups, and classes. Associations are sometimes organized by primary groups seeking to achieve a specific goal, and some primary groups will in all likelihood be found within most associations, even the most bureaucratic. Since members of ethnic groups, by virtue of their common culture, and of classes, because of their similar economic or social position, are likely to be thrown together frequently, they typically give rise to a multitude of primary groups which may play a significant role in the organized life of these larger groups.

Classes and ethnic groups provide a "recruiting field," in Ginsberg's phrase, for the emergence of associations. The existence of associations limited to members of one class or ethnic group may be merely a matter of happenstance; they may be confined to one group merely because the members live close together or are thrown into frequent and regular contact. A businessmen's club in a predomi-

nantly Irish or Jewish section of a large city, for example, is obviously likely to be confined to members of one ethnic group, even if they are not drawn together by ethnic interests. Their ethnic character, however, may then affect the aims and activities of the organization. Class and ethnic associations may, on the other hand, represent group efforts to protect themselves or to advance their common interests, as in the case of trade unions, or any of the many organizations formed by the numerous ethnic groups in the United States.

Relations between classes and ethnic groups are often complex, for they substantially affect one another. Discrimination against a particular ethnic group may largely determine its class position; the majority of American Negroes are confined to poorly paid manual or service occupations. Exclusion from opportunities for education or from desirable occupations for racial or ethnic reasons confines members to a low class position. On the other hand, an ethnic group's class position affects the way in which it is treated by the rest of the society. Collective action as well as personal interaction among members of different groups may then be based on a complex intermingling of both ethnic and class interests and attitudes.

The groups we have thus far examined function within a larger territorially defined whole in which men pursue their various activities. This large, inclusive group, when defined in territorial terms, is the *community*. Unlike other groups, it is defined in part by its physical location, which also provides a significant bond of solidarity.

There is an obvious overlap between community and society, and in small cohesive societies they are virtually identical. But within most societies there are usually the geographically distinguished subdivisions which we call towns, villages, hamlets, cities, and, sometimes, neighborhoods within cities. As parts of a larger whole these communities are usually not independent, yet it is possible for men to live out their lives within their borders. Even in the metropolis one finds areas in which many local residents were born and reared, in which they work, find their leisure, marry, have families, and expect to be buried.[24]

In describing and analyzing the community one necessarily examines the diverse groups which take form within it and their relations to one another. One considers the relations of the community to other communities and to the larger whole of which it is a part. But there are also distinctive qualities of the community as such that affect the groups within it, their relations to one another and to the whole. In such conventional terms as *urban, rural, small town,* and *suburban* we obviously recognize the existence of overall differences which warrant close inspection. Some of these differences are readily apparent: sheer size and number, the physical concentration or dispersion of the population, and characteristic occupations. The relevance of these—and other characteristics—to social organization, however, constitutes more difficult and complex problems, to which we shall turn in Chapter 11.

Types of societies

As one considers the diverse groups and the complex combinations and interrelationships to be found among them, one is likely to ask whether it is possible to sort out some overall pattern of social organization characteristic of whole societies. Sociologists since virtually the beginnings of their discipline have, in fact, repeatedly differentiated two broad types of societies within the seemingly endless diversity. Herbert Spencer labeled these types the *militant* and *industrial*; Sir Henry Maine distinguished between a society based on *status* and one based on *contract*; Ferdinand Tönnies differentiated *Gemeinschaft* (community) from *Gesellschaft* (society); Émile Durkheim contrasted societies held together by *mechanical solidarity* and those held together by *organic solidarity*; Howard Becker has identified the two types as *sacred* and *secular*; and Robert Redfield employs the categories of *folk* and *urban* society.

Each of these pairs of categories calls attention in different ways and with varying emphasis to approximately the same social and cultural differences. We can bring together these various contrasts within the more recently coined concepts of *communal* and *associational* societies.

A communal society is typically small, with a simple division of labor and consequently only a limited differentiation of roles. The role of the adult male among the Nunivak Eskimos, to take an extreme case, is roughly the same for almost all men, with some differences only among those who are married, single, or widowed; the only important economic differentiation is between men and women; the shaman alone performs a distinct religious role; and except for chiefs with limited authority and older men who exercise an unofficial and informal leadership, there is no formal structure of political roles. Families and other (informal) primary groups make up the important units within the society as a whole. Social roles are therefore inclusive rather than segmental; they include many aspects of behavior rather than merely some limited segment of an individual's activities.

Because members of a communal society generally perform inclusive rather than segmental roles, they necessarily interact with one another in a wide variety of contexts. Social relationships are therefore long-lasting, inclusive, and intimate or personal. They take on intrinsic significance rather than being instrumental; they are valued (positively or negatively) for themselves rather than as means to other ends. The reciprocal expectations of persons involved in these primary relationships are diffuse and generalized; one must live up to standards of respect, loyalty, affection, or love, for example, rather than merely fulfill specifically defined obligations.

Immediate families and often larger kin groups, small cliques, and perhaps a handful of other subdivisions exhaust the group memberships in the communal type of society. There may be various kinds of organizations based on age, sex, or marital status, though even these are likely to be small primary groups rather than special interest associations. Thus among the Samoans were the *Fono,* the assembly of headmen of the village households; the *Aumaga,* the organization made up of younger men and those not yet recognized as headmen; and the *Auluma,* a loose organization of umarried women, widows, and wives of men not yet in the *Fono.*

In such a social structure behavior is regulated largely by custom; the many facets of everyday life are governed by a complex array of rules and regulations covering the activities of eating and sleeping, hunting and fishing, praying and dancing, and love-making. Action flows fairly smoothly through conventional grooves. With mores exercising a strong hold upon behavior, there is little need for formal law. Law, we might say, is part of the tradition; it is not codified or rationalized, not enacted or dictated but,

emerging from the cumulative experience of the society, is incorporated in the customs known and accepted by its members. The strong grip of tradition does not mean, however, an identity of behavior among men. As Redfield has pointed out, the individual is not a "sort of automaton in which custom is the mainspring. . . . Within the limits set by custom there is invitation to excel in performance. There is lively competition, a sense of opportunity, and a feeling that what the culture moves one to do is well worth doing." [25]

To summarize, in the communal society social roles are inclusive rather than segmental, social relationships are personal and intimate, and there are comparatively few subgroups other than family and kinship units. In this typically "small, isolated, nonliterate, and homogeneous [society], with a strong sense of group solidarity," [26] tradition permeates all aspects of life and the range of alternative patterns of behavior open to individuals is inevitably restricted.

The *associational society,* which is epitomized by the great modern metropolis, is characterized by a marked division of labor and a proliferation of social roles. Individuals must fit into a complex social structure in which they occupy many statuses and play many different and frequently unrelated roles. Whether one is a Catholic, a Protestant, or a Jew is (in principle, though not always in fact) irrelevant to the particular occupation one follows; treatment in a court of law is supposedly unaffected by one's political affiliations and activities, the clubs to which one belongs, and one's economic position. A man's wage or salary is not influenced by whether he is single or married, childless or father of a large brood. The various roles men play are usually segmental; they are limited to specific contexts, confined to a narrow range of activities, and involve the personality of the actor to a limited extent only.

Social relationships in the associational society therefore tend to be transitory, superficial, and impersonal. Individuals associate with one another for limited purposes and social interaction tends to be confined to the specific interests involved.

The prototype is the narrowly contractual relation of buyer and seller in an open market exchange transaction, in which everything is formally irrelevant to the relation except considerations of price, quantity, and quality of the goods being exchanged. The rights and obligations of the parties are specific and definite—neither more nor less than explicitly agreed upon for the specific occasion—and the establishment of any particular associational relation does not imply any other social relations between the participants.[27]

Such relations are essentially instrumental; they are important not in themselves but for the goals or ends which they bring closer to realization. As a result there is less possibility of strong emotional involvement with other persons than in primary relationships.

Life in the associational society loses its unitary, cohesive character. The job and family life are seemingly separated, religion is apt to be confined to particular times and places instead of permeating the whole of human existence, work and leisure are sharply distinguished. As a result, the family does not occupy the same central place in the social structure that it possesses in a communal society. Men belong to various groups, and many of these are bureaucratically organized associations, each devoted to and pursuing its own goals and interests.

In this complex, diversified society, with its myriad groups and competing interests, the pervasive hold of tradition has been largely broken, and the compar-

ative uniformity of thought has been replaced by an almost endless variety. There are relatively few universally accepted beliefs, values, and standards of behavior; the mores have been weakened, and formal law has emerged to regulate behavior and govern social intercourse. Change is therefore rapid; indeed, sophistication and innovation are positively sanctioned in many areas of life. Instead of the tight integration characteristic of communal society, the associational society is loosely articulated and the degree of consensus tends to diminish.

These ideal types suggest some of the ways in which the various elements of social organization are related to one another: As roles change from inclusive to segmental, social relationships tend to become more formal and impersonal; as interests multiply with the division of labor, associations proliferate; as the size of a society—or an association—increases, the tendency toward formal organization is encouraged. Such generalizations provide a useful starting point in the analysis of specific societies.

The distinction between communal and associational society also provides the basis for a historical interpretation of modern society. The long-run trend, some students argue, has been from communal to associational society. The growth of cities, the presumed decline in the importance of the family, the multiplication of associations and the extension of bureaucracy, the weakening of tradition, and the lessened role of religion in everyday life are all adduced as evidence of this transformation. These changes lead on the one hand to disorganization, conflict, instability, anxiety, and psychological strains, on the other hand to freedom from controls and coercion and to new opportunities for individual growth and creativity. This historical interpretation, therefore, is closely linked to both theoretical assertions and moral judgments about the importance of intimate relations, tradition, and common values, and their place in modern society.

The problems that are thus raised not only concern sociology, but also deal with crucial issues in the future of modern society. On what basis can consensus and stability be achieved in an urban industrial society? Is it necessary, in order to solve the social and economic problems of such a society, to return to traditional values and older modes of organization? Are the alternative social and cultural forms appropriate to a complex modern society consistent with such values as freedom, opportunity, and individuality?

Notes

[1] Charles H. Cooley, *Human Nature and the Social Order* (New York: Scribner, 1902), p. 33n.

[2] Adam Ferguson, *Essay on the History of Civil Society* (7th ed.; Boston: Hastings, 1809), p. 4.

[3] For a review of the literature on feral man see M. F. Ashley Montagu, *The Direction of Human Development* (New York: Harper, 1955), Ch. 11. For a detailed description and analysis of a case of a completely rejected child see Kingsley Davis, "Extreme Social Isolation of a Child," *American Journal of Sociology*, XLV (January, 1940), 554–65; and "Final Note on a Case of Extreme Isolation," *American Journal of Sociology*, LII (March, 1947), 432–47. A more recent report on a case of feral man is found in William F. Ogburn, "The Wolf Boy of Agra," *American Journal of Sociology*, LXIV (March, 1959), 449–54. A suggestive psychological interpretation of feral man is offered by Bruno Bettelheim, "Feral Children and Autistic Children," *American Journal of Sociology*, LXIV (March, 1959), 455–67.

[4] For a detailed review of the meanings assigned to "culture," both past and present, see Alfred L. Kroeber and Clyde Kluckhohn, *Culture, a Critical Review of Concepts and Definitions* (New York: Random House Vintage Books, n.d.). For an account of the various ways in which "culture" has been used since the end of the eighteenth century and of its applications in social criticism rather than social science, see the stimulating and suggestive study by Raymond Williams, *Culture and Society* (New York: Doubleday Anchor Books, 1959).

[5] Gladys Bryson, *Man and Society* (Princeton: Princeton University Press, 1945).

[6] Jay Rumney and Joseph Maier, *Sociology: The Science of Society* (New York: Schuman, 1953), p. 74.

[7] Georg Simmel, *Sociology*, trans. by Kurt H. Wolff (New York: Free Press, 1950), p. 10.

[8] Ralph Linton, *The Study of Man* (New York: Appleton, 1936), p. 91.

[9] Ralph Linton, *The Cultural Background of Personality* (New York: Appleton, 1945), p. 125.

[10] R. R. Marett, *Anthropology* (rev. ed.; London: Oxford, 1944), p. 183.

[11] Talcott Parsons, *Essays in Sociological Theory* (New York: Free Press, 1949), p. 203.

[12] William Graham Sumner, *Folkways* (Boston: Ginn, 1906), pp. 53–4.

[13] See Kingsley Davis, *Human Society* (New York: Macmillan, 1949), p. 71.

[14] Robert M. MacIver and Charles H. Page, *Society: An Introductory Analysis* (New York: Rinehart, 1949), p. 24.

[15] John Kenneth Galbraith, *The Affluent Society* (Boston: Houghton Mifflin, 1958), p. 9.

[16] Ernst Cassirer, *An Essay on Man* (New York: Doubleday Anchor Books, 1953), pp. 53–5.

[17] A. L. Kroeber and Talcott Parsons, "The Concepts of Culture and of Social System," *American Sociological Review*, XXIII (October, 1958), 582–3.

[18] See, for example, the selections by William Archer, Constant Coquelin, and Konstantin Stanislavsky in Toby Cole and Helen Krich Chinoy (eds.), *Actors on Acting* (New York: Crown, 1949).

[19] Mirra Komarovsky, "Cultural Contradictions and Sex Roles," *American Journal of Sociology*, LII (November, 1946), 184–9.

[20] Ely Chinoy, "Local Union Leadership," in Alvin W. Gouldner (ed.), *Studies in Leadership* (New York: Harper, 1950), p. 168.

[21] Talcott Parsons, *The Social System* (New York: Free Press, 1951), pp. 439–47.

[22] For an amusing characterization of the *tummler* see David Boroff, "The Catskills: Still Having Wonderful Time," *Harper's Magazine*, July, 1958, pp. 56–63.

[23] Morris Ginsberg, *Sociology* (London: Butterworth, 1934), pp. 40–1.

[24] For a description of such an urban neighborhood, see Michael Young and Peter Willmott, *Family and Kinship in East London* (New York: Free Press, 1957).

[25] Robert Redfield, "The Folk Society," *American Journal of Sociology*, LII (January, 1947), 300.

[26] *Ibid.*, p. 297.

[27] Robin M. Williams, Jr., *American Society* (2nd ed.; New York: Knopf, 1960), pp. 479–80.

Suggestions for further reading

GOFFMAN, ERVING. *The Presentation of Self in Everyday Life.* Garden City: Doubleday Anchor Books, 1959.
A sensitive and perceptive analysis of role-playing and social interaction seen from the perspective of a "dramatic performance."

GREER, SCOTT. *Social Organization.* New York: Random House, 1955.
A suggestive discussion that sees social organization as both structure and process.

HUGHES, EVERETT C. "Dilemmas and Contradictions of Status," *American Journal of Sociology*, L (March, 1945), 353–9.
A good brief description of problems stemming from situations in which men are placed in incompatible roles.

KLUCKHOHN, CLYDE, AND WILLIAM H. KELLEY. "The Concept of Culture," in Ralph Linton (ed.), *The Science of Man in the World Crisis.* New York: Columbia University Press, 1945, pp. 78–106.
A conversation in which several anthropologists explore the concept of culture.

KOMAROVSKY, MIRRA. "Cultural Contradictions and Sex Roles," *American Journal of Sociology*, LII (November, 1946), 184–9.
An analysis of the difficulties faced by college women because of the competing demands of different roles they play.

LINTON, RALPH. *The Study of Man.* New York: Appleton, 1936.
A classic textbook. Chapter VII deals with "Society" and the processes that sustain it. Chapter VIII, "Status and Role," introduced these concepts into sociology and anthropology. Both chapters are still worth careful study.

MACIVER, ROBERT M. *The Web of Government.* New York: Macmillan, 1947, pp. 421–30.
A penetrating summary of the chief characteristics of the "multi-group" (associational) society.

REDFIELD, ROBERT. *The Little Community.* Chicago: University of Chicago Press, 1960.
A seminal analysis of the folk (communal) society by a noted anthropologist.

SUMNER, WILLIAM GRAHAM. *Folkways.* Boston: Ginn, 1906.

The pioneer description of folkways and mores. The gist of the analysis is found in Chapter I; the remainder of the book is largely illustrative and based on materials now substantially out of date.

WILLIAMS, ROBIN M., JR. *American Society.* 2nd ed. New York: Knopf, 1960, Ch. 12.
A statement of the chief characteristics of social organization and an attempt to describe the outlines of social organization in the United States.

ZNANIECKI, FLORIAN. *Social Relations and Social Roles.* San Francisco: Chandler, 1965.
A segment of an unfinished treatise by one of the major figures in the development of sociology that explores in detail the nature and variety of social relationships and social roles.

3

Diversity and uniformity

The variety of social forms

Both culture and social organization display an almost endless variety of forms, a fact that raises many questions and suggests numerous hypotheses of great importance in sociological inquiry. In an age when the rest of the world is daily brought close by modern means of transportation and communication, the enormous diversity of customs, beliefs, habits, and forms of social organization found in human society hardly seems to need elaborate documentation. The veiling of Moslem women, the strange customs of the Eskimos, love in the south seas, Communist political and economic arrangements—these and many other examples of traditions, practices, and social structures that differ from our own are continually reported in the press, radio, and television and, for those who are interested, described in books that are easily available. Yet the prevailing tendency to measure all other customs against our own is so strong that the extent and manner of diversity require constant emphasis.

The full range of cultural and social variation can be found in the vast library of anthropological studies, the reports of perceptive travelers and journalists, and the accounts of the past offered by historians. One is tempted to choose examples of either the trivial or the exotic, the very commonplace and familiar or the most unusual and bizarre, in order to demonstrate how widely human behavior can vary and, incidentally, to stimulate the reader to develop and sustain objectivity in examining his own culture and society. For unusual examples of what others take to be normal or conventional may lead us to look with fresh eyes upon those customs generally taken for granted.

The Andaman Islanders in the Bay of Bengal are not supposed to whistle at night because they believe it will attract spirits; among Americans whistling is supposed to be one way of keeping up one's spirits while walking alone past a graveyard at night. Among the Comanche, brothers may, under certain circumstances, lend their wives to each other for sexual purposes, and certain Eskimo groups characteristically offer their wives for the night to a visitor, practices that Americans and many others would look upon as highly immoral. Hindus refuse to eat beef and Moslems to eat pork, whereas Christians, except for a small group of vegetarians, enjoy both. Among the Toda of South India, to thumb one's nose at another person is a sign of respect; in Western Europe and the United States, to do so is a gesture that expresses defiance and disrespect. Americans and Europeans shake hands by way of greeting; Polynesians rub noses.

These striking illustrations should not lead us to ignore more familiar but less obvious social and cultural differences, which at close range seem to be matters merely of individual preference and personality characteristics. Interest in symphonic music is widespread among some groups in the United States, but Kentucky mountaineers, urban Negro workers, and teen-agers are likely to prefer other kinds of music. Rural folk tend to identify the evening meal as "supper" and urbanites as "dinner," although some city dwellers, particularly in the working class, may retain the rural usage. Class consciousness seems to be more pervasive among the very rich than among other economic groups. Americans with high incomes tend to be Republicans whereas those with low incomes are more frequently Democrats.

The existence of marked differences in the norms, values, and social arrangements found in societies scattered around the world—and within societies—not only raises the scientific question of how to account for social and cultural diversity; it also poses ethical or moral problems that require at least brief comment here. People everywhere tend to consider their own values and beliefs absolute. But if there are marked differences in the rules and values governing family life, sexual behavior, political relationships and practices, economic activities, religious ritual and dogma, and so on, can there be any absolute standards? "The mores," wrote William Graham Sumner, "can make anything right and anything wrong." On what grounds—if any—is it

possible to conclude that one set of norms and beliefs is right and another wrong? One possible answer would be the existence of universally held standards. Perhaps the closest approximation to a universal norm is the incest taboo; yet even though sexual relations between siblings and between parents and children are always forbidden (except in a few special situations), there is considerable variation in the other relatives who are included within the taboo.

From the facts of cultural variation has emerged the principle of cultural relativity, that beliefs and norms valid in one society may be looked upon as false or immoral in another. The principle clearly conflicts with any assertion of absolute truth and has sometimes been attacked as subversive of established belief and even of the maintenance of social order. As is so often the case, however, the same ideas can be used in very different ways. From one point of view, it is true, cultural relativity can provide the basis for a radical critique of existing practices and beliefs. If other peoples seem to live adequately and happily under different norms and with different beliefs, then perhaps one's own culture is not the best or free from defects. If the Samoans allow or encourage premarital sexual intercourse without disastrous results or even with desirable consequences, then perhaps the conventional sexual mores of American society could be changed for the better. If economic activities can be pursued without the stress of competition, then perhaps the widespread assumption that competition is inevitable and is the source of progress is not true.

This kind of radical critique, which was once widespread, has been tempered by recognition of the fact that single beliefs or practices can not be properly interpreted or evaluated without reference to the total context in which they are embedded. If Samoan sexual practices did not produce destructive consequences, it was because of other aspects of Samoan culture and social structure. Borrowing of individual cultural traits is difficult because of the close interdependence of the elements of a culture. From these considerations it would appear that cultural relativity can also lead to a conservative attitude toward norms and values. If culture is relative, then whatever exists in one's own society is clearly appropriate—for that society—and need not be questioned. If the Samoans believe in and practice premarital sexual exploration, then it may be good for them, but it has no implications for appropriate practice elsewhere. The desirability of American Puritanical sexual mores then can only be assessed within the confines of American culture and society; the experience of other societies would appear to be irrelevant. This inference from the doctrine of cultural relativity is as limited as the radical critique which rejected some norms or values out of hand without reference to the total context in which they were located.

The resolution of the conflict between any type of cultural absolutism and cultural relativity and an evaluation of all the moral or ethical implications of cultural relativity clearly pose such complex issues that we can hardly explore them here in any detail. But cultural relativity does lead to at least one important conclusion upon which there may be considerable agreement: that each society, with its norms and values, is one of many, capable of change—in various directions— and is a product of man's effort to come to terms with the world around him and with the needs of an ongoing social order. The awareness of cultural diversity is thus an antidote to ethnocentrism and the basis for a fuller understanding of mankind's common humanity.

Social uniformities

Within the diversity and variety, however, are many kinds of uniformities. On the basis of data in the Human Relations Area Files at Yale University, George Murdock has compiled a list of those features

which occur, so far as the author's knowledge goes, in every culture known to history or ethnography: age-grading, athletic sports, bodily adornment, calendar, cleanliness training, community organization, cooking, cooperative labor, cosmology, courtship, dancing, decorative art, divination, division of labor, dream interpretation, education, eschatology, ethics, ethnobotany, etiquette, faith healing, family, feasting, fire making, folklore, food taboos, funeral rites, games, gestures, gift giving, government, greetings, hair styles, hospitality, housing, hygiene, incest taboos, inheritance rules, joking, kin-groups, kinship nomenclature, language, law, luck superstitions, magic, marriage, mealtimes, medicine, modesty concerning natural functions, mourning, music, mythology, numerals, obstetrics, penal sanctions, personal names, population policy, postnatal care, pregnancy usages, property rights, propitiation of supernatural beings, puberty customs, religious ritual, residence rules, sexual restrictions, soul concepts, status differentiation, surgery, tool making, trade, visiting, weaning, and weather control.[1]

This list, of course, represents a set of abstractions within the broad category of culture, although it includes, clearly, forms of social organization as well (family, kin-groups, status differentiation, division of labor). The list could be both expanded and contracted, and other types of uniformities could be substituted;

there is no final classification of the elements of culture and social organization. Clark Wissler, for example, describes the universal components of culture as consisting of speech, material traits, art, mythology and scientific thinking, religion, family and social systems, property, government, and war.[2] In their classic descriptions of "Middletown," a midwestern American community, Robert and Helen Lynd utilized a set of categories derived from Wissler: getting a living, making a home, training the young, using leisure, engaging in religious practices, and participating in community activities (including government).[3] Couched in other terms, one finds in all societies a family system, a structure of power and authority, religious beliefs and practices, and institutions which govern the allocation and use of scarce resources (economic institutions). The universal elements in culture and society can therefore be identified at different levels of abstraction; the varieties of social life can be categorized or conceptualized in different terms. The explanations which are consequently offered for the regularities and patterns found in social life may then depend on which categories are used.

In addition to universal social and cultural patterns there are also those forms which recur only in some cases. Bureaucracy as a type of social organization is found in all modern industrial societies and, to a limited extent, in some "primitive" societies. Historically it has also appeared in ancient Egypt, classical China, the Roman Empire, and the medieval (and modern) Catholic Church. Similarly, the institutions labeled as "feudal" have existed in many times and areas: medieval Europe, modern Islam, premodern Japan, parts of Latin America. Monogamy is a widespread pattern, but many societies encourage other forms of marriage. Age-grading occurs in a number of societies, as do the levirate (the requirement that a man marry his dead brother's widow), cross-cousin marriage, and inheritance only through the mother's (or only the father's) family. Though some are frequent, none of these patterns is universal.

A major task of sociology is to account for both the diversity to be found in social life and for the recurrent elements in culture and social organization. Why is an incest taboo universally found? Or religion? Or magic? Or status differentiation? Or the division of labor? Why do groups differ from one another in the objects which they worship? In their sexual practices? In the distribution of power and authority? In the organization of economic activities? But societies that differ in many respects also exhibit similar cultural patterns and forms of social organization. The United States and the Soviet Union are dissimilar in many ways, yet both possess highly developed technologies, elaborate bureaucratic organization, and a steadily increasing concentration of the population in urban areas. Virtually all the countries of western Europe and the United States experienced a rise in the birth rate after the end of World War II, yet their family systems differ in many respects. The similarities, as well as the differences, call for explanation.

Human history is full of alternative theories that try to interpret these facts. In the chapters that follow we shall develop a sociological explanation that, we contend, is the most fruitful way of accounting for both the recurrent features of social life and for the differences among and within societies. But so widespread and pervasive are nonsociological theories, particularly those which emphasize biological and geographical facts, that they should be reviewed and evaluated.

Biology and society

The universal recurrence of certain types of cultural patterns and forms of social organization suggests the possibility of a close relationship between them and the biological nature of man. Even if culture is learned, rather than inherited, it is possible that what is learned depends upon innate characteristics? Phrased somewhat differently, to what extent or in what ways are culture and social organization determined, shaped, or influenced by man's biologically inherited equipment, impulses, and drives? Is there an "instinct" for family life? Or for religious belief and practice? Does the incest taboo occur universally because of some innate revulsion against sexual contact with members of one's own family? Are people inherently modest about their biological functions? Do men naturally seek to acquire possessions or to gain power over others?

Given their diversity, culture and social organization can hardly be shaped or molded by inherited tendencies, except perhaps in the most general fashion. Although all societies have some kind of family system, the variations in size, marital arrangements, and division of responsibilities among members, and in the norms governing descent, inheritance, residence, and relations among kin rule out the likelihood that innate characteristics *determine* the nature of family organization. The fact that there are only two sexes and not three or four obviously sets limits on the forms of marriage: monogamy, polygyny (one man and more than one woman), polyandry (one woman and more than one man), and group marriage (a menage of several men and several women, a pattern found so infrequently that some scholars deny its existence). But which of these forms a group adopts depends upon culture, not inherited impulses. The family is rooted in biological fact, to be sure, but its forms cannot be explained biologically.

The enormous range of sacred beliefs, objects, and practices similarly demonstrates the lack of specific inherited patterns of religious behavior. All kinds of objects are worshiped or given religious significance: animals, trees, plants, the sun and moon, particular persons, ancestors, spirits, and many kinds of gods. Religious observances encompass all manner of action and ritual. But, it may be argued, even if no specific religious forms are inherent or instinctive, the prevalence of religion in all societies would surely seem to demonstrate some innate need or impulse in man's nature. The Soviet Union, it has been claimed, provides a test case which demonstrates the inherent need for some religion, for the Soviet government has tried to extinguish religion, only to fail. Not only is there evidence of continued religious faith and practice, but Communism itself, it is argued, has become a new "secular" religion. It seems clear, however, that traditional religion maintains its hold chiefly among older Soviet citizens, and it is still possible that continued antireligious agitation eventually may virtually eliminate traditional religion in the Soviet Union; deep-rooted beliefs are hardly to be destroyed in a short time. The presumed religious character of Communism itself remains to be fully demonstrated. Communism cannot be considered a religion if it merely serves the same functions; for if religion is defined simply by the functions it serves, it becomes impossible to distinguish religious from other beliefs and practices that explain or interpret the character of human life and its relations to the divine, or that bind men together in a morally united community.

In any case, there are in many, perhaps in all, societies nonbelievers who reject or deny the prevailing religious views; despite the popular aphorism, there are atheists in fox-holes. (In a survey of American soldiers during the Second World War, 17 per cent of a group serving in the Pacific and 8 per cent of a group in Italy reported that prayer did not "help at all when the going was rough." [4]) It seems more consistent with the facts available to us, therefore, to conclude that there is no biologically determined inevitability about the emergence of religious belief and practice. In the long run there is, perhaps, a strong tendency for religion to emerge from man's search for answers to certain fundamental problems of human existence, answers usually shared within a group, but at any time and place the extent, degree, and form of religious belief may vary enormously.

From these illustrations and from the knowledge provided by psychology and biology, it seems clear that the impulses or drives, the potentialities for emotional response and learning, are so general and diffuse that they can be molded or channeled in the innumerable ways which an inspection of human societies reveals. As we have pointed out earlier, the *absence* of specific inherited modes of behavior makes possible the development of culture and the substantial variation in the means by which men insure their survival and regulate their relations with one another. The social insects—ants, bees, and others—cannot vary their behavior because their responses and the roles they play are rooted in instinct; in the complex social life of the bee hive, each participant

obeys the dictates of his genetic character. Nonhuman primates—chimpanzees, howler monkeys, baboons, and others—are less constrained by instinct than insects and possess a considerable capacity for learning. But they are limited in their behavior and social development by the absence of culture, a lack which stems largely from their inability to learn or acquire an abstract language. Most primates possess or learn a substantial vocabulary of signs by which they can communicate, although both the range of sounds they can utter and their capacity for abstraction are greatly limited. The biological characteristics which distinguish man from other animals—the upright stance, opposable thumb, larger and more highly developed brain, and the capacity for language—are conditions necessary for culture; they do not account for it.

Other biological facts, however, provide "points of reference" or "foci" around which cultural patterns and social structures inevitably develop. These foci consist of the structural and functional differences between the sexes; the fact that human infants are dependent for a comparatively long time upon others for survival; the organic drives generated by hunger, thirst, and sex; the processes of maturation and aging; and the fact of death. Around these points of reference develop standards governing the relations between the sexes, practices of child care, techniques for securing and preparing food and drink, funeral practices, puberty rites, and so on. In every society men and women, children and adults, have different roles to play. But the norms men obey and the roles they perform—the foods they eat, whether women are modest or flaunt their charms, techniques of child care, how readily children obey their parents, and whether the dead are cremated or buried, worshiped or merely mourned—depend not upon instinct but upon the nature of the society in which men live and its institutional prescriptions. "Human biology," Clyde Kluckhohn has said, "sets limits, supplies potentialities and drives, provides clues which cultures neglect or elaborate." [5]

Race

If biological facts cannot in themselves adequately explain the universally found types of institutions and social structures in human society, perhaps they may account for the differences which exist. It can be argued that the social and cultural differences among the peoples of the world stem from inherent biological differences, that the distinctive qualities of particular groups are hereditary. The lower level of education and economic achievement among American Negroes, some advocates of white supremacy have claimed, stems from an inevitable, biologically based inferiority. Americans and Englishmen possess and value democratic political institutions, it has been asserted, because of an innate predisposition and talent for self-government.[6] Chinese, Russians, French, Germans, and other nations presumably inherit particular talents and characteristics. "Through *my* race," wrote an eminent Mexican painter about one of his works, "will speak the Spirit."

The idea that cultural and social differences stem from or are determined by biological differences, an idea that came to a tragic harvest in recent years, has a long history, although its fullest, most systematic and influential elaboration is hardly more than a century old. Aristotle saw the differences between rulers and ruled, between Greeks, Asiatics, and

northern Europeans, as inherent and natural. "For some men are by nature formed to be under the government of a master; others, of a king; others, to be the citizens of a free state, just and useful." [7] The explicit formulation of a theory which divides mankind into distinctive races, however, came only in the eighteenth century, when the great Swedish botanist Linnaeus identified four races on the basis of skin color: *Americanus rufus, Europaeus albus, Asiaticus luridus,* and *Afer niger.* In addition he established a category which he labeled "monstrosus," to include abnormal types with which he was not familiar.[8] These categories, of course, have since been refined and elaborated by biologists and physical anthropologists. The attempt to link these biological differences to social and cultural variations occurred in the nineteenth century, largely in the work of Count Arthur de Gobineau, a French aristocrat who, with his follower, Houston Stewart Chamberlain, inadvertently provided the theoretical foundations for Nazi-racist doctrine and practice.

As a biological concept, race refers to a number of people who possess common inherited characteristics. Most racial classifications are based on external physical traits: color of the skin, hair, and eyes, head form, type of hair, contours of the nose and jaw, height, body build, amount of body hair. The racial interpretation of social and cultural variation asserts that these biological characteristics account for the level and nature of a particular culture, the form of government, or the frequency of various patterns of behavior. According to such theories, European civilization was superior to that of the rest of the world because of the innate superiority of the white man. Negroes have a higher rate of venereal disease and illegitimacy in the United States than whites, such a theory holds, because of their innate immorality. Whatever distinct qualities are attributed to the Jews (who have been identified both as evil capitalists and evil Communists, as a menace to others because they are superior or because they are inferior) are traced to hereditary capabilities. Such theories gain a seeming plausibility because there are some empirical correlations between racial characteristics and cultural and social forms. It is possible to point to actual differences in behavior, beliefs, values, and social organization between groups that are racially more or less distinct, between tall, blond, blue-eyed Nordics and short, dark, brown-eyed Mediterraneans, between white Europeans and black Africans, between yellow-skinned Chinese and white-skinned Americans. It is then an easy, though not legitimate, step from these obvious facts to the conclusion that racial traits *determine* cultural and social characteristics.

The evidence against this racial determinism is extremely strong. There are, first, serious technical problems in establishing racial classifications and in placing individuals in these categories. The biological traits used in identifying races vary widely, within groups as well as between them. Some nominally "white" Europeans are darker than some presumably "black" Africans. Many "tall" Nordics are actually shorter than the generally shorter Mediterranean. "With each character chosen for measurement, though the averages differ, the extremes overlap." [9] In addition, the physical features used for racial classification do not occur in stable relationships. Black-skinned peoples are among the shortest and tallest; white-skinned people have both very long heads (dolichocephalic) and very round heads (brachycephalic). In a study done in Sweden

in 1897–1898 it was found that only 11 per cent conformed to the "pure" tall, blue-eyed, blond, long-headed Nordic type, although the Swedes are considered to be one of the most Nordic of European populations.[10]

Human history is full of racial mixing and the present racial categories typically include many individuals who are not racially "pure." The great migrations in human history frequently brought one physical type into close contact with another, with inevitable intermixture. No European nation is racially distinct; "white" Americans are a complex mixture of darker and lighter groups, all of whom nominally belong to the same race. Many, probably most, Americans who are labeled as Negro (and many "whites" as well) actually possess a mixed racial ancestry, for there has been considerable miscegenation in the past. "Because of the complexity of human history," a recent statement on race by a group of distinguished physical anthropologists and biologists concluded, "there are . . . many populations which cannot easily be fitted into a racial classification." [11]

Despite the existence of racially mixed populations, or *clines*, as they are technically identified, a large proportion of the world's population probably falls into recognizable racial categories. A recent major study, which sought to describe the world's races, assigned over 90 per cent to the Caucasoid and Mongoloid races and the remaining to the Negroid, Australoid, and Capoid. Clinal populations were distributed on the basis of their "parent races." Both the numerical and geographical distribution and many of the attributes of these races were looked upon as historical as well as biological products, with "distinctive genetic attributes" emerging "through the selective forces of all aspects of the environment, including culture." [12]

Even though it may thus be possible to establish clearly differentiated races and to place each person unambiguously in one or the other of these races, there is still no evidence of any connection between racial traits and the forms of social life. Anthropological, sociological, and historical data provide overwhelming testimony that similar cultures can be found among peoples with very different physical characteristics, and that culture and social organization can change quickly without any corresponding change in racial identity. Nordics have lived under totalitarian political institutions and under democratic ones. During the period around World War I many American writers maintained that the Teutonic peoples have peculiar instinctive talents for self-government; during the 1930s, Hitler created a totalitarian state and justified his actions on the grounds of the innate superiority of the Nordic race. In Africa, hitherto primitive peoples have been transformed under our very eyes into modern national states that are increasingly playing an important role on the world scene.

To put the matter in homelier and perhaps more concrete terms, French cuisine is different from American or English not

United Nations from Monkmeyer

United Press International Photo

United Press International Photo

United Nations

United Press International Photo

The differences among these well-known American Negroes provide evidence that in the United States "race" refers primarily to a social rather than to a biological category. FROM TOP: *Ralph Bunche, United Nations Under Secretary for Special Political Affairs. Sammy Davis, Jr., entertainer. James Baldwin, author. Mahalia Jackson, singer. Lena Horne, singer.*

because of innate culinary talents but because of different cultural and social backgrounds. Hindus refuse to eat beef not because they are naturally superstitious and ignorant, but because they hold cows to be sacred. The permissive or approving attitudes toward premarital sexual experience found in many societies are not the product of innate immorality or of a lower stage of human development but of social and cultural circumstances. If most Negroes in the United States have comparatively little education and hold inferior jobs, it is not because they possess little aptitude for education or are less capable of skilled work and of assuming responsibility, but because of the disabilities to which their social position in American society exposes them.

If skin color, shape of the head, size, and other presumably racial traits do not *determine* what people eat or think or how they are ruled, yet these physical characteristics cannot be totally excluded from sociological analysis. They can provide some of the biological "clues" that a culture seizes upon and uses. Men may develop attitudes and feelings toward skin color; they may respond favorably or unfavorably to the shape of the eyelid. They may order their relationships on the basis of racial differences, confining those with dark skins to menial jobs, or excluding them from schools, or from certain forms of social intercourse. They may justify such behavior with complex theories of race, or with Biblical citations to prove that God intended white and black to be separate. Physical appearance, then, becomes an element the sociological significance of which depends upon the sentiments and values assigned to it. (Not only racial characteristics but other physical traits as well, it should be noted, often come to have social meaning. The present standards of feminine attractiveness in

America, for example, emphasize relatively svelte, sleek lines: among the Ibo of West Africa, feminine beauty "is all but identified with obesity." A society may seek to cultivate the physical aptitudes of the warrior or athlete, or it may minimize these attributes in favor of artistic or intellectual abilities, or it may stress both to varying degrees.)

Popular conceptions of race must therefore be distinguished from the tested knowledge arrived at through scientific investigation. The sociological analysis of racial ideas is different from the biological analysis of racial characteristics. Sociologists are concerned with the opinions and attitudes of people with regard to race and toward specific racial groups and how they affect behavior and social structure. Biologists and physical anthropologists seek to discover the genetic character of human races, insofar as they exist, and to find out whether each race possesses any distinctive traits or abilities. There are, it appears, racially linked traits; for example, only Negroes can suffer from a disease called sickle cell anemia, but as we have seen, there is little evidence that skin color, hair form, or any of the many other biological attributes that have been thus examined exert any determining influence on culture or social organization.

The ideas to which men have subscribed, however, have played a very important historical role. Although they do not constitute the total explanation for the extermination of six million Jews by the Nazis, who considered Jews an inferior race, or of racial segregation in the United States, England, the Union of South Africa, and elsewhere, racial—or perhaps more accurately, racist—ideologies can justify or rationalize the treatment of particular racial and ethnic groups. In time, scientifically established facts and theories may gain popular currency, as they seem to be doing in some areas and among some groups, replacing myth, tradition, and folklore. Such a transition will, of course, have its own sociological consequences.

Sex differences

We have thus far reduced biological facts to a secondary role in the explanation of sociological phenomena—to the status of relevant conditions rather than determining factors. Can we also minimize in this fashion the differences between men and women? To what extent is their behavior determined by inherited characteristics linked with their sex? The considerable variation in the roles played by men and women in different societies suggests the possibility that, except for childbearing, there are no inherent differences, that maleness and femaleness, male roles and female roles, depend solely upon what the culture makes of them. The differences that do exist in attitudes, interests, and behavior seem in many instances readily explicable by reference to cultural facts—the ways in which children are reared and the expectations attached to men and women. American girls are given dolls, encouraged to be "little mothers" and to behave like "little ladies." They are rewarded when they behave in a "feminine" fashion and are likely to be scolded if they try to ape their male playmates or siblings. Boys, on the other hand, are given toy guns or mechanical gadgets and are expected to be aggressive; they are more likely to be allowed to get dirty without being scolded, to run, jump, climb, and in various other ways to behave like a "real boy." Failure to live up to these expectations leads to the unpleasant epithet of

"sissy" and to other pressures to conform to the appropriate masculine behavior. Little wonder that women usually behave like ladies and men usually behave like men.

Yet despite the evidence that sex differences are apparently in many ways cultural rather than biological products, there remain enough recurrent and widespread differences between men and women to refute an all-embracing cultural determinism. In every society different roles are assigned to men and women, and there is some sexual division of labor. The care of young children is almost everywhere the task of women, who rarely participate in military combat, metalworking, hunting, or fishing. Although the father often gives children a great deal of attention—playing with them, fondling them, looking after their needs—the nurturing role, described explicitly in our society as "mothering," is characteristically filled by the mother. There are cases of female soldiers—in Russia and Israel in recent times, in parts of Africa in the past, and the legendary Amazons—but they are very much the exception.

Levels and types of achievement are also significantly different among the sexes. History has seen comparatively few women of great distinction in art, letters, politics, science, and philosophy. There are—and have been—many women of talent who have made significant contributions to these fields, but the towering figures—Dante, Newton, Goethe, Kant, Picasso, Freud, Einstein—have been almost without exception men.

Differences in the expected behavior of men and women are often linked to obvious contrasts in personality. Although there are "masculine" women and "effeminate" men, as well as a few societies in which women take over what we would define as the masculine role and personality,[13] men are on the whole more aggressive and dominating, and many cultures expressly consign women to a subordinate and inferior status.

Finally, despite the greater strength and endurance of the male, women seem to be in some respects biologically superior. Not only do they mature earlier, physically, emotionally, and intellectually, but they are also less susceptible to disease, have lower mortality rates, and enjoy a longer life expectancy.

Are all these differences due solely to culture and society, or do they stem, at least in part, from the complex interaction between inherent characteristics and cultural patterns? There is no clear answer to these questions. We do not know the extent to which—and how—physiological and anatomical characteristics of each sex and their accompanying psychological traits, if any, shape sex roles. In a suggestive essay, Erich Fromm argues that there is a "coloring of character which is rooted in sex differences" derived from such things as the fact that sexual intercourse is always a test of a man's capacity, whereas a woman need not demonstrate anything but must only be willing to participate. Fromm adds, however, "This coloring is insignificant in comparison with the socially rooted differences, but it must not be entirely neglected." [14] There is indeed evidence that the psychological differences derived from biological characteristics can be so overlaid with cultural demands that their influence may not be readily apparent, at least to superficial observation, or is reflected only at deep psychological levels. Culture may virtually reverse the usual roles of men and women, though possibly at some psychological cost to both. The perhaps "natural" submissiveness of women, for example, may be re-

placed by culturally sanctioned aggressiveness, but if women are in fact passive and receptive, as some writers have claimed, then one might anticipate widely ramifying psychological and sociological consequences.

The debate over the "natural" differences between men and women and the "true" characteristics of each is not purely academic. Just as race may be a socially significant idea, so may varying definitions of "femininity" and "masculinity" affect sex roles and the relations between the sexes. Thus Betty Friedan argues, in her widely read and controversial *The Feminine Mystique*, that various sociological and psychological theories that define feminine fulfillment as essentially and naturally sexual and domestic are "self-fulfilling prophecies" that ignore the other activities and interests of which women are capable.[15]

It seems clear, then, that no sociological explanation can disregard such biological facts as race and sex or the conceptions that people have of these facts—but that sociology cannot be reduced to biology. Though the distinctive features of the human species make culture possible, they do not determine its content. Though nature imposes requirements of food, drink, shelter, and sexual gratification, it does not determine how they shall be met. Racial characteristics may influence men's behavior, but only because of the values men assign to them, and not because they are biologically tied to any precisely defined modes of action.

Climate and geography

A second major alternative to a sociological analysis of patterned behavior and group life emphasizes the role of the physical environment. Climatic and geographic interpretations of social life have a long history, dating back, as do most theories of man and society, at least to the ancient Greeks. For a full illustration of a theory which assigns primary importance to climatic variation we may turn to the eighteenth-century French philosopher Montesquieu:

> We have already observed that great heat enervates the strength and courage of men, and that in cold climates they have a certain vigour of body and mind, which renders them patient and intrepid, and qualifies them for arduous enterprises. This remark holds good, not only between different nations, but even in the different parts of the same country. In the north of China people are more courageous than those in the south; and those in the south of Corea have less bravery than those in the north.
>
> We ought not, then, to be astonished that the effeminacy of the people in hot climates has almost always rendered them slaves; and that the bravery of those in cold climates has enabled them to maintain their liberties. This is an effect which springs from a natural cause. . . .
>
> These facts being laid down, I reason thus: Asia has properly no temperate zone, as the places situated in a very cold climate immediately touch upon those which are exceedingly hot—that is, Turkey, Persia, India, China, Corea, and Japan.
>
> In Europe, on the contrary, the temperate zone is very extensive, though situated in climates widely different from each other; there being no affinity between the climates of Spain and Italy and those of Norway and Sweden. But as the climate grows insensibly cold upon our advancing from south to north, nearly in proportion to the latitude of each country, it thence follows that each resembles the country adjoining it; that there is no very extraordinary difference between them, and that . . . the temperate zone is very extensive.
>
> Hence it comes that in Asia the strong nations are opposed to the weak; the warlike, brave, and active peoples touch immediately upon those who are indolent, effeminate, and timorous; the one must, therefore, conquer, and the other be conquered. In Europe, on the contrary, strong nations are opposed to the strong, and those who join each other have nearly the same courage. This is the grand reason for the weakness of Asia, and of the strength of Europe; of the liberty of Europe, and of the slavery of Asia. . . .[16]

The facts upon which this interpretation rests can, of course, be challenged in the light of modern knowledge, but there remain a good many empirical correlations between climate and culture and social organization which lend credence to climatic determinism. Crime, suicide, and marriage rates vary during the year, being higher in some seasons and lower in others. Obviously life in the Arctic is different from that in Bali; life in the Sahara from that in tropical jungles.

The facts of topography, soil conditions, and natural resources supply yet another possible explanation of cultural and social differences. Thus a distinguished geographer has explained the form of most of the world's cities by reference to the topography and soil of the places where they have been built.[17] The presence of the English Channel has been cited frequently as the cause of many of England's distinctive features. The presence or absence of natural resources has been taken as the crucial factor in determining a nation's character and standing in the world of nations.

The evidence against both climatic and geographical determinism is clear and convincing. Widely dissimilar climates and geographical conditions have seen much the same pattern of culture and social organization. The perhaps apocryphal story of the Englishman dressing for dinner in the tropics illustrates this point, as does the historical evidence on the extent to which Europeans and, more recently, Americans have brought their ways of life to the various parts of the globe in which they have settled. June is the favored month for marriage in the United States, but some European peasant societies have preferred November. Conversely, climate and geography have remained the same in many areas in which marked changes have occurred in culture and social organization. The rapid transformation of societies as different as Russia and that of the Manus of the Admiralty Islands of the Pacific may serve as examples. Russia has changed in less than fifty years from a largely peasant society with only the beginnings of industrialization into a heavily urban, industrial society of the first rank. Within a period of barely ten years the Manus gave up a large part of their traditional culture and social structure as they adopted new customs, beliefs, and practices derived primarily from Americans brought to the Southwestern Pacific by World War II.[18]

Like biological facts, however, geographic and climatic facts cannot be dismissed from the analysis of social and cultural life. People everywhere have some form of dress or bodily adornment, but the Eskimos wear furs to protect themselves from the cold while Tahitians wear only a loincloth or kilt of tapa cloth made from the bark of the mulberry tree. Climate and topography may not determine how people behave, but they set problems that must be solved. There is no necessary uniformity in how these problems are met; one can endure tropical climate by stripping to a loin cloth, by sleeping through the hottest part of the day, or by developing and utilizing air-conditioning apparatus.

How people respond to heat or cold, mountainous terrain or level plains, how they utilize the resources they have or meet the problems created by the absence of resources, depends on their cultural equipment—their knowledge, skills, and values—and their social organization. A recent Air Force investigation of responses to climatic conditions reported that ". . . studies of Eskimos produced no evidence that their bodies were better equipped for the cold than those of the white men who are infiltrating their domain. The Eskimos' ability to endure extremely low temperatures seems to be based solely on acquired skills and excellently adapted clothing and diet." [19]

As we examine the world political scene, such geographic facts as the presence of oil deposits, the availability of tin, rubber, and uranium, and the amount of cultivable land possessed by each nation are of obvious significance. But it is important to note that they take on significance because of the values assigned to them. Their usefulness depends upon the knowledge and technology possessed by men. The Middle East was much less important in world affairs when navies did not burn oil; it may become less important as we develop atom-powered ships. The coal deposits of Pennsylvania and the iron ore of the Mesabi range in Minnesota had no significance or value for the aboriginal American Indians; modern Americans have erected an industrial civilization upon them.

Not only is geography unable to determine the form of society or shape its culture, it may itself be affected by human action, for men can change to some degree the physical environment in which they live. Agricultural practices can lead to the erosion of once fertile soil; witness the present state of the Tigris and Euphrates valleys, once the center of a flourishing agriculture and a great civilization. Unrestrained leveling of forests can lead to excessive run-off of water and damaging floods. But if men can create deserts they can also make the desert bloom, as the Israelis have done in once barren areas of their tiny nation. Rivers can be rechanneled, dams built, arid lands irrigated, mountains lowered, and tunnels built. As man leaves his imprint on soil, topography, and the flow of waters, the impact of these natural circumstances upon society is changed.

Conclusion

Biology, geography, and climate therefore have no independent significance in any explanation of the form and content of culture and social organization. They are clearly relevant, socially and culturally, at many points as necessary conditions and as circumstances which impose limits, set problems, provide opportunities. But the central focus of any analysis of the differences and uniformities found as one compares or examines cultural norms and social structures must remain on a distinctively sociological level. "We must . . . seek the explanation of social life in the nature of society itself," wrote

the influential and distinguished French sociologist, Émile Durkheim.[20] Sociology, we have said, cannot be reduced to biology; nor can it be translated into either geography or meteorology. It contains a variety of theories within itself, but these all share the premise that sociology possesses a distinctive subject matter and point of view which are independent of the theories and perspectives of other disciplines.

There remains, however, one final problem to which we must address ourselves before we can accept this premise as the basis for all of our subsequent discussion and analysis. Is it possible that society and culture are merely projections of the individual? Will a knowledge of psychology enable us to account for social phenomena? From our discussion thus far it would seem clear that sociology cannot be reduced to psychology, but it is still necessary to examine the problem and to consider the relationship between individual and society.

Notes

[1] George Peter Murdock, "The Common Denominator of Cultures," in Ralph Linton (ed.), *The Science of Man in the World Crisis* (New York: Columbia University Press, 1945), p. 124.

[2] Clark Wissler, *Man and Culture* (New York: Crowell, 1923), p. 74.

[3] Robert S. Lynd and Helen M. Lynd, *Middletown* and *Middletown in Transition* (New York: Harcourt, 1929 and 1937).

[4] Samuel A. Stouffer *et al.*, *The American Soldier, II: Combat and Its Aftermath* (Princeton: Princeton University Press, 1949), 174.

[5] Clyde Kluckhohn, "Universal Categories of Culture," in Alfred L. Kroeber *et al.*, *Anthropology Today* (Chicago: University of Chicago Press, 1953), p. 513.

[6] See, for example, John W. Burgess, *Political Science and Comparative Constitutional Law*, I (Boston: Ginn, 1896), 37–9.

[7] Aristotle, *Politics*, trans. by William Ellis (London: Dent Everyman's Edition, 1912), p. 103.

[8] For a review of the development of racial categories until 1900 see Gustav Retzius, "The Development of Race Measurements and Classification," in Alfred L. Kroeber and Thomas T. Waterman (eds.), *Source Book in Anthropology* (rev. ed.; New York: Harcourt, 1931), pp. 94–102.

[9] Raymond Firth, *Human Types* (rev. ed.; New York: New American Library, 1958), p. 20.

[10] *Ibid.*

[11] *The Race Concept* (Paris: UNESCO, 1952), p. 11.

[12] Carleton S. Coon, with Edward E. Hunt, Jr., *The Living Races of Man* (New York: Knopf, 1965), pp. 9–10.

[13] See Margaret Mead, *Sex and Temperament in Three Primitive Societies* (New York: Morrow, 1935), Part I: "The Mountain-Dwelling Arapesh."

[14] Erich Fromm, "Sex and Character," in Ruth N. Anshen (ed.), *The Family: Its Function and Destiny* (New York: Harper, 1949), pp. 375–92.

[15] Betty Friedan, *The Feminine Mystique* (New York: Norton, 1963).

[16] Charles-Louis de Montesquieu, *The Spirit of Laws*, I, trans. by Thomas Nu-

gent, rev. by J. V. Pritchard (New York: Appleton, 1900), pp. 315, 317–8.

[17] Griffith Taylor, *Urban Geography* (New York: Dutton, 1949).

[18] See Margaret Mead, *New Lives for Old* (New York: Morrow, 1956).

[19] *The New York Times,* July 23, 1957. The story described an attempt by the Air Force to test pills that would help men keep warm under Arctic conditions. It included the fact that researchers had some evidence that Negroes tended to chill more easily than whites, although the reasons for this difference were unclear.

[20] Émile Durkheim, *The Rules of Sociological Method,* trans. by Sarah A. Solovay and John H. Mueller (Chicago: University of Chicago Press, 1938), p. 102.

Suggestions for further reading

BIERSTEDT, ROBERT. *The Social Order.* Revised edition. New York: McGraw-Hill, 1963, Chs. 2, 3, 12.
A useful, well-written discussion in a recent textbook of the influence of geographical and biological factors on society. Chapter 10 examines the nature and source of differences between men and women.

COON, CARLETON S., WITH EDWARD E. HUNT, JR. *The Living Races of Man.* New York: Knopf, 1965.
An effort to describe and account for the characteristics and distribution of races.

DUNN, L. C., AND THEODOSIUS DOBZHANSKY. *Heredity, Race, and Society.* New York: Penguin, 1946.
A brief analysis of individual and group differences in hereditary characteristics by two distinguished geneticists.

HUNTINGTON, ELLSWORTH. *Mainsprings of Civilization.* New York: Wiley, 1945.
"An attempt to analyze the role of biological inheritance and physical environment in influencing the course of history." Written by a distinguished ge-

ographer who overemphasizes the importance of geographical factors.

MEAD, MARGARET. *Male and Female.* New York: New American Library, 1955.
A full-scale attempt by a noted anthropologist to determine what is inherent and what is acquired in sexual roles and behavior.

MONTAGU, M. F. ASHLEY. *The Direction of Human Development.* New York: Harper, 1955.
A detailed examination of the biological bases of personality and social life. The author argues the innate goodness of human nature and attributes human flaws—moral and otherwise—to "human nurture."

MONTAGU, M. F. ASHLEY. *Man's Most Dangerous Myth: The Fallacy of Race.* New York: Columbia University Press, 1942.
A criticism of the concept of race as "An Ugly Human Error" and an examination of the relationship between group differences in physical characteristics and society and culture.

MURDOCK, GEORGE PETER. "The Common Denominator of Cultures," in Ralph Lin-

ton (ed.), *The Science of Man in the World Crisis.* New York: Columbia University Press, 1945, pp. 123–42.
An attempt to explain cultural universals by reference to the ways in which people learn.

SERVICE, ELMAN R. *A Profile of Primitive Culture.* New York: Harper, 1958.
Brief summaries of the culture and social structure of twenty societies: primitive bands, tribes, "primitive states,"

and peasant communities. *A useful review of the great variety found in human institutions, beliefs, and forms of organization.*

SOROKIN, PITIRIM. *Contemporary Sociological Theories.* New York: Harper, 1928, Ch. 3.
A critical review of geographical theories and interpretations of society and behavior.

4

Culture, society, and the individual

Sociological and psychological perspectives

Human life, we have said, is group life. The isolated individual is a philosopher's fiction—Rousseau's "noble savage" and Hobbes's presocial man engaged in a perpetual war against others—or a tragic accident, as in the case of feral man. Men do not live apart, each seeking a private solution to the problems of survival. They live together, sharing a common way of life (a culture) that regulates their collective existence and provides methods for adapting to the world around them and for controlling and manipulating to some degree the forces of nature.

In viewing human experience from a sociological perspective which emphasizes the collective features of social life and the shared and patterned aspects of behavior, we seem to neglect the individual person. Sociologists study society and culture, social relationships and social norms, shared beliefs and common values, social structure and patterned behavior, as distinct from the individuals who conform to or deviate from social norms, subscribe to beliefs and values prevalent in their group, and participate in relationships embodied in social structures. Yet society and culture, as well as all the other abstractions we have used, do not, except in a metaphorical sense, live, behave, respond, adapt, adjust. Only

individuals, alone or with others, act. All that we can observe is these individuals—who differ in some respects from one another—as they attend school, take marriage vows, look after children, work, vote, make political decisions, write books, go to church, and engage in the myriad other activities that make up a way of life. Culture and society become tangible only in the minds and actions of individuals.

Because the abstract character of sociological concepts and sociological analysis seems to contrast sharply with the concreteness of human behavior, it is necessary to consider the relationship between the individual and culture and society. The warrant for a point of view that seems to disregard the individual is both substantive and methodological; it lies not only in the nature of that relationship but also in the fact that it is possible to distinguish, for analytic purposes, between psychological and sociological aspects of behavior.

In its use of abstractions, sociology, as we noted earlier (see Chapter 1), is no different from other scientific disciplines. Psychology, which focuses upon the individual and his personality, also uses abstractions—ego, attitude, drive, stimulus, repression, learning, reinforcement—and psychological propositions are general statements about the relationships among variables. It is precisely the process of abstraction and the manipulation of the resulting ideas that constitute the core of any science.

Society and culture on the one hand and personality and the individual on the other are not sharply differentiated entities; they simply represent different conceptual foci for exploring the nature and sources of human behavior. Edward Sapir has graphically distinguished these alternative perspectives:

If I see my little son playing marbles I do not, as a rule, wish to have light thrown on how the game is played. Nearly everything that I observe tends to be interpreted as a contribution to the understanding of the child's personality. He is bold or timid, alert or easily confused, a good sport or a bad sport when he loses, and so on. The game of marbles, in short, is merely an excuse, as it were, for the unfolding of various facts or theories about a particular individual's psychic constitution. But when I see a skilled laborer oiling a dynamo, or a polished mandarin seating himself at the dinner table in the capacity of academic guest, it is almost inevitable that my observations take the form of ethnographic field notes, the net result of which is likely to be facts or theories about such cultural patterns as the running of a dynamo or Chinese manners.[1]

The same item of behavior can thus be conceptualized from either a psychological or sociological point of view. Human conduct may be seen in relation to the structure and dynamics of the individual personality, or it may be viewed in relation to the organization and functioning of culture and society. The purchase of a mink coat, for example, may be looked upon as an action providing some kind of ego gratification for the buyer (or her husband), or as behavior contributing to the status of the woman (or her family). These perspectives are obviously those of psychology and sociology. They may be linked together, of course, in the observation that the buyer derives her ego gratification in part from the status she gains.

In conceptualizing the same phenomenon differently the sociologist and psychologist are led to ask different questions. Each approach enables us to explain some aspects of behavior; neither alone can explain the totality of behavior. The sociologist seeks to explain, for example, why the rate of alcoholism is low among Jews and high among Irish Catholics. The relevant questions would be: What are the differences in experience, values, attitudes, and social relationships that might be related to drinking? If one were to try to explain why any one individual—Jew or Irish Catholic—was an alcoholic, the answer would have to consider the structure of the personality, emotional stresses and tensions, and prior personal experience. Alcoholism can thus be considered as an affliction of an individual or as a patterned form of behavior occurring at a given rate in each group.

The distinctive perspectives and preoccupations of psychologist and sociologist have frequently led to distorted interpretations of human behavior against which each must guard. In his concern for the individual the psychologist has on occasion lost sight of the influence of social norms and social structure on personality. On the other hand the sociologist has sometimes reified such concepts as culture, society, institution, and role, transforming them from bloodless abstractions based on observation of repeated actions into concrete, active entities that presumably coerce individuals to ends or purposes distinct from those of living, acting, human beings.

Nor should the fact that it is both possible—and fruitful—to distinguish sociological and psychological perspectives from one another obscure the obvious interdependence of individual and society. Each person is simultaneously a carrier of culture, a participant in group life, and a distinctive personality—as well as a sentient biological organism. Personality is to a large extent a social product, while psychological traits are related in complex and subtle ways to culture and social structure.

The individual as a social product

Yet in a sense culture and society transcend the individual, for they are not dependent upon any specific person or persons in whose attitudes and actions they find expression. As Ralph Linton has observed:

Unpleasant as the realization may be to egotists, very few individuals can be considered as more than incidents in the life histories of the societies to which they belong. Our species long ago reached the point where organized groups rather than their individual members became the functional units in its struggle for survival.[2]

Culture possesses an obvious continuity that extends beyond the lifetime of those who possess, create, and utilize it, and the structure of a society persists despite the continual replacement of its members.

Without society, the individual cannot survive. As we saw earlier, men possess no instinctive skills or knowledge, and no inherited patterns of behavior other than such automatic responses, or reflexes, as grasping, sucking, the knee jerk (*patellar*) response, blinking, and so on. The instruments with which men cope with their environment and organize their collective existence are derived from culture. Moreover, the infant requires not only the satisfaction of physical needs by others for a relatively long time, compared to

other animals, but also their attention and care. This observation is hardly new; in the thirteenth century the Emperor Frederick II conducted an experiment that demonstrated the point clearly:

His second folly was that he wanted to find out what kind of speech and what manner of speech children would have when they grew up, if they spoke to no one beforehand. So he bade foster mothers and nurses to suckle the children, to bathe and wash them, but in no way to prattle with them or to speak to them, for he wanted to learn whether they would speak the Hebrew language, which was the oldest, or Greek, or Latin, or Arabic, or perhaps the language of their parents, of whom they had been born. But he laboured in vain, because the children all died. For they could not live without the pettting and the joyful faces and loving words of their foster mothers. And so the songs are called "swaddling songs," which a woman sings while she is rocking the cradle, to put a child to sleep, and without them a child sleeps badly and has no rest.[3]

This conclusion has gained empirical support from modern research, particularly studies by René Spitz, who compared infants in a foundling home with children in an isolated fishing village where physical conditions were difficult, with a group of middle-class infants, and particularly with babies in a nursery attached to a penal institution for delinquent girls.[4] In the foundling home nutritive, hygienic, and medical care were good, but the children received little personal attention from the nurses. (Each nurse, however motherly she might be, could spend little time with one child while responsible for eight.) In the penal institution, physical conditions were equally adequate, but the children were looked after much of the time by their mothers. The conclusion drawn from comparison of these groups was that the absence of "maternal care, maternal stimulation, and maternal love" led not only to limited physical and emotional development, but also to a high mortality rate. Or, in the words of a distinguished psychoanalyst, "Babies who aren't loved don't live." [5] (This conclusion applies, however, chiefly to the latter half of the first year of life.) Spitz's specific findings have been challenged, chiefly on methodological grounds, but other research has generally sustained the verdict that "adequate 'mothering' or 'parenting' has vital significance for development." [6]

Each individual is born with a more or less distinctive physical equipment that will grow and mature. He enjoys a capacity for learning which distinguishes him from other animals. He has drives and needs—hunger and food, thirst and drink, libido (to use the Freudian term) and sexual gratification, as well as potentialities for emotional response—anger, fear, love, hate. But genetic traits and individual potentialities unfold and take on form only in the course of experience in a social environment. The individual learns to satisfy his needs in a socially approved fashion. What he eats and how often, whether he drinks cow's milk, goat's milk, or the fruit of the vine, whether he has a single sexual partner or many—all depend upon the culture. His likes and dislikes, hopes and ambitions, his interpretations of society itself and of the supernatural (if he comes to believe in the latter) are derived from the social world around him. In short, he becomes a social being as he absorbs a culture that enables him to survive and to live in society and that guides his actions and gives meaning to his existence.

Even such ostensibly "private" experiences as emotional response and perception are influenced by culture, as mediated through the activities of other persons with whom one interacts. In a perceptive study of hospital patients, for example, Mark Zborowski found that members of various ethnic groups responded very differently to the experience of physical pain. "Old Americans" tended to maintain a stoical attitude, although they might give way to crying or groaning—if no one was present—when the pain became acute. Both Jews and Italians, on the other hand, were likely to be "very emotional," complaining, groaning, moaning, or crying without any sense of shame. The Italian, however, when relieved by drugs "easily forgets his suffering and manifests a happy and joyful disposition." The Jew, on the other hand, remained concerned about the source of his pain and often was reluctant to take analgesic drugs for fear they might hide important symptoms.[7]

The influence of culture on perception may be illustrated by the "moralistic story of the countryman and the cricket."

Walking down a busy city street one day the countryman seized his city-bred friend by the arm, crying, "Listen to the chirp of the cricket!"

The urbanite heard nothing until the bucolic friend led him to a crack in the face of a building where the cricket was proclaiming his presence unheard by the passing throngs.

"How can you hear such a little sound in the midst of all this noise?" the city man wondered.

"Watch," his friend replied as he tossed a dime upon the sidewalk. Whereupon a dozen people turned at the faint click of the coin.[8]

Sociological explanation and the individual

The close dependence of the individual upon his social milieu makes it possible to account for some aspects of human behavior without direct reference to psychological characteristics. Since people tend to follow the norms of the groups to which they belong, knowledge of an individual's group affiliations and of the attributes of those groups is likely to be sufficient to predict and account for his actions. If one knows the social class of an Englishman, one can predict quite accurately whether he will say "house" or "home" when referring to his residence (the former is upper class, the latter is not), or whether he will say "rich" or "wealthy" when referring to his—or anyone else's—economic circumstances (the former is upper class, the latter is not).[9] It is a safe prediction that middle-class Americans—who may have very different personalities—have only one wife; call their evening meal "dinner"; own a car, washing machine, dryer, and television set; and hope to send their children to college.

One can also assume that persons who have shared similar experiences and possess common social characteristics will behave, on the whole, in approximately the same fashion in the same situations, even when their behavior is not institutionally prescribed or when alternatives are left open to them by the culture. Because their values and perspectives are alike, they tend to see the world and react to it in much the same way. If Americans share a common economic status, place of residence, and religious background, for example, it is possible to predict, with a reasonable degree of reliability, how they will vote in national elections. (The degree of predictability is increased if one excludes the largely one-party South.)

The same explanatory model can help to account for variations in behavior. If one finds differences in language, dress, voting, eating habits, relations between parents and children, attitudes, beliefs, and so on, one need not explore the psychological attributes of each individual but can find an adequate explanation in the varied social experiences people have had and the contrasting norms and social structures of the groups to which they belong.

It must be understood, however, that the specific empirical conclusions which follow from these propositions are always statements of relative frequency or probability. Manual workers, on the whole, tend to think of themselves as belonging to the working class, but one nationwide study found that only 77 per cent of urban manual workers identified themselves in this fashion.[10] Most persons "swear" to perform their duties faithfully when they take an oath of public office in the United States, but a small number only "affirm" that they will do so. Or, to take a different type of finding, morale of industrial workers tends to be high when there are well-established work groups in the factory; when workers have not established personal relationships with one another morale is likely to be low.[11]

These empirical findings are couched in statistical terms in part because of the complexity of social life. Manual workers possess, in addition to their occupations, many other attributes that may influence their class identifications. For example, those manual workers who do not consider themselves members of the working class tend to have more education and to come from white-collar families more frequently than those who accept a working-class identification.[12] Those who "affirm" their responsibilities are Quakers whose religious beliefs keep them from "swearing" in a conventional manner. Many other factors in addition to relations with fellow workers may influence morale in the factory; low wages or an unpleasant foreman can offset a congenial group of co-workers, and an interesting job can make up for the absence of pleasant social relationships. As it is virtually impossible to take into account all the social and cultural variables that affect human behavior, there must always be some margin of error in sociological analysis and prediction. In this, of course, sociology is not peculiar, for all empirical research suffers, to a greater or lesser degree, from the same disability.

The fact that the individual is largely a social product and that it is therefore possible to account for many aspects of his behavior by reference simply to culture and social organization does not mean that he is merely a passive instrument of his society. The relationship between society and the individual is not that of puppeteer and puppet, with the individual pulled hither and yon as the strings are manipulated. "No anthropologist [or sociologist]," wrote Ruth Benedict, "with a background of experience of other cultures has ever believed that individuals were automatons, mechanically carrying out the decrees of their civilization." [13] The individual is not merely a tape recording of his culture, if we may shift the metaphor, even if he sometimes plays back parts of the recording as various occasions require. He must be seen as an active being who is likely to behave in a more or less standardized fashion, but who also possesses the capacity for innovation and deviation and may through his actions significantly influence and change the nature of his culture and society.

The tendency to conform to cultural requirements and social expectations cannot be seen as "normal," but must be taken as problematical; it is not something to be assumed, but a fact to be explained. We need to explore, therefore, the process by which the organism becomes a person capable of participating actively in the life of society and to examine the relevance of personality and psychological dynamics for the structure and functioning of society.

Agencies of socialization

The process of *socialization*, which transforms the raw human material into a social being, serves two major functions. On the one hand, it prepares the individual for the roles he is to play, providing him with the necessary repertoire of habits, beliefs, and values, the appropriate patterns of emotional response and modes of perception, the requisite skills and knowledge. On the other hand, by communicating the contents of the culture from one generation to the other, it provides for its persistence and continuity.

The chief agency in this process is usually the family or kinship group. In ministering to the needs of the helpless infant, the parents—initially, in most cases, the mother—establish a relationship with him that is of central importance in his future development. The child discovers how to secure satisfaction of his bodily requirements by communicating, through sound and gestures, with others. First as a largely passive member of the family and then more actively, he learns to play appropriate roles and acquires the abilities, attitudes, and modes of response that enable him to participate in social life outside the family circle. Because one's earliest and closest ties are usually with parents, siblings, and sometimes other kinfolk, family experience and expectations carry a special emotional weight and are therefore of particular importance in shaping personality and transmitting cultural demands and expectations.

Everywhere, however, there are also other persons or groups that participate in the socialization process. Occasionally other agencies may almost replace the family. The Israeli kibbutz, for example, assigns care of small children to a communal nursery, except for the few hours each day that they spend with their parents. When children are old enough to leave the nursery they still remain with their age-mates in a communal setting rather than with their families. Peer groups, in fact, are found in most societies, and in some they serve important functions in defining appropriate behavior, setting standards, and inculcating goals. Through various institutionalized sanctions they may also enforce conformity to established norms, including those specific to their age group.

In contrast with the family, which is typically more authoritarian (and, from the child's viewpoint always so in some degree) and more likely to transmit traditional values, the peer group usually offers a more egalitarian experience, although it too may on occasion become rigidly authoritarian in its demands upon its members. Within the peer group there are often opportunities to explore topics tabooed in relations with adults, and to secure support from others as young people seek to break away from parental constraints and establish an independent identity.

The family alone cannot adequately train children for many adult roles in a complex industrial society, and other agencies, particularly the school, therefore also contribute significantly to preparation for adult life. Not only is the school expected to transmit skills and practical knowledge, but important cultural values as well: patriotism, ambition,

concern for others, and so on. The impact of the school is affected, of course, by family attitudes and behavior, which can facilitate formal educational efforts or impede them. The school itself includes both the formal organization, with prepared curriculum and established procedures, and the teachers, with whom students can establish personal relationships that may significantly affect their attitudes and behavior. It also provides a convenient center for the development of informal, though often important, peer groups. (For a full discussion of education, see Chapter 15.)

Finally, in contemporary society, the mass media contribute to the socialization of the child—and the continuing socialization of the adult. In the information they make available, the models of behavior they provide, the values they express and illustrate, the experiences—vicarious thrills, entertainment, horror, and so on—they offer, the mass media can reinforce the efforts of family and school, or weaken and dilute them. Children can learn directly from the media, which also communicate to parents and peers standards of behavior they then transmit. The media may be deliberately utilized for education and indoctrination, as in educational television in the United States or in the exploitation of all forms of mass communication in authoritarian societies where the regimes systematically try to spread and sustain the values that they approve.

In a complex and heterogeneous society lacking "official" values and with no central direction and control, the influence of the mass media is usually unplanned and uncertain, potentially dysfunctional in relation to prevailing standards of some groups, or to those of the whole society. Even in a totalitarian society there may be a gap between intention and result, with unanticipated and unwanted consequences flowing from both the content and the techniques of the media.

Unlike a traditional and relatively stable society in which the agencies of socialization are limited and tend to function together harmoniously, a complex modern society subjects the individual to a diverse array of socializing influences that are not likely to be consistent with one another. The child hears in Sunday School that "the meek shall inherit the earth," but he may also witness admiration for the strong and powerful on the part of his parents and in the mass media. The eleven-year old whose parents are reluctant to discuss "the facts of life" may see a photograph of an unborn foetus on the cover of *Life* magazine and be able to read a detailed, fully illustrated account of its development. The expectations of parents and peer groups often conflict, and the schools may demand more—or less—from the child or young adult than his parents have prepared him for. (The contemporary unwillingness of American college and university administrators to serve *in loco parentis*, in part because of student pressure, creates difficulties for some students not yet ready for a fully independent adult role.)

The consequences of such inconsistency are complicated and varied. On the one hand the individual may find himself uncertain and ill-prepared for playing the roles expected of him, or even, in some instances, with serious internal conflicts. On the other hand, as he learns to cope with diverse influences and pressures, he may become more autonomous, that is, more capable of making independent judgments about the desirability of conforming to cultural norms. The conditions that determine the outcome have yet to be adequately delineated.

In a changing society, both the techniques for training a child and the substance of that training usually combine the new and the traditional. Mothers may rely upon what their mothers told them and also upon the latest advice from the child-care specialist. The schools seek to inculcate and reinforce many of the traditional moral verities while teaching new skills and exploiting modern techniques. To some extent parents and teachers inevitably express in the methods they use a carry-over from their own earlier experience at the same time that they are responding to the changes that have taken place in the world in which they live.

The socializing agencies themselves are continually subject to external forces that affect their socializing function. Modern science, communicated through the schools and the mass media, has influenced the ways in which parents look after their children, take care of their needs, and respond to their behavior. Governmental bodies impose controls over the contents of the mass media and governmental programs determine the resources available to the schools. For families that are unable to provide adequately for their children, for either economic or psychological reasons, there may be aid and support from welfare agencies of various kinds. A changing economic order and expanding technology lead to changes in the schools and to a redefinition of the qualities encouraged in children as prerequisites for success.

The process of socialization

Socialization is a complex and multifaceted process. As he grows, each individual's biological impulses are directed into culturally patterned channels. Appropriate responses are "reinforced," inappropriate ones "extinguished" by a system of rewards and punishments. He learns which gestures or actions elicit food, cuddling, or elimination of discomfort, and how he is expected to respond to the actions of others. Eventually, he comes to eat three meals each day rather than two, to handle food with implements rather than stuffing it into his mouth with his fingers, to perform his bodily functions at the appropriate time and in the appropriate place. Much of this learning, then, consists of the development of habits that conform to the customs of the society.

The channeling of drives and the acquisition of acceptable habits are not mechanical processes but are linked with judgments of right and wrong, good and bad. One not only learns to do something in a particular way, but also that it is the right or correct way. Values, which reinforce and sustain many habits, are learned chiefly from parents, sometimes didactically through direct instruction, in part through expressions of approval or disapproval for conformity or nonconformity. A middle-class child in the United States who takes something that does not belong to him is told to "give it back," and is informed that one does not take another's property. If he fails to complete some assigned task—homework, mowing the lawn, piano or violin practice—he will be reminded of the importance of persistence and of doing things well. Slovenliness, carelessness, and procrastination are criticized in middle-class homes, whereas neatness, precision, and doing chores on time are rewarded. In other societies, of course, and to some extent in other social classes, different values and standards are encouraged. For example, modesty, usually stressed in American families, is relatively unimportant among the Trobriand Islanders; respect for elders, traditionally strongly emphasized among the British middle and upper classes, is much less emphatically stressed in the United States; equality, a major American value, is much less important in most Western European societies.

Children acquire values—and attitudes and beliefs—not only through explicit precept and overt reward or punishment, but also through suggestion, implication, and example. Nothing need be said explicitly for the child to recognize qualities that are valued highly and those that are not. Sensitive to emotional nuances in parental behavior, he can often recognize implicit approval or disapproval of his own or some one else's actions even when it is not openly expressed. Models for conventional (or unconventional) forms of behavior are found in the mass media and among peers as well as in the family.

The individual, however, is more than a mere bundle of habits and values, attitudes and beliefs, all of them learned and culturally patterned. This bundle of psychological elements is organized into a structure, the "personality," in which the parts are related to one another and not randomly organized. A personality, therefore, possesses attributes that render it more than the mere sum of its parts.

The term *personality* is difficult to define and is as variously used as *society* —perhaps even more so. Yet most psychologists would agree, no matter how they use the term, that it refers to some kind of psychological structure or organization. They disagree among themselves about what elements constitute the personality and the mechanisms through which the psychological system functions.[14]

Of central importance in personality is the *self*, the individual's awareness of and feeling about his own personal and social identity. The self serves an integrating function for the personality; the significance of habits, attitudes, values, and beliefs depend largely upon their relationship to one's feelings about one's self. One responds more readily and more intensely to those external events that impinge upon one's self-image and self-evaluations than to those in which one's self is not involved. The participant in a group conversation pricks up his ears at a vaguely heard reference to himself from a distant corner, though he "hears" nothing else. He remains calm and objective as various topics are discussed, only rising angrily—or pleasantly—at comments which might be taken as referring to *his* personality, *his* relations to others.

Our understanding of the nature, origins, and functions of the self and its relations to social life rests to a large extent upon the contributions of Charles Horton Cooley, an economist turned sociologist and one of America's seminal sociological theorists, and George Herbert Mead, Cooley's contemporary and a philosopher and social psychologist.

Building upon earlier work by William James and the psychologist James M. Baldwin, Cooley emphasized the interdependence of self and society. Although he felt that "the emotion or feeling of self may be regarded as an instinct" (a view not shared by many other students of personality), it was only "defined and developed by experience." [15] The most significant types of experience, he asserted, took place within "primary groups": family, play group, and neighborhood. Necessarily a member of these groups during childhood, the most plastic period of his development, the individual acquires basic human characteristics and sentiments within them. These groups were "primary" because they were "fundamental in forming the social nature and ideas

Each child brings to his life outside the home a personality largely shaped by the family, but the child's experience with others, particularly in the peer group, also contributes to continued growth and development.

of the individual"; they were "the nursery of human nature." [16] (For a full discussion of primary groups, see Chapter 6.)

Through the medium of language, which is obviously social in character, the individual derives the ideas that he adopts as his own. The attitude one takes toward one's own character—physical, psychological, and social—is significantly affected by the attitudes of others. If they approve of his actions or appearance, or he thinks they do, then he too approves of them, and vice versa. Cooley called this self-image the "looking-glass self," which, he said, "seems to have three principal elements: the imagination of our appearance to the other person; the imagination of his judgment of that appearance; and some sort of self-feeling, such as pride or mortification." [17]

Mead's contribution, which he and many other scholars viewed as an extension and elaboration of Cooley's analysis, also focuses upon the self as a social product.

The self [he wrote] has a character which is different from that of the physiological organism proper. The self is something which has a development; it is not initially there, at birth, but arises in the process of social experience and activity, that is, develops in the given individual as a result of his relations to that process as a whole and to other individuals within that process.[18]

The distinctive quality of the self is that "it is an object to itself"; it can achieve distance and objectivity of some sort in looking at and evaluating itself.

Through language and gestures the individual learns to put himself in the place of others and to act as they might—to play their roles. By continually doing so he develops the capacity to look at himself from their standpoint and comes to orient his behavior to the expectations of others, both directly and through the points of view he has *internalized*, that is, incorporated into his own personality.

The individual experiences himself as such, not directly, but only indirectly, from the particular standpoints of other individual members of the same group, or from the generalized standpoint of the social group as a whole to which he belongs.[19]

Mead's work was largely speculative, based upon his observations of his own behavior and of others around him and upon his study of philosophical and psychological literature. Yet similar conclusions have also been derived from careful empirical research. On the basis of a careful and painstaking study of children, for example, Jean Piaget, the distinguished Swiss social psychologist, concluded that "Social life is necessary if the individual is to become conscious of his own mind."[20]

While Cooley and Mead saw clearly the extent to which the self was a social product and emphasized the importance of language and communication, Sigmund Freud, the founder of psychoanalysis and the most influential student of human behavior of the past century, stressed the emotional dynamics of socialization and personality development. Despite a strong belief in the instinctive and unchanging nature of human drives, Freud saw in family relationships a crucial factor in the formation of personality. Although he largely ignored the institutional character of the family, he examined in great and perceptive detail the complex interaction of mother, father, and children, and the psychological consequences of these relationships. From his analysis came significant additions to our knowledge of both personality dynamics and the processes by which people come to follow—or to ignore—the dictates of society.

Emerging from the interaction between parents and children, according to Freud, are emotional attachments that contribute in strategic ways to the personality. Because of the intimacy and emotional ties, children tend to *identify* with their parents, to want to become as much like them as possible. Sons are apt to identify with their fathers, daughters with their mothers, although the process is sometimes only partially completed, sometimes never, and sometimes takes unusual or distorted forms. Eventually the standards of the parents—which are usually also the standards of the society—become part of the child's personality, an internalized guardian that watches over and judges his actions. This "introjected" or internalized parent—the parental image which becomes part of the child's personality—Freud called the *superego*. One of the latter's functions, he pointed out, is to serve as "the vehicle of tradition and of all the age-long values which have been handed down . . . from generation to generation." [21] In a sense, the parent is always present and failure to live up to parental standards can generate a more or less painful sense of guilt, for these internalized norms constitute the conscience. (Like Mead, Freud also noted that "the ego can take itself as an object, it can treat itself like any other object, observe itself, criticize itself, and do Heaven knows what besides with itself." [22]) One may, of course, for various reasons fail to obey these rules and suffer the pangs of guilt, but in most instances, it would appear, the fear of guilt serves to induce conformity to those social norms embodied in parental precepts.

In addition to those values in terms of which the person judges his self, or ego, the superego incorporates goals and conceptions of achievement which the individual strives to realize—in Freudian terms, the *ego-ideal*. In seeking to be like the parent and to live up to his expectations, now internalized and part of the personality, the individual is driven to pursue socially approved goals. Thus, unless his model or mentor is himself a criminal, rebel, or eccentric, the individual learns to want what the culture says he should want—to become rich and famous, to perform some socially valued tasks, to be a respectable and law-abiding citizen. Goals and ideals, then, as well as norms and moral standards, derive from the social and psychological interaction between parents or parent-substitutes and the child. The person is not simply hedged about with internalized restrictions or coerced into required modes of behavior by his conscience, but also acquires the springs of action that can channel impulses and energies into lines of effort that are potentially both socially useful and personally gratifying.

This highly generalized process of personality development is subject, of course, to endless variations. Families are broken and the usual sequence cannot take place. Other adults replace parents, who may be rejected by their own children. In a society in which all children are looked after by women, the son's initial attachment to his mother may be so strong that he finds it difficult to establish a close relationship with his father and to identify with him. For various reasons, the son may remain closely attached to his mother and the daughter to the father. In these varied circumstances, the child may never come to internalize the values of the culture or may not assign to particular values and goals the same importance they assume for others. Alternatively, he may acquire values or psychological tendencies appropriate to the prevailing social and cultural demands through these less typical sequences; as Warner and Abegglen point out, for example, many mobile business executives appear to lack strong attachments to their fathers but are deeply influenced by their mothers.[23] If there are differences in family structure, relatives other than either father or mother may play a central role in personality development.[24]

Finally, some of the components of personality that affect social action and that may, indeed, be of considerable importance in determining how men play various social roles derive from the methods of child care and child training. Psychoanalytically oriented scholars have tried to demonstrate a relationship between how children are fed, toilet trained, and disciplined, on the one hand, and various institutions, beliefs, and values on the other.[25] Although there seems to be little conclusive evidence of a direct connection between child-rearing techniques and specific patterns of behavior, general personality traits do appear to be significantly affected by how children are looked after and trained.

The type of discipline imposed upon the child, for example, generates an attitude toward authority in general that may be important in shaping adult response to the exercise of authority. Children brought up in rigid, authoritarian families without a great deal of warmth and affection, it has been argued on the basis of at least some empirical evidence, tend to become rigid personalities who are submissive toward constituted authority and at the same time delight in ordering others about.[26] (Under some circumstances, however, these "authoritarian personalities" revolt violently because their own feelings are in fact deeply ambivalent, and their ready acceptance of authority conceals a deep hostility toward and resentment against the rigid discipline to which they were once subject.) Other important personality traits—aggressiveness, restraint, competitiveness, distrust, acceptance—also reflect not simply the explicit values of the culture, but the modes of child-rearing as well.

Adult socialization: continuities and discontinuities

Although there is now general agreement that the most important elements in socialization take place during childhood, there is no point at which one can say that the process is complete. As the individual matures he enters—or passes through—new roles, each with its own requirements. Many of these roles build upon the physical capacities that come with maturation—adolesence, motherhood, military service—and upon the skills, knowledge, values, and motivations

gained earlier. The child starts school only when he has reached an age at which society feels that his physical, social, and intellectual skills will enable him to cope with the new demands made upon him—at five in England, six in the United States (if one ignores nursery school and kindergarten), and seven in the Soviet Union. He enters the occupational world after he has acquired at least some of the prerequisites for employment or undergone the training needed for a specific job.

Part of the preparation for many adult roles consists not only in learning necessary skills, but also in instilling appropriate motivations and values. Unlike Peter Pan, most children want to grow up and become parents, workers, soldiers, citizens. They are ready to make the effort necessary to learn how to play these roles and have often already incorporated the values linked with them. Under such conditions, that is, where there has been "anticipatory socialization," learning proceeds easily and effectively.

Adult roles, however, on occasion do not rest upon motivations, values, and abilities already acquired, and childhood experience provides little preparation for what is expected later. Among the Manus of New Guinea, for example, boys are free and unrestrained, bearing little responsibility and subject to little or no authority. Yet upon maturity they are suddenly thrust into a complex system of debts, obligations, and responsibilities which they are expected—and forced—to accept.[27] Such discontinuities might be expected to produce strain and tension, perhaps even efforts to escape from new demands being made. Yet acceptance of the role is often rapid because of the pressures brought to bear by others and the absence of a significant group upon which the individual can call for support in resisting the new role requirements. (For a discussion of means of social control, see Chapter 18.)

In a complex and changing society there are perhaps inescapable discontinuities in the successive roles that people learn to play. Because of the diversity of occupational roles, for example, the ability of parents and schools to prepare people adequately for the tasks they will perform and the problems they will face is limited, and the process of socialization must therefore continue through adult life. Rapid social change requires new patterns of behavior and difficult emotional adjustments that could hardly have been anticipated. Whites who have always thought Negroes inferior must learn to accept them as equals as patterns of race relations change. Men who grow up with fixed ideas as to masculine superiority may have to learn to accept orders from women superiors as barriers to the advancement of women are lowered and more of them pursue professional careers. The solitary scholar may have to accommodate himself to organized research programs and the worker whose know-how is replaced by modern technology must acquire new skills.

Educational institutions, the mass media, and peer groups continue to serve as agencies of socialization for adults, supplemented by the complex organizations in which people carry on many of their activities. Within these organizations efforts are made not only to familiarize the newcomer to established routines but also to inculcate the particular values and loyalties that maintain the structure and lead to conformity to the demands of the new role. These efforts involve explicit instruction, the promise of rewards for conformity and penalties for nonconformity, and the give-and-take of personal interaction with others who express the values and expectations of the organization.[28]

The potentialities for adult socialization, however, may be limited as a result of prior experience. Early social relationships and the events of childhood have lasting effects upon personality, as Freud so clearly showed, and upon the individual's capacity to adapt to changing circumstances and learn new ways. Children who are allowed to express their feelings—including hostility and violence—freely and openly may find it difficult in later life to exercise emotional restraint. Thus lower-class children who come from an emotionally unconstrained background often are not able to take on readily the restraint characteristic of the middle class that is expected of them in school and later on the job.

The lasting effects of early socialization should not be overemphasized, though there is continuing disagreement as to just how persistent they are. There are institutions such as mental hospitals, welfare agencies, courts, and prisons that are intended to secure major changes in values, personality, and the ability to cope with social situations. Whenever the individual can be removed from familiar social contexts, the possibility of *resocialization*—major changes in personality and values—is increased, as cases of political "brainwashing" in various countries reveal. (There is some evidence, however, that return to familiar routines tends to restore the older patterns of thought, feeling, and action.)

Without minimizing the relevance of the basic personality attributes established in early childhood, it is necessary to remember that the individual is engaged in an ongoing social process. He is always a "focus of group affiliations"[29] that entail various expectations concerning behavior and are enforced by diverse

social sanctions. His response to these social requirements and the persons with
whom he comes into contact will be affected by the personal characteristics he
brings to the situation, though his personality may in turn be changed in various
ways by his new experiences.

Social character and social structure

Because the individual is to such a large
extent a product of his social experience,
those who have been brought up in the
same fashion can be expected to be much
like one another and to differ from those
reared under another regimen. Culture
not only provides the values and attitudes
transmitted to children but also defines
the patterns of child-rearing that affect
the structure and dynamics of the personality.[30] The psychological traits common
to those who have been socialized in the
same fashion constitute a "social character" which is potentially related in diverse
ways to values and beliefs as well as the
institutionalized system of social relationships.

Efforts to generalize about the character of social groups is not new. Aristotle,
for example, compared the "Asiatics,
whose understandings are quick and who
are conversant in the arts, [but] are deficient in courage; and therefore are always conquered and the slaves of others"
with the Greeks, who were "both courageous and sensible," and therefore "free,
and governed in the best manner possible." [31] In recent times the question of
"national character" has been dealt with
in diverse fashion by historians, novelists,
and others. Leo Tolstoy once characterized various Europeans as follows:

Germans are self-confident on the basis of an
abstract notion—science, that is, the supposed
knowledge of absolute truth. A Frenchman is

self-assured because he regards himself personally, both in mind and body, as irresistibly
attractive to men and women. An Englishman
is self-assured, as being a citizen of the best-
organized state in the world, and therefore as
an Englishman always knows that all he does as
an Englishman is undoubtedly correct. An Italian is self-assured because he is excitable and
easily forgets himself and other people. A Russian is self-assured because he knows nothing
and does not want to know anything, since he
does not believe that anything can be known.[32]

(Tolstoy's generalizations can, of course,
be challenged, yet with characteristic
acuity, he focused upon an important psychological attribute, the basis for self-
evaluation.) In a perceptive account of
the Russians, a contemporary British
writer observed:

The average Russian can be plunged for long
periods into moods of either pessimism or opti-
mism, either apathy or concentrated effort, and
under the stimulus of persons around him he
can also change his moods rapidly and show
that they are changed, yet he cannot be called
volatile or superficial. . . . [There is also] the
well known tendency of many Russians to
break out, at long intervals, into wild outbursts
of joy or grief, anger, drunkenness, cruelty.[33]

Although generalizations about national character are often couched in stereotyped terms that ignore both the range
of variation and the existence of individual differences, they cannot be casually
dismissed. There is little doubt, despite
great differences within a nation, that
Englishmen and Americans, Russians and
Frenchmen, Cubans and Chinese do differ
from one another not only culturally, but
also psychologically—in self-conceptions,
modes of response, definitions of masculinity and femininity, attitudes toward
sex, and so on. Our knowledge of the
character, extent, and consequences of
such differences is as yet crude and often
inadequate, although the theories and
methods needed to enlarge our understanding are steadily developing.[34]

National traits and the differences

among members of various societies and social groups have been variously attributed to race, climate, geography, and history. We have already noted the inadequacies of a racial explanation of group similarities and differences and the limitations of climatic and geographic interpretations (see Chapter 3), although weather and the physical habitat obviously can enter into the experiences that affect personality. The impact of history, while unquestioned, must be precisely defined; it may refer to awareness of and reverence for the past as such, to traditions derived from earlier times and carried down through the generations, to those institutions shaped in the past that define how children shall be looked after and what they shall be taught.

Our growing understanding of the agencies and processes of socialization now makes it possible to explore more systematically the relationship between social character and specific institutions and social structures. A number of studies, chiefly of small, relatively homogeneous communities, have tried to identify the type of social character produced by particular methods of socialization and to relate it to specific values, beliefs, and forms of social organization. A detailed analysis of the people of Alor, a small island in what is now Indonesia, for example, found that mothers, busily at work in the fields, tended to neglect their children, who characteristically developed into anxious and suspicious adults ready to participate in a harsh, competitive society. Their religion and folklore also revealed distrust and uncertainty, which might both reflect the basic personality structure and contribute to its formation.[35]

The close link between personality and culture found in communities such as Alor and the high degree of consistency between them are not paralleled in larger, more complex societies in which methods of child-rearing are more varied, the influences to which children are exposed more diverse, and the roles open to individuals more numerous and more differentiated. Rather than a single "social character" there may be several, or many. Distinctive methods of socialization among subgroups—the middle class, Negroes, and Jews, for example—may generate identifiable character or personality types. In a multigroup society there may be both values that become part of the personalities of most people and psychological attributes peculiar to members of particular groups. Despite some systematic inquiry and a good deal of speculation, the psychological dimensions of a complex society have yet to be adequately delineated.

Even without a clear-cut definition of social character it is possible to identify psychological traits that affect patterns of response in social situations. Some of these traits—emotional needs, drives, feelings, orientations to others—are clearly related to the process of socialization. In a perceptive and influential analysis of American character, David Riesman focused upon changing "modes of conformity," those "components of personality that . . . play the principal role in the maintenance of social forms."[36] (For a discussion of these modes of conformity, see Chapter 18.) A major study by Adorno, Frenkel-Brunswik, Levinson, and Sanford examined in great detail the sources of the "authoritarian personality" and its relationship to prejudice.[37] Other psychological attributes are products of the culture and social structure within which individuals carry on their daily lives. In a study of a one-day radio campaign by Kate Smith during World War II in which she sold $39 million worth of war bonds, it was found that one reason for her success was her apparent sincerity. It was this quality that appealed to people who, because of their position in American society, felt a "craving for reassurance, an acute need to believe, a flight into faith." [38]

As these studies of the authoritarian personality and mass persuasion suggest, psychological characteristics generated by social experience are important not only because they account for conformity to social norms and group expectations, but also because they enter in various ways into the dynamics of the social system and, frequently, into the process of social change. It has been pointed out, for example, that American culture encourages feelings of guilt and self-blame among those who do not achieve economic success, because it assigns to each individual the full responsibility for his own economic fate. These feelings in turn serve a significant social function for they focus criticism upon the individual rather than upon those institutions and social structures which make success difficult for members of some groups to achieve. [39]

By repressing men's desires and enforcing modes of behavior which run counter to impulses and drives, both innate and acquired, the process of socialization and the demands society frequently makes of its members create psychological problems for society. One of Freud's chief contributions to our understanding of the dynamics of personality is his demonstration of an inevitable degree of tension between inherited impulses and drives of the organism and the requirements of social life. It is possible to accept the conclusion that men pay a psychological price for the acquisition of culture without accepting Freud's theory that culture is merely the product of sublimated sexual urges, a reward for renouncing instinctual gratification or a substitute for such gratification. The organism is con-

strained by its social experience in manifold ways; the individual must learn to control at least some of his impulses and to channel his drives along accepted lines.

The very nature of the social process itself adds to the inevitable tension between individual and society. No society is so fully integrated that the individual is free from uncertainty and conflicting demands. Sentiments or feelings generated by social life often must be restrained or inhibited. Demands for novelty or excitement are unfulfilled in a routine and unchanging way of life. Sacrifices may be required for the welfare of others without regard to personal wishes. "*Dulce et decorum est pro patria mori,*" Linton has noted, "expresses the social point of view. The individual who has to do the dying may acquiesce in its propriety, but it can hardly seem sweet to him." [40]

One significant aspect of culture and social structure, therefore, is the way in which they deal with the emotional needs of individuals. "If society is to survive," Linton observes, "culture must not only provide techniques for training and repressing the individual, it must also provide him with compensations and outlets. It if thwarts and suppresses him in certain directions, it must help him to expand in others . . . [and] must also provide the individual with harmless outlets for his socially repressed desires." [41] Failure to do these things will stimulate both deviation from social norms and social change. (For a discussion of "institutionalized safety valves" that offer opportunities to release socially generated tensions, see Chapter 18.)

Individual differences

That individuals resemble one another because of their social backgrounds or even that they possess common psychological attributes does not mean that individuals do not differ—often greatly—from one another. Indeed, differences among individuals persist for many reasons—biological, psychological, and sociological. Socialization produces people capable of playing social roles; it does not lead to identical personalities indistinguishable from one another.

Man is not a *tabula rasa* upon which culture writes; nor, to change the figure, is he a lump of clay to be molded by society. The unique biological equipment that each person possesses necessarily enters into the formation of his personality, which is not simply the sum derived from the addition of culture to organism but a result of a complex interaction between individual and society. What is sometimes called temperament, for example, that is, the generalized mode of response —rapid or slow, phlegmatic or lively— seems to be essentially inherited and closely related to biological functioning. "No culture yet observed," Ruth Benedict has commented, "has been able to eradicate the differences in the temperaments of the persons who compose it." [42]

No single individual incorporates in his personality the whole of his culture, or even all of those segments of it that enter into his experience. The middle-class American child is hardly likely to be exposed to the same cultural patterns or social experience as the child of a steel-worker or a Hollywood movie star. Although they may all see the same television programs and read some of the same books, the specific content of each is interpreted differently, at least in some degree, and has somewhat different consequences.

Even though the socialization process is roughly similar for those in comparable social circumstances, it inevitably differs in individual cases in subtle, yet often important details. Insofar as the self emerges out of interaction with a limited number of other people, its character will reflect the idiosyncratic attributes they possess. The composition of the family or household, the complex interaction among parents, the specific events that occur during the impressionable years of childhood, and many chance factors contribute to the characteristics that distinguish each individual from others.

Adherence to the same social norm, therefore, does not necessarily carry the same emotional weight for each person. The child may be forced to remain clean at a very early age or he may gradually and easily learn that it is considered better to be clean than dirty. In each case he has learned the social norm, but the emotional concomitants are not likely to be the same. Any element derived from the culture may therefore have various functions in the psychic economy of individuals.

These distinctive personality attributes affect individual responses to the prescriptions of the culture and the expectations and demands of others. Temperamental variations, for example, can affect the reaction to the culture in which individuals happen to be born. A phlegmatic person in a strenuous, fast-moving society will respond quite differently from a lively, active one; the roles he will choose (when he has a choice), and how he performs required social roles may well be affected by his temperamental characteristics. Suggestible persons may readily be persuaded by the latest television commercial while others remain unmoved; aggressive children participate readily in some kinds of games while shy ones seek other activities. Out of these complex modes of response emerge patterns of behavior the explanation for which must inevitably include the psychological traits of individuals, although the sociologist relates these traits to the facts of social organization rather than to the structure or functioning of the individual personality.

Postscript

The problem with which this chapter has dealt, the relations between individual and society, clearly is of interest not only to social scientists. It is a persistent question which has also preoccupied men throughout human history, from the earliest philosophers and religious leaders to present-day scholars and moralists, for the answer inevitably possesses moral and political implications. It is a question of particular relevance in the modern world, where large-scale organization and totalitarian regimes threaten ruthlessly to subordinate the individual to group purposes and to control and manipulate his daily activities, his beliefs and attitudes, and even his conception of himself, without that respect for the individual which constitutes one of the richest strands in the Western cultural tradition. The contemporary cultural themes of alienation, anomie, and disenchantment so prevalent in literature, philosophy, and theology, as well as in social science, focus upon the individual's relations to his society and the forces that limit his freedom.

We cannot explore the many answers that have been given to these questions in the past or their implications. To do so would lead us into problems of intellectual history and the sociology of ideas and knowledge. The lessons of modern social science concerning the interdependence of individual and society, however, can make some contribution to our understanding of the moral and political issues inherent in the continuing discussion and debate about the possibilities of individual freedom and the extent of the individual's dependence upon and subordination to the society in which he lives.

Although our analysis will focus upon the available reliable knowledge, the reader should remind himself—as we shall occasionally remind him—that theoretical controversies and empirical findings have a wider than scientific import, and that sociology, like any other human activity, cannot be extracted from its social context. The student of society must try to disassociate himself from the values of his society in his scientific endeavors, but nevertheless he can hardly forget that he is a member of society and that his findings and conclusions have social consequences.

Notes

[1] David Mandelbaum (ed.), *Selected Writings of Edward Sapir* (Berkeley: University of California Press, 1949), p. 590.

[2] Ralph Linton, *The Cultural Background of Personality* (New York: Appleton, 1945), p. 12.

[3] James B. Ross and Mary M. McLaughlin (eds.), *The Portable Medieval Reader* (New York: Viking, 1949), pp. 366–7.

[4] René A. Spitz, "Hospitalism: An Inquiry Into the Genesis of Psychiatric Conditions in Early Childhood," *Psychoanalytic Study of the Child*, I (1945), 53–74; and René A. Spitz, "Hospitalism: A Follow-up Report," *Psychoanalytic Study of the Child*, II (1946), 113–7.

[5] Sandor Ferenczi, quoted in Linton, *op. cit.*, p. 9.

[6] L. Joseph Stone and Joseph Church,

Childhood and Adolescence (New York: Random House, 1957), p. 63. See pp. 58–66 for a review of the literature on this problem.

[7] Mark Zborowski, "Cultural Components in Responses to Pain," *Journal of Social Issues*, IV (1952), pp. 16–30.

[8] E. Adamson Hoebel, "The Nature of Culture," in Harry L. Shapiro (ed.), *Man, Culture, and Society* (New York: Oxford, 1956), pp. 175–6.

[9] These examples are drawn from Nancy Mitford (ed.), *Noblesse Oblige* (New York: Harper, 1956). A comparable, though much briefer, list of class differences in the use of language in the United States is offered in E. Digby Baltzell, *Philadelphia Gentlemen* (New York: Free Press, 1958), p. 51. Baltzell's list is much shorter, in part because he does not attempt the elaborate exploration reported in Mitford, in part because class differences in language are not so great in the United States as in England.

[10] Richard Centers, *The Psychology of Social Classes* (Princeton: Princeton University Press, 1949), p. 86.

[11] See Elton Mayo and G. F. F. Lombard, *Teamwork and Turnover in the Aircraft Industry of Southern California* (Boston: Harvard Business School, 1944); and Elliott Jacques, *The Changing Culture of a Factory* (New York: Dryden, 1952).

[12] Centers, *op. cit.*, Table 68, p. 164, and Table 77, p. 180.

[13] Ruth Benedict, *Patterns of Culture* (New York: Pelican, 1946), p. 234.

[14] See Calvin Hall and Gardner Lindzey, *Theories of Personality* (New York: Wiley, 1957).

[15] Charles H. Cooley, *Human Nature and the Social Order* (New York: Scribner, 1902), p. 139.

[16] Charles H. Cooley, *Social Organization* (New York: Scribner, 1929; originally published in 1909), p. 23.

[17] Cooley, *Human Nature and the Social Order*, p. 152.

[18] George Herbert Mead, *Mind, Self, and Society* (Chicago: University of Chicago Press, 1934), p. 135.

[19] *Ibid.*, p. 138.

[20] Jean Piaget, *The Moral Judgment of the Child*, trans. by Marjorie Gabain (New York: Free Press, 1948), p. 407.

[21] Sigmund Freud, *New Introductory Lectures on Psycho-analysis*, trans. by W. J. H. Sprott (New York: Norton, 1933), p. 95.

[22] *Ibid.*, p. 84.

[23] W. Lloyd Warner and James Abegglen, *Big Business Leaders in America* (New York: Harper, 1955), Ch. 5. See also Franz Alexander, "Educative Influence of Personality Factors in the Environment," in Clyde Kluckhohn, Henry A. Murray, and David M. Schneider (eds.), *Personality in Nature, Society, and Culture* (2nd ed.; New York: Knopf, 1953), pp. 431–2.

[24] See Bronislaw Malinowski, *Sex and Repression in Savage Society* (New York: Meridian, 1955).

[25] See, for example, Abram Kardiner *et al.*, *The Psychological Frontiers of Society* (New York: Columbia University Press, 1945).

[26] Theodore Adorno *et al.*, *The Authoritarian Personality* (New York: Harper, 1950).

[27] Margaret Mead, *Growing Up in New Guinea* (New York: Morrow, 1930).

[28] See Stanton Wheeler, "The Structure of Formally Organized Socialization Settings," in Orville G. Brim, Jr., and Stanton Wheeler, *Socialization After Childhood: Two Essays* (New York: Wiley, 1966), pp. 51–116.

[29] Robert M. MacIver and Charles H. Page, *Society: An Introductory Analysis* (New York: Holt, 1949), p. 217.

[30] See John W. M. Whiting and Irvin L. Child, *Child Training and Personality: A Cross-Cultural Study* (New Haven: Yale University Press, 1953).

[31] Aristotle, *Politics*, trans. by William Ellis (New York: Dutton, 1939), p. 213.

[32] Leo Tolstoy, *War and Peace*, trans. by Louis and Aylmer Maude (New York: Simon & Schuster, 1942), p. 709.

[33] Wright Miller, *Russians as People* (New York: Dutton, 1961), pp. 88–9.

[34] See Alex Inkeles, "Personality and Social Structure," in Robert K. Merton, Leonard Broom, and Leonard S. Cottrell, Jr. (eds.), *Sociology Today* (New York: Basic Books, 1959), pp. 249–76.

[35] See Kardiner, *op. cit.*, Chs. 5–9. The report of the field research is in Cora Du Bois, *The People of Alor* (Minneapolis: University of Minnesota Press, 1944).

[36] David Riesman, with Reuel Denny and Nathan Glazer, *The Lonely Crowd* (New Haven: Yale University Press, 1950), p. 4.

[37] Adorno, *et al.*, *op. cit.*

[38] Robert K. Merton, *Mass Persuasion* (New York: Harper, 1946), p. 143.

[39] See, for example, Ely Chinoy, *Automobile Workers and the American Dream* (New York: Random House, 1955), Ch. 10.

[40] Ralph Linton, *The Study of Man* (New York: Appleton, 1936), p. 413.

[41] *Ibid.*

[42] Benedict, *op. cit.*, p. 234.

Suggestions for further reading

BRIM, ORVILLE G., JR., AND STANTON WHEELER. *Socialization After Childhood: Two Essays*. New York: Wiley, 1966.
Two essays dealing with adult socialization, the first on general problems, the second on socialization within formal organizations.

COHEN, YEHUDI. *Social Structure and Personality: A Casebook*. New York: Holt, 1961.
An excellent collection of research studies tied together by the author's theoretical analysis and interpretation.

COOLEY, CHARLES H. *Human Nature and the Social Order*. New York: Scribner, 1902.
An early discussion of the interdependence of individual and society that is still in some respects a classic.

DAVIS, KINGSLEY. *Human Society*. New York: Macmillan, 1947. Ch. 7, "Jealousy and Sexual Property: An Illustration."
A sociological analysis of a psychological response that examines the social conditions under which the expression of jealousy is expected or permitted and the social functions it performs.

DURKHEIM, ÉMILE. *Suicide*. Trans. by John A. Spaulding and George Simpson. New York: Free Press, 1951 (first published in 1897).
A classic example of sociological analysis of a phenomenon usually thought of in psychological terms. A major contribution to sociological theory.

ELKIN, FREDERICK. *The Child and Society: The Process of Socialization*. New York: Random House, 1960.
A brief analysis of the forms and agencies of socialization and of subcultural differences in patterns of socialization.

ERIKSON, ERIK H. *Childhood and Society*. New York: Norton, 1950.
Using a psychoanalytic approach, coupled with anthropological observation, the author explores in rich and suggestive fashion the relationship between culture and personality.

LINTON, RALPH. *The Cultural Background of Personality*. New York: Appleton, 1945.
An excellent introduction to the ways in which culture and social structure affect the development of personality.

MEAD, GEORGE HERBERT. *Mind, Self, and Society*. Chicago: University of Chicago Press, 1934.
A very difficult but rewarding analysis of the processes by which the self develops. An extraordinarily influential book among American sociologists.

PARSONS, TALCOTT. *Social Structure and Personality*. New York: Free Press, 1964.

A collection of essays on the interrelations of social structure and personality. See particularly Ch. 1, "The Superego and the Theory of Social Systems," which seeks to link together systematically the formation of personality and the functioning of the social order.

PIAGET, JEAN. *The Moral Judgment of the Child.* Trans. by Marjorie Gabain. New York: Free Press, 1948.

An intriguing study by a noted Swiss social psychologist of the process by which the child acquires moral standards. One of a number of important studies of socialization by the same author.

5
Modes of sociological analysis

The sociological "why?"

The task of sociology, we have said, is to explain those aspects of human behavior encompassed in the concepts of culture and society. These concepts define the foci of sociological interest; they direct our attention to patterned and repetitive forms of acting, thinking, and feeling and to the organized relations among individuals and groups.

A great deal of sociological and anthropological investigation results in merely systematic description of the recurrent behavior and social relationships found in different societies or among different groups. Such factual reports, though obviously essential, constitute only the initial step in sociological inquiry, since the latter's ultimate aim is to explain or account for the facts.

In common discourse, explanation frequently means simply making some phenomenon more understandable; it is "simplification, paraphrase, and description," [1] and may be achieved by analogy, example, or by restatement in other words. Scientific explanation, on the other hand, consists in showing or identifying the conditions under which events take place, or their relations to other events. It seeks to answer the question: "Why?"

"Why?" is perhaps as much a weasel word as any in our entire vocabulary.

The question is usually asked with some implicit expectation of the kind of answer desired, of the terms in which the answer is to be given. For example, the question, "Why do people commit suicide?" is not the same for the psychologist and the sociologist. The former wants to know why a particular individual takes his own life. The latter is asking why suicide is more frequent in some groups than in others and what conditions account for changes in the frequency with which it occurs. (For a fuller discussion of the difference between psychological and sociological perspectives, see Chapter 4.) "Why?" states the existence of a question; it does not specify its precise character. Our immediate task, therefore, is to spell out the nature of the sociological "Why?" [2]

Within sociology itself there are as many answers to the question "Why?" as there are alternative sociological theories. Among the substantial array of sociological explanations, however, two major approaches may be distinguished, each resting upon different assumptions, asking different kinds of questions, and expecting different answers. We shall call these approaches the "functional" and the "historical." The older terms by which they have been identified are "static" and "dynamic," terms which go back to Auguste Comte, the founder of sociology as a distinctive discipline, although the latter term has now come to have a different meaning. On occasion these alternative approaches have also been described as "synchronic" and "diachronic."

In the continuing process of conceptual analysis and development, all of these terms have undergone refinement and redefinition. Like most other sociological concepts, *social function* has been considerably revised and elaborated upon since it first appeared in systematic form in Émile Durkheim's *The Rules of Sociological Method* in 1895. The term *dynamics*, which for Comte meant social change and social evolution, has now come to have a significant place in the usually ahistorical approach of functionalism, referring to the processes by which a social system is maintained. Early sociologists were greatly concerned with history and the evolution of society; after a long period during which the idea of evolution was largely ignored, it has recently reappeared in sociological discussion, albeit in a somewhat revised form.[3]

The functional approach, although sometimes defined in special ways and containing difficult and important problems yet to be resolved, has come to possess a generally understood and accepted meaning.[4] It sees a society as a more or less integrated whole. Explanation consists in showing the place of social norms, beliefs, patterns of behavior, social relationships, and values in the entire structure and in relation to one another. Functionalism's fundamental question has to do with the maintenance of social order or of a "social system."

The historical approach, though it too may view a society as a whole, is concerned chiefly with change, with the development and transformation of institutions, beliefs and values, patterns of behavior, and forms of organization. In-

stead of asking how a society hangs together and what keeps it going as a more or less integrated whole, it seeks to define the processes of change, the conditions under which it occurs, and the consequences of various kinds of change for the social order.

The functional and the historical are not contradictory approaches to sociological phenomena; rather they complement one another, and will in all likelihood become more and more closely linked together as our understanding of both the structure and functioning of society and the changes taking place within it is extended.

Functional analysis

Society, we have noted, is a totality made up of interrelated and interdependent parts. From one point of view it is a complex structure of groups and individuals held together in a web of social relationships. From another, it is a system of institutions related to and reacting upon one another. From either perspective, society may be thought of as a functioning whole, as an operating system. Analogies in scientific analysis can be misleading, yet it is sometimes helpful to conceive of society as an organism, or at least as possessing some organic characteristics. The different components of society should be seen in relation to the whole; apart from that whole they lose their sociological significance. They are constantly acting and reacting upon one another, adapting themselves or being adapted in various ways to changes or processes occurring in other segments of society. An essential task of sociology, therefore, is to explain the functioning of society and to explore the relations between the parts and the whole and among the parts themselves.

The concept of *function*, which has

come in recent years to play an increasingly important role in performing this task, is "neither new nor confined to the social sciences." [5] It occupies a significant position in such varied disciplines as biology, psychology, physics, and architecture. In the social sciences the concept has developed in an uneven fashion, "in shreds and patches," to use Robert Merton's phrase, with now one, now another, aspect emphasized. But the presupposition upon which the concept—and the mode of analysis associated with the concept—is based, namely that phenomena must be seen "in terms of interconnection of operation rather than in terms of separate . . . units" [6] has remained unchanged and unchallenged.

The idea contained in the pioneer formulation of Émile Durkheim, of course, was not new. It can be found frequently in the work of Karl Marx and of Herbert Spencer, the nineteenth-century evolutionary thinker against whose ideas Durkheim was contending. As an organism or aggregate (individual or social) becomes more complex, Spencer asserted, "that combination of actions which constitutes the life of the whole makes possible the component actions which constitute the lives of the parts." [7] Durkheim's contribution lay in his clear differentiation of the analysis of social functions from the analysis of the development and evolution of social forms. "When . . . the explanation of a social phenomenon is undertaken," he wrote, "we must seek separately the efficient cause which produces it and the function it fulfills." [8]

The concept of function refers to the "observable objective consequences" of social phenomena as they relate to social structure, institutional systems, and culturally patterned sentiments, values, and beliefs. The phenomena with which sociology is concerned are those encompassed by the concepts thus far examined: cultural patterns, institutions, values, roles, social relationships—as well as other more precisely defined and conceptualized social phenomena. Any regularity, that is, any patterned or repetitive behavior, interaction, or emotional response, can therefore be subjected to functional analysis.

The explanatory significance of "function" can be simply stated. If we seek to account for some social fact in functional terms we try to identify its relations to other elements in society, conceived of as an ongoing system of interdependent parts in which the item studied has positive results, that is, it makes possible other activities or sustains other patterned, repetitive social or cultural forms. In effect, we ask: What are the consequences of the item studied for other elements of the structure, or for the structure as a whole?

Such analysis may be carried on at different levels. On the most general level one may consider the contribution of any social or cultural item to the survival, persistence, integration, or stability of a society as a whole. The functions of the family in any society include, at least, bringing new members into the society, providing for their physical maintenance, transmitting to them a large part of the culture which they need to know (the process of "socialization"), and giving them their initial position, or status, in the social structure. (For an analysis of the family see Chapter 8.) This general level of functional analysis has sometimes been stretched to include the satisfaction of those needs of individuals—food, shelter, sexual gratification, and emotional response—without which human life could not persist. The warrant for this extension of the concept of function to physiological and psychological categories lies in the fact that in some measure all societies focus their social and cultural organization upon the satisfaction of these needs. The family, for example, almost always provides an approved channel (though not necessarily the only appropriate one) for satisfying sexual desires, as well as offering the possibility of other significant emotional experience.

Analysis of the functions of institutions and social structures for society as a whole has often been coupled with efforts to identify and delineate the *functional requisites* that must be met if a society—any society—is to persist and survive.[9] Sociologists have defined these requisites in various ways, although they tend to agree that every society must provide for biological reproduction and survival, for socializing new members and motivating them to carry out socially necessary roles, and for maintaining some degree of social order. In addition to these minimum requirements, others have been suggested about which there is little agreement. The importance of the definition of functional requisites (a theoretical task not yet adequately performed) lies in part in the attempt to account for the presence of universal culture patterns and social structures—family, religion, political controls, and so on—by relating them to the fundamental requirements for sustained group life.

The attempt to explain specific cultural and social phenomena on the basis of the functional requisites they satisfy often rests upon an implicit definition of the limits or boundaries of a particular society. Such a definition is clearly necessary in order to examine the functions of institutions and social structures for the total social order. But various criteria can be used in order to establish limits of an inclusive social system. In a "primitive" tribe the limits are likely to be fairly clear-cut, set by shared cultural patterns and a system of social relationships largely or totally confined within the group. The social unit is adequately set off by the shared loyalties to a total social code. In modern societies, however, the limits are likely to be defined in most cases by political organization and boundaries. That this can be theoretically justified stems from two facts: Power and politics play a particularly important role in the life of modern societies, and political boundaries usually coincide with significant cultural divisions. Yet in some instances, in parts of Europe and the Near East, for example, ethnic and political boundaries are not congruent. Thus in Belgium the division between Flemish and Walloons has been for many years a constant source of friction and antagonism, which appear now to be increasing. In Iraq a dissident Kurdish minority resists the central authority, and in Morocco efforts to create a modern state and society have run into difficulties because of a sizeable Berber minority in an otherwise largely Arab population. Failure to recognize these facts may lead to inaccurate or misleading conclusions about the total societies in which these divisions exist.

Functional analysis therefore often focuses upon "subsystems," or subgroups, or subcultures, within the larger whole—upon the economy, or polity (the institutions and collectivities relevant to the structure of power), for example, or upon the kinship system, the value system, or some complex organizational structure. It is often fruitful to look upon each of these components or aspects of a total social order from a functional point of view, inquiring into its dynamics and how it is sustained, as well as examining its relationships to other subsystems or to the society as a whole.

Concern with functional requisites may lead—indeed in some cases has led—to assumptions about the inevitability of specific institutions and forms of organization. These assumptions derive from the neglect of *functional alternatives*, that is, those institutions or social structures which can perform the same or similar functions. In addition, if attention is concentrated chiefly on the ways in which a specific rule or belief or structure serves the society as a whole, the full range of its consequences may remain unexamined. Concepts and questions, we pointed out earlier, focus attention upon some phenomena and consequently tend to exclude other matters from observation; they are ways of not-seeing as well as of seeing. By focusing attention upon the contributions of religion to social stability, for example, many writers have ignored alternative ways of maintaining stability and the frequently divisive and disruptive effects of religion as well.[10] Similarly, a general analysis of government as an institutional system, the principal functions of which are to maintain social order by resolving disputes and to enforce conformity to important social norms, may result in the neglect of the problem of what kind of order: authoritarian or democratic, hierarchical or equalitarian, traditional or rational.

The analysis of the functions of any feature of a society must include not only its contribution to the total social order but also its consequences for particular groups and institutions within the society. The careful scheduling of railroad operations, to cite a familiar illustration, obviously contributes to the efficient performance of essential social tasks in an industrial society. But the functional significance of the careful timing and ordering of operations must also be seen in relation to diverse groups and a variety of institutionalized activities. For some industries reliable train schedules are necessary in order to maintain the continuous flow of production; if, for example, a large nylon plant does not receive regular shipments of the chemical ingredients it needs the whole manufacturing process would be interrupted. For the stockholder, the more efficient the performance of the railroad, the higher may be his return. For the commuter, adherence to railroad timetables makes possible a regular and predictable pattern of daily behavior: He can shower, shave, drink his morning coffee, and kiss his wife good-by secure in the knowledge that if he arrives at the station as late as 8:29½ A.M. he will still be able to beat the boss to the office. For small-town cab drivers, the scheduled arrival of trains passing through may dictate a regular feature of their daily routine and provide a source of fares. For the railroad employee, the rigorous demands of train schedules influence his working hours and his whole pattern of life. He becomes enormously sensitive to time and is likely to demand punctuality in all contexts. Since he must adapt himself to timetable requirements, he may not be able to follow the normal day-by-day routines of other people; he will frequently have to spend nights as well as days away from home and may have to work on Saturdays, Sundays, and holidays when others are enjoying time off from their labors. These facts may in turn affect his family life and participation in community affairs.[11]

Manifest and latent functions

As a close examination of this illustration will indicate, some of the functions of railroad schedules are intended and desired while others are either unintended or unknown to the persons directly involved. It is essential, therefore, in examining the functions of social and cultural forms to distinguish between the purposes or goals they are supposed to achieve and the actual consequences which flow from them. The effects of regular train schedules on railroad employees and small-town taxi-drivers are clearly unanticipated consequences of rules made in order to achieve other objectives. Or, to take another illustration, we buy clothing to protect us from the elements, to satisfy our own standards of taste, to please or impress our family, friends, and perhaps, our neighbors. Whatever our aims, however, our clothing in fact identifies and contributes to our status, or standing, in the community, as do many of the activities we normally carry on for a wide variety of reasons.

Purpose and result frequently do not completely coincide: What is intended is often not achieved. There is no evidence, for example, that rain dances by the Zuñi bring rain, or that many of the rites and ritual incantations of healers in primitive societies cure disease, despite the beliefs and intentions of dancers and watchers, of healers and their patients. That this is so, however, does not mean that such patterned activities have no important social functions.

A distinction must therefore be drawn between *manifest* and *latent* functions. Manifest functions are those consequences for society or any of its subsystems or segments that are "intended and recognized by participants in the system." Latent functions are those consequences that are "neither intended nor recognized." [12]

The line between these two types of functions is neither fixed nor always easy to draw. Latent consequences may at times become quite apparent. Several years ago women in a university dormitory were offered the total elimination of curfew restrictions. To the surprise of the Dean, they refused. They had suddenly realized the advantages inherent in a rule that gave them a legitimate excuse for an early good night to an unsuccessful date.

The functions of particular institutions or values may be manifest to some persons and not to others. Edward Gibbon, for example, in describing the various religions prevalent in ancient Rome, observed that they "were all considered by the people as equally true; by the philosopher, as equally false; and by the magistrate, as equally useful." [13] While most American Catholics at the turn of the century probably did not conceive of their religion as an instrument for minimizing social or political discontent, President Taft described it as "one of the bulwarks against socialism and anarchy in this country." [14] Two leading businessmen, "a Nordic Protestant, James J. Hill, and a Semitic skeptic, Max Pam, gave generous sums to Catholic institutions for the avowed purpose of helping to spread discipline over the restive working classes of the land." [15] Similarly, as Liston Pope reported in his study of a North Carolina mill town in the 1930s, some Baptist and Methodist manufacturers helped support dissident Protestant sects because they provided a noneconomic and nonpolitical outlet for the frustrations generated by low wages and poor working conditions, [16] a function that sect members could hardly be aware of.

Despite the occasional inability to identify specific functions as either manifest or latent, formulating the distinction leads us consciously to explore in every case the unnoticed consequences of institutions, beliefs, and forms of organization. As Merton has pointed out, by examining the latent functions of "seemingly irrational social patterns"—magic and superstition, for example—it is possible to explain their place and persistence in the social scheme of things. Although a rain dance is not likely to produce rain, it may well relieve anxiety and bring more closely together the members of the society, and reinforce—or raise—the social status of some of the participants as well. These more or less latent functions may provide a reasonably adequate explanation for the persistence of such ritual, despite its failure to achieve its manifest aims.

Similarly, the persistence of illicit patterns of action such as political corruption or gambling can also be explained in considerable measure by reference to the latent functions they serve in American society. Political corruption, as it develops in political machines, for example, often "humanizes" and "personalizes" the operation of government. In addition to its less applauded consequences, such as increasing the cost of government and favoring private interests at the expense of the public interest, it offers an avenue of social mobility to some persons, and provides a source of income not only for party hacks but also for businessmen and racketeers who can do business with the machine.[17] Gambling, when it is not institutionally sanctioned, often thrives among persons whose lives are otherwise closely ordered; it provides them with variety and excitement usually unavailable to them. Among those with few opportunities for wealth or even occasional affluence, gambling, in the numbers racket, for example, offers a chance for gain otherwise not possible for them.

The social consequences of institutional patterns and social structures, as even cursory examination discloses—and as our illustrations suggest—are not always advantageous for the whole society or for some of its component parts. Any single pattern may have both negative and positive results. The American belief that anyone who has "what it takes" can "get ahead in the world," for example, may stimulate ambition (a quality valued by Americans) and reinforce loyalties to American institutions (which provide the opportunities ostensibly open to everyone), but it may also encourage vain hopes and lead to frustration, guilt, and self-blame among those who fail to succeed, whether because of personal limitations or social obstacles. Informal limitation of output among factory workers, a fact frequently documented in industrial studies, may perform significant functions for the workers: protection against the "speed-up" and against layoffs because of fulfilled contracts, as well as direct satisfactions simply from participation in the group. But workers' restriction of output obviously limits the efficiency of industrial operations. The use of terror by a totalitarian regime helps it to maintain power but clearly creates difficulties for many of its citizens—and may inhibit the growth of spontaneous social groups outside the "official" bureaucratically organized structure.

In order to focus attention systematically upon the negative consequences of social patterns, as well as the positive, the concept of *dysfunction* is often employed to refer to those consequences that tend to diminish the integration or stability of a society or any of its component parts and to lessen the possibility of survival and persistence.

To summarize, functional analysis, we may then say, consists of the exploration of the full range of social and cultural consequences, both manifest and latent, positive and negative (which may be either manifest or latent), of any institutional pattern or social structure. Marion Levy has suggested that because the term *function* encompasses all of these possibilities, one should distinguish between *eufunction* (the positive contribution to the success or stability of a structure) and *dysfunction* (the negative consequences).[18] As the meaning is usually clear from the context, these neologisms are not always necessary, although the distinction they imply should be kept clearly in mind.

In order to discover the functions—and dysfunctions—of any social pattern it is necessary to locate it in the specific social and cultural context in which it occurs. Frequently the social structure and culture generate the very problems or needs to whose resolution or satisfaction the item contributes. Without an understanding of the nature and sources of economic or political discontent, for example, it would be difficult to assay the way in which religion meets that discontent. Further, the same pattern can serve different functions in different contexts. Emphasis upon individual advancement in a rapidly expanding society encourages innovation and creativity; in a relatively stable society with limited opportunities it may lead only to considerable frustration and illegal experiments—or to revolutionary change.

Functional analysis: three cases

We may illustrate more fully the nature of functional analysis with three cases drawn from very different social contexts.

"RITUALS OF REBELLION" AMONG ZULU WOMEN   In his analysis of South African rituals, Max Gluckman describes agricultural rites performed by women at the time when planting is begun each year.

The young unmarried girls donned men's garments and carried shields and assagais [spears]. They drove the cattle out to pasture and milked them, though cattle were normally taboo to females. Meanwhile their mothers planned a garden for the goddess [Nomkubulwana] far out in the veld, and poured a libation of beer to her. Thereafter this garden was neglected. At various stages of the ceremonies women and girls went naked, and sang lewd songs. Men and boys hid inside the huts, and might not go near the women. If they did, the women and girls could attack them.[19]

These rituals were felt to be of positive value, and to be important in securing a good crop.

The functions of these rituals, in which women "committed public obscenities and acted as if they were men," can be understood only in relation to the position of women in Zulu society.

. . . a woman was in law—in law, not always in practice—subject to the control of some man—either her father or brother, or after marriage her husband. The prime effect of this subordination was to give these men control over the woman's capacities as wife and as child-bearer. In exchange for transferring to the husband a woman's capacity as a wife, including her work in the gardens, and her capacity as a bearer of children, the husband handed over to her male relatives cattle which were taboo to her—she could not touch them or go into their corral. . . .

. . . the approach of marriage was a period of great distress for Zulu girls: they were subject to frequent attacks of hysteria which were ascribed to the love-magic of their suitors. Marriage itself was a difficult relation, requiring adjustment to a strange family where the girl was hedged with many taboos. She had to avoid important parts of her husband's home village and even parts of her own hut. She had to alter her language so as not to use any word containing the root of her husband's name or the names of her senior male relatives-in-law. Her stressed function was to be a dutiful, hard-working, faithful, and decorous wife, bearing children for her husband, and caring for those children. Only when they grew up could she become independent, as the mother of grown sons.[20]

The difficulties in the woman's position were further complicated by the peculiarities of the Zulu system for reckoning descent and determining inheritance.

The annual rituals, therefore, provided an opportunity to engage in normally prohibited behavior. "Allowing [the women] to herd the cattle would be a reward and a release, especially while they were also allowed to go naked and sing lewd songs and attack wandering men. This statement, that performing these normally tabooed actions is a reward and release, seems to be justified by the descriptions we have. But part of its interpretation involves psychological analysis for which there is [as yet] no evidence."[21] Although there has been no systematic research into the psychological aspects of this interpretation, there does appear to be evidence, largely clinical in character, that an emotional catharsis does enable people to continue to function effectively in situations in which there are built-in sources of tension.

In addition to these social-psychological functions, "the lifting of the normal taboos and restraints obviously serves to emphasize [the conventional rules] . . . this particular ritual, by allowing people to behave in normally prohibited ways, gave expression, in a reversed form, to the normal rightness of a particular kind of social order."[22] The functions of these rituals, then, included at least the resolution of tensions created by the social structure, and the reinforcement of existing norms and relationships; in generating these results the rituals help to sustain the whole system of family roles and relationships, which in this case meant virtually the entire fabric of the society.

THE TOLKACH IN SOVIET SOCIETY   In 1959, *Izvestia*, the official government newspaper in the Soviet Union, published a lengthy article excoriating the *tolkachi* (literally "pushers"), who worked as agents for plant managers, locating scarce materials they needed and making arrangements for their delivery. Many of the activities of the *tolkachi* resembled those of expediters in American industry, whose task is to assure the delivery of needed supplies. But in order to secure the raw materials or components that were required by his client, the *tolkach* often had to persuade officials to ignore the plans they were supposed to be following, either through persuasion, personal influence, or *sub rosa* gifts and exchanges. According to *Izvestia*, one factory in the Urals had sent out 2,762 *tolkachi* in an eleven-month period, a steel mill had dispatched 2,813 and one factory in the Gorki district had been host to approximately 3,000 *tolkachi* within an eight-month span.[23]

In an economy in which production is carefully planned, with each plant required to achieve a given output and with careful provision for deliveries of required supplies, the widespread phenomenon of the *tolkach*, who operated on the thin edge of legality, would seem to be something of an anomaly. Yet he survived despite the official criticism, for he served important functions. No over-all plan can foresee all the problems that might interfere with the operations of a complex economy, in which failure to achieve a set goal in one plant may precipitate a sequence of failures in other plans when needed supplies are not forthcoming. As the Soviet Union has sought to achieve a continued high rate of industrialization and economic growth, building new plants, training a labor force, introducing new techniques, some such failures have been perhaps inevitable. Yet little allowance is made for the many exigencies that can develop, and plant managers are held responsible for the quotas they have been assigned. In these circumstances, it would hardly be surprising if plant managers had recourse to the quasi-legal *tolkach* who might be able to secure the necessary supplies.

The consequences of the frequently criticized activities of the *tolkach* could be both functional and dysfunctional for the economy as a whole. Barrington Moore sums up these consequences as follows:

By interfering with the intricate system of priorities he performs a definite disservice to the regime. On the other hand, by scaring up supplies that may be useless where they are, but are badly needed by his employer, he performs a definite service for the economy. Possibly his positive contributions outweigh his disadvantages in the eyes of the authorities, who therefore continue to tolerate his existence.[24]

The steadily increasing productivity of the Soviet economy, which is probably eliminating chronic shortages of some materials, and the various changes that have been made in the organization and administration of the economy since 1959, however, may have diminished the need for the free-wheeling *tolkach*. In any event, there has been little mention of the *tolkach* in recent years in either the Soviet press or the writings of students of the Soviet Union.

AMERICAN "BABY MANUALS"   *A Manual of Child Care*, by Benjamin Spock, was first published in 1946 and then reprinted in a paperback edition which went through 58 printings. A revised paperback edition subsequently went through

150 printings by 1965, and according to its publishers the book had sold over 16 million copies since its first appearance. The Children's Bureau published *Infant Care*, a somewhat briefer guide book, in 1914, and has since revised it ten times, more recently in 1963. An estimated 40 million copies have been distributed. These are only the most popular and widely used of a large array of baby-care manuals that provide American mothers (and fathers) with suggestions and directions for looking after children and for dealing with the many problems they face: health, feeding, toilet training, sex education, discipline, and so on.

Why this extraordinary and by now steady and familiar pattern of using published child-care manuals? One obvious explanation would be the growth of scientific knowledge in both medicine and psychology in recent decades and the mounting public respect for science. But this explanation in itself is incomplete, for it overlooks those changes in family structure that lead people to seek such knowledge. Why do so many parents not rely, as their parents did before them, upon time-tested and traditional methods of child care handed down from mother to daughter, with such modifications as creep into traditional routines from time to time? The answer lies in large measure in the structure of the contemporary American family. (For a fuller discussion of the American middle-class family, see Chapter 8.)

The modern American household is typically limited to parents and their children; resident in-laws are, on the whole, strongly disapproved of. Moreover, in our highly mobile society, many of these "nuclear" or "elementary" families, as they are called, are likely to live some distance from their respective parents, and from uncles, aunts, and cousins. In addition, the typical family is relatively small and the intervals between children short. Many girls, consequently, have little opportunity to witness or learn traditional methods of caring for small children. The shifting roles of women now include, in addition to childbearing and child care, other activities looked on as necessary, proper, and desirable; there are, therefore, no strong incentives and only limited opportunity in many cases to acquire in advance the skills of motherhood. As a result the young mother is likely to have little practical knowledge when her own children arrive, and parents or relatives who might be helpful are not easily accessible. She must, therefore, secure information, advice, and aid from other sources. In a society that places so much stress upon science, suggestions from appropriately qualified professionals are likely to carry heavy weight. The function of these baby-care manuals, then, is to fill the gap in knowledge left by the particular structure of the modern-day family. They provide methods for dealing with recurrent problems for which there are few traditional solutions available and hardly any other sources of aid.

The use of such child-care literature, however, is more frequent in the middle class than in the working class. In a recent study, Zena Blau found that 77 per cent of a sample of white middle-class mothers had read Dr. Spock's book, compared with only 48 per cent among working class mothers.[25] This difference reflects class differences in family structure, values, and knowledge. Middle-class families have typically been smaller (though this difference has been diminishing). More significantly, they are better educated (91 per cent of the middle-class women had graduated from high school or attended college, compared with

only 45 per cent of the working-class women) and more approving of the findings of modern medical and psychological science. They are also more likely to see child-rearing as "problematic" and therefore to seek out expert aid and advice than are working-class parents, who are inclined to be quite satisfied with traditional methods of child care.[26]

Social change and the "historical" approach

Functional analysis in general and each of the specific concepts we have thus far introduced presume a considerable degree of stability and constancy in human behavior. One cannot examine a social role without assuming that the norms governing behavior persist over a period of time. An assertion that a particular belief contributes to the persistence of some institutional system obviously implies that both belief and institutions have some measure of continuity. Yet it is also readily apparent that though many things seem to remain the same, other aspects of society are continually changing. In a world so frequently described as revolutionary, this point hardly needs emphasis. Sociological analysis, therefore, must account not only for stability and continuity, but also for the transformation of society and culture and for the introduction of new ideas, new habits, new relationships, new forms of organization.

The problems of change, of course, are not new to sociology, which has deep roots in eighteenth- and nineteenth-century philosophies of history. Beginning with Comte and his predecessors—for example, Henri de Saint Simon—and continuing through the rest of the nineteenth century and into the twentieth, most sociologists devoted their attention chiefly to problems of social change. The central questions for Comte, Herbert Spencer, and Lester F. Ward concerned the processes and the sequences through which society had evolved. These evolutionary theories made frequent assumptions about the inevitability of progress, the superiority of modern society, and the proper place of sociological knowledge itself. They began with origins: How did the family first come into being? Or religion? Or the state? Having established theories of origins, they then sought to trace the successive stages through which institutions had developed. Often they applied the concepts and theories of biological evolution: natural selection, survival of the fittest, adaptation.

These problems are of comparatively little interest to contemporary scholars. As Robert M. MacIver and Charles H. Page have observed: "The seed of society is in the beginnings of life, and if there were . . . beginnings [of society] in any absolute sense we know nothing of them." [27] The theory of unilineal social evolution, which held that each society passes through the same stages of development, has been entirely abandoned. Evolution, as a guiding principle, no longer has much currency among sociologists or anthropologists, except for a few scholars who continue to use the concept, albeit in a refined and sophisticated form. One of these contemporary scholars, Julian Steward, sums up his version of evolutionary theory as follows: "The methodology of evolution . . . postulates that genuine parallels of form and function develop in historically independent sequences or cultural traditions. Second, it explains these parallels by the independent operation of identical causality in each case." [28] By examining the emergence of roughly similar social forms in different societies it might then be possible to arrive at valid

conclusions concerning the development of institutional systems and social structures. This type of formulation does not differ very much from prevailing theoretical views except in its assumption that it may eventually be possible to develop a general theory of evolution applicable to all social groups.

The general failure of evolutionary theory—and its rejection—stemmed from two related weaknesses. The mechanical application of ideas derived from one field of inquiry to another (a tactic utilized by some students of man and society in order to create a seemingly scientific discipline) almost inevitably distorted the facts by coercing them into preconceived schemes. More significantly, perhaps, evolutionary theorists could not reach agreement on the criteria that distinguished the more evolved from the less evolved, the more complex from the less complex, particularly in the light of new knowledge concerning non-Western societies and cultures. A seemingly simple society among the Australian aborigines, for example, possessing a crude technology and subsisting on hunting and food gathering, was found to have an extremely complex kinship system and elaborate ceremonials. [29]

The development of functional theory was in part a reaction to the inadequacies of evolutionary thought and an effort to explore the interrelations of social institutions and social structures. There now appears to be a swing back toward a renewed interest in evolution, though within the context of the knowledge we now possess of the structure and functioning of society. Talcott Parsons, for example, perhaps the leading sociological "functionalist," in a paper which he defined as a "contribution to the revival and examination of evolutionary thinking in sociology," has sought to identify, in a very general fashion, a sequence of "evolutionary universals," each of which constitutes a necessary prerequisite for the development of new and more complex levels of social organization.[30] In a much less abstract formulation, Wilbert Moore has asserted that "there has been a long-term increase in man's ability to adapt to and control his environment." There are several "long-term trends" which, he argues, are "consistent" with this assertion: the increase in the size of human populations, the "additive or accumulative character of objective knowledge and rational technique," the accelerating rate at which knowledge can be acquired and stored, and the incorporation of all men into a *"single* system," despite persisting conflicts and differences among human groups.[31]

These new evolutionary formulations, however, though raising important long-run questions, are so general that they still have only limited value in accounting for the specific complex changes that take place in institutions, values, beliefs, social structures, and patterns of social behavior. Yet an historical approach must seek to explain these changes. While the functional approach focuses upon the mechanisms by which an existing social order is maintained, the historical directs attention to the forces and processes that contribute to the flux and variation of social life.

The contrast between the functional and historical approaches, however, is sometimes mistakenly described as a distinction between the static and the dynamic. Both approaches must deal with social processes taking place over a period of time even though they order and interpret their observations differently. To see a society as a functioning whole is not to see it as unmoving or standing still; if we may borrow an image from

biology, the vital processes of social life, the complex reciprocal adjustments and responses of individuals, organizations, and institutions to one another, continue wherever men live together in society. Within any social order there are processes of varying degrees of complexity, more or less regular sequences of events in which men conform to established norms and fit into some existing social structures. Functional analysis deals with such processes within a relatively stable structure in which the participants may change and individuals may move from one role or status to another. The historical approach is concerned with the processes by which the structure itself is changed.

Before one can deal with problems of social change, it has been argued, one must first understand the functional dynamics of society. There seems to be little warrant for this asserted priority; insofar as inquiry begins with facts to be explained one can as readily begin with the facts of change as with the facts of stability. But wherever one begins, one must eventually deal with both sets of facts, to maintain, as it were, a double focus. Both views, the historical and functional, presuppose that society is a whole or system made up of interrelated and interdependent parts.

Many theories of social change have emphasized one factor—or one part in the total complex—while underestimating or neglecting others: Karl Marx's economic determinism, Thorstein Veblen's technological determinism, theories that assign crucial importance to ideology or religion or to geography and climate. These monistic interpretations attribute an independent and dynamic character to a single factor; as it is transformed other elements in the society are affected and eventually change their form or function.

These theories have frequently called attention, when first put forward, to previously ignored or underestimated historical forces, but they all inevitably oversimplify the causes and processes of change. So interconnected are the various elements of society that no one set of institutions or social structures, no matter how important it may be, can be said to be unaffected by others—self-caused, so to speak. (The gross "factors" in these theories—Marx's "economic base," Veblen's technology, for example—are so conceived, in any case, that in effect they include several readily distinguished variables.) The course of economic development can be and frequently is markedly influenced by political or religious institutions. Ideas and beliefs do not exist in an ivory tower free from the influence of the market place or the political arena. The pursuit of power and authority is often directed to ends defined by economic or religious values, which can in turn affect the very nature of political organization. What is important in one era may be more or less important in another: Strictly economic factors probably played a much greater role in the nineteenth century than they do in the mid-twentieth. As C. Wright Mills commented: "We do not know any universal principles of historical change; the mechanisms of change we do know vary with the social structure we are examining. For historical change *is* change of social structures, of the relations among their component parts. Just as there is a variety of social structures, there is a variety of principles of historical change." [32]

In the absence of any over-all theory of social change, we shall suggest only some general perspectives to guide our discussion. Sources of change may be exogenous, that is, come from outside the society, or endogenous, that is, from within.

The latter can be either institutionally sanctioned types of innovation or the tensions, strains, and conflicts generated within the society itself.

Diffusion

As the world has become more closely knit together, with greater frequency of contact among members of different societies and an increased flow of information and ideas from one to another, the diffusion of cultural forms has increased. Americans dance the tango, Frenchmen drink Coca-Cola, and the Japanese play baseball.

The concept of *diffusion*, the spread of cultural traits from one society to another (or from one place or group to another within the same society), was first proposed as an alternative to the evolutionary explanation for the appearance of similar characteristics in different societies. That such transfer has always been frequent is indisputable, despite the strongly nationalistic biases which lead citizens of some countries, including our own, to ignore the extent of their cultural indebtedness to others. As Ralph Linton has pointed out in a much-quoted passage:

Our solid American citizen awakens in a bed built on a pattern which originated in the Near East but which was modified in Northern Europe before it was transmitted to America. He throws back covers made from cotton, domesticated in India, or linen, domesticated in the Near East, . . . or silk, the use of which was discovered in China. All of these materials have been spun and woven by processes invented in the Near East. He slips into his moccasins, invented by the Indians of the Eastern woodlands, and goes to the bathroom, whose fixtures are a mixture of European and American inventions, both of recent date. He takes off his pajamas, a garment invented in India, and washes with soap invented by the ancient

Gauls. He then shaves, a masochistic rite which seems to have been derived from either Sumer or ancient Egypt.

Returning to the bedroom, he removes his clothes from a chair of southern European type and proceeds to dress. He puts on garments whose form originally derived from the skin clothing of the nomads of the Asiatic steppes, puts on shoes made from skins tanned by a process invented in ancient Egypt and cut to a pattern derived from the classical civilizations of the Mediterranean, and ties around his neck a strip of bright-colored cloth which is a vestigial survival of the shoulder shawls worn by the seventeenth-century Croatians. Before going out for breakfast he glances through the window, made of glass invented in Egypt, and if it is raining puts on overshoes made of rubber discovered by the Central American Indians and takes an umbrella, invented in southeastern Asia. Upon his head he puts a hat made of felt, a material invented in the Asiatic steppes.

On his way to breakfast he stops to buy a paper, paying for it with coins, an ancient Lydian invention. At the restaurant a whole new series of borrowed elements confronts him. His plate is made of a form of pottery invented in China. His knife is of steel, an alloy first made in southern India, his fork a medieval Italian invention, and his spoon a derivative of a Roman original. He begins breakfast with an orange, from the eastern Mediterranean, a cantaloupe from Persia, or perhaps a piece of African watermelon. With this he has coffee, an Abyssinian plant, with cream and sugar. Both the domestication of cows and the idea of milking them originated in the Near East, while sugar was first made in India. After his fruit and first coffee he goes on to waffles, cakes made by a Scandinavian technique from wheat domesticated in Asia Minor. Over these he pours maple syrup, invented by the Indians of the Eastern woodlands. As a side

In many parts of the world, concern is expressed about the "Americanization" of local culture. Here is a street scene in Ghana.

Marc Riboud from Magnum

dish he may have the egg of a species of bird domesticated in Indo-China, or thin strips of the flesh of an animal domesticated in Eastern Asia which have been salted and smoked by a process developed in northern Europe.

When our friend has finished eating he settles back to smoke, an American Indian habit, consuming a plant domesticated in Brazil in either a pipe, derived from the Indians of Virginia, or a cigarette, derived from Mexico. If he is hardy enough he may even attempt a cigar, transmitted to us from the Antilles by way of Spain. While smoking he reads the news of the day, imprinted in characters invented by the ancient Semites upon a material invented in China by a process invented in Germany. As he absorbs the accounts of foreign troubles he will, if he is a good conservative citizen, thank a Hebrew deity in an Indo-European language that he is 100 per cent American.[33]

Diffusion is a selective process. As much or more may be rejected as is accepted by a society which comes in contact with new and different social and cultural patterns. Alien ideas and practices that run counter to well-established beliefs and values are rejected, and those imported cultural traits that are adopted must "fit" in some fashion into the culture, or answer some felt need derived from existing circumstances. Japan, for example, adopted much of Western technology, which enabled them to achieve desired goals, without simultaneously taking over Western political beliefs, institutions, art forms, philosophy, or eating habits. Only recently, as traditional verities have been challenged in the years after the Japanese defeat in World War II, have Japanese youth adopted many Western habits, attitudes, and leisure interests.

Not all exogenous change, of course, occurs gradually as new ideas are introduced through the various media of communication or through commercial, cultural, or political exchanges among members of different societies. History records many conquests in which one group of nation has forcibly imposed its power and might upon others, though even conquerors have usually had to take into account the culture and social organization of the conquered to avoid endless resistance and difficulty. In their colonial endeavors the British often exploited indigenous political arrangements, using local chiefs or rulers for their own administrative purposes. Many parts of the world even now have just emerged from colonial domination, though not without having experienced significant changes in their culture and social structure. Some of the former French colonies in Africa, for example, have adopted French parliamentary forms and carry on their debates in French, punctuated on occasion with references to classical French literature.

As nations have been incorporated into an international system of power and elaborate networks of trade and commerce, they have found it difficult to escape from the play of international political and economic forces. Even the most powerful now feel the impact of events that take place outside their boundaries.

Equilibrium and change

Yet many of the changes that occur within a society stem from internal sources, from the normal workings of its own institutions. In seeking out these endogenous sources of change, it is sometimes useful to conceive of society as a system whose equilibrium is constantly being disturbed and in some degree re-established. By equilibrium is meant a state of affairs in which institutions, values, and social structures are functionally interrelated to form a more or less integrated whole. Religious institutions sustain the existing forms of political authority and family relationships; educational institutions inculcate accepted moral standards and train individuals to undertake the adult roles they are to perform; beliefs concerning the nature of human life are fairly consistent with existing patterns of social relationships; individuals are able to achieve the goals which are sanctioned by the culture as important; and so on.

In a comparatively well-integrated traditional society, the influence of external forces, peaceful or warlike, is apt to be the major, though not the exclusive, source of change. Within such a society, innovation is likely to be looked at askance, and invention is infrequent, although it occasionally occurs.

Since no society is absolutely static or ever fully integrated, this equilibrium should be conceived of as dynamic or moving and always as only partial. As changes occur and their repercussions are felt, adjustments are made that tend to restore the equilibrium of the system. (If appropriate adjustments are not made, the system, of course, may fall apart.) Within the social system of the factory, for example, introduction of new procedures or new machines frequently disturbs established routines and breaks up informal social groupings among workers, requiring sometimes complex and often difficult readjustments.

There is nothing immediate or automatic about these readjustments. They may be long delayed or long avoided, leading in some instances to pressures that explode in violent revolution or drastic, though less violent, change, followed by a new integration differing in many significant respects from the old. Thus workers who are disturbed by abrupt changes or by unresolved grievances may organize, strike, and force substan-

tial revisions of the structure of labor-management relations.

The focus upon equilibrium or integration should not lead to a disregard of conflict or to the assumption that it merely reflects lack of integration or consensus within society. In the more extreme forms of conflict, civil war or race riots, for example, the consensus upon which society rests is challenged or destroyed. In its less violent forms, however, conflict represents a mechanism for resolving differences, thus contributing to the stability of the social order. Conflict may be an institutionalized feature of social structure: strikes or political opposition, for example; it may be tolerated as in the case of religious contentions; or it may be an inevitable consequence of the structure of society, particularly when there are many groups each seeking to realize its own ends. It has been suggested recently that a "conflict model" of society would be more fruitful than an equilibrium model;[34] certainly, as Lewis Coser has demonstrated in some detail, conflict has been ignored or underestimated in much recent sociological work.[35] But it is doubtful that there is as yet an adequate formulation of a model that can offer greater theoretical advantages than an appropriately qualified approach to society as a more or less integrated system.

In the discussion of equilibrium, as in other sociological analysis, there is sometimes a tendency to reify the concept of society, to speak of it as a "boundary-maintaining system" continually attempting to maintain its equilibrium, and of its responses to irritations or strains. Such usages normally mean that groups of persons respond in patterned ways to difficulties they face in their social lives in order to protect their established way of life or to provide for the basic necessities of collective life. To slip from this appropriate sociological shorthand into the assumption that it is the concept that acts, thinks, feels, responds, is so easy that it is important to renew the injunction against reifying what are otherwise necessary or useful abstractions.

In most modern societies, some kinds of invention and innovation, which inevitably disrupt the equilibrium of the system, are not only welcomed, but are also stimulated and encouraged. Innovation in some fields represents conformity with significant social values. Thus American society is usually receptive to new gadgets, tools, and implements (though some technical and mechanical innovations meet resistance for economic and other reasons). Efficiency and invention in industry are constantly stimulated by economic pressure. Technological innovation is encouraged in many ways: through the patent system, suggestion schemes in factories, and through a cultural emphasis upon such values and beliefs as those embodied in the traditional saying, "If a man make a better mouse trap the world will make a beaten path to his door." The scientific progress upon which technology increasingly has come to rest is fostered through research laboratories and scientific institutes. Few other fields in the United States are equal to technology and science in their encouragement of new ideas, new devices, new routines, although in such varied segments of social life as leisure and business procedure there is a wide range of permissiveness and tolerance, as well as actual encouragement, for new techniques.

Because of the interdependence of the elements of society, change at any one point is likely to precipitate changes elsewhere. (This proposition, it should be noted, occupies a key place in the relations between functional and historical analysis.) Science and technology are

therefore in effect built-in disturbers of the peace. The innovations they create are usually accepted as desirable without reference to all of their possible consequences, some of which therefore come unheralded, unpredicted, and, frequently, from the point of view of many groups, unwanted. For example, the automobile, when it first appeared, was adopted chiefly by a few members of the leisure class as a new means of recreation and display. When its practical value became apparent and its cost was reduced, largely as a result of rapid technological progress, it quickly became a standard possession for many, eventually most, American families. By the mid-1960s more than 80 million motor vehicles crowded American highways; the number is expected to increase to well over 100 million within less than twenty years.

The consequences of this readily accepted change for American culture and society have been virtually incalculable. The automobile industry became one of the nation's greatest and a dominant component of the economy; the recession of 1958 was widely labeled an "automobile recession" because of a substantial dip in the industry's fortunes and its impact on the rest of the nation's business and economy. The automobile has played a major role in influencing the nature of urban and suburban growth. Leisure patterns have been changed; family life, religion, and politics influenced; birth rates and death rates affected. Few if any of these consequences were foreseen or expected; many were not desired. In gaining fame and fortune with his mass-produced Model T, Henry Ford helped to destroy the peaceful rural world he himself valued so highly.

The equilibrium of a social system, however, can be disrupted not only by cultural innovations, but also by dynamic processes generated by its own institutions. One of Karl Marx's chief contributions to the development of social science lay in his demonstration that accepted institutions could create the conditions that would eventually lead to their transformation. Conventional and approved capitalist behavior, for example, has contributed to the transformation of capitalism: Unrestricted competition in a free market has steadily reduced the extent of competition in many industries; the elimination of an employer's responsibilities for his workers left them to the mercies of the market and led to labor organization and the eventual reconstruction of worker-employer relations. In some peasant societies, to take an alternative illustration, inheritance rules calling for equal division of land among sons may eventually create such miniscule plots of land for farming that they will be unable to support the families living upon them.

With changes continuously taking place in various sectors of society, tensions, strains, and pressures for further shifts are built up. Under some conditions, the readjustments necessary to resolve the difficulties which exist come about relatively easily, through a democratic political process or by the efforts of those who recognize the need for some changes. If groups of people are stimulated or provoked by some difficulty for which there does not appear to be a ready solution—if they cannot achieve their goals, or their security or status is sharply challenged, or incompatible or excessive demands are made upon them—they may deliberately seek to transform the existing state of affairs by creating a *social movement*. Many of the changes that do occur in society are at least in part the outcome of more or less organized action on the part of such movements—for example, the prohibition movement, the Granger

movement, Naziism in Germany, the Mau Mau in Kenya, the civil rights movement, the "Ban the Bomb" movement in England of several years ago. Not all movements are successful in achieving their goals; their efforts in fact often lead to opposition movements that confront each other in the political arena. Even if social movements do not accomplish their stated aims, they can nevertheless play an important role in the shifting social order. (For a fuller discussion of social movements, see Chapter 20.)

In the analysis of change, then, to summarize our discussion thus far, we must include influences from without, contact with other groups, institutionalized sources of change, the latent consequences of existing institutions and social structures, tensions generated by the lack of complete integration, and organized efforts to effect change. These are not unrelated forces, and their interrelations must be examined systematically in sociological study.

Recognition of the complexity of social change and of the forces which initiate or provoke it should not lead to the conclusion that because a great many variables are involved "it does not make much differences which variable one starts with." [36] The equilibrium-interdependence approach that we have suggested undoubtedly leads, if systematically pursued, to the inclusion of almost the entire range of relevant variables. "In the end," as Kingsley Davis points out, "in order to explain the total change in a society, one would have to consider the main variables constituting the social equilibrium." [37] But specific changes can often be accounted for adequately without necessarily considering all aspects of the society. Even though a developed explanation of any change eventually encompasses a wide range of variables, it is necessary to assess the relative importance of each. In explaining the increasing professionalization of many occupations, for example, shifts in family organization or in religious beliefs seem to be much less significant than the development of new skills and the nature of the social and economic rewards available to those who successfully claim professional status.

Sociology and history

The analysis of specific types of social organization and of institutions and other cultural forms, we have suggested, must deal with problems of change as well as those of function and order. Throughout the following chapters, therefore, social change will be a recurrent theme—the transformation of the modern family, the shifts in patterns of social stratification and of race relations, the expansion of cities, the elaboration of bureaucracy, the increasing importance of science, the growth of population. In addition, we shall devote Chapter 20 to a consideration of some general problems relating to change that transcend these specific changes.

We wish to emphasize this concern with change because too much sociological work, particularly in the United States, has been directed to static studies, too little to problems of change. Any analysis, of course, necessarily emphasizes some facts and problems at the expense of others. Many sociological studies have merely sought to establish relationships among a given set of facts at a particular time and place—between size of organization and forms of authority, for example, or between class position and reading habits. Functional analysis has tended to emphasize problems of order and the maintenance of a given social system. But

in a world of rapid and frequently revolutionary change, failure to give adequate attention to the shifts constantly taking place in the ways in which people live, in the ideas they live by, and in their relations with one another, must seriously limit the utility and applicability of sociological inquiry. As C. Wright Mills put it in a provocative and stimulating discussion of "The Uses of History," "Only by an act of abstraction that unnecessarily violates social reality can we try to freeze some knife-edge moment." [38]

We have chosen to call our approach to the study of social change "historical" for two reasons. First, we wish to emphasize the fact that all sociological inquiries refer to persons and action at some specific time and place. Although sociologists try to derive propositions not limited by time or place, their analytic, ahistorical studies, whether of voting behavior, mental health, community power structure, class differences in behavior, or family disorganization, almost inevitably assume, implicitly, a given historical context. The greater the awareness of that context, the sources from which it is derived, and the tendencies toward change inherent in it, the greater the likelihood that more of the relevant variables will be taken into account and the less the possibility that generalizations derived from such studies will be extended to other circumstances where they do not apply.

Mills has argued that "There is . . . no 'law' stated by any social scientist that is trans-historical, that must not be understood as having to do with the specific structure of some period. Other 'laws' turn out to be empty abstractions or quite confused tautologies." [39] Mills seems to dismiss too cavalierly the possibility of generalizations that apply beyond specific historical situations, but he is correct in discounting many, perhaps most, of the "laws" that are now asserted to define universally found relationships among sociological variables. At best we can point at present to variables to be taken into account in dealing with particular problems and, at a very general level, to the conditions which must exist for certain events to take place or for various structures to survive. These are not unimportant contributions, but they remain still at some distance from general theory readily applicable to any and all societies. Some of our most useful sociological theories have, in fact, been explicitly confined to particular places and periods: theories of the American character and of the origins of modern capitalism, for example. Others, which were initially formulated in general terms—theories of the city, of bureaucracy, of industrial organization—have turned out to be far more historically confined than originally thought. Even if—or, perhaps more optimistically, when—adequate general sociological theory is available, the problem of its applicability to specific historical situations will still have to be resolved.

Second, we wish to stress the link between sociology and history. In so doing, however, it is necessary to distinguish between the two fields as well as to identify their affinities. These disciplines mean different things to the practitioners of each, and it is therefore difficult to draw clear lines and assign neatly demarcated fields of inquiry. There are many historians who might legitimately be identified as sociologists—and vice versa. Nevertheless, some rough distinctions can be drawn, for the historian's interests and focus of attention are, on the whole, different from those of the sociologist.

The historian is typically concerned with the past, but unless he is a pure antiquarian, he is also interested in its relevance to the present. The sociologist, on the other hand, is much more likely to focus his attention upon the present, although there are some—and there should be more—exceptions to this self-imposed limitation.

Many historians disclaim any identification as scientists; their aim is narrative, to describe *wie es eigentlich gewesen ist* (as it really was), in the oft-quoted phrase of the great German historian Ranke. They are "scientific" only insofar as they seek the most reliable data. Much of the narrative deals with concrete persons and presumably unique events. The sociologist, on the other hand, as we noted earlier, is centrally concerned with generalizations. Individuals and events are important chiefly as they fit into categories or patterns. Abstraction, inevitable in any intellectual discourse (including history), is explicit, self-conscious, and typically at a higher level than in historical scholarship.

The English economic historian Michael Postan has argued, however, that the "uniqueness" and the "concreteness" of historical study are essentially "fictitious," for if historical investigations were truly unique and concrete, actually limited to specific persons and events, they would be dull and uninteresting. Only when comparisons or generalizations are suggested or implied does historical study become truly valuable. Nevertheless, he asserts, the historian must maintain these fictions, else he will lose his distinctive identity and fail to make his distinctive contribution. Despite—or perhaps because of—this mild and, if Postan is right, fruitful self-deception, the creative historian does have something to contribute to the effort to create a "science of society." [40]

In addition, a good deal of historical inquiry actually deals not with individual persons and unique events, but with institutions, organizations, beliefs, and ideas—that is, with social structure and culture. In these areas the historian obviously deals with materials and problems similar to those of the sociologist. The differences lie in the extent to which explicit general concepts are used, in the emphasis upon the concrete and unique in one case and on the general and recurrent in the other, and in a greater concern with change on the part of the historian. Each, therefore, has something to contribute to the other, although at present it appears that more historians are benefiting from their exposure to sociology than the other way around.

Conclusion

The contrast between the functional and historical approaches is itself in all likelihood merely a phase in the history of sociology. If this now barely maturing discipline is to achieve its goals and fulfill its youthful hopes, these approaches—and the theories they have engendered—must be brought together into a unified whole. Already they share several common perspectives. They both entail an awareness of the complex interrelationships which exist within society and of the limitations of any simplified one-factor interpretation of social behavior. They are both concerned with generalization rather than with the individual and unique, and they utilize similar concepts for catching the recurrent aspects of social life. Finally, they both recognize the importance and value of a comparative approach, for whatever the problems selected for study the systematic comparison of different societies, past and present, provides both the basis for suggestive hypotheses and the material for testing them.

Notes

[1] Ralph Ross, *Symbols and Civilization* (New York: Harcourt, 1962), p. 64.

[2] For a full analysis of the "modes of the question 'Why?'" see Robert M. MacIver, *Social Causation* (Boston: Ginn, 1942), especially Part III.

[3] See, for example, the articles by Talcott Parsons, Robert N. Bellah, and S. N. Eisenstadt, *American Sociological Review*, XXIX (June, 1964).

[4] For an essay that argues that sociological analysis *is* functional analysis, see Kingsley Davis, "The Myth of Functional Analysis," *American Sociological Review*, XXIV (December, 1959), 757–72.

[5] Robert K. Merton, *Social Theory and Social Structure* (rev. and enlarged ed.; New York: Free Press, 1957), p. 46. Much of the following discussion of functional analysis is derived from Ch. 1.

[6] Gerhart Niemeyer, *Law Without Force* (Princeton: Princeton University Press, 1941), p. 300, quoted in Merton, *op. cit.*, p. 46n.

[7] Quoted in Lewis A. Coser and Bernard Rosenberg (eds.), *Sociological Theory* (2nd ed.; New York: Macmillan, 1964), p. 622.

[8] Émile Durkheim, *The Rules of Sociological Method*, trans. by Sarah A. Solovay and John H. Mueller, ed. with an intro. by George E. G. Catlin (Chicago: University of Chicago Press, 1938), p. 95.

[9] See David Aberle *et al.*, "The Functional Prerequisites of a Society," *Ethics* IX (January, 1950), 100–11, for an effort to spell out a minimum set of functional prerequisites (or, more precisely, requisites).

[10] For a useful analysis of the risks of a functional analysis of religion, see Merton, *op. cit.*, pp. 28–30.

[11] William F. Cottrell, "Of Time and the

Railroader," *American Sociological Review*, IV (April, 1939), 190–8.

[12] Merton, *op. cit.*, p. 51.

[13] Quoted in Louis Schneider, "Problems in the Sociology of Religion," in Robert E. L. Faris (ed.), *Handbook of Modern Sociology* (Chicago: Rand McNally, 1964), p. 783.

[14] *Ibid.*, p. 784.

[15] Charles A. Beard and Mary R. Beard, *The Rise of American Civilization*, II (New York: Macmillan, 1930), 778.

[16] Liston Pope, *Millhands and Preachers* (New Haven: Yale University Press, 1942), pp. 84–91 and Ch. VIII.

[17] For a suggestive exposition of the latent functions of the political machine, see Merton, *op. cit.*, pp. 72–82. For an attempt to place Merton's analysis in an historical context, see Eric L. McKitrick, "The Study of Corruption," *Political Science Quarterly*, LXXII (December, 1957), 502–14.

[18] Marion J. Levy, *The Structure of Society* (Princeton: Princeton University Press, 1952), pp. 76–83.

[19] Max Gluckman, *Custom and Conflict in Africa* (Oxford: Blackwell, 1955), p. 111.

[20] *Ibid.*, pp. 113–4.

[21] *Ibid.*, p. 115.

[22] *Ibid.*, pp. 115–6.

[23] *The New York Times*, April 19, 1959.

[24] Barrington Moore, Jr., *Terror and Progress: U.S.S.R.* (Cambridge, Mass.: Harvard University Press, 1954), p. 62.

[25] Zena S. Blau, "Exposure to Child-Rearing Experts: A Structural Interpretation of Class-Color Differences," *American Journal of Sociology*, LXIX (May, 1964), 596–608.

[26] Melvin L. Kohn, "Social Class and Parent-Child Relationships: An Interpretation," *American Journal of Sociology*, LXVIII (January, 1963), 471–80.

[27] Robert M. MacIver and Charles H. Page, *Society: An Introductory Analysis* (New York: Holt, 1949), p. 589.

[28] Julian H. Steward, "Evolution and Progress," in Alfred L. Kroeber *et al.*, *Anthropology Today* (Chicago: University of Chicago Press, 1953), p. 315.

[29] W. Lloyd Warner, *A Black Civilization* (New York: Harper, 1937).

[30] Talcott Parsons, "Evolutionary Universals in Society," *American Sociological Review*, XXIX (June, 1964), 339–57. See also Parsons, *Societies: Evolutionary and Comparative Perspectives* (Englewood Cliffs: Prentice-Hall, 1966).

[31] Wilbert E. Moore, *Social Change* (Englewood Cliffs: Prentice-Hall, 1963), p. 116.

[32] C. Wright Mills, *The Sociological Imagination* (New York: Oxford, 1959), p. 150.

[33] Ralph Linton, *The Study of Man* (New York: Appleton, 1936) pp. 326–7.

[34] Ralf Dahrendorf, "Out of Utopia: Toward a Reorientation of Sociological Analysis," *American Journal of Sociology*, LXIV (September, 1958), 115–27.

[35] Lewis A. Coser, *The Functions of Social Conflict* (New York: Free Press, 1956).

[36] Kingsley Davis, *Human Society* (New York: Macmillan, 1949), p. 634.

[37] *Ibid.*

[38] Mills, *op. cit.*, p. 151.

[39] *Ibid.*, pp. 149–50.

[40] Michael M. Postan, "History and the Social Sciences," in *The Social Sciences: Their Relations in Theory and in Teaching* (London: LePlay, 1936), pp. 60–70.

Suggestions for further reading

BIERSTEDT, ROBERT. "Toynbee and Sociology," *British Journal of Sociology*, X (June, 1959), 95–104.

A brief summary of the differences between sociology and history and of their interrelationships.

DURKHEIM, ÉMILE. *The Rules of Sociological Method.* Trans. by Sarah A. Solovay and John H. Mueller. Edited with an introduction by George E. G. Catlin. 8th ed. Chicago: University of Chicago Press, 1938, Ch. 5, "Rules for the Explanation of Social Facts."
The classic formulation of the difference between functional and causal (historical) analysis.

KOMAROVSKY, MIRRA (ED.). *Common Frontiers of the Social Sciences.* New York: Free Press, 1957, Part I, "History and Social Research."
A series of essays, theoretical and substantive, dealing with and illustrating the relations between historical analysis and sociological research.

LINTON, RALPH. *The Study of Man.* New York: Appleton, 1936, Chs. 18, "Discovery and Invention," and 19, "Diffusion."
Brief but useful discussions of innovation and diffusion based upon anthropological research.

MACIVER, ROBERT M., AND CHARLES H. PAGE. *Society: An Introductory Analysis.* New York: Holt, 1949, Book III, "Social Change."
A critical review of alternative theories of social change, a reinterpretation of the nature of social evolution, and a brief summary of some long-run trends in the development of modern society.

MERTON, ROBERT K. *Social Theory and Social Structure.* Revised and enlarged ed. New York: Free Press, 1957, Ch. 1, "Manifest and Latent Functions."
A comprehensive and critical discussion of the concept of function, including a paradigm for functional analysis that seeks to avoid many of the pitfalls it contains.

MILLS, C. WRIGHT. *The Sociological Imagination.* New York: Oxford, 1959, Ch. 8, "Uses of History."
An excellent discussion of the relevance of history for sociological analysis.

MOORE, WILBERT E. *Social Change.* Englewood Cliffs: Prentice-Hall, 1963.
A very useful short book that attempts to formulate an approach to and interpretation of problems of social change.

PART TWO

Social organization

PHOTO CREDITS:
United Press International Photo,
Sam B. Tata from Black Star,
National Cotton Council,
Sybil Shelton from Monkmeyer, Dalmas—Pix

6

The primary group

Nature of the primary group

In a much-quoted passage in which he introduced the concept, Charles H. Cooley defined primary groups as:

✳ . . . those characterized by intimate face-to-face association and cooperation. They are primary in several senses, but chiefly in that they are fundamental in forming the social nature and ideals of the individual. The result of intimate association, psychologically, is a certain fusion of individualities in a common whole, so that one's very self, for many purposes at least, is the common life and purpose of the group. Perhaps the simplest way of describing this wholeness is by saying that it is a "we"; it involves the sort of sympathy and mutual identification for which "we" is a natural expression. One lives in the feeling of the whole and finds the chief aims of his will in that feeling.

It is not to be supposed that the unity of the primary group is one of mere harmony and love. It is always a differentiated and usually a competitive unity, admitting of self-assertion and various appropriative passions; but these passions are socialized by sympathy, and come, or tend to come, under the discipline of a common spirit. The individual will be ambitious, but the chief object of his ambition will be some desired place in the thought of the others, and he will feel allegiance to common standards of service and fair play.[1]

The essential attributes of the primary group then, according to this definition, are: "intimate face-to-face association," the "we" feeling or sense of belonging together, and the "common spirit" with its standards of "service and fair play."

Cooley's seminal discussion is ambiguous on several important points. Although intimacy is an essential element of the primary group, face-to-face association obviously need not be intimate nor, conversely, is intimacy limited to face-to-face relations. The direct contact of salesgirl and customer, foreman and worker, employment service interviewer and unemployed worker, even prostitute and customer (in most cases), are formal and impersonal, while the long-range correspondence of Oliver Wendell Holmes and Harold Laski, or the relations between Peter Ilyitch Tchaikovsky and his beloved Madame Nadezhda von Meck, whom he never saw, bespeak intimacy sustained over both time and distance. Close contact may—and frequently does—provide the foundation for primary relationships, but it need not lead to such relationships.

A second ambiguity stems from the fact that "we" feeling is in some measure characteristic of any social group; as Kingsley Davis has suggested, Cooley himself implies this fact in his discussion of the "necessary extension of 'primary ideals' [loyalty, kindness, sympathy, truth] to larger groups."[2] In the primary group, as Cooley observes, the sense of group identity and loyalty is strong, involving the person deeply, and resting upon the "mutual identification" of members with one another. In this way the group becomes an end in itself: "One lives in the feeling of the whole and finds the chief aims of his will in that feeling." In impersonal groups, in contrast, objectives are limited and specific, the relations within the group are valued largely for the goals whose realization they make possible rather than for their own sake. The "we" feeling is therefore less encompassing, imposes fewer responsibilities or obligations, and entails a more limited commitment by the individual to the group.

Intimacy, inclusive and intrinsically valued relationships, and shared values deriving from experience within the group itself are, then, the principal marks of the primary group. But like all groups it possesses a structure, an organization of roles and relationships—"the sometimes differentiated and . . . competitive unity," in Cooley's phrase—that requires analysis.

In this chapter we are concerned with more informal and spontaneous groups—the autonomous circle of friends who come together by choice and in pursuit of fellowship and to share common interests, the collection of workers in a factory or office out of whose daily interaction has emerged a network of personal relationships that bind them into a recognizable collectivity, the band of advocates who pursue a course that unites them into a dedicated "ideological primary group," to use Edward Shils' phrase. (We shall examine the family, with its institutionally defined structure, in Chapter 8.)

For almost two decades after Cooley's original formulation in 1909, little atten-

tion was given to the primary group by sociologists, other than to emphasize its presumed tendency to disintegrate in a commercialized urban society. During the 1930s and 1940s there was a revival of interest that stemmed from studies of workers in industry and slum gangs, research into the social psychology of group behavior, sociometric analysis of patterns of attraction and rejection in group settings, and group psychotherapy.[3] We can perhaps best begin the analysis of the structure and functions of the primary group by descriptions drawn from two of the studies that contributed to its "rediscovery."

Case studies of primary groups

THE HAWTHORNE, OR WESTERN ELECTRIC, STUDIES [4]   During the 1920s and continuing until 1932, the Western Electric Company pursued in its Hawthorne, Illinois, plant a series of investigations into fatigue, monotony, and morale in relation to production. In the course of their research the investigators were led from a concern for the physiological consequences of work to the structure and functioning of primary groups in the factory. Although our central interest here is in the last of these studies, the entire series warrants a brief review, for it demonstrates the interplay of fact and theory in scientific inquiry as well as the uses and importance of an explicitly sociological approach.

The several investigations known as the Hawthorne studies were undertaken because of unexpected results in an experiment testing the influence of lighting on output. The researchers had been experimenting with changes in illumination, expecting to find that production increased when illumination was improved and decreased when it was cut down. Instead they found that output in the experimental room went up or remained at relatively stable levels not only when the lighting was improved, but also when it was sharply reduced. Clearly, it seemed to the investigators, other factors, probably psychological in nature, were at work. To explore these "human" factors, as they called them, a new inquiry, the Relay Assembly Test Room, so called because it involved a group of girls assembling electrical relays used in telephones, was initiated. Six girls were set to work in a separate room where detailed records could be kept of their output, behavior, and physical condition while the conditions of work were systematically changed. At the outset the six girls chosen for the experiment were told of the research plans, and

great care was taken to convince the girls that the purpose of the test was not to "boost" production but rather to study different types of working conditions so that the most suitable environment for work could be found. They were urged not to hurry or "drive," but to work at a natural pace, as only in this way would the results have any significance.[5]

Different rest periods were tried and then the length of the working day and working week was varied. During a period of more than two years, as various changes—for better and for worse—were made, output on the whole continued to go up. After a careful examination of a great mass of data, the hypotheses that the behavior of the group of girls could be attributed to economic incentives, to less monotony because of rest periods, or to lessened fatigue because of improved physical conditions of work were rejected. It appeared clear that the attitudes of the girls and their feelings about their work were of strategic importance. More-

over, good relations with supervisors and the positive atmosphere inadvertently created in the experimental situation by soliciting cooperation and paying close attention to the girls had so improved their morale that they continued to increase their production even when rest periods were taken away and other advantages provided at various stages of the inquiry were eliminated. Finally, the relations among the girls themselves seemed somehow to be related to their feelings and their behavior. This last observation however, remained fallow for a while before its importance was recognized and its implications explored.

The investigators had thus been led from a largely physiological interpretation of workers' behavior on the job to a psychological point of view. They therefore embarked upon a large-scale interviewing program designed to discover the attitudes and feelings of workers toward their job, particularly toward supervisory practices, and the conditions which affected these judgments and sentiments. In the course of this investigation, in which more than 20,000 employees were interviewed over a three-year period, the interviewers were at first struck by the extent to which complaints about the job were related to the personal problems of workers. But it soon became increasingly evident that the hypothesis that had emerged in a tentative fashion from the Relay Assembly Test Room, namely that it was necessary to see workers' comments and behavior in the context of the work group, was of major importance.

Having arrived at a point of view which focused upon the relations of workers to one another (social organization) as a determinant of both attitudes and behavior, the investigators undertook an intensive study of one small group of fourteen workers engaged in the assembly of switches for use in telephone switchboards. Nine of the workers were "wiremen" whose task consisted of attaching wires in rows, or banks (hence the name Bank Wiring Room), to a component used in telephone switchboard equipment. Three other workers soldered the terminals (soldermen), and two others inspected the finished product for defects.

The data were secured by an observer who remained in the room while the men worked, noting their actions and their conversation, keeping a record of their output, and interviewing each of the workers several times. The presence of an outsider, it was thought, might affect men's behavior and therefore limit the value of the data thus gained, but the evidence, both from this and other studies, indicate clearly that workers' actions were not substantially affected and that the data gained in this fashion were reliable. Perhaps the clearest indication that the observer's presence did not affect workers' behavior is the fact that after a time they did not hesitate to break company rules in his presence.

The technical requirements of the tasks performed by these fourteen men, the physical layout of the room, the method of payment (group piecework, in which each man's wages depended upon total output of the group as well as his own contribution), and company rules all influenced the relations of workers to one another and the frequency and forms of social interaction. Since each man's income depended upon the output of the whole group, there was, understandably, more interest in one another's efforts than had they been paid individually. The speed with which each group of workers could operate depended upon the others: if wiremen were slow, soldermen would be held up; if inspectors were slow, wiremen would not be able to keep going. The

company assigned each man a job and did not approve exchanging tasks. The physical layout of the room and the location of workers affected their opportunities for contact with each other; wiremen, for example, were supposed to stay at their designated work positions, unless they were waiting for an inspector or were performing other tasks sometimes expected of them, while both inspectors and soldermen had to move from place to place.

From the close and continued observation of this group of fourteen men, several significant facts emerged. First, the men shared a set of norms which were not officially defined; indeed the norms ran counter to the rules and expectations of management. Although management had set up a group wage-incentive system designed to increase production, the workers had established their own definition of a reasonable day's work—and stuck to it quite consistently so that, from management's point of view, they were restricting production. The workers felt that no one should "squeal" to management about anything that occurred in the workroom; that no one should work too hard, that is, be a "rate buster," even though they would all presumably profit by the increased output; that no one should be a "chiseler," that is, do too little; and finally, that one should not be too standoffish or superior.

Second, these norms were enforced by the group in various ways. Violation resulted in criticism and an open display of hostility. If someone worked too hard, for example, it was considered appropriate for another worker to "bing" him, that is, to hit him on the arm, to remind him that he was transgressing. Violent reaction to this symbolic punishment would have been out of place and resented by the others.

Third, the workers came to have more or less regular or patterned relationships with one another. Inspectors were looked upon as somewhat superior to the others, and soldermen as somewhat inferior, although the wiremen themselves were divided into higher and lower categories on the basis of their type of equipment. Action tended to follow these hierarchical lines; it was more likely to be initiated from above than below. This was true, for example, in the job-trading that went on despite the company rule prohibiting it. Wiremen and soldermen occasionally switched jobs for a while, although always on the initiative of the wiremen. A regular pattern of mutual aid in which most workers participated existed within the group. The group itself was divided into two smaller cliques, which included eleven of the fourteen workers, although one man in each clique was a marginal member, in the sense that he did not participate in all the activities of his group such as "horsing around," buying candy, betting, and talking.

These facts may appear trivial. Their sociological importance lies in the clear demonstration that even in a highly organized work situation governed by formal rules presumably enforced by an official hierarchy, there is likely to develop an "informal organization," as the investigators called it. Relationships among workers were not confined to the tasks they performed; in fact, their work performance was clearly influenced by the social organization which had emerged on the job. The norms shared by the group largely determined their response to company rules and requirements, while supervisors found it necessary to take into account the group's values and internal structure. For its members, the group provided accepted methods for coping with the demands of the job and for gov-erning relations among themselves, as well as offering important intrinsic gratifications which in themselves made the jobs more—or occasionally less—satisfying.

All these conclusions were hardly new or revolutionary; a student of Cooley or, for that matter, anyone familiar with workers and working conditions might have reported the same facts. Their importance stems, as Michael Olmsted has pointed out, from

. . . the way in which the conclusions were reached. They were "discovered" by prestigeful and practical people who were looking for something else. Consequently, the studies could not be dismissed as mere idle speculation or as being of no interest or applicability to "real life." Nor could the emphasis on the social organization of the small group be ascribed to the preconceptions of professional social scientists bent on proving the relevance of their discipline.[6]

The Western Electric studies, therefore, provided a new impetus to the study of the primary group and its functions, particularly in those large bureaucratic organizations so pervasive in modern society. (For an analysis of bureaucracy see Chapter 11.) The Hawthorne investigations were followed by a large number of studies exploring the role of the primary group in diverse contexts: other industries, service trades, department stores, research laboratories, the armed services. The point of view which emerged from the Western Electric inquiries, sometimes called the "human relations approach" has also gained adherents among industrial executives and has had widespread effects upon personnel policies and managerial ideologies.

THE CORNER BOYS   Unlike the Bank Wiring Room, in which a primary group developed within a larger formal organization, the Norton Street Gang described

by William F. Whyte [7] was the product of
life in an Italian slum neighborhood in
Boston. Moreover, Whyte's research
procedure was very different from that
followed in the Hawthorne plant, for it
entailed several years of residence in the
area and participation within the group [8]
rather than the detached observation of
an outsider.

The "Nortons," whose corporate name
derived from the street corner where
members regularly assembled, included
thirteen young men aged twenty to twenty-
nine who had grown up in the neighborhood. A few of them had once belonged to the same adolescent gang. Most
were unemployed—the study was made
during the last years of the depression of
the 1930s—and all were unmarried.
Were it not for the depression it is unlikely that they would have become part
of the gang or that their common activities would have been what they were—or
that they would have become well known
in sociological literature.

The Nortons displayed group characteristics very similar to those of the Bank
Wiring Room: They engaged in patterned
activities, shared a body of norms and
values that regulated their behavior, and
were tied together in a structure of interrelated roles. They met regularly, although usually without formal planning,
at conventional places—the corner, or a
cafeteria where they gathered each evening for coffee or beer. One evening each
week they bowled. Membership entailed a
set of mutual obligations and expectations
that, although rarely mentioned, were on
the whole well understood; these became
explicit only when they were ignored or
disregarded.

While Alec and Frank were friends, I never
heard either one of them discuss the services
he was performing for the other, but when
they had a falling-out over the group activities

with the Aphrodite Club [a group of young
women], each man complained . . . that the
other was not acting as he should in view of
the services that had been done for him. In
other words, actions which were performed
explicitly for the sake of friendship were revealed as being part of a system of mutual
obligation.[9]

Implicit in this situation is what Alvin
Gouldner has called the "norm of reciprocity," that one must return benefits to
those from whom benefits are received.[10]

Attitudes and behavior toward outsiders as well as toward members of the
group itself were regulated by shared
norms. For example, they had similar attitudes toward women. "Anglo-Saxon"
women outside the Italian community—
and a few from within—were legitimate
targets for sexual advances, with the
amount of prestige accruing from a successful conquest depending upon the social status of the woman, an Anglo-Saxon
Protestant eliciting the greatest respect.
Most women in the neighborhood were
off-limits; not only were some of them
sisters of friends and therefore tabooed,
but they constituted potential wives, who
were expected to be virgin when married.[11]

The structure of roles that defined relations of members to one another within
the group took an hierarchical form with
a leader, "Doc," and several lieutenants,
each with influence over some of the remaining members, as indicated in Figure
1. The importance of the hierarchy lay in
the fact that the higher the individual's
position, the greater freedom he possessed
to initiate action for those below him. The
group itself maintained the structure by
acting in such a way as to prevent
changes in the established relationships.
When Alec, who ranked at the bottom of
the Nortons, challenged the established
leaders in a bowling match, enough psy-

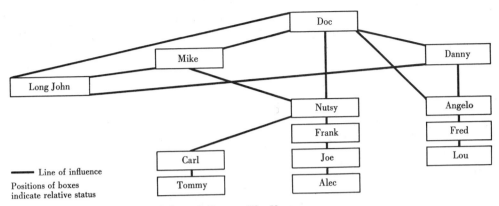

Figure 1. *Organization of an Informal Group: The Nortons*

William F. Whyte, *Street Corner Society*, enlarged ed., p. 13 (Copyright 1943, 1955 by The University of Chicago). Reprinted by permission of The University of Chicago Press.

chological pressure was brought to bear through razzing and heckling to result in his defeat.

The hierarchy, however, was not a one-way affair. Information and suggestions from the low-ranking members were not ignored, although they could only become effective when sanctioned by Doc or one of his lieutenants. The leader himself had to live up to the demands of his role in order to maintain his superiority. He was expected to lend others money if he had any, for example, but was not expected to borrow himself, except from those close to him in the group. His position rested upon his aptitudes and skills, his resourcefulness and judgment, his "fair-mindedness" in dealing with others, and his effectiveness as a spokesman for the group in its relations with outsiders. Failure to live up to these role-expectations would effectively weaken or even destroy the leader's status.

When informal groups like the Nortons tried to establish a formal organization, complete with constitution, pro-

gram, and elected officers, their efforts, Whyte found, met with little success. The importance of the group for its members lay, not in any explicit goals it might try to pursue, but in the intrinsic satisfactions derived from their shared activities and their relations to one another.

Whyte's analysis of "street corner society" possesses a double significance. It demonstrates clearly that even in a primary group, with its close personal relations, strong sense of unity, and shared values, leadership may be of great importance in determining how the group as a whole functions. Second, it reveals again the ubiquity of the primary group by showing how even in a slum neighborhood, frequently described by sociologists as "disorganized," group loyalty and the bonds of intimacy persist and, indeed, play a major role in organizing and channeling the social life of its residents.

The characteristics of the primary group, as illustrated in these two cases, may be summarized as follows: The bonds which hold the group together are *affective,* that is, emotional rather than rational or traditional—although there may be rational and traditional elements present. Relations among members are *diffuse,* encompassing behavior in diverse contexts, and therefore permitting some degree of spontaneity. The group is an end in itself for its members rather than an instrument for the achievement of other ends. Each member therefore in some measure identifies his interests with those of the whole. As a result, he is not apt to pursue his private advantage if it conflicts with the values of the group or entails the possibility of losing his place within it.

The intimacy and emotional warmth characteristic of the primary group do not necessarily preclude the possibility of internal conflict; indeed, these attributes may in fact increase the likelihood of tension and disagreement. To assume that all was harmony and consensus even within a cohesive and tightly knit group would falsify the realities of social life. As leader of the Nortons, Doc frequently found it necessary to resolve internal conflicts in order to prevent defection of some member or to keep the group from splitting. Yet even his position was occasionally challenged. Individual disagreements may be shelved when outside pressure pushes members closer together, but in the continuous round of group activity friction and conflict should be considered normal occurrences.

One might even anticipate that conflict would be more likely to occur in primary groups than in others. "There is more occasion," Lewis Coser suggests, drawing upon Georg Simmel and Sigmund Freud, "for the rise of hostile feelings in primary than in secondary groups, for the more the relationship is based upon the participation of the total personality—as distinct from segmental participation—the

more it is likely to generate both love and hate." [12] Hostile feelings may be repressed, in the interest of group solidarity, but even if they explode into open conflict they need not lead to dissolution of the group unless the point at issue "affects the basic layers of common belief on which the solidarity of the social body lastly rests." [13] Indeed, conflict in the group may occur only because relationships are stable and members feel that they need not restrain themselves. Under such conditions, the venting of hostility may in fact serve to strengthen the group by preventing the accumulation of hostility that may lead to action destructive of the structure of relationships within it.

Emergence, growth, and dissolution

Unlike the family, whose existence and organization are institutionalized in every society, other primary groups made up of friends, neighbors, playmates, coworkers, and so on, emerge gradually during the course of daily life under appropriate conditions. If men are thrown together in frequent association over a period of time, as in the Bank Wiring Room, or in a college dormitory, an office, or an army company, they are likely to develop a structure of roles and relationships, with mutual obligations and expectations, shared norms and values, and some sense, however tenuous or implicit, of collective identity.

The emergence of friendly and intimate relations is not, of course, the only possible outcome of constant association with others. As Lawrence Wylie points out in a perceptive description of life in a French village, the villagers, who have ample opportunity to know one another, may have "nothing between them" and hardly notice one another's existence, or may be *brouillé* (hostile) or *bien* (friendly) with one another.

> If you are *brouillé* with someone it means . . . that you have quarreled and are now "on the outs." You have broken off relations. You avoid passing each other in the street, and when you cannot avoid passing you turn your head to avoid having to speak. You try not to be caught in a social situation in which you would normally be expected to shake hands. . . . If by chance you cannot avoid meeting, you appear to lose your temper. You threaten physical or legal sanctions against each other. . . . Even though you do not injure your opponent through physical or legal action, you may still harm him by attacking him orally. . . .
> Being *bien ensemble* means being "in" with each other, being on friendly terms. You play games together. You have your apéritif together. Your families often spend the evening together. You support each other in your *brouillés,* and you may even participate in them. When you need someone to do a favor you can count on the friend with whom you're *bien.*[14]

As this description suggests, hostility and antagonism may be regulated by custom and convention just as are friendship and intimacy, and both types of relationships may emerge from the same circumstances.

Whether friendship or hostility—or both—develops between persons thrown together frequently, or whether they merely disregard each other's presence—insofar as that is possible—depends not only upon their social characteristics and the kinds of situations in which they find themselves, but also on their personal attributes and psychological traits. Within the Bank Wiring Room, for example, there were several men who either did not want or were unable to develop personal relationships with other workers, to become part of the group. Clashes of personality are particularly likely to occur when individuals come in contact with others in situations where they cannot choose their associates.

Although small size and face-to-face relations have often been taken as essential characteristics of the primary group, it is "more appropriate," as Edward Shils has written, "to treat them as conditions affecting the formation of primary groups."[15] As the number of members in a group increases, the possibility of frequent interaction among them all diminishes and the range of behavior that is possible is narrowed. Evidence from some of the studies of social groups seems to suggest that on the whole "the more frequently persons interact with one another, the stronger their sentiments of friendship for one another are apt to be."[16] Hence, although a small group may not become a primary group, it is more likely to do so than one made up of a large number of persons. There is no simple or direct correlation, however, between the size of a group or the frequency of interaction, on the one hand, and the extent or scope of the personal relationships that may develop on the other. Too many other conditions affect the nature of the relationships that may emerge from continued interaction.

Within the large organizations in which primary groups so often develop, the possibilities of interaction that may lead to intimate and personal ties are often affected by managerial policy, physical layout, or demands of the job. In some large plants there are—or have been, on occasion—rules against talking on the job. This rule, which may seem needlessly arbitrary or inhuman, is based upon the assumption that men work better if not distracted by talk, and upon the fear, based in part on fact, that if employees develop relations on the job beyond those formally required they may work to the detriment of the organization. Men who are physically separated from one another by a machine, or by a long distance, or who work in so noisy a place that communication is difficult are not likely to establish social relationships on the job. The rapid movement of personnel, whether sanctioned by company policy or imposed by technological or organizational necessities, may also effectively prevent the emergence of informal relations.

When frequent interaction is possible, men may come together on the basis of shared values or interests; "birds of a feather," as the familiar saying has it, "flock together." Within a large organization or in a community, similar ethnic or religious or educational backgrounds may provide the initial foundation upon which the primary group takes shape. The mere existence of common values or interests, however, only provides a necessary rather than a sufficient condition for the emergence of a primary group; people may, of course, maintain their distance for diverse reasons, despite cultural similarities and frequent association. There remains therefore the task of identifying the conditions under which "birds of a feather" do "flock together"—or do not. Congeniality, or the lack of it, among the personalities involved may constitute one important variable, but it is certainly not the only one—and in any case the nature of "congeniality" itself requires analysis.

That members of a primary group share particular values or beliefs—that matrons who play bridge together are all Republicans, that members of a teen-age gang are all devoted to the same popular singer, or that workers in a factory agree that one should not work any harder than is absolutely necessary—does not necessarily mean, however, that they came together *because* of these shared judgments.

Shared values may result from membership in a group as well as providing the basis upon which it is built. If people with different values do establish close relations with one another, they will in all likelihood either reconcile their differences or avoid conflict by keeping away from any discussion of issues that divide them. Unless some such accommodation is achieved the relationship may well break down unless the differences are of only minor importance or the ties become very strong before the differences become apparent.[17]

Numbers, frequency of interaction, and shared values, then, constitute conditions that make possible or inhibit the formation of primary groups, but the key factor would appear to be the function or functions they serve for their members. Workers thrown together in a work situation, for example, find that informal social organization offers methods for coping with the demands of management and for dealing with unforeseen or uncontrolled circumstances, as well as providing the intrinsic gratifications that come from friendly social relationships and participation in a pleasant and congenial group. The need for satisfying relations with others leads men and women to seek out friends and to try to become members of small groups within which they can readily and openly express their feelings and secure emotional response—in which they can "be themselves."

Once formed, the primary group is likely to persist as long as it provides its members with personal satisfaction and as long as no external forces interfere with its activities. In some respects the group might be termed a "self-maintaining system," for the very round of activities in which its members engage serves to sustain the bonds among them and to reinforce the group's structure.

The leader, when there is such a relatively well-defined role, maintains his position in part by resolving internal clashes and maintaining internal solidarity. When the group is engaged in performing explicit tasks, as in the case of an airplane crew whose work relations have become overladen with personal ties, the continued achievement of collective goals also contributes to continuing stability.

In the normal course of social life, however, primary groups develop, persist for a while, change their character perhaps, as members leave or new ones enter, then dissolve, only to have their members come together in new contexts with other people and form new groups. Some may be long-lasting—the lifelong ties of children who grow up together, the persisting friendships found from time to time among schoolmates, professional colleagues, or neighbors—but others are temporary and fleeting. In a group bound together by emotional ties, there always exists the possibility of personal clashes and disagreements that may lead to the disruption of the social unity. But the fate of the group depends not only upon its internal dynamics and the personalities of its members, but also—and perhaps more importantly—upon external forces.

The high rate of mobility characteristic of modern society—from job to job, place to place, up or down the social ladder—continually breaks into established relationships. One out of every five Americans changes residence each year. If a departing member does not play a strategic role in the group he leaves, his going may have no important consequences, resulting only in a minor shuffling of roles and relationships. If, on the other hand, he occupies a key position in the group, his absence may lead to the virtual dissolution of the group.

Insofar as a primary group's structure reflects the social position of its members outside its confines, changes in an individual's external status may affect his position within the group and his relations with others. When Doc, for example, had no money and could not adequately perform his role as leader, the entire group was affected. When he found a job and was kept away from the group for long periods of time, the whole structure, which had depended so heavily upon him, fell apart.

As men make new friends, marry, join clubs, improve their circumstances, or develop new interests, needs once satisfied by a particular primary group may weaken or change, with a resulting shift in the attitude toward and, perhaps, participation in the group. Since men are judged socially in part by the company they keep, changes in status in the larger community may lead to a balancing of the pleasures—and obligations—of old friendships against the consequences of continued association with persons on a different status level. The dropping of old friends—or the less typical holding on to them—is by now a familiar feature in the stories of worldly success so prevalent in our literature. On the other hand, as Whyte points out in his study of Cornerville, loyalty to the group constituted for some of the boys one of the important factors inhibiting social mobility.

The continuing process of group formation and dissolution characteristic of a mobile and changing society does not necessarily mean, however, that relationships slowly built up over a period of time are all destroyed. They may persist as significant and meaningful relationships, but only if there is more than nostalgic sentiment about the past to hold them together. The momentary reliving of college life at an alcoholic reunion weekend does not bespeak significant primary relationships among one-time college friends, but rather futile and pathetic efforts to revive what passing years and little contact with one another have in effect destroyed. A lapse of time without the day-by-day shared experience upon which close ties almost inevitably rest leaves the relationship only a shadow of its former self, for intimacy tends to generate new and further intimacy, "As if increase of appetite had grown/By what it fed on." If one-time friends have pursued related careers so that past ties can be reinforced by common interests and similar experiences, then the once-close bonds may be sustained, or even enriched, despite only occasional meetings over the years.

Social functions of the primary group

The importance of the primary group stems from its prevalence and from the functions it performs for both individuals and larger social groups—including society as a whole. As MacIver and Page have pointed out:

The simplest, the first, the most universal of all forms of association is that in which a small number of persons meet "face to face" for companionship, mutual aid, the discussion of some question that concerns them all, or the discovery and execution of some common policy. The face-to-face group is the nucleus of all organization, and . . . is found in some form within the most complex systems—it is the unit cell of the social structure. The primary group, in the form of the family, initiates us into the secrets of society. It is the group through which, as playmates and comrades, we first give creative expression to our social impulses. It is the breeding ground of our mores, the nurse of our loyalties. It is the first and generally remains the chief focus of our social satisfactions. In these respects the face-to-face group is primary in our lives.[18]

Whether innate or, more likely, as a result of the fact that humans are reared by other humans, the need for emotional response from others and intimate association with them is a persisting human quality. The central elements of personality are acquired in the bosom of the family, and men continue to need the warmth, security, and intimacy they experience as children. The primary group—especially, although not exclusively, the family—provides for these psychological needs. In doing so, it also contributes to the stability of the social order by enabling individuals to maintain their personal equilibrium and to perform adequately their accustomed social roles.

Now all the evidence of psychiatry . . . [George Homans writes] shows that membership in a group sustains a man, enables him to maintain his equilibrium under the ordinary shocks of life, and helps him to bring up children who will in turn be happy and resilient. If this group is shattered around him, if he leaves a group in which he was a valued member, and if, above all, he finds no new group to which he can relate himself, he will, under stress, develop disorders of thought, feeling, and behavior. His thinking will be obsessive, elaborated without sufficient reference to reality; he will be anxious or angry, destructive to himself or to others; his behavior will be compulsive, not controlled; and, if the process of education that makes a man easily able to relate himself to others is itself social, he will, as a lonely man, bring up children who have a lowered social capacity.[19]

Suicide rates and the frequency of mental illness are higher among those who lack close ties to others than among those who are members of intimate social groups: The divorced and the unmarried show higher frequencies of both suicide and mental disturbance than do the married. And those who live in the more impersonal environment of the city—and particularly those parts of the city where individuals are likely to be socially isolated —are more prone to self-destruction and, it would appear, to psychological breakdown than those from farms, small towns, or suburbs. (Lower reported rates of mental disease in rural areas and small towns, however, may merely represent a tendency not to report or to hospitalize the emotionally disturbed.)

The need for sociability, intimacy, and emotional response is not, of course, a fixed quantity. It varies from person to person, perhaps even from group to group. Insofar as this need is created or emerges from the early experience of the individual, it can be affected by idiosyncratic experiences, thus leading one person to demand more close ties with people and another to require less. Insofar as child-rearing practices vary from one group to another, there may be differences in the amount or form of intimacy and emotional response required by members of different groups. Just as some individuals are more capable of standing alone against collective opinion or with minimal emotional support from others, so it seems likely that whole groups may vary along these psychological lines.

Because of its emotional tone and the close ties that bind it together, the primary group also serves as an important instrument of social control. Men are sensitive to the judgments of others, particularly those whose opinions they value and whose approval they desire; they are therefore likely to conform to the norms of the group and to avoid any actions that might elicit disapproval or criticism from their friends. By adhering to the standards of the group they also gain the approval and respect that contribute in turn to the group's continued stability and unity.

Other, more direct mechanisms are also available to ensure conformity to group norms. In both the Bank Wiring Room and among the corner boys it was apparent that any potential—or actual—disregard of accepted rules of behavior would lead to reprisal or punishment: heckling, razzing, or even a symbolic physical punishment. The extreme penalty, always available to the primary group, is total rejection or exclusion, sending someone to Coventry, as it is sometimes called, after the citizens of Coventry, who, it is said, "had at one time so great a dislike to soldiers that a woman seen talking to one was instantly tabooed; hence, when a soldier was sent to Coventry he was cast off from all social intercourse." [20]

The role of the primary group in the large organizations in which it is found or in the society as a whole depends partly upon which norms and values it incorporates into its structure. If conformity to the rules of the factory or office or military organization become part of the expected actions of the primary group, then it serves a positive function for the formal structure. If, on the other hand, the primary group sanctions behavior that runs counter to the formal rules its members are supposed to obey then it may be dysfunctional for that organization, although, as we shall see in Chapter 11, deviations from the rules may also contribute in various ways to efficient operations and the achievement of organizational goals.

In the Bank Wiring Room the informal organization, from management's point of view, was dysfunctional. It maintained a standard of production that was clearly below what the group was capable of doing; by enforcing that standard it was directly opposed to the principles underlying the company's wage incentive scheme. There is considerable evidence from other studies of factory workers that this "restriction of output" is a wide-spread phenomenon. The recurrence of this pattern among work groups in industry suggests the possibility that cultural aspects of working class life or recurrent features of economic and industrial organization affect the norms and values that workers incorporate in their informal social organization. The primary group, that is, does not stand apart from institutional and structural features of the society in which it functions, but is inextricably linked in its internal workings as well as its larger consequences to that society.

In those instances in which management, by its over-all policies and practices or through the day-by-day activities of the foreman, who represents management to the workers, has been able to enlist the loyalties of its employees, adherence to company rules and achievement of company objectives become part of the primary group structure and facilitate the functioning of the larger organization. But the primary group may contribute to effective operations of a large organization in other ways as well. Merely by providing men with the satisfactions derived from membership in a congenial group, it can enhance morale and increase efficiency. Or, as we shall see in the discussion of bureaucracy in Chapter 11, the primary group frequently provides informal mechanisms for solving problems bypassed by the formal organization—or created by it.

The primary group, democracy, and totalitarianism

The primary group, then, mediates, in a sense, between the individual and the society in which he lives. The larger implications of this fact, however, are by no means clear or agreed upon by scholars. During the Enlightenment freedom from local and traditional bonds was strongly emphasized and highly valued.[21] Loyalty to persons and the group ran counter to the universal values of justice, freedom, and progress. A democratic government, for example, is supposed to ignore the claims of family and friendship in administering the law; in principle, at least, it dispenses an even-handed justice on the basis of general rules to which all subscribe. The emergence of a centralized state and of rational organization presume and rest upon a diminished role for the primary group.

The extension of formal organization, the growth of impersonal social relationships, and the weakening of primary bonds have been noted frequently by observers of the modern world, sociologists and others. The extension of governmental functions, the proliferation of giant corporations and mass organizations, the emergence of the "multiversity," and the urbanization of the population constitute the principal visible evidence of the changes. In the eyes of some observers these facts—particularly the disintegration of the primary group—are the source of many of the ills that confront modern society, including the emergence of totalitarianism and its associated ideologies. The breakdown of primary groups would leave society, in Homans' terms, "a dust heap of individuals without links to one another."[22] "A society composed of an infinite number of unorganized individuals," wrote Émile Durkheim, "that a hypertrophied state is forced to oppress and contain, constitutes a veritable sociological monstrosity."[23] Even Marx, writing from a very different perspective, attacked capitalism for destroying all ties among men except the "cash nexus."

When men lack membership in primary groups that can provide intimacy, emotional response, and an ordered way of life, some writers have argued, they may turn to messianic, revolutionary, and authoritarian movements in which they can lose themselves and escape the burden of their isolation. Within such a movement they form "ideological primary groups," characterized by "a very intense solidarity, which demand[s] far-reaching individual renunciation on behalf of the group" and by "an extreme 'we-consciousness.'"[24] In such groups, the intrinsic satisfactions of membership are much less important than pursuit of the ideological objective which is the essential unifying bond.

Within the totalitarian society to which such movements can lead the destruction of primary ties continues, for the totalitarian state is jealous of any competing loyalties. As in all societies, some primary groups may persist, but only those that fit into the apparatus of the state. Others are suppressed or, if they cannot be totally eliminated, like the family, they are continually subject to constraints. In the Soviet Union, Barrington Moore observes, "the regime tries to destroy all social bonds except the ones that it has itself created, and through which it can manipulate the population."[25] In his autobiography, Wolfgang Leonhard, a product of Soviet training as a Party functionary expected to operate in a Russian satellite, describes in fascinating detail the efforts made—and needed—in order to prevent students from becoming too friendly with one another.[26]

The view that sees the decay and destruction of primary groups as the chief source of the ills of modern society (a view that frequently leads to assertions of the need for tradition and for greater respect for authority and to attacks on "liberalism" and the "welfare state") rests upon both fact and supposition, and is flawed in several ways. The impact of isolation upon the individual can be readily seen, and the emergence of fanatacism and of a commitment to radical ideologies and social movements are apparent among persons who have lost roots in a cohesive social group (though not all radicalism derives from this source). Yet Soviet totalitarianism did not emerge in a society that had experienced the liberating—and destructive—effects of the Enlightment, democracy, or rationalism; most pre-Revolutionary Russians lived within the confines of traditional villages organized in "primordial primary groups," to use Shils' phrase, those based upon "blood" and a common territory. Moreover there is an increasing body of evidence that sociologists may have overestimated the extent to which urban life and bureaucratic organization destroy the primary group or prevent its emergence. As Homans observes, new groups are always forming, unless strong measures are taken to prevent people from coming together. "The seed of society is always fertile."[27]

Notes

[1] Charles H. Cooley, *Social Organization* (New York: Scribner, 1929; first published in 1909), pp. 23–4.

[2] Kingsley Davis, *Human Society* (New York: Macmillan, 1949), p. 290.

[3] For an account of the "rediscovery" of the primary group, see Edward Shils, "The Study of the Primary Group," in Daniel Lerner and Harold D. Lasswell (eds.), *The Policy Sciences* (Hoover In-

stitute Studies, No. 1 [Stanford: Stanford University Press, 1951]), pp. 44–69.

[4] The full description of the Hawthorne studies is found in Fritz J. Roethlisberger and William J. Dickson, *Management and the Worker* (Cambridge, Mass.: Harvard University Press, 1939).

[5] *Ibid.*, p. 32.

[6] Michael S. Olmsted, *The Small Group* (New York: Random House, 1959), pp. 30–1.

[7] William F. Whyte, *Street Corner Society* (enlarged ed.; Chicago: University of Chicago Press, 1955).

[8] For a detailed account of Whyte's research procedures, see *ibid.*, Appendix, pp. 279–358.

[9] *Ibid.*, p 257.

[10] Alvin W. Gouldner, "The Norm of Reciprocity," *American Sociological Review*, XXV (April, 1960), 161–78.

[11] William F. Whyte, "A Slum Sex Code," *American Journal of Sociology*, XLIX (July, 1943), 24–32.

[12] Lewis Coser, *The Functions of Social Conflict* (New York: Free Press, 1956), p. 62.

[13] José Ortega y Gasset, *Concord and Liberty* (New York: Norton, 1946), p. 15.

[14] Lawrence Wylie, *Village in the Vaucluse* (Cambridge, Mass.: Harvard University Press, 1957), pp. 196–7, 200.

[15] Shils, *op. cit.*, p. 44.

[16] George C. Homans, *The Human Group* (New York: Harcourt, 1950), p. 133. See also pp. 113–7, 181–7, and 241–52 for some elaboration and some of the necessary qualifications to this general proposition.

[17] Robert K. Merton and Paul F. Lazarsfeld, "Friendship as a Social Process," in Morroe Berger, Theodore Abel, and Charles H. Page (eds.), *Freedom and Control in Modern Society* (New York: Van Nostrand, 1954), pp. 29–37.

[18] Robert M. MacIver and Charles H. Page, *Society: An Introductory Analysis* (New York: Holt, 1949), pp. 218–9.

[19] Homans, *op. cit.*, pp. 456–7.

[20] Brewer's *Dictionary of Phrase and Fable* (rev. and enlarged ed.; New York: Harper, n.d.), p. 245.

[21] For a fuller analysis of the problem dealt with in this section, see Olmsted, *op. cit.*, Ch. 4. Much of my discussion rests upon Olmsted's analysis.

[22] Homans, *op. cit.*, p. 457.

[23] Émile Durkheim, *The Division of Labor in Society*, trans. by George Simpson (New York: Free Press, 1947), Preface to 2nd ed., p. 28.

[24] Edward Shils, "Primordial, Personal, Sacred and Civil Ties," *British Journal of Sociology*, VII (June, 1957), 138.

[25] Barrington Moore, Jr., *Terror and Progress: U.S.S.R.* (Cambridge, Mass.: Harvard University Press, 1954), p. 158.

[26] Wolfgang Leonhard, *Child of the Revolution*, trans. by C. W. Woodhouse (London: Collins, 1957).

[27] Homans, *op. cit.*

Suggestions for further reading

COOLEY, CHARLES H. *Social Organization.* New York: Scribner, 1909, Part I.
The classic statement on the nature and functions of the primary group.

GANS, HERBERT J. *The Urban Villagers.* New York: Free Press, 1962.
A study of an urban neighborhood dominated by a "peer group society."

HARE, A. PAUL, EDGAR F. BORGATTA, AND ROBERT F. BALES. *Small Groups: Studies in Social Interaction*, 2nd ed., rev. New York: Knopf, 1965.
A collection of papers and research reports, although largely oriented in a psychological direction. Contains an extensive annotated bibliography.

HOMANS, GEORGE. *The Human Group.* New York: Harcourt, 1950.

A suggestive attempt to construct a systematic theory of the nature and functions of the social group, largely focused upon small groups and communal societies.

OLMSTED, MICHAEL S. *The Small Group.* New York: Random House, 1959.
An excellent summary and evaluation of research and theory.

ROETHLISBERGER, FRITZ J., AND WILLIAM J. DICKSON. *Management and the Worker.* Cambridge, Mass.: Harvard University Press, 1959, especially Parts IV and V.
The ground-breaking study of informal organization and the primary group in the context of large-scale formal organization, part of which is reviewed in this chapter.

SHILS, EDWARD A. "The Study of the Primary Group," in Daniel Lerner and Harold D. Lasswell (eds.), *The Policy Sciences.* (Hoover Institute Studies, No. 1.) Stanford: Stanford University Press, 1951, pp. 44–69.
A useful account and appraisal of the diverse sources from which have emerged the systematic study of the primary group.

WHYTE, WILLIAM F. *Street Corner Society,* enlarged ed. Chicago: University of Chicago Press, 1955.
The study, partly summarized in this chapter, which demonstrated the importance of the primary group in ostensibly disorganized slum areas of a large city. An excellent example of the analysis of the social structure of the small group.

7

Family, kinship, and marriage

Family, kinship, and marriage: some basic distinctions

The family, it is frequently said, is the basic social unit. The immediacy of our involvement in family life, the intensity of the emotions which it generates, the sexual and other satisfactions that it provides, the demands it makes upon our loyalties and efforts, and its functions with respect to childbearing and child care seem to offer ample evidence of its priority as the fundamental social group. For each individual the family may indeed be "almost without question . . . the most important of any of the groups that human experience offers." [1] But what is of central significance for most individuals may not be of comparable importance for society. Despite its presence in all known societies, the form of the family and its relations to the society around it vary widely.

In some societies each individual's life is bound up almost totally within the family, while in others many roles and relationships are relatively independent of it. In a communal society (described in Chapter 2) the family—or some larger kinship group—is typically the most significant social unit to which men belong. The allocation of political power is often linked with family institutions; among the Ashanti of West Africa, for example, the ruler maintained the allegiance of

many of his subjects by taking a wife from each of the numerous clans, thus binding them to him by ties of kinship as well as political loyalty. Economic activities are frequently organized along family or kinship lines; among the rural Irish—as in many other societies—economic obligations traditionally have been part of the family structure (although this situation is changing rapidly), and marriages are arranged with a sharp eye to their economic consequences. Indeed, to distinguish economic, political, and religious institutions and roles from those of marriage and the family is often very difficult, for primitive and peasant peoples do not usually differentiate as sharply as we do among the diverse areas of social life—the political, economic, religious, familial, and so on.

In an associational society, in contrast, a multiplicity of groups enlist men's loyalties, each helping to establish their place in society. Individuals rather than families are the units within most associations, and many roles and relationships—most importantly, perhaps, those linked with job or occupation—have little connection with the family. If the family is less extensive and inclusive in its demands and its functions than in most communal societies, it nonetheless usually plays an enormously important role in almost everyone's life. Moreover it is still in diverse ways related to other institutions and structures. One's income is not affected by ones' marital status, but one's income tax is. Voting is open to most adults, no matter what their family position, but most family members tend to vote the same way. Individuals own property, although inheritance usually goes from parent to child.

Many generalizations about the family, including some of those frequently made about its place and functions, suffer from considerable ambiguity because of the diverse groups to which the term is often applied, both in everyday discourse and scientific analysis. In one dictionary, for example, which represents conventional usage, the family is defined as "parents and their children, dwelling together or not," as "any group of persons closely related by blood, as parents, children, uncles, aunts, and cousins," as "all those persons descended from a common progenitor," and as "the group of persons who form a household under one head, including parents, children, servants, etc." [2] Clearly these four definitions refer to different forms of social structure; although they all include persons related by so-called blood ties, or *consanguinity*, and marital ties, or *affinity*, they vary both in number and in the relationships among their members. In order to assess the actual importance of the family in any society—or in society in general—it is therefore necessary to give the term a precise meaning and to distinguish it from other types of groups and structures to which it is related.

The family must be seen as part of a larger whole, the *kinship* system. The latter consists of a structure of roles and relationships based upon blood ties (consanguinity) and marriage (affinity) that bind men, women, and children into an organized whole. Various positions in our own kinship system reveal the complex interlocking of consanguine and affinal bonds. Siblings are bound to one another by virtue of their common parentage. First cousins are related because the father or mother of one is a sibling of a parent of the other. More distant cousins have siblings among their grandparents, or among more remote ancestors. In-laws are related to one another because one has married a child or sibling of the other. Most other societies have much more complex kinship terminology than our own, but in all cases each identifiable position is related to other positions either by blood or marriage.

From the point of view of the individual, kinship refers to "any relationship . . . to another through his father and mother. All kinship ties thus derive from the family, that universal and fundamental group which everywhere and in some way or another incorporates the institution of marriage." [3]

The *family*, as distinct from the more embracing kinship structure, consists of a group made up of "adults of both sexes, at least two of whom maintain a socially approved sexual relationship, and one or more children, own or adopted, of the sexually cohabiting adults." [4] Usually the family shares a common residence and its members cooperate in meeting their economic needs.

The two central institutional elements of the family are *marriage* and *parenthood*. The former, which sociologically must be distinguished from the family, consists of the rules which govern the relationship between husband and wife (or husbands and wives). These rules define how the relationship shall be established and how it may be ended, the expectations and obligations it entails, and the persons who may—or may not—enter into such a relationship. Although sexual access is usually an essential element in marriage, not all stable sexual unions constitute marriages. Many western Europeans recognize the possibility of a lasting relationship between man and mistress, and other societies have institutionalized forms of concubinage.

A continuing sexual relationship is an important part of marriage chiefly because of its connection with childbearing and child care. As Bronislaw Malinowski points out, "marriage cannot be defined as the licensing of sexual intercourse, but rather as the licensing of parenthood." [5] A recurrent feature of the many varieties of marriage arrangements is the fact that they all provide the approved context for having children and define the social parenthood of the offspring; they identify those who have prescribed rights, duties, and responsibilities relating to the child's care. Although the father's biological role in parenthood ceases with conception, yet every society follows what Malinowski defines as *the principle of legitimacy*, "that no child should be brought into the world without a man—and one man at that—assuming the role of sociological father, that is, guardian and protector, the male link between the child and the rest of the community." [6]

So closely tied are marriage and parenthood that the former is sometimes not considered to be consummated until a child is born, as among the Andaman Islanders in the Bay of Bengal, for example, or the Kalinga of the Philippine Islands. Even in our own society, refusal of one partner to have children is a legitimate reason for annulling a marriage. Conversely, of course, marriages may take place because a child has been conceived. William J. Goode reports that in many parts of Europe in the eighteenth century, and well into the nineteenth, there existed a widespread pattern of permitted premarital sexual relations, with marriage normally following conception—or even birth of the child—without imposing any social stigma upon the couple. [7]

The universality of the family

Some form of family is found in virtually all human societies, although its position within the larger kinship system varies greatly, from a central and dominating place, as in middle-class American society, to minimal importance among many primitive people who emphasize the larger kin group rather than the unit of husband, wife, and children. Many explanations have been suggested for the apparent universality of the family. Some of these explanations take the form of "conjectural history" [8] in which origins are derived from "known principles of human nature," and the evolution of social institutions is traced from presumptive beginnings. Robert Briffault, for example, found the primal source of the family in the biological tie between mother and child. The "original" family was therefore matriarchal and all other forms emerged from this beginning. He found evidence for this interpretation in the prevalence of matrilineal kinship systems among primitive tribes and in the apparent ignorance of physical paternity in a few of the simplest societies. [9] The weight of anthropological evidence does not support this interpretation; some exceedingly simple societies have patrilineal kinship systems and the ignorance of biological paternity does not result in the absence of a socially recognized father.[10] It seems likely that the search for the origin of the family—as in the case of other basic institutions—in the ultimate sense must remain forever confined only to speculations that excite debate, intrigue the mind, and suggest the mysteries of human existence.

A second explanation for the near universality of the family stresses the importance of sexual needs and the requirements of human reproduction. Yet the institutionalization of sex relations, found in all societies, cannot suffice to explain either the marital relationship or the importance of kinship ties. Although no society leaves the expression of sex desires or the selection of sexual partners totally unregulated, there are, as noted above, many cases in which sexual intercourse before or outside marriage is permitted or even positively sanctioned. Of 250 societies for which George Murdock found data, "65 allow unmarried and unrelated persons complete freedom in sexual matters, and 20 others give qualified consent, while only 54 forbid or disapprove premarital liaisons between non-relatives, and many of these allow sex relations between specified relatives." [11] Behavior, in any case, can frequently run counter to the express sexual conventions of a society, as Alfred Kinsey and his colleagues have so fully demonstrated for the United States.[12]

The effects of pregnancy and childbirth upon the woman and the prolonged infancy of the child have also been cited as the basis for the universality of family. Mother and child require support and care which marriage ensures. But these needs can be met without marriage or a husband-father, since blood kin of the woman can provide for her needs and those of her children, as indeed they do in many cases described by anthropologists. The presence of a husband, it would seem, is therefore essentially a result of social and cultural inducements and pressures rather than of biological requirements.

The explanation for the almost universal presence of the family must then be found in the nature of society itself. A widely accepted theory centers upon the functions performed by the family for the maintenance and continuity of organized social existence. "This universal social structure," Murdock writes, "produced through cultural evolution in every human society [is] presumably the only feasible adjustment to a series of basic needs" [13]—needs identified as sexual, economic, reproductive, and educational.

The major social functions of the family, according to Kingsley Davis, are reproduction, maintenance, social placement, and socialization of the young. The bearing of children is rarely approved of outside the family, although sexual gratification outside of marriage is often permitted. Physical and social paternity need not be the same and in some societies little is done to ensure their congruence. But no society lacks a group of adults who serve as parents of the child. By insisting that parenthood be confined within the family, society provides for attention and care for both mother and child. The family transmits to the child, both directly through teaching and indoctrination, and indirectly through the methods of child care and training, the content of the culture (socialization). The individual's position in society initially comes from membership in a family (the function of social placement) from which he also acquires attitudes, values, skills, and knowledge that will affect his later status.

These are not the only functions served

by the family. It may play an important role in relation to the economic life of a society, constitute a significant mechanism in the structure of political authority, and occupy an important place in religious activities. The family typically provides an accepted and approved channel for satisfying personal needs—for sexual gratification, emotional response, and social support. But, Davis argues, reproduction, maintenance, placement, and socialization are the "core functions with which the family is always and everywhere concerned. There may be great variation from one society to another in the precise manner and degree of fulfillment of these functions, but the four mentioned seem to be the ones which universally require a family organization." [14]

The combination of these functions in one social structure, Davis holds, accounts for the universal presence of the family. As he is careful to point out, each of these functions can be performed by other groups. But once linked together, he argues, there inevitably follow certain structural consequences; "from a sheer analysis of the concurrent functions themselves, we can deduce the kind of group which performs them."

The family, Davis writes,

must, in the first place, be a biological group because reproduction requires that there be sexual relationships between two, and biological relationships between all members of the group. It must, in the second place, be a working group with economic solidarity and division of labor between the members, because the care and support of children demand this. It must, in the third place, be a group whose initial and later members have a similar class status with common class sentiments and advantages, because status ascription and training for a status require such homogeneity. It must, in the fourth place, be an intimate group having a common habitation and enduring for a long time, because the human reproductive span and the period of dependency in the offspring are both long, capable of occupying together as many as forty years of the parents' lives. After the long period of procreation and child care the group partly breaks down by the withdrawal of the offspring to found similar groups of their own; but in the meantime the biological interconnection between the members, the cooperative labor, the common class status, the long and close living together, and the shared sorrows and gratifications must have increased the primary solidarity and deepened the sentimental ties until the group is one of the most fundamental in the lives of its members and in the society of which it is such an essential part. [15]

The efficiency that results from combining these "core" functions in one social unit seems clear enough, but need they always be linked together? There are cases in which one or another function is largely removed from the family. In the Israeli kibbutzim, for example, care of children is turned over to communal nurseries and schools where trained nurses and teachers take over many of the duties usually assigned to parents or other relatives. Except for the six weeks after the child's birth, when the mother can spend as much time as she likes with her child, and the time required for nursing before the child is weaned, parents can spend only Saturday and an hour or two each week day with their children, plus such other brief visits as their daily work may permit. Sexual gratification, childbearing, a partial contribution to the socialization of the child, and the emotional gratifications derived from these activities are the chief functions of the kibbutz family; maintenance and social placement are no longer its province, except insofar as membership in a family does define relationships to some other members of the community. If then the family persists in the kibbutz, as it has—it cannot be because of the presence of all of the core functions.

One might still argue, despite this

evidence, that the combination of functions in the family is a continuing and consistent tendency rather than a universally found fact. If the core functions are not all combined in a single structure, then perhaps strains and tensions develop that lead men eventually to re-establish the functional unity of the family. A continuing study of the kibbutz family might test this hypothesis, and there is evidence that in some of the kibbutz communities parents are playing an increasingly important role in relation to their children.[16] Although various utopian experiments in Europe and the United States that sought to eliminate the family entirely have failed, there are reliable recorded cases in which the family as a recognized group of sexually cohabiting adults and their children did not exist (although some form of kinship and some institutionalized definition of parenthood was always present). One cannot assume, therefore, that the family will always and inevitably re-emerge from efforts to change its character radically or even, perhaps, to eliminate it entirely.[17] Instead it is necessary to inquire into the diverse forms of kinship and family organization and to examine the conditions that sustain the family and those that transform it.

Forms of kinship and family structure

The many forms of family and kinship organization are recorded in a rich library of anthropological and sociological works. The value of this library is twofold. So deeply ingrained are the perspectives derived from one's own experience in a particular type of family that it is especially difficult to examine family and kinship systems in an objective and de-tached fashion. In studying different systems, one may come to see more clearly and objectively the distinctive character of one's own kind of family, as well as its similarities with others. Second, the existence of a full and growing comparative literature provides an opportunity—as yet only partially exploited—to establish a general theory of family and kinship structure.

Three different types of families have been distinguished in comparative studies. (1) The *nuclear,* or *elementary,* family consists of husband (father), wife (mother), and children. The latter may be biological offspring of the couple or adopted members of the family; the distinction between biological and social paternity, which has considerable importance in American society, has little or no significance in many others. (2) The *extended* family is made up of more than one nuclear unit and extends across more than two generations—for example, the three-generation family that includes parents, their married and unmarried children, children-in-law, and grandchildren. (3) The *compound* family rests upon polygamous marriage. In *polygyny,* one man and more than one wife, the most frequently found and generally the most popular form of compound family, the man "plays the role of husband and father in several nuclear families and thereby unites them into a larger familial group." [18] The opposite case of *polyandry,* one woman and two or more husbands, is rarely reported; where it does exist it appears to be associated with meager economic resources, as among some of the poorer Tibetans, and sometimes takes the form of fraternal polyandry, with brothers sharing a single wife.

The nuclear family is found almost everywhere, either as the predominant family type, or as a component in both extended and compound families. From a Western perspective, with its insistence upon monogamy, polygamous unions may appear strange or immoral, yet they flourish widely. Of 192 societies for which he was able to secure data, George Murdock found that "47 have normally only the nuclear family, 53 have polygamous but not extended familes, and 92 possess some form of the extended family." [19] These data, however, must be cautiously interpreted, for a society's approval of polygamy, and the prestige earned by those who can afford more than one wife does not necessarily mean that most marriages are in fact polygamous. In many instances only a relatively small number of men are able to afford more than one wife, and in polygamous societies most marriages are in fact monogamous.[20]

The family, whatever its form, is always embedded in a larger kinship system, although the marital relationship, which is so heavily emphasized in American society, is sometimes submerged in the larger scheme of kinship ties. A system in which the conjugal ties are given preponderant importance is called a *conjugal family system;* one in which ties to blood kin are emphasized is called *consanguine.* Or, as Ralph Linton has described these two types:

In societies organized upon the conjugal basis we can picture the authentic functional family as consisting of a nucleus of spouses and their offspring surrounded by a fringe of relatives. In those organized on the consanguine basis we can picture the authentic family as a nucleus of blood relatives surrounded by a fringe of spouses.[21]

The nuclear family is essentially a transitory group; it is formed by marriage, grows as children are born, diminishes as children marry and form their own families, and disappears when the married couple die. The consanguine family is long-lived; it is constantly replenished and achieves continuity and persistence despite the death of older members and the loss of those who are required to leave upon marriage.

The American "middle-class" family is an extreme case of the conjugal type in the extent to which it emphasizes marital ties and the conjugal unit. The preferred household consists of the married couple and their children; the presence of the parents—or a parent—of either spouse is likely to be looked upon as a potential source of friction and difficulty. Children are expected to become independent and establish their own homes and families. The tie between husband and wife is viewed as the most important bond holding the family together.

In contrast, many other societies relegate the married couple to a secondary position and assign much greater importance to consanguine relationships. In the traditional Chinese family, for example, the man was expected to be much more concerned with his responsibilities to his father and mother than to his wife. The difference between American and Chinese family patterns in this respect is clearly illustrated in the following observations by a Chinese-American sociologist:

Recently I went to a movie in which a young couple had a quarrel. The wife, in a huff, ran out of the apartment carrying a packed suitcase. The husband's mother, who lived on the next floor, then appeared on the scene. The elderly woman consoled her son by saying, "You're not alone, son. I am here." The audience roared with laughter. The sequence of events and that particular remark left little doubt in the minds of the audience that the elder woman was at the back of the young couple's quarrel. . . .

A Chinese audience would have found hardly anything amusing in these events. In the Chinese view, the younger woman, and not the older one, would have been the culprit. For whether or not a man has reached majority, his tie with his parents customarily has priority over that of the marital bond. Only a bad woman would leave her husband because of the conflict between the two responsibilities. Under the circumstances, the mother who consoled her son was doing nothing out of order.[22]

Changes taking place in China are transforming the traditional family, however, and with greater independence for women, increasing equality between husband and wife, and diminished parental authority, the interfering mother-in-law may eventually appear in China, too—if she has not already done so.

Perhaps the most extreme form of consanguine kinship is that of the historic Nayar, who virtually eliminated the nuclear family. A Nayar woman went through a marriage ceremony with a man whom she rarely, if ever, saw again, and in whom she had no further interest, except for the need to perform the appropriate ritual should he die. The woman then took to herself a series of lovers. Children were looked after in the maternal household, to which they owed their allegiance. The presumptive biological father had no responsibility toward his offspring, but was expected to acknowledge his paternity by a payment to the midwife who attended the mother in childbirth.[23]

Kinship systems differ not only in the relative importance they assign to conjugal and consanguineous relations, but also in the ways they order or arrange blood relationships. The key concepts here are *lineage* and *descent*. Members of a lineage are linked together because they derive from a common ancestor. A lineage may be *patrilineal* or *matrilineal*, based upon descent respectively in the male or female line. In such unilineal descent systems, attitudes, sentiments, and behavior toward father's kin and mother's kin are likely to be different. In Western society, in which both lines of descent are recognized (a *bilateral* system), no major institutionalized distinctions are made between mother's and father's relatives, although there may in practice be consistent or frequent differences. Because American women typically have closer emotional ties to their parents than do men, for example, relations with the woman's family are often closer and more frequent than are those with the husband's family.

Emphasis upon one line of descent, or even the existence of clearly marked descent groups living together, does not eliminate significant kinship ties with persons outside one's lineage. In a matrilineal system, for example, the child belongs to his mother's lineage, but he also has well-defined relationships with his father's kin. Conversely, the individual in a patrilineal system also maintains ties with his mother's kindred. In American society it is taken for granted that each person belongs in effect to several families: his own, the family of *procreation*, consisting of husband, wife, and their children; the family into which he is born—his *family of orientation*— to which he owes some allegiance even after he marries and, customarily, leaves home; his wife's family, or even his wife's mother's and wife's father's families, as well as his father's and mother's families. In fact, however, it is probably more accurate to say that the individual maintains *relations* with members of all these familes, and that he *belongs* only to his own families of procreation and orientation. From the point of view of the observer this array of families constitutes an interlocking structure of family groups. From the point of view of each individual member the system looks different—is different—for the persons who belong to it stand in diverse relations with one another; one man's cousin is another's brother or sister, one's mother is someone else's aunt, or daughter, or cousin, or mother-in-law, and so on.

Kinship terminology is frequently a useful clue to the structure of the system. Failure to differentiate among cousins, for example, except by degree of relationship—first, second, and so on—or among aunts and uncles, reflects the bilateral character of the American kinship structure; no institutionalized distinction exists between mother's and father's relatives. In the unilineal kinship systems found in many primitive societies different terms are applied to mother's brother and father's brother, reflecting the different relations with these "uncles" and the different roles they play in the individual's family.

Analysis based solely upon kinship terminology, however, can be misleading, for application of the same term may coincide with substantial differences in behavior. Anthropologists have often made errors with respect to "classificatory" relatives, that is, those to whom an individual applies a common term even though they are not biologically related to him in the same way—classificatory mothers, for example, who may include both the person's biological mother and other females of her generation in the larger kin group. Even though there is usually some common element in the relationship with persons who are similarly identified, distinctions are often made among them; the difference between one's "real" mother and all others is known and is usually the basis for different behavior and a distinctive relationship.

The location of authority within the kinship group or family constitutes another important element in the structure. One may distinguish the *patriarchal* family dominated by the father-husband, epitomized in the Old Testament, the *matriarchal* family (found rarely, if ever),

and the *equalitarian* family characteristic of contemporary middle-class America. These are of course ideal types; in practice the structure of authority is always a complex matter depending upon the situation, the particular actions or issues involved, and the diverse ways in which men and women influence each other's behavior. In suburban America, for example, the prolonged absence of the father during the working day necessarily shifts much of the authority over children and household to the mother, even though the father remains nominally the final authority. The wife and mother in the ostensibly patriarchal Jewish family of Eastern Europe frequently played a dominant—even domineering—role. Despite strenuous efforts, Jews often found it difficult to eke out more than a bare subsistence, and the woman's task of making do with what there was augmented her household influence, which was already substantial because emotional ties between mother and children were much closer than those between the father and his offspring. Men who immersed themselves in talmudic study in the synagogue escaped the difficulties at home without loss of face— indeed, if they were good talmudic scholars they even gained prestige—but in so doing they ran the risk of abdicating much of their patriarchal authority.[24]

As these examples suggest, the structure of the family, as defined by the categories of size or extension, lineage, and authority, is linked in diverse ways to other social structures and institutions. As we shall see in the discussion of the family in industrial society and specifically in the United States, family structure is affected by economic, educational, and political institutions, even when familial roles are clearly differentiated from occupational or political roles. It does, in turn, have a significant effect upon the functioning of the larger social structure within which it exists.

Marriage

The structure of the family and the larger kinship system is also, of course, crucially affected by the institutions governing marriage. Of these, three are of particular importance, those defining how many spouses one can have, where the married group (a pair or larger) shall establish residence, and which persons are permitted to marry or are ineligible as potential mates.

We have already referred to the difference between monogamous marriage, polygyny, and polyandry. In most cases of polygyny, by far the more frequent form of plural marriage, all the spouses do not live in one establishment but each woman has a separate domicile to which the man may come at regular times or as it pleases him. Although polygyny may seem to some readers a difficult scheme of things for men and women to endure, not only does it function effectively in many societies without generating serious problems for either sex, but it often provides what the women—as well as the men—define as positive advantages. The several wives of one man often share—and therefore lighten—their domestic burdens. Since the number of wives a man can afford usually displays his economic and social status, the women themselves frequently encourage further marriages. And the possibility of sexual jealousy is usually limited by careful definition of rights and duties of both husband and wives.

As is so often the case with general concepts, the categories usually applied to patterns of residence oversimplify the complex realities found in some societies. The conventional distinctions are between *patrilocal* residence, in which the husband and wife stay with the man's family; *matrilocal* residence, when they live with the woman's family; and *neolocal* residence, in which the marital group establish their own independent domicile. There are, however, also cases of *avunculocal* residence, in which the couple remain with a maternal uncle of the groom, and *matri-patrilocal* residence in which the couple live first with the bride's family and then, after the birth of a child, with the groom's, or else they alternate between their respective families of orientation periodically during the course of their married life.

Patterns of residence, however, like other forms of behavior, reflect not only the cultural prescriptions but also other circumstances. Thus, in American society neolocal residence is generally preferred, but where a family actually lives may be affected by economic fluctuations or by the economic level of the couple, particularly in the early years of married life. During a depression newly married couples are more likely to live with the parents of one or the other. If a couple lacks the resources to establish their own household they are likely to choose that pair of parents best able to afford and to accommodate them, although according to a study made in 1946, three out of five couples chose to live with the wife's family [25] (and there is little reason to think such a pattern would have changed). With the relatively sustained prosperity of the postwar period, the number of couples who live with the parents of one or the other has declined from 1,314,000 in 1952 to less than three-quarters of a million in 1964, even though the total population and the number of families have increased.[26]

Residence rules are important elements of kinship organization because of their influence upon the nature of the household or domestic group. This group is not identical with the kinship system or the family, for many persons among whom there are recognized and important relationships do not share a common home. The household often constitutes a significant group within the larger kinship structure, possessing its own loyalties, values, obligations, and problems. Its size and composition vary widely, including, for example, the physically separate nuclear family common in American society, various forms of extended or compound families living together, and complex residential patterns that cut across family lines—as among the Ashanti, for example, where husband and wife frequently reside separately and only spend occasional nights together. Differences in the type of household may have important consequences for relationships within the family and kinship system; proximity or distance can affect the intensity of relations, the extent to which persons may aid or assist one another, the problems they share, and the adjustments that are required in the course of day-to-day social life.

The third important component of marital institutions consists of rules that govern the selection of marriage partners. These rules define who shall choose a spouse and the criteria in terms of which a choice shall be made. No society permits a totally free choice, even in contemporary America where few formal restraints are placed upon the operation of the marriage market and where love is supposed to overcome all obstacles. Yet despite the values calling for independent choices by men and women of their marriage partners, there are clearly various kinds of pressures and controls that create discernible patterns of marital selection along class, ethnic, religious, and even regional lines. In sharp contrast, however, to the relative freedom of choice in American society are the arranged marriages familiar to any reader of history who has followed the careers of Western European royal families. Many societies, notably the traditional Chinese and Indian, left little freedom in the hands of young people and explicitly vested in the family elders the choice of a husband or wife for a child.

Two types of norms may limit the selection of a husband or wife, no matter who makes the decision, *endogamous* and *exogamous*. Endogamous rules require marriage within a group—a clan for example, or social class, or religious community. Violations of such rules call forth serious penalities; thus an orthodox Jew may perform the ritual for the dead for a child who marries a non-Jew, and marriage across racial lines can lead to exclusion from the ordinary social life within either race. There still remain some states in the United States that legally prohibit miscegenation, that is, marriage between members of different races, often defined absurdly in mathematical genetic terms, that is on the basis of the number of grandparents of a particular race.

Endogamy, however, is sometimes simply the result of conventional patterns of social intercourse rather than the product of explicitly recognized and enforced norms. Class endogamy, for example, results in large part from the fact that most people tend to associate with others of about the same income and educational level, although cross-class marriage may on occasion lead to informal sanctions; for example, an American upper-class woman who marries beneath her station is likely to be shunned socially by her erstwhile friends (men have somewhat greater freedom in this regard), but no formal rules *require* intraclass marriage.

Exogamous rules prohibit marriage within a group. Thus many primitive societies require their members to marry outside their tribe or clan, thus maintaining a continuing network of relationships with other groups based upon marriage. In every society there are incest taboos that prohibit sexual congress and marriage between members of the nuclear family, that is, between father and daughter, mother and son, brother and sister, and grandparent and grandchild. Although sexual relations are sometimes allowed between persons who would not be permitted to marry one another, the two types of prohibitions usually coincide. Frequently the taboos extend beyond the nuclear family. In Massachusetts, for instance, there are "legal impediments to marriage between a man and his son's wife, grandson's wife, wife's mother, wife's grandmother, wife's daughter, wife's granddaughter, brother's daughter, sister's daughter, father's sister, or mother's sister," and between a woman and comparable male relatives.

The incest taboo

Many explanations have been proffered for the incest taboo, but any adequate analysis must account not only for its presence in all societies, but also for the following facts: (1) "incest taboos do not apply universally to any relative of opposite sex outside of the nuclear family"; (2) "incest taboos are never confined exclusively to the nuclear family"; (3) they "apply with diminished intensity to kinsmen outside the nuclear family"; (4) they "are highly correlated with purely conventional groupings of kinsmen"; (5) they are "characterized by a peculiar intensity and emotional quality"; (6) "violations of incest taboos do occur." [27]

Several common-sense explanations for the incest taboo are frequently offered. First, it is often asserted that incest and intermarriage will lead to a biological deterioration that incest taboos and exogamous marriage requirements serve to prevent. There are several sources of difficulty in this widespread view. In the first place, it requires both reliable knowledge about heredity and genetics, which is hardly likely to be found among Australian aborigines, the illiterate tribesmen of Africa, or Indian peasants, and a rational approach to sex and marriage, which does not usually characterize human behavior. In the second place, the genetic facts themselves do not necessarily bear out the prediction of biological deterioration; the consequences of inbreeding depend upon the characteristics of those persons who are the forebears of the group. Characteristics which may appear in all members of the group eventually may be either desirable or harmful—witness the breeding of cattle, horses, dogs, and poultry, on the one hand, and, on the other, the spread of hemophilia (a genetically carried disease) through Europe's intermarrying royal families—or irrelevant. Third, some societies encourage or even require marriage between such close relatives as first cousins (usually cross-cousins, the children of a man and his sister). There are also a few known cases in which there was no incest taboo, or at least substantial exceptions. Thus there are recorded instances of tolerated—or perhaps encouraged—exceptions to the taboo against brother-sister marriage among the Pharoahs of ancient Egypt, and even among commoners during the period of Roman domination,[28] as well as in the royal families of Hawaii and the Incas of Peru. Finally, even if men had rationally established the incest taboo on good scientific grounds, there would be little reason for the strong emotional reaction which the thought—or event—of violation of the taboo frequently elicits.

The feelings so often generated by incestuous relations have led to the theory that there is an inherent revulsion against intimate relations between family members. The existence of some violations, apparently in all societies, testifies to the absence of such innate or inherited feelings. Nor does this instinct-explanation account for the various ways in which the taboo is extended beyond the nuclear family. These extensions follow no fixed order, sometimes including paternal kin, sometimes maternal, frequently various relatives on both sides of the family, and almost always including kin by both marriage (affinity) and blood (consanguinity).

A third interpretation, offered by Edward Westermarck, a noted Finnish anthropologist and author of a multivolume history of marriage, attributes the incest taboo to the dulling of sexual appetite because of constant association between members of the elementary family and occasionally other relatives as well. This theory is not consistent with continuing relations between husband and wife, the findings of depth psychology which frequently reveal intense attractions between persons with long intimate association— including siblings, and parents and children—and the extent to which marriages occur between persons who have long known one another.

The inadequacies of these various explanations of the apparent universality of incest taboos lend support to a sociological explanation that focuses upon the functions of the incest taboo in maintaining a relatively stable social structure. In order to persist and to perform its usual functions the family requires a fairly clear definition of roles and relationships within it. Incestuous relationships would seriously disturb the structure and interfere with its continued effectiveness. Should relations occur between father and daughter, for example, what would be the appropriate relations between the child of such a union and his half-sister-mother? In general, children of incestuous unions would occupy an unclear and uncertain position in any family system, creating serious internal problems that would tend to disrupt the structure. Moreover, sexual relations are also likely to be incompatible with other kinds of mutual expectations and obligations. In a matrilineal system in which mother's brother was tabooed, for instance, what would be the effect upon the authority usually exercised by a man over his sister's daughter should they become sexually intimate? It seems improbable that the combination of sexual intimacy and relations of superiority and authority could be institutionalized for any extended period.

If this functional interpretation has validity, then, as Murdock points out, the extensions of the incest taboo beyond the nuclear family would tend to follow the structure of the particular kinship system. By prohibiting relations within the socially important kinship group, potentially disruptive conflict or competition is prevented. In a matrilineal family, mother's relatives are more likely to be tabooed than father's kin; in a patrilineal society the reverse holds true.[29]

In addition to preventing difficulties within the family, the incest taboo also serves more positive functions. By requiring marriage outside the kinship group, it establishes a network of relationships that tie together families into the larger social unit. Multiple loyalties that cut across family lines sustain the unity of the larger group. From a psychological point of view, Talcott Parsons has argued, the incest taboo not only regulates and controls erotic relationships within the family but also makes possible those erotic ties necessary for marriage and the establishment of new families.[30]

The emotional intensity usually attached to incest taboos and the strong response to their violation can thus be explained in social-psychological terms. Instead of dulling sexual appetite, constant intimacy between men and women seems to stimulate it. This assertion is substantially supported by clinical evidence and much psychological theory. In order to maintain the taboo, therefore, it becomes necessary to impose severe repressions, which in turn account for the strong emotional response to either the possibility of incest or its actual occurrence. Each mention or incident of incestuous relations, it can be argued, stimulates deeply repressed desires, whose continual repression requires an intense concentration of emotional energy. (This interpretation clearly rests upon psychological premises whose validity cannot be demonstrated here. Without some such psychological assumptions, however, social-psychological problems, such as the institutionalized recurrence of particular emotions, could not be analyzed.)

The problem of functional integration

Insofar as it applies to members of the nuclear family, the incest taboo, then, is an ever-present feature of family structure; otherwise, as we have seen, the taboo itself, like most other structural aspects of family and kinship systems, shows great variation from society to society. Yet the seemingly endless variety is in fact limited, not by instinctive or hereditary predispositions, and not simply by the biological nature of human beings, but by the need for some measure of unity and coherence in this, as in any, social structure. Within the obvious limitations imposed by the fact of only two rather than three or four sexes, and by the nature of the reproductive process and of the prolonged dependence of the human infant, men have managed to create an impressive array of alternative social arrangements.

Despite the fact that men are enormously plastic, however, the institutions which regulate their behavior and order their relations to one another cannot maintain their hold indefinitely if they create contradictory situations or impose competing demands. In this respect there is, as noted earlier, "a strain toward consistency," a tendency for the elements of a social structure to fit together into a coherent system.

The "strain toward consistency" in family and kinship structure can be illustrated in the close relationship between residence rules and the calculation of descent, and in the connection between the approved pattern of mate selection and the general type of family structure. Of the 96 patrilineal societies for which Murdock found data, 78 had patrilocal residence; of the remaining eighteen, four usually followed patrilocal rules but also allowed a choice between husband's and wife's family or permitted the couple to set up a separate establishment, six allowed separate homes or a choice of residence, and eight alternated between the two families.[31] The relatively consistent connection between patrilocal residence and patrilineal descent reflects the likelihood that matrilocal residence would create difficulties for a patrilineal system. If children were brought up in their mother's family, they might well focus their loyalties upon the household in which they lived and upon the male members of their mother's family or kin group rather than upon the father's lineage. (In contrast to this situation, loyalty to the mother's lineage in a matrilineal system frequently seems to hold up well despite patrilocal residence and no consistent relationship holds between matrilineal descent and matrilocal residence.)

Once a particular pattern of residence has been established, Murdock argues, other features of family and kinship structure must almost inevitably change.

So different are the circumstances of life for the individual under these several arrangements that it should occasion no surprise that the adoption by a society of a new rule of residence normally leads to far-reaching internal readjustments.

Patrilocal residence involves a man in lifelong residential propinquity and social participation with his father's patrilineal kinsmen; matrilocal residence associates him with the matrilineal relatives of his mother before marriage and with those of his wife after marriage; . . . neolocal residence isolates him before marriage with his family of orientation and thereafter with his family of procreation; avunculocal residence aligns him physically and socially with his male matrilineal kinsmen and their families. Not only do his relations with his parents, his children, and other relatives differ profoundly under these various arrangements, but so do those with his wife. Either she or he may be isolated from his own relatives, while the other is surrounded and supported by sympathetic kinsmen, or both may be isolated together and made primarily dependent upon one another, or in special cases both may be amongst friendly kinsmen.[32]

The method of selecting marriage partners is in turn affected by the size and nature of the kinship group. In the consanguine family the individual is likely to have less freedom of choice than in the conjugal family. Arranged marriages or preferential mating—in which, for example, cross-cousins, the son and daughter of a sister and brother, are expected to marry one another—are frequently found in consanguine families, particularly when the residential group is large and inclusive. Even when the expression of some choice is possible, firm controls are often exercised in order to prevent marriage with someone who is not wanted by the larger group or with a member of a family or kinship group with whom no formal ties are desired. Since a new wife in, say, a patrilocal consanguine family becomes a member of a group to which she is expected to make some kind of contribution, her qualities are very important not only to her spouse but also to the rest of her husband's family. In many cases marriage also establishes ties between the married couple's families, who can then be called upon by one another to live up to stipulated obligations. Each family must therefore inquire into the character of the potential new member in order to avoid a disadvantageous connection. The existence of controls over marriage does not necessarily mean, however, that strong emotional ties may not be present, for love and passion are perhaps universal human emotions. But they are not necessarily tied to marriage; instead they may emerge after marriage or outside of it.

The free choice of mates, which is accepted and approved in American society —although in fact limited in various formal and informal ways—is consistent with, if not made possible by, the conjugal nature of the family. Since each newly married couple is expected to establish its own home and to be relatively independent, the choice of a marriage partner is much less important to the partners' parents and families than in the typical consanguine group. The ostensible freedom of choice, however, is in fact limited in diverse ways. Despite the relative independence of each nuclear unit, the marriage of a son or daughter may affect a family's social standing or even, in some cases, its economic position; marriages between members of families with large property holdings is clearly not without potential economic consequences. Moreover, the small size of the conjugal family, as we shall see later, also tends to increase the emotional ties among its members and to make any child's action—particularly marriage, with its far-reaching effects upon individual happiness—a matter of great concern to the parents. Finally, the range of available marriage partners is obviously limited by the normal patterns of social interaction; young men and women associate, for the most part, with others of the same educational background, class, religion, race, or ethnic group. Free choice, therefore, is always to some degree choice among a limited range of potential spouses subject to various characteristically subtle, albeit often not ineffective, controls.

The internal structure of the family and the functional integration of its elements are frequently affected by changes that take place elsewhere in the society. When traditional practices or established roles and relationships are disrupted by external forces, structural changes are likely to take place as family members adapt themselves to new situations. Tensions may not be eliminated—indeed, no social structure is ever likely to be so well-integrated that there are no points of strain—but a sufficient measure of integration to enable family members to satisfy their needs and to get along with one another may be re-established after older patterns are upset.

The Tanala of Madagascar, for example, were once organized as large patrilineal groups. Their economy was based upon dry-rice cultivation, a technique that quickly depleted the soil and required frequent movement from place to place. The large family provided an effective means of organizing the effort needed to clear land every few years and to tend the crops. When some of the Tanala learned from adjacent tribes how to grow rice in swampy soil, the entire structure of the society, including the family, underwent change. Wet-rice cultivation required smaller work groups and did not exhaust the soil. Encouraged by an existing emphasis upon private property, small families soon separated themselves from the larger patrilineal group and took ownership of their particular piece of fertile land. Lineages came to have limited importance, chiefly for ceremonial occasions, rather than comprising, as they once had, large groups whose members were tied together in a network of relationships that governed a large share of their activity.[33]

Economic changes have also initiated important shifts among the Bemba of Northern Rhodesia. At one time descent in this society was matrilineal, and residence matri-patrilocal. When he married, a man went to live with his wife's family. After several children were born he and his wife returned to his village, although older children were usually sent to the mother's village to be brought up. Now that many men go to work in the copper mines instead of moving in with their wives' families, the traditional residence pattern has broken down. Since a man can now support himself by working for wages, he can also avoid the one-time dependence upon his wife's family after marriage. By providing goods that his earnings enable him to buy, he has also improved his position in relation to his children. Moreover, the local European

*The American middle-class
conjugal family has become smaller,
less tied to earlier generations,
and more equalitarian, and its
style of life—as with much of
American life—has become more
casual, as evident in these family
portraits past and present.*

residents, because of their wealth and power, now offer new models of behavior; men who are increasingly removed from traditional surroundings "believe it to be more English, and therefore more fashionable, to claim their father's clan instead of their mother's, and some missions have definitely encouraged this change." [34] The shifting emphasis, however, was not totally new, for there had been important ties between the father and his children despite the matrilineal descent pattern: A man took his father's name, father and child normally had close ties to one another, and a father had to be consulted about his daughter's marriage.

The family in urban industrial society

The expanding industrialism which produced changes in the kinship structure of the Bemba has affected family life wherever it has taken hold. On the basis of a meticulous assessment of the available data, William J. Goode has concluded that everywhere in the world there is now a trend toward "some type of *conjugal* family system," at least in part as a result of industrialization, although other factors such as values and ideologies are also contributing independently to the changes taking place.[35] Because the family systems that antedate modernization vary so greatly, the rates of change and the specific patterns of change may differ significantly. But since industrial technology and the organization that usually accompanies it characteristically impose some similar demands in any society, they seem to produce similar results wherever they appear, at least in the long run, despite differences in culture and social organization.

By removing occupational roles and relationships from the family, an industrial economy lessens the need for an extended or compound family, which typically had important functions in an agricultural or pastoral economy. The geographical and social mobility characteristic of an industrial society encourages a neolocal conjugal pattern, although in many, perhaps most, instances, significant relationships persist between the nuclear unit and its kindred.

The conjugal family itself becomes smaller as urbanization and longer schooling, both characteristically concomitants of advancing industrialization, contribute to a declining birth rate. In traditional societies, most families hope or expect to have many children; they are often economically helpful or are valued for religious or other reasons. The newer values of an urban, often commercial, culture—rationality, material success, social advancement, fashion, cultivation of arts or learning—assign less importance to large families and encourage activities and interests outside the family circle. (For a discussion of urbanism and urban values, see Chapter 12.)

Since the skills required by modern technology require extended education, parents cannot effectively train their children for their economic roles or provide relevant models for them to emulate. The family therefore is unable to perform in any large degree one of its traditional functions, that of preparing children for adult roles as productive members of society. This loss further weakens family bonds as children pursue interests acquired from the school or from the newly emerging mass media rather than from their parents or kinfolk, or nearby elders.

As domestic duties diminish or seem less important, women are increasingly attracted—or in some cases, particularly in the working class, pushed by economic pressures—into the industrial and commercial world. The entry of women into the labor market is facilitated by new household technology—gas or electric stoves, vacuum cleaners, refrigerators, dishwashers, washing machines, dryers— and by commercial services that perform tasks once done at home—canning, laundry, baking, sewing, even housecleaning. (In some advanced industrial societies, however, the introduction of labor-saving devices is partially offset by the virtual disappearance of a servant class.)

Gainful employment increases women's independence from their husbands; domesticity is no longer the only respectable outlet for a woman, nor is she totally dependent upon a husband for support. This new independence—actual or potential—contributes to the emergence of an equalitarian relationship between husband and wife that is also encouraged by other trends both within the family and in the larger society. Since the family is no longer a significant productive unit with a recognized division of labor, family roles change. New ideologies— feminism or equalitarianism—contribute to a new pattern of relationships within the family, often through legislation that changes the legal obligations of husband and wife, and their respective rights to own or dispose of property.

Relations between husband and wife are also affected by the changing emotional tone of family life. The impersonality of a predominantly bureaucratic, urban world increases the importance of the family as a repository of human warmth and response. The intimacy that human beings need in order to maintain their personal stability and, indeed, their sanity is found chiefly within the family, whose limited size seems to increase even more the emotional freight carried by family relationships. Such emotional intensity appears to be far more compatible with equality within the family than with traditional patterns of masculine authority. As Elizabeth Bott clearly shows in a study of a small number of English families, those with few close ties with persons outside the family are more likely to draw closely together and to develop an equalitarian relationship than those who are involved in a lively or active social life outside the family.[36]

The increased importance of the conjugal unit and of the emotional bonds that hold it together not only diminishes the likelihood of close control over the individual's choice of a marriage partner, but even transforms the relatively free choice of a mate into a functional necessity. Members of a traditional family are part of a cooperative whole in which each person has defined tasks to perform; husband and wife in a small conjugal family must increasingly adjust to one another's personal needs and qualities without reference to an explicit and generally accepted set of role requirements. Under these circumstances, both personal preference and, perhaps, "romantic" love are more effective bases from which to launch a marriage than are the judgments of one's parents.

The changes in family and kinship structure occasioned by industrialization can create serious problems both for those who have to adjust to new circumstances and for society as a whole. The attenuation of kinship ties frees the individual from some traditional constraints and responsibilities, but it also detaches him from obligations and attachments that help give life order and meaning. The lessened importance of the family as a cooperative economic venture is coupled with greater demands upon the marital relationship itself and, therefore, upon the individual's capacity to adapt himself to the personal needs and qualities of his spouse. These changes expose men and women to uncertainties and personal conflicts and contribute to an increased frequency of family disorganization and divorce. Although many persons learn to cope successfully and creatively with the new problems of the "modern" family, to make the many personal adjustments required by roles that are no longer clearly defined, even to take in stride divorce or extramarital affairs, various forms of personal and social disorganization appear to be linked with the disruption of family ties or the failure of the family to live up to the emotional demands that are now characteristically made of it. It would be incorrect to assign full, or even major, responsibility for such social problems as deliquency, mental illness, or suicide to the family, although many persons do so, particularly moralists and some publicists. Yet since the family is one of the major instruments of social control, the weakening or breakdown of established family or kinship ties and the loss of some of its traditional functions may diminish the hold of society over the individual, thus allowing for both greater freedom and greater license, unless other forms of control are substituted for it.

The fact that the family is significantly affected by economic changes should not obscure the influence that family structure itself may, in turn, have upon the course of economic development. As Goode has shown, the differences in the rate of economic modernization of China and Japan, for example, are probably attributable at least in part to differences in the structure of the family and its relations to economic and political institutions. In Japan only one son inherited the property owned by the family, thus allowing for the accumulation of capital, while in China capital was dispersed because all sons were equally entitled to a share in the father's estate. Although the possibilities of mobility were greater in China, a successful man was expected to carry his family along with him. In Japan, in contrast, a man with an incompetent son could adopt an able young man, who then became part of the family, in order to continue the enterprise and "those who rose did not need to help the undeserving members of the family." [37]

The American middle-class urban family

The effects of industrialization and of urban growth can be clearly illustrated in the case of the American middle-class urban family. No two family systems, of course, are identical, for the processes by which the urban industrial family has emerged have varied from one society to another, and distinctive values and customs are inevitably reflected in the patterns of family life. Because of the fluid nature of American society and its particular values and ideologies, the family, usually more resistant to change than other institutions and structures, seems to have been more susceptible to external forces in the United States than elsewhere, and therefore reflects more fully the demands and pressures of an industrial society.

The United States, we noted earlier, has apparently gone further than most other societies in emphasizing the importance of the isolated conjugal unit. Husband, wife, and children constitute the middle-class urban family, both in myth and reality. A separate residence for each conjugal family is the preferred pattern, once pictured in a vine-covered cottage with a white picket fence, but now more often in a split-level ranch house or Cape

Cod cottage complete with picture window, breezeway, and outdoor grill—but in either case with no relatives. If a newly married couple must live with the family of either spouse, their plight is looked upon as either temporary or unfortunate. (The decline in the number of husband-wife families living with another family in the years between 1952 and 1963 suggests that now fewer newlyweds do not immediately establish their own households.)

For parents—or a widowed parent—to have to live with the family of a married child is also apt to be looked upon by both parents and children as a substantial misfortune, despite the advantage of a built-in baby sitter or additional tax exemption. The oft-repeated mother-in-law jokes, with their image of a meddlesome intruder, reflect popular conceptions; a resident parent, it is feared, may affect the relations of husband and wife, interfere with the rearing of children, and often impose difficult economic burdens.

Although emphasis upon the conjugal unit inevitably lessens the importance of ties with other relatives, it does not eliminate them. Among middle-class families, parents often assist their children in establishing a home after marriage and continue to contribute through gifts on birthdays, anniversaries, or at Christmas time, or when children are born. If they are not too far away, grandparents often provide some help in caring for children.[38] Among working-class families, social life may in fact continue to focus around relatives of either husband or wife—or of both—if they are close by.[39] And in upper-class families, pride of ancestry and sense of kinship are of much greater importance than in most other segments of American society.

In all families there remain emotional ties with kin outside the nuclear unit—

between grandparents and grandchildren, for example, between married couples and their parents- and siblings-in-law. Not only do these ties persist, but also, as Goode points out, "it is impossible to eliminate these additional kin ties without disrupting the nuclear family itself." [40]

Nevertheless, most American families are in fact isolated conjugal units made up of husband, wife, and children. In 1964, of some 41 million conjugal families, more than 32 million or almost 80 per cent were established in their own households, while almost nine million had other relatives in their homes. Of the latter group, a good many included unmarried sons and daughters over eighteen. (The source from which these figures are drawn did not distinguish between adult children and other kin, but in 1960 about three-fifths of adult relatives living with families were unmarried children.) As noted earlier, there were fewer than three-quarters of a million married couples living with relatives. There were in addition about six million other family groups made up of a single parent with children, of adult with a child or children of a relative, and of adults who were related to one another. [41]

Limited to husband, wife, and children, the conjugal family is relatively small. In 1964 the average size of American families was 3.7. [42] In 1790 the average had been 5.4, and in 1890, the average family had 4.5 members. Family size has risen since 1950, largely because of a fairly high birth rate, but held down by an increase in the number of small independent family groups.

In some respects, however, the over-all average is misleading, since the size of each conjugal unit necessarily changes in the course of its existence. In 1964, for example, the average size of husband-wife families in which the head of the family was under forty-five was 4.4, while the size of families in which the head was forty-five to sixty-four years old was only 3.4. [43] Among those families headed by a person over sixty-five, the average size was only 2.4.

These data suggest the existence of a family "life cycle" whose present and past character is shown in Table 1. The average age of marriage in 1960 was 22.3 for men and 20.2 for women. (In 1964 these averages had risen to 23.1 and 20.5, the first increase in these figures in many years and a reversal of a trend toward a lower age of marriage that has persisted since 1890. [44] Almost three-quarters of married women have their first child within two years of marriage and half have their last by the time they are twenty-six. The last child is usually married before the father is fifty years old, the mother forty-seven. The couple can then look forward to between fifteen and twenty years together before the husband dies, and his wife will then survive him by a decade or more. In other words, the (nonexistent) "average" couple may expect to live together for more than forty years, with no children in the home for about one-third of this time.

Some of the changes this family life cycle has undergone are shown in Table 1. In addition to the long-run decline in the age at marriage, the length of time the couple will live together increased by about one-third from 1890 to 1960. The period of childbearing has decreased, the likelihood that both husband and wife will survive to see the marriage of their last child has increased, and the number of years the couple will have together without any direct responsibility for children has been extended.

Both the present cycle and the changes that have taken place are, of course, averages, and there is substantial variation in

Table 1

MEDIAN AGE OF HUSBAND AND WIFE AT SELECTED STAGES OF THE LIFE CYCLE
OF THE FAMILY, 1960, 1950, 1940, and 1890

Stage of the life cycle of the family	Median age of husband				Median age of wife			
	1960	*1950*	*1940*	*1890*	*1960*	*1950*	*1940*	*1890*
A. First marriage	22.3	22.8	24.3	26.1	20.2	20.1	21.5	22.0
B. Birth of last child	27.9	28.8	29.9	36.0	25.8	26.1	27.1	31.9
C. Marriage of last child	49.2	50.3	52.8	59.4	47.1	47.6	50.0	55.3
D. Death of one spouse *	65.7	64.1	63.6	57.4	63.6	61.4	60.9	53.3
E. Death of other spouse †	—	71.6	69.7	66.4	—	77.2	73.5	67.7

* Husband and wife survive jointly from marriage to specified age.
† Husband (wife) survives separately from marriage to specified age. No data for 1960.

Data for 1890, 1940, and 1950 from Paul C. Glick, *American Families*, Table 33, p. 54; reprinted by permission of John Wiley & Sons, Inc. Data for 1960 from Ben J. Wattenberg and Richard M. Scammon, *This U.S.A.* (Garden City: Doubleday, 1965), p. 42.

all of the specific elements of timing—age of marriage, spacing and number of children, age at which children marry or leave home, and so on—among both individuals and, more significantly from a sociological point of view, among groups. For example, age at marriage is higher among college graduates than among those who have not gone to or completed college. Farm families have more children than urban families and manual workers more than white-collar salaried employees or independent businessmen. Life expectancy is greater for whites than for Negroes.

These differences reveal the continued existence in American society of other types of families in addition to the one characteristic of the urban middle class. Except for a small upper class among whom extended kinship ties and a strong sense of family continuity and tradition are found, most variations in family structure occur among lower-class ethnic and racial minorities—Italians, Puerto Ricans, Japanese, French Canadians, Mexicans, and Negroes. Peasants who came to the United States from Quebec, Italy, Mexico, and many other nations

usually brought with them a traditional, closely knit, patriarchal family system which persisted for some time in the new world.

The most distinctive deviation from the middle-class pattern, however, has been the lower-class Negro family which emerged in the aftermath of slavery. Centered around the mother, the most significant bonds linked her with the children while the father, if present at all, characteristically occupied a peripheral position. As the Negroes moved cityward after World War I and World War II, this female-centered family, which had functioned with some modicum of adequacy in the rural South, often became disorganized and unstable, with high rates of illegitimacy and desertion.[45] In a controversial report published in 1965 by the United States Department of Labor, it was argued that this instability had been perpetuated and increased among lower-class urban Negroes because of the high rate of unemployment among Negro men. Their inability to secure and hold a job seriously inhibited any possibility that they might play a positive role in the family. In 1962, almost one-quarter of

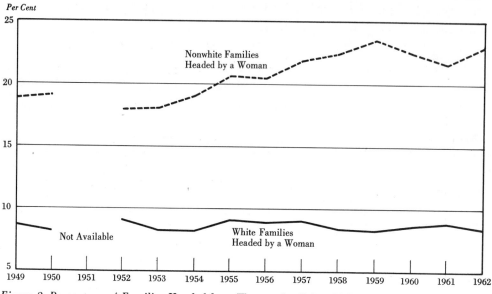

Figure 2. *Percentage of Families Headed by a Woman, by Color, 1949–1962*

U.S. Department of Labor, *The Negro Family: The Case for National Action* (Washington, D.C.: U.S. Government Printing Office, 1965), p. 11.

nonwhite families were headed by women, compared with less than 10 per cent among whites (see Figure 2).

As members of minority groups have acquired middle-class occupations, income, and education, they have tended to model their family life upon the conventional middle-class pattern, although they sometimes continue to possess some distinctive characteristics. Negroes who escape from the confines of the lower-class ghetto often "overconform" to middle-class ways and insist upon the strictest "respectability" as they seek to maintain their uncertain status, particularly in relation to the white community.[46] Oriental families in the "younger" generation have broken sharply with traditional patterns, whereas peasant families stemming from the south of Italy have taken three generations to make the change, often only at the cost of considerable disorganization and internal conflict.

Family functions and family structure

The facts revealed in the family cycle of the typical middle-class urban family have far-reaching implications for both its structure and its functions. The diminished size of the family and its transitory character indicate its lessened importance as a productive economic unit. In a farm economy, like that which included most American families until almost the end of the nineteenth century, most members contribute to a collective enterprise and children are helpful. In an urban industrial or commercial economy, occupational pursuits are removed from the home and neither children nor wife nor other relatives can contribute directly to the husband's economic efforts, except in the case of very small business. (In some corporations, universities, and other large organizations, however, the wife does play an important, albeit unofficial, role in relation to her husband's career.) Economically the family has become essentially a consumption unit; family interests —concern for status, well-being of children, maintenance of harmonious relationships—largely govern patterns of expenditure.

Childbearing and child care, however, remain the responsibility of the family, although increasingly parents look for outside assistance and often expect the schools and other agencies to carry much of the burden of socializing the child and preparing him—or her—for adult roles. As we saw in Chapter 5, the widespread use of child-care manuals (and, it should be added, the growth of child-study organizations and increased reliance upon pediatricians and other child-care experts) reflect the changing structure of the family. The decline of the extended family and the relative isolation of the conjugal unit have thrown parents upon their own resources. Isolation and diminished size have concomitantly limited the opportunities available for girls to learn the rudiments of child care before becoming mothers themselves, although the new role of baby sitter, so prevalent in middle-class America, enables these temporary parent-surrogates to gain experience with children.

During the first years of life, when basic characteristics of personality are being formed, the child is almost totally in the hands of his family. (In some upper-class homes and among families in which both parents work, a nursemaid or relative may in large measure replace the mother.) Patterns of feeding, techniques of toilet training, control of aggression, and most of the other components of child care that shape personality are controlled by parents whose actions reflect not only their own personalities but also the influence of both tradition and the modern knowledge that comes from child-care experts.

For the middle-class child, however, school begins early. The age at which most children are sent to school has steadily gone down, and many middle-class children now enter nursery school by the age of three or four. Sometimes the nursery school is simply a custodial institution designed to provide time off for the mother or to enable her to hold a job; in other cases it is expected to supplement the family, to provide, in an age of small families, directed and controlled relationships with other children, or to offer experiences no longer readily available within the family.

Since few fathers can train their sons for the complex and changing occupational roles of industrial society, the school has taken over almost full responsibility for this task. Even in farming, schools have come to supplement—if not displace—parental instruction. For women, who play an increasingly important role in the life of society outside the home—in politics, business, industry, education, civic affairs, and so on—and who have escaped Victorian restraints and are now credited with the ability and desire to pursue interests beyond those of pure domesticity, more and more formal education has also become a necessity. (Indeed, more girls complete high school than boys; in 1960, 42.5 per cent of all women over twenty-five years of age had completed four years of high school, compared with only 39.5 per cent of all men over twenty-five. Only three-fifths as many women had completed college, however, 5.8 per cent compared with 9.6 per cent of the men.[47])

As an ever-larger proportion of young people receive more and more formal education (see Table 2), additional functions have been turned over to the

Table 2

RETENTION RATE PER 1,000 STUDENTS ATTENDING SCHOOL FROM FIFTH GRADE THROUGH FIRST YEAR OF COLLEGE FOR SELECTED YEARS, 1942–1950 TO 1954–1962

Period of school attendance	*5th grade*	*8th grade*	*10th grade*	*High school graduate*	*Year of high school graduation*	*First year college*
1942–1950	1,000	847	713	505	1950	205
1947–1955	1,000	919	748	559	1955	286
1952–1960	1,000	936	835	621	1960	328
1954–1962	1,000	948	855	636	1962	336

U.S. Bureau of the Census, *Statistical Abstract of the United States, 1963* (Washington, D.C.: U.S. Government Printing Office, 1963), p. 120.

schools. Courses in home economics, consumer buying, foods, and sewing supplement, or perhaps in some cases replace, the traditional modes of teaching girls needed skills. Schools are expected to inculcate political loyalties, contribute to character building, teach good manners, and give driving instruction as well. Even preparation for marriage and family life—including sex education—has been condensed into formal courses. So-called "functional marriage" courses abound in colleges and universities, and problems of family life are frequently taught in secondary schools, sometimes as part of home economics or social studies classes, sometimes in separate courses. Such formal efforts to prepare young people for marriage, whatever their degree of success, emphasize the personal adaptability now required for a successful marriage because of the changing functions of the family and the concomitant shifts in its structure.

In allowing or encouraging the schools to assume these tasks, the family has by no means relinquished altogether its responsibility for socializing children and preparing them for adult roles. Instead, the family and schools—as well as the child's peer group and now the mass media—constitute a complex system of pressures and counterpressures, now facilitat-

ing one another's efforts, now inhibiting them; sometimes sustaining one another, sometimes generating tension or conflict, or precipitating change. From their parents, children acquire attitudes and social values that affect their interest in learning and their responsiveness in the classroom. Teachers must constantly cope with attitudes toward specific subjects and subject matter that derive from the family. Parents may insist that children do their homework, or may pay little attention to school work; they may sustain or subvert school discipline; they may encourage respect or disrespect for the teacher. Indeed, so dependent is the school upon the family that strenuous efforts are constantly made through the creation of parent-teacher associations, the institution of visiting days for parents, and numerous other devices to prevent conflict or disagreement and to keep school and home working harmoniously together.

Schools not only educate children but also, through the children, they often train the parents. In the past, millions of immigrants learned something about their new country from their children, who brought home with them language, information, values, and habits that were presumably better adapted to life in the new world. In many instances, of course, there were conflicts between children educated in American schools and on American streets and parents who were still tied to their traditional culture. There are relatively few foreign-born immigrants in America now (only 5 per cent in 1960 compared with 11 per cent in 1930), but a similar problem exists in the contrast between predominantly middle-class schools and the values and beliefs of many working-class families, a large number of whom are Negro or Puerto Rican or Mexican, only recently arrived in the metropolis.

As its economic functions have declined, the family's importance as a source of emotional response, its "affectional" function, as it has been called, has increased. The nature of modern industrial society, we noted earlier, leaves little room for intimacy and emotional response from others outside the home or groups of close friends. Love becomes a major preoccupation and a predominant value, partly because it presumably offers a warm and comfortable haven in a cold and bureaucratic world. Matthew Arnold's famous lines, written in 1867, seem peculiarly modern:

Ah, love, let us be true
To one another! for the world, which seems
To lie before us like a land of dreams,
So various, so beautiful, so new,
Hath really neither joy, nor love, nor light,
Nor certitude, nor peace, nor help for pain.

And in America, love and marriage are inextricably linked; they "go together," as a once-popular song had it, "like a horse and carriage." Other societies have also placed great emphasis upon love, but few have insisted so emphatically that it must be confined to the marriage bed. Americans are supposed to marry for love, and not merely in order to have children, to link families together, or to avoid the possibility of sin.

The emphasis upon love as the basis

for marriage necessarily exerts strong pressure upon each individual to choose his own spouse, for no one else can share his feeling, or readily select a person with whom an intimate and persisting relationship can be established. In practice, as noted earlier, there are substantial limits upon freedom of choice. Marriages tend to be confined within classes, religious groups, races and ethnic groups, and even within neighborhoods, although the frequency of some forms of intermarriage seems to be increasing. As immigrant groups have become Americanized and have achieved middle-class status, they have increasingly ignored ethnic lines in marriage. According to many reports 30 per cent or more of all marriages in which a Catholic is a party are with non-Catholics. The rate of intermarriage for Catholics, which varies widely, from 13 per cent in New Mexico to 70 per cent in North Carolina, is low in areas in which the cultural differences between Catholics and non-Catholics are great, as in New Mexico and Texas, increases as the number of Catholics in an area decreases, and is higher among the upper social and economic levels.[48]

"Romantic love" has often been caustically criticized for blinding young people to the prerequisites for a successful marriage. But there is ample evidence that many young people are, in fact, quite sensible about their choices, although there are inevitably errors made, errors that can perhaps hardly be avoided when successful marriage rests upon the interaction of two personalities in situations where guide lines are no longer clearly marked. Formal courses in marriage and family, for which more is often expected or claimed than they can provide, try to ready young people for the many adjustments required as they seek to work out for themselves a pattern of family life.

Hays from Monkmeyer

Sybil Shelton from Monkmeyer

With increased equalitarianism in the family, greater economic independence of women, and the importance now assigned to the emotional satisfactions to be derived from family life, the husband has assumed greater domestic responsibilities.

A relationship based upon love is not easily confined within clearly marked out traditional roles, the nature of which, in any event, has changed as the functions of the family have altered. Lighter domestic duties, fewer children, and longer schooling free women from the endless press of maternal responsibilities while they—and their husbands—are still relatively young. By the time children are in high school—and certainly soon afterward—household demands have diminished and women may be free, if they so desire, to pursue other interests.

Little wonder, then, that there has been a steady increase in gainful employment among married women and a marked change in the characteristic chronology of employment among women. Until relatively recently, most working women were single. When they married they withdrew from the labor market and confined their energies to the care of their home, husband, and children. This pattern has changed, however. In 1962, one-third of all married women were gainfully employed. Of almost 24 million women in the labor force, three-fifths were married, 5.5 million were single, and slightly less than 4 million were widowed, divorced, or separated. Increasingly, women go to work upon completing their education —whether high school or college—and continue to hold a job until marriage or even until close to the arrival of the first child. Although there were more than 2 million working women with children under six in 1960, most women do not return to work for several years after they have had their children. But with the declining age of marriage and a relatively small family, women are ready to return to work—or even to find a job for the first time—by their mid-thirties or early forties.

Relationships within the family have

inevitably been affected by the changing role and status of women. Their greater economic independence and their political and legal equality have contributed to a relative equality within the family. The traditional patriarchal pattern, which made considerable sense in a productive unit that required direction and leadership, can hardly survive in a family that has come to play an important role as a repository of affection. The traditional division of labor within the home, which reflected the superior status of the male, has also been substantially changed. Although there is still a rough division between men's and women's tasks, men often wash the dishes, change diapers, run the vacuum cleaner, and do the shopping, although probably more frequently at some stages of the family life cycle than at others. Both the decline in traditional patterns of authority and the blurred distinctions between men's and women's duties are reflected in the frequent jokes about "who wears the pants."

Divorce and family disorganization

In the relatively fluid structure of the modern family, the members of which are held together largely by emotional attachments rather than by mutual services and collective goals, there is considerable room for friction. Lacking clear-cut and mutually agreed-upon definitions of marital roles, husband and wife may find themselves disagreeing about their respective duties and obligations, or about how to bring up a child, or the kind of relations they should maintain with their respective parents. Some men still retain traditional conceptions of masculine authority and feminine domesticity and subordination which their wives may find difficult to accept. In working out a pat-

tern of family life where there is no clear, firm set of rules to follow, many couples discover that they are incapable of making the many adjustments required of them. Since marriages, after all, are made on earth, husband and wife may turn out to be personally incompatible, despite their initial feeling that they were "made for each other." And many such marriages, of course, end in divorce.

The divorce rate in the United States, which is higher than in most other countries, increased steadily from the middle of the nineteenth century (the earliest period for which reliable data are available) until the years following the Second World War. In 1860 there were only 7,380 divorces, or .3 per 1,000 people. The number and rate rose slowly to 1 per 1,000 people prior to World War I and 2 per 1,000 people in 1940. After the war there was a rapid increase, with over 600,000 divorces granted in 1946, a rate of 4.4 for each 1,000 persons. By 1950 the rate had dropped to 2.5 per 1,000 and since early in the 1950s has remained at about 2.3. Another measure of the frequency of divorce, the number for each 1,000 married women, shows roughly the same pattern, from a low of 1.2 in 1860 to 8.7 in 1940, a peak of 18.2 in 1946, and a relatively constant figure between 9 and 10 per 1,000 married women since 1950.[49] These figures, of course, describe only the visible peak of the iceberg, for there is a less readily perceptible volume of desertion, conflict, and marital maladjustment.

There are, of course, variations in the frequency of divorce among different groups. Different attitudes toward divorce are reflected in the lower divorce rate among Catholics than among Protestants and Jews. Couples with different cultural backgrounds are more prone to divorce than those with similar backgrounds, and the younger people are when they marry the greater the likelihood of divorce. The divorce rate is higher among childless couples than among those with children, though perhaps chiefly because divorce-prone couples are less likely to have children than because the presence of children keeps the family together. Finally, divorce occurs more often among Negroes than among whites and is more frequent in the lower classes than in the upper.

Many of these variations in the divorce rate stem from differences in the likelihood of tension in marriage and in the ability of husband and wife to cope with the problems of married life. Yet each of these variations requires careful analysis, for they may be affected by many other factors. Thus, as Goode points out, when divorce is difficult and expensive to secure, it occurs more frequently among the upper classes. When divorce procedures are liberalized, this pattern is reversed and divorce is more prevalent in the lower classes.[50]

The high divorce rate has sometimes been taken as evidence of the inadequacy of love as a basis for marriage, but it is probably more accurate to say that "the figure reflects not so much the failure of love as the determination of people not to live without it" [51]—hence the prevalence of "romantic divorce" and remarriage. Concomitant with, and in part as a result of, the increasing frequency of family friction and the lessened willingness to accept an unsatisfactory marital relationship has come a change in the public attitude toward divorce and, in many states, a greater ease in dissolving a marriage. In 1966 the New York state legislature finally rewrote the divorce law, which had remained unchanged since 1787. Rather than put up with a bad situation, couples secure divorces and then in most instances find other mates. Younger divorcées are more likely to remarry than

are older ones, and Protestants tend to find new spouses more frequently than do Catholics, but other variables also affect the likelihood, timing, and frequency of remarriage. In fact, most divorced people—two-thirds to three-quarters of them—do marry again, and more than nine-tenths stay married on the second try. (In England, a similar proportion of the divorced remarry.[52])

Given the nature of the contemporary American family and its functions, and the demands men and women make upon marriage, there is little likelihood that the rate of divorce and the frequency of desertion and of other evidences of family instability can be eliminated or even substantially cut. The potentially deleterious effects of an overcommitment to "romantic love" can perhaps be minimized by better preparation for marriage. New institutional facilities—marriage counseling services, for example—may enable couples experiencing difficulties in their relationship to work through their problems without destroying their marriage. External circumstances that sometimes create friction between husband and wife—poverty or crowded housing, for instance—may be corrected. But these and other preventive steps are at best meliorative; some measure of divorce and marital conflict is the price to be paid for the freedom of choice, the emphasis upon personal compatibility and emotional satisfaction, the equality of husband and wife—and in recent years in some measure of children as well—to be found in the modern family. Short of a quixotic insistence upon a return to the traditional family, there is little choice for American society but to seek to cushion the undesirable consequences of the type of family that historical forces and individual preferences have conspired to bring about.

Notes

[1] Robert Bierstedt, *The Social Order* (2nd ed.; New York: McGraw-Hill, 1963), p. 379.

[2] *American College Dictionary* (New York: Random House, 1957).

[3] E. E. Evans-Pritchard, *Kinship and Marriage among the Nuer* (Oxford: Oxford, 1951), p. 49.

[4] George P. Murdock, *Social Structure* (New York: Macmillan, 1949), p. 1.

[5] Bronislaw Malinowski. "Parenthood—The Basis of Social Structure," in Rose Coser (ed.), *The Family: Its Structure and Functions* (New York: St. Martin's, 1964), p. 15.

[6] *Ibid.*, p. 13.

[7] William J. Goode, *World Revolution and Family Patterns* (New York: Free Press, 1963), p. 38.

[8] The phrase "conjectural history" was first suggested by an eighteenth-century writer and recently revived by A. R. Radcliffe-Brown, "The Study of Kinship Systems," *Journal of the Royal Anthropological Institute*, LXXI (1941), 1–18.

[9] Robert Briffault, *The Mothers* (New York: Macmillan, 1927).

[10] For an analysis of the significance of ignorance of paternity in a primitive society, see M. F. Ashley Montagu, *Coming into Being among the Australian Aborigines* (New York: Dutton, 1938).

[11] Murdock, *op. cit.*, p. 5.

[12] Alfred C. Kinsey, Wardell B. Pomeroy, and Clyde E. Martin, *Sexual Behavior in the Human Male* (Philadelphia: Saunders, 1948); and Alfred C. Kinsey, Wardell B. Pomeroy, and Clyde E. Martin, *Sexual Behavior in the Human Female* (Saunders, 1953).

[13] Murdock, *op. cit.*, p. 11.

[14] Kingsley Davis, *Human Society* (New York: Macmillan, 1949), p. 395.

[15] *Ibid.*, p. 396.

[16] For a detailed account of child-rearing in the kibbutz, see Melford E. Spiro, *Children of the Kibbutz* (Cambridge, Mass.: Harvard University Press, 1958).

[17] For a challenging essay that denies the universal necessity of the family, see Barrington Moore, Jr., *Political Power and Social Theory* (Cambridge, Mass.: Harvard University Press, 1958), Ch. 5.

[18] Murdock, *op. cit.*, p. 2.

[19] *Ibid.*

[20] For a summary of several studies of the Chinese family that document the prevalence of monogamy in a potentially polygamous family system, see Olga Lang, *Chinese Family and Society* (New Haven: Yale University Press, 1946), pp. 136–7. For a review of data on the Moslem Arab family, which allows as many as four wives but in which monogamy is the most frequent pattern, see Goode, *op. cit.*, pp. 101–4.

[21] Ralph Linton, *The Study of Man* (New York: Appleton, 1936), p. 159.

[22] Frances L. K. Hsu, *Americans and Chinese* (New York: Schuman, 1953), pp. 125–6.

[23] For recent studies of the Nayar, see E. Kathleen Gough, "Changing Kinship Usages in the Setting of Political and Economic Change among the Nayars of Malabar," *Journal of the Royal Anthropological Institute*, LXXXII, Part II (1952), 71–88; and Gough, "The Nayars and the Definition of Marriage," *Journal of the Royal Anthropological Institute*, LXXXIX (January–June, 1959), 23–34.

[24] For accounts of the Jewish family in Eastern Europe prior to World War I, see Mark Zborowski and Elizabeth Hertzog, *Life Is With People* (New York: International Universities Press, 1952); and Ruth Landes and Mark Zborowski, "Hypotheses Concerning the Eastern European Jewish Family," *Psychiatry*, XIII (November, 1950), 447–64.

[25] Reported in Paul C. Glick, *American Families* (New York: Wiley, 1957), pp. 44–5.

[26] These data from U.S. Bureau of the

Census, *Current Population Reports*, Series P-20, No. 44 (September 6, 1953), "Marital and Household Characteristics: April, 1952," Table 5, p. 14; and No. 139 (June 11, 1965), "Household and Family Characteristics: March, 1963," Table 3, p. 15.

27 Murdock, *op. cit.*, pp. 284–8. Much of the ensuing discussion follows Murdock's analysis.

28 Russell Middleton, "Brother-Sister and Father-Daughter Marriage in Ancient Egypt," *American Sociological Review*, XXVII (October, 1962), 603–11.

29 Murdock, *op. cit.*, p. 307.

30 Talcott Parsons, *Social Structure and Personality* (New York: Free Press, 1964), Ch. 3, "The Incest Taboo in Relation to Social Structure and the Socialization of the Child."

31 Murdock, *op. cit.*, Table 65, p. 235; Table 66, p. 237; Table 67, p. 239; Table 68, p. 240.

32 *Ibid.*, p. 202.

33 Linton, *op. cit.*, pp. 348–55.

34 Quoted in Raymond Firth, *Human Types* (rev. ed.; New York: New American Library, 1958), p. 97.

35 Goode, *op. cit.*

36 Elizabeth Bott, *Family and Social Network* (London: Tavistock, 1957).

37 William J. Goode, *The Family* (Englewood Cliffs: Prentice-Hall, 1964), p. 115.

38 Marvin B. Sussman, "The Help Pattern in the Middle-Class Family," *American Sociological Review*, XVIII (February, 1953), 22–8.

39 Floyd Dotson, "Patterns of Voluntary Association Among Urban Working-Class Families," *American Sociological Review*, XVI (October, 1951), 687–93.

40 Goode, *World Revolution and Family Patterns*, p. 371.

41 These figures are from U.S. Bureau of the Census, *Current Population Reports*, Series P-20, No. 139, *passim*.

42 *Ibid.*, p. 5.

43 *Ibid.*, Table 8, p. 22.

44 Ben J. Wattenberg and Richard M. Scammon, *This U.S.A.* (Garden City: Doubleday, 1965), p. 35.

45 E. Franklin Frazier, *The Negro Family in the United States* (rev. and abridged ed.; New York: Dryden, 1951), Part IV.

46 See E. Franklin Frazier, *Black Bourgeoisie* (New York: Free Press, 1957).

47 These percentages are calculated from U.S. Bureau of the Census, *Statistical Abstract of the United States, 1963* (Washington, D.C.: U.S. Government Printing Office, 1963), Table 153, p. 120.

48 See John L. Thomas, "The Factor of Religion in the Selection of Marriage Mates," *American Sociological Review*, XVI (August, 1951), 487–91; Loren E. Chancellor and Thomas P. Monahan, "Religious Preference and Interreligious Mixtures in Marriages and Divorces in Iowa," *American Journal of Sociology*, LXI (November, 1955), 233–9; and Harvey J. Locke, Georges Sabagh, and Mary M. Thomes, "Interfaith Marriages," *Social Problems*, IV (April, 1957), 329–33.

49 Paul H. Jacobson, *American Marriage and Divorce* (New York: Holt, 1959), Table 42, p. 90.

50 Goode, *World Revolution and Family Patterns*, p. 86.

51 Morton M. Hunt, *The Natural History of Love* (New York: Knopf, 1959), p. 342.

52 Ronald Fletcher, *Britain in the Sixties: The Family and Marriage* (Baltimore: Penguin, 1962), p. 143.

Suggestions for further reading

ANSHEN, RUTH NANDA (ED.). *The Family: Its Function and Destiny*, rev. ed. New York: Harper, 1959.
A collection of articles. See especially the theoretical essays by Ralph Linton and Talcott Parsons and the studies of the family in different societies.

BELL, NORMAN W., AND EZRA F. VOGEL. *A Modern Introduction to the Family.* New York: Free Press, 1960.
An excellent collection of papers on the family.

BERNERT, ELEANOR H. *America's Children.* New York: Wiley, 1958.

GLICK, PAUL C. *American Families.* New York: Wiley, 1957.
Two excellent statistical analyses of the composition and structure of the family and of trends in family life. Based upon census data.

EHRMANN, WINSTON W. *Premarital Dating Behavior.* New York: Holt, 1959.
A rich study of dating and courtship practices among college students.

FLETCHER, RONALD. *Britain in the Sixties: The Family and Marriage.* Baltimore: Penguin, 1962.
An analysis of the family in contemporary Britain.

FRAZIER, E. FRANKLIN. *The Negro Family in the United States,* rev. and abridged ed. New York: Dryden, 1951.
An excellent historical account of the development of the Negro family in the United States.

GOODE, WILLIAM J. *After Divorce.* New York: Free Press, 1956.
The best single study of the after-effects of divorce.

GOODE, WILLIAM J. *World Revolution and Family Patterns.* New York: Free Press, 1963.
A major contribution to the analysis of trends in family structure in China, Japan, India, sub-Saharan Africa, the Arab countries and the West.

KINSEY, ALFRED C., WARDELL B. POMEROY, AND CLYDE E. MARTIN. *Sexual Behavior in the Human Male.* Philadelphia: Saunders, 1948.

KINSEY, ALFRED C., WARDELL B. POMEROY, AND CLYDE E. MARTIN. *Sexual Behavior in the Human Female.* Philadelphia: Saunders, 1953.
These two books, which have become cultural landmarks, are biologically oriented studies of the frequency and form of "sexual outlets" of Americans —and not of men or women in general. They do not deal directly with family life but do provide useful data on erotic behavior at different levels of American society.

KOMAROVSKY, MIRRA. *Women in the Modern World.* Boston: Little, Brown, 1953.
A sociological analysis of the problems of middle-class American women, with particular reference to the influence of education upon careers, marriage, and family life.

LEWIS, OSCAR. *The Children of Sanchez.* New York: Random House, 1961.
A detailed account of the family life of a slum family in Mexico City based upon intensive transcribed interviews with all its members.

MURDOCK, GEORGE P. *Social Structure.* New York: Macmillan, 1949.
An attempt at a comparative sociology of the family based upon the data available in the Human Relations Area Files. Although much criticized by some anthropologists, it remains a major piece of work.

SIRJAMAKI, JOHN. *The American Family in the Twentieth Century.* Cambridge, Mass.: Harvard University Press, 1953.
A semipopular account of the evolution and present form of the American family. A readable and informed discussion.

YANG, C. K. *The Chinese Family in the Communist Revolution.* Cambridge, Mass.: M.I.T. Press, 1959.
A description of changes taking place in the Chinese family as a result of the Communist revolution.

YOUNG, MICHAEL, AND PETER WILLMOTT. *Family and Kinship in East London.* New York: Free Press, 1957.
A detailed description of working-class families in a relatively self-contained London neighborhood.

8
Social stratification

The nature of social stratification

In every society some men are identified as superior and others as inferior: patricians and plebians, the twice-born and once-born, aristocrats and commoners, masters and slaves, the classes and the masses. Except perhaps where everyone lives at a bare subsistence level, some individuals are likely to be rich, others well-to-do, and still others poor. Everywhere some rule and others obey, although the latter may possess varying degree of influence or control over the rulers. These contrasts—between higher and lower, rich and poor, powerful and powerless—constitute the substance of social stratification.

So complex and multifaceted are the facts of social stratification that they have been described and interpreted in many diverse ways. Some writers have assigned greater importance to rank, others to wealth, power, or privilege as the crucial dimension of stratification. The differences between aristocrats and commoners, prosperous and poor, ruling and ruled, have been viewed as a result of inherent differences among men, as a product of institutional forces over which men have little control, as social patterns that contribute to the functioning of society, as a source of conflict and strain. Stratification may be considered a proc-

ess, a structure, a problem; it may be seen as one aspect of the differentiation of roles and statuses in society, as a division of society into social groups or quasi-groups, as the social arena in which the problem of equality and inequality presents itself—or as all of these.

Consensus among sociologists as to the best or most appropriate definition of *social class*, the key concept in the analysis of social stratification, has not yet been achieved. This continuing disagreement is based in part upon the fact that different scholars have focused their attention upon different aspects of stratification. The resulting confusion can be largely dispersed by distinguishing *class, status,* and *power*. These categories of stratification are based upon different criteria, derive from different sources, and the phenomena to which they refer have varied consequences. The three are usually closely related to one another, and one of the central problems in the study of social stratification is the nature and extent of their interrelationships.[1]

Class

Although the definition of a class as a group possessing the same economic position in society is usually identified with Marxist theory, it has in fact a long history that begins well before Karl Marx wrote *The Communist Manifesto*. Aristotle, for example, noted that "in all states there are three elements: one class is very rich, another very poor, and a third is a mean," and then assessed the relevance of these divisions for government and politics. Many centuries later (in 1788), in a much-quoted passage in *The Federalist*, James Madison wrote:

Those who hold and those who are without property have ever formed distinct interests in society. Those who are creditors, and those who are debtors, fall under a like discrimination. A landed interest, a manufacturing interest, a mercantile interest, a moneyed interest, with many lesser interests, grow up of necessity in civilized nations, and divide them into different classes, actuated by different sentiments and views. The regulation of these various and interfering interests forms the principal task of modern legislation, and involves the spirit of party and faction in the necessary and ordinary operations of the government.[2]

By the early decades of the twentieth century, American scholars, with only a few exceptions (among whom were the principal pioneers of American sociology[3]), had come to ignore these views of the Founding Fathers; the prevailing viewpoint held that American society was "classless" or "middle class." The very mention of class, in part because of its association with Marxist doctrine, was identified as what some persons would now call "subversive" or "un-American," although problems of stratification were not totally ignored. Only in the 1940s did it once again become respectable for American social scientists to recognize explicitly the existence of class differences in the United States and to carry on systematic research in this field. The history of the concept of class is itself, therefore, a fascinating problem in

the sociology of ideas and knowledge yet to be fully explored.[4]

In the development of the concept of class, Marx's theory has been of major importance, despite its demonstrable limitations. Marx defined classes in terms of their relationship to property.

The owners of mere labor-power, the owners of capital, and the landlords, whose respective sources of income are wages, profit, and ground-rent, in other words, wage laborers, capitalists, and landlords, form the three great classes of modern society resting upon the capitalist mode of production.[5]

This definition, as Marx himself observed, was not original.

No credit is due to me [he wrote] for discovering the existence of classes in modern society nor yet the struggle between them. Long before me bourgeois historians had described the historical development of this class struggle and bourgeois economists the economic anatomy of the classes.[6]

In 1776 Adam Smith had written in *The Wealth of Nations*, the basic contribution to laissez-faire "capitalist" economics:

The whole annual produce of the land and labour of every country . . . naturally divides itself . . . into three parts; the rent of land, the wages of labour, and the profits of stock; and constitutes a revenue to three different orders of people; to those who live by rent, to those who live by wages, and to those who live by profit. These are the three great, original and constituent orders of every civilized society, from whose revenue that of every other order is ultimately derived.[7]

By virtue of their position in the economic order, members of each class, according to Marx, share common experiences, a more or less distinctive way of life, and certain political and economic interests. The bourgeoisie (owners of the means of production) and the proletariat (wage laborers) are inevitably led into conflict because of their contradictory interests. Other classes, whose existence

Marx recognized, were given little attention because, he thought, they played only a minor role on the contemporary historical stage. Group awareness (class consciousness) and collective political and economic action develop, Marx asserted, in the course of political and economic conflict. Proletarian class consciousness is particularly likely to emerge because its members all face serious difficulties and are thrown into close daily association in their work.

This interpretation has frequently been vulgarized by both Marxists and anti-Marxists into a crude economic determinism that reduces all issues to matters of economic interest, and leaves no room for alternatives and human choice. Marx himself recognized that class consciousness does not *automatically* arise simply because men share a similar objective position in society. In his own analysis he clearly demonstrated that ideas, the strategy and tactics of political and economic action, and human effort necessarily play an important role in determining how each class acts, although he also believed that history was on his side. He assigned to a revolutionary party the task of stimulating the requisite class awareness and creating the political organization needed to effectuate the revolution he both desired and labored to bring about. (Lenin, building upon Marx, but more the man of action than the scholar or theorist, insisted that without the Party there could not be the revolutionary class consciousness which Marx sometimes described as inevitable and sometimes suggested could only be created by positive action that took into account the concrete historical situation.)

Modern history demonstrates both the errors and the inadequacies of Marx's analysis. Many of his specific predictions have not been fulfilled: The middle class

has not disappeared, although its character has changed. The working class has not been progressively pauperized; instead its standard of living has risen with advancing industrialization. Ownership has not been concentrated in fewer and fewer hands in capitalist society, but has been quite widely dispersed through the medium of stock ownership, although it is true that giant corporations directed by men who often own little, if any, stock in the enterprises they manage have come to occupy a dominant place in the capitalist economy. Revolutions led by Communists have not taken place in the more advanced industrial nations where Marx expected them, but in the less-developed areas where Communism has become the basis for industrialization rather than its product.

In concentrating on economically based classes, Marxist theory overlooked other forms of stratification, underestimated the consequences of other divisions in society, and seriously neglected the ubiquitous problem of political power. Class membership is only one attribute of a person; other social characteristics inevitably enter into behavior. Class position may on occasion exercise a predominant influence upon men's actions, but its effects may be diminished or changed by the other characteristics men possess: religion, ethnic affiliation, national loyalty, and so on.

Despite these shortcomings, some of Marx's sociological premises are still valid. In most societies there are divisions or classes with an economic base, which are significant components of social structure. Men who occupy similar places in the economic order are very likely to face the same problems, go through comparable life experiences, have common attitudes and values, and therefore behave in much the same fashion. Their relations with members of other classes are also likely to follow the same pattern. A class may, under appropriate conditions, coalesce into a group—or groups—that plays an important part in the organized life of the society. Even if a class remains only a social category without group consciousness or an organized structure, the fact that its members may act in roughly the same way—for example, in voting, or in accepting or rejecting new ideas or practices—has important consequences for the society as a whole.

We may define a class, then, as a *number of persons sharing a common position in the economic order*. For Marx that position was based upon man's relations to the means of production—ownership or nonownership of property, that is— and, among owners, upon the type of property. Not only is property ownership usually a source of income and therefore of the things that money can buy, but, as we shall see in Chapter 12, it also carries with it power or control over economic resources, and, therefore, to a considerable extent, over other persons.

The crude separation between owners and nonowners, however, grossly oversimplifies the complex economic divisions found in modern industrial society. Moreover, whatever validity property may once have possessed as the central determinant of class structure in Western society has been diminished—although not eliminated—by changes that have taken place since Marx's time in the nature of property institutions (see Chapter 12). Occupational distinctions—among skilled, semiskilled, and unskilled workers, clerks, salespeople, independent entrepreneurs, officials, managers, and professionals—now appear to be more significant criteria of class than mere ownership or nonownership of property not only in Western Europe and North America but also in industrial societies elsewhere. "Life chances," that is, the opportunity to secure those things valued by a society—income, goods, power, prestige—are significantly affected by the ways in which men earn their livelihood, although in "capitalist" society wealth and occupation are still closely related to one another.

Status

Although wealth and occupation are often significant bases for prestige or social standing, they are not the only criteria in terms of which men assess one another's social worth, or even necessarily the most important. Other values such as ancestry, education, race, power, or style of life may provide alternative, or additional, bases of social ranking. The system of status—the ranking of roles and their incumbents—therefore constitutes a dimension of social stratification which must be considered both independently of and in relation to the division of society into economically based classes. (For a discussion of the concept of status and this particular usage, see pp. 39–40.)

In any society with more than a minimal division of labor based upon age and sex, roles vary in the prestige they carry and the rewards they provide. These differences in status derive from many sources: the power or authority attached to some roles, the relative importance assigned to alternative roles by society, the number of persons capable of performing the requisite tasks, the rewards they carry. The existence of institutionalized inequality, it has often been claimed, serves to motivate men to prepare themselves for difficult and responsible tasks and to perform them adequately enough to meet the needs of collective social life.

There is undoubtedly a tendency for prestige and other rewards to increase sufficiently to enlist requisite manpower for difficult and important tasks. In recent years, for example, scientists have gained greater income and enhanced respect, and the salaries of college professors have risen steadily as the demand for college and university teachers has grown. Yet clearly there is no direct or simple relationship between rewards and the contributions to society of movie stars and professional athletes, some of whom are among the best paid and most admired members of American society.

Since each person plays many roles, it is necessary to distinguish between the differential evaluation of roles and the hierarchical ranking of individuals. The social standing of those who teach, for example, is not identical with the status of teachers in general. Despite their common occupation, teachers whose parents are small businessmen or skilled workers—as many of them are—typically move in somewhat different circles and possess somewhat lower status than those who come from professional or executive families. Some roles, of course, are more important than others in determining status; in American society, as in most industrial societies, occupation is usually the chief determinant.[8] Empirical studies of status-ranking therefore often use occupation as the chief index of status, even though other attributes may also be included in such analyses.

Each person acquires his position in the status structure initially from his family. Indeed, as we noted earlier, the family and not the individual is characteristically the essential unit in social stratification. As part of their role parents are expected to care and provide for their children; in many instances this includes placing them as high in the social order as possible. Those who already hold high positions are able because of their prestige or wealth or power to guarantee a higher rank for their offspring than the latter might be able to achieve on their own.

The status of individuals, then, may be *ascribed* or *achieved,* based upon relatively fixed criteria over which they have no control—ancestry, inherited wealth, or ethnic affiliation—or upon qualities or attributes that can be gained by some direct action—or luck. Even ascribed status, however, puts strong pressure upon the individual to acquire the appropriate manner and skills so as to remain at the social level to which he is born. The aristocrat who inherits his rank and is brought up to follow the requirements of his position may fall from his elevated station if he fails to conform to the requirements of his status or disregards the obligations placed upon him.

Societies differ in the relative importance they assign to ascriptive and achievement criteria of status. The traditional Indian caste system, for example, involved a hierarchy based almost entirely upon ascription, while most industrial societies place great emphasis upon achievement. The many criteria which can provide grounds for judgment— wealth, occupation, ancestry, education, religion, race, ethnic affiliation, power, social behavior—are not randomly assorted, for they are often closely linked to one another. Education, for example, helps to determine one's occupational level as well as serving directly as the grounds for social ranking. One's occupation clearly affects the amount of income one may earn, as well as carrying some status value itself.

Whatever the accepted prerequisites of

status, it normally must be ratified by behavior. Wealth and power, for example, are usually prerequisites for very high status in the United States, but by themselves they may not lead to prestige or acceptance into certain exclusive social circles. Toward the end of the nineteenth century, a number of horny-handed prospectors who had struck it rich in the West sought access to New York City "Society," but they lacked the manners, speech, and social skills, as well as the ancestry, required for entry to Mrs. Astor's drawing room. Eventually they secured acceptance to such groups for their children by sending them to the "correct" schools and dancing masters, outfitting them at the proper dressmakers and tailors, and providing them with the appropriate accouterments. English history, too, is full of successful merchants and manufacturers whose wealth eventually enabled them to secure entry to the upper classes. Such entry came about after they had bought land, possession of which was more prestigeful than ownership of a factory or business, changed their style of life, and managed to obscure their origins in "trade." Yet mere possession of the requisite social skills without the support of wealth and power is not likely to sustain a high social position unless men can parlay their status into access to income and influence. These facts suggest that one task in the study of social stratification is the analysis of the complex interrelations among the many criteria of status.

A great deal of a person's behavior, whatever his motives, carries status connotations. His actions may merely identify his position or they may help to change—or reinforce—his standing. Whether a woman wears mink or mouton, an original creation designed by Dior or Balenciaga or a copy bought in Macy's, not only indicates how much money she can afford to spend, but also contributes to her—or her family's—status. One's vocabulary and accent may not only provide a social identification, but may also affect one's rank. In a study of class differences in speech, an English linguist identified the following words as either *U* (upper class) or *non-U* (not upper class) : [9]

U	*Non-U*
luncheon	dinner
house	home
false teeth	dentures
sick	ill
looking glass	mirror
master	teacher

Of perhaps greater importance than choice of words is accent; "a misplaced 'h'" one writer has observed, "is sufficient to betray a man's breeding, his education, his social class." [10]

Although class differences in speech are much less marked in the United States than in Britain (and in both cases there are also regional variations that cut across class lines), they are not totally absent. An American sociologist studying the upper ranks of Philadelphia society reported that upper-class persons say that they *"live* in a *house, employ servants* to *wash* the *curtains* and clean the *furniture,* including a *sofa;* they use the *toilet,* the *porch, library,* or *playroom."* Members of the middle class say that they *"reside* in a *home, hire help* or *domestics* to *launder* the *drapes* and clean the *house-furnishings* which include a bedroom *suite* (like in suit) and a *davenport;* they use the *lavatory,* the *veranda, den,* or *rumpus room."* [11] These expressions were common in 1940; it is possible that the mass media and the increasing general level of education may have eliminated some of these differences, although these—or other —words and idioms may still carry status value: "how do you do?" as contrasted with "pleased to meet you," for example, or "dinner jacket" as against "tuxedo."

The fact that many actions possess status connotations does not necessarily mean that men are continually motivated by a desire for the approval of others or by a chronic concern with their social

So pervasive are success values and the emphasis on mobility in American society that advertisers often focus upon them in their efforts to sell their products, undoubtedly helping to reinforce these values at the same time that they play upon them.

standing. Behavior that affects men's status often results from complex motives that may not include any concern with status. The extent and form of status-striving varies from group to group and must therefore be examined anew in each class or society. Many studies, as well as the observations of perceptive novelists, agree that the middle class and the *nouveaux riches* are particularly status-conscious and far more anxious about their position than other groups.[12] Men are usually attentive to the judgments of others and interested in their social standing. But the nature and extent of these concerns and their sociological consequences are very likely to differ in different kinds of societies.

Prestige, or status, as C. Wright Mills points out, "involves at least two persons: one to claim it and another to honor the claim."[13] Unless both agree upon the appropriate grounds for prestige there can be no consistent status structure. When there is no consensus upon status values, particular groups may find themselves in an ambiguous position, their claims to status accepted by some and denied by others. In a study of a midwestern city, for example, Mills found that small businessmen were ranked relatively low by high-status business and professional men and relatively high by manual workers.[14] Individuals, families, or entire occupational or other groups who are moving up or down in the class structure often occupy an uncertain status, for they may possess attributes appropriate for several different levels of prestige.

A changing distribution of wealth and power may also lead to status competition in which the newly rich and recently powerful challenge the very credentials upon which the established upper class has maintained its status, by emphasizing wealth, for example, rather than ancestry, or by developing a cosmopolitan mode of life rather than a traditional one. But a rising class, rather than rejecting the values of an established social elite, often tries merely to follow them. In eighteenth-century pre-Revolutionary France, as Elinor Barber has shown, the rising bourgeoisie did not challenge the status values of the nobility, but instead sought to live up to them. Similarly, the rising merchants and manufacturers of eighteenth- and nineteenth-century Britain frequently tried to copy the style of life of the landed aristocracy and to gain admittance to their social circles.[15]

Persons who occupy a common rank tend, on the whole, to associate with one another, particularly in more narrowly "social" activities, rather than with persons of higher or lower status. Because they share the same status values, they approve of one another and disparage those who fail to live up to their standards of behavior. To the extent that they set themselves off from others, limit participation in certain social activities to those of similar prestige, and establish and maintain social relationships with one another, they can be said to constitute a *status group*.

Power

Power, the capacity to control the actions of others, and the frequently (but not always) correlative phenomenon, authority (or legitimate power), a recognized right to command, are features of most if not all social structures. Many roles and statuses carry with them some prescriptions of authority or an approved freedom of action that affects the behavior of others. Foremen in industry, whether in Britain, the United States, or the Soviet Union, can enforce their orders to their subordinates; their right to give such orders is usually accepted, even though it may be limited by union rules, legal restrictions, or, in the U.S.S.R., by Communist Party functionaries. The managers of giant corporations in a capitalist economy, though somewhat constrained by labor unions and, on occasion, government policy, can determine the fate of thousands of persons, indeed, in some respects, of a whole society by their decisions on financing, pricing, production schedules, wages, and the location of plants. Those who hold public office are the most obvious examples of persons possessing both power and authority, for, in passing or enforcing laws and in adjudicating among individuals or between individuals and the state, they decide what others can or must or cannot do.

Since we shall examine political institutions later, we may defer most of our discussion of power and authority until Chapter 13. Here only two further observations need be made. First, because the state possesses the legal monopoly of force in all modern societies, all other forms of power and authority are presumably subject to political control. The right of businessmen, labor leaders, or others to make decisions that affect the whole society or large numbers of persons within it can be limited or confined by political action and legislation. Second, close and significant relations are likely to exist between political institutions and the activities of government, on the one hand, and both the class structure and the status hierarchy, on the other. Except for analytic purposes, government and politics are not separate and independent features of society. Although the state may control other aspects of social life, it is itself subject to the influence of social groups operating through accepted institutions or, occasionally, through direct revolutionary action.

Although the study of power is essential in *political* analysis, power is by no means confined to government. There is the illegitimate power of the gangster; the often hidden or obscured power of the party boss and, at times, of the business leader; the recognized but informal power of the local social arbiter; not to speak of the combined authority and power of parents, priests, and even professors. Here we are concerned, however, with power, naked or sustained by myth or law, as an ever-present feature of social stratification.

Class, status, and power: their interrelations

The three major dimensions of stratification tend, on the whole, to hang together, feeding into and supporting one another. Wealth, occupation, and power may all serve as criteria of status. Occupational roles often carry authority and power, and ownership of property makes possible control not only over things but in some measure over people. Status may provide—or block—access to opportunities for wealth and power. Economic groups and interests almost inevitably play an important part in the political process, where status values may also be reflected. But each form of stratification, as noted earlier, has its own proponents.

Some writers, chief among them Marx, assign priority to the economic bases of class and ignore or minimize other aspects of social stratification. Others argue that power constitutes the essential element in class structure.[16] Many American sociologists have focused their attention chiefly upon status-ranking, thereby, by

implication if not explicitly, relegating economic and political factors to a secondary position. These contrasting views raise three related problems: Are these three dimensions of stratification—class, status, and power—of equal significance in the life of society? In their mutual interrelations, is one or another of them of greater or lesser importance? Under what conditions do they become more or less important?

The answers to these questions often reflect the diverse concerns and political orientations of social scientists. Those concerned with social change have tended to focus their attention largely upon the economic aspects of stratification, or upon the group consciousness that often arises among those who share a common class position, and have explored the connection between economic interests and political power. Those concerned with the forces making for stability in the social order have tended to emphasize the importance of status and of patterns of consumption rather than the place people have in the process of production.

Whether class, status, or power is of greater significance, therefore, depends at least in part upon the questions being asked as well as upon the historical situation being studied. This means that broad generalizations, such as the following, are inevitably risky. Tentatively, however, several propositions seem to be in order. In exploring the forms and process of *interpersonal relationships* the dimension of status probably is of greater immediate importance in shaping conduct than either power or class. The "gold digger" may weigh her escort's purse, but most women judge him by his manners and style of life, though in all likelihood the financial implications are also drawn. Who visits with whom, is invited to dinner, or is carefully excluded from the list of eligibles for marriage and from dinner and cocktail parties depends upon prevailing views of social (status) acceptability.

If, on the other hand, one is chiefly interested in studying the processes of *social change*, then there is considerable evidence that the facts of class and power are on the whole of greater importance than those of status. The status structure itself in the long run is so dependent upon class divisions that it will more often play a secondary rather than a primary role. Max Weber has set this problem in large historical perspective:

When the bases of the acquisition and distribution of goods are relatively stable, stratification by status is favored. Every technological repercussion and economic transformation threatens stratification by status and pushes the class situation into the foreground. Epochs and countries in which the naked class situation is of predominant significance are regularly the periods of technical and economic transformations. And every slowing down of the shifting of economic stratifications leads, in due course, to the growth of status structures and makes for a resuscitation of the important role of social honor.[17]

The close connections among class, status, and power, however, may be challenged and destroyed by forces other than technological and economic innovations. New claims to status may come from a nascent political group as well as a rising economic class. Just as new classes usually seek to acquire the status symbols that will mark their superiority, so rising political elites try to legitimize their status and to secure the deference and respect appropriate to their new-found power. In pursuing this goal they may also preëmpt the requisite economic resources. But as status is recognized and secured, the claims of honor may come to take on added importance, achieving an equal place in the hierarchy of values with economic and political interests.

Systems of stratification

From one point of view, class, status, and power represent the principal interests found in any system of stratification. Men pursue economic gain, protect and aspire to social standing and reputation, and seek control over others or freedom from control. These interests, of course, are not mutually exclusive; they tend to coalesce, realization of one leading to realization of the others, although a society may emphasize one at the expense of the others. These interests, however, take form and become operative within a structure of classes, status groups, and a hierarchy of power that divide members of society into an array of frequently overlapping groups or categories.

Analysis of the structure or system of stratification in any society requires consideration of at least the following conditions:

(1) the number and size of classes and status groups;

(2) the amount of movement of individuals and families from one group to another (social mobility);

(3) the sharpness of the lines between groups, as evident in readily apparent differences in behavior or style of life and in the extent of class consciousness;

(4) the specific bases for division— the kind and amount of property men own, the occupations they follow, and the values from which status derives;

(5) the distribution of power among the several classes and status groups.

Of these conditions, two—the amount of mobility and the sharpness with which class and status lines are defined—have been used to distinguish types of stratification systems. The United States, the Soviet Union, and indeed most industrial societies possess a relatively *open* class structure in which status is based primarily upon achievement, and movement up and down the social scale is possible and relatively frequent. In India and in most traditional societies, the stratification system is relatively closed (although this situation appears to be changing rapidly) ; for the most part status is ascribed and individual mobility is limited. Open and closed stratification systems are sometimes described by the terms *class* and *caste*.[18] *Inheritance* and *competition* have been used in much the same fashion as ascription and achievement.[19]

The actual situations to which these distinctions are applied (as with so many distinctions in social science) do not offer sharp or rigid contrasts. In open societies status and class position are often affected by family connections or inheritance; sons of wealthy parents are more likely to be wealthy than sons of poor parents— even though there are opportunities for the poor to rise, or the well-to-do to sink. And in closed or caste societies there is some room for individual achievement, especially in new occupations, and also the possibility that an entire group may change its position. Even though we characterize societies as open or closed, as class or caste, each case inevitably represents some mixture or combination of the principles of ascription and achievement, of inheritance and competition.

Stratification systems differ in the clarity with which classes, status groups, and political divisions are defined by group attitudes and practices. Parsons has suggested that stratification in the United States, for example, is characterized by

its relative looseness, the absence of a clear-cut hierarchy of prestige except in a very broad sense, the absence of an unequivocal top elite or ruling class; the fluidity of the shadings as well as mobility between groups, and, in spite of the prestige-implications of the generalized goal of success, the relative tolerance of many different paths to success.[20]

In more traditional societies, status is more clearly visible in dress or speech, in accepted patterns of deference or domination among superior and inferior, in clear-cut distinctions between different occupational groups. In medieval Europe, the feudal *estates*—clergy, nobility, and peasantry—were separated not only by customs and attitudes but also by legal prescriptions that defined the relations of groups to one another and the obligations of each within the social structure. When class and status lines are relatively clear-cut, they also tend more often to coincide; one can more often predict a person's status from his class position and vice versa in a "tight" or closely integrated system of stratification than in a loosely structured system where the relations between occupation or property and social standing are modified by many other criteria of status.

Although the "openness" and "looseness" of a stratification system seem to be related to one another, there is some evidence that they can be relatively independent. For example, the rate of social mobility in the United States appears to be approximately the same as that in Great Britain and in some other European countries, although European class and status divisions are usually more clear-cut and more openly recognized.[21]

The interrelations among the many attributes of stratification systems can be illustrated by examination of three cases: the Indian caste system, with clear-cut divisions, little individual mobility, and the domination of inherited status; the relatively open Soviet class structure that has emerged in a totalitarian society dominated by a political bureaucracy and subscribing to an ideology that denies the existence of classes; and the relatively open system of the United States, with fluid and vaguely defined class and status lines, a considerable volume of social mobility, and an equalitarian ideology that coexists with recognized class and status distinctions.

The Indian caste system

Caste in India—with its rigid rank order, clear-cut differences among the castes, status ascribed at birth and virtually unchanging and unchangeable, minimal or nonexistent individual mobility, and institutionalized relationships among the castes—has provided the model for the sociological definition of caste in general. (The term *caste* originally had only a local meaning; the Portuguese who came to India in the sixteenth century applied their word *casta* [race or lineage] to the different Indian groups they encountered, perhaps as a translation of the Indian *varna*, meaning color but also applied to caste. In time the attributes of Indian caste gave the term a general significance, releasing it from its Indian context and allowing its application to other more or less similar social structures.)

Indian society is usually divided into four inclusive castes—the *Brahmins*, or priests, the *Kshatriya*, or warriors, the *Vaisya*, or merchants, and the *Sudra*, or peasants and workers. There are, in addition, the *outcastes* or *untouchables*, those who have been expelled from their caste, either in their own persons or in that of their ancestors, for violations of the rigidly enforced codes of caste behavior. In 1931, the most recent date for which figures are available, approximately 6 per

cent of India's Hindu population were Brahmins, just over 70 per cent belonged to other castes, and over 20 per cent were untouchables.

This gross division provides only an initial approximation to a very complex hierarchical ordering of society. The Census of 1901, the last to give reasonably full data by caste, listed more than 2,300 main castes. Even this large number does not adequately suggest the elaborateness or complexity of the structure, for most castes, including the outcastes, are further subdivided into subcastes. In 1891, two castes alone were reported to have 1,700 subcastes each. In 1931 a small state with a population of only 350,000 reported almost 400 subcastes among the Brahmins and more than 1,000 castes of Rajputs (one of the larger castes among the Kshatriya). A recent study estimated that there were more than 10,000 caste groups, "the members of which regard themselves as of the same blood and ritual status." [22]

This proliferation in part reflects the size and diversity of India itself. In each region and locality the caste structure has developed distinctive forms; the essentially local character of Indian society left each village or area quite free to follow its own lines of development. Few castes therefore extend throughout all of Indian society. The actual, functionally significant structure of caste can therefore be seen best in the forms it assumes in specific villages. Table 3 shows the caste hierarchy of Bispara, a village of 685 people in eastern India, as it existed in 1953.

A very different structure has emerged in Shamirpet, a village in Central India with a population in 1951 of just under 2,500, of whom 340 were Moslems. Shamirpet's caste hierarchy is shown in Table 4.

Although the caste system is closely

Table 3

APPROXIMATE HIERARCHY OF CASTES
IN BISPARA

A. High Hindus	1	Brahmin
	2	Warrior
	3	Herdsman
		or Distiller*
		or Writer
		or Oriya
	4	Fisherman
	5 † Kond § Potter
	6 † Kond Herdsman
	7 † Christian
	8 † Moslem
B. Low Hindus	1	Templeman
	2	Barber
	3	Washerman
	4	Weaver

Line of Pollution

C. Untouch-ables	1	Outcaste
	2	Basketmaker
	3	Sweeper

* The word *or* indicates that caste-groups under this number dispute for precedence.
† These caste-groups are considered non-Hindu. However, informants could allot them a place in a table of precedence. In the case of converts to Christianity and Islam, their rank depends on the caste of their pagan ancestors. Converted Outcastes, for instance, are still untouchable.
§ *Kond* refers to the aboriginal residents of the area who were conquered by invading Hindus.

F. G. Bailey, *Caste and the Economic Frontier* (1958), p. 8. Reprinted by permission of Manchester University Press.

tied to Hinduism, its influence in Indian society is so pervasive that it tends to incorporate other religious groups—Moslems and Christians, for example—into the hierarchical structure. In Shamirpet the Moslems constitute a castelike group at about the level of the agricultural castes. In Bispara, Christians and Moslems have also come to occupy rela-

tively clearly defined positions in the structure, although there are individual exceptions. Since many Moslems and Christians are converts from Hinduism, they usually simply keep their place in the caste order despite their changed religion.

Caste provides the fundamental organizational framework of Indian society, particularly in the villages. The extent of its influence can be seen in the following facts:

1. Membership in a caste is hereditary; apart from those who lose caste it is fixed for life.

2. Marriage is usually confined within the caste, although *hypergamy*, marriage of a man of higher status and a woman of lower status, is sometimes permitted.

3. Most relationships between members of the several castes are defined and limited by caste rules. Social intimacy between higher and lower castes is usually enjoined, particularly eating and drinking together. Any contact with outcastes—the untouchables, or *harijans*—is defined as polluting; that is, it renders the caste Hindu ritually unclean and requires appropriate remedial purification ceremonies.

4. As Tables 3 and 4 illustrate, caste is usually tied closely to occupation, which is transmitted from father to son, although less so in the cities than in the villages. "*Dharma* (that is, rules for righteous conduct and living) require members of a caste to stick to their caste's traditional or hereditary calling or callings." [23] Yet not all men do so. In one village in Central India that was studied intensively, three quarters of the adult men followed the traditional occupations of their caste. Most of the others were in farming, an occupation that, with cattle-rearing, is open to members of all castes. Other occupational shifts that were tolerated were between callings at the same

Table 4

APPROXIMATE HIERARCHY OF CASTES IN SHAMIRPET

1. High Hindus	Brahmin (Priests)	
	Traders (Komti)	
2. Occupational Castes *	{ Agriculturists { Potters { Shepherds	(Kapu-Reddi) (Kummari) (Golla)
	Agriculturalists	(Kapu-Mattarasi)
	{ Weavers { Toddy-tappers	(Sale) (Gaondla)
	{ Washermen { Barbers	(Sakali) (Mangali)
	{ Stone-workers { Hunters and matmakers { Minstrels	(Vaddar) (Erkala) (Pichha-Kuntla)
3. Untouchable Castes	Mala	
	Madiga	

* Bracketed castes are at approximately the same level.

S. C. Dube, *Indian Village* (1955), pp. 36–7. Reprinted by permission of Routledge & Kegan Paul Ltd., London.

level of "ritual purity" or "impurity." [24]

Intercaste relations frequently include established obligations between persons of different castes who provide each other with specific services. In Shamirpet, for example, the carpenter repairs the implements of farmers and periodically provides new ones; in return, twice each year, he is given a share of the crops. Similarly a barber is attached to a weaver's family from which he regularly receives some cloth in return for his services. Castes are thus sometimes bound together in a complex network of economic interdependence.

5. Failure to conform to caste requirements can result in expulsion from the caste and severance of all the ties that stem from membership in the group. Over the centuries, the outcastes, who transmit to their children their own deprived status, have been divided into their own castes, based largely on the occupations they perform—usually the least desirable, ritually impure, and most poorly rewarded, although some *harijans* have taken advantage of new occupations to amass wealth and seek power.

6. Each caste has an organized central body that enforces caste rules. Although caste authorities vary in their effectiveness, they do serve to control behavior of their members by punishing—or threatening to punish—violations. For example, in one village a high-ranking Rajput was accused of illicit sexual relations with

Sam B. Tata from Black Star

Dorien Leigh Ltd. from Black Star

a Moslem woman; he was expelled from his caste and only allowed to return after giving up his relations with the woman and agreeing to pay for repairs to the temple and the cost of a new marble floor.

7. Mobility in caste society, except for those who lose caste, is typically a collective rather than an individual matter. Within a caste a person may improve his standing, but usually he can change his caste position only if the entire group— lineage or caste—manages to raise itself. Castes move up in the hierarchy by copying behavior expected of higher castes, particularly with respect to what is eaten. The upwardly mobile group also refuses to eat with or to have other intimate contact with those whom they now claim to outrank. Such mobility typically rests upon prior economic improvement, which permits greater freedom of action and in itself elicits respect from others.

This brief sketch merely describes some of the principal structural features of the traditional caste system in India. It does little justice to the extraordinary complexity of this system, of the myriad ways in which it molds the thought, sentiment, and conduct of the Indian people, or of the numerous changes that have taken place, both locally and nationally, over the many centuries during which it has survived.

The remarkable persistence of this system, the origins of which are uncertain, stems from several sources. The major outlines of the system, which has persisted for some three thousand years, changing continually in its internal constitution but persisting in its fundamental features, is defined in the ancient sacred writings of Hinduism, which offer mythical accounts of the differentiation of castes. Hinduism also contains a belief in reincarnation; one's place in the caste order is determined by the individual's adherence to caste requirements in the preceding life and by his religious devotion—and is therefore unchangeable. A major function of religious belief—in this case as in many others—is therefore to sustain the existing order. The dominant Brahmins derive their superiority in large part through their control over religious ritual.

In any firmly established system, there is substantial inertia among those in the lower strata who might be expected to try to initiate changes. These groups lack knowledge, an awareness of specific alternatives, and enough command over resources to make effective action possible. Among an illiterate and ill-informed people, tradition, no matter how cruelly it may bear upon them, exercises a strong and inflexible hold. Even though grossly exploited and suppressed, they also develop some "vested interests" in a system that provides a kind of status security and a psychological orientation which largely precludes either individual efforts to change one's status or collective action aimed at broad social reform or revolution.

Should the untouchables, who suffer serious disabilities, disregard the religious justification of their status and seek to change the system, they run into the resistance of those in the higher levels of the hierarchy who have large vested interests in maintaining things as they are. And since there is a substantial correlation between status, economic position, and political power, the upper groups are in a strategic position to resist efforts at change. In one village, the untouchables were beaten up and their huts burned when they refused to carry out the tasks they were usually expected to perform, such as "removing the carcasses of dead cattle from the houses of the higher castes, beating the tom-tom at the festi-

vals of village deities, and removing the leaves on which the high castes had dined during festivals and weddings." In another village, the untouchables complained that the village Headman had not given them money appropriated by the Provincial Government to improve their huts. The higher-ranking caste of Peasants justified the disregard of government policy by claiming "that the Untouchables had spent the money given to them on toddy, and that this showed that Untouchables could not be improved." [25]

The past hundred years have seen new forces at work, however, that seem to be affecting significantly the ancient patterns. The British, on the whole, made no efforts to change the system, tending to work with it rather than against it, utilizing existing institutions whenever possible in order to maintain their own power and control. Some of the changes introduced by the British served to stimulate caste feeling and to increase the relevance of caste within Indian society. Thus greater ease of communication and the breakdown of old territorial units stimulated caste organization and led to the establishment of caste journals designed to encourage caste loyalty and pursue caste interests. On the other hand, introduction of a uniform criminal code weakened the authority of caste councils; various measures were taken to protect the rights of untouchables and to remove many of their disabilities.

Economic changes initiated during the period of British rule and more recently accelerated by Indian efforts to industrialize and raise standards of living set in motion processes that are having a substantial impact upon caste. New industries, new jobs, and new techniques inevitably affect traditional roles and relationships and create new ones, although many of these innovations can be—and have been—readily incorporated into the system. Increased movement from villages to cities removes people from traditional constraints, although there is some tendency for members of the same caste to cluster together in urban centers and for caste membership to become the basis for organized social and political activity.

Largely through the efforts of Mahatma Gandhi and his successor, Jawaharlal Nehru, legislation to improve the lot of the untouchables was passed, guaranteeing them access to education, jobs, and religious observances. The Constitution adopted when India gained independence in 1947 included protection and safeguards for those at the bottom of the caste structure. Although such measures have some affect, they have made their way only slowly into the villages in which most Indians live, where tradition is very strong, power is most likely to be concentrated in the higher castes, and innovations are apt to be staunchly resisted.

The values upon which the ancient hierarchy rested have themselves been affected by the large-scale changes taking place, including particularly the extension of educational opportunities. Those who acquire education are more likely to acquire important positions in the corporate life of the village, whatever their caste. In raising their own position they improve that of their caste, and they are also likely, because of their experience outside the local community, to be receptive to economic and political innovations, which can have long-run effects upon the caste system.

Despite these forces at work, however, the hardiness of the caste order and its resistance to change should not be underestimated. Indian society is so heavily dominated by the caste system—it provides a place in society for almost everyone, it defines important relationships

among people, it is closely linked to religion, to economic organization, and to political institutions—that it cannot easily be replaced. And its persistence for several millennia testifies to its adaptability to the pressures of changing circumstances.

Class in a "classless" society: the Soviet Union

One professed aim of Marxism is a classless society. Immediately upon gaining power in Russia in 1917, therefore, the Communists abolished by decree "all the classes of society existing up to now in Russia, and all divisions of citizens, all class distinctions and privileges, class organizations, and institutions." [26] Social structures do not respond readily to decrees, however, and the Soviet rulers pushed toward their professed goal by confiscating private property, equalizing wages, and defining new roles for the Communist party, the trade unions, the Soviets, and other freshly established organizations. The official drive toward equalitarianism continued, although with occasional steps backward, until 1931, when Stalin reversed his field, attacked "equality mongering," and initiated a series of measures that greatly helped to re-establish and reinforce class differences.

This reversal was precipitated by difficulties stemming from the forced industrialization that had been started in 1928 with the First Five Year Plan. A shortage of skilled labor, high labor turnover, and the ambiguous position of managers and technicians—suspect in a "proletarian" state—were pressing problems. In order to create incentives for acquiring skills, increasing output, and accepting authority and responsibility, piece rates were introduced both in industry and on the

farms, and higher salaries and other perquisites were offered to trained professional and technical personnel. In time
further rewards were offered to skilled
workers, industrial managers, professionals, and other groups for whose efficient
and reliable services there was pressing
need.

The restoration of inequality was justified by the Soviet regime as a temporary
measure in keeping with the transition
from socialism ("from each according to
his ability, to each according to his ability") to Communism ("from each according to his ability, to each according to his
needs"). This ideological justification, according to some sociologists and other
writers, should not obscure what they
view as the functional necessity of stratification in any complex industrial society.
The Soviet leaders, however, faced the
enormous problem of quickly industrializing a largely rural, illiterate society. In
this difficult situation Stalin enunciated a
policy that promised quick results. In a
different society other forms of inequality, or perhaps less of it, might serve
similar functions. And even if some form
of inequality is an inevitable outcome in
a society with a complex division of labor—as it probably is—its nature and
extent remain open questions.

By Communist lights, however, there
are no significant class differences in the
Soviet Union. Since classes are based, according to Marxist theory, upon the ownership or nonownership of property, there
can be no classes in a society in which, as
in the Soviet Union, all productive property is owned by the state. In 1936, in a
report on the proposed and subsequently
adopted new Constitution, Stalin distinguished between the classes of peasants
and workers, on the one hand, the boundaries between which, he asserted, had disappeared, and, on the other hand, a

stratum (and explicitly *not* a class) of
"toiling intelligentsia"—the professionals,
technicians, and administrators. This formulation is generally accepted as the
official Soviet view.

The importance of this official view,
however, lies not in its reliability as a
description of Soviet society, but in the
role it plays in Soviet life itself. Just as
some of the dynamic forces of American
life can be traced to the discrepancy between the democratic doctrine of equal
opportunity and the facts of institutionalized inequality, so it is possible that the
differences between the facts of Soviet social structure and the official picture of
that structure may constitute an important source of action and policy. This
would be the case, for example, if the
regime recognized the contradiction between ideology and reality and therefore
sought to do something about it, or if it
denied the inconsistency but nevertheless
had to face its consequences.

As an industrial society, with its technological demands, its needs for particular skills, and its organizational requirements, the Soviet Union has developed
occupational groups similar to those of
the United States, England, and France.
With increasing industrialization the proportion of peasants in a once preponder-
antly rural society (more than 80 per cent
of Russians were peasants in 1914) has
steadily fallen and in 1959 constituted
slightly over half the population—and it
has continued to decline. As the number
of peasants has diminished, the number
of industrial workers has multiplied, the
latter somewhat more rapidly than the
former. Table 5 (taken from a Soviet
source) indicates the extent of the
changes in these classes that took place
between 1939 and 1963; these probably
are long-range trends, which can be expected to continue.

Table 5

CHANGES IN CLASS STRUCTURE IN THE U.S.S.R., 1939–1963

Occupational group	*Percentage of the gainfully employed*		
	1939	*1959*	*1963*
Workers (urban and rural)	32.19	48.2 ⎫	
Nonmanual (urban and rural)	17.54	20.1 ⎭	73.6
Collective farmers	44.61	31.4	26.3
Individual peasants and artisans not in cooperatives	2.60	0.3	0.1
Totals	96.94 *	100.0	100.0

* The remaining 3.06 per cent are not accounted for.

A. I. Aitov, "Some Peculiarities of the Changes in Class Structure in the U.S.S.R.," *Soviet Sociology*, IV, No. 2 (Fall, 1965), 3. Reprinted by permission of International Arts and Sciences Press.

Within these large categories, however, there are important subdivisions. In an analysis of social stratification in the Soviet Union in 1950, Alex Inkeles divided the population as follows:

1. The ruling elite, a small group consisting of high Party, government, economic, and military officials, prominent scientists, and selected artists and writers.

2. The superior intelligentsia, composed of the intermediary ranks of the categories mentioned above, plus certain important technical specialists.

3. The general intelligentsia, incorporating most of the professional groups, the middle ranks of the bureaucracy, managers of small enterprises, junior military officers, technicians, etc.

4. The white collar group, largely synonymous with the Soviet term for employees, which ranges from petty-bureaucrats through accountants and bookkeepers down to the level of ordinary clerks and office workers.

The working class was also markedly differentiated, incorporating:

1. The working class "aristocracy," that is, the most highly skilled and productive workers . . .

2. The rank and file workers, those in one of the lesser skill grades earning slightly above or below the average wage for all workers.

3. The disadvantaged workers, estimated to include as many as one-fourth of the labor force, whose low level of skill and lack of productivity or initiative kept them close to the minimum wage level.

The peasantry, although relatively homogeneous, also was divided into distinguishable sub-groups:

1. The well-to-do peasants, consisting of those particularly advantaged by virtue of the location, fertility, or crop raised by their collective farms—i.e., those living on the so-called "millionaire" farms—and those whose trade, skill, or productivity pushes them into the higher income brackets even on the less prosperous farms.

2. The average peasant, shading off into the least productive or poor peasant groups.

There was, in addition, a residual group of those in forced labor camps who are really outside the formal class structure. . . .[27]

Despite changes in the relative size of some of these groups (and the probable elimination of forced labor), these categories in all likelihood still describe adequately the divisions within Soviet society—or at least as adequately as may be possible without close on-the-scene study. The differences among the intelligentsia, workers, and peasants are closely related to variations in income and prestige, although the working-class "aristocracy" appears to rank higher and to earn more than some white-collar employees, much as in the United States, and a few collective farmers are better off than the average worker. The range of income is as great, or perhaps even greater, than in the United States and in some other Western countries. Not only are there substantial differences in earnings between an ordinary worker and a top industrial manager or leading academician, but no progressive income tax narrows the gap; the maximum tax is 13 per cent, compared with 70 per cent in the United States. Moreover, the higher circles of Soviet society have additional perquisites: chauffeurs and cars, better housing, *dachas* (country homes), vacation retreats, shops not accessible to the general public, and special awards of various kinds for distinguished achievement.

With these differences in income and occupation there emerge varying styles of life, reflected in any scene of a Soviet department store or city street: visiting peasant women in rough clothes and a babushka; well-dressed, carefully made-up wives of professionals and managers; workers' wives not so poorly attired as peasants but still far removed from the trim, almost stylish intelligentsia. As mass-produced commodities are only slowly becoming available at low prices to most workers, income differentials lead to marked variation in styles of life—in housing, dress, and leisure. These differences are partially mitigated, however, by free medical care, pensions for the aged, available social services, and low costs for such public services as transportation.

In a study based upon interviews with Soviet émigrés in 1950 and 1951, Inkeles, Bauer, and Kluckhohn found that there were also class differences in attitudes toward the regime, the party, the work they do, and other aspects of Soviet society.[28] (See Table 17, Chapter 13.) Although there have undoubtedly been some changes since that time, there is some evidence that differences in attitudes among the peasants, workers, and intelligentsia remain. Important as these differences are, however, they are not necessarily a sign of marked class consciousness or of effective class organization. The regime makes strenuous and apparently successful efforts to prevent any free organizational activity that is not under its control, for independent groups are a potential basis for political opposition.

The fundamental division in Soviet life, some scholars have claimed, is between the Communist Party, with about 7 million members in 1952 and almost 9 million in 1961, and the rest of Soviet society—or between the small group that dominates the society and the rest of the population. Since power is concentrated in the hands of the party, particularly its leadership, differences between classes that stem from existing institutional arrangements—income differentials, preferential access to shops or vacation resorts, income tax rates, and so on—can potentially be changed. What the regime gives, it can take away, and at least during the first quarter century after the 1917 Revolution policy toward the different groups in Soviet society fluctuated widely.

Membership in the party, however, is not evenly distributed; peasants are poorly represented, the intelligentsia heavy represented. This situation is in large measure a result of a systematic effort that began in the mid-1930s to enlist the leading figures in Soviet society—engineers and scientists, administrative officials in government and industry, soldiers, scholars, and the most productive workers. Despite efforts to broaden the social base of the party membership, it still contains a disproportionate, though slowly diminishing number drawn from the administrative-managerial bureaucracy.[29]

Whether or not the social composition of the party will in the long run affect its policies is highly problematic. The distinctive interests of the upper groups, to the extent that they exist or become manifest, may conflict with the needs of the party and the regime, and with the ideology they profess. In the event of such differences, what might happen is an open question, particularly because other groups may also pursue their own interests—the military and the secret police, for example. The removal in 1956 of tuition requirements for higher education, which had been introduced in 1940, and the introduction of various other equalizing measures that lessened the advantages of the well-to-do intelligentsia would seem to indicate that factors other than "class" interests were at work. In the long run the interests of the party and of the upper ranks may coincide, and where they diverge the practical needs of the regime in all likelihood will predominate. (A recent [1966] book argues, however, that the professional, scientific, and technical elite is asserting its autonomy from party controls and threatens—or promises—to play a much stronger and more independent role in the future.[30])

The possibility of class-based political differences, however, is lessened by the high degree of social mobility found in the Soviet Union. Although children of the intelligentsia possess obvious advantages—they secure readier acceptance in advanced educational institutions and in the better schools, they acquire knowledge, skills, and acquaintances that give them an advantage in the competition for place—rapid industrialization has opened up many new opportunities for able and aspiring Soviet youth. The extension of education to the entire population has made it possible for many children of peasants and workers to achieve high places in the party, in industry, and in the professions. As the process of industrialization proceeds and the rural population decreases, considerable mobility will undoubtedly persist, together with the greater likelihood that children of those already in the upper groups will do better than others. The "self-made man" is a Soviet reality, although his achievement takes place within the complex organizational apparatus of a planned and centrally controlled society.

Class in the United States

Unlike India, where the system of stratification has retained its chief characteristics for many centuries, and unlike the Soviet Union, which overthrew a class system only relatively recently emerged from feudalism in a violent revolutionary outburst, the United States has experienced a gradual but continuing shift in both class and status structures. Some indication of the major outlines of the class structure and its changes can be seen in Table 6, which presents the occupational distribution for 1870, 1910, 1950, and 1960.

The central change in the class structure has been the transformation of the middle class. During most of the nineteenth century this group was made up chiefly of independent farmers and businessmen. The proportion, and in recent years even the absolute number, of farmers has declined steadily; at present less than 4 per cent of the labor force consists of farm-owners and managers. The proportion of independent entrepreneurs,

Table 6

OCCUPATIONAL DISTRIBUTION OF THE LABOR FORCE IN THE UNITED STATES, 1870, 1910, 1950, AND 1960

Occupation	Percentage of the labor force			
	1870	*1910*	*1950*	*1960*
White Collar				
Professional, technical, and kindred workers	3.0	4.4	8.5	10.8
Proprietors, managers, and officials	6.0	6.5	8.6	8.1
Clerks, salespeople, and kindred workers	4.0	10.2	18.9	21.1
Manual Work				
Skilled workers and foremen	9.0	11.7	13.8	13.6
Semiskilled workers	10.0	14.7	21.7	21.7
Laborers, except farm	9.0	14.7	8.3	8.0
Servants	6.0	6.8	6.3	5.6
Farm				
Farm owners and managers	24.0	16.5	7.3	3.7
Farm laborers	29.0	14.5	4.3	3.3
Not reported			2.3	5.1
Number in labor force	12,924,000	37,271,000	56,239,000	67,799,000

Data for 1870, 1910, 1950 from Joseph A. Kahl, *The American Class Structure*, p. 67 (Copyright 1953, 1954, 1955 and © 1957 by Joseph A. Kahl). Reprinted by Permission of Holt, Rinehart and Winston, Inc., and the author. The original sources of these data are for 1870, Alba M. Edwards, *U. S. Census of Population, 1940: Comparative Occupation Statistics, 1870–1940* (Washington, D.C.: U.S. Government Printing Office, 1943), p. 101, plus C. Wright Mills, *White Collar* (New York: Oxford, 1951), pp. 63–5; for 1910, Edwards, *op. cit.*, p. 187; for 1950, *U.S. Census of Population, 1950*, Vol. II, Part I (Washington, D.C.: U.S. Government Printing Office, 1951), Table 53; for 1960, *U.S. Census of Population, 1960*, Vol. I, Part I (Washington, D.C.: U.S. Government Printing Office, 1961), Table 201. In 1950 and 1960 service occupations were counted separately; they were allocated half to servants, one-fourth to semiskilled, and one-fourth to laborers.

who are included in the census category of "proprietors, managers, and officials," has remained fairly constant over the years, although their importance in the economy and their status in society have declined as large corporations have come to dominate the nation's economic life.

While the "old middle class" of independent farmers and businessmen has diminished in size (particularly the farmers) and importance, the "new middle class" of white collar employees—clerks, salespeople, salaried professionals, technicians—has steadily grown. Clerks, salespersons, and similar employees now com-

prise about one-fifth of the total working population; together with the professionals, officials, and managers they include well over one-third. It is the rise of this new middle-class—in most Western societies, as well as in the United States—that has in large measure confuted the Marxist prognosis. The decline of the farm population, which first contributed chiefly to the industrial labor force, has been offset in recent years by the increase in white-collar employment.

The occupational character of the working class, the relative size of which has remained roughly the same for half a century (except for farm laborers, who now constitute less than 5 per cent of the labor force), has also changed. The proportion of unskilled laborers has steadily declined as mechanization has eliminated heavy manual tasks; indeed, the actual number of unskilled workers has decreased in recent years, despite over-all increases in population and the size of the labor force. For many decades the relative number of both skilled and semi-skilled workers grew, and only in the years since World War II has the proportion of workers in these two categories remained relatively constant. One result of these shifts is readily apparent; over the years the general level of skill and education, and with them of income and status, of the working class has improved. (This general improvement, however, should not obscure the fact that in 1963 more than 5 million families—over 10 per cent of all families—and 6 million individuals without families earned less than $2,000.)

The upper class, which late in the nineteenth century had come to consist chiefly of industrial and business magnates, includes today many men whose position is not based upon ownership, but upon *de facto* control of the giant corporations that now dominate the economy. The importance of such control (frequently not based upon possession of corporate stock) lies in the power to manipulate great accumulations of wealth, and also to acquire some of it through stock bonuses and other means. In addition to these top-level corporate executives and those who still own a great deal of property are a number of leading professionals, military leaders, and politicians. This upper-class group, which has always been very small, is probably a mere 2 or 3 per cent of the labor force.

This description sketches the broad outlines of class in American society. But it must often be modified when one examines a particular community and seeks to explore the relevance of stratification for local community life. The relative proportions of each class change from place to place. Washington, D.C., for example, has no heavy industry and is an overwhelmingly middle-class city dominated by white-collar employees, its lower class consisting chiefly of servants and service workers. Heavy-industry cities like Gary, Indiana, and Flint, Michigan, have a larger concentration of workers than more diversified cities like Lansing, Michigan, and Fort Wayne, Indiana. In 1960, two-thirds of Gary's male labor force and 64 per cent of Flint's consisted of skilled, semiskilled, and unskilled workers, compared with 46 and 47 per cent respectively in Lansing and Fort Wayne. Class lines tend to be more sharply drawn in the Detroit area, where General Motors, Ford, and Chrysler confront the United Automobile Workers, than in sprawling, diversified middle-class Los Angeles.

Except for certain communities with only a small middle class, the lines between classes are usually not clearly or sharply drawn. And many occupations do not lend themselves easily to placement in one or another class. Is the self-employed artisan who works alone—painter, plumber, electrician—a skilled worker (working-class) or an independent entrepreneur? Shall his skill or his independence provide the basis for classification? Is the office employee who is increasingly likely to become a machine operator in a mechanized office a white-collar employee or a blue-collar worker? Shall his task (frequently indistinguishable from that of workers in modern automated factories), the method of payment (salaried rather than an hourly wage), or the work-

Table 7

MEDIAN TOTAL MONEY INCOME OF FAMILIES IN THE UNITED STATES BY
OCCUPATION OF HEAD OF FAMILY AND OF INDIVIDUALS BY OCCUPATION
AND SEX, 1964

Occupation	Median family income	Median income of individuals	
		Male	Female
Professional, technical, and kindred workers	$ 9,977	$ 7,950	$4,417
Self-employed	13,646	12,524	2,096
Salaried	9,638	7,722	4,550
Managers, proprietors, and officials	9,289	7,463	3,425
Self-employed	7,326	5,862	2,589
Salaried	10,428	8,510	4,367
Clerical and kindred workers	7,163	5,719	3,507
Sales workers	8,170	5,764	1,911
Craftsmen, foremen, and kindred workers	7,670	6,268	3,141
Operatives and kindred	6,542	5,130	2,758
Laborers, except farm and mine	5,086	3,259	*
Private household workers	2,367	*	659
Service workers	5,525	4,065	1,626
Farm managers and owners	3,329	2,376	*
Farm laborers	2,423	1,300	*

* No available data; too few cases.
U.S. Bureau of the Census, *Current Population Reports: Consumer Income*, Series P-60, No. 47 (Washington, D.C.: U.S. Government Printing Office, September 24, 1965), Table 9, p. 29, and Table 23, pp. 41–2.

ing environment (office instead of factory) be the major criterion of class position? Or should workers in automated factories who watch instruments and manipulate dials be considered as middle-class persons despite their hourly wage and factory work environment? These ambiguous cases—and there are many others—testify to the absence of clear-cut divisions between classes.

Despite some overlapping, however, fairly definite differences in income and wealth separate occupational groups. Table 7 gives the median total money income in 1963 of families by occupation of the family head (many families have more than one wage earner) and of individuals by occupation and sex. (The me-

dian is the figure that divides the total group into equal segments; half of the families earn more than the median, half earn less.) These figures show clearly the greater average income of professionals and managers and the lower incomes of the unskilled, the semiskilled, farm laborers, and servants and other service workers. These data also reveal those areas in American society where class lines are most likely to be blurred and ill-defined. That skilled workers earn more on the average than do clerks, salespeople, and self-employed businessmen suggests that the differences in styles of life and status between the upper reaches of the working class and the lower levels of the middle class are more uncertain and confused than those between any other levels in the class structure.

As income levels have increased steadily, particularly since World War II, a substantial proportion of manual workers now earn "middle-class" incomes and can afford to buy many of the consumer goods made available by a highly productive technology. (A similar pattern is also evident in other advanced industrial societies.) Thus in 1964 almost three-quarters of all families headed by a skilled worker enjoyed an annual income of over $6,000, as did almost three-fifths of those of semiskilled workers and about one-third of laborers' families. (The median family income in 1964 was $6,569.)

Despite steadily rising standards of living, however, there remains a substantially disadvantaged minority, variously estimated at from thirty to fifty million, depending upon the definition used. In 1962 the President's Council of Economic Advisers drew the "poverty line" at an annual income of $3,000 for a family and $1,500 for an unrelated individual; others have used sliding scales adjusted for size of the family, age of its head, and farm residence. The great majority of those who fall into the "poor," no matter where the line is drawn, are farm workers and service workers, those in families headed by women, the elderly, and Negroes. By and large they are badly educated and lack useful job skills. Many of them possess several of these attributes.

The plight of this "underclass," as it has been called, has drawn much attention and the "war on poverty" initiated in 1964 has tried—and is trying—various expedients to improve its circumstances. But the problems of this "war" have not allowed easy solutions, for they involve complex issues of civil rights and the status of the Negro, as well as questions of economic policy and social welfare. The

poor in an otherwise affluent society do not fit easily into conventional categories of class; their problems are those of race, age, residence, and family structure, as well as of occupation, income, and wealth.[31]

Status in the United States

Class structure is closely tied in American society to the status hierarchies of towns, cities, and regions. Despite variations in the nature of the status hierarchy from place to place, many empirical studies consistently reveal a close correlation between status and occupation and, correlatively, between status and source (property, wages, or salary) and amount of income. A widely used *Index of Status Characteristics* devised by W. Lloyd Warner that was validated against direct measures of status (that is, how members of a community ranked one another) was based upon occupation, source of income, house type, and place of residence.[32] An Index of Social Position used by A. B. Hollingshead in a study of New Haven utilized occupation, education, and residence to locate people within the status hierarchy.[33] In these, as in other studies, occupation is given more weight than the other attributes.

An index, however, is merely a measure of another variable; from occupation, for example, one infers social standing. Its validity is based upon a statistical correlation; on the basis of past experience one can make a reliable prediction of status. But such correlations must be explained. Why is there the persisting close relationship between occupation and status?

In almost all the available studies, occupation is reported as a major *determi-*

Table 8

PRESTIGE SCORES OF OCCUPATIONAL GROUPS, 1947

Occupational group	Number of occupations	Average score
Government officials *	8	90.8
Professional and semiprofessional workers	30	80.6
Proprietors, managers, and officials	11	74.9
Clerical, sales, and kindred workers	6	68.2
Craftsmen, foremen, and kindred workers	7	68.0
Farmers and farm managers	3	61.3
Protective service workers	3	58.0
Operatives and kindred workers	8	52.8
Farm laborers	1	50.0
Service workers (except domestic and protective)	7	46.7
Laborers (except farm)	6	45.8

* Includes Supreme Court justice, state governor, Cabinet member, mayor of a large city, United States Representative, diplomat, county judge, head of a department in a state government.

Paul K. Hatt and C. C. North, "Jobs and Occupations: A Popular Evaluation," in Reinhard Bendix and Seymour M. Lipset, *Class, Status and Power*, p. 414 (Copyright 1953 The Free Press). Reprinted by permission of The Macmillan Company.

nant of status. The judgments men make about one another are strongly influenced by awareness of the other's job. The skills, responsibility, and authority inherent in different occupations lead to differential evaluations. Occupation also contributes to status indirectly through the income it provides, the style of life it makes possible, and the social relations in which it involves people.

When occupations are themselves ranked, they tend to follow an order that is closely tied to income, wealth, and, on the whole, the amount of formal education and skill they require, and the degree of authority and responsibility they carry. Table 8 reports the average prestige scores of the several occupational groups as found in a national survey of jobs and occupations conducted in 1947. The almost 3,000 adults who were interviewed were asked to evaluate ninety occupations as "excellent," "good," "average," "somewhat below average," and "poor." A single general score for each

occupation was derived from the answers. A replication of this study in 1963 found small differences in the rating of specific occupations, but no major change.[34] A comparison of these occupational ratings and the income distribution shown in Table 7 shows a close correlation.

Different occupations also entail different styles of life, illustrated, for example, by the hours at which men go to work. "Banker's hours," for example, is both a descriptive term and a reflection of the mixed envy, respect, and criticism directed toward men of wealth, power, and seemingly greater leisure. More significantly, one's occupation makes possible, or even requires, social contacts with different kinds of people; insofar as "a man is judged by the company he keeps"—as he frequently is—occupation is again indirectly a source of status.

Despite the close relationship between class and status position, the prestige effect of occupation, income, and wealth can be offset or modified by other circumstances. Most studies of status report at least some persons whose status is higher than their class position would seem to warrant, and vice versa. Ancestry or family affiliation, education, residence, community participation, power, or "manners and morals," or several or all of these factors, may contribute to the standing of an individual or family in the community. Thus the no longer affluent but still socially accepted upper-class family, on the one hand, and the newly rich but not yet accepted family, on the other, are familiar figures in many communities. In most cases, however, inconsistency between class and social status appears to reflect the fact of social mobility: Outward signs of high standing persist after the economic base upon which it rested is gone or, alternatively, status-associated manners and style of life do not change as rapidly as occupation, income, or wealth. In the long run, class and status tend to come together again in the United States as in most other "open-class" societies.

Except for national "celebrities" whose status rests upon publicity and public relations, the general ranking of occupations, and distinctions based upon ethnic and racial characteristics—a problem we shall examine in the next chapter—there can hardly be said to be a national status order. Each community has its own prestige hierarchy, though those who move from place to place normally find it relatively easy to fit in at approximately the same level. Thus in "Yankee City," a New England community of about 15,000, W. Lloyd Warner and his associates described in the 1930s six classes or, in our terminology, status groups:

Upper-upper, made up of "Old Families," predominantly the most successful business and professional men, living on or near Hill Street, the "best" neighborhood in town.

Lower-upper, similar to the Upper-upper economically but not "Old Family."

Upper-middle, chiefly business proprietors and professional men, active in civic affairs, not as well-to-do as the two upper classes, resident in Homeville, a clearly defined neighborhood in one part of the city.

Lower-middle, "Sidestreeters," divided between the lower levels of white-collar employees and skilled workers.

Upper-lower, the "respectable" working people, predominantly semiskilled workers in the city's factories.

Lower-lower, "Riverbrookers" living on the flats near the harbor, notorious for their disregard of moral conventions and their casual way of life, though most of them were "guilty of no more than being poor and lacking in the desire to get ahead." [35]

In his investigation of New Haven in 1951, Hollingshead found only five classes, which corresponded closely to the divisions in Yankee City, except for the absence of an "upper-upper" class (though he did identify a "core group" of "old families" within the highest category) and differences in the proportion within each group. In a rural community in New York, Harold Kaufman reported eleven status groups. Some investigators, however, have argued that there is no consistent and clear-cut division into status groups, but only a complex set of overlapping, continuous status hierarchies.[36]

These differences in findings and interpretations may stem from various sources. Individuals and groups within a community may base their judgments upon different criteria, or they may draw different distinctions within the status order. Table 9 shows the status perspectives found among the white members of different status groups in a Mississippi community in the late 1930s. The "upper-upper" class, for example, made no distinctions among lower-class whites, while the lower-middle, upper-lower, and

Table 9

THE SOCIAL PERSPECTIVES OF STATUS GROUPS, OLD CITY, MISSISSIPPI, 1936

Upper-upper		Lower-upper
"Old aristocracy"	UU	"Old aristocracy"
"Aristocracy," but not "old"	LU	*"Aristocracy," but not "old"*
"Nice, respectable people"	UM	"Nice, respectable people"
"Good people, but 'nobody' "	LM	"Good people, but 'nobody' "
	UL	
"Po' whites"		"Po' whites"
	LL	

Upper-middle		Lower-middle
"Society" ⎧ "Old families"	UU	"Old "Broken-down
⎨ "Society" but		aristocracy" aristocracy"
⎩ not "old families"	LU	(older) (younger)
"People who should be upper class"	UM	"People who think they are somebody"
"People who don't have much money"	LM	*"We poor folk"*
	UL	"People poorer than us"
"No 'count lot"		
	LL	"No 'count lot"

Upper-lower		Lower-lower
	UU	
"Society" or the "folks with money"	LU	"Society" or the "folks with money"
	UM	
"People who are up because they have a little money"	LM	"Way-high-ups," but not "Society"
"Poor but honest folk"	UL	"Snobs trying to push up"
"Shiftless people"	LL	*"People just as good as anybody"*

Allison Davis, Burleigh B. Gardner, and Mary R. Gardner, *Deep South*, p. 65 (Copyright 1941 the University of Chicago). Reprinted by permission of The University of Chicago Press.

lower-lower saw significant differences among the bottom levels. This status structure appears to be similar to that found in Yankee City, although each status group sees the community in somewhat different terms. Because of this variation, the number of status divisions reported may therefore reflect the observer's judgment as to the important distinctions rather than a community consensus.

The relative importance of the several criteria of status may vary from one community to another, or from group to group within a community, or may change with the passage of time as the objective class structure changes. In large communities, for example, with their impersonality and numerous secondary relationships, visible signs of status are more important determinants of social standing than the less tangible personal qualities that may be of crucial importance in smaller communities. Again, in many cities in which large corporations have established branch plants, the old upper class based upon ancestry, inherited wealth, and a traditional style of life has been challenged by newcomers who emphasize achievement, occupational standing, education, and the demands of fashion.

The sociological demonstration of the existence of a status hierarchy and its impact on both behavior and the attitudes of Americans toward themselves and others has frequently been contrasted with the pervasive American emphasis upon equality. Yet, despite the seeming contra-

diction, the concern for status itself, as many foreign observers have noted, is at least in part a result of the prevailing equalitarianism.

European observers, from Harriet Martineau and Frances Trollope in the 1830's to James Bryce in the 1880's and Denis Brogan in recent years, have pointed out that the actual strength of equality as a dominant American value—with the consequent lack of any well-defined deference structure linked to a legitimate aristocratic tradition where the propriety of social rankings is unquestioned—forces Americans to *emphasize* status background and symbolism.[37]

What is significant about the desire for status, however, is not merely the effort to gain repute, but the values upon which reputation rests. Lacking a traditional aristocracy or elite which might set standards, American society has, on the whole, emphasized pecuniary values. Wealth has been taken as evidence of achievement and achievement is, to a substantial degree, measured by its economic return. The priority of pecuniary values has been challenged, however, not only by subgroups such as artists and writers, but also by those who, having earned or inherited wealth, have sought to legitimate their superior position by emphasizing nonpecuniary values—ancestry, style of life, acceptance of civic responsibility, the furtherance of "good causes."

Correlates and consequences

Both class and status are correlated with many other social facts, including, for example, population differentials, family characteristics, membership in associations, religion, patterns of leisure, and politics. But a correlation, as we noted earlier, is not an explanation; in each case it is necessary to inquire into the exact nature of the relations between class and status and, say, birth rates or reli-

An affluent mass-consumption society blurs some of the visible evidences of status differences, as in this "line-for-line" copy by Macy's of an original French design. The Patou original is on the right.

Macy's New York

gious affiliation, and to explore the consequences of class and status differences.

The fact that many variables are closely correlated with *both* class and status stems from the intimate connection between these two dimensions of stratification in the United States. Since class and status may not be equally important in every case, however, their relative significance must be assessed. We can illustrate these complex problems of analysis and interpretation by examining briefly the relations between class and status differences and population, family life, and membership in voluntary associations.

POPULATION   In all Western industrial societies consistent class differences in both mortality and fertility have persisted for many decades. Generally, infant death rates decrease as the income of the father increases, and there is a longer life expectancy than among members of the lower class. This difference may be explained in larger part by differences in nutrition, physical conditions of life, and availability of medical care on the one hand, and less tangible and less readily demonstrated variations in health practices and information on the other.

Both class (income, occupation, wealth) and status (styles of life), then, are clearly related to differences in mortality, although not in any simple fashion. Low income may preclude adequate medical care and account for some of the higher mortality in the lower classes, but it cannot in itself account for undesirable health habits that also affect death rates. Differences in education, which may explain greater or less willingness to seek or accept modern health and medical practices, are themselves related both to class and status differentials. As the general levels of income and education increase,

and as medical care becomes more easily available, the differences in life expectancy should diminish, as they have already begun to do.

Until quite recently there was a clear inverse relationship between class and fertility: The highest birth rates were in the lower segments of the class structure. The differences increased during the late nineteenth century as middle- and upper-class birth rates dropped rapidly. The divergence narrowed between the two World Wars when lower-class birth rates fell more quickly, and has apparently continued to diminish as the birth rates increased faster in the middle than in the lower classes during the post-World War II "baby boom." There is no simple explanation for these fertility differentials and their changing pattern.[38] But the influence of middle-class values and their gradual extension into the lower classes, status striving, increasing education, and urbanization, and the high rates of social mobility are all no doubt of considerable importance.

SOME FAMILY ATTRIBUTES   Families in the several classes differ not only in size. Age of marriage increases as class and status rise, in part because of the extended schooling of the middle and upper classes, in part because working-class youth is less likely to learn to postpone present gratifications—sexual and otherwise—for future gains. Working-class boys characteristically begin their heterosexual experiences earlier—and continue to have them more frequently—than do middle- and upper-class boys, though these differences may be diminishing as middle-class sex mores become "freer." In some working-class communities, a boy who has not had sexual intercourse by the age of sixteen or seventeen, Alfred Kinsey has commented, is "either physically incapacitated, mentally deficient, homosexual, or earmarked for moving out of his community and going to college." [39] Both early marriage and the insistent search for present pleasures contribute to the persistence of lower-class status by interfering with extended schooling or other training, preventing the long-range planning needed for advancement in a bureaucratized society (see Chapter 10), and by imposing family responsibilities that limit freedom of action and leave little money for investment in either business or education.

Divorce rates also vary by class, decreasing as class and status level rise, except for the "new upper class" and a small number of celebrities in "cafe society" and the world of entertainment. The sources of these differences are not to be found directly in the economic position of the several classes but exist in their values and cultural traditions. The established upper class, for example, places heavy emphasis upon the "family" and emphasizes extended kinship ties, often at the expense of the conjugal unit. These close kinship ties are clearly related to the importance of ancestry as a basis for high status position. Concern with family position also results in a careful selection of marriage partners, so careful, indeed, that there appears to be a relatively high rate of spinsterhood among upper-class women who will not marry "beneath" them. (Upper-class men have somewhat greater freedom of choice, for it is easier for a man to gain social acceptance for a wife from a lower status level than for a woman to bring a lower-status husband into her social circle.) As Hollingshead points out, "The degree of kinship solidarity, combined with intra-class marriages, found in this level results in a high order of stability in the upper class. . . ." [40]

In the working class, on the other hand, some of the factors associated with a greater likelihood of divorce such as earlier age at marriage and shorter courtship are part of the prevailing pattern. Moreover, working-class persons focus their social life much more around home, family, and relatives than do members of the middle class; they have fewer friends and participate less frequently in both friendship groups and formal organizations. They therefore lack the "external group supports" that might enable a marriage to survive despite difficulties that develop in the relationship between husband and wife. [41]

MEMBERSHIP IN ORGANIZATIONS Studies in New York, Detroit, Los Angeles, Denver, and New Haven, in Yankee City and other smaller communities, and data from several national surveys consistently demonstrate that membership in voluntary organizations increases as class and status level rise. [42] Using almost any index of stratification—whether income, education, interviewer's rating, home ownership, or occupation—investigators report that the proportion of persons belonging to two or more associations increases and the proportion with no such membership decreases the higher the class and status position.

These differences reflect the costs of participation, educational differences, and the functions that voluntary associations serve for their members. A single labor union suffices, it would seem, to look after the manual worker's economic interests; he possesses few other interests that he seeks to satisfy through a formal organization, although he may join a fraternal organization for sociable reasons or because it offers some kind of insurance benefits. With their greater education, middle-class people have wider interests—civic, political, recreational— which they pursue through voluntary associations. For business and professional persons, membership in voluntary organizations is highly useful, if not essential, in order to become better known, to make contacts, or to increase the number of clients or customers. By banding together they may also pursue their collective interests more effectively. Finally, voluntary associations frequently acquire a status identification; membership may then be sought at least in part for the prestige it brings, acquiring new standing or reinforcing the old. Membership in the Knickerbocker Club in New York City, the Rittenhouse in Philadelphia, or the Somerset in Boston testifies to elite status, whereas belonging to the Rotary Club or Kiwanis marks the middle-class man. In each community, membership in the country club (or one of the several such clubs) reflects and sustains the social standing of its members.

Class consciousness, class organization, and politics

Class and status-group membership provide potential bases not only for differences in behavior but also for group consciousness and collective action. According to Marx, common experience and interests lead almost inevitably to class consciousness and political action: The course of history therefore is shaped by the conflict of classes in the struggle for power. Similarly, James Madison, as we have noted, and other early Americans as well, singled out class interest as the chief basis of political conflict.

It is quite clear that political differences do in some measure follow class lines, in the United States as elsewhere.

Workers are more likely to be liberal or radical in their views on economic issues, middle-class people to be more conservative. Workers more frequently vote Democratic, middle-class members more frequently vote Republican. The higher in the class structure, the greater the Republican strength, the lower in the structure, the stronger the Democrats. (For a fuller analysis of the class basis of politics see Chapter 13.)

Despite these contrasts, there appears to be comparatively little corporate class consciousness—the feeling within a class that its members are tied together by common interests—in the United States comparable to that found in England, say, or in France. Even those organizations that represent different classes —for example, the United States Chamber of Commerce or the A.F.L.- C.I.O.—do not differ sharply on many basic issues, accepting on the whole the rights of private property, the existence of a relatively free economy, and the prevailing political arrangements and practices. The conflicts that do emerge focus around modifications of existing institutions and relationships rather than any drastic changes, although over a long period of time the cumulative result may be a substantial transformation of American society. The history of the United States therefore cannot be written simply as a record of class conflict, although it cannot be written accurately without recording the struggles between farmers and bankers, labor and management, small business and big business, status-seekers and status "elites."

The extent of class consciousness in the United States has varied from time to time, emerging strongly in some periods, as in the early 1880s and the 1930s, years of depression and hardship, and subsiding at other times, as in the 1950s. In 1881 the assembled delegates to the first convention of the American Federation of Labor adopted a Declaration of Principles whose Preamble began.

A struggle is going on in the nations of the civilized world between the oppressors and the oppressed of all countries, a struggle between capital and labor, which must grow in intensity from year to year and work disastrous results to the toiling millions of all nations if not combined for mutual protection and benefits.[43]

The Preamble to the Constitution adopted in 1955 by the united American Federation of Labor–Congress of Industrial Organizations begins:

The establishment of this federation . . . is an expression of the hopes and aspirations of the working people of America. We seek the fulfillment of these hopes and aspirations through democratic processes within the framework of our constitutional government and consistent with our institutions and traditions.[44]

The absence of a revolutionary class consciousness, such as Marx expected to emerge, stems from diverse sources. A key feature of American social history has been the absence of a feudal aristocracy, a circumstance that eliminated the need for a revolutionary overturn or a radical ideology in order to remove traditional restraints. Conflicts of interest have been present from the beginning, but America nevertheless began as a predominantly middle-class society with widespread ownership of property and without the deep-rooted cleavages characteristic of settled European society.

The continuing transformation of American life under the impact of technological growth and mass immigration has inhibited the coalescence of class and status hierarchies into a single consistent whole. Membership in other groups and social categories cuts across both class membership and status identification, creating competing pressures and complex patterns of allegiance that affect the ebb and flow of political forces. Thus regional, religious, racial, ethnic, and community loyalties impose demands that can modify or minimize the relevance of class or status interests and preclude strong class consciousness. Southerners in recent years have frequently asserted that they were white southerners first and Democrats second, particularly when civil rights issues were at stake. Samuel Lubell has shown how ethnic and religious identifications affected the pattern of class divisions in American politics from the New Deal to the 1950s.[45] Belonging to other groups often takes priority over allegiance to one's class, particularly since the very nature of the stratification system, with its stress upon individual and not group striving, inhibits the growth of class consciousness.

Even the emergence of great fortunes and the growth of giant corporations have not produced lasting and deep-rooted class consciousness. The democratic political system has provided machinery through which class battles could be fought without violence or mass action; there has been no need to throw up the barricades in the streets of New York or Philadelphia as there may have been in Paris. Industrial growth has also made possible a fairly steady rise in the standard of living and the visible differences between working- and middle-class styles of life have been diminished by the wide availability of mass-produced goods. Real wages in the United States have steadily risen, with only occasional setbacks during depressions or unusual inflation. During these reversals class consciousness has tended to grow, only to be pinched off again when a revival of industry and trade and the steadily increasing productivity of American industry provided new goods at prices that made them available to a mass market. The resulting material abundance in which most Americans have shared needs no elaboration; the plethora of cars, television sets, washers and dryers, air conditioners, refrigerators, and so on is readily apparent. More than three-fifths of all American families own their own homes—or are paying off a mortgage. Those who live on the edge of poverty, though still a fairly large number (we noted earlier that in 1964, 5 million families and 6 million individuals earned less than $2,000 per year), constitute special groups who are unlikely to generate a common solidarity and pursue collective action: old people surviving on pensions that dissolve as inflation continues; a number of unskilled workers who lack the knowledge and ability to organize effectively; and families supported by one woman's earnings. Only the Negroes have made concerted efforts to remove the disabilities under which they labor.

Social equalitarianism and a belief in equality of opportunity, both sustained by a considerable amount of upward mobility, have also tended to soften the effects of class differences. Americans have always scoffed at social pretensions and boasted an "equalitarianism of manners." "Why, I swear we don't make any great manner of distinction in our state between quality and other folks," says Jonathan, the comic—and democratic—Yankee character in *The Contrast,* the first comedy by an American, produced on the American stage in 1787. Today, despite recognized differences in status, putting on airs is looked upon as snobbery; one man is "just as good as another," wealth and social position notwithstanding. Europeans have commented frequently on the absence of undue deference to superiors and the emphasis upon personal qualities that characterize American life. Alexis de Tocqueville, in his classic *Democracy in America,* written

more than a century ago, considered equality the chief characteristic of Americans and American society and explored its complex ramifications into many areas of social life. Here we need only observe that the persistence of equalitarian manners and values lessens class antagonisms and thereby diminishes the likelihood of the growth of class consciousness, even as it stimulates status-striving.

Writing in the 1780s, the Frenchman Michel de Crèvecoeur, in his *Letters from an American Farmer,* dwelt upon the "decent competence" of every American and the absence of great contrasts of wealth and poverty. Revolutionary times saw the feudal inheritance rules of primogeniture and entail swept away, reforms designed to prevent the growth and perpetuation of great hereditary fortunes. Although there have been efforts to lessen differences in wealth and income through progressive taxation and inheritance taxes (the latter relatively unsuccessful [46]), America's chief equalitarian concern appears to be equality of opportunity, a principle identified by some Americans as a description of reality, and accepted by most as a goal to be achieved and maintained. As long as men believe that America is the "land of opportunity" where any one who "has what it takes" can "get ahead in the world," where, in Edward Everett's words, "the wheel of fortune is in constant operation and the poor in one generation furnish the rich in the next," they are hardly likely to develop class solidarity and engage in revolutionary—or radical—politics.

Social mobility in American society

Social mobility and equality of opportunity, however, have probably never been as widespread as Americans have believed.

"Poor immigrant boys and poor farm boys who became business leaders," the historian William Miller has commented, "have always been more conspicuous in American history books than in the American business elite." [47] The facts concerning the rate of mobility, particularly in the past, are difficult to ascertain and their meaning is subject to diverse interpretations. The student assessing the amount of mobility is in the position of a thirsty drinker looking at a half-bottle of whiskey—if he is an optimist it is half full, if he is a pessimist it is half empty. Measured against a standard of equal opportunity for all, one might conclude that social mobility has been seriously limited. Compared with a society in which social position is usually inherited, America has always offered rich and unusual opportunities.

Ample evidence is available to demonstrate that inherited class position makes an important difference in the opportunities people have. In a 1952 study of big business leaders, 4.5 per cent were sons of unskilled and semiskilled workers and 10.3 per cent of skilled workers, although manual workers constitute almost half the labor force. On the other hand, 17 per cent of the business leaders were sons of major executives or owners of large businesses.[48] Almost two-thirds of the members of the House of Representatives in 1941–1943 and 55 per cent of the United States Senators in 1949–1951 were sons (and daughters) of professionals, proprietors, and officials.[49]

Access to higher education is significantly affected by class. Children of nonmanual workers are far more likely to go to college than are children of manual workers, even when intelligence is held constant. This situation reflects not only the limited income of lower-class children and the economic and social advantages of those in the middle and upper classes, but also the existence of contrasting cultural patterns that encourage or discourage continued education. With many exceptions, of course, especially in certain ethnic groups, working-class children receive less parental encouragement and less prompting from teachers, they are more likely to be concerned with present satisfactions than future gains, and they have less familarity with the possibilities and prerequisites for advancement than other children.

Class differences in access to continued schooling are of particular importance, for in an increasingly specialized industrial society education has come to be a major prerequisite for advancement. Fifty-seven per cent of the business leaders studied in 1952 were college graduates and an additional 19 per cent had had at least some college education.[50] The proportion will probably increase in the future. Even those with family advantages cannot usually expect to achieve high positions if they do not go to college or secure some specialized training.

These facts, however, are not inconsistent with a high rate of mobility. As we pointed out earlier, ascription plays some role in determining both class and status positions as long as family institutions require or encourage parents to aid their children to find their place in the world, and as long as other institutions make it possible for them to do so. But in American society birth and family status are not the sole—or even the essential determinants—of class position. There are paths upward that are traveled by many men and, except for dark times like the extended depression of the 1930s, there has been sufficient mobility to sustain the image of an open society.

How much mobility there actually is in any society, however, is difficult to measure. Most students of the problem have focused their attention upon movement in the occupational hierarchy, a procedure warranted for several reasons: Occupation is both an index and determinant of status, it is usually related to income and property ownership, and no other data are as readily accessible. Since the correlation with other dimensions of stratification, although close, is not complete, occupational mobility cannot provide a fully adequate measure of either status mobility or enlarged power. Findings derived from analysis of occupational mobility may also be affected by the particular lines drawn between occupational groups. For example, in their detailed comparative analysis of mobility in industrial societies, Lipset and Bendix have considered only movement from manual to nonmanual occupations, disregarding mobility within the working class (unskilled or semiskilled to skilled or vice versa) and within the middle class (from clerical to managerial or professional). [51] That the use of other categories might produce other results can be illustrated by data drawn from a careful study of social mobility in Indianapolis. In 1910, 21.2 per cent of sons of semiskilled workers became white-collar workers, compared with 26 per cent in 1940. If movement up to the ranks of skilled workers is included in calculating the mobility of sons of semiskilled workers, the proportion who rise above their fathers' level drops from 53 per cent in 1910 to only 44.4 per cent in 1940. [52]

Despite these difficulties, the empirical studies of social mobility suggest several general conclusions. In recent decades, more sons find themselves at the same level as their fathers than at any other level. [53] Each study also reports that a substantial proportion of its sample experienced some upward mobility. In a na-

tional sample survey in 1945, 35 per cent had moved up, while 29 per cent had moved down. [54] Most mobility, as reported in the various studies, involves shifts only to occupational levels adjacent to those of the individual's father.

Because of the uncertainty of the evidence it has been difficult to determine whether there has been any long-run change in the rate of social mobility. The view widely held during the depression decade and for some time afterward, that there had been a narrowing of opportunity and a slowdown in the rate of mobility, has been seriously challenged. The present consensus among specialists holds that there has been no decline, and that there may well be a continuing increase. So complex are the problems of measurement, however, and so numerous the variables that must enter into an equation that might express the rate of social mobility, that it is unlikely that a precise answer can be found or that agreement can be reached on the meaning of the available evidence.

Much of the analysis of social mobility has therefore focused upon institutional and structural changes that have affected the opportunities to move up—and down—and the channels and prerequisites of mobility. Of particular importance, obviously, are long-run technological and industrial trends. The increasing mechanization of production and the growing scope and size of organizations have led to a steady growth in the proportion of professionals, managers, technicians, and other white-collar employees. This growth has provided rich opportunities for upward mobility from both the lower-middle class and from the ranks of industrial workers. Differential birth rates and the prevailing patterns of migration also contributed to the possibilities for mobility. Until very recently, middle- and upper-middle-class birth rates were comparatively low, hardly enough to reproduce themselves and certainly not high enough to fill all the important posts in an expanding economy. Able and ambitious persons from the lower class were therefore able to move upward. In postwar years the rise in middle-class birth rates makes problematical the continuation of this demographic spur to upward mobility.

The steady flow from farm to city which began early in the nineteenth century also contributed to a continuing process of mobility, for many migrants brought few skills with them and became part of the industrial labor force. Together with the large number of immigrants from abroad they provided a ready supply of labor for industry, making it possible for those who had arrived earlier—from farms or from abroad—to rise into the middle class. Mass immigration ceased in 1924, and there are few rural folk left to join the urban trek. In recent years Negroes and Puerto Ricans have filled a similar role, but as they seek to rise, as a good many already have, the question of a continuing source of recruits for the bottom of the ladder may acquire a crucial significance.

Changes in industry may provide the answer. By 1956 white-collar workers for the first time outnumbered skilled, semiskilled, and unskilled workers. With continuing automation and an increasing proportion of the labor force engaged in services, communication, and distribution, the working class may fall off substantially in relative size; by the mid-1960s there were already five professional, managerial, and clerical employees for each four blue-collar workers. These changes may increase competition for desirable positions, particularly as the prerequisites for mobility, chiefly education, become more widely available.

The changing nature of industry and of American society as a whole has in some measure changed the form and character of both the image of success and the channels for securing it. The self-made man operating his own business, once the ideal form of achievement, has been replaced by the man who climbs the bureaucratic ladder. Although small business remains a viable institution, it has lost its central place and provides few opportunities for substantial achievement. Workers and salesmen dream of—and often start—their own businesses; college graduates enter one of the larger bureaucracies in which achievement and ability count for more than in small- or middle-sized organizations. Education, therefore, as we observed earlier, has come to play the central role in social mobility and in providing opportunity for those from the lower levels of society. To the extent that education becomes more widely available, therefore, opportunities for advancement will increase.

The continuing volume of mobility, whether higher, lower, or about the same as in the past, is clearly sufficiently large to sustain belief in the existence of rich—even if not "equal"—opportunities and to encourage hope among Americans that they or their children will some day do better. But it may have other consequences as well. For those who fail, as some must, in a society that encourages all to strive and that promises success to those who are capable, failure is evidence of personal inadequacies. Upward mobility requires adjustments that many men find difficult, evident both in research findings and in the prevailing folklore of the rich and successful but unhappy man; and downward mobility may be even more difficult to take. A society with *carrières ouvertes aux talents* must therefore pay a price for the freedom and opportunities it offers to its members, just as a caste society which provides security of status limits men's freedom and prevents many of its members from exploiting their capabilities.

Notes

[1] The general outlines of the theoretical orientation of this chapter are derived largely from Max Weber, *From Max Weber: Essays in Sociology*, trans. and ed. by H. H. Gerth and C. Wright Mills (New York: Oxford, 1946), Ch. VII.

[2] *The Federalist* (New York: Random House Modern Library, 1941), p. 56.

[3] See Charles H. Page, *Class and American Sociology* (New York: Dial, 1940).

[4] For one general effort at such an analysis, see Stanislaw Ossowski, *Class Structure and the Social Consciousness* (London: Routledge, 1963). For accounts of the development of theories of stratification in the United States, see Milton M. Gordon, *Social Class in American Sociology* (Durham: Duke University Press, 1958); and Page, *op. cit.*

[5] Karl Marx, *Capital*, III, trans. from the 1st German ed. by Ernest Untermann (Chicago: Kerr, 1909), 1031.

[6] Karl Marx and Friedrich Engels, "Letter to Georg Weydemeyer, Mar. 5, 1852," in *Correspondence, 1846–1895* (New York: International Publishers, 1935), p. 57.

[7] Adam Smith, *The Wealth of Nations* (London: Dent Everyman Edition, 1910), p. 230.

[8] Alex Inkeles and Peter H. Rossi, "National Comparisons of Occupational Prestige," *American Journal of Sociology*, LXVI (January, 1956), 329–39.

[9] Alan S. C. Ross, "U and Non-U," in Nancy Mitford (ed.), *Noblesse Oblige* (New York: Harper, 1956), pp. 55–93.

[10] Ralph Pieris, "Speech and Society: A Sociological Approach to Language," *American Sociological Review*, XVI (August, 1951), 500.

[11] E. Digby Baltzell, *Philadelphia Gentlemen* (New York: Free Press, 1958), p. 51.

[12] See, for example, John Dollard, *Class and Caste in a Southern Town* (3rd ed.; Garden City: Doubleday Anchor Books, 1957); C. Wright Mills, *White Collar* (New York: Oxford, 1951), Ch. 11; and W. Lloyd Warner and Paul S. Lunt, *The Social Life of a Modern Community* (New Haven: Yale University Press, 1941).

[13] Mills, *op. cit.*, p. 239.

[14] C. Wright Mills, "The Middle Classes in Middle-Sized Cities," *American Sociological Review*, XI (October, 1946), 520–9.

[15] See Elinor G. Barber, *The Bourgeoisie in 18th Century France* (Princeton: Princeton University Press, 1955); for England, see R. H. Gretton, *The English Middle Class* (London: Bell, 1917).

[16] See, for example, the suggestive essay by Ralf Dahrendorf, *Class and Class Conflict in Industrial Society* (Stanford: Stanford University Press, 1959).

[17] Weber, *op. cit.*, pp. 193–4.

[18] Robert M. MacIver and Charles H. Page, *Society: An Intoductory Analysis* (New York: Holt, 1949), pp. 348–58.

[19] Charles H. Cooley, *Social Organization* (New York: Scribner, 1912), Ch. 18. Cooley's discussion, although frequently overlooked, remains a useful analysis of the structural conditions that determine the relative importance of achievement and ascription as bases of status. In this connection, see Page, *op. cit.*, Ch. 6, especially pp. 189 ff.

[20] Talcott Parsons, "A Revised Analytical Approach to the Theory of Social Stratification," in Reinhard Bendix and Seymour M. Lipset (eds.), *Class, Status and*

Power (New York: Free Press, 1953), p. 122.

[21] Seymour M. Lipset and Reinhard Bendix, *Social Mobility in Industrial Society* (Berkeley: University of California Press, 1959), Ch. 2; David Glass (ed.), *Social Mobility in Britain* (London: Routledge, 1954).

[22] K. S. Mathur, *Caste and Ritual in a Malwa Village* (New York: Asia Publishing House, 1964), p. 67.

[23] Mathur, *op. cit.*, p. 160.

[24] *Ibid.*, pp. 148–9.

[25] M. N. Srinivas, "The Dominant Caste in Rampura," *American Anthropologist*, LXI (February, 1959), 3–4.

[26] Quoted in Alex Inkeles and Raymond A. Bauer, *The Soviet Citizen* (Cambridge, Mass.: Harvard University Press, 1959), p. 67.

[27] Alex Inkeles, "Social Stratification and Mobility in the Soviet Union, 1940–1950," *American Sociological Review*, XV (August, 1950), 466. Also reprinted in Bendix and Lipset, *Class, Status and Power*, pp. 609–22.

[28] Alex Inkeles, Raymond A. Bauer, and Clyde Kluckhohn, *How the Soviet System Works* (Cambridge, Mass.: Harvard University Press, 1957), Part IV; and Inkeles and Bauer, *The Soviet Citizen*.

[29] For an analysis of trends in the recruitment and social composition of the Communist Party, see Merle Fainsod, *How Russia Is Ruled* (rev. ed.; Cambridge, Mass.: Harvard University Press, 1963), Ch. 8; and T. H. Rigby, "Social Orientation of Recruitment and Distribution of Membership in the Communist Party of the Soviet Union," *The American Slavic and East European Review*, XVI (October, 1957), 275–90.

[30] Albert Parry, *The New Class Divided* (New York: Macmillan, 1966).

[31] For discussion and analysis of the problem of poverty, see Ben B. Seligman (ed.), *Poverty as a Public Issue* (New York: Free Press, 1965); Margaret S. Gordon (ed.), *Poverty in America* (San Francisco: Chandler, 1965); and Michael Harrington, *The Other America* (New York: Macmillan, 1962).

[32] W. Lloyd Warner *et al.*, *Social Class in America* (Chicago: Science Research Associates, 1949).

[33] August B. Hollingshead and Frederick C. Redlich, *Social Class and Mental Illness* (New York: Wiley, 1958), Ch. 4.

[34] Robert W. Hodge, Paul M. Siegel, and Peter H. Rossi, "Occupational Prestige in the United States, 1925–63," *American Journal of Sociology*, LXX (November, 1964), 286–302.

[35] Warner and Lunt, *op. cit.*; Warner *et al.*, *op. cit.*, pp. 11–8.

[36] See, for example, John F. Cuber and William F. Kenkel, *Social Stratification* (New York: Appleton, 1954), Chs. 7, 13.

[37] Seymour Martin Lipset, *The First New Nation* (New York: Basic Books, 1963), p. 112.

[38] For a penetrating analysis of class differentials in fertility in the Western world, see Dennis H. Wrong, "Trends in Class Fertility in Western Nations," in Reinhard Bendix and Seymour Martin Lipset (eds.), *Class, Status, and Power* (2nd ed.; New York: Free Press, 1966), pp. 353–61.

[39] Alfred C. Kinsey, Wardell B. Pomeroy, and Clyde E. Martin, *Sexual Behavior in the Human Male* (Philadelphia: Saunders, 1948), p. 381.

[40] August B. Hollingshead, "Class Differences in Family Stability," in Bendix and Lipset, *Class, Status and Power* (New York: Free Press, 1953), p. 286.

[41] See William J. Goode, *Women in Divorce* (New York: Free Press, 1956; first published as *After Divorce*), pp. 66–7.

[42] See Mirra Komarovsky, "The Voluntary Associations of Urban Dwellers," *American Sociological Review*, XI (December, 1946), 686–98; Floyd Dotson, "Patterns of Voluntary Association among Urban Working-Class Families," *American Sociological Review*, XVI (October, 1951), 687–93; Morris Axelrod, "Urban Structure and Social Participation," *American Sociological Review*, XXI (February,

1956), 13–8; Wendell Bell and Maryanne T. Force, "Urban Neighborhood Types and Participation in Formal Associations," *American Sociological Review*, XXI (February, 1956), 25–34; and Charles R. Wright and Herbert H. Hyman, "Voluntary Association Memberships of American Adults: Evidence from National Sample Surveys," *American Sociological Review*, XXIII (June, 1958), 284–94.

[43] *Report of the First Annual Session of the Federation of Organized Trades and Labor Unions of the United States and Canada*, Pittsburgh, Pa., December 15–18, 1881 (published by the Federation), p. 3.

[44] *The New York Times*, May 3, 1955, p. 24.

[45] Samuel Lubell, *The Future of American Politics* (2nd ed., rev.; Garden City: Doubleday Anchor Books, 1956).

[46] See John C. Bowen, "The Tax That Doesn't Tax," *The Nation*, June 27, 1959, pp. 575–7.

[47] William Miller, "American Historians and the Business Elite," *Journal of Economic History*, IX (November, 1949), 208.

[48] W. Lloyd Warner and James C. Abegglen, *Occupational Mobility in American Business and Industry* (Minneapolis: University of Minnesota Press, 1955), p. 38.

[49] Donald R. Matthews, *The Social Background of Political Decision Makers* (Garden City: Doubleday, 1954), p. 23.

[50] Warner and Abegglen, *op. cit.*, p. 96.

[51] Lipset and Bendix, *Social Mobility in Industrial Society*.

[52] Natalie Rogoff, *Recent Trends in Occupational Mobility* (New York: Free Press, 1953), Tables 52 and 53, pp. 118–9.

[53] See Percy E. Davidson and H. Dewey Anderson, *Occupational Mobility in an American Community* (Stanford: Stanford University Press, 1937), p. 23; Richard Centers, "Occupational Mobility of Urban Occupational Strata," *American Sociological Review*, XIII (April, 1948), 197–203; Rogoff, *op. cit.*, p. 62; and Elton F. Jackson and Harry J. Crockett, Jr., "Occupational Mobility in the United States: A Point Estimate and Trend Comparison." *American Sociological Review*, XXIX (February, 1964), 5–15.

[54] Centers, *op. cit.*, p. 201.

Suggestions for further reading

BALTZELL, E. DIGBY. *The Protestant Establishment*. New York: Random House, 1964.
A critical analysis of the history, nature, and functions of the "white, Anglo-Saxon, Protestant" elite in the northeastern United States.

BENDIX, REINHARD, AND SEYMOUR MARTIN LIPSET (eds.). *Class, Status and Power*. New York: Free Press, 1953; 2nd ed., 1966.
A valuable collection of theoretical and empirical writings. The second edition, subtitled "Social Stratification in Comparative Perspective," contains a considerable amount of additional material on other societies.

DAHRENDORF, RALF. *Class and Class Conflict in Industrial Society*. Stanford: Stanford University Press, 1959.
A stimulating effort to focus the analysis of social stratification around problems of conflict.

DJILAS, MILOVAN. *The New Class*. New York: Praeger, 1957.
This interpretation of Communism, written by a political prisoner and spirited out of a Yugoslav jail, argues that the Communist party has become the new ruling class in the Soviet Union and the nations of eastern Europe.

DUBE, S. C. *Indian Village*. London: Routledge, 1955.
A close study of the workings of caste

in a village in central India. Particularly good in its treatment of ritual.

HOLLINGSHEAD, AUGUST B. *Elmtown's Youth.* New York: Wiley, 1949.
A detailed study of the impact of class differences on adolescents in a small midwestern community.

HOLLINGSHEAD, AUGUST B., AND FREDERICK C. REDLICH. *Social Class and Mental Illness.* New York: Wiley, 1958.
A major study of the connections between social class and mental illness, which shows class differences in rates of mental illness, the frequency and form of treatment, and the responses to psychiatric problems and practitioners.

KAHL, JOSEPH A. *The American Class Structure.* New York: Holt, 1957.
A useful, straightforward summary of much of our knowledge of social stratification in the United States.

KUPER, LEO. *An African Bourgeoisie.* New Haven: Yale University Press, 1964.
An analysis of an emerging African middle class.

LENSKI, GERHARD. *Power and Privilege.* New York: McGraw-Hill, 1966.
An interesting and important effort to formulate a theory of social stratification.

MILLS, C. WRIGHT. *White Collar.* New York: Oxford, 1951.
A challenging and suggestive analysis and interpretation of the emergence and role of the new middle classes by a maverick sociologist who was critical of much modern sociological research.

PAGE, CHARLES H. *Class and American Sociology.* New York: Dial, 1940.
A summary of the analyses of class found in the work of the important early American sociologists.

SCHUMPETER, JOSEPH. "Social Classes in an Ethnically Homogeneous Environment," in *Imperialism and Social Classes.* New York: Meridian, 1955.
A penetrating essay on the nature, functions, and evolution of social classes.

SHOSTAK, ARTHUR B., AND WILLIAM GOMBERG (eds.). *Blue-Collar World.* Englewood Cliffs: Prentice-Hall, 1964.

A collection of essays that explore patterns of culture and social organization in the American working class.

SOROKIN, PITIRIM A. *Social and Cultural Mobility.* New York: Free Press, 1959.
This book contains the whole of Social Mobility, first published in 1927 and still the most inclusive study of social mobility, as well as a chapter on spatial mobility from another of the author's works.

THERNSTROM, STEPHAN. *Poverty and Progress.* Cambridge, Mass.: Harvard University Press, 1964.
An historical account of social stratification and social mobility in Newburyport, Massachusetts ("Yankee City") in the nineteenth century. An excellent example of historical sociology.

TOCQUEVILLE, ALEXIS DE. *Democracy in America.* 2 vols. New York: Vintage, 1954.
This classic study, written in the 1830s, examines the influence of equalitarianism upon all aspects of American culture and society. Not only is it a model of sociological analysis in its treatment of social facts, but it also remains remarkably up-to-date both in the sociological generalizations it advances and in its analysis of American society.

WARNER, W. LLOYD, AND JAMES C. ABEGGLEN. *Occupational Mobility in American Business and Industry, 1928–1952.* Minneapolis: University of Minnesota Press, 1955.
A detailed analysis of social origins and career patterns of American business leaders. The data, collected in 1952, are compared with the findings of a study by F. W. Taussig and C. S. Joslyn, *American Business Leaders,* New York: Macmillan, 1932, based upon data collected in 1928.

WARNER, W. LLOYD, MARCIA MEEKER, AND KENNETH EELLS. *Social Class in America.* Chicago: Science Research Associates, 1949.
An attempt to construct objective measures of status in American society.

9

Racial and ethnic groups

Race, culture, and social structure

In many societies racial and ethnic groups constitute important components of the social order, and the relations among them create significant social problems. White-Negro relations in the United States, long a chronic source of difficulty, have in the 1950s and 1960s become a major social and political issue. In the nations of Southeast Asia the presence of substantial Chinese minorities with—or without—continuing ties to the homeland engenders persisting anxiety and tension. Israel faces complex problems in assimilating Jews from Europe, Africa, and Asia into a single nation. Belgium has experienced acute conflicts between its Flemish- and its French-speaking population. In South Africa a sharp and potentially explosive division between whites and blacks is complicated by other differences: almost 400,000 Asians, more than a million Cape Colored who spring from a massive intermixture of whites and Hottentots in the eighteenth century, and an ethnic cleavage that separates the whites into Afrikaaners, English (themselves split on the racial issue), and a relatively small number of Jews.

Membership in racial and ethnic groups can affect men's status and their relations with others. Skin color or distinctive cultural traits often fix men's place in their society and constitute grounds for differential treatment, or *discrimination*. Possession of distinctive physical traits or of unique values, beliefs, and customs frequently provides a focus for common loyalties and the basis for collective action, particularly if a group is singled out for discriminatory attention. American Negroes, first brought as slaves and then severely disadvantaged even though legally free, have gradually become more and more concerned with the advancement of the "race" and more active and aggressive in seeking to eliminate discrimination, improve their economic circumstances, and secure full civil rights. Jews, Italians, Greeks, Irish, and many other ethnic groups possess, to varying degrees, their own communal organizations, themselves both a product and a source of collective identity—the American Jewish Committee and the American Jewish Congress, the Order of the Sons of Italy, the American Hellenic Educational Progressive Association (AHEPA), the Ancient Order of Hibernians.

Like any major division of the social order, however, racial and ethnic groups, though often partially congruent with other social divisions, may also cut across them. Perhaps the most significant linkage with other dimensions of social structure is the close connection that often

In Belgium the hostility of the 5 million Flemish-speaking Belgians toward the 4 million French-speaking Walloons has led to repeated demonstrations and protests in order to secure better political representation, greater use of the Flemish language, and other improvements. The result has often been violence between members of the two groups.

obtains between racial or ethnic identity and class. Most American Negroes, for example, are manual workers or are employed in poorly paid service occupations, although there are also small and growing Negro middle and upper classes. Jews are now largely concentrated in white-collar, business, and professional occupations in the United States, although some Jews are still to be found at almost all class levels in American society. In most parts of Latin America a close correlation exists between physical traits such as skin color and class position; persons with dark skins and Negroid features are more likely to be in the lower classes. Chinese residents in Southeast Asia are engaged primarily in commerce and light industry while the natives are predominantly farmers. In the Hawaiian Islands, on the other hand, the many racial and ethnic groups—native Polynesians, Japanese, Chinese, Filipinos, Puerto Ricans, Portuguese, Koreans, Spaniards, and others—are now quite thoroughly scrambled and play a minor role, as ethnic groups, in Hawaiian life. Only a small number of upper-class whites (*Haoles*, as they are called) remain apart and distinct.

The fact that racial and ethnic groups frequently overlap or merge with other social divisions complicates analysis of their nature and their relations to one another. Moreover, it is sometimes difficult to disentangle the influence of distinctive physical or cultural attributes from that of other characteristics. The frequently close tie between racial and ethnic divisions and class structure has encouraged some writers to interpret prejudice and discrimination chiefly, or even exclusively, in economic terms.[1] Although the importance of economic factors should not be minimized, such an interpretation ignores other important aspects of intergroup relations and in itself is incapable of explaining many of the complex existing patterns.

Physical and cultural differences are often closely linked, but they can also vary independently; racially distinct groups sometimes share a common culture, and different ethnic groups are often derived from the same biological stock. In South Africa, whites and blacks by and large are set apart by both appearance and ways of life. Chinese, Japanese, and Filipino immigrants to the United States were both racially and ethnically different from both native-born Americans and other immigrants; their descendants have been increasingly assimilated into American society. But even if they lost completely the language, religion, and customs they brought with them, they would be marked off by their appearance. American Negroes, too, on the whole, are readily identifiable, but they possess no traditional way of life derived from African ancestors; their culture is indigenous to American society and reflects their social and economic position. ("The process of sloughing off African culture," E. Franklin Frazier has written, "has been so thoroughgoing that at the present time only in certain isolated areas can one discover what might be justly called African cultural survivals." [2]) In Hawaii, both

cultural and physical differences among many groups (the Japanese are somewhat of an exception) appear to be disappearing as a relatively high rate of miscegenation produces new physical types.

The fact that race is frequently unrelated to cultural differences is clearly demonstrated in Europe, where the distribution of ethnic patterns generally is independent of biological attributes. So mixed are Europe's peoples that no nation is clearly marked off from others in appearance, even though there are, of course, gross differences between northern and southern Europeans. Many Frenchmen, Italians, Spaniards, Germans, Swiss, and others are physically much alike, but they speak different languages, subscribe to different political beliefs, order their daily lives in diverse fashion, and think of themselves as distinct from one another. Similarly, no clear-cut biological contrasts separate the many European immigrant groups who came to the United States at the end of the nineteenth and beginning of the twentieth centuries: Poles, Greeks, Hungarians, Bulgarians, Russians, Czechs, Jews (who derive from several nations), and so on. Jews, who are usually physically indistinguishable from many other white-skinned persons, have nevertheless remained in some measure set apart socially in the several European countries in which they have found a place.

Cultural differences are often attributed to biological variation, but, as we noted earlier, culture is learned and not inherited. There is no evidence to support the view that the biological mechanisms that determine physical characteristics—color of the skin and eyes, head shape, type of hair, stature, and so on—also control values, beliefs, customs, or forms of social organization. Racial traits (that is, inherited physical attributes common to a group of people) enter into social life *insofar* as men develop feelings and make judgments about them, or construct theories about culture and society in which they play a part. Otherwise these traits are of interest primarily to physical anthropologists and biologists and not to students of culture and society.

Where skin color and other racial characteristics have come to play an important role in group relations, they have usually been associated with cultural differences. European conquerors who subjugated native peoples often justified their economic, political, and military domination with high-sounding ideologies—the "white man's burden," for example—or with beliefs in the inherent superiority of whites over colored races, although this superiority usually rested on the fact that, as the well-worn couplet has it:

Whatever happens we have got
The Maxim gun and they have not.

Racial attributes often have come to possess independent significance as social facts. Even when contrasts in language, dress, religion, occupation, education, or some or all of these diminish or disappear, attitudes and feelings toward skin color, type of hair, shape of lips, and other biological characteristics tend to persist—"visibility," as Robert E. Park expressed it, has social consequences. Similarly, a pattern of intergroup relations, once established, is often not readily changed, particularly if it serves some function, or provides some gains, for the dominant group. To the extent that persons with a similar biological endowment conceive of themselves as a race, whether more or less spontaneously or because they are so considered by others, they become an ethnic group as well, for their conception of themselves now binds them together into a social whole, even if they possess few other distinctive cultural traits.

In recent years racial identity itself has come to play an important role in international, as well as national, affairs. People of color have joined in a common hostility toward the white Europeans who have dominated so much of Asia and Africa. Indians, Chinese, Japanese, Indonesians, Africans, and others express their dislike for the ways in which American Negroes are treated—or the ways in which they think Negroes are being treated. Some of the latter in turn currently claim some kinship with Africans of whose culture they have little knowledge or understanding. Just as racist dogma may have significant social consequences even when it has no basis in fact, so a common loyalty to an image of a race acquires a reality apart from the biological characteristics upon which it presumably rests.

The study of racial and ethnic groups therefore demonstrates with particular clarity the validity of W. I. Thomas' theorem: "If men define situations as real, they are real in their consequences." Racial ideologies have often contained assertions that were demonstrably false, but their historic role, particularly in the past century, has been far-reaching. The Nazis' extermination of 6 million or more Jews rested upon doctrines of racial superiority and inferiority that can be traced back to such nineteenth-century writers as Arthur de Gobineau and Houston Stewart Chamberlain. In the United States, theories of racial superiority put forward by both reputable scholars and popular propagandists have had widespread acceptance. These racist doctrines provided a large part of the theoretical justification for adoption of the national quotas incorporated in the legislation of the early 1920s that halted mass immigration, and they have been widely used to justify various forms of racial discrimination. Images of the various ethnic groups in the United States have affected the treatment immigrants have received, and persistent, often highly inaccurate, stereotypes of Jews, Irishmen, Italians, Puerto Ricans, Mexicans, and others continue to influence the relations of these with other groups.

Critical, derogatory, or hostile feelings and attitudes cannot in themselves, however, account for the relations among racial and ethnic groups. Prejudice is only one variable among many, and perhaps it is as likely to result from discrimination as to produce it. Later in this chapter we shall consider the nature, sources, and functions of prejudice; here we are concerned with the various patterns of ethnic group relations—with how members of different groups behave toward one another—and the structural and cultural facts that determine their form.

Patterns of ethnic group relations

Many racial and ethnic groups are often described as "minorities" when they occupy a subordinate position in society. Yet on occasion minorities are not discriminated against—the French and Italians in Switzerland, for example—and sometimes the "minority" is in fact larger than the ostensible "majority"; the blacks in the Union of South Africa, for example, constitute about two-thirds of the population. Nor is any group intrinsically a minority, in the social sense; changing political boundaries and the flow of migration often changes the status of groups from superior to subordinate, from minority to majority. As Louis Wirth points out:

In pre-war Poland under the Czarist regime the Poles were a distinct ethnic minority. When they gained their independence at the end of the first World War, they lost their minority status but reduced their Jewish fellow Poles to the status of a minority. As immigrants to the United States the Poles again became themselves a minority. During the brief period of Nazi domination the Sudeten Germans of Czechoslovakia reveled in their position of dominance over the Czechs among whom they had only recently been a minority. . . . It is not the specific characteristics, therefore, whether racial or ethnic, that mark a people as a minority but the relationship of their group to some other group in the society in which they live.[3]

Relations between majority and minority, or superior and inferior, are often—but not always—marked by conflict and hostility. The differences that set groups apart from one another contain the seeds of such conflict, for commitment to one set of values and institutions can readily render others suspect. Both the extent of conflict and the intensity of hostility may, of course, vary widely. In some instances, ethnic groups have achieved a fairly stable and harmonious equilibrium, or racial differences have been reduced to a minimal social role. In Switzerland, for example, four distinct language groups—French, German, Italian, and Romansh—have worked out an amicable and stable *modus vivendi* despite marked differences in numbers. (German-speaking Swiss constitute almost three-quarters of the population, the French-speaking about one-fifth, the Italian one-twentieth, and the Romansh just over 1 per cent.[4]) In Brazil, as we shall see in more detail, physical traits by themselves are of little importance in determining a man's status, opportunities, or social relationships.

At the other extreme, racial and ethnic minorities have sometimes been brutally treated. The extreme case, of course, was the mass murder of millions of Jews by the Germans under Hitler during World War II. In the Union of South Africa, the Nationalist Party, which has been in power since 1948, has pursued a policy of *apartheid* or "separate development," the enforced segregation of the races under white domination.

In most situations, however, conflict and hostility are contained within a system that holds members of ethnic groups to a particular place in the social order and regulates their relations with others. For many years a recognized "racial etiquette" governed white-Negro relations in the American South; under the impact of basic changes taking place in Southern society as well as the challenge of the civil rights movement, these established patterns have been crumbling. In some nations, including the United States, various aspects of racial and ethnic relations are governed by law: Some states prohibit miscegenation, and others outlaw racial or religious discrimination in hiring employees. In South Africa, nonwhites have few political rights and are constrained in many ways by both legislation and administrative rulings.

Many types of circumstances affect the structure of ethnic group relations, of which three appear to be of particular importance: first, the number and size of the several groups; second, the nature and extent of both physical and cultural differences; and third, the "arena of competition—i.e., the resources and values for which the minority and majority compete, the advantages which the majority seeks to derive from the presence of the minority and the perpetuation of its subordinate status, the general opportunities or barriers to upward mobility inherent in the larger society's economy, social organization, and ideological setting." [5]

When several ethnic groups are contained within a single society, a complex hierarchy often emerges in which each group may occupy a somewhat different social position. In the United States, Wirth noted in 1945, "There is little doubt but that the Negro . . . has become the principal shock absorber of the antiminority sentiment of the dominant whites." [6] Despite the changes that have taken place since the end of World War II, this statement is still substantially correct. Other ethnic groups possess fewer disabilties and are more readily able to become full-fledged members of American society. Indeed, they often share anti-Negro sentiment and follow the usual patterns of discrimination and exclusion. In pursuit of full acceptance they may even outdo others in their hostility and prejudice toward the Negro. In contrast, in societies with only one or two ethnic divisions, lines are likely to be rigidly drawn and resistant to efforts to break them down.

Small groups less often meet with hostility from a dominant majority than large. A few Negroes or Jews or Catholics may be accepted in a predominantly white Protestant community, whereas a larger number are often defined as a threat and therefore rejected and excluded from full participation. The greatest hostility to colored immigrants in Britain has developed in those urban areas in which large numbers of them have settled. When the subordinated group outnumbers the superior, the typical colonial or once colonial situation, relations are often sharply exacerbated. In the United States, Negroes have been most fully discriminated against, least likely to be allowed to vote, and most rigorously kept in an enforced submissive status in those areas of the Deep South where whites are a numerical minority.

The relevance of number and size, however, depends in part upon other conditions.

No inherent antipathies shape relations between racial and ethnic groups, but the nature and extent of the differences between them inevitably contribute to the ways in which they respond to one another. When contrasts are minimal, the dissimilarities are less apt to be seized upon as grounds for differential treatment. Some similarities may override the variations; for example, in the United States persons of the same religion often disregard ethnic lines in choosing a husband or, especially, a wife.[7] Physical differences, however, often have an effect, even among persons with similar cultural characteristics; visibility reinforces—or even helps to create—cultural variation and the likelihood of discrimination. Cultural differences can be gradually eliminated, but physical contrasts as such can only be removed through a long process of miscegenation and physical amalgamation, which is itself often strenuously resisted. But this fact does not account for—nor should it be used to justify—a racist interpretation of social and cultural patterns.

Cultural contrasts—in language, religion, traditions, customs—are not in themselves inevitably grounds for hostility and conflict. Many groups and persons, notably in the United States, deplore ethnic differences and look favorably upon the "melting pot" (a phrase coined by Israel Zangwill in 1906) in which distinctive cultural traits are merged to form a new whole. Others— Horace Kallen and Louis Adamic, for example—saw great virtue in a "pluralistic" society, a "nation of nations," in which each group maintains its own culture in a complex and varied whole. A dominant ethnic group—for example, the Haoles in

Hawaii a few decades ago, and now the Afrikaaners in South Africa—may reject both these solutions and seek to maintain its own superiority by keeping all others from gaining entry to its ranks or access to its privileges. The particular pattern that emerges depends in large part upon the social, economic, and political structure in which these varied groups find themselves.

When any group's wealth, power, or status can be challenged by others, or when members of different ethnic groups are competing for scarce values such as power or wealth, conflict is likely to develop and racial or ethnic differences easily become a basis for hostility. By excluding others from access to political power, by confining them to menial occupations, or by stigmatizing their color or culture, a dominant group monopolizes political, economic, or status values, or all of them, for itself. Patterns of discrimination and subordination are often created in order to gain such values, and once a system of superior-inferior relations between ethnic groups is created, any change usually threatens established prerogatives. This fact helps to explain the extent of resistance to equal status for Negroes in the United States, despite pervasive equalitarian values; the unwillingness or refusal of many whites to give political rights to Africans in Rhodesia and South Africa; the long resistance of French *colons* in Algeria to any proposals to change existing political arrangements, despite the violent rebellion of the Algerians against continued French domination.

So complex and varied are the interrelations among the factors that shape ethnic and racial relations, however, that we can best explore their relevance by examining in some detail three contrasting situations that are both sociologically illuminating and socially important: race relations in Brazil, Negro-white relations in the United States, and the position of American Jews.

Brazil: a racial "melting pot"

Brazil's population consists of whites, blacks, and—perhaps the largest group —those of mixed racial ancestry. The aboriginal Indians have almost disappeared except in more remote areas where some isolated tribes are found, although they did contribute in the early years of settlement to the present mixed population. Among the whites, predominantly Portuguese in origin, there are substantial groups of Europeans who have come to Brazil during the past seventy-five years—Germans, Italians, Poles, Spaniards, and more Portuguese. Although there was for a time some resistance to assimilation among these immigrants, particularly among the Germans, Charles Wagley, long a student of Brazil, has observed, "Nowadays . . . the descendants of Europeans would like to be Brazilians." [8] In addition, approximately 200,000 Japanese have come to Brazil since 1908.

Despite this multiracial population and a history of Indian and Negro slavery, Brazil has developed a society in which there is little racial hostility and conflict. Racial distinctions are made, but they play only a secondary role in defining the relations of persons and groups to one another.

Official Brazilian statistics use four racial categories: *branco* (white), *pardo* (brown), *prêto* (black), and *amarelo* (yellow). In common discourse, however, other and often finer distinctions are made. In one small town in the Northeast,

for example, the whites were divided into blonds and brunets and those with some Negro ancestry. The nonwhites were divided into eight different groups on the basis of their appearance, in addition to those of Indian background.[9] The importance of such complex and refined distinctions, which vary from region to region, lies in the fact that they preclude any rigid separation of clear-cut racial groups.

Racial characteristics are not ignored, but in themselves they do not determine an individual's status or class position. Indeed, there is often a seeming confusion between racial identification and class position. In one region, Donald Pierson reports, "A common expression was . . . a rich Negro is a white man and a poor white man is a Negro." [10] In an analysis of 500 persons in the city of Bahia, for example, all of them officially listed as *brancos*, Pierson found that about a quarter possessed obvious Negroid characteristics.[11] Wagley reports a case in which townspeople refused to identify the town drunk as "white," despite his appearance, and insisted that the leading woman in the town was white rather than a dark mulatto.[12]

Although "European physical traits [have] definite prestige and aesthetic values among all ranks of society," [13] racial traits in themselves do not constitute a major barrier to opportunity or to social intercourse. *Prêtos* or those of mixed ancestry who rise in the social order change both their social and economic position and in some measure the racial terms applied to them. "Money whitens the skin" is a Brazilian saying.[14] "Once risen, [lighter mulattoes] are no longer considered 'mulattoes' but 'brancos,' it being thought 'inelegant and impertinent' to remind such persons of their racial origins." [15]

Color prejudice is readily expressed in Brazil and there are many invidious stereotypes of Negroes comparable to those present in the United States. In addition, discrimination on the basis of color does occur occasionally. Prejudice and discrimination, however, are characteristically directed toward individuals rather than groups, and these facts do not contradict the image of Brazil as a racial "democracy."

. . . there is obviously a wide gulf in Brazil [Wagley writes] between what people say and what they do, between verbal and social behavior. The emotional tone surrounding color prejudice is generally lighthearted and amused, and mixed with a liberal sprinkling of earthy appreciation. [One observer] records the heckling of a football team by fans in racial terms so strong that they would have caused a race riot in the United States. Marvin Harris tells of a white man . . . who stoutly maintained that a Negro, even if he was a *doutor* (a professional) should not be associated with, but who bowed and scraped when he actually met a Negro engineer. Also, set against the derogatory attitude, there is a certain pride in the "Brazilian race" and even in the *prêto* (Negro). . . . Derogatory attitudes and stereotypes remain in the Brazilian tradition and can be called upon in any competitive situation (if there is no other way to get at your competitor you can always call him a *prêto*), but they generally lack conviction as determinants of behavior.[16]

Racial characteristics, however, are closely linked with class position. *Prêtos* typically occupy a low position in the class order and *brancos* a high one; most of the middle and upper classes are white, and dark-skinned Brazilians have probably experienced less social mobility than have Negroes in the United States. But these facts reflect the history of the country and the relatively static Brazilian economy rather than racial discrimination.

Barriers between persons with different racial characteristics are those of class rather than of color—and class distinctions are very sharply drawn. But those who do overcome these barriers are socially accepted, whatever their racial traits. Members of the middle and upper classes who do have some Negro ancestry are not excluded or significantly limited in their social intercourse. Thus at least one President of Brazil has been what in the United States would be called a "Negro." Pierson reports several cases of ostensibly white, upper-class persons of definite Negro ancestry. Discovery by others of such facts "will lead . . . to no alteration in the social standing of the individual involved, to no modification in the social esteem in which he or she is held . . . a significant indication of the character of the Brazilian racial situation as compared with that in the United States, for example, where a similar revelation would create a scandal."[17]

These marked differences between Brazil and the United States reflect important contrasts in their history and social structure. Brazil was colonized originally by Portuguese who brought with them little concern for racial differences—and no women. A long period of Moorish domination in Portugal had produced a relatively dark-skinned population, a liking for dusky beauties, and a readiness for miscegenation in their overseas adventures. As has often been the case when colonization has been predominantly by men rather than by families, they took Indians as wives or mistresses, even as they ruthlessly exploited the natives. Later, they frequently chose their women from among the Africans who were imported as slaves.

Miscegenation quickly became a widespread pattern. The 1950 census reported that 61.6 per cent of the population was white, 11 per cent black, and 26.6 per cent brown, with the remainder yellow.

But, as Wagley points out, "It should be remembered that the census data reflect racial identity as reckoned by the respondents and sometimes by the census taker; a survey by objective anthropological standards would certainly show a larger percentage of mixed types." [18] Many Brazilians now believe that a progressive racial homogenization is taking place, eliminating chiefly the darker-skinned group and "lightening" the entire population. That there may be some basis for this belief is evident in the fact that the proportion of those classified as *prêto* declined by almost one-third between 1940 and 1950.

Slavery, which began early because the Indians were neither numerous nor easily adaptable to the labor needs of a plantation economy, was not legally abolished until 1888, but the process by which it was eliminated began much earlier, was much more protracted, and was much less violent than the traumatic events that put an end to slavery in the United States. From early in the colonial period there existed various devices by which slaves could be freed. Men frequently set free their own illegitimate offspring of slave mothers, and often manumitted others in their wills or as part of customary yearly celebrations. In addition, slaves could purchase their own freedom, and both law and public opinion required owners to accept payment when offered by a slave. Emancipation societies bought freedom for many slaves, and some owners voluntarily set their chattels at liberty. By the time slavery was officially abolished, most blacks and *mestiços* were already free. The release of some 600,000 slaves did not create an upheaval comparable to that generated by both the Civil War and the emancipation of the Negroes in the United States. Nor was the colored population defined as an immediate threat to

the existing social and political order as Negroes were in the South after the Civil War—and as some white southerners still believe them to be today.

These facts—widespread miscegenation, the blurring of physical differences in the population, the gradual freeing of Negro slaves—have prevented the growth of a racist ideology. Instead Brazilians often express pride in the absence of racism and in the relative disregard of racial differences. Physical attributes like skin color are not ignored, but they do not provide the basis for significant group divisions.

Negroes in the United States

Unlike Brazil, where racial variations are so great that no clear distinction is made between white and black, American society draws a sharp line between the races. Negroes are set off by both color and ancestry. Identification as a Negro is based not only upon visible attributes but also upon knowledge of who one's parents—or grandparents or great-grandparents—were. Even when appearance is ostensibly Caucasoid, known Negro ancestry is usually enough to identify an individual as a Negro. In 1960 the United States Census classified all those of mixed ancestry as Negro, including "persons of mixed American Indian and Negro descent, unless the Indian ancestry very definitely predominates or unless the individual is regarded as an Indian in the community." [19]

Thus identified, Negroes have often been described as a caste marked by an unchangeable—and inferior—status. The warrant for considering Negroes to be a caste lies in the presence of restraints upon intermarriage and of barriers to intimate social intercourse with whites. The laws of twenty-nine states prohibit racial intermarriage, defined in various ways, and there is a very widely accepted and deeply rooted belief that it is undesirable. Apart from a few groups and individuals, especially within certain of the professional, entertainment, and artistic occupations, who draw no color line, Negroes and whites rarely exchange the intimacy of home-to-home visits, or come together in other than formal situations. A few light-skinned persons with some Negro ancestry are able to "pass" permanently into the "white" world and many more with similar physical credentials become "temporary whites" in recreational, consumer, and occupational activities. But most Negroes, whatever their abilities or accomplishments, are unable to cross the caste barrier, and many whose appearances would allow them to are unwilling to do so. The way in which the Negro is identified, as Myrdal points out, helps maintain the social division between the races. "Had the caste line been drawn differently—for example, on the criterion of predominance of white or Negro ancestry or of cultural assimilation—it would not have been so possible to hold the caste line so rigid." [20]

Unlike the Hindu caste system, however, no accepted religious ideology sanctions Negro inferiority, although a few staunch advocates of "white supremacy" continue to quote Scripture in support of their views. Many forms of discrimination limit the Negroes' political rights, their economic and educational opportunities, access to good housing, and the use of public and quasi-public facilities, but these constraints are neither as widespread nor as difficult to break through as the norms governing marriage and personal relationships. And from the point of view of the dominant American values,

discrimination against Negroes is an anomaly that must constantly be rationalized and justified—or must eventually be eliminated.

In the years since the Supreme Court declared in 1954 in *Brown vs. Board of Education of Topeka* that "separate but equal" schools were unconstitutional, there have, in fact, been substantial changes in the position of the Negro and in the structure of Negro–white relations. Indeed, so substantial have been these changes that many observers have characterized what has happened and what continues to happen in the mid-1960s as the "Negro Revolution."

In any social revolution, specifying a starting point is inevitably in some measure arbitrary. Behind the 1954 decision lay a series of cases that began with one decided in 1938 in which the University of Missouri Law School was required to admit a qualified Negro applicant. Many other events, it could be argued, were of equal and perhaps of even greater importance. The Montgomery bus boycott of 1955 led by Martin Luther King, for example, was the first instance of organized mass resistance to the pattern of race relations in the South. Passage of the Civil Rights Act of 1957 was the first legislation by Congress seeking to protect the rights of Negroes since 1875. The importance of the *Brown* case lay in the fact that it applied to schools at all levels, and not merely to professional or graduate schools. It was, therefore, clearly evident to both whites and Negroes that it signaled a massive change, as well as providing a legal—and ultimately contributing to the moral—basis for a challenge to the entire fabric of Negro-white relations.

If we are to understand these events and other dramatic and important actions—the student sit-ins in 1960, the "freedom rides" in 1961, the March on Washington in 1963, the Watts riots in 1965, the voter-registration march through Mississippi initiated by James Meredith in 1966—they must be located in the structural and cultural context out of which they emerged. There are elements of continuity as well as of change in the relations between whites and Negroes and in the position of the Negro in American society, as well as in the sociological variables that affect them— the structure of political power, economic institutions, varying and often conflicting values, attitudes, and interests. Both whites and Negroes act within a complex social setting, their actions often affected by how they define the frequently unclear and ill-defined situation in which they find themselves.

There is considerable debate over the speed with which the Negro Revolution is taking place. For many Negroes it is far too slow; for many whites much too fast. There can be little doubt that in some respects the position of the Negro has improved. But it is equally true that Negroes in American society remain substantially disadvantaged.

The disadvantages suffered by Negroes are clearly demonstrated in a comparison of their occupations, income, and education with those of whites. Table 10 gives the occupational distribution of whites and nonwhites (over 90 per cent of whom are Negroes) for 1960, as reported in the decennial census of that year. Almost three-quarters (74.4 per cent) of male nonwhites were unskilled or semiskilled laborers or service workers, compared with less than one-third (32.7) per cent of the white male population. Among employed nonwhite women, over 70 per cent were service workers or held unskilled or semiskilled jobs, more than twice as many, relatively, as among white women, only

33.6 per cent of whom were in these categories. In the South, Negroes are even more heavily concentrated in menial, poorly paid occupations.

Yet these figures represent substantial improvement over the past, for in 1930, 60 per cent of Negro men were unskilled laborers compared with 36.5 per cent in 1960. The proportions of professionals, clerical workers, and skilled workers have grown, although slowly, from 1.5 to 3.9 per cent, from 1.7 to 5.0 per cent, and from 4.8 to 10.2 per cent, respectively.[21]

No such progress is evident in the rate of unemployment, which has consistently been much higher among Negroes than among whites. In 1950, 5 per cent of whites were unemployed, compared with 8.5 per cent of nonwhites. In 1960, the comparable figures were 5.6 and 10.2, and in March, 1965, when unemployment was finally diminishing after a long period of relatively high unemployment, 5.1 per cent of whites were without work compared with 9.2 per cent of nonwhites.[22]

In education, Negroes are also much worse off than whites, although there has been some progress in recent decades. In 1960, 41.9 per cent of all nonwhite males over twenty-five years of age had less than an eighth-grade education, compared with only 17 per cent of whites. Among females, the figures were 36.1 and 14.9. Only 25.8 per cent of nonwhite males and 28.8 of nonwhite females had completed four years of high school, compared with 49.3 per cent of white males and 51 per cent of white females. Only 5.6 per cent of nonwhite males had completed four years of college, half as many as among whites.

With the over-all improvement in education in the United States, the number of Negroes with relatively few years of schooling has been substantially diminished, although a marked differential re-

Table 10

OCCUPATIONAL STATUS OF WHITES AND NONWHITES * IN THE UNITED STATES, BY SEX, 1960

	Male		Female	
	White	*Nonwhite*	*White*	*Nonwhite*
Professional, technical, and kindred	11.0%	3.9%	13.8%	7.5%
Managers, officials, and proprietors, except farm	11.5	2.3	4.0	1.2
Clerical and kindred	7.1	5.0	32.7	8.5
Sales workers	7.4	1.5	8.7	1.7
Craftsmen, foremen, and kindred	20.5	10.2	1.3	0.7
Operatives and kindred	19.5	23.5	15.7	12.8
Private household workers	0.1	0.7	4.1	34.3
Service workers, except private household	5.2	13.7	12.4	20.7
Farmers and farm managers	5.6	4.4	0.5	0.7
Farm laborers and foremen	2.3	7.1	0.9	2.9
Laborers, except farm and mine	5.6	19.4	0.5	1.0
Occupation not reported	4.2	8.4	5.3	8.1
Total Number	39,461,680	4,005,266	18,548,577	2,623,724

* Nonwhites include Indians and Orientals, although Negroes constitute over 90 per cent of the total.
U.S. Bureau of the Census, *U.S. Census of Population: 1960, General Social and Economic Characteristics, United States Summary*, Final Report PC(1)–1C (Washington, D.C.: U.S. Government Printing Office, 1962), Table 87, pp. 1–216.

mains. In 1960 only 13.9 per cent of all nonwhites between the ages of twenty-five and twenty-nine had not completed the eighth grade, compared with 29.3 per cent among those thirty-five to forty-four years old. Yet these figures are still twice as high as among whites, only 5.5 per cent of whom in the twenty-five to twenty-nine-year-old group had less than eight years of schooling.[23]

Moreover, there is a marked differential in the quality of education that is available. A substantial proportion of Negroes are still in states in which the per capita expenditure on schools is low— and in those states expenditures for Negroes have usually been lower than for whites. Many other Negroes are in city slums in which the schools are old, facilities inadequate, and provision for the problems created by poverty and limited cultural backgrounds minimal.

In view of the kinds of jobs they have (if any), the amount of unemployment, and the level of education, it is hardly surprising that income levels among Negroes are much lower than among whites. Table 11 shows the incomes of white and nonwhite families from 1947 through 1965. Although there has been a consistent upward trend for both groups, in March, 1965, a much larger proportion of nonwhite families (38.6 per cent compared with only 15.3 per cent) was earning incomes of less than $3,000. Almost one-quarter of white families had incomes of $10,000 or more, but only 6.6 per cent of nonwhites earned that much.

Low occupational status, limited education, and inadequate income—and the

Table 11

MONEY INCOME—PERCENTAGE DISTRIBUTION OF FAMILIES BY INCOME LEVEL, BY COLOR OF HEAD, 1947–1965*

	Total	Under $1,000	$1,000 to $1,999	$2,000 to $2,999	$3,000 to $3,999	$4,000 to $4,999	$5,000 to $5,999	$6,000 to $6,999	$7,000 to $9,999	$10,000 to $14,999	$15,000 and over	Median income
White families												
1947	100.0	9.0	14.9	22.3	20.8	12.4	8.1	9.5		3.0		$3,157
1950	100.0	10.0	12.2	17.3	21.3	14.4	9.6	5.5	6.1	3.5		3,445
1955	100.0	6.6	8.7	10.4	14.3	16.0	13.4	9.9	13.9	5.3	1.5	4,605
1960	100.0	4.1	6.9	8.1	9.4	10.5	13.3	11.2	21.3	11.2	4.1	5,835
1961	100.0	4.2	6.6	7.8	9.1	10.3	12.1	10.6	22.0	12.0	5.1	5,981
1962	100.0	3.3	6.3	7.4	8.6	9.8	11.8	11.3	22.3	13.7	5.3	6,237
1963	100.0	3.2	5.8	6.9	8.2	8.8	11.3	10.5	23.8	15.6	5.9	6,548
March, 1965	100.0	2.7	5.4	7.2	7.7	8.3	10.0	10.1	23.6	24.1		6,858
Non-white families												
1947	100.0	28.8	33.5	18.8	8.4	4.4	3.1	3.0		0.1		1,614
1950	100.0	28.1	25.3	23.5	13.5	4.3	1.9	1.5	1.7	0.3		1,869
1955	100.0	19.0	20.7	17.6	17.2	11.1	5.8	4.8	3.1	0.6	†	2,549
1960	100.0	13.4	18.3	14.8	14.0	10.4	8.7	6.7	8.7	4.3	0.6	3,233
1961	100.0	12.7	18.0	16.8	12.7	11.7	8.0	5.8	9.0	4.4	1.2	3,191
1962	100.0	10.9	17.3	16.3	15.1	11.4	9.2	6.2	8.2	4.3	0.8	3,330
1963	100.0	9.2	16.3	17.6	13.5	10.9	8.7	7.3	10.8	4.1	1.6	3,465
March, 1965	100.0	7.9	14.3	16.4	14.9	11.6	8.8	7.7	11.9	6.6		3,724

* Beginning in 1960, figures include Alaska and Hawaii.
† Less than 0.05 per cent.
U.S. Bureau of the Census, *Statistical Abstract of the United States: 1965* (Washington, D.C.: U.S. Government Printing Office, 1965), Table 470, p. 342; and *Current Population Reports*, Series P-20, No. 145 (Washington, D.C.: U.S. Government Printing Office, December 27, 1965).

problems and pathologies that characteristically accompany such conditions—reflect historical circumstances and prevailing patterns of discrimination. Torn from their native cultures, Negroes were brought to an alien world as slaves. After emancipation, various efforts were made to assist them, but many, perhaps most, Negroes were soon left to their own resources. With the exception of a relatively small number, most of whom were of mixed ancestry and had been freed before the Civil War, they were quickly reduced to a crude existence in the South as farm tenants (chiefly sharecroppers), domestic servants, and unskilled laborers.

By the early years of the twentieth century, most of the 90 per cent of the Negroes who lived in the South were effectively disfranchised, constrained, and segregated by a complex set of "Jim Crow" laws and customs that "extended to churches and schools, to housing and jobs, to eating and drinking . . . to virtually all forms of public transportation, to sports and recreations, to hospitals, orphanages, prisons, and asylums, and ultimately to funeral homes, morgues, and cemeteries." [24] Dependent upon the landlords from whom they rented land and the employers for whom they worked, politically impotent, with minimal opportunities for education, incapable of resisting the rigorous and sometimes violent pressure that sought to keep them in their inferior position, Negroes were at the bottom of a rural and economically undeveloped region that was itself almost an internal colony of the commercial and industrial North.

This system of discrimination and segregation persisted with only small changes for several decades, part of a social order in which "white supremacy" was a key feature. The structure of Negro-white relations was sustained by a complex and interlocking set of sociological and social–psychological factors.

For the dominant whites, the subordination of the Negro has always provided important gains. Slavery was not only profitable to slaveholders, but it also provided other, less easily calculated, advantages: Negro mistresses, avoidance of heavy labor, numerous servants to make life easier, the sense of power and self-aggrandizement that inevitably comes from the ability to give orders and be obeyed. Even after the abolition of slavery, the whites were able to derive substantial benefits by maintaining a pattern of discrimination and segregation. In his detailed analysis of the social and psychological structure of a town in the Deep South in the mid-1930s, John Dollard demonstrates in detail the economic, prestige, and sexual gains accruing to the whites from their superior position. Negroes provided cheap and submissive labor, their deference and respect for whites were gratifying and ego-enhancing, and, although white women

were off-bounds for Negro men, Negro women were legitimate objects of sexual advances for white men. [25]

The several aspects of the Negroes' position formed an interrelated whole, a "vicious circle" in which each disability helped to justify and sustain the others. Because of their limited education, most Negroes were (as many still are) unprepared for any but menial jobs. Low income meant low standards of living and poor health and often precluded any but the briefest schooling for children, even if it were available. And in the pre-World War II South, particularly during the Depression, there were few jobs of any sort available and only extremely limited educational facilities.

Without education, too, there was little likelihood of any participation in political life, which, in any case, was closed to Negroes through a variety of devices—legal and extralegal. Unable to vote, Negroes could bring little pressure to bear to increase educational opportunities, to improve the educational facilities open to them, or to establish public policies that might raise their economic level. Indeed, Negroes received less than their proportionate share of the aid made available to the South during the Depression of the 1930s by the Federal government because of their lack of both political power and political know-how.

For lower-class Negroes, at least, there were some compensating gratifications to be found in their way of life. [26] With their lower status came greater freedom of emotional expression. Aggressive impulses were openly expressed, although they had to be directed within the Negro group and not against the whites, and sexual desires could be more freely satisfied, as they were not constrained by middle-class cultural prohibitions. Because whites expected them to be unreliable, lazy, and careless, Negroes could often exploit these images to their own advantage by avoiding work and shirking responsibility. "The Negro had learned a thousand subtle and disguised ways to express his natural resentment—the slovenly broom stroke, the crooked nail, the idiotic 'yassuh,' the misplaced tool, the Uncle Remus story—in which the defenseless Br'er Rabbit outwits all the powers, thrones, and dominions arrayed against him." [27] These patterns of behavior did not make the Negro "happy," but they did help him to endure his disadvantaged status.

The image of the "happy Negro," derived from the absence of middle-class restraints, and the facts of ignorance and poor living standards were linked by whites with theories of inherent Negro inferiority, innate laziness, and a presumed desire to submit to white authority, in order to rationalize and justify the exploitation and subordination of the Negro. In the face of the democratic and equalitarian values of American culture, defenders of the system of discrimination and segregation called upon folk tales, jokes, personal experiences, scientific reports whenever possible, and even Scripture to support their view that Negroes were inferior and incapable of improvement and wanted no change.

But at bottom a system of discrimination that offers relatively few gratifications to a minority group rests upon force and the threat of force. Control of the power of the state permitted whites to enforce the laws—which they wrote—that imposed segregation or denied access to public facilities or provided wholly inadequate financing for Negro schools. When legal or conventional norms were ignored or challenged, lynching, bombing, cross-burning, beating, and threats were used—as they have been in recent years—in order to stem Negro efforts to break down racial barriers, gain new opportunities, and achieve equal status.

The Negro Revolution has challenged many features of this system, but the system itself had already begun to change before the dramatic events of the 1950s and 1960s. Improvement in the position of the Negro, which contributed to the emergence of the Negro Revolution, was due to a substantial extent to large-scale changes taking place in the South as well as in the rest of the nation. Continued industrialization and urban growth have altered the geographical distribution of the Negroes, the opportunities open to them, the needs of the dominant whites, and the whole tenor of southern life. Drawn by the prospect of better jobs and greater opportunities, Negroes began leaving the South in substantial numbers after World War I. By 1940 almost a quarter of the Negro population lived in other parts of the country, and by 1960 over two-fifths. By 1975—and perhaps sooner—it has been estimated, more than half of all Negroes in the United States will be living outside the South. [28]

In both the South and elsewhere, the Negroes have also become urban residents. By 1960 three-fifths of Southern Negroes were living in cities; in other parts of the nation almost all Negroes were urban—fourteen of every fifteen in the Northeast, sixteen of every seventeen in the north central states, ten of every eleven in the West. A third of all Negroes in 1960 were living in the twenty-five largest American cities. Indeed, Negroes were slightly more urban (73 per cent) than whites (70 per cent).

Movement out of the South and into cities has not freed Negroes from their disabilities, and the problems of Negro–white relations have become acute

in many urban centers. But urban employment, in the South and elsewhere, has meant higher wages, better living standards, access to better education than that available in the rural South. Outside the South, at least, Negroes were freed from legal and customary constraints. As their numbers in cities grew, particularly in the North and Midwest and more recently on the West Coast, Negroes have been able to organize their efforts more effectively and to secure political concessions, both locally and nationally.

Social and economic programs initiated during the New deal—unemployment compensation, social security, minimum wage standards, farm relief—have been of special value for Negroes who were, and in large measure still are, concentrated at the bottom reaches of the economy. The elimination of segregation in the military services after World War II and the impact of military experience upon both Negroes and whites who served with them contributed further to the lowering of barriers facing Negroes and to increasing unwillingness to tolerate a subordinate status. Except for the recurrent recessions of the 1950s, during which Negroes were typically hardest hit, the post-World War II prosperity and economic expansion have provided opportunities for many Negroes to secure better jobs, earn more

Large-scale economic and technological changes in the rural South, particularly the introduction of cotton-picking machines and other elaborate farm equipment, have made many Negro farm workers superfluous and forced them into the city.

money, achieve a higher standard of living, and offer their children greater educational opportunities.

Improvements in the Negroes' lot, rather than muting their demands, have stimulated organized efforts to break down legal, political, educational, economic, and social barriers. Leadership of this effort has come on the whole from the better educated: Martin Luther King, Jr. for example, with a doctorate in philosophy from Boston University; Stokely Carmichael, who became head of the Student Nonviolent Coordinating Committee (SNCC) in 1966, with a degree from Howard University; James Farmer, founder of the Congress of Racial Equality (CORE), son of a college professor and a theology student at Howard University. For the bulk of the Negro population, the improvements that have occurred have only awakened the desire for futher progress—for equal treatment, equal opportunities, the right to vote, access to the goods and services and facilities of an affluent society. What once may have seemed distant and out of reach now appears possible; traditional restraints can no longer be tolerated or accepted, and there are even demands that Negroes be compensated for three centuries of exploitation.

Negro efforts to gain equal status and opportunity in American society have taken many forms, from the modest self-help program advocated by Booker T. Washington at the turn of the century, the activities of the National Association for the Advancement of Colored People founded in 1909 by Negro intellectuals and white liberals, and the Back to Africa Movement led by Marcus Garvey during the 1920s to the various civil rights and "black nationalist" groups of the 1950s and 1960s. The programs and even the explicit goals of these groups have varied,

reflecting the diverse responses of Negroes to the complex difficulties facing them. For the NAACP and the Southern Christian Leadership Conference headed by Dr. King, the objective has been equality and full integration into American society. In the summer of 1966 the theme of "black power," interpreted in various ways by different groups, became a key issue. For such extremist groups as the Black Muslims, the goal has been complete separation from the "white devils" under an ideology of black superiority.[29]

Much of the struggle for Negro equality has focused upon legislation and political activity. For many years it had been argued, not least by some sociologists,[30] that race relations could not be changed by legal action, but only by the gradual transformation of attitudes and customs. Laws cannot change folkways or mores, it was claimed, or eliminate prejudice. Yet in fact much of the structure of race relations in the South had been imposed by "Jim Crow" legislation, and it is clearly evident that discrimination can be affected by legal action. Under pressure from Negro leaders who threatened a mass march on Washington, President Roosevelt issued an executive order in 1941 forbidding racial discrimination in companies holding government contracts, and some progress was made. Executive orders issued by President Truman led to the desegregation of the armed services. The first effective Fair Employment Practices Law was passed by New York State in 1945, and many other states and many cities have since passed similar legislation, as well as laws forbidding various other forms of discrimination. The omnibus Civil Rights Act of 1964 strengthened machinery and procedures established in earlier legislation to secure and protect Negro voting rights, prohibited discrimination in public accommodations and public facilities, banned discrimination in employment, and in various other ways sought to improve the methods for assuring Negroes equal rights.

The effectiveness of legislation, however, depends heavily upon how it is enforced. There has been considerable complaint by Negroes that civil-rights legislation has not been carried out with sufficient energy and aggressiveness. Inevitably there is room for administrative discretion, the exercise of which may be affected by legal and political considerations—as well as by the attitudes of the administrators. One result of the fact that by and large civil-rights legislation has not lived up to the expectations of its advocates and supporters has been the pressure for both more legislation and stronger political action to ensure strict enforcement of the law.

Yet it is also evident that many of the disabilities and difficulties of Negroes do not yield readily to direct government action, but are dependent upon the state of the economy, welfare measures, patterns of urban growth, educational policies and practices, and even international relations. Because these elements are also governed or affected by public policy, some Negro groups have extended their advocacy to political issues seemingly unrelated to race relations, such as the war in Viet Nam, or have challenged established institutions such as the neighborhood school.

Passage of civil-rights legislation and some of the changes that have occurred in the position of the Negro are the result not merely of his greater aggressiveness but also of the wider acceptance of the legitimacy of his claim to equal status and treatment. This acceptance in turn reflects the fact that the gains once derived from Negro subordination are not as important as they once were to substantial segments of American society. New agricultural technology has eliminated the need for a great deal of cheap labor. Modern industry no longer requires unskilled labor, and its demands for better-trained and more skilled workers—white or black—have increased. With its bureaucratic organization, industry can largely ignore racial etiquette in its employee relations; maintenance of racial distinctions may actually prove costly and inefficient. Changing patterns of sex behavior among both whites and Negroes have diminished the extent and importance of sexual contact between white men and Negro women. Economic growth in the South and continued prosperity and high wages elsewhere have eliminated some status anxieties and made some whites less concerned about associating with Negroes on an equal basis—at least on the job or in formal circumstances.

Changes in the functions of the system of discrimination have not occurred equally in all segments of the social structure, and considerable resistance to further Negro progress remains. Whereas some groups can accept the breakdown of established patterns of segregation and discrimination without feeling that their interests and status are being endangered, others find a serious threat in the advances Negroes have made and are making. There is ample evidence to suggest that the staunchest opposition and hostility to the Negroes' efforts to break down legal and conventional barriers are found among lower-middle-class and working-class whites,[31] whose feelings are often exploited by politicians seeking election to public office. Not only do they see an increasing number of Negroes who are achieving middle-class occupations, income, and style of life, but in areas once monopolized by whites they now find growing Negro competition. As this competition comes from persons who are defined as inferior, it is looked upon as a substantial danger to their own status. The Negroes' drive to break down restrictions, to pursue their ends by political means, and to reject any evidence of social inferiority because of their race is therefore met not only with intense hostility but also, on occasion, with violence.

As the number of Negroes in cities outside the South has grown, anti-Negro attitudes and actions have also spread. Although free from legal constraints outside the South, Negroes in large cities have experienced low wages, widespread unemployment, because of the limited number of jobs either open to them or for which they were qualified, inadequate housing, and often inferior educational facilities. As it became evident that solutions to these problems might require drastic measures, those whites most directly affected began to offer resistance. Lower-middle-class whites objected to Negroes moving into their neighborhoods for fear that property values might decline. White parents were reluctant to see school children bused from one neighborhood to another in order to equalize racial distribution in the schools; for Negroes such a measure meant equalizing opportunities, while for whites it meant both intimate social relations and, perhaps more significantly, the danger of lowered educational standards. Whether warranted or not, these fears generated tension and hostility among whites, with resulting resentment and anger among Negroes. When the frustrations and resentment among Negroes became too great, they burst into violence and rioting—in Los Angeles, Chicago, Omaha, Cleveland, Rochester, Philadelphia, New York City—with predictions of further

outbursts if measures were not taken to improve the situation of the urban Negroes.

The Negro problem, Gunnar Myrdal pointed out in his classic study, *An American Dilemma* (published in 1944), is in large measure a problem for whites.

It is . . . the white majority group that naturally determines the Negro's "place." The Negro's entire life, and, consequently, also his opinions on the Negro problem [as well as his actions] are, in the main, to be considered as secondary reactions to more primary pressures from the side of the dominant white majority.[32]

As the Negro Revolution has grown, this assertion has probably become somewhat less accurate a description. Whites, it is true, still control the major institutions of American society; they can yield, resist, temporize; they can accept or initiate some changes and reject others. But the decisions whites must make are increasingly influenced by Negro actions and efforts, and their freedom of action is increasingly limited by the pressures emanating from the Negro community.

Jews in the United States

Unlike Negroes, Orientals, and other racially identifiable groups, the Jews along with many ethnic minorities are marked only by their distinctive cultural traits. Racial theories have sometimes been used to justify differential treatment of such ethnic groups, some of which occasionally develop a spurious but nonetheless real "race consciousness," but the differences that do exist between them and others are social and cultural in character and in origin, and not biological. In these ethnic groups the absence of readily identifiable physical attributes, in fact, is frequently of considerable sociological importance, for it makes possible a more rapid assimilation and even physical amalgamation of minority groups into the larger society.

Despite their lack of readily visible physical traits, however, Jews in the United States are set apart by a deeper and less easily bridged "fissure line" [33] than any other white ethnic group. Both hostility and discriminatory practice from without and strong loyalties within the group keep the Jews persistently and clearly separate. Group identity, which was to some degree thawing in the congenial American social climate, was markedly stimulated by the rise of Nazism and has gained further strength from the post-World War II revival in religious interest and participation.

Jews came early to the New World; the first small contingent arrived in New York in 1654. These early newcomers encountered little prejudice or discrimination, and before the end of the eighteenth century the few thousand Jews in the United States already possessed religious freedom and civic equality. Although their numbers grew steadily—by 1880 there were about a quarter of a million Jews in this country—they met with little difficulty until the last decades of the nine-

teenth century, when overt anti-Semitism appeared and discrimination against Jews became accepted practice in some segments of American life.

The emergence and growth of anti-Semitism resulted basically from the changing nature of American society and the changing character and size of the Jewish population. Before 1880, most Jews in America had come from Germany or from Eastern Europe via Germany. The revolutionary changes that had taken place in Western Europe in the nineteenth century had already released them from some of the restrictions of the ghetto before they migrated, and in America they continued the process of change already underway in their culture by quickly discarding much of the old ritual and tradition. The mass immigration that began in the 1880s was not only larger than any that had preceded it but was also strik-

Efforts of Negroes confined to urban ghettoes to break out into white middle-class areas have generated a great deal of opposition. Here a Negro demonstration for "open housing" in a white suburb of Chicago stimulated such strong and open expression of hostility that massive police protection for the demonstrators was necessary.

United Press International Photo

ingly different culturally. Between 1870 and 1914, more than two million Jews arrived in the United States, of whom more than three-fifths came from Russia and more than one-fifth came from Austria-Hungary. These eastern European Jews brought with them a way of life that differed in many ways from that of their predecessors: They spoke Yiddish rather than German; many of them were deeply attached to a religious orthodoxy that prescribed elaborate daily rituals; those who were not religiously committed shared, like the others, a self-conscious folk culture; and they came in such numbers that they could sustain traditional forms of communal life in the great urban centers where most of them settled.

Discrimination had begun, however, even before the mass immigration of the end of the nineteenth century. It started with the exclusion of well-to-do Jews from resort hotels and social clubs, and it reflected the efforts of a newly rich upper class uncertain of its own status to define and protect their prerogatives by blocking "Jewish entry into the 'social life' of the upper class and thereby [restricting] Jewish ability to compete." [34] The social, economic, and political tensions and conflicts of the late nineteenth and early twentieth centuries, coupled with the mass immigration, led to the spread of anti-Semitism to other groups and to other forms of discrimination.

During the years of mass immigration, a widespread hostility developed toward all groups from Eastern and Southern Europe, and new racist theories were formulated that argued the innate inferiority of these new immigrants and were used to support severe restrictions upon further immigration. The Jews, who were different from both native-born Americans and other immigrants not only in their language, dress, and manners but also in

religion, came in for special attention. The prominence of some Jews in European financial capitals lent support to an increasingly accepted myth of a Jewish financial conspiracy to dominate the world; and a pervasive rural and small-town hostility toward Wall Street was readily focused upon the Jews, particularly by certain frustrated Populists like Tom Watson of Georgia, for whom predominantly city-dwelling Jews also symbolized urban corruption. The speed with which many Jews were able to establish themselves in business aroused jealousy and contributed further to the image of the Jew as a sharp and ruthless businessman who offered unfair competition to others.

What began largely as social exclusion spread into occupational and educational discrimination and occasional violence or the threat of violence: the lynching of a Jew in Atlanta in 1915, the activities of the revived Ku Klux Klan in the Twenties, the "lunatic fringe" or "hate" groups of the 1930s and 1940s.[35] Efforts were made at various times to imitate the political anti-Semitism found in Europe—in France at the turn of the century, pre-Revolutionary Russia, Nazi Germany—but these attempts met with only minimal success, although they undoubtedly contributed to anti-Semitic prejudice.

Despite the prejudice and discrimination directed toward them, Jews have had extraordinary economic success in the United States. Warner and Srole reported that in "Yankee City" the Jews had moved up from their original working-class position more rapidly than had any other immigrant group. Recent studies of the class composition of American Jews finds them heavily—and increasingly—concentrated in the middle class, in either business or the professions, and above the national average in income.[36] Some of this mobility is due to what Nathan Glazer has called "a passion for education that was unique in American history." [37] (In the mid-1960s over three-quarters of Jewish college-age youths were attending some college or university, compared with a national figure of roughly 40 per cent.)

Relatively sustained prosperity since the end of World War II and the prevailing emphasis upon tolerance for religious differences have substantially reduced overt expressions of anti-Semitism, yet Jews remain in large measure set apart, despite the marked success with which they have found a place in economic and political life. They continue to be excluded from many clubs, from intimate social intercourse with others of the same class levels, from some desirable residential communities—and they find some persisting evidence of occupational discrimination, particularly in the higher levels of some types of business and industry.

The social barriers, however, are in part reciprocal. Jews possess the lowest rate of intermarriage of any religious group; in a 1957 study, "about $3\frac{1}{2}$ per cent of married Jews were married to non-Jews." [38] An elaborate communal apparatus built up to meet collective needs sustains the separate identity and indeed in some respects encourages it. But the continued separation of Jews and non-Jews also reflects both active discrimination and the persistence of a polite anti-Semitism that often excludes Jews from "social" intercourse and concomitantly engenders among them a strong defensive desire to remain within the comfortable confines of their own group—hence the numerous Jewish hotels, camps, resorts, and so on.

Even when such social barriers are lowered, there persists among many Jews as a heritage from their historical experience of more than two millennia and, particularly from recent European experience, the lurking fear that beneath the surface there lies a latent reservoir of anti-Semitism ready to burst forth once again as it has in the past. (German Jews, for example, were the most fully assimilated Jews of Europe before the Nazis began their campaign to exterminate them completely—a fact that has been used by some Jewish leaders to oppose assimilation.) The "swastika epidemic" of 1960, which began in Germany but which saw over 600 incidents in the United States of desecration of synagogues and Jewish cemeteries with crudely painted swastikas and anti-Semitic epithets, and similar attacks on Jewish homes and businesses produced another reminder of the persistence of anti-Semitism.

A Jewish writer has posed the dilemma that American Jews often feel they face as follows:

For to a Jew the problem essentially is this: how can the Jewish people survive in the face of hostility which threatens to destroy us, and on the other hand, in the face of a friendliness which threatens to dissolve our group ties and submerge us as a whole by absorbing us individually. [39]

One result of this dilemma has been a considerable amount of self-searching among Jews about the problems of identity in a multigroup society, and their contributions to these problems inevitably throw light not only upon their own difficulties but those of other groups as well.

Prejudice

These cases demonstrate clearly the inadequacy of the popularly held view that the origins of discrimination and of racial and ethnic conflict are to be found in prejudice. The complex circumstances which give rise to and sustain both anti-Semitism and anti-Negro discrimination and prejudice provide ample evidence of the inadequacy of any theory that focuses exclusively, or even heavily, upon attitudes and feelings as the basic determinants of intergroup relations. But the importance of prejudice in helping to maintain certain social patterns should not be underestimated; as we noted earlier, it has often played an important role in racial and ethnic relations and warrants attention in this chapter. Our task here is to examine the nature, sources, and functions of prejudice.

The nature of prejudice is difficult to define; one man's prejudice is another man's gospel. It can perhaps be best understood as consisting of rigid and hostile attitudes directed toward a group or toward an individual because he is a member of a group, or, as Gordon Allport puts it, prejudice is "thinking ill of others without sufficient warrant." [40] These attitudes typically rest upon inaccurate or unsupported beliefs concerning the character of those against whom they are focused. Prejudice then has both *affective* and *cognitive* elements, that is, feelings toward others and ideas about what they are like. Because these ideas are emotionally charged, they are often resistant to change; prejudiced persons are often immune to even the most firmly established evidence that the presumed facts upon which their attitudes rest are false.

The line between prejudice and criticism is sometimes difficult to draw. Do objections to the policies of the National Association for the Advancement of Colored People reflect anti-Negro feeling? Is disapproval of Jewish efforts to aid Israel a manifestation of anti-Semitism? Is

doubt about the desirability of having a Catholic President evidence of prejudice? The marks of prejudice are the feelings that accompany critical judgments, acceptance of erroneous or unsupported assertions about another group, and the rigidity with which opinions are held. Like most other sociological and psychological categories, therefore, prejudice is a *variable* rather than a fixed entity.

Prejudice is learned; it is neither inherent nor automatically acquired. It stems from social experience and is often derived from others. As the individual acquires his own social identity and establishes group loyalties—as American, white Protestant Anglo-Saxon, Negro, Jew, Italian, or Frenchman—he learns to differentiate between himself and his ethnic compatriots on the one hand and those who are socially defined as different on the other. The very nature of organized society, therefore, contains the seeds of prejudice, for allegiance to the in-group and its values constitutes one of the preconditions for hostility toward other groups. Indeed, prejudice toward the outsider often serves to strengthen the bonds of solidarity within the group.

But awareness of differences between oneself and others need not lead to prejudice. An individual's attitudes toward other groups depend in large measure upon the culture in which he is reared and in which he lives. From that culture and through the groups to which he himself belongs, particularly his family, he acquires images, feelings, and beliefs with respect to persons who possess different values or a distinctive appearance. Parents and other adults—teachers, ministers, relatives, friends—may communicate their own attitudes and opinions through jokes, stories, ephithets, and expressions of opinion in informal conversation: for example, that Negroes are dirty, innately musical, but highly emotional and simple-minded, and that it would be degrading to accept them as equals in social situations; or, alternatively, that skin color is of little importance and that each individual should be judged for his own actions, abilities, and character. Or, again, parents—or others—may encourage children, directly or indirectly, to believe that Jews are sharp businessmen, too clannish, not to be trusted and therefore that one should have little to do with them; or, that Jews have different beliefs and customs, some attractive and others not, and like other groups will have their own share of rogues, villains, heroes, saints, and average people.

Conceptions of other groups are often deeply rooted in cultural traditions that contribute, often subtly, to racial and ethnic prejudices. Our traditional literature, for example, contains racial and ethnic figures who symbolize prevalent invidious stereotypes: Shylock, the rapacious and scheming Jew; Fagin, the rascally, greedy Jew; Uncle Tom, the subservient and loyal Negro; the treacherous and stealthy Injun Jim. A recent study of the relationship between Christian belief and attitudes toward Jews has shown clearly that "religious outlooks and religious images seem to be at the root of the anti-Semitism of millions of American adults." [41]

Prejudices—or nonprejudicial attitudes and feelings—can also be communicated through the mass media: books, magazines, newspapers, movies, radio, and television. Newspapers may contribute to the persistence of racial images by identifying muggers and murderers and drug addicts as Negroes or Puerto Ricans; white criminals are normally not identified by race in news stories. Radio, movies, and television have projected such stereotypes as the simple-minded Negro servant, the Negro "mammy," the Italian gangster, the Irish drunkard, the scheming Oriental. In a careful study of magazine fiction in 1946, Bernard Berelson and Patricia Salter discovered that members of ethnic minorities were usually assigned subservient roles, were often pictured in stereotyped, even caricatured terms, and were more frequently given low status or illegitimate occupations than the "white Protestants" who made up most of the fictional characters.[42] Treatment of ethnic minorities in the mass media has changed substantially since that study was done, however, as the result of pressure from ethnic organizations and an apparent shift in the cultural atmosphere. In movies and television, at least, crude stereotypes are now avoided, and members of minorities have either disappeared or are now often sympathetically portrayed, although often as unrealistically, if not as critically, as before.

In any society, stereotyped conceptions of members of other groups are perhaps inevitable; without some shorthand method of identifying and classifying people it would be impossible to get along. In this respect, stereotypes—generalized "pictures in our heads"—are of considerable importance. But stereotypes often rest upon unwarranted generalizations and are frequently applied indiscriminately to individual cases: Every Jew is a potential Fagin or Shylock; each Negro an Uncle Tom, or a carefree irresponsible, and unreliable child, or a dangerous, hostile, and aggressive savage intent on raping white women; each Russian is a Raskolnikov swept away by uncontrollable emotions or an agent—or victim—of the Soviet secret police; every

Frenchman is a debonair, worldly gentleman devoted mainly to *l'amour*.

Prejudices, then, and the stereotypes that help to sustain them are cultural products, acquired by those who share the culture. Prejudiced people are therefore conforming to the norms of their own groups and the expectations of their fellow members; expressions of prejudice reaffirm their membership and their unity with others. Failure to conform exposes them to criticism and social pressure, as illustrated in extreme cases by such epithets as "nigger lover."

To account for culturally patterned prejudice, one must examine the context in which it takes shape and the functions it performs. In some measure, as we have already noted, prejudice reflects reality; it is built upon some facts, however unrepresentative or misinterpreted. Negroes, for example, are physically different, on the whole they occupy a distinctive position in the class structure, and their educational and cultural level is lower than that of whites. But the more significant sources of prejudice are the functions it serves. Collective ideas emerge because they answer some needs, and one can therefore usually assume that when ideas are widely accepted they provide answers to problems with which people are concerned.

Because the "American Creed" of equality, freedom, and democracy is contradicted by the discrimination to which Negroes are subject, white Americans face a moral dilemma from which anti-Negro prejudice and the beliefs that sustain it provide an escape. By asserting that Negroes like to be ordered about, whites justify their power. By belittling Negro abilities, they excuse occupational discrimination. By assuming that Negro men invariably have designs upon white women, they provide a presumably legiti-

mate reason for their hostility and for the violence with which actual or imagined Negro advances toward white women are treated; only drastic measures, it is felt, will keep the Negro "in his place."

Prejudice may serve both economic and political functions. Anti-Semitism, for example, often serves to justify restrictions upon competition; by excluding Jewish competitors, some businessmen secure their own advantage. Jews—perhaps more than members of any other minority group—have also at times served as scapegoats upon whom the evils of the times or the difficulties of a particular group are blamed. The Nazis blamed the Jews for defeat in World War I and for the many serious problems faced by Germany during the period of the Weimar Republic. By focusing responsibility upon the Jews, they offered a simple explanation for a complex situation, thus relieving themselves of responsibility for their circumstances and making understandable, so it seemed to many, the harsh fate that had befallen many Germans during years of military defeat, inflation, and depression.

The hostility that is usually characteristic of prejudice is also part of each affected individual's personality, and its origins and functions in the psychic economy of the prejudiced individual cannot be ignored. Much recent research has sought to uncover the psychological sources of prejudice, and there appears to be some evidence that those persons who conform rigidly to prevailing values, who are submissive to authority and critical of those who flout conventional norms, and who are preoccupied with problems of power and status are likely to be prejudiced.

A chief source of such traits is to be found in the relations between child and parent. Strict and overbearing parents who are inconsistent in their disciplinary demands and do not express love and affection easily and freely are apt to foster resentment, emotional rigidity, and acceptance of authority, coupled with an underlying hostility toward both those who wield authority and those who are capable of resisting it and enough personal insecurity to develop a tendency toward rigid conformity to social norms. These traits are accompanied by a reservoir of aggression and hostility that are likely to be focused upon those who have no power and do not represent authority—typically minorities and "outgroups." [43] For these people, then, prejudice serves important psychological functions by providing an outlet for bottled-up impulses generated by their life experience.

When prejudice is culturally sanctioned, as among many white southerners, for example, the psychological needs met by prejudice can be fulfilled in an approved and legitimate fashion, and personality and culture move in coordinated channels, each sustaining the other. When prejudices are not an approved part of a culture, those whose hostility toward other groups is so deep-seated as to defy cultural constraints may become members of the "lunatic fringe" or followers of reactionary—or radical—leaders whose ideological stock in trade is hatred focused upon Jews, Negroes, Catholics, or less specifically defined groups such as "foreigners" or "subversives."

For the most part, however, overt behavior toward other groups is not simply a product of personality but emerges in a complex social situation. There is a good deal of evidence, some scrappy and anecdotal, some systematically collected, that people with little prejudice often discriminate when it is customary or expedient to do so and that people who are

strongly prejudiced will sometimes refrain for similar reasons from overt hostility or discrimination toward the objects of their dislike. Patterns of interaction are often guided by custom and law and take place within organizational contexts that affect their shape and frequency. Prejudiced people may not discriminate because the law prohibits it, public opinion frowns upon it, or economic or other interests may be threatened by it.

The implications of the distinction between prejudice and discrimination, between attitude and sentiment on the one hand and overt action on the other, are far-reaching, particularly for those who seek to affect intergroup relations. If prejudice is emotionally rooted and serves important psychological functions, rational efforts at education and persuasion are not likely to be very effective. But the persistence of prejudice is not in itself a permanent block to changing the ways in which people act, for sometimes they can be led to ignore their prejudices—or lack of prejudice—in concrete situations in which institutional requirements preclude hostile or discriminatory action.

Finally, just as discrimination can stem from prejudice, so can prejudice be affected by the actual patterns of interaction among members of different groups. Men can learn to be unprejudiced, as well as prejudiced, and the experience of satisfactory relations with members of other groups may serve that educational purpose. But in all the programs for changing the relations of white and Negro, Jew and gentile, the native-born and the immigrant, the relevance of the functions of discrimination, as of prejudice, are perhaps of paramount importance. For as long as men possess vested interests in the maintenance of differential treatment, they are unlikely willingly to change their actions.

Notes

[1] See, for example, Oliver C. Cox, *Class, Caste, and Race* (Garden City: Doubleday, 1948.

[2] E. Franklin Frazier, *The Negro in the United States* (New York: Macmillan, 1949), pp. 3–4.

[3] Louis Wirth, "The Problem of Minority Groups," in Ralph Linton (ed.), *The Science of Man in the World Crisis* (New York: Columbia University Press, 1945), pp. 351–2.

[4] For an analysis of some of the conditions that make possible the stable ethnic equilibrium in Switzerland, see Kurt Mayer, *The Population of Switzerland* (New York: Columbia University Press, 1952), Ch. 8.

[5] Charles Wagley and Marvin Harris, *Minorities in the New World* (New York: Columbia University Press, 1958), p. 264.

[6] Wirth, *op. cit.*, p. 353.

[7] Ruby Jo Reeves Kennedy, "Single or Triple Melting Pot? Intermarriage Trends in New Haven, 1870–1940," *American Journal of Sociology*, XLIX (January, 1944), 331–9.

[8] Charles Wagley, *An Introduction to Brazil* (New York: Columbia University Press, 1963), p. 87.

[9] Harry W. Hutchinson, "Race Relations in a Rural Community of the Bahian Recôncavo," in Charles Wagley (ed.), *Race and Class in Rural Brazil* (Paris: UNESCO, 1952), pp. 27–31.

[10] Donald Pierson, "Race Relations in Portuguese America," in Andrew Lind (ed.), *Race Relations in World Perspective* (Honolulu: University of Hawaii Press, 1955), p. 439.

[11] Donald Pierson, *Negroes in Brazil* (Chicago: University of Chicago Press, 1942), p. 129.

[12] Wagley, *An Introduction to Brazil*, p. 142.

[13] Pierson, "Race Relations in Portuguese America," p. 437.

[14] Wagley, *An Introduction to Brazil*, p. 142.

[15] Pierson, "Race Relations in Portuguese America," p. 443.

[16] Wagley, *An Introduction to Brazil*, pp. 139–40. The reference is to Marvin Harris, *Town and Country in Brazil* (New York: Columbia University Press, 1956), p. 125.

[17] Pierson, *Negroes in Brazil*, p. 128.

[18] Wagley, *An Introduction to Brazil*, pp. 134–5.

[19] Quoted in Peter I. Rose, *They and We: Racial and Ethnic Relations in the United States* (New York: Random House, 1964), p. 9.

[20] Gunnar Myrdal, *An American Dilemma* (New York: Harper, 1944), p. 669.

[21] For a summary of changes up to 1950, see E. Franklin Frazier, "The Negro in the United States," in Andrew W. Lind (ed.), *Race Relations in World Perspective* (Honolulu: University of Hawaii Press, 1955), pp. 348–57.

[22] U.S. Bureau of the Census, *Statistical Abstract of the United States: 1965* (Washington, D.C.: U.S. Government Printing Office, 1965), Table 470, p. 342.

[23] *Current Population Reports*, Series P-20, No. 138 (Washington, D.C.: U.S. Government Printing Office, May 11, 1965), pp. 10, 11.

[24] C. Vann Woodward, *The Strange Career of Jim Crow* (new and rev. ed.; New York: Oxford, 1957), p. 8.

[25] John Dollard, *Caste and Class in a Southern Town* (Garden City: Doubleday Anchor Books, 1957), Chs. 6–8.

[26] *Ibid.*, Ch. 17.

[27] Robert Penn Warren, *Who Speaks for the Negro?* (New York: Random House, 1965), p. 374.

[28] Ben J. Wattenberg and Richard M. Scammon, *This U.S.A.* (Garden City: Doubleday, 1965), p. 270.

[29] For sociological accounts of these groups, see C. Eric Lincoln, *The Black Muslims in America* (Boston: Beacon, 1961); and Essien Udosen Essien-Udom, *Black Nationalism* (Chicago: University of Chicago Press, 1962). A valuable contribution to the understanding of these groups is *The Autobiography of Malcolm X* (New York: Grove, 1964).

[30] For a discussion of such sociological interpretations, see Myrdal, *op. cit.*, pp. 1048–51.

[31] See Melvin M. Tumin, *Desegregation: Resistance and Readiness* (Princeton: Princeton University Press, 1958).

[32] Myrdal, *op. cit.*, pp. 75–8.

[33] See Robert M. MacIver, *The More Perfect Union* (New York: Macmillan, 1948), pp. 28 *ff*.

[34] George Eaton Simpson and J. Milton Yinger, *Racial and Cultural Minorities* (3rd ed.; New York: Harper, 1965), pp. 214–5.

[35] For a careful study of the nature of "lunatic fringe" hate groups, see Leo Lowenthal and Norbert Guterman, *Prophets of Deceit: A Study in the Techniques of the American Agitator* (New York: Harper, 1949).

[36] For a discussion of some of the evidence, see Nathan Glazer and Daniel P. Moynihan, *Beyond the Melting Pot* (Cambridge, Mass.: M.I.T. Press and Harvard University Press, 1963) pp. 143–55.

[37] *Ibid.*, p. 155.

[38] *Ibid.*, p. 160.

[39] Ben Halpern, "America is Different," in Marshall Sklare (ed.), *The Jews: Social Patterns of an American Group* (New York: Free Press, 1958), p. 25.

[40] Gordon Allport, *The Nature of Prejudice* (Cambridge: Addison-Wesley, 1954), p. 6.

[41] Charles Y. Glock and Rodney Stark, *Christian Belief and Anti-Semitism* (New York: Harper, 1966), at 205.

[42] Bernard Berelson and Patricia J. Salter, "Majority and Minority Americans: An Analysis of Magazine Fiction," *Public Opinion Quarterly*, X (Summer, 1946), 168–90.

[43] The major study in this field is T. W. Adorno, Else Frenkel-Brunswik, Daniel J. Levinson, and R. N. Sanford, *The Authoritarian Personality* (New York: Harper, 1950). For a useful summary of this and other research into the psychology of prejudice, see Selma Hirsh, *The Fears Men Live By* (New York: Harper, 1955).

Suggestions for further reading

ADORNO, T. W., ELSE FRENKEL-BRUNSWIK, DANIEL J. LEVINSON, AND R. NEVITT SANFORD. *The Authoritarian Personality.* New York: Harper, 1950.
An elaborate attempt to determine the psychological roots of prejudice. A very influential study, which has stimulated a good deal of follow-up research, as well as criticism.

FRAZIER, E. FRANKLIN. *The Negro in the United States*, rev. ed. New York: Macmillan, 1957.
A sociological history of Negro life, culture, and institutions and of Negro–white relations. A comprehensive survey.

GLAZER, NATHAN. *American Judaism.* Chicago: University of Chicago Press, 1957.
An account of the religion and community life of American Jews. Especially interesting for its analysis of the mixture of religious and nonreligious group sentiment among Jews.

GLAZER, NATHAN, AND DANIEL P. MOYNIHAN. *Beyond the Melting Pot.* Cambridge, Mass.: M.I.T. Press and Harvard University Press, 1963.
An important study of Negroes, Puerto Ricans, Jews, Italians, and Irish in New York City.

GORDON, MILTON. *Assimilation in American Life.* New York: Oxford, 1964.
Problems and processes of assimilation of ethnic groups in American society.

HANDLIN, OSCAR. *The Newcomers: Negroes and Puerto Ricans in a Changing Metropolis.* Cambridge, Mass.: Harvard University Press, 1959.
A recent analysis of the position and problems of Negroes and Puerto Ricans in New York City that compares them with earlier immigrant groups.

HANDLIN, OSCAR. *The Uprooted.* Boston: Little Brown, 1952.
A sensitive and penetrating account of immigration and immigrants in the United States.

HIRSH, SELMA. *The Fears Men Live By.* New York: Harper, 1955.
A summary and interpretation of studies of prejudice, especially The Authoritarian Personality *and several related volumes.*

HUGHES, EVERETT C., AND HELEN M. HUGHES. *Where Peoples Meet: Racial and Ethnic Frontiers.* New York: Free Press, 1952.
A comparative analysis of the consequences of contact among different racial and ethnic groups.

LIND, ANDREW W. (ed.). *Race Relations in World Perspective.* Honolulu: University of Hawaii Press, 1955.
A collection of papers on race relations in different parts of the world.

MASSING, PAUL W. *Rehearsal for Destruction.* New York: Harper, 1949.
A study of political anti-Semitism in imperial Germany.

MYRDAL, GUNNAR. *An American Dilemma.* New York: Harper, 1944.
Despite the substantial changes that have taken place since publication of this book and the need to bring up to date much of the data it contains, this remains a major study of the Negro and the problem of Negro-white relations

in the United States. It has been abridged in Arnold Rose, The Negro in America, *New York: Harper, 1944.*

ROSE, PETER I. *They and We: Racial and Ethnic Relations in the United States.* New York: Random House, 1964.
A very useful brief synopsis and evaluation of our knowledge of racial and ethnic relations in the United States.

SILBERMAN, CHARLES E. *Crisis in Black and White.* New York: Random House, 1964.
A journalist's perceptive analysis of the pressing problems and issues in Negro-white relations in the United States.

SIMPSON, GEORGE EATON, AND J. MILTON YINGER. *Racial and Cultural Minorities,* 3rd ed. New York: Harper, 1965.
A comprehensive review and interpretation of work in the field of racial and ethnic relations, focused largely on American problems and data.

SKLARE, MARSHALL (ed.). *The Jews: Social Patterns of an American Group.* New York: Free Press, 1958.
A comprehensive collection of papers on the Jews in the United States.

THOMPSON, VIRGINIA M., AND RICHARD ADLOFF. *Minority Problems in Southeast Asia.* Stanford: Stanford University Press, 1955.
A fact-crammed survey of ethnic problems in an area of great ethnic diversity.

WAKEFIELD, DAN. *Island in the City.* Boston: Houghton Mifflin, 1957.
A journalist's description of "Spanish Harlem," a predominantly Puerto Rican part of Manhattan.

WARREN, ROBERT PENN. *Who Speaks for the Negro?* New York: Random House, 1965.
An extraordinarily perceptive report and interpretation of detailed interviews with leaders of the Negro Revolution by a Pulitzer Prize-winning novelist born, reared, and educated in the South.

10
Bureaucracy

The problem of large-scale organization and the bureaucratic solution

As men come together in large groups in order to pursue collective goals they inevitably face new and complex problems of organization. Traditional methods for directing, controlling, and coordinating the efforts of many persons performing various tasks, frequently in different locations, are no longer adequate. As the size and complexity of the association increases, the amount of internal administration—that is, the activities necessary to maintain the organization itself and to carry out its prescribed tasks—grows. The existence of these problems and the need for new methods of combining and coordinating the efforts of a large number of persons were noted many centuries ago by a Graeco-Roman historian, Dio Cassius. In discussing the Roman Empire of the first century A.D., he wrote:

> The cause of our troubles is the multitude of our population and the magnitude of the business of our government; for the population embraces men of every kind, in respect both of race and endowment, and both their tempers and their desires are manifold; and the business of the state has become so vast that it can be administered only with the greatest difficulty.[1]

One major solution to the problems of large-scale organization has been the development of *bureaucracy*, which Robert K. Merton defines as "a formal, rationally organized social structure [involving] clearly defined patterns of activity in which, ideally, every series of actions is functionally related to the purposes of the organization."[2] This sociological definition, which we shall follow, contrasts sharply with the widespread use of "bureaucracy" and "bureaucrat" as political epithets often applied to government agencies and officials, for whom the conventional stereotype is the officious, rule-conscious, responsibility-dodging clerk entangled in red tape and preoccupied with busy-work. Some political scientists have even distinguished between bureaucracy on the one hand and honest, efficient, and democratic administration on the other, between bureaucrats—unpleasant inefficient people—and responsible and reliable civil servants. "A passion for routine in administration, the sacrifice of flexibility to rule, delay in the making of decisions, and a refusal to embark upon experiment," evils inherent in bureaucracy, according to Harold Laski,[3] are undoubtedly to be found in bureaucratic bodies—public and private—but the efficiency and realiability desired in the operations of any large organization are also the *product* of what sociologists call bureaucracy. One task of sociological analysis, therefore, is to iden-

tify both the conditions that produce bureaucratic red tape and inflexibility and
those that lead to efficient performance in
pursuit of collective goals.

Bureaucracy is a form of social structure to be found not only in government
but also in many other large-scale organizations. Full-scale bureaucracy probably first emerged as an answer to problems of political and military organization
in ancient Egypt, China at about the time
of Christ, and imperial Rome. With the
growth of other large bodies—the Catholic Church, modern corporations, national
and international trade unions, organizations like the Rotary International and
the American Legion—and the increasing
size and scope of educational institutions, philanthropic agencies, professional
groups, and the myriad other associations
found in modern society, bureaucracy has
come to characterize more and more of
contemporary life.

The pervasiveness of bureaucracy is
reflected in many ways. An increasing
proportion of persons are employed in
bureaucratic positions. As we saw in
Chapter 8, the number and proportion of
white-collar workers, many of them engaged in administering large organizations or in performing routine bureaucratic tasks, have increased steadily and
substantially. Millions of others in various kinds of work are subject to bureaucratic controls on their jobs.

The extension of governmental functions brings men frequently into contact
with government officials: tax collectors,
draft boards, plumbing inspectors, unemployment interviewers, license clerks,
county agents, and so on. In many other
areas of life in which men are involved
with large-scale organizations, they are
also continually affected by formal rules
that limit or guide behavior. When regis-
tering in a college or university, for ex-

ample, forms must be filled out, regulations followed, the appropriate signatures
secured. Rules govern attendance, examinations, grades. Specified officials must
decide which regulation applies and when
exceptions can be made. If a hospitalized
individual carries medical insurance, his
physician must file the necessary forms in
order to ensure benefits—which will be
paid only under carefully prescribed conditions. When we travel we must follow
explicit regulations: A dog (other than a
seeing-eye dog) cannot be taken on a
train; baggage on board ship must be
marked in a specified fashion; one cannot return to the United States without
having been vaccinated against smallpox
in the preceding three years; and so on
ad infinitum.

In some totalitarian societies bureaucratic controls are maximized. The state
extends its powers into areas once left
free or only partially dominated by political regulations: It exercises control
through rules dictated and enforced by
bureaucrats employed in centrally directed agencies. But bureaucracy is by no
means confined to totalitarian states, for
modern democratic societies—of both
capitalist and welfare-state varieties—
make extensive use of what Max Weber
called "man's greatest social invention."

Bureaucracies may differ widely in the
details of their organization and operations, but in general outline they are sufficiently alike to construct an *ideal type*
of bureaucratic structure. This ideal type,
derived largely from the work of Weber,[4]
is a model of a rationally ordered structure, and therefore provides a useful
starting point for the analysis of the nature and functioning of any concrete bureaucracy.

Essential bureaucratic characteristics,
each contributing to the efficient operations of the organization and each func-

tionally related to the others, include: (1) carefully defined positions or *offices*; (2) a *hierarchial order* with clear-cut lines of authority and responsibility; (3) selection of personnel on the basis of *technical* or *professional qualifications*; (4) *rules and regulations* governing official action; (5) *security of tenure* and the possibility of a *career* by promotion in the hierarchy. Each of these traits requires some comment.

(1) The prerequisites and perquisites of each office in a bureaucratic hierarchy, the tasks expected of its incumbent, and his formal relationships to superiors and subordinates are all clearly and explicitly defined. All offices exist, in principle, independently of their incumbents, but unlike family roles, for example, which are informally or traditionally defined and can be filled only by particular persons, bureaucratic roles are formally established and can be occupied by anyone with the appropriate qualifications. The nature of bureaucratic offices is illustrated by a United States Civil Service Commission announcement of openings for patent examiners:

Persons appointed to positions [at the lowest rank] will perform elementary professional, scientific, or technical research in the examining of applications for patents; determine what is claimed to be new; see that the disclosure is complete; and investigate the prior art as represented by patents already granted in the United States and various foreign countries, and by the description in technical literature.

Persons appointed to positions at [higher grades] will examine, study, and interpret the technical aspects of patent applications, determining independently in most cases whether petitions, oaths, drawings, specifications, and claims meet formal requirements. . . . The degree of supervision will vary with the grade of position.

In order to qualify for the lowest rank, applicants are required to have completed one of the following:

A. A full curriculum of study in an accredited college or university, leading to a bachelor's degree in a pertinent field of engineering, or . . . [various other educational alternatives equivalent to a four-year college program].

B. An adequate experience background which has included at least 4 years of successful and progressive experience in a pertinent field of engineering, chemistry, or physics. . . .

C. Any time-equivalent combination of A (Training) and B (Experience) above.[5]

Important consequences flow from the sharp separation of office from incumbent. It frees the organization from dependence upon particular individuals in particular positions. Where offices are not formally defined each person may make his job into whatever his abilities and energies permit; although this may prove useful when the incumbent is particularly able, it requires substantial adjustment every time there is such a change in personnel. The need for such adjustment is minimized by explicitly defining and limiting what each officeholder is expected to do. In effect, the separation of office and person applies the principle of interchangeable parts to human material; the organization continues to operate effectively as long as the posts are held by qualified persons.

(2) Offices are usually arranged in hierarchial order with a formal chain of command. The archetype of this kind of social structure is, of course, military organization, with its ranks of commissioned and noncommissioned officers, its enforced recognition of the duties and responsibilities of those with authority, its insistence upon obedience to superiors. In any large organization, however, some form of coordination of effort is required beyond that which may emerge from a shared commitment to common goals, for there may be divergent views on how best to pursue those goals. Hierarchy locates

responsibility in specific hands and allows for clear-cut determination of policy. By establishing lines of authority it makes possible control over the array of offices and effective coordination of effort. Finally, and we shall return to this point shortly, it sets up a line of advancement for persons seeking a career.

(3) Bureaucratic offices are filled in principle by persons who demonstrate their competence to perform the required duties. This contrasts sharply with the situation in nonbureaucratic organizations, in which various roles are apt to be filled on the basis of traditional or personal relationships—relatives, friends, or political supporters exercise their claims to preferred posts. The value of selecting professionally or technically qualified personnel is clear enough; trained officials are more likely to do their jobs well—particularly in view of the greater specialization required in a complex, industrial society—than those whose positions rest upon family ties, inheritance, personal friendship, or political favors.

Methods of selection in a bureaucracy, therefore, are of crucial importance. Formal examinations provide an impersonal and systematic procedure for testing applicants and have been widely used, although other methods are sometimes utilized such as personal interviews, perusal of records, recommendations from others, and completion of specified training. Examinations were employed in China before the Christian era, although the Chinese examination system did not come to full flower until the seventh century. The British Civil Service has relied upon formal examinations, as have federal, state, and local governments in the United States. What is tested, however, depends upon the prevailing conception of relevant skills. In China, a literary education and familiarity with the classics of

Confucianism were taken as evidence of competence to perform the tasks required of government officials. A liberal education and its appurtenances were long defined as requirements for administrative posts in the British civil service; general intellectual and personal competence was more highly valued than practical skills. American civil service examinations have characteristically focused upon the precise skills required for particular positions.

(4) A body of explicit rules, usually codified, governs the official actions of officeholders. The existence and application of these rules give rise to the frequent complaints about red tape, yet without them there would be confusion and inefficiency in any large organization. Formal regulations that dictate appropriate behavior provide for relative uniformity of action and minimize the disruptive effects of personal interests, predilections, preferences, and biases. Because their formal relations to one another are established by the rules, officeholders can work together, at least in theory, whatever their personal feelings toward fellow employees may be. In addition, as Merton points out, "In this way, the subordinate is protected from the arbitrary action of his superior, since the actions of both are constrained by a mutually recognized set of rules." [6] Finally, for those who come in contact with the bureaucratic apparatus —for bureaucracy's "clients"—the rules provide for uniform treatment, a point to which we shall return.

(5) In order to assure competent and unbiased performance by bureaucratic officeholders, they are often given security of tenure—usually after a probationary period. This security renders them less susceptible to outside pressures. Continued efficiency is encouraged by offering possibilities for advancement in the

hierarchy. Promotion may be based simply on length of service or upon demonstrated achievement, as measured by formal examinations or by the less formal judgments of superiors.

The sources of bureaucracy

These attributes, which constitute the skeletal principles of bureaucratic organization, are achieved only to varying degrees in any concrete case. They emerge and develop as responses to specific problems in particular historical situations. The conditions that give rise to bureaucracy in the United States, the Soviet Union, ancient Egypt, classical China, and imperial Rome obviously differ in many respects. But in all cases, as Max Weber points out, "The decisive reason for the advance of bureaucratic organization has always been its purely technical superiority over any other form of organization. . . . Precision, speed, unambiguity, knowledge of the files, continuity, discretion, unity, strict subordination, reduction of friction and of material and personal costs—these are raised to the optimum point in the strictly bureaucratic organization." [7]

Efficiency alone, however, as Weber recognized, hardly accounts for the growth of bureaucracy. Men must recognize the technical advantages of bureaucracy, be ready to give up traditional procedures, and possess the values and institutions necessary to create and maintain a bureaucratic organization.

As was noted earlier, the increased size and scale of organization and the range and complexity of the activities being pursued have made traditional administrative procedures and structures inadequate. The growth of the nation-state,

with which bureaucracy is frequently identified, and of large-scale economic enterprises has strongly encouraged tendencies toward bureaucratic organization.

In democratic societies, bureaucracy, with its uniform rules and careers open to talent, promises both fair and equitable procedures and efficiency. Thus the passage of civil service legislation in the United States reflected an effort not only to secure qualified personnel, but also to eliminate partisanship in the administration of government. By guaranteeing tenure to government employees selected on the basis of merit, civil service regulations made it possible to carry out their duties honestly and efficiently without danger of political reprisal or loss of a job. Citizens, therefore, can insist upon uniform treatment by government officials, according to the law and official regulations. In this respect, bureaucracy is intimately related to democratic values.

In the Soviet Union, bureaucracy not only promised efficiency but also provided an instrument for directing and controlling the entire nation in its efforts to achieve predetermined goals. Despite the initial hostility toward bureaucracy, which the revolutionary leaders identified with Tsarist rule, the Soviet regime soon found it necessary to adopt bureaucratic methods in order to carry on government business. With the introduction of national economic planning, rational organization became essential in order to ensure the appropriate use of available resources, including manpower. Centralized authority, bureaucratic rules, and impersonal standards of competence and performance provided the institutional machinery for enforcing the discipline required by an industrial society upon a labor force unaccustomed to its demands.

The willingness to use bureaucratic methods rests upon appropriate values and attitudes. In Western society, a strong emphasis upon rationalism in science, philosophy, and religion (particularly Calvinism) encouraged a rational approach to organization. In addition, Calvinism, by encouraging hard work as a moral virtue, provided a cultural and psychological foundation for the order and discipline required in a bureaucratic structure. In the Soviet Union, the rational "scientific" bias of Marxism, which severely criticizes the "irrationality" of a competitive capitalist economy, justified the extreme bureaucratization of Soviet society.

Adoption of bureaucratic devices has also been closely linked to the growth of a money economy. Bureaucracy has existed in the absence of such an economy, but it has developed more fully when money has become the conventional medium of exchange. Money possesses an abstract quality that encourages rational calculation. It permits the payment of regular salaries, a method of remuneration that facilities the maintenance of control over officeholders. Volunteer workers can be independent of their supervisors. Those who possess traditional rights can also more readily resist direction from above. Salaried officials, on the other hand, are more likely to be dependent on their earnings, and they can also see the possibilities of advancement in terms of constantly increasing income. The emergence of bureaucracy has frequently been accompanied by the transformation of traditional obligations into monetary terms, thus encouraging formal and rational relations between the official and the client, customer, or subject.

The underlying social and cultural conditions upon which bureaucracy rests cannot account, however, for the emergence of specific forms of organization at particular times and places. The inadequacies or limitations of existing procedures and relationships must be apparent and there must be some perceptible advantage in establishing new arrangements. Although efficiency and rational administration are presumably the goals of bureaucratic reorganization, other interests may also be at work. Thus Civil Service rules have on occasion been extended to employees in the Federal government in order to make secure jobs first acquired through political influence. By blanketing incumbent jobholders under civil service, political appointees are assured of permanent tenure. One long-run result of this politically motivated extension of bureaucratic rules is the extension of the merit principle to more employees, for further replacements then must be selected according to usual bureaucratic procedures.

Since various interests may be affected by the administrative policies that are established, the particular procedures that are set up, and the way in which authority is allocated, there are often substantial conflicts both within the organization and among those affected by its actions over specific organizational decisions. When the British Civil Service was reorganized in the latter half of the nineteenth century and became a bureaucratic apparatus much admired for its efficiency, a separate relatively small high-level "administrative class" was established, with very high standards for entry. The methods for choosing members of this class were designed not only to secure men of great ability, but also to limit recruitment to those "from the social strata monopolizing the great public schools and universities."[8] Criticism of the Civil Service has often focused upon the interests therefore represented—and unrepresented—among the senior public servants in the government.

The processes by which bureaucracy is extended are not confined to government, for any large-scale organization is subject to similar pressures. In a suggestive study of a gypsum plant, Alvin W. Gouldner has delineated some of the circumstances that give rise to specific bureaucratic characteristics.[9] Shortly after a new plant manager had been appointed, he had introduced new rules and a more rigid enforcement of the old ones. His predecessor had been a casual fellow, on good terms with his subordinates and easy to get on with. Discipline in the plant under him had been lax and rules had not been strictly enforced. The transition to more formal and bureaucratic administration came about under the new manager because of "institutionally derived pressures, convergent on the position of a new plant manager, which made him accept and initiate bureaucratic patterns."[10]

Having been transferred from another plant, the plant manager had no personal ties with his subordinates. In order to gain control of the situation, he found it necessary to make greater use of formal machinery than had his predecessor. Lacking informal channels of communication, for instance, he instituted regular reports from his subordinates in order to keep informed about what was going on in the plant. Many company rules had been ignored by the previous manager— for example, one that prohibited employees from taking gypsum board home for personal use. When the new manager, concerned about costs and wanting to impress his superiors, insisted upon enforcing this regulation, he generated considerable irritation and hostility. As he could not count upon personal loyalty to ensure efficiency and cooperation, he bore

down even harder upon bureaucratic prescriptions. Gradually, subordinates who had been carried over from the earlier regime were replaced by newcomers whose outlook was closer to that of the new manager, contributing further to an emphasis upon adherence to rules and regulations as a means of increasing efficiency.

Analysis of this particular case suggests two general conclusions. First, the circumstances that give rise to particular bureaucratic forms—new rules, greater insistence upon adherence to them, sharper definition of the responsibilities of office—stem from specific situations. In the gypsum plant the problems created by the advent of a new manager precipitated bureaucratic reforms. Similarly, in many companies, efforts to cut costs lead to new procedures or clearer lines of authority; if profits are high enough, however, there may be a willing acceptance of things as they are in the organization. Again, in government agencies, charges of favoritism may lead to new rules or revised regulations that define more explicitly the responsibilities of office.

A second conclusion is that the actual operations within organizations are not wholly determined by the bureaucratic blueprint. The ideal bureaucracy, in Weber's terms, "succeeds in eliminating from official business love, hatred, and all purely personal, irrational, and emotional elements which escape calculation."[11] But no organization achieves this ideal; no blueprint describes all of its activities. In order to explore the actual functioning of bureaucracy we must therefore examine the kinds of social relationships that do appear, the methods by which policy is translated into practice, and the recurrent problems or dilemmas inherent in the operations of a bureaucratic organization.

Informal organization, or "bureaucracy's other face"

People who regularly work together are not likely to remain on the impersonal and formal terms prescribed by the organization chart. From continued association there emerges an "informal structure" of roles and relationships that plays an important part in determining daily activities. Within this structure, as Charles H. Page suggests, "can be observed the development of friendships and cliques, the interplay of love and hate. . . . The intense impersonality of the official bureaucracy is frequently matched in degree by the highly personal quality found unofficially within it." [12] The informal structure, "bureaucracy's other face," in Page's suggestive phrase, sometimes runs parallel to or supplements the formal organization, and sometimes runs counter to it. Secretaries in an office characteristically develop primary group relations that incorporate mutual obligations of aid and assistance, even though formal regulations may proscribe such behavior. A group of employees may come to define the location of desks in an office as symbolic of relative status; physical rearrangement of the desks will then be interpreted as a shift in their relative standing in the hierarchy even when no such change is intended. The effects of informal patterns of organization could be illustrated at length; here a few cases will suffice.

In a detailed study of a law enforcement agency, Peter Blau found that agents who were expected to take serious problems to their superiors had instead established a system of informal consultation among themselves despite regulations prohibiting exchanges of information about particular cases. Agents were reluctant to bring their problems to their supervisors because such actions might suggest that they were unable to handle difficult cases and therefore might affect their merit ratings and future advancement. [13]

A study of the naval disbursing officer reveals that he frequently ignored regulations governing payments of salary. These violations, however, were clearly patterned and based upon three different types of relationships: those with personal friends who based their requests upon the obligations of friendship; those with other officers with whom a systematic exchange of favors took place—pay given out ahead of time in exchange for some favor in the dining room, or privileged access to the storeroom; and those with superior officers who might, in turn, do some kind of favor—or refrain from doing an ill turn. [14]

Spontaneous—that is, unplanned—roles and relationships and the presence of primary groups functioning within the larger whole pose significant problems in the analysis of bureaucratic organization. Although not accounted for in the formal scheme of things, "bureaucracy's other face" clearly affects its overall operations. Does the informal structure, one might ask, weaken the organization, lessen its efficiency, and prevent fulfillment of its official goals? Or may it, perhaps, contribute, directly or indirectly, to the organization's stability and to the successful achievement of its objectives?

There are no final answers to these questions, for the informal structure may be *both* functional and dysfunctional for the organization. It may, for example, increase the stability and efficiency of a bureaucracy by its indirect effects upon morale. Consistent and effective performance of any task depends not only upon skill and effort, but also upon the feelings men have toward their work. In a bureaucracy, as in any group, efficiency is usually related to morale, and there is substantial evidence that morale is affected by the relations among persons who work together. To the extent that informal structure in a bureaucracy provides satisfying primary group relationships on the job, then, it can serve positive functions for the organization as a whole.

Informal arrangements worked out on the job frequently improve employees' efficiency directly by providing mechanisms both for dealing with problems not foreseen by the officials who establish and control the formal structure and for solving problems created by the structure itself. The system of informal consultation in the law enforcement agency studied by Blau contributed not only to the agents' morale, but also to their knowledge, self-confidence, and skill:

It transformed an aggregate of individuals who happened to have the same supervisor into a cohesive group. The recurrent experience of being dependent on the group, whose members furnished needed help, and of being appreciated by the others in the group, as indicated by their solicitations for assistance, created strong mutual bonds. . . . Second, this practice made more effective law enforcement possible because it improved the quality of the decisions of agents. Every agent knew that he could obtain help with solving problems whenever he needed it. This knowledge, reinforced by the feeling of being an integrated member of a cohesive group, decreased anxiety about making decisions. Simultaneously, being often approached for advice raised the self-confidence of an investigator. The very existence of this practice enhanced the ability of all agents, experts as well as others, to make decisions independently.[15]

Paradoxically, the informal structure may help to achieve organizational goals precisely *because* it ignores the formal requirements. In the Navy, Page points out, as in any highly bureaucratized organization,

. . . the circumvention of this regulation [that "all official communications . . . must . . . be routed through the 'chain of command' "—"channels"] appears as precisely the solution of a pressing problem. When such a development occurs the individuals involved, if they are sophisticated in the ways of their organization, will operate on the level of the informal structure wherein a solution is usually possible, and will thereby avoid that bureaucratic frustration so frequently felt by those who are strict followers of "the book."[16]

So important are informal groups and practices that one of the wisest students of large-scale organization, a former top-ranking executive, has argued that informal organization is not only an inevitable feature of any large bureaucratic structure, but an essential one: it is "necessary to the operation of formal organizations as a means of communication, of cohesion, and of protecting the integrity of the individual."[17]

In order to secure the maximum efficiency, then, the able administrator or executive must make use of the relationships, norms, and sentiments not incorporated in the formal table of organization and the rules. The ways in which these informal procedures can be systematically used have been explored by Blau,[18] who points out that relaxation of formal requirements—the use of first names, establishment of personal relations, overlooking violations of minor regulations —establishes a network of obligations upon which the executive can sometimes call in order to secure special efforts from his subordinates. The possibility of enforcing a rule that is usually ignored also gives the supervisor an additional sanction, although continued disregard of a rule may become so widely taken for granted that sudden enforcement may be looked upon as unfair and a "dirty trick." If the personal ties that emerge, the practices that spontaneously develop, and the shared values and attitudes of small groups are not taken into account by the administrator or executive, they may become dysfunctional, leading to resistance to policy, blocked lines of communication, and even deliberate sabotage of organizational goals.

Despite the substantial body of evidence upon which it rests, however, this analysis of informal relationships within formal organization must be cautiously applied. All the studies cited, it should be noted, were carried out by American sociologists in American settings. The analysis may therefore not apply to all bureaucracies, it has been argued, because it rests upon cultural premises not found in all societies. A recent study of bureaucracy in France by Michel Crozier reports that there was no comparable tendency there toward the development of close personal relationships among coworkers. In the government office he studied:

Girls remained isolated, although this entailed hardship for many of them who were strangers in the city and had been abruptly severed from families and friendship ties. They reported that they very rarely had friends in the agency. They reiterated that they preferred having their friends outside. Even among those who had friends, the friendships never seemed to develop into articulate groups. There were very few associations of any sort—no culture, educational, or leisure joint activities worth mentioning.[19]

In the factory he investigated "more friendships were reported . . . but they did not develop into cliques or even into stable informal groups. Cliques were viewed with great disfavor, and groups that could cut across several categories were inconceivable."[20]

The reason for these failures to establish personal ties Crozier found in French cultural traits: "the low state of free group activities and the difficulty that Frenchmen experience in cooperating on a formal basis" and the fact that informal activities tend to be "negative, instable, and never expressed openly."[21] Such traits, Crozier suggests, may indeed provide one of the cultural reasons for the development of the particular kinds of formal organization and bureaucratic behavior found in France.

The dilemmas of formal organization

According to the bureaucratic blueprint, policy is made at the top and the rest of the organization is the technical instrument that puts it into practice. The government civil service, for example, presumably is nonpartisan; it is expected to carry out efficiently whatever policies are set by the legislature and by the chief executive and his policy-making aides. Officials of a large corporation are also expected to follow the policies of the top executives. A scientific staff may be encouraged to range widely or to stick to limited projects; plant managers may be told to hold labor unions closely to the contract or they may be allowed to go along with most union requests; sales managers are encouraged to push one product rather than another; and so on. These policies are presumably to be carried out according to the rules laid out by the policy makers and according to the formal allocation of responsibility and authority.

As we have seen, however, there may in fact be an informal structure that exists within the bureaucratic organization. The administrator or executive must therefore continually balance the advantages of hierarchy, authority, and conformity to the rules against the benefits to be derived by recognizing and making use of practices and relationships not allowed for in the rule book and organizational chart.

A second dilemma to which the informal organization also contributes centers around the need for an effective system of communication. As has frequently been pointed out, policy making requires a reliable flow of information from the bottom to the top of the organization, and of policies and orders from the top down. Facts and ideas are expected to move up the hierarchy until they reach the policy makers. Once a policy has been arrived at, commands and instructions must then move down to the level of operations. The bureaucratic dilemma lies in the fact that hierarchy, highly standardized procedures, and formal relationships are likely to inhibit the free flow of information, while a looser, more informal structure facilitates the flow of information. Crozier reports that in the French bureaucratic organizations he studied the existence of rigid divisions between the several levels of the hierarchy made it very difficult for information to move either up or down.[22] According to Peter Blau and W. Richard Scott,

Studies of experimental and work groups have shown that status differences restrict the participation of low-status members, channel a disproportionate amount of communication to high-status members, discourage criticism of the suggestions of the highs, encourage rejecting correct suggestions of the lows, and reduce the work satisfaction of the lows and their motivation to make contributions.[23]

Control over the flow and content of communication is difficult to achieve, and subordinates can often exercise considerable influence over both the formulation of policy and its execution. By holding back information, they can affect their superiors' definitions of the situations in which they must act, and in so doing affect the final decisions. Under some conditions there may even be a built-in pressure to doctor the facts sent to higher officials; if an accurate report may reflect upon the officeholder (or his friends), for example, he may not give an unvarnished picture of the situation.

Those who direct the flow of information within the structure are in a strategic position to affect both policy and action. Sidney Webb once reported that as President of England's Board of Trade he received on the average more than 8,000 letters every day, few of which he ever saw. The permanent civil servants who screened his mail therefore controlled in some measure his daily activities as well as the information and problems that came to his attention. By allowing too many communications and too many problems to reach the administrator's desk, subordinates can submerge him so completely in details that he may never get around to issues with which he might—or should—be dealing. Unless strong external pressures are at work (or the executive can rely upon informal channels of communication), the particular problems brought to him for decisions are in large part chosen for him by his subordinates. The extent to which permanent civil servants can influence policy is clearly a problem of particular importance in government, where officialdom may constitute a distinctive social group with its own interests and viewpoints that it may hope to see reflected in public policy.

Lines of communication and the flow of information are also of crucial importance in carrying out policy after it has been formulated. Again, the top executive is to some degree at the mercy of his subordinates. General directives issued at the top must be translated into concrete decisions governing day-by-day activities.

An insistence upon careful control of ex- penditures, for example, may have little effect upon actual disbursements; expense accounts are hard to keep track of, and fiscal controls may not be sufficient to prevent padding, the latter a procedure which, in any case, nowadays seems to be sanctioned by the going conventions of expense-account life. In a study of a So- cialist government in Saskatchewan, Can- ada, Lipset reported that "One cabinet minister decided that certain government work that had previously been contracted out to private concerns should be done by government employees whenever possible. His deputy minister [a top-ranking civil servant], however, continued sending the work out to private concerns." [24] If orders and policies from above are not accu- rately transmitted down the hierarchy, what is done may not conform to official plans and expectations. And if executives cannot secure reliable information about what is actually happening in the lower ranks of the organization, they cannot effectively control its operations. Whether the needed facts are available depends upon both the formal machinery available for securing them and the informal chan- nels through which information can be transmitted—or held back. The inherent and perhaps unavoidable difficulty is that the formal machinery necessary for di- recting operations and ensuring responsi- bility and predictability can inhibit the flow of information necessary for policy making and for maintaining effective con- trol.

In order to minimize the necessity of direct control, bureaucracy encourages the *professionalization* of its personnel.[25] Competence rests upon appropriate train- ing, during which the doctor, lawyer, ac- countant, engineer, scientist, or other professional masters a recognized body of knowledge, acquires appropriate skills,

and incorporates universalistic criteria of performance. Governed by these criteria, which are independent of personal or local considerations, the professional can presumably be counted upon to do his job with relatively little direction or surveil- lance. Failure to carry through his res- ponsibilities would result not only in sanctions imposed by the organization but also in criticism and loss of standing among his professional peers, as well, per- haps, as in feelings of guilt because he has violated his own standards of profes- sional performance.

The tendency toward professionali- zation in large organizations, clearly evi- dent in the increasing numbers of special- ized experts of all kinds now employed by them, creates another recurrent bu- reaucratic dilemma. Any organization necessarily encourages loyalty to its values and goals, while the essence of professionalism is adherence to the norms established by the professional group. As Blau and Scott point out, "studies of professionals and semiprofessionals in formal organizations have consistently found that the conflict between bu- reaucratic and professional orientations is a fundamental issue." [26] There may be occasions when the interests of the or- ganization and the requirements of professional practice conflict. Shall a company doctor send home on sick leave a worker who is suffering only a mild physical disturbance? Shall a college professor focus his energies chiefly upon his students and the problems of his col- lege or university, or shall he devote him- self to scholarly efforts that will lead to wider recognition? Shall a social worker stick closely to the formal rules and with- hold aid from a client whose eligibility is uncertain, or should he be centrally con- cerned with the human needs upon which his professional training leads him to focus? "Although a professional orientation motivates a person to do better work in terms of professional standards," Blau and Scott observe on the basis of their close study of a public-assistance agency, "it also gives him a basis for ignoring administrative considerations and thus may lead to poorer performance in terms of the standards of the organization." [27] Emphasis upon professionalism may therefore diminish organizational loyalty and diminish the authority of the bureaucratic official. Stress upon commitment to the organization and its goals, on the other hand, may lower professional standards and the level of performance.

The dysfunctions of bureaucratic organization

As these dilemmas suggest, bureaucracy is not a fixed or precisely defined entity, but a way of organizing human effort faced with a set of constantly recurring problems that allow of no final solution. The bureaucratic model defined by Weber ostensibly provides a rational organization that maximizes predictability, reliability, and efficiency. In fact, of course, as our earlier observations indicate, the dynamics of bureaucracy are far more complex than allowed for in the Weberian model. Moreover, as Merton points out in a penetrating analysis, the organizational devices ostensibly designed to maximize efficiency may backfire, generating the evils that are conventionally associated with bureaucratic structures.[28]

Many years ago these "congenital defects" were described by an English writer as Red Tape, Mystery Mongering, Jack-in-Office, and Gentlemanly Malingering.[29] Red tape is too well known to

require much elaboration. It consists of an overemphasis upon rules, procedures, and paper work. It is epitomized in the story related in the Soviet Union during the Stalin regime of the worker who went to a government office to secure some firewood. A friend who saw him returning with a heavy sack on his back congratulated him on his success in securing the wood so quickly, only to be told that the sack merely contained the forms to be filled out. Mystery Mongering—a tendency to conceal administrative procedures from outsiders, thus leaving them in some measure at the official's mercy—is not confined to bureaucrats; it is found among many groups whose members seek to sustain power and prestige by emphasizing how difficult their tasks are and how much one must know in order to perform them. Jack-in-Office is the officious bureaucrat whose power and security have gone to his head. The Gentlemanly Malingerer no longer feels called upon to work very hard because of his secure job tenure.

These evils might be attributed to ordinary human frailties, the corrupting effects of power, or the debilitating consequences of too much security, were it not for the fact that they do not appear universally, and that their prevalence seems to vary with specific conditions. Such facts suggest that their origins lie in the bureaucracy itself rather than in personal (individual) qualities.

To secure "reliability of response and strict devotion to regulations" bureaucracy promises security and advancement to those who conform to its norms. In inculcating a proper respect for rules and procedures, Merton suggests, the organization almost inevitably leaves the official with an exaggerated concern with routines and regulations.[30] Eventually means become ends in themselves. Goals of the organization become less important to its members than maintenance of the organization itself—and particularly those of its features that have acquired a patina of age and tradition or have become incorporated into the informal structure.

Insistence upon rigid application of rules creates difficulties not only within the organization, where it may slow down operations and increase costs, but also in the relations between the organization and its "clients." Many bureaucratic positions require the official to apply rules to specific situations and persons. Is an applicant for unemployment insurance or an old-age pension entitled to payments, and if so, how much? Which of the many job applicants in an employment office shall be sent out in answer to an employer's request? Should a student who lacks the formal prerequisites be allowed to enter a course he wants to take? Is a particular request for hospitalization benefits under a medical insurance plan legitimate? Rules, we pointed out earlier, are essential in order to ensure uniform treatment, to avoid the intrusion of the official's personal feelings, and to increase the speed with which cases are handled. But overly strict adherence to the rules can easily lead to rigidity and inflexibility; the widespread equation of red tape with bureaucracy suggests the frequency with which it does.

One should not belittle the problems of officials who must conform to a complex body of rules and apply them to diverse situations, or to expect them to maintain a batting average of 1.000. The bureaucratic assumption is that any situation can be—indeed must be—handled according to regulations. Each client, however, typically sees his problem as unique. As Everett Hughes observes in his discussion of work, one man's

emergency is another's routine; the person who feels that he has particular needs or peculiar problems is not likely to be pleased if he is treated in a routine fashion.[31]

Almost inevitably, of course, some cases that come across a bureaucrat's desk are unusual, and the available rules or procedures may not readily apply. The confirmed bureaucrat who cannot see beyond the rules transforms them into a Procrustean bed wherein the special case is cut to size. For example, a clerk in the office of a group medical plan had to deal with the following case: A man and woman working for the same company had carried individual hospitalization insurance. For two years after they were married, they failed to change their individual policies to a joint policy; the company personnel office did not call the matter to their attention or take any action itself. A month after they did shift to joint coverage, the woman became pregnant, her child arriving on time. The clerk refused to allow the maternity benefits usually provided because the rules required a couple to be covered by the plan for twelve months. The argument that they had been paying hospitalization insurance individually for several years previously (ten years, in the case of the man) did not impress the clerk or, subsequently, any of her superiors. The frustrated couple fulminated against the inflexibility of the bureaucrats; the officials pointed out that they were merely applying the rules. When unusual situations of this type arise, a new rule or a policy decision of some kind is obviously required. Fear of making a mistake, or of taking unresolved difficulties to superiors, encourages rigidity, and the superiors themselves may be so committed to a bureaucratic point of view that it is difficult to secure the constant modifications that life in a complex and changing society requires.

The "congenital defects" of bureaucracy, however, are tendencies rather than inherent qualities; they are potential and not inevitable. They may be mitigated by the informal practices and relationships that emerge within the organization: for example, the informal consultation of law-enforcement agents, the patterns of mutual aid that may develop in an office secretarial pool, the occasional disregard of "channels" among the more knowing naval officers—each described above. These defects are perhaps less likely to develop among professional persons—doctors, teachers, social workers, engineers, scientists—whose sense of duty and standards of performance, as noted earlier, are in some measure independent of the organization than among bureaucrats confined to more or less routine tasks.

Much, of course, depends upon the policies and practices of both top executives and the supervisors at each level of the hierarchy, for they must tread a fine line between too much bureaucracy and too little. As we pointed out earlier, if they disregard "bureaucracy's other face" they may generate dissatisfaction, friction, and lowered efficiency. On the other hand, if they do not formulate consistent and clear-cut policies they create confusion and uncertainty that employees may resolve by even greater and more rigid adherence to such rules as there are. If they reward and encourage initiative on the part of subordinates they can prevent rigidity and inflexibility; but too little control and direction can lead to the loss of the uniformity and predictability that constitute two of the virtues of bureaucratic organization.

As Blau points out, however, potential dysfunctions may be minimized by structural devices as well. He suggests, for example, that a "split in managerial authority"—separation of day-to-day supervision from control over wages, working conditions, and procedures governing advancement—would improve relations between superior and subordinate and contribute to concentration upon the tasks at hand. The use of rating scales based upon "clearly specified results" rather than upon mere conformity to regulations, Blau argues, would also help to prevent the ritualism and rigidity potentially found in bureaucracy.[32]

These suggestions for improving the formal structure of bureaucracy testify to the need for its continuing rationalization. Many of the deficiencies attributed to bureaucracy stem from the failure to carry out the logic of its organization. For example, failure to allocate authority commensurate with responsibility can lead to buck-passing, avoidance of responsibility, and overdependence upon rules. In one medium-size organization in which the writer was once employed the chief executive was reluctant to permit department heads to make certain kinds of decisions, particularly those relating to the staff—requests for special leave required her approval, as did the routine scheduling of working hours and time off. Even when the department heads could make decisions on their own, they were almost always reviewed, although in practice rarely changed. These executives soon became unwilling to make decisions without prior approval from above. Personnel procedures were slowed down as a result, morale was weakened, and turnover was high, so that the staff was overloaded with new and only partially trained personnel.

Students of administration are continually engaged in working out formal devices and rules of procedure designed to increase organizational efficiency—defining the proper number of subordinates who can be effectively controlled by one man (the span of control), improving the flow of paper work, refining processes of selection, and so on. Detailed empirical researches during the past two or three decades have demonstrated clearly, however, that purely formal procedures and organizational devices, no matter how refined and helpful, will not in themselves produce the desired results.

The problem of central concern is the expeditious removal of the obstacles to efficient operations which recurrently arise. This cannot be accomplished by a preconceived system of rigid procedures . . . but only by creating conditions favorable to continuous adjustive developments in the organization. To establish such a pattern of self-adjustment in a bureaucracy, conditions must prevail that encourage its members to cope with emergent problems and to find the best method for producing specified results on their own initiative, and that obviate the need for unofficial practices which thwart the objectives of the organization, such as restriction of output.[33]

Social consequences of bureaucracy

Interest in the internal problems and complex workings of bureaucratic organization should not obscure its wider social consequences. For Weber, the growth and spread of bureaucracy were part of the "disenchantment of the world"—the decay of tradition, an interest in efficiency rather than a concern for ultimate values, the replacement of myth and imagination by rationality and routine. Bureaucracy, for Weber, was not the only source of this "disenchantment," nor was it peculiarly modern; the progressive rationalization of life has a long history and can be found not only—or, perhaps

even centrally—in the forms of organization by which men pursue their interests, but also in philosophy, religion, law, and science.

More concretely, the critics of bureaucracy see its pervasive influence extending into hitherto relatively free and unregimented areas of social life: the free professions of law and medicine, higher learning, the church, scientific research, recreation, and sports. The physician is increasingly dependent upon the hospital, with its bureaucratic order as well as advanced facilities. Now more often a specialist than a general practitioner, the physician must in some measure become an administrator as well as a healer. His success depends in part upon his ability to come to terms with the hierarchical formal structure of the hospital and to make effective use of the various skilled assistants available to him: nurse, laboratory technician, pharmacist, dietician, social worker.

The lawyer, too, more and more becomes part of the great "law factories," as they have been called, with an established hierarchy, standardized procedures, and a clear division of labor—each lawyer specializing in some particular area of the law and aided by law clerks, secretaries, and occasionally bookkeepers, accountants, and investigators. In addition, the great law firms are closely tied to the corporate hierarchies that dominate the economy, and the legal career frequently entails entering one of them in order to climb the ladder as a corporation lawyer or as an administrator whose legal skills stand him in good stead.[34]

In education, as Robert and Helen Lynd once observed, there is a tendency for "the administrative horse [to] gallop off with the educational cart."[35] Teachers complain that they must spend more time filling out forms than teaching. In higher education as in the lower school years, tests are often standardized and the distribution of grades must follow a predetermined statistical curve. In a savage attack on the higher learning in America, Thorstein Veblen over half a century ago described its "underlying presumption" as the view that learning was

a merchantable commodity, to be produced on a piece-rate plan, rated, bought and sold by standard units, measured, counted and reduced to staple equivalence by impersonal, mechanical tests. In all its bearings the work is hereby reduced to a mechanistic, statistical consistency, with numerical standards and units; which conduces to perfunctory and mediocre work throughout, and acts to deter both students and teachers from a free pursuit of knowledge, as contrasted with the pursuit of academic credits.[36]

The explosive events on the University of California campus in Berkeley in 1964 and 1965 and the discontent evident there and elsewhere among students in the United States in the mid-1960s have been attributed at least in part to the bureaucratization of the large university in recent years.[37] (For a fuller discussion of education, see Chapter 15.) One of the central features of the ideology of the "new left" among students is "down with bureaucracy."

Within the academic profession, salaries follow a regular pattern and increase not only with seniority, but also with the acquisition of degrees, so much more for an M.A., or for a Ph.D. So formal have the academic requirements for promotion become in some universities that the doctorate is often familiarly known as the "journeyman's (or union) card." Even academic careers have in some measure been changed. For many, scholarly achievement is still the measure of success, but for others there are now new possibilities in the administrative hierarchy, the two career lines—scholarly and bureaucratic—closely linked by the profusion of committees that spring up in colleges and universities.[38]

The Roman Catholic Church has long possessed an elaborate bureaucratic structure, with its clear-cut hierarchy, division of labor—incorporating, among others, parish priests, missionaries, teachers, scholars, diplomats—formal rules and regulations, and a necessarily elaborate system of internal administration. "This great organization," Page comments, "both suffers the consequences of all close-knit bureaucracies—conservatism, formalism, ritualism, etc.—and enjoys their advantages—order, predictable ac-

Without the elaborate bureaucratic apparatus evident in this characteristic registration scene, no large university could function. Its cost to the participants— students, faculty, and administration— they themselves know.

Sybil Shelton from Monkmeyer

tion, dispatch of business (even when the 'business' is soul-saving)." [39] The Church has avoided or minimized some of the potential bureaucratic disabilities because of the frequently close ties between parish priest and parishioner, the influence of the central religious commitment, and a remarkable adaptability to the concrete problems it faces.

Even in less formal and less hierarchical religious bodies bureaucratic tendencies have emerged. The increasing size of some churches and the widening range of their activities have led to an extensive division of labor—teaching, fund-raising, preaching, supervising the young, counseling the married, visiting the old and sick—that has produced an array of ministerial specialists. A telephone call to a modern urban church for the "minister" is likely to elicit the response: "Which one?" Many ministers and many churches escape this tendency because of their limited size or their poverty; bureaucracy, although perhaps efficient, is also expensive. But the elaboration of church organization, with centralized bodies and specialist services, inevitably gives rise to some measure of bureaucratic organization, possessing its defects as well as its virtues.

In some respects the demands that every bureaucracy makes upon its members are the same—an ability to work well with others, respect for the rules, and technical competence. These continuing requirements upon personality and upon the values men accept create, it is claimed, the "organization man"—well trained, efficient, loyal, bland, restrained, conformist, and concerned with getting along as well as getting ahead.[40] Persons with these attributes can fit easily and smoothly into bureaucratic grooves where teamwork and cooperative effort are required. Corporate recruiters tend to seek out persons who resemble—or can be molded into—this form. Increasingly, therefore, William H. Whyte has argued, the educational institutions that produce the future executives, technicians, administrators—and most college and university graduates see their future as members of some large organization rather than as independent entrepreneurs or professionals—have geared their efforts to creating the appropriate type.

The organization man accepts values that differ from those of the past: "belongingness," "togetherness," and reliance upon the group rather than individualism and self-reliance; from "morality to morale," in David Riesman's phrase, and "from the bank account to the expense account," in Paul Lazarsfeld's words. However appropriate—or functional—these values and the personal characteristics associated with them may be for the usual operations of a bureaucratic organization, they inevitably intrude into areas where they are, in some respects, destructive, or dysfunctional. In the research laboratory, as Whyte points out, the chief prerequisites for success are imagination and originality rather than the ability to get on well with others; the qualities of the administrator are not necessarily combined with those of the creative scientist, but in many instances the relevant values have been reversed in the selection of personnel. Similarly, university departments, in selecting new members of their staff, may choose the pleasant, amiable, and competent person over the difficult, perhaps prickly, personality who shows signs of unusual imagination and ability.[41]

These diverse consequences of the spread of bureaucracy—its impact on medical and legal practice, education, religion, social values—have occasioned a great deal of alarm. They seem to bespeak fundamental changes that run counter to widely accepted values and foreshadow a different and less attractive world. But such changes as have occurred—or are occurring—are part of the price that has been paid for the advantages offered by bureaucracy. The rationalization of organization helps make possible the marvels of mass production and distribution that in themselves may contribute to new kinds of freedom. By using human resources effectively, bureaucracy can increase their collective contribution to the society and make possible achievements that less carefully controlled effort would find out of reach. Bureaucratic rules and regulations ensure uniform treatment for those who come in contact with large-scale organizations as customers or clients, or as citizens in relation to their government. In some measure democracy itself rests upon rational bureaucratic forms. Any final assessment, therefore, must also weigh these consequences and, indeed, the many others the scope, extent, and implications of which have yet to be explored.

Bureaucracy and power

Of perhaps more persistent concern than the social consequences of bureaucracy has been the problem of power that bureaucrats come to wield. The increasing functions of government in Europe and America in the nineteenth and twentieth centuries led to a substantial growth of government bureaucracy. Advocates of increased governmental responsibilities insisted upon the need for political action to counter the growth and power of private enterprise and to provide solutions for the social problems created by urban and industrial expansion. They emphasized the rational aspects of bu-

reaucratic administration and argued that it was possible to maintain effective political controls over public officials.

Stressing the advantages they saw in unregulated private enterprise, the critics of government bureaucracy expressed fear of the growing power of bureaucratic officials to exercise control over the actions of others, particularly over individual entrepreneurs. They focused upon the dysfunctions of bureaucracy—red tape and officiousness—that left the citizen at the mercy of officialdom, and upon the possibilities of inefficiency and irresponsibility that might stem from secure tenure and the absence of competition.

Although bureaucracy is supposed to be the efficient instrument of the policy makers, there can be little doubt, as the earlier discussion of communication suggests, that those who direct the activities of a bureaucratic organization are to some degree at the mercy of their subordinates. Those who possess important skills, particularly if they are professionals, are able to maintain some measure of autonomy and to reduce the effectiveness of hierarchical controls. The "higher civil servants," in particular, occupy an important place in relation to the formulation and execution of policy.

Inevitably, perhaps, government bureaucracy, like others, is marked by a tension between "service" and power. Officially committed to anonymous and impersonal service in pursuit of goals set for the organization by its policy-making heads, they also pursue their own interests. Bureaucratic self-interest, however, need not be defined expressly in terms of power per se, nor is it likely to be. But in order to protect themselves from outside intereference and to avoid changes that might disturb established routines and relationships, officials may try to free themselves from superior authority. Informal organization can provide mechanisms for doing so, as can manipulation of the channels of communication. To the extent to which bureaucratic employees manage to escape from control from above they can impose their judgments on others in the ways in which they interpret the rules and exercise the authority inherent in the offices they occupy.

Officials in the higher ranks are in a particularly strategic position to influence the definition and execution of government policy. Their special skills and knowledge are useful—even, on occasion, essential—in determining what should be done, but the line between offering detached advice and pushing for a specific course of action is not readily drawn or is easily overstepped. A dramatic example of the problems implicit in this situation is to be found in the recurrent question of how to maintain effective control over the United States Central Intelligence Agency. Other examples can readily be drawn from the experience of many other nations.

In any organization, even the most democratic, Robert Michels has argued in his classic *Political Parties*, there is an inevitable tendency for top-level officials to take over and maintain effective control. According to this "iron law of oligarchy," they achieve this domination because of their technical skills and knowledge and their mastery of the administrative machinery and the channels of communication. They justify their actions by identifying the organization with themselves and by emphasizing their experience, capabilities, and service.[42]

Although there can be little doubt that there are "oligarchical" tendencies in organization, there is serious question as to their inevitability. In a detailed study of the International Typographical Union,

unique because of its institutionalized and effective two-party system, Lipset, Coleman, and Trow have identified some of the factors that inhibit the operation of Michels' "iron law"—the structure of the industry, the "culture" of the printers, the institutions regulating access to power, the availability of knowledge about policy questions.[43] Similar factors are probably relevant in any public bureaucracy—the nation's social structure, its prevailing values, the organization of the bureaucracy and its relations to the legislature, elective officials, and the judiciary, the complexity of the issues that arise, the extent of public participation in politics.

The extent to which bureaucracy can affect policy—directly or indirectly—has given rise to considerable discussion of its role in relation to social change. As long as the bureaucracy shares the values of those who dominate the state, it is likely to be the dedicated instrument of the government, whatever its goals, conservative or radical. As J. Donald Kingsley has shown, the British Civil Service that developed during the nineteenth century was drawn from and shared the values of the British ruling class and it functioned assiduously and effectively in building and administering the Empire.[44] In a period of rapid social change, however, when governments change—or are overthrown—the role of the bureaucracy becomes more problematic.

An established bureaucracy, it has been asserted, is intrinsically conservative. If drawn from social groups which no longer dominate public policy, its own values may be out of harmony with the new rulers and its actions may be governed accordingly. Thus "the administration of land-reform measures has been a stumbling block in countries where the top groups of the bureaucracy were linked with the large landholders." [45] More fundamentally, bureaucracy, it has been asserted, is intrinsically conservative.

As a going concern [writes Fritz Morstein Marx, for many years a student of governmental bureaucracy] it bears a distinctly conservative streak. It responds to the present in the light of the past, confining the future to the immediately foreseeable. It has an operational interest in stability, in an undisturbed working rhythm, in today's repetition of yesterday. Not unnaturally, the higher civil service usually favors a firm structure of political power as something to lean against. Expressed differently, administrative systems normally have a professional predilection for the status quo. Higher civil servants often emerge as emotional defenders of the given order of things. [46]

Bureaucracy, according to Karl Mannheim, has a tendency "to turn all problems of politics into problems of administration." [47] From this point of view, the test of any policy is whether it can be carried out within the existing administrative machinery. If not, it can be defined as "impractical," thus limiting any goal to what fits into the existing structure and inhibiting the possibilities of change.

In fact, however, bureaucracy has not followed a consistent pattern in its responses to change. There have been many cases in which bureaucrats have effectively inhibited or sabotaged new programs, either by blocking their execution or by persuading their superiors that their plans for change were unreasonable or impractical. On the other hand, civil servants have accepted innovations on many occasions and have faithfully performed their duties as neutral instruments of the state.

Our understanding of what accounts for bureaucratic responses to social change—with reference to both immediate circumstances and underlying factors—is as yet very limited. Yet the problem is not only of historical interest but also of growing importance, particularly as the world's new nations seek to establish themselves, and, in most cases, to modernize their economy and their social structure. In these efforts, the bureaucracy, often of colonial origin and in many cases one of the chief middle-class groups, occupies a strategic position. Without its effective support and contribution, little progress can be made toward modernization. Yet its traditional status and self-interests may be jeopardized by the possibilities of substantial change, and it often lacks the tradition of service and commitment that might lead it to serve as the instrument of a radical program, whatever its own sentiments. Under such circumstances, transformation of the bureaucracy itself may be both a part and prerequisite of modernization.

Notes

[1] Quoted in G. H. Stevenson, "The Imperial Administration," in *The Cambridge Ancient History*, X (Cambridge, Eng.: Cambridge University Press, 1934), 182.

[2] Robert K. Merton, *Social Theory and Social Structure* (rev. and enlarged ed.; New York: Free Press, 1957), p. 195.

[3] Harold Laski, "Bureaucracy," in *Encyclopedia of the Social Sciences*, III (New York: Macmillan, 1930), 70.

[4] Max Weber, *From Max Weber: Essays in Sociology*, trans. and ed. by H. H. Gerth and C. Wright Mills (New York: Oxford, 1946), Ch. 8.

[5] United States Civil Service Commission, Announcement No. 130B, November 12, 1957.

[6] Merton, *loc cit.*

[7] Weber, *op. cit.*, p. 214.

[8] R. K. Kelsall, *Higher Civil Servants in Britain* (London: Routledge, 1955), p. 3. See also J. Donald Kingsley, *Representative Bureaucracy* (Yellow Springs: Antioch Press, 1944).

[9] Alvin W. Gouldner, *Patterns of Industrial Bureaucracy* (New York: Free Press, 1954).

[10] *Ibid.*, p. 98.

[11] Weber, *op. cit.*, p. 216.

[12] Charles H. Page, "Bureaucracy's Other Face," *Social Forces*, XXV (October, 1946), 91.

[13] Peter M. Blau, *The Dynamics of Bureaucracy* (Chicago: University of Chicago Press, 1955), Ch. 7.

[14] Ralph H. Turner, "The Naval Disbursing Officer as Bureaucrat," *American Sociological Review*, XII (June, 1947), 342–8.

[15] Blau, *op. cit.*, p. 113.

[16] Page, *op. cit.*, p. 90.

[17] Chester A. Barnard, *The Functions of the Executive* (Cambridge, Mass.: Harvard University Press, 1938), p. 123.

[18] Peter M. Blau, *Bureaucracy in Modern Society* (New York: Random House, 1956), pp. 70–4. See also the discussion of the "indulgency pattern" in Gouldner, *op. cit.*, Ch. 2.

[19] Michel Crozier, *The Bureaucratic Phenomenon* (Chicago: University of Chicago Press, 1964), p. 214.

[20] *Ibid.*, p. 215.

[21] *Ibid.*, pp. 216, 219.

[22] *Ibid.*, pp. 51–3.

[23] Peter M. Blau and W. Richard Scott, *Formal Organizations* (San Francisco: Chandler, 1962), p. 243.

[24] Seymour M. Lipset, *Agrarian Socialism* (Berkeley: University of California Press, 1950), pp. 266–7.

[25] For an analysis of the professions, see Talcott Parsons, *Essays in Sociological Theory* (rev. ed.; New York: Free Press, 1964), Ch. 2.

[26] Blau and Scott, *op. cit.*, p. 246.

[27] *Ibid.*

[28] Merton, *op. cit.*, Ch. 6.

[29] Ramsey Muir, *Peers and Bureaucrats* (London: Constable, 1910), pp. 48 ff.

[30] Merton, *op. cit.*, pp. 198–202.

[31] Everett C. Hughes, *Men and Their Work* (New York: Free Press, 1959), pp. 54–5.

[32] Blau, *Bureaucracy in Modern Society*, pp. 64–6.

[33] *Ibid.*, pp. 60–1.

[34] For brief trenchant discussions of bureaucratization in the legal and medical professions, see C. Wright Mills, White Collar (New York: Oxford, 1951), pp. 115–29. See also Erwin O. Smigel,. *The Wall Street Lawyer* (New York: Free Press, 1964).

[35] Robert S. and Helen M. Lynd, *Middletown in Transition* (New York: Harcourt, 1937), p. 206.

[36] Thorstein Veblen, *The Higher Learning in America* (Stanford: Academic Reprints, 1954; first published in 1918), pp. 221–2.

[37] See the frequent references to bureaucratization in Seymour M. Lipset and Sheldon S. Wolin (eds.), *The Berkeley Student Revolt* (Garden City: Doubleday Anchor Books, 1965).

[38] For a suggestive discussion, see Charles H. Page, "Bureaucracy and Higher Education," *The Journal of General Education*, V (January, 1951), 91–100.

[39] Charles H. Page, "Bureaucracy and the Liberal Church," *The Review of Religion*, XVI (March, 1952), 144–5.

[40] See William H. Whyte, Jr., *The Organization Man* (New York: Simon & Schuster, 1956).

[41] For a good analysis of recruiting practices in large universities, see Theodore Caplow and Reece J. McGee, *The Academic Marketplace* (New York: Basic Books, 1958).

[42] Robert Michels, *Political Parties*, trans. by Eden and Cedar Paul (New York: Free Press, 1949; first published in 1915).

[43] Seymour M. Lipset, Martin A. Trow, and James S. Coleman, *Union Democracy* (Garden City: Doubleday Anchor Books, 1962).

[44] J. Donald Kingsley, *Representative Bureaucracy* (Yellow Springs: Antioch Press, 1944).

[45] Fritz Morstein Marx, "The Higher Civil Service as an Action Group in Western Political Development," in Joseph La Palombara (ed.), *Bureaucracy and Political Development* (Princeton: Princeton University Press, 1963), p. 86.

[46] *Ibid.*, p. 87.

[47] Karl Mannheim, *Ideology and Utopia*, trans. by Louis Wirth and Edward Shils (New York: Harcourt, 1946), p. 105.

Suggestions for further reading

BARNARD, CHESTER A. *The Functions of the Executive.* Cambridge, Mass.: Harvard University Press, 1938.
A thoughtful discussion of problems of organization by an executive with wide administrative experience. One of the first books to emphasize the importance of informal relations within large-scale formal organization.

BERGER, MORROE. *Bureaucracy and Society in Modern Egypt.* Princeton: Princeton University Press, 1957.
A study of the role of the higher civil servants in modern Egyptian society. Concerned with the social role of this group rather than its administrative activities.

BLAU, PETER M. *Bureaucracy in Modern Society.* New York: Random House, 1956.
An excellent brief review and evaluation of both theory and important empirical studies of bureaucracy.

BLAU, PETER M., and W. RICHARD SCOTT. *Formal Organizations.* San Francisco: Chandler, 1962.
A very useful summary and analysis of a large body of research and theory on the structure and functioning of complex organizations.

CROZIER, MICHEL. *The Bureaucratic Phenomenon.* Chicago: University of Chicago Press, 1964.
A study of French bureaucracy that throws a good deal of light on variations in bureaucratic organization.

EISENSTADT, S. N. "Bureaucracy and Bureaucratization: A Trend Report and Bibliography," *Current Sociology*, VII, No. 2 (1958), entire issue.
A summary of the status of research and theory on bureaucracy and a classified and annotated bibliography.

GOULDNER, ALVIN W. *Patterns of Industrial Bureaucracy.* New York: Free Press, 1954.
An interesting, although overwritten, study of the emergence of bureaucratic forms in a gypsum plant.

KINGSLEY, J. DONALD. *Representative Bureaucracy.* Yellow Springs: Antioch Press, 1944.
An analysis of the relations between the British Civil Service and British politics and social structure.

LA PALOMBARA, JOSEPH (ed.). *Bureaucracy and Political Development.* Princeton: Princeton University Press, 1963.
A collection of essays on the role of bureaucracy and bureaucrats in the process of political development and modernization now going on in many parts of the world.

MERTON, ROBERT K., et al. (eds.). *Reader in Bureaucracy.* New York: Free Press, 1952.
A collection of writings on bureaucracy that contains both theoretical and empirical (historical and modern) materials. See especially the essays by Merton and Reinhard Bendix.

MOORE, WILBERT. *The Conduct of the Corporation.* New York: Random House, 1962.
A lively, perceptive discussion of the nature of the modern corporation.

SELZNICK, PHILIP. *TVA* and the *Grass Roots*. Berkeley: University of California Press, 1949.
A study of the way in which relations of an organization to outside forces affected its operations.

WEBER, MAX. *From Max Weber: Essays in Sociology.* Trans. and edited by H. H. Gerth and C. Wright Mills. New York: Oxford, 1946, Ch. VIII.
The classic essay on bureaucracy, which has been the starting point for most of the recent theoretical and empirical work.

WHYTE, WILLIAM H. *The Organization Man.* New York: Simon & Schuster, 1956.
A lively account by a perceptive journalist of life in the large organizations that dominate American society and of their impact upon the values and behavior of their salaried employees.

11

Communities: ecology and urbanization

The small community

Communities, we have said (in Chapter 2), are inclusive, territorially defined social groups within which men can pursue the total round of life. Although they may contain internal divisions—families, clans or lineages, classes, ethnic groups, associations—communities provide a common social identity and enlist loyalties that transcend the demands of many other groups. Within a community, MacIver points out, men "develop in some kind and degree distinctive common characteristics—manners, traditions, modes of speech . . . the signs and consequences of a common life." [1]

Since "all community is a matter of degree," and the larger frequently encompasses the smaller, its limits are often difficult to draw. Villages and cities are contained within regions, neighborhoods within cities, regions within nations, and even nations within an international community. Each area can be said to constitute a geographical or territorial whole whose members are, in some respects, tied together by significant bonds. "Even the poorest in social relationships," MacIver writes "is a member in a chain of social contacts which stretches to the world's end. In the infinite series of social relationships which thus arise, we distinguish the nuclei of intenser common life, cities and nations and tribes, and think of them as *par excellence* communities." [2] Here we shall be concerned only with small communities—tribe, village, the rural neighborhood—and cities, and with their interrelation. As a nation is essentially a political unit—actual or potential—we shall defer consideration of its sociological characteristics until Chapter 13.

For most of his history man has lived chiefly in small communities, tied closely to the land or water from which he derived his sustenance. Even today perhaps two-thirds of the more than 3 billion humans who populate the earth are tribesmen or villagers. Unless they have become part of a national or world economy they maintain themselves at hardly more than a minimum level of subsistence, producing little of the surplus needed to build an increasingly complex and differentiated culture.

The social structure and culture of the small community typically are portrayed in terms resembling the communal society described in Chapter 2. Limited size and relative isolation are associated with homogeneity, stability, and resistance to change. There can be only a limited division of labor with a minimal proliferation of social roles. The family or kinship group is likely to be of paramount importance and there are relatively few other groups functioning within the society. Life flows along traditional channels and a strong sense of solidarity binds together the whole.

These gross, yet largely accurate, generalizations cover a wide variety of customs, social structures, and beliefs. Despite their over-all similarities, tribes and villages often differ as much from each other as from large communities with respect to kinship and family organization, religious beliefs and practices, technology and economic arrangements, and so on. The historical origins of the distinctive institutional, cultural, and structural characteristics of many small communities are lost in an unrecorded past, particularly among isolated and illiterate peoples. The relations of these attributes to one another and their functions in the social order can often be explained without reference to the community as such. But in some respects—and it is these that concern us here—the culture and social organization of a community, small or large, are linked to the territorial base, that circumscribed area within which men pursue their common life.

The nature of the territorial base affects a community's social structure and modes of life in many ways. Geographical conditions may account in part for local variations: Desert communities will differ in some ways from those in the jungle, in temperate wooded areas, or in the Arctic. But terrain, resources, and climate, as noted earlier, set problems, impose limits, and create opportunities; they do not in themselves determine the cultural response. Some areas may be incapable under any conditions of supporting more than a sparse population, but in most instances the size of a community depends upon its ability to cope with the natural environment and to utilize and exploit its

resources. Many small communities have not yet developed a culture or, particularly, a technology that enables them to provide much more than the basic needs of food and shelter for a limited number of people.

Geographical conditions may also affect the *ecology* of a community—that is, the way in which it distributes its personnel and activities in space. Many villages, for example, are located along a single axis, giving the impression of "a long, one-streeted village winding its way across the landscape." [3] The origins of these line villages, as they are called,

seem to lie in peculiar geographic features of the landscape which combine with cultural needs and practices in a way to place a premium upon river frontages, alluvial fans [sedimentary deposits left by rivers] at the foot of sharp escarpments, intervals along the beds of streams that flow through narrow mountain valleys, "dry points" along ancient dunes and levees of a marshy country, etc.[4]

Within this geographic setting, however, the interests and values of the members of the community lead to a lineal arrangement of houses and farms. Since the best soil for cultivation in such areas is limited, each family can be sure of having some desirable land only if it is divided into narrow strips running back from the river edge or away from the escarpment.

Often communities follow traditional models, values, and practices derived from and perhaps more appropriate to other locations. Local topography and resources are ignored and conventional patterns are arbitrarily imposed upon the land. Line villages have occasionally been established where geographical conditions did not require them, and conversely, other settlement patterns have been followed in areas where line villages would have been more practical.

Ecology itself is an aspect of social

The small community assumes many forms, reflecting its own traditional patterns and contributing in various ways to social structure and local customs. TOP: Nahalal, Israel, a settlement laid out in a regular pattern with the farm land totally outside the community. CENTER: Inman, Kansas, a small town containing stores and services, surrounded by farms, each with its own house and outbuildings, laid out in a rectangular pattern. BOTTOM: A small Pennsylvania town, similar in some respects to Inman but divided by the main street (the highway passes along the edge of Inman) and with a somewhat more varied dispersion of farms in the countryside.

structure the development and consequences of which deserve—and have
gained—sociological study. Spatial patterns often reflect and result from the
culture and social organization of a community. In Jordan, for example, each
village

is usually divided into a number of sections or
quarters (*harah*), and each of these tends to be
occupied by people belonging to the same lineage. Ordinarily, there are no visible demarca-
tions between the several sections of the village, which is typically a jumble of houses
connected by narrow paths. The whole gives
no appearance of plan beyond the tendency for
the houses to be similarly oriented with relation to the dominant topographical features of
the site.

Most villages have an open space (*sahah*)
where biweekly or monthly markets are held
and which serves as a gathering place on social
occasions generally. The village mosque is apt
to be situated at or near the *sahah*, as are
whatever stores or coffeehouses the village may
possess. In larger villages, or in those in which
more than one religious sect is well represented, there may be more than one *sahah*,
each with its own mosque or church.[5]

In the Punjab of Northwest India,

villages are subdivided whether their inhabitants are mainly Jat, or Hindu, or Muslim. And
the inhabitants know the boundaries of the
divisions within the village though they are
well aware that families belonging to division A
may be living in division B because of such
circumstances as overcrowding and availability
of housing. The subdivisions of the villages have
both boundaries and recognized membership,
even though these may not exactly correspond.
Each subdivision may also have its own meeting place, its own shops and its own holy
places. I have been told . . . that even dogs
know the boundaries of the *pattis* [quarters] to
which they belong and will not allow canine
trespassers.[6]

Nomads or migrant tribes who move
from place to place without a fixed place
of residence nevertheless usually locate
their habitations in a manner that reflects

their social structure. Among the Comanche, for example, the layout of the camp
followed an established pattern. The
leader first located his tipi, and other
families then took positions in some predetermined relationship to it. Places
would be kept open for families who were
not present when camp was pitched. Although the topography of the site inevitably influenced the arrangement of tipis,
"next-door neighbors in one camp would
be next-door neighbors in all camps." [7]

In sharp contrast to the concentrated
villages found in most parts of the world
is the pattern of dispersed or open settlement found in many American rural communities. Early settlers brought a tradition of village life with them which they
quickly reproduced, but these forms disappeared with the movement toward the
frontier. Farmers found economic advantages in settling on their own land; they
could be close to the livestock and free
from the daily trek from home to fields.
Land on the frontier was often acquired
simply by "squatting" long enough to
claim possession. (The Homestead Act of
1862 endorsed this pattern by requiring
residence on the land in order to gain
legal title to it.) A rigid checkerboard
system of surveying that ignored terrain
and divided land into square sections
contributed further to haphazard settlement; in the absence of any economic or
cultural pressures for a concentrated village each farmer was free to put up his
buildings wherever he pleased, and encouraged to do so by the prevailing emphasis upon individualism.

Once established, spatial arrangements
can in turn affect culture and social structure. The concentrated village, for example, makes possible a close community
life which is more difficult to achieve in
a dispersed rural "neighborhood." In
India, M. N. Srinivas has pointed out, the

village as a whole can assume responsibility for protection against both wild beasts and human enemies, while separate families in the areas of open settlement found in some regions must see to their own defense. (Srinivas also suggests the possibility, for which he offers no empirical evidence, that large unilineal kinship groups and a martial tradition are likely to be more prevalent among isolated families than among village inhabitants.[8])

Possible consequences of dispersed settlement were suggested early in the nineteenth century by Timothy Dwight, a preacher and at one time president of Yale University:

> . . . the farmer [resident on his own land] can more advantageously manage his own property, can oversee it more readily, and labour on it with fewer interruptions. . . .
>
> But scattered plantations are subject to many serious disadvantages. Neither schools nor churches can, without difficulty, be either built by the planters or supported. The children must be too remote from the school, and the families from the church, not to discourage all strenuous efforts to provide these interesting accommodations. . . . [If they are built] trifling infirmities, foul weather, and the ill state of the roads, will prevent a regular attendance. . . .
>
> At the same time, persons who live on scattered plantations are in a great measure cut off from that daily intercourse which softens and polishes man. When we live at a distance from every neighbor, a call demands an effort, and a visit becomes a formal enterprise. . . . Social intercourse, therefore, exercised too little to begin to be pleasant, will be considered as an incumbrance; and the affections which cherish it, and which it cherishes and refines in its turn, will either sleep or expire. The gentle and pleasing manners, naturally growing out of it, can never be formed here. On the contrary, that rough and forbidding deportment, which springs from intercourse with oxen and horses, or with those who converse only to make bargains about oxen and horses, a rustic sheepishness, or a more awkward and provoking impudence, take possession of the man, and manifest their dominion in his conduct. The state of the manners, and that of the mind, are mutually causes and effects. The mind, like the manners, will be distant, rough, forbidding, gross, solitary, and universally disagreeable.[9]

This no doubt overdrawn picture disregards the "visiting" and "neighboring" often found in such rural communities and the forms of mutual assistance they developed—cooperative barn-raising, husking and quilting bees, and so on. Nevertheless, it is quite probable that the sense of community and the involvement in a collective community life are much less prevalent in areas of open settlement than in villages, and that levels of "refinement" may differ.

Isolation for individuals or communities is a matter of degree, dependent upon distance and the means of transportation and communication and upon the existing structure of social relationships. Few communities are totally lacking in relationships with others. Even small, relatively isolated primitive tribes often have significant ties with other communities that affect their internal organization and influence their ways of life. Exogamy, for example, necessarily links together small communities, or groups from different communities, creating networks of mutual obligation and expectation among them. Among the Wataita of East Africa, blood pacts between elders from different villages establish effective bonds not only among the particular individuals but also among their lineage groups and even their entire communities.[10] Trading relationships, as among the Trobriand Islanders of the Western Pacific, may also bring together members of different communities in a network of mutual obligations that significantly affects life within each village.

With the expansion of Western culture and the improvement of the means of transportation and communication, many once relatively isolated communities have been drawn into a larger, increasingly interdependent world. Contact with outsiders brings new techniques, implements, and ideas within the purview of the tribesman and the peasant. African natives, for example, who have gone to work in gold and diamond mines or on European-owned plantations have taken—or sent—back to their tribes new goods or wealth that have affected the traditional order of prestige and influence; their absence has itself led to changes in the social structure of their villages.

Conquest, political domination, or economic exploitation of isolated primitive communities by Europeans and Americans have almost inevitably influenced the local structure of power and weakened the hold of traditional values. (Occasionally, however, primitive communities respond to external pressures with an intense revival of traditional beliefs, as in the Ghost Dance among American Indians, or the Mau Mau among the Kikuyu of Kenya, who mounted violent attacks upon both foreigners and those natives who accepted English domination.) In those new—or old—nations in Africa, Asia, and Latin America now undergoing "modernization," once isolated communities are being drawn into larger political contexts within which they are subject to forces emanating from rapidly expanding urban centers.

The relative isolation and independence of peasant communities in Europe and Asia and of the independent farmer in the United States have been so substantially diminished by technological, economic, and political trends that Max Weber as long ago as 1906 could write: "A rural society, separate from the urban social community, does not exist at the present time in a great part of the modern civilized world." [11] Agriculture has become so much a part of the world economy that the ups and downs of the market inevitably have substantial repercussions in the rural community, often leading to significant changes in its culture and social organization. Easier access to the city and new modes of communication have led to the introduction of new ideas, implements, customs, and values, and have weakened the hold of tradition, affected the existing structure of prestige and influence, and often diminished the solidarity of the community.

The village in Europe and Asia, the rural neighborhood or country town in the United States, may still constitute the focus of social life for the peasant and farmer, but these small communities can no longer realistically be considered apart from their ties with the world around them. Indeed, in the more "advanced" industrial societies, the number and proportion of farmers has steadily diminished. So far has this process gone in some nations that Kingsley Davis has suggested that they can be described as almost totally urbanized, as in Great Britain, where almost two-fifths of the population live in cities of over 100,000 and over four-fifths are designated as urban.

The growth of cities

Cities first took form around 5000 B.C. in Egypt, India, and Mesopotamia, but the number of urban dwellers in the world remained relatively small until the nineteenth century. Ancient Rome, probably the largest city to have developed until nineteenth-century London, at its peak held no more than one million inhabitants (although some estimates reduce this number to a quarter of a million), but perhaps no more than one or two per cent of the people of the ancient world lived in cities. Few of the great cities of prenine-teenth-century Europe were very large: Fifteenth-century Venice had somewhat more than 100,000 inhabitants, Elizabe-than London between one and two hun-dred thousand, and Paris during the reign of Louis XIV, when it was the greatest city of Europe, only about 200,000. Despite their comparatively small populations, the cities of Europe—and of Asia and Africa—exerted a great influence upon their societies. History, it is sometimes said, is made in cities; the rural countryside and isolated tribes play a historical role only by virtue of their relations to the city. Tied to the land, strongly rooted in tradition, and with per-spectives limited to the narrow focus of rural or tribal life, the small community enters world history, one might say, only when it is thrust there by external forces.

In 1800, Davis has estimated, about 2.4 per cent of the world's population lived in cities of 20,000 or more.[12] Since the be-ginning of the nineteenth century there has been a striking increase in the num-ber and proportion of urban people. As Table 12 indicates, the proportion of per-sons living in cities of more than 20,000 has roughly doubled every fifty years since 1800; between 1800 and 1950 the proportion in cities of more than 100,000 increased almost eightfold; by 1960 more than a quarter of the world's population was in such urban centers. In 1800 there were no cities with more than 1 million inhabitants. In 1950 there were almost fifty and nearly 900 cities had popula-tions of more than 100,000. By 1960 nearly 1,400 cities had more than 100,000 residents. If present trends continue, by the year 2050 more than four-fifths of the world's population will live in cities of more than 20,000 and more than half in cities of 100,000 or more.

Urban growth in the United States has

Table 12

PERCENTAGE OF WORLD POPULATION LIV-ING IN CITIES, 1800–1960

	Cities of 20,000 or more	Cities of 100,000 or more
1800	2.4	1.7
1850	4.3	2.3
1900	9.2	5.5
1950	20.9	13.1
1960	28.1	19.9

Data for 1800, 1850, 1900, 1950 from Kingsley Davis, "The Origin and Growth of Urbanization in the World," *American Journal of Sociology*, LX (March, 1955), 433; reprinted by permis-sion of The University of Chicago Press. Data for 1960 from Gideon Sjoberg, "The Rural-Urban Dimension in Preindustrial, Transitional, and Industrial Societies," in Robert E. L. Faris (ed.), *Handbook of Modern Sociology* (Chi-cago: Rand McNally, 1965), p. 134.

proceeded at a far more rapid tempo than in most other parts of the world (see Table 13). In 1790 only 5 per cent of the nation's population were urban dwellers. At the beginning of the Civil War there were almost as many city dwellers, pro-portionately, as there are in the entire world today. By 1920 more than half the population lived in cities, and by 1960 more than two-thirds were urban resi-dents. In 1790 no city had as many as 50,000 inhabitants; a century later there were twenty-three cities with between 100,000 and 500,000 residents and three cities with more than 1 million. By 1960 five cities contained more than a million inhabitants and sixteen between 500,000 and 1 million.

Until recently, larger cities grew more rapidly than smaller cities, and an in-creasing proportion of the population was concentrated in cities of more than 100,000 population. In 1860 only 8.8 per cent of the population lived in cities of

Table 13

URBAN GROWTH IN THE UNITED STATES, 1790–1960

Urban territory	1790 5.1	1800 6.1	1820 7.2	1840 10.8	1860 19.8	1880 28.2	1900 39.7
Places of							
1,000,000 or more	—	—	—	—	—	2.4	8.5
500,000 to 1,000,000	—	—	—	—	4.4	3.8	2.2
250,000 to 500,000	—	—	—	1.8	0.8	2.6	3.8
100,000 to 250,000	—	—	1.3	1.2	3.2	3.6	4.3
50,000 to 100,000	—	1.1	1.3	1.1	1.4	1.9	3.6
25,000 to 50,000	1.6	1.3	0.7	1.4	2.1	2.9	3.7
10,000 to 25,000	1.2	1.0	1.3	2.4	2.8	4.4	5.7
5,000 to 10,000	1.2	1.8	1.6	1.9	3.1	3.4	4.2
2,500 to 5,000	1.1	0.9	1.0	1.0	1.9	3.2	3.8
Rural territory	94.9	93.9	92.8	89.2	80.2	71.8	60.3
Places of							
1,000 to 2,500	—	—	—	—	—	—	4.3
Percentage of total population							
United States	100.0	100.0	100.0	100.0	100.0	100.0	100.0
Total population							
United States	3,929,214	5,308,483	9,638,453	17,069,453	31,443,321	50,155,783	75,994,575

Class and size	1910	1920	1930	1940	1950 * Old urban definition	1950 * New urban definition	1960 † Old urban definition	1960 † New urban definition
Urban territory	45.7	51.2	56.2	56.5	59.6	64.0	63.0	69.9
Places of								
1,000,000 or more	9.2	9.6	12.3	12.1	11.5	11.5	9.8	9.8
500,000 to 1,000,000	3.3	5.9	4.7	4.9	6.1	6.1	6.2	6.2
250,000 to 500,000	4.3	4.3	6.5	5.9	5.5	5.5	6.0	6.0
100,000 to 250,000	5.3	6.2	6.1	5.9	6.5	6.3	6.4	6.5
50,000 to 100,000	4.5	5.0	5.3	5.6	6.1	5.9	7.8	7.7
25,000 to 50,000	4.4	4.8	5.2	5.6	6.6	5.8	8.2	8.3
10,000 to 25,000	6.0	6.7	7.4	7.6	8.5	7.9	9.9	9.8
5,000 to 10,000	4.6	4.7	4.8	5.1	5.2	5.4	5.2	5.5
2,500 to 5,000	4.1	4.1	3.8	3.8	3.7	4.3	3.5	4.2
Places under 2,500	—	—	—	—	—	0.4	—	0.4
Unincorporated parts of urbanized areas	—	—	—	—	—	4.9	—	5.5
Rural territory	54.3	48.8	43.8	43.5	41.0	36.0	37.0	30.1
Places of								
1,000 to 2,500	4.6	4.5	3.9	3.8	3.6	4.3	3.1	3.6
Percentage of total population United States	100.0	100.0	100.0	100.0	100.0	100.0	100.0	100.0
Total population United States	91,972,266	105,710,620	122,775,046	131,669,275	150,697,371	150,697,371	179,323,175	179,323,175

* Before 1950 all persons in politically incorporated places of 2,500 or more and certain other special cases were classified as urban. A new definition introduced in 1950 included unincorporated places of 2,500 or more and densely settled areas, incorporated or unincorporated, outside cities with a population of 50,000 or more.

† Figures are for continental United States, excluding Alaska and Hawaii.

U.S. Bureau of the Census, *Statistical Abstract of the United States* (Washington, D.C.: U.S. Government Printing Office), for 1790–1940 (79th ed.; 1958), Table 15, p. 21; for 1940, 1950, and 1960 (84th ed.; 1963), Table 13, p. 21.

more than 100,000. By 1900 the figure had risen to 18.9 per cent and by 1930 to almost 30 per cent; since 1930 the proportion in cities over 100,000 has remained relatively constant. In 1860 only 4.4 per cent of the nation's people dwelt in cities of more than half a million; by 1930 the proportion had risen to 17 per cent and by 1950 to 17.6 per cent. Between 1950 and 1960 this figure dropped to 16 per cent as smaller cities and suburbs grew more rapidly than the centers of the great metroplitan areas.

The figures in themselves still underestimate the urban impact, for around the larger cities have grown up hinterlands that include nearby farm areas, residential and industrial suburbs, and satellite cities dominated by the center. In 1900 less than one-third of the population lived in these "metropolitan areas"; by 1960, 63 per cent were included. And as cities grew in number and size, the contrast between rural and urban life was substantially diminished. New modes of transportation and communication brought farmers and small-town residents more easily and more frequently into the city and exposed them continually to cultural influences emanating from urban centers even when they remained at home.

Before men could come together in cities, agricultural techniques had to be efficient enough to provide for both the tillers of the soil and an urban population. The growth of cities has paralleled and in large part has rested upon the increase in the production of foodstuffs. Agricultural surplus, however, is not necessarily measured by the adequacy of the diet it provides or even by what its producers might wish to consume. Conquerors or an emerging ruling group have often imposed their exactions without regard for the standard of life peasants have

had to accept. "The growth of city life [in the ancient world]," write MacIver and Page, "rested on the precarious foundations of slavery, forced labor, and taxation by the conquering or ruling class; and in some modern civilizations, such as the Chinese and Indian [and, one might add, the Russian], the exploitative factor remains highly significant in the maintenance of large cities." [13]

Two further conditions were required before cities could be built or could grow. First, food and the other raw materials upon which urban life rests had to be made available. Crops are of little value if they cannot readily be moved to the cities where they are needed. The increase in agricultural output therefore had to be paralleled by improvements in the technology of transport: the domestication of the horse and other pack animals, the invention of the wheel, the boat, and eventually of the modern means of transportation. Second, since new problems were created when large numbers of people came together in a single community, new knowledge, skills, techniques, and materials were required. In the ancient cities of the Near East trade and commerce were of major importance in resolving these problems. The story of urban growth in ancient Egypt, Mesopotamia, and the Indus valley "is one of accumulating wealth, of improving technical skill, of increasing specialization of labor, and of expanding trade." [14] All these conditions contributed in turn to increase in population from which the city drew recruits.

Urban centers of considerable size were found in many parts of the world prior to the nineteenth century, but the rapid growth of cities since 1800 is essentially a product of modern industrialism. Heavily urbanized nations are those with an advanced industrial technology which can turn out the goods to be exchanged for agricultural products, furnish the means for bringing these products to the city, and provide the techniques and materials for building and maintaining urban centers. From industry and the scientific knowledge upon which it increasingly rests have also come the machines, chemicals, and know-how that have increased agricultural output. In 1790 the work of more than nine farm families was required to sustain one urban family in the United States. In the 1960s, less than 10 per cent of the American labor force produces enough foodstuffs and other agricultural products not only to sustain the entire population, but also to export large quantities and to pile up surpluses in government warehouses.

Images of the city

From its earliest days, the city as a place and as a way of life has been the object of hostility and criticism. The double themes of urban sinfulness and decadence and rural virtue and vigor can be traced from at least the Old Testament to the present. Sodom and Gomorrah remain vivid symbols of urban vice and decay, against which the industrious and virtuous farmer is set in sharp contrast. "From out of the populous city men groan, and the soul of the wounded cries out," says the Old Testament. "Great cities are but a large sort of prison to the soul, like cages to birds," declared a sixteenth-century Frenchman. Jean Jacques Rousseau described cities as "the sink of the human race," and a seventeenth-century English poet wrote, "God the first garden made, the first city Cain." Thomas Jefferson argued that "The mobs of great cities add just so much to the support of pure government as sores do to the strength of the

human body," and Ralph Waldo Emerson asserted that "Cities give not the human senses room enough." In recent times the higher death rates and lower birth rates of the cities, in comparison with rural areas, have been widely interpreted as signs of moral and physical degeneration.

Complementing this unhappy picture of the artificial, immoral, and degenerate city is the still widespread image of rural virtue, health, and happiness. This image has perhaps had a wider currency in America than in most other parts of the world, for the American farmer has not been a peasant, "bowed by the weight of centuries," but an independent landowner in an individualistic, fluid society without a feudal past. In an editorial in 1956 *The New York Times*, commenting on the decline in the number of farmers and the changing—or disappearing—rural way of life, concluded:

We trust the farmer image will never completely die out in our national life. We hope the picture of the little white house; the big red barn; the contented cows, horses, sheep, hens and pigs; the waving fields of wheat, corn, potatoes, radishes, tomatoes, cucumbers, and parsley; the happy, well-behaved little family, arising at 4:30 A.M. and going to bed soon after 8, will never vanish from our dreams.[15]

Cities, however, have not been without their defenders. "The city is the teacher of the man," said Plutarch. "In all ages and areas, from ancient Egypt to modern America, the highest development of human mentality, initiative, and achievement has been in urban communities," wrote an American scholar for the *Encyclopedia of the Social Sciences*.[16] The sophistication, cultivation, and creativity of the city are contrasted with the "idiocy of rural life"; the city has its slickers, but the countryside has its rubes and hayseeds. While Jefferson worried about urban "mobs," the nineteenth-century

American preacher and writer Theodore Parker wrote: "Cities have always been the fireplaces whence light and heat radiated out into the dark."

These contrasting attitudes constitute in themselves facts of considerable sociological importance. Urban sociology itself, particularly in the United States, has been seriously affected by the implicit acceptance of critical attitudes toward the city. Much of the early work in American sociology focused attention upon the prevalence of immorality, decay, and social disorganization in the city. In studies of the suburban communities that emerged after World War II, on the other hand, some sociologists displayed an urban bias, emphasizing the tendencies toward standardization, the absence of urban stimulation, and the pressures for conformity.

Images of the city have other, perhaps more important consequences as well. Both the virtues and the vices attributed to the city draw rural and small-town migrants who contribute so heavily to the increase in urban population. It is difficult to demonstrate the actual impact of the image of the "golden city," as Thomas Wolfe called it, upon migration, but it seems likely that the promise of wealth and luxury, of sensual delights and cultural opportunities, even of the actuality or hope of forbidden fruit, contributes to the movement to the city.

Politically, the widespread attitudes toward the city and the farm have been of considerable importance in the United States, for they provide rationalizations and justifications for or against particular political institutions. In some eyes, the "farmer image" presumably so dear to the heart of *The New York Times* provides a rationale for the overrepresentation of rural areas in state legislatures as well as in the United States Senate. Farmers have drawn heavy subsidies

while cities, until quite recently, have received relatively little aid in dealing with their increasingly difficult problems. Responses to recent legislative and judicial actions—the establishment of a new cabinet post to deal with urban problems and the Supreme Court decisions affecting legislative apportionment—have undoubtedly been affected by such images as well as by considerations of economic and political self-interest.

Finally, the images men have of what a city is or ought to be also affect the ways in which men seek to build or rebuild their urban communities. They may try to capture the virtues—real or imagined—of the countryside or small town or, alternatively, may endeavor to create cities that possess the qualities that defenders of urban life claim a great city should achieve.

Urbanism: culture and social structure

Of the many statements about the city one may distinguish those that claim merely to describe urban life and society and those that contain judgments of value. The low urban birth rate is a fact the truth of which can be objectively and reliably tested. That such a fact demonstrates the decadence of the city is a judgment that rests upon value premises about which men may disagree. Our task here is not to judge but to explore the nature of the city and the social and cultural consequences of urban growth. (This task, however, is not irrelevant to problems of value, for value judgments often rest upon assertions that may or may not be true.)

Size and density of population are usually hallmarks of the urban community, but there is little agreement about where the line between rural and urban should be drawn. In the United States— and in Mexico and Venezuela—any settlement with a population of 2,500 or more is classified as urban. (This is not the full definition in the United States Census, which also includes reference to areas adjacent to cities with sufficient density of population but not legally incorporated as cities.) In India, Ceylon, Belgium, and Greece the dividing line is set at 5,000; several other countries draw the line at 2,000; and New Zealand considers 1,000 as the minimal size of an urban community. These definitions are inevitably arbitrary and tell us nothing about the characteristic ways of life or forms of social structure found in the city. Nevertheless, the facts of size and density constitute basic characteristics from which a theory of urban society has been derived.[17]

With growing numbers comes a greater hetereogeneity of population. The city continually recruits its residents from elsewhere—farms, villages, perhaps other cities or even other societies or nations— and these migrants bring with them diverse beliefs, values, and ways of life. Increasing size requires a greater division of labor and the emergence of new, often highly specialized roles. Both size and heterogeneity preclude the pervasive familiarity with others characteristic of the small community. More and more of one's social life is organized in formal and impersonal relationships that discourage the possibility of intimacy; the formal association supplants the primary group as the context in which one pursues many of the routines of daily life.

Cultural shifts accompany these changes in social relationships. As Georg Simmel points out, the variety and number of external stimuli and of social contacts are likely to increase. Psychic demands therefore become greater and only

by developing a protective layer of sophistication (indifference, a blasé attitude) and of rationality can the individual protect himself from the incessant pressures of the social environment. The money economy characteristic of the city contributes further to the rationality and objectivity of the urban dweller, for money is an abstract medium that minimizes personal criteria of judgment and gives to social interaction its own formal character. Thus, Simmel writes:

> Punctuality, calculability, exactness are forced upon life by the complexity and extension of metropolitan existence and are not only most intimately connected with its money economy and intellectualistic character. These traits must also color the contents of life and favor the exclusion of those irrational, instinctive, sovereign traits and impulses which aim at determining the mode of life from within.[18]

Urban impersonality, rationality, and diversity also engender tolerance of differences and a lack of concern with the behavior of others that make possible— even encourage—innovation and a disregard for tradition. Each individual can pursue his own interests, adopt new beliefs, and follow new lines of action, for he can escape the coercions inherent in close relations with others. If others disapprove of his behavior he can change both his residence and his associates, seeking out those who share his inclinations and point of view. Hence a myriad of social worlds—neighborhoods, the professions, the theater, academic circles, exclusive social clubs, political clubs, the underworld—can emerge in the city, each with its own distinctive beliefs, values, and modes of action—within the limits imposed by urban forms of social control.

Tradition and the opinions of family and friends lose some of their force in the urban community, for it is easy to escape from close surveillance, to become lost in the anonymous urban crowd. Instead, the formal machinery of law and of bureaucratic rules and regulations, as well as the stirrings of self-interest, constitute the means by which social order is maintained. Formal organizations rather than the family catch up and provide outlets for the diverse interests of a variegated population. These organizations become significant elements in the organized life of the community, shaping its form and affecting the public policies that influence or direct its collective fate.

A reality as complex as the city can be contained only imperfectly in these—or any other—sweeping generalizations. Despite their plausibility, therefore, as a description and interpretation of urban society and culture, they must necessarily be tested by systematic observation, modified or rejected whenever the facts reveal a different pattern of social life. Cities differ from one another not only with respect to size and density, but also in many other salient attributes: population composition, economic characteristics, forms of government, topography, and so on. Moreover, as Gideon Sjoberg has shown, preindustrial cities differ in significant ways from industrial cities,[19] and most theories of urban society and culture have dealt with the latter. At best then, the theory of the city so briefly summarized above can be descriptive only of prevailing tendencies or dominant patterns; it offers hypotheses to guide research and not tested empirical generalizations.

There is, however, some confirming evidence for several of the generalizations about rural-urban differences and the nature of urban society. Bernard Berelson and Gary Steiner report in their "inventory of scientific findings" on human behavior that there is substantial basis for concluding that there is "more political and religious tolerance in the cities than in rural areas," that there is "less religious observance in the cities than in rural areas, especially in the form of church attendance by men," that there is "more change in the cities, more stability in the country," and more divorce, crime, and suicide in the urban areas than the rural.[20] Moreover, many presumably urban attributes do vary with the size of the community. On the basis of a careful analysis of data from the Census of 1950, Otis D. Duncan and Albert J. Reiss conclude:

> Generally speaking, the larger the community the smaller is the proportion married, and the larger are the indicators of family disruption. In large places, the labor force participation of women is high, comparatively, and effective fertility low. . . . The study finds a direct correlation between community size and the proportion of the labor force engaged in white collar occupations. . . . One may surmise that the high proportion of clerical workers in large urban centers represents a tendency toward large-scale organization of human activities. . . . Perhaps the proportion of clerical workers is the best single occupational indicator of the complexity of the division of labor.[21]

These facts also testify to the likelihood that as the size of the community increases, formal, impersonal relationships gain in relative frequency in comparison with primary, and particularly family, ties.

As these data suggest, urbanism, the interrelated set of attributes that characterize the city, is a matter of degree. Many urban social relationships are formal and impersonal, but primary groups and relationships also persist. Supermarkets with self-service carriages and cashiers who merely punch the cash register replace the corner grocer who knew his customers—their tastes, preferences, children, and often their personal problems—but here and there the neighborhood store remains. Most urban medicine is carried on by specialists who often seem to be more interested in the heart, appendix, or throat than the patient, but some general practitioners concerned with the whole patient are still at work. Most men are employed in bureaucratic structures, but primary groups develop, as pointed out in Chapter 10, within any large-scale organization.

Many of the patterns of interaction in the city, however, do not seem to fit into either of these alternative categories of primary or impersonal. One might speak of "neighborly" relations that entail mutual aid but do not achieve the closeness of the primary group, or of "personalized contacts" which allow for friendliness without intimacy.[22] The character of such relationships has been perceptively described by Jane Jacobs in a staunch defense of certain features of urban life:

. . . it is possible in a city street neighborhood to know all kinds of people without unwelcome entanglements, without boredom, necessity for excuses, explanations, fears of giving offense, embarrassments respecting impositions or commitments, and all such paraphernalia of obligations which can accompany less limited relationships. It is possible to be on excellent sidewalk terms with people who are very different from oneself, and even, as time passes, on familiar public terms with them.[23]

When primary relationships are found in the city, they are not typically based upon geographical propinquity, as they frequently are in the small town or rural countryside. Neighborliness is not usually an urban virtue; indeed, from the point of view of many urbanites it becomes a vice, translated as nosiness, disregard for privacy, and butting into other people's business. "Spatial proximity and social distance" is a sociological cliché often applied to urban life, for even when men are deeply enmeshed in significant networks of primary relationships, their associates are likely to be chosen on the basis of common interests or shared experience rather than because they live close by. Neighborliness is not necessarily absent, but it emerges only under special conditons—after long residence in one place, when families with children live near one another, when physical barriers set off a distinctive area within which local loyalties develop, when residents of an area share the same cultural background, or when common interests bring neighbors together in a concerted effort to cope with a local problem such as elimination of a neighborhood eyesore or agitation for better police protection.

Differences among cities in the activities that engage their residents complicate the problem of formulating generalizations about urban culture and social structure. Although few cities of any substantial size are devoted exclusively to a single activity—their size alone requires some diversification simply to meet local needs—many cities do tend toward some degree of specialization. Washington is overwhelmingly a political city, as is Brasilia. Atlantic City and Miami Beach, England's Brighton, and Nice in France are resorts. Pittsburgh and Detroit, Lille and Lyons, Leeds and Manchester are predominantly industrial cities.

There has been little systematic inquiry into the consequences of specialization or of the presence or absence of distinctive organizations and activities upon the culture and social structure of urban communities.[24] But it seems clear that political centers, for example differ significantly in their population composition, associational life, leadership, and political interest and values from industrial centers or resorts. The presence of a university not only brings a special group of both students and scholars, but may also provide opportunities and stimulation (as well, perhaps, as creating problems) not found in other places. The social structure and tenor of life in a city like St. Augustine, Florida, or Santa Cruz, California, are undoubtedly affected by the presence of a large number of elderly people who have retired there, just as New York City reflects the presence of the nation's leading financial exchange and Chicago and Omaha the presence of the stockyards.

Even within a city, however, the differences among the many groups it contains—classes, ethnic groups, races, religious communions, neighborhoods—make generalization difficult. As noted in Chapter 8, for example, there are substantial variations in the frequency with which members of different classes belong to the voluntary associations considered to be characteristic of urban society. In a study in 1946 in New York City, Mirra Komarovsky found that 60 per cent of male industrial workers did not belong to any voluntary organization, compared with 53 per cent of white-collar workers earning less than $3,000 per year and 21 per cent of professionals.[25] Ten years later Morris Axelrod found that the proportion of people belonging to voluntary associations in Detroit fell from 81 per cent of those earning $7,000 per year or more to only 42 per cent of those earning less than $3,000.[26] Other studies show that the urban working class confines a larger share of its off-the-job social life within the family and peer group than the middle class.[27]

In many types of neighborhoods in the city there are diverse modes of social life: the anonymity of the rooming house district, the hectic street life of the slum, the violent frustration of the racial ghetto, the busy round of social engagements on the Gold Coast, the discreet respectability of the middle-class residential area, the friendly but detached neighborliness of the well-to-do in an area of one-family homes and sweeping lawns. In some measure, therefore, urban social life and social structure reflect the ecological form of the city, a form which is itself a product of complex economic, cultural, and political forces operating with a geographical context.

Ecology of the city

Many efforts have been made to discover regular ecological patterns in the city, but each set of generalizations seems to apply only to a limited number of cases. In 1925 Ernest Burgess suggested that American cities could be described as a series of concentric circles radiating out from the central business district, within each of which distinct neighborhoods could also be identified.[28] (See Figure 3.A.) Based on a careful study of Chicago, that pattern was the result of distinctive local circumstances as well as pervasive institutional forces. Chicago is built upon flat land running back from Lake Michigan and centering around the "Loop," the central business district. Its growth was rapid and largely shaped by the free play of private economic interest. Under similar geographical and social conditions, other cities often reveal a similar pattern, but when these conditions do not obtain, marked deviations from the concentric-circle form appear.

A second "theory," proposed in 1939 by Homer Hoyt, modified Burgess's scheme by calling attention to the movement of types of neighborhoods within "sectors" carved in wedge-shapes from the center outward.[29] (See Figure 3.B.) Of central importance in defining these sectors and channeling growth are the major travel arteries. This description too, although an accurate rendering of

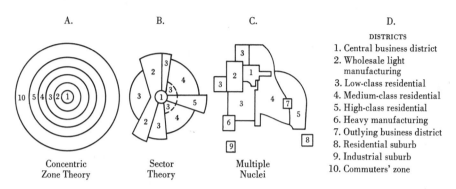

The concentric-circle theory has been advanced as a generalization applicable to all cities. The arrangement of the sectors in the sector theory varies from city to city. The diagram for multiple nuclei represents one possible pattern among innumerable variations.

Figure 3. Generalizations of Internal Structure of Cities

Chauncey D. Harris and Edward L. Ullman, "The Nature of Cities," *The Annals of the American Academy of Political and Social Science*, CCXLII (November, 1945), 13. Reprinted by permission of The American Academy of Political and Social Science.

some cities, does not apply to all. A third pattern noted by geographers Edward Ullman and Chauncey Harris consists of "nuclei" around each of which a particular type of growth takes place.[30] (See Figure 3.C.) Eventually more or less differentiated areas—commercial, light industry, heavy industry, low-cost residential, medium- or high-cost residential—appear. This nucleated structure develops under several different conditions: when separate communities expand until they become a single urban mass, when proximity is an advantage to persons engaged in similar activities, when different activities do not go well together—heavy industry and high-cost residential, for example.

Although none of the empirical generalizations about the spatial froms of urban communities—concentric circles, sectors, multiple nuclei—stands up when applied to cities with varying topography, history, and economy, several types of ecological areas do recur with considera-

ble frequency. Some of these areas are listed in Figure 3.D., which contains a guide to 3.A., 3.B., and 3.C. In the central business district are concentrated office buildings, department stores, and a diverse array of other retail establishments and professional and business services. Few private residences are found here, although there are likely to be hotels for transients. The area surrounding the business core, which contains wholesale establishments and light manufacturing, is often described as a *zone of transition*, for it was once a residential locality but has been abandoned by its residents and is characterized by mixed land uses. Because its old homes are deteriorating, it frequently contains—or contained, for the situation is changing rapidly—rooming houses used by a floating population made up largely of single persons and the residential slums of the ethnic or racial groups who find themselves at the bottom of the class structure. This zone's avenues are lined with pawnshops, cheap restaurants, taverns, and stores selling used clothing, second-hand furniture, and cheap household goods. This is the home of skid row and the cheapest honkytonks, the locale for "bohemia," the part of the city visited by middle-class "slummers" seeking life in the raw, and the racial ghetto avoided by outsiders. In the 1920s, it was also the field of many sociological investigations, Harvey Zorbaugh's *The Gold Coast and the Slum*, Paul Cressey's *The Taxi Dance Hall*, Frederick Thrasher's *The Gang*, and others. Now it is an area that in some cities is undergoing renewal or redevelopment.

Within each of the residential zones described by Burgess there are often important sociological differences. The lower-class residential district, for example, may include some neighborhoods of small one-family homes, and others with multiple-dwelling-unit buildings, and may contain more or less distinct ethnic subcommunities. Similarly, high-class residential areas may encompass streets of high-rent apartment buildings (sometimes, in New York City and other metropolitan centers, cheek by jowl with slum tenements) and equally expensive secluded areas of one-family homes. The commuter zone defined by Burgess has now come to include both residential and industrial suburbs as well as outlying commercial or business districts.

In a "free economy" land values play an important role in determining the uses to which an area is put. Owners tend to devote their land to whatever use will produce the greatest return; if they can gain more by building stores or factories than by building residences, they will try to do so. The desirability of property for various uses depends in turn upon transportation facilities, topography, and the activities carried on nearby. If industry or some

types of business move into a residential neighborhood, it is likely to decline because it becomes less attractive as an area in which to live. It is not, however, mixed land use *per se*, as Jane Jacobs and others have shown, that causes the deterioration of an urban neighborhood, for diversity can in fact be very desirable if it offers a lively environment, a variety of readily available services, and imposes no risk or hardships upon local residents.[31] It is rather the presence of certain kinds of land use—parking lots, junk yards, gas stations, enterprises that draw heavy traffic—that leads to blight or urban decay or that serves as evidence that an area is already becoming run down.

That part of the city with incompatible land uses is likely to become a slum, with ill-kept buildings and inadequate public facilities, providing low-rent housing for those with limited incomes. Slums persist, however, not only because of a demand for low-cost housing but also because they can be profitable to the owners. Many families can be crowded together and total rent collections increased, particularly among racial or ethnic groups who cannot freely find housing elsewhere in the city.

Although land values and economic competition play the major role in determining ecological patterns in a free-market economy, noneconomic variables also enter into the patterns of land use and the spatial distribution of groups and activities. As Walter Firey demonstrated (in a study published in 1947), the spatial pattern of Boston has been significantly affected by traditional values.[32] Boston Common, for example, like many other comparable parks in the center of large cities, has remained inviolate, despite the high return it could produce were it to be utilized for business purposes. Even a proposal to build a parking garage under the Common to accommodate some of the cars filling the narrow streets of downtown Boston was initially rejected for sentimental reasons, and only finally built in 1961. As building and rebuilding goes on in the older sections of American cities, campaigns are frequently mounted to save some old landmark or unusual structure.

The movement of various groups within the city often rests upon cultural values of various kinds. In Boston's North End, Walter Firey pointed out, many Italians who could afford better housing elsewhere refused to move from the neighborhood because they preferred to remain close to their own ethnic group, and Herbert Gans found the same response among Italians in Boston's West End.[33] Barriers to Negro residence usually rest upon racial prejudice, and the ecological distribution of other groups is affected by both in-group commitments and hostility from without.

Ecological theories of the past tended to emphasize impersonal forces and social processes that expressed themselves, characteristically, through a multitude of individual decisions—to build, to move, to buy, to sell. Yet history, of course, records many cities that were built according to some preconceived scheme or that were rebuilt according to some design, as Baron Haussman reconstructed Paris during the reign of Napoleon III. Even in American cities, the context within which individual decisions concerning land use have been made has typically been a predetermined gridiron street layout, a pattern that goes back in urban history at least as far as Mohenjo-Daro, a city in the Indus valley of India built several millennia before the birth of Christ. The gridiron plan was imposed upon Manhattan in 1811 on the basis of the recommendation of a commission appointed by the state legislature. The commission observed that in considering the layout of the city they "could not but bear in mind that a city is to be composed of the habitations of men, and that strait sided and right angled houses are the most cheap to build and the most convenient to live in." [34] The physical or ecological structure of a city, then, is clearly affected by such complex factors as prevailing architectural fashions and the images of what a city or an urban neighborhood can or ought to be.

Increasingly, the outlines of American cities rest in the hands of public officials and large-scale developers rather than in a multitude of separate individuals each going his own way. Zoning rules seek to control future growth and change. Public housing projects, "downtown" developments, neighborhood rebuilding plans such as that for Lincoln Square in New York City or Scollay Square in Boston, and private schemes such as the insurance company-sponsored Fresh Meadows in Queens are now defining the shape of much of the future city. Economic interests embodied in individual decisions, though not irrelevant, must now often operate through the sometimes open, sometimes devious, channels of urban politics and public administration.

These empirical generalizations and theoretical interpretations about urban ecology derive mostly from American cities, and their relevance to urban development elsewhere in the world has yet to be determined. One effort to apply the concentric circle scheme to Paris and its environs identified seven zones, though they possessed neither sharply defined boundaries nor a clear-cut circular form. Moreover, it was necessary to recognize the extent to which Paris was divided along class lines, predominantly middle class toward the west and heavily working class toward the east.[35] The shape of many French cities differs in several significant respects from American cities. There are less likely to be central business districts comparable to those found in most cities in the United States. Because of controlled building heights, land values have not risen and similar activities are likely to be spread out rather than concentrated in a single location. The ecological segregation characteristic of the United States has not developed to the same degree. Instead of the high population density found in some areas of American urban centers, the population is more evenly distributed. The much slower growth and the longer history of French cities have produced a much greater variety of urban forms. Finally, the *quartier* has demonstrated much more viability as a significant social unit than the urban neighborhood has in the United States.[36]

Metropolis and suburbs

Traditional urban patterns have changed as more and more metropolitan centers have incorporated a growing proportion of the population. This process has occurred not only in the United States, where, as we noted earlier, two-thirds of the nation now (1966) reside in 224 metropolitan areas, but also in other nations. In England, for example, more than 40 per cent of the people live in six large metropolitan areas, or conurbations, as the English call them, around London, Liverpool, Manchester, Birmingham, Leeds, and Newcastle. Although the trend is most pronounced in England and the United States, metropolitan areas have multiplied and incorporate more and more of the populations of such diverse countries as Australia, Canada, Denmark,

France, Italy, the U.S.S.R., Japan, and India, and even in some measure parts of Latin America and Africa.[37] The widespread increase of metropolitan areas means not only the increase of urbanism, but also of *suburbanism,* in one form or another, in many parts of the world.

Within metropolitan areas in the United States, the "rings" surrounding the central cities have grown steadily for more than half a century, and since 1930 even more quickly than the central cities (see Table 14). Although metropolitan areas continue to grow faster than other parts of the country, their increase is chiefly in the outlying sections. In many places the central city is now barely holding its own, or is even experiencing a decline in population, as many of its residents move to the suburbs. Between 1950 and 1960, the rings in over one-third of the metropolitan areas grew more rapidly than the central cities, which, in almost one-quarter of the cases actually lost population. Milwaukee, for example, increased by 16.3 per cent while its suburbs added 41.7 per cent. St. Louis declined by one-eighth at the same time that its suburbs more than doubled.

Outside the central city the metropolitan area includes various types of communities: satellite cities, frequently with their own internal differentiation and their own suburban fringe; industrial towns; dormitory suburbs for well-to-do business or professional men, for industrial workers, and for the several levels of the middle class. The expansion of the areas outside the central city, particularly since the end of World War II, is in part simply the result of population growth—between 1950 and 1960 the nation's population increased by almost 30 million and by the mid-1960s had added more than half again as many. In some measure this metropolitan expansion is

Table 14

STANDARD METROPOLITAN AREAS, UNITED STATES, 1900–1960

All S.M.A.s	Number of S.M.A.s	Popu- lation (mil- lions)	In S.M.A.s	In central cities	In rings	In U.S.	In S.M.A.s	In central cities	In rings
		Percentage of U.S. total				Rate of growth during preceding decade			
1960	212	112.9	63.0	32.4	30.6	18.5	26.4	10.8	48.5
1950	162	85.6	56.8	32.8	24.0	14.5	21.8	13.9	34.7
Principal S.M.A.s *									
1950	147	84.3	56.0	32.3	23.8	14.5	21.8	13.7	34.8
1940	125	67.1	51.1	31.6	19.5	7.2	8.3	5.1	13.8
1930	115	61.0	49.8	31.8	18.0	16.1	27.0	23.3	34.2
1920	94	46.1	43.7	28.9	14.8	14.9	25.2	26.7	22.4
1910	71	34.5	37.6	28.0	12.7	21.0	32.6	35.3	27.6
1900	52	24.1	31.9	21.2	10.7	20.7	—	—	—

* Principal S.M.A.s are those with more than 100,000 inhabitants.

Data through 1950 from Donald J. Bogue, "Urbanism in the United States, 1950," *American Journal of Sociology*, LX (March, 1955), Tables 4 and 5, p. 480; reprinted by permission of The University of Chicago Press. Data for 1960 from U.S. Bureau of the Census, *Statistical Abstract of the United States, 1963* (84th ed.; Washington, D.C.: U.S. Government Printing Office, 1963), p. 13.

also a product of economic forces: high land values push industries out to the fringes where costs are less, bringing workers and then the services they need in their wake. Both residential movement and industrial migration rest upon the automobile and truck, which have made possible full use of suburban areas, away from easy access to railroads and other means of public transportation.

But the move to the suburbs also reflects an effort to realize values not easily achieved in the city. A growing emphasis upon family life, the desire for home ownership, and a distaste in at least some cases for urban life have pushed many people out to the suburbs. This exodus is not a simple rejection of the city, but rather of the state to which many cities have fallen (see Figure 4). Adequate housing for families at reasonable prices is often difficult to secure. Because of high land values, taxes, and the cost of building, little housing is erected in the city for middle-income families, who therefore have little choice but to move out. (In New York City in 1960, apartments renting for from $80 to $120 per month—presumably middle-class housing—accounted for only about 25 per cent of all dwelling units. Among those who were renting such apartments, one-third were paying more than one-quarter of their incomes for rent, while almost one-fifth were committing more than one-third of their incomes for housing. Of the almost 30,000 new rental units built in 1959 and the first few months of 1960, over 60 per cent rented for more than $120 per month.[38] The situation has probably not improved since that time and may, indeed, have worsened.) Even if housing were available, the schools are often old and overcrowded, a fact of great importance to education-conscious middle-class parents, and other public facilities are also likely to be inadequate and neglected.

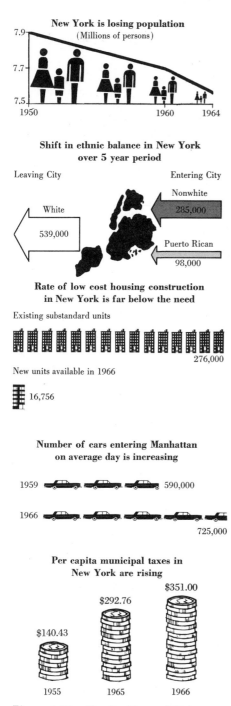

New York is losing population
(Millions of persons)

**Shift in ethnic balance in New York
over 5 year period**

Leaving City   Entering City

Nonwhite

White   285,000

539,000

Puerto Rican

98,000

**Rate of low cost housing construction
in New York is far below the need**

Existing substandard units

276,000

New units available in 1966

16,756

**Number of cars entering Manhattan
on average day is increasing**

1959   590,000

1966

725,000

**Per capita municipal taxes in
New York are rising**

$351.00

$292.76

$140.43

1955   1965   1966

*Figure 4. Five Key Problems of Cities
(Using New York City as an Example)*

Suburban growth itself contributes to the growing problems of the metropolitan area. The heavy volume of commuting traffic chokes city streets and renders urban residence even less desirable. As shopping in the city becomes more difficult and crowded, new centers spring up in the suburbs that cut into the city's economic health and accelerate the rate of decay. Those most likely to flee the disabilities of urban life are middle-class families, from whom civic leadership to deal with urban problems is often recruited.

In the place of those who leave the central cities come migrants from rural areas and small towns, more and more of them Negroes from the South and Puerto Ricans. By 1960 more than half of Washington's population was Negro, 35 per cent of Baltimore's, almost a quarter of Chicago's, almost one-third of Detroit's. These proportions have continued to increase, and the size of the Negro communities in many other cities has grown as well. Between 1950 and 1960, the twenty-four largest metropolitan areas, those with a population of 500,000 or more, lost 2,399,000 white residents and acquired 2,641,000 Negroes. Few Negroes managed to escape from the city even though in some of them the Negro middle class was growing steadily. (In 1960, one-third of the Negro families in Chicago had incomes of $6,000 or more.) But only 4 per cent of the residents of the suburbs of the twenty-four largest metropolitan areas were Negro.

The changing class and ethnic character of cities creates new problems and adds new burdens. Racial tensions often sharpen, and when relief for the difficulties facing racial minorities are not forthcoming violence can erupt, as it has in Los Angeles, Philadelphia, Rochester, and other cities in recent years. The problems inherent in adjusting to an urban environment throw many new arrivals onto relief rolls or into the hands of social service agencies, expanding governmental costs at a time when the tax base is not increasing and may even be declining. And as these various problems become more and more severe, the exodus to the suburbs is further stimulated.

The suburbs, it is sometimes suggested, constitute the new "frontier," where old values can be regained and new ones achieved. Family life becomes more important; families are larger. The relative uniformity of most suburban communities ensures enough similarity of values and interests to encourage the growth of neighborliness; relations with others are based in large measure upon propinquity. The lower size and density of the population not only provide more open space but also encourage increased participation in community life.

This view is challenged by the argument that the friendly, congenial, homogeneous suburb offers less opportunity for a "private" life than does the city. The advantages of anonymity and the opportunity to choose one's friends and associates without regard to possibly irrelevant criteria of residence and physical proximity are lost. In addition, critics assert, the suburbanite lives in a uniform environment and is less exposed to the variety, color, and excitement of urban life; the cultural and institutional facilities of the metropolis are so far away that they are not easily exploited.

These assertions contain both fact and value, and we should distinguish between the actual character of suburban life and the judgments made of it. The growth of the suburbs does constitute something new, an effort to combine the best of two worlds: from the countryside, a more cohesive community, greater opportunities for a family-centered way of life, more

space for living and readier access to nature; all this, however, within easy access of the amenities of the city, but without its disadvantages—crowding, dirt, noise, deteriorating public facilities, anonymity, inability to participate in or control the centers of community power, and, presumably, higher taxes. This combination itself is not new; the older suburbs offered these advantages to a relatively limited number of well-to-do families who could afford them. In the more recent opportunity for millions of families to pursue these values lies the novelty of the situation.

This effort to achieve a suburban utopia for the "masses" is perhaps open to question, but its value or desirability is not our immediate concern. Whether or not men do in fact gain the goals they pursue, and the consequences of both their pursuit and their realization are sociological problems *par excellence*. There is already considerable evidence that this utopian effort has come upon hard times and that even harder times may lie ahead. If the patterns of suburban growth are left to the relatively free play of economic forces in which each for himself and no one for everyone is the rule, then important requirements of collective life are likely to be ignored and as a result the needs of private life are not met. Open space is often gobbled up by developers unconcerned with the necessity or desirability of open space for parks, woods, walks, fields. Each new development adds to the suburban tax burden, which soon equals that of the city. Access to the amenities of the city—shops, theaters, museums, professional services, special schools, and so on—becomes increasingly difficult, and as a result urban facilities may even deteriorate for lack of an effective and interested public. The virtues of the suburb— its lesser density, greater space, limited size and therefore smaller resources—preclude transporting many of the urban advantages to the outlying areas.

The suburbanite often seeks to protect his new way of life by insisting upon the independent political existence of his community and by denying any responsibility for either the metropolitan center or the metropolitan area as a whole. Limited size, homogeneity, and freedom from the more obvious urban flaws make the suburb seem not only a pleasanter place to live, but also a more manageable and more comfortable world. But although it may indeed constitute a nucleus "of intenser common life," in MacIver's phrase, it is now part of a larger community as well, in which each individual's fate, as well as that of each community, is inevitably tied up with the larger whole.

The dimensions of that larger community have steadily expanded and one may now identify in several parts of the country an incipient *megalopolis*, a continuous urbanized and suburbanized strip that encompasses many cities, as metropolitan areas have begun to overlap at their margins and to grow together. The French geographer Jean Gottman has analysed this process in great detail on the northeastern seaboard from north of Boston to south of Washington, D.C.[39] Similar trends, though much less advanced, can be seen elsewhere—along the northern shores of the Great Lakes, from Dallas to Fort Worth in Texas, in southern and nothern California, as well as in parts of Europe such as the Ruhr, Holland, and in nothern England. As the open spaces within and between metropolitan areas are built up, Gottman argues, it becomes necessary for many purposes to think of the megalopolis as the important sociological entity, rather than the central city, the suburb, or even the metropolitan area.

How significant the megalopolis may be is open to question; one recent critic discounts its present importance. "Each of the metropolitan areas along the [Eastern] seaboard," he asserts, "remains strongly oriented to its own center." [40] Yet many questions remain concerning the actual nature of the metropolitan community and its relations to the diverse smaller communities contained within it. Can the central city maintain the services it makes available to the entire area and provide those amenities from which both urbanite and suburbanite benefit? Will the city continue to become the home for the upper and lower classes, with racial minorities segregated in lower-class ghettoes and the middle class in homogeneous suburbs? What would be the long-run consequences of such an ecological pattern? Can suburbs avoid an increasing and perhaps oppressive tax burden and still maintain the type of community life and services they want? Will the older suburbs lose the advantages of location that they possess—the proximity to open fields and the absence of heavy traffic, for example—as the wave of suburban growth spreads further and further from the central city? Can the problems that face the entire metropolitan area—water supply, roads and traffic, maintenance of parks and recreational areas, coordinating police and fire protection—be solved without decreasing or eliminating the separate political identity of the suburban communities? Indeed, is it possible that some of these problems require action on a large scale, that of the megalopolis? In this complex welter of problems, one sociological and political fact at least seems unchallenged: that many of the crucial problems of community life for both city and suburbs take shape within a larger area and that the smaller units within that area cannot independently cope with them.[41]

Notes

[1] Robert M. MacIver, *Community*, (London: Macmillan, 1920), p. 23.

[2] *Ibid.*

[3] T. Lynn Smith, *The Sociology of Rural Life* (3rd ed.; New York: Harper, 1953), p. 214.

[4] *Ibid.*, pp. 233–5.

[5] George L. Harris *et al.*, *Jordan* (New York: Grove, 1958), p. 61.

[6] Marian L. Smith, "Social Structure in the Punjab," in *India's Villages* (Calcutta: West Bengal Government Press, 1955), p. 148.

[7] Ralph Linton, *The Study of Man* (New York: Appleton, 1936), p. 212.

[8] M. N. Srinivas, "Introduction," in *India's Villages* (Calcutta: West Bengal Government Press, 1955), p. 3.

[9] Quoted in T. Lynn Smith, *op. cit.*, pp. 219–20.

[10] Alfred Harris, "The Political Role of Blood Pacts in Taita" (unpublished paper).

[11] Max Weber, *From Max Weber: Essays in Sociology,* trans. and ed. by H. H. Gerth and C. Wright Mills (New York: Oxford, 1946), p. 363.

[12] Kingsley Davis, "The Origin and Growth of Urbanization in the World." *American Journal of Sociology,* LX (March, 1955), 433.

[13] Robert M. MacIver and Charles H. Page, *Society: An Introductory Analysis* (New York: Holt, 1949), p. 314.

[14] V. Gordon Childe, *Man Makes Himself* (London: Watts Thinkers' Library, 1948), pp. 146–7.

[15] *The New York Times*, January 29, 1956.

[16] William B. Munro, "City," in *Encyclopedia of the Social Sciences*, III (New York: Macmillan, 1930), 474–82.

[17] The development of this theory is found largely in two influential essays: Georg Simmel, "The Metropolis and Mental Life," in Simmel, *The Sociology of Georg Simmel,* trans. by K. Wolff (New York: Free Press, 1950), pp. 409–24; and Louis Wirth, "Urbanism as a Way of Life," *American Journal of Sociology*, XLIV (July, 1938), 1–24.

[18] Simmel, *op. cit.*, p. 413.

[19] Gideon Sjoberg, *The Preindustrial City* (New York: Free Press, 1960).

[20] Bernard Berelson and Gary Steiner, *Human Behavior: An Inventory of Scientific Findings* (New York: Harcourt, 1964), pp. 606–7.

[21] Otis Dudley Duncan and Albert J. Reiss, Jr., *Social Characteristics of Urban and Rural Communities, 1950* (New York: Wiley Census Monograph Series, 1956), pp. 4–5.

[22] Ernest W. Burgess and Donald J. Bogue (eds.), *Contributions to Urban Sociology* (Chicago: University of Chicago Press, 1964), pp. 231–2, editors' prefatory comments to Marion Wesley Roper, "The City and the Primary Group."

[23] Jane Jacobs, *The Death and Life of Great American Cities* (New York: Random House, 1961), p. 62.

[24] For one such effort that focuses largely upon economic, demographic, and occupational data, see Albert J. Reiss, Jr., "Functional Specialization of Cities," in Paul K. Hatt and Albert J. Reiss, Jr. (eds.), *Cities and Society* (New York: Free Press, 1957), pp. 555–75.

[25] Mirra Komarovsky, "The Voluntary Associations of Urban Dwellers," *American Sociological Review*, XI (December, 1946), 686–98.

[26] Morris Axelrod, "Urban Structure and Social Participation," *American Sociological Review*, XXI (February, 1956), 13–8.

[27] Floyd Dotson, "Patterns of Voluntary Association among Working-Class Families," *American Sociological Review*, XVI (October, 1951), 687–93; and Herbert Gans, The *Urban Villagers* (New York: Free Press, 1962).

[28] Ernest W. Burgess, "The Growth of a City: An Introduction to a Research Project," in Robert E. Park, Ernest W. Burgess, and Roderick D. McKenzie, *The

City (Chicago: University of Chicago Press, 1925), pp. 47–62.

[29] Homer Hoyt, *The Structure and Growth of Residential Neighborhoods in American Cities* (Washington, D.C.: U.S. Federal Housing Administration, 1939).

[30] Chauncey D. Harris and Edward L. Ullman, "The Nature of Cities," *The Annals of the American Academy of Political and Social Science*, CCXLII (November, 1945), 13.

[31] Jacobs, *op. cit.*, Part Two.

[32] Walter Firey, *Land Use in Central Boston* (Cambridge, Mass.: Harvard University Press, 1947).

[33] Gans, *op. cit.*

[34] Quoted in Christopher Tunnard and Henry Hope Reed, *American Skyline* (New York: New American Library, 1956), p. 57.

[35] P. H. Chombart de Lauwe *et al.*, *Paris et L'Agglomération Parisienne* (Paris: Presses Universitaires de France, 1952), Part I.

[36] Theodore Caplow, "Urban Structure in France," *American Sociological Review*, XVII (October, 1952), 544–9.

[37] For data on the extent of metropolitan growth in various parts of the world, see Jack P. Gibbs and Kingsley Davis, "Conventional versus Metropolitan Data in the International Study of Urbanization," *American Sociological Review*, XXIII (October, 1958), 504–14.

[38] Data from U.S. Bureau of the Census, *U.S. Census of Housing, 1960*, II, *Metropolitan Housing*, Part 5 (Washington, D.C.: U.S. Government Printing Office, 1963), Table B-2, pp. 128–33.

[39] Jean Gottman, *Megalopolis* (Cambridge, Mass.: M.I.T. Press, 1961).

[40] Hans Blumenfeld, "The Modern Metropolis," in Scientific American, *Cities* (New York: Knopf, 1965), p. 53.

[41] Robert C. Wood, *Suburbia: Its People and Their Politics* (Boston: Houghton Mifflin, 1959).

Suggestions for further reading

CENTER FOR URBAN STUDIES. *London: Aspects of Change*. London: Macgibbon & Kee, 1964.
Essays dealing with the recent growth of London, its changing shape, new communities in the London area, and two ethnic groups.

DOBRINER, WILLIAM (ed.). *The Surburban Community*. New York: Putnam, 1958.
A collection of papers on the growth, social organization, and style of life of American suburbs. A wide range of quality.

DUNCAN, OTIS D., AND ALBERT J. REISS, JR. *Social Characteristics of American Cities*. New York: Wiley Census Monograph Series, 1956.
A detailed analysis of American cities based upon census data.

EDITORS OF FORTUNE. *The Exploding Metropolis*. Garden City: Doubleday Anchor Books, 1958.

Assorted essays on the changing character of metropolitan areas in the United States. Contains provocative and suggestive sociological writing on American cities, although written primarily by journalists.

GANS, HERBERT J. *The Urban Villagers*. New York: Free Press, 1962.
A penetrating account of "peer group society" in a lower-class Italian neighborhood in Boston.

HATT, PAUL K., and ALBERT J. REISS, JR. *Cities and Society: The Revised Reader in Urban Sociology*. New York: Free Press, 1957.
An excellent collection of writings on the nature of the urban community and urban life.

JACOBS, JANE. *The Death and Life of Great American Cities*. New York: Random House, 1961.
A challenging view of the advantages

of closely textured urban life and how
to achieve it, as well as a lively attack
on many of the traditional ideas of
urban planning.

LYND, ROBERT S., and HELEN M. LYND. *Middletown*. New York: Harcourt, 1929.

LYND, ROBERT S., and HELEN M. LYND. *Middletown in Transition*. New York: Harcourt, 1937.
Two detailed studies of an American community, done ten years apart. Landmarks in American sociology.

MUMFORD, LEWIS. *The City in History*. New York: Harcourt, 1961.
A major contribution to the history of the city from its earliest beginnings. See also his earlier treatise. The Culture of Cities, *New York: Harcourt, 1938*.

PARK, ROBERT E. *Human Communities*. New York: Free Press, 1952.
A collection of essays by the man who gave the chief impetus to urban sociology in the United States and whose suggestions provided the basis for many of the empirical studies of urbanism and the city.

SCIENTIFIC AMERICAN. *Cities*. New York: Knopf, 1965.
A useful collection of essays on problems of urbanization in the United States and elsewhere.

SIMMEL GEORG. *Sociology*. Trans., ed., and with an introduction by Kurt H. Wolff. New York: Free Press, 1950, pp. 409–24, "The Metropolis and Mental Life."
An enormously suggestive and influential essay.

SJOBERG, GIDEON. *The Pre-Industrial City*. New York: Free Press, 1960.
A description and analysis of the nature of cities in nonindustrialized parts of the world.

VIDICH, ARTHUR, and JOSEPH BENSMAN, *Small Town in Mass Society*. Princeton: Princeton University Press, 1958.
An attempt to show how the small community in America is increasingly dominated by external forces emanating from metropolitan and national centers of power.

WEBER, MAX. *The City*. Trans. and ed. by Don Martindale and Gertrud Neuwirth. New York: Free Press, 1958.
A historical and comparative analysis of the institutions that characteristically grow up in the city.

WEST, JAMES (pseud.). *Plainville, U.S.A.* New York: Columbia University Press, 1945.
A study of the culture and social structure of a small rural American community.

WOOD, ROBERT C. *Suburbia: Its People and Their Politics*. Boston: Houghton Mifflin, 1959.
A penetrating analysis of the emerging problems of American suburbs that seeks to relate suburban values and ways of life to political institutions.

PART THREE

Social institutions

12
Technology and economic institutions

Scarcity and economic man

Ever since Adam's mythic fall, man has had to work in order to provide food, shelter, and clothing and to secure those other material amenities he has come to desire. He has done so not as an isolated creature but as a participant in a social order; Robinson Crusoe is a novelist's creature and the economist's fiction, not a prototype of man in society. From the culture of his group, man acquires the knowledge and skills required to make use of the resources available to him; as a member of the group he participates in the cooperative effort to meet material needs.

Needs themselves, however, are not simply biological requirements. Men come to want *particular* types of food and *specific* materials with which to make clothing and build shelters; they acquire many other appetites for things beyond those required for subsistence: ornaments, implements, and miscellaneous accouterments. Men's wants, as well as their needs, provoke their efforts; and wants are readily expanded from bare requirements for survival to a host of other goods. Reflecting the values of the culture, they may range from the relatively

limited demands of a savage headhunter or primitive peasant, concerned with little more than essentials, to the seemingly unending desires of a modern American, continually encouraged by a massive apparatus of persuasion to buy, to own, to enjoy, to spend.

Since men's energies and the resources available to satisfy their wishes are limited, they must inevitably choose among alternative values.

Some values such as those of religious devotion, group pride, community recreation are inherently nondistributive; they are participated in rather than divided up. One person's enjoyment does not diminish another's participation in the same value complex—indeed, the value may *require* that others share it. But other values are distributive: they are divisible, and what one person appropriates diminishes what otherwise would be available to others.[1]

When not enough of these distributive values are available to satisfy all of men's wants freely or completely, some institutional mechanisms must be available to allocate resources and distribute goods, or else society would be replaced by that "war of every man against every man" described by Thomas Hobbes. "The basic economic problem . . . is thus the allocation of scarce means to alternative ends."²

Economics, as a distinct discipline concerned especially with the use of scarce resources, has focused its attention chiefly upon such things as prices, profits, wages, rent, interest rates, and gross national product. The "behavior" of these variables is, of course, the product of human decisions, but economic analysis, for the most part, does not explore the complex social and cultural forces which shape these decisions. For many years, economics generally took for granted a social order within which men could pursue freely the most profitable use of available materials, including labor. Men were assumed to be rational, their wants chosen at random. On the basis of such premises economists were able to study the interrelations among their highly abstract economic variables. The theories they have developed are frequently subtle, complex, even elegant, and, within the limits imposed by their assumptions, of considerable value.

The fiction of the rational "economic man" found in classical economic theory—a man who can perhaps be described as a human calculating machine that disregards all sentiment and tradition as it totes up possible profits and losses—has been severely and justifiably criticized. Bankers, managers, workers, foremen, salesmen, and many others are often influenced by social values, traditional customs, and personal ties with others. That the "propensity to truck, barter, and exchange" postulated by Adam Smith is not inherent is demonstrated by its frequent absence among primitive peoples, who also display little evidence of what we view as economic rationality. Moveover, their economic behavior and their economic insitutions are not readily distinguished—

either by themselves or by visiting anthropologists—from other aspects of social life.

When economists apply models of rational economic behavior to concrete situations, they are often forced to entertain additional variables; as Wilbert Moore observes, such concepts as "the propensity to consume [and] the propensity to save . . . represent an attempt by economists to take into account social and psychological factors not derivable from economic theory but appropriate to economic policy."³ In dealing with immediate situations that are inevitably more complex than even the most sophisticated theories allow—for example, in the study of labor relations in which problems of sentiments and organization are often found, in the analysis of economic growth, particularly in so-called underdeveloped areas, and in the exploration of consumer behavior—economists have had to recognize the presence and the importance of institutions, values, and social structures. The resulting overlap in the work of different social sciences is proving of benefit to all.⁴

Despite its limitations, however, classical economic theory and its "economic man" retain a double importance. First, the concept of the economic man can be used as a legitimate scientific abstraction, as long as it is not reified and treated as a concrete entity. Second, and more significant from a sociological perspective, it also reflects a characteristic and peculiar aspect of Western society, which has to an unusual degree given an "independent" existence to economic values, activities, and institutions. Occupational and kinship roles are segregated, a pattern not often found in most other societies. Money, the abstract nature of which makes possible and encourages limited, formal, and impersonal relationships, is the universal medium of exchange. Traditional obligations between master and servant, employer and employee, seller and buyer, are replaced by a "cash nexus." Men are expected to seek the greatest possible profit in their economic transactions, and sentimental considerations are deemed irrelevant; the principle of *caveat emptor* still applies widely. And the most important measure of a businessman's success remains in the profit he turns.

Western society has institutionalized the "economic man" by encouraging rational economic action, by sanctioning an unremitting acquisitiveness, and by treating labor and land—man and nature—as commodities. These presuppositions—economic rationality, acquisitiveness, and a narrowly economic approach to the world—have become, in some measure, part of the perspective from which Westerners see the economic life not only of their own but also of other societies.

Comparative studies of other peoples have demonstrated not only the peculiar nature of these presuppositions but also the uniqueness of many Western economic institutions and the precariousness of the conventional distinctions between the economic and the social. An understanding of both the nature of economic institutions and their relations to other aspects of culture and social structure requires recognition of the fact that "man's economy, as a rule, is submerged in his social relationships." [5]

Property institutions

Of central importance in determining how scarce resources shall be utilized are the institutions of property—those social norms that define who owns what. As is often the case, however, so bemused are we by the connotations of the words we employ and the conceptions of reality they suggest, that we may find it difficult to establish the general character of property either in our own society or in others. As Walton Hamilton and Irene Till have noted, "A creature of its own intellectual history, the word [*property*] belongs to a culture, to a society, and to a vocabulary. The hazard of reading the associations of the word into the subject of inquiry constantly attends its use; at best it is a darkened glass wherein to exhibit passing systems of ownership." [6]

The term *property* is usually applied to the things men possess, but it also refers to the system of "rights and duties of one person or group (the owner) as against all other persons and groups with respect to some scarce good." [7] The European and American idea of private property, with its suggestion of unfettered rights for the owner to do as he pleases with his possessions, seems to imply an antithesis between individual and society with respect to ownership—as though the individual held his rights *against* the claims of society. This antithesis, which is reinforced by a sharp dichotomy often drawn between public and private ownership, is grossly misleading; for private property, like any other kind, is not only inevitably subject to various social controls but it exists only by virtue of accepted social institutions. Men can own private property only because society allows them to. Moreover, as Hamilton and Till point out, "Among every people convention limits the opportunities which property affords; the law, resting upon custom, disburses ownership between individuals and the community; and morality restrains even the pleasure of a man 'to do as he will with his own.' " [8]

In the United States, for example, what is defined as private property is hedged about with restraints of various kinds. Men can, on the whole, do as they will with their personal possessions and presumably spend their money any way they like, but a man who bought jewelry for another man's wife might be inviting trouble. In many cities zoning ordinances prevent urban landowners from doing certain kinds of things with their property; they are not allowed, for example, to build a tannery or gas station or even, perhaps, a multistory apartment house in some residential areas. Many suburbs in recent years have imposed limits on the number of houses to be constructed on a piece of land, requiring, in some instances, several acres for each home. Custom and social pressure often keep the suburbanite at work maintaining a neat, trim front lawn, whereas he might prefer to let it go to seed, or to solve his crabgrass problem by paving the whole thing. A great many regulations govern where and how men can drive the cars they own, and where they can park. Possession of corporate shares entitles the owner to vote at the annual shareholders' meeting and to make a claim on any profits, but it gives no direct control over the physical assets for which the stock presumably stands.

Property institutions, then, define the *rights* men have over their possessions, the *persons* or groups who possess rights, privileges, and powers over valued objects, and the *things* over which property rights are extended.[9]

No society permits men unlimited freedom in the use of the things they own. To do so, as a German scholar once observed, "would result in the dissolution of society," [10] for it would enable men to disregard the requirements of organized social life. Ownership of property is not merely, or even primarily, a relationship between persons and things; it also establishes relations among persons. The owner's rights are to be respected by others and sustained by the community against any who might challenge them. The many laws against theft and trespassing, for example, contain not only the codified rules, but also sanctions imposed by society against any who violate the rights of property.

Ownership also carries with it power over other persons, as well as socially accepted and protected rights over things. Insofar as others are affected by how property is used, they are subject to the power of those who control it. Indeed, since the way in which scarce resources are utilized affects the entire society, those who determine how they shall be allocated to alternative purposes may possess considerable power, depending in large part upon the distribution of ownership and the conventional limits imposed upon property rights.

In Western society the rights of use and of disposal are usually linked closely to one another; owners can not only decide what to do with their possessions, subject to customary or legal restraints, but can transfer them to others if they see fit to do so. Although we therefore tend to assume that these rights invariably are linked together, comparative evidence reveals that they are often separated and assigned to different persons. In autonomous villages in Indonesia, for example, all land belongs to the village as a whole, which usually consists of members of a single clan. Any villager can undertake to cultivate as much unused communal land as he can manage after informing the village headman, securing his permission, and performing the requisite ritual sacrifice. As long as he works the land, he maintains exclusive rights over it, and it remains his to farm until he allows it to be overgrown by the jungle. Although he can use the land as collateral for loans, he cannot sell it; nor could his creditors ever gain complete possession should he forfeit his collateral. The land cannot be alienated from the community.[11]

The unity of property rights in the United States has in recent decades been substantially affected by fundamental economic trends. As corporations have grown in size and the number of shareholders has increased, control over corporate assets and operations increasingly has come into the hands of the top executives. Although usually possessing some stock in the companies they head, these corporate managers rarely own more than a very small proportion of the total. The stockholders who "own" the corporation therefore possess little or no control over its operations; their "ownership," as noted earlier, entitles them merely to a vote for directors and on such issues as are presented to the annual stockholders' meeting, and to a claim on the profits. This separation of ownership and control was described by A. A. Berle and Gardner Means in their classic study *The Modern Corporation and Private Property* as the "splitting of the property atom." [12]

When one inquires into the complex structure of property rights contained in the modern corporation—or in many primitive or peasant societies—one can see readily the inadequacy of such simple classifications of ownership as private and public, of individual ownership versus that of the community or state or society. As our illustrations thus far have suggested, there is no untrammeled right of private ownership, even in American society where, presumably, it is highly regarded. And many forms of property in the United States are held in diverse ways: by individuals; by partners; by families; by such collectivities as the corporation, church, trade union, and educational institution. Much property is owned by the various political entities, ranging from school districts to the Federal government. One may fairly realistically still describe the system of ownership as a whole as "private," for much of it—and perhaps the strategic portion, namely industry—is free from direct state controls, and individually owned property can be transmitted from parents to children, subject only to moderate taxation.

Complex structures of property rules and relations are found in most societies; individual ownership of some things coexists with various kinds of group controls over other valued objects, and rights are structured in diverse and often intricate patterns. Even where public ownership presumably dominates, individuals frequently possess both the right and the responsibility to determine how various kinds of property are to be used. In the Soviet Union, for example, some forms of private ownership are allowed, chiefly of those personal things required in daily life—clothing, furniture, books, automobiles, jewelry, and so on. In recent years some individuals in the U.S.S.R. have also been allowed to build their own homes, but the land they are assigned remains public property, and no building can be carried on for speculative or profit-making purposes. Productive property—factories, tools, machines, land—remains publicly owned, but merely to describe these things as the property of the state or of the people, without reference to the complex ways in which control over their use is allocated and determined, would be to oversimplify and distort significant economic institutions of Soviet society. Insofar as the Soviet minister or plant manager possesses the legitimate right to determine how land or equipment or other resources shall be used, within the limits and subject to the constraints imposed upon him, he is in a position very similar to that of his American counterpart or of the private owner of productive facilities.[13]

For both the definition of property rights and their allocation to individuals or groups, distinctions are frequently made among various kinds of property. One set of rules may apply to land, another to the buildings upon it, still others to tools or machines, personal possessions, or to such "incorporeal" or intangible property as copyrighted trade marks, a business' "good will," the magical charms sold in West Africa, or the personal names claimed as family property in the Marquesan Islands of the South Pacific. The most significant distinction among types of property, perhaps, is that between productive facilities such as land, tools, and machines, or what economists call *capital*, and those things used directly for personal satisfaction, or what economists call *consumer goods*. Possession of the latter is of obvious importance for individuals, for they make possible satisfaction of important wants. But the use to which capital is put clearly affects the entire society; those who own productive facilities are often able to acquire considerable power and influence, for their decisions can have far-reaching consequences in determining the kind and quantity of goods produced, the general level of economic activity, and the opportunities for employment available to others as well.

Technology

The materials with which a society meets its needs include both resources and the technology that transforms resources into the things men want. Technology includes, however, not only tools, machines, and other implements, but also the accu-

mulated knowledge and skill required to utilize whatever instruments are available. Without the requisite know-how, complex machinery is of little value; with it even crude tools can be very efficient. A simple cutting tool in the hands of a skilled practitioner may produce extraordinary results, whereas modern machinery in the hands of illiterate or semiliterate peasants or tribesmen may soon become useless—as many nations now trying to industrialize are discovering, to their sorrow. (Sometimes, however, as among the Manus of the South Pacific, natives previously unfamiliar with modern technology take to complex machines and new devices with great enthusiasm and considerable facility.) A full description of technology, therefore, should include not only the specific implements men use, but also the traditional lore, the practical skills, and, where it exists, the relevant background of scientific principles or generalized knowledge.

The level of technological development achieved by any society depends upon many factors. There is an obvious relationship between technology and the geographical environment, which sets many of the most important problems men must cope with and provides the resources they can use. The Bedouin desert dweller needs skills, techniques, and equipment different from those required by the Tibetan peasant, the jungle-dwelling African, or the urban European. The constraints of the environment, however, although they pose problems and limit men's options, "do not dictate in any precise way the lines on which an economy [technology] shall develop. Man by his skill and labor produces a kind of secondary environment, which is a function of techniques as well as resources."[14] Nevertheless, when Nature offers few resources, technology characteristically has been crude or confined to limited fields. In areas where abundant resources are found—coal and iron, for example, or great rivers, forests, and alluvial plains—a more complex and productive technology is possible.

But the presence or absence of nature's bounty is only part of the story. Rich resources do not in themselves guarantee a rich technology; witness the cultures of the American Indians prior to the white man's coming. Resources, like human needs, are not fixed entities; the earth and its products become "resources" only when men learn how to use them. Petroleum was an elixir hawked by traveling mountebanks until someone discovered how to refine it. Even after scientists had established the existence of uranium, it was of little more than academic interest until it became the essential ingredient in the atomic bomb and its value as a potential source of power was recognized. Waterfalls are merely scenic wonders or obstacles to navigation or, at times, objects of worship unless men learn to harness their energy. "The march of invention subdues waste land with dry farming, converts a flash of lightning into a great industry, and keeps the catalogue of natural resources in perpetual flux." [15]

Technology, then, rests upon knowledge. All technical advances, as well as all scientific knowledge, are built upon what is already used or known. During most of human history, the knowledge and skills relevant to the industrial arts were handed down from one generation to another as fathers taught their sons, masters trained apprentices, or elders saw to the education of their juniors. Now and then a few imaginative persons, typically pursuing a process of trial and error, invented new tools or techniques or discovered new facts upon which further technological progress could be built.

In recent times technology has increasingly come to rest not upon traditional knowledge, or even upon a rational empiricism focused upon practical problems, but rather upon abstract scientific knowledge. The practical inventor, such as Thomas Edison or George Westinghouse, and the hardheaded mechanic—for example, Henry Ford—are replaced by the technically trained engineer and the scientist in his laboratory or study. The marvels of modern industry are more and more the results of the elaboration of such abstract conceptions as $E = MC^2$, and the products of the test tube, slide rule, microscope, electronic computer, and other instruments of contemporary scientific inquiry. (For a discussion of science as a social institution, see Chapter 16.) Science, of course, can make up for absent resources, an atomic power plant may substitute for coal or water power, and scientifically based methods for the desalinization of water may yet help the desert bloom.

In some measure, technology is also self-generating; its component parts are often so closely linked that a breakthrough at one point leads to advances elsewhere. Of particular importance in technological development are the source and amount of power available for productive uses. Many things are out of reach as long as man must rely upon his own energy alone or even upon that of domestic animals. Men equipped with axes and their own broad shoulders can fell only a few trees each day; a mechanical saw markedly increases their productivity. For this reason such achievements as the invention of the steam engine, the conquest of electricity, and the harnessing of great rivers have had great impact upon technological development in general, and promise to have equally significant effects upon the future of technology and society in all lands.

Acceptance of new tools, machines, or processes, however, is not automatic, but depends in large part upon prevailing ideas and values. In modern industrial society, technological change and innovation are not only usually welcomed, but they are also positively encouraged, both by our prevailing values and by such institutionalized incentives to creativity as the patent system. So receptive are men in industrial society to technical innovations that they often adopt new techniques or products without concern for the possible social consequences that may follow—for workers, for the community, for accepted practices and values.

The rational attitude toward technology characteristic of urban, industrial life—an attitude that considers chiefly the sheer technological efficiency promised by something new—has not been found historically in most other societies. In many groups, new tools or techniques or implements may be adopted if they promise to make traditional tasks easier or to produce greater or better quantities of the things men want. But, as Linton points out, "a society will not accept a new invention simply because it works better than something which they already have if it lies in a field which the society considers unimportant." [16] The advantages to be gained are not enough to compensate for the annoyance and difficulties such changes often entail.

A society that accepts the inevitability or desirability of hand labor does not seek out labor-saving devices. And unless there is considerable desire for new instruments and techniques, the occasional failures and breakdowns that often occur when inventions are first put to work may destroy whatever interest may have once existed. When innovations run into deeply held preconceptions, or threaten established values, they may well be re-

jected, despite the advantages they possess. For example, the cast-iron plow invented in 1814 was feared by many American farmers because they thought it would poison the soil; only after such fears were allayed did this efficient implement come into wide use.

In small, relatively homogeneous, traditional societies in which the individual finds it difficult to evade the controls imposed by the group, acceptance of any technological innovation depends upon its evident utility, its compatibility with prevailing values, its potential effect upon the social structure, and the power or persuasiveness of the innovator. In larger, more complex and differentiated societies there are significant differences among groups and individuals in their attitudes and responses toward both new and old techniques of production. New tools, machines, or methods are often adopted only after long and difficult struggles in which innovators, supporters, resisters, and others who are passive or uninterested—although in many instances not unaffected—act out a complex drama on the historical stage. Riots occurred frequently in the early days of the Industrial Revolution in England, where workers attacked the machines that were changing their way of life and affecting their source of livelihood. Contemporary trade unions sometimes resist technological changes that threaten to disrupt the work routines of their members or that may lead to lower earnings. (If changes cannot be prevented, unions try to control their introduction, cushion their effects upon members, and reap some of the profits they make possible.) On occasion, inventions have been adopted only after personal dramas of proposal, rejection, perseverance, and final success. In 1913 Lee De Forest was almost convicted of using the mails to defraud for selling shares in the audion tube, a device that subsequently turned out to be a major step in the development of modern electronics. The automobile was at first looked upon as simply a plaything for the rich, and only after Henry Ford had pioneered the production of a cheap, standardized car ("you can have it any color you want as long as it's black") did it become a standard means of transportation.

The institutional system, the structure of power and control, and the character of the participants help to shape the outcome of these dramas. Those who possess power over property and persons can insist upon the use of new devices despite the opposition of others. Thus British manufacturers in the early nineteenth century moved relentlessly ahead despite the workers' resistance. As technology becomes more elaborate, the ability to marshal resources and manpower becomes increasingly important as a prerequisite for further advance. Much contemporary discussion concerns the relative capacities of a planned society like the Soviet Union and of the more loosely organized society of the United States to achieve a rapid rate of technological progress. In order to achieve a high rate of economic growth, many of the leaders of the new nations of Africa and Asia, as well as those in older but economically backward countries, are seeking ways of organizing their economies that will facilitate the use of modern technology. But power may also be used to inhibit change, for those who control capital and resources can refuse to make use of new inventions or can place obstacles in the path of the inventor; corporations have sometimes bought up new inventions in order to prevent economic losses, have set aside new methods or products because they would not fit in effectively with the going mode of production, or have simply clung to tradi-

tional methods (though, in a competitive economy, at the risk of failure).[17]

In summary, then, the uses of technology and its growth must be seen in a context of existing knowledge and skill and of supporting or inhibiting values—and in relation to the prevailing system of power and control.

The complex interrelationships between technology and social and cultural factors can be seen in stark outline in the problems of those underdeveloped areas now seeking to industrialize. These predominantly agricultural societies face the purely economic problems of accumulating a sufficient capital surplus to make possible the purchase or manufacture of the tools and machines they need, but this economic task is affected by many cultural and social conditions. Traditional values and beliefs often generate resistance to new techniques. Arab villagers, for example, resisted the installation of a village pump because it would eliminate the traditional female task of carrying water, and Puerto Rican sugar cane workers opposed the use of mechanical devices because "the cane needs the human touch to grow well."[18] Peasants and tribesmen are frequently unwilling or unable to accept the demands imposed by sustained factory work, and in some cases too few technicians, managers, and skilled workers possessing the knowledge and abilities needed to operate an industrial plant are available.

Despite opposition—not to the fruits of industrialization, for which there is often heavy demand, but to its requirements—those who possess political and economic power are usually able, directly or indirectly, to impose their decision to introduce modern technology. But they may be constrained in their detailed policies and programs by the situations they face—by the pressure of a rising population upon the available resources (see Chapter 17); by discontent among those who are unable to secure present gratifications because their labor must go into the manufacture of tools, machines, and factories rather than into the goods they want; by the unwillingness of businessmen to invest in risky but socially necessary fields of production, or of peasants to change their traditional agricultural methods or to go to work in the new factories. Occasionally, as in contemporary China or in the past in the Soviet Union, the rulers may cut through these inhibiting forces with a mailed fist, not counting the immediate human cost that must be paid in order to create an industrial technology in a short period of time.

Technological determinism

So widespread are the effects of technology that some social analysts have been led to a monistic technological interpretation of society and history. According to this view, of which Thorstein Veblen is the outstanding proponent, technology inevitably determines men's habits and ways of thinking. Changes in technique require continual institutional readjustment and cultural adaptation, for new tools and machines impose new routines, require fresh skills, and shape the "intellectual and spiritual attitude on the part of the workman." The "machine industry," in sharp contrast with the antecedent handicraft system, requires long schooling and the "ready apprehension of opaque facts, in passably exact quantitative terms"; it runs counter, Veblen argues, to "the suffusion of . . . knowledge with putative animistic or anthropomorphic subtleties, quasi-personal interpretations of the observed phenom-

ena and of their relations to one another." Moreover, the "routine and . . . discipline [imposed by the machine] extend beyond the mechanical occupations as such, so as in great part to determine the habits of all members of the modern community." [19]

Not all groups are equally exposed to the "constraining forces of the environment," that is, to both technology and the concrete problems of survival and maintenance. Those who are engaged in "business" rather than "industry" are most removed from "economic exigencies," and have little contact with the hard requirements of technology. They are therefore more resistant to change than workers and engineers who must constantly meet the requirements of a mechanical, scientifically based technology. Unlike Marx, however, who saw an endless conflict between the proletariat and the bourgeoisie that would end in the triumph of the presumably technologically progressive working class, Veblen, more pessimistically, pointed out how the "leisure class," because it possesses power and prestige, could often inhibit or restrain the changes required by—and for—technological progress.[20] In the long run, however, Veblen—and others—assume that technology contains the dynamic forces making for social change, and that other components of culture and social structure inevitably adapt themselves to the new circumstances created by technology. (Despite the basic importance he assigned to technology, Veblen himself, it should be noted, devoted much of his attention in his published work to the role of habit, instinct, and interests in social and economic life.[21])

The technological interpretation of social change and social structure, despite the subtlety and complexity with which Veblen elaborated it, possesses obvious limitations. As we have already noted, the progress of technology, although in some measure self-generated, is also influenced, sometimes strongly, by other variables: values, knowledge, social institutions, and social structure. Choices among technological alternatives may be based simply upon criteria of efficiency or upon such other grounds as their effects upon workers, possibilities for profit and loss, their consequences for the community as a whole, or even desire to keep up with technological fashion—witness tractors on farms too small for their economic use and computers that cost their purchasers more than the white-collar workers whom they replace.

The impact of technology is always conditioned to some extent by the social and cultural context. An assembly line can be used to drive workers at an incessant, back-breaking tempo, or it can be run at more moderate and reasonable speeds. Both social values and the relations between workers and employers, union and management, and other considerations as well enter into the final outcome. The impact of the modern media of mass communication upon values, beliefs, and action depends upon the images, ideas, information, and values the media communicate, and many factors enter into their content. Nuclear weapons have enormous destructive power, but the decision to use them will rest upon political and moral considerations as well as purely technological ones.

In rejecting technological determinism, however, one should not ignore or minimize the substantial impact of technology upon social life. In societies with a primitive technology, life remains close to the level of bare subsistence. "Preoccupation with the daily or seasonal food supply, the frequency of hardship, and the risks of hunger are obvious characteristics of a primitive economy [and technology]." [22] With improved techniques for coping with the world around them, men can escape the constant concern with immediate needs; surplus makes possible leisure, foresight, and planning, and a diversification of interests and activities, all of which in turn are likely to contribute to further technological advance and to changes in culture and social relations.

In a general way the impact of new techniques and products must be readily apparent to anyone living in a world in which each day brings news of some new or forthcoming technical marvel: factories without workers, machines that "think," new methods of food preservation and packaging, "aromarama," three-dimensional television, space travel, and so on. Columnists and political pundits continually speculate about the effect of television on traditional political practices and the results of substituting the jet plane for the campaign train. Warfare is revolutionized by new weapons and the shifting balance of productive facilities.

The revolutionary technological developments usually referred to as "automation"—electronic control systems and high-speed data processing—have had far-reaching results, the extent and nature of which are still unclear and in some areas vigorously debated. Economists, industrialists, and labor leaders have argued about the extent to which automation has increased unemployment. The traditional issue—are those displaced by the new technology eventually absorbed as a result of continued economic growth?—is being redefined to some degree because of the possibility that the complex machines and processes now being used may eliminate one whole class of workers, those without skill. There is the possibility that there will soon be no useful place left in the economy for the

Modern automated production, widely found in such industries as chemicals, automobiles, steel, and now its own industry, electronics, has also spread out into many other fields. This highly automated production line turns out crackers.

whose skills are either inadequate or no longer needed. Many corporate executives, on the other hand, see no need for positive action, but would prefer to leave the outcome to the "free play" of economic forces—that is, to the multitude of individual decisions by workers, owners, and managers within the context of prevailing economic institutions.[23]

In addition to the problems of unemployment, automation may affect the nature of the work men do, the class structure (through its impact on the occupational distribution), education, corporate and political decision-making, even ultimately, both directly and indirectly, the values of modern society. Computers create alphabetical indexes of the words in a literary work that either took many years to do before or that were never done at all, and they make possible the calculations needed for space exploration and the building of intercontinental ballistic missiles.[24]

The full impact of technology, both in general terms and with respect to specific innovations, requires, of course, much more detailed analysis than is possible here, for the ramifications spread widely through the social order. Family life is affected as new products alter the daily tasks of husband and wife, the methods of child-rearing, the frequency and timing of childbearing. The productivity of modern industry opens up the "new frontier" of leisure, changing the traditional values assigned to work. Life expectancy is lengthened as new techniques and materials make possible both medical advances—plastic replacements for human tissues and computers that produce more reliable diagnoses than were possible in the past—and improved material conditions of life. Rulers find new techniques with which to maintain their power or crush opposition, and some of them now

many millions whose education has gone no further than the eighth or even the tenth grade.

How men see the consequences of automation and the proposals that have been made for dealing with the problems that have emerged reflect the perspectives and interests of various groups. An automobile company executive showing Walter Reuther, President of the United Automobile Workers, through an automated factory observed that machines do not need to be paid for overtime and do not pay union dues, to which Reuther rejoined, "And you will have a hard time selling them cars." Union leaders advocate severance pay for those displaced by the new technology and emphasize the need for substantial programs sponsored by business and government to retrain those have at their disposal instruments that may destroy us all. Military leadership is transformed from those qualities required by the battlefield to the ability to use the products of advanced technology based on modern science. Men's values, habits, and expectations, as well as their social roles, are inexorably transformed by novel ways of performing old tasks, fresh opportunities available to them, and new vistas opened by more powerful tools for acquiring new knowledge, more efficient methods of communication, and faster means of travel.

Various efforts have been made to relate types of technological systems to forms of culture and social structure, as yet, however, without clear-cut or consistent findings. But even if no overall pattern emerges, there do appear to be consistent relationships between some technological variables and particular characteristics of social life. All industrial societies, whatever their economic or political complexion, resemble one another in important respects: the jobs men pursue; the knowledge and skill required of workers, technicians, and managers; important aspects of factory organization; even, as noted in Chapter 7, trends in family structure. Our knowledge of these similarities and the extent to which industrial technology sets limits within which only certain social and cultural developments can take place, however, is still tentative and uncertain, for until very recently industrialization was almost entirely limited to "capitalist" societies—England, the United States, France, Germany, and other nations of western Europe. The relative importance of economic institutions and the means of production is, therefore, not easily assessed. As we discover more about the Soviet Union, and observe the changes to which industrialization gives rise in other parts

Automation in the steel industry has increased productivity and changed manpower requirements. TOP: *Men at work in an old rolling mill.* BOTTOM: *A modern mill in which the same number of men tend two machines at tasks that are obviously less demanding physically.*

of the world where economic and political systems vary, we may learn more about the effects of modern technology, as *such,* upon society and culture.

The division of labor

Industrialization has brought with it— and rests upon—a marked specialization and division of labor. More refined tools, more complex machines, and the elaborate organizational apparatus required to operate modern technology create an almost endless number of new tasks. The third edition of the *Dictionary of Occupational Titles,* published in 1965 by the United States Department of Labor, describes 21,741 occupations "which are known by 13,809 additional titles, making a total of 35,550 titles defined." [25] This edition contained 6,432 jobs not contained in the second (1949) edition, although the total number of occupations actually was slightly lower.

The extent of specialization is suggested in the following illustrations:

ASSEMBLER FOR PULLER-OVER, HAND (boot and shoe [industry]) . . . Inserts cement covered counter between lining and shoe upper to prepare upper for further lasting operations: Places counter on wire screen, dips screen in liquid cement and drains excess cement from counter. Positions last on pin jack. Inserts counter between lining and upper. Pulls shoe upper onto last and alines back seam of upper with guide marks on last. Tacks upper to last, using tool.

ASSEMBLER FOR PULLER-OVER, MACHINE (boot and shoe [industry]) . . . Tends machine that tacks shoe parts to last to prepare shoe upper for further lasting operations. Places counter and tip support (box toe) on rack, immerses rack in liquid cement, and drains excess cement from parts. Inserts pre-cemented parts between lining and upper. Pulls and alines upper on last. Sets last on pin jack of machine. Pushes pin jack and upper into machine that tacks upper to last at heel seam and heel seat.[26]

Six pages of the *Dictionary* are devoted to assemblers of various kinds, differing in what they assemble or what specific part of the assembly process they perform.

Other examples of specialization, drawn almost at random from the *Dictionary,* are:

CHICKEN SEXER . . . Examines genital organs of baby chicks to determine their sex by turning back fold of skin on the anus or by inserting illuminated viewer into anus. Places chicks in boxes according to sex.[27]

MATTRESS PLUGGER . . . Cuts rubber tubing into specified lengths with scissors and inserts cut pieces into holes in rubber mattresses to reinforce them and give them elasticity.[28]

SPOOLER, SEQUINS . . . Winds strings of plastic sequins on spools preparatory to shipment. Pulls string of sequins through yardage indicator and cuts off specified length. Examines string for broken threads, knots, and irregular lay of sequins. Feeds string into winding machine that winds it on spool.[29]

Similar specialization is also found among white-collar workers and professionals. The *Dictionary* describes twenty-four different kinds of editors and contains reference to thirty-two other job titles among editors. In the description of a "general office clerk" the *Dictionary* notes that such a clerk "May be designated according to field of activity as DEATH-CLAIM CLERK (insurance); or according to location of employment as AIRPORT CLERK (Air. trans.); CAMP CLERK; COLLIERY CLERK (mining and quarrying)." Six specific types of clerks are then defined in detail.[30]

Although this extraordinary proliferation of occupational categories is relatively recent, the division of labor is not confined to industrial society but can be found in some form everywhere. Even in the most primitive societies men and women are assigned different tasks, and in many nonindustrial cultures there is considerable specialization in specific crafts. In many parts of Africa, for instance, ironworking is a highly developed skill carried on by recognized craftsmen, and among the Polynesians, Melanesians, and other island and coastal dwellers boatbuilding is a specialized craft. But only in industrial societies have men carried the division of labor to such elaborate lengths that Henry Ford once defined the goal of mass production as the reduction of the assembly line worker's task to doing "as nearly as possible one thing with only one movement." [31]

The division of labor produced by modern technology and the complex organization of the modern economy results not only in the simplified tasks of the factory worker (many of which, as we noted earlier, are now being eliminated by continued technological advance) but also in an increasing number of jobs requiring a great deal of highly specialized skill and knowledge. The degree of specialization among doctors, lawyers, scientists, and engineers is perhaps a commonplace, but there are also those who specialize, for example, in mail-order selling, the use of audio-visual aids in education, the editing of college textbooks, the determination of the cause of airplane accidents or of the amount of damage suffered by crops because of a hailstorm.

Occupational specialization leads to a multiplicity of differentiated social roles that require not only technical expertise but also social skills, values, and attitudes. In addition to knowledge of the manufacturing process, the factory manager must be able to elicit cooperation and effort from his staff and his workers; he may have to bargain with union leaders, cope with government inspectors, deal with customers, and get along with his corporate superiors. The complex and

often subtle personal qualities demanded in some occupations are illustrated clearly in the advertising executive. The *"public* side" of the occupation includes "administrative skill, judgment, and business sense," in addition to "talent and technical skill." To succeed, however, the executive must also possess "nerve," that is, the ability to work "under the constant pressure of volume, deadlines, possible criticism, and the ever-present image of total failure," as well as "calmness, tact, deference, good humor, and loyalty to the right people." And he must often maintain these latter qualities in extremely difficult situations.

In a business where costs are a factor, where pressures are greater than one can absorb by oneself, the ability to resist pressures which are destructive to the individual is a necessary trait for success and for survival. For instance, a client may make demands that are too expensive, too time-consuming, or are impossible of fulfillment. The account executive in this case must either talk the client into modifying his demands or convince him that his demands have been fulfilled when they have not. At times he may be able to convince the client that the demands are totally unreasonable. But whatever he does, the account executive must do so in a manner that gains the respect or the liking of the client.[32]

Some occupations, particularly those that require special knowledge and training or impose distinctive requirements—doctors, printers, sailors, railroadmen, traveling salesmen—develop subcultures of their own, complete with jargon, customs, and values. Technical vocabularies, which are found in most kinds of work, provide a useful verbal shorthand that facilitates quick and easy communication, as well as serving other important functions. Because an occupation's argot cannot be understood by the uninitiated, it impresses them with the complexities and difficulties of the job, eliciting respect and simultaneously excluding the outsider. Becoming a member of an occupational group often entails learning its customs—technical and nontechnical. There are often "initiation ceremonies" that both demonstrate the superior knowledge and skill of the older and more experienced workers and test the newcomer's ability to fit into the work group. "A new man in a lumber planing mill is sent after the board-stretcher, the new apprentice in a glass factory is told to secure a mold-stretcher from the stock room, and from time immemorial mechanics' helpers have been told to go and fetch a left-handed monkey wrench." [33]

As men pursue different occupations, with different values and interests, the ties that bind them together become more tenuous. These tendencies can be seen not only in the differences between workers and managers, or farmers and industrial laborers, but also among—or within—the professions, or in the ranks of executives. Among scholars, for example, concentrated efforts in some narrow area of inquiry sometimes render them unable to comprehend one another's studies or to converse in an informed manner about any but the most elementary aspects of the social life they presumably share. When men cease to share common values, or when the parochial values and interests of the occupational group, whether it be trade union, professional society, or business organization, take precedence over or run counter to those of the whole, society faces a weakening of the ties that bind its members together.

The division of labor itself, however, as the French sociologist Émile Durkheim pointed out in a classic analysis, can also be an important source of solidarity.[34] As men take up new and different tasks, they necessarily become increasingly dependent upon one another. The "mechanical" solidarity of a primi-

tive society which rests to a great extent upon the similarities among its members is replaced, Durkheim argues, by the "organic" solidarity of a complex society based upon mutual need and the contribution each man makes to the collective life in which he has a distinctive part.

But the fact of interdependence in itself is not always—or perhaps ever—enough to hold a society together. As Durkheim himself pointed out before the end of the nineteenth century, the individualism, economic rationality, and impersonality of Western society were gravely threatening its unity and coherence. Consensus and solidarity rest upon shared understandings and common values, as well as upon rationally adjusted interests and the awareness of interdependence. Individuals, therefore, lack a source of moral unity, which might be supplied, Durkheim suggested, either by the state or perhaps by occupational or professional groups that could be so organized as to create a moral power men respect.[35]

One source of the "abnormal" form of the division of labor—that is, the form that weakens social solidarity—Durkheim found in the worker's inability to find meaning in his limited activities; failing to see his place in the scheme of things, he is unable to establish significant relations with others or to participate in the moral unity basic to social order. This problem—the impact of industrial labor upon workers—has preoccupied students of industrial society from its very beginnings. Thus Adam Smith, in *The Wealth of Nations*, published in 1776, commented:

The man whose whole life is spent in performing a few simple operations, of which the effects are perhaps always the same, or very nearly the same, has no occasion to exert his understanding or to exercise his invention in finding out expedients for removing difficulties which never occur. He naturally loses, therefore, the habit of such exertion, and generally becomes as stupid and ignorant as it is possible for a human creature to become.[36]

About a half century later, Alexis de Tocqueville, a French visitor to the United States whose *Democracy in America* remains one of the most penetrating analyses of American society and culture ever written, observed:

When a workman is unceasingly and exclusively engaged in the fabrication of one thing, he ultimately does his work with singular dexterity; but at the same time he loses the general faculty of applying his mind to the direction of the work. He every day becomes more adroit and less industrious; so that it may be said of him that in proportion as the workman improves, the man is degraded. What can be expected of a man who has spent twenty years of his life in making heads for pins? And to what can that mighty human intelligence which has so often stirred the world be applied in him except it be to investigate the best methods of making pins' heads? When a workman has spent a considerable portion of his existence in this manner, his thoughts are forever set upon the object of his daily toil . . . he no longer belongs to himself, but to the calling that he has chosen. . . . In proportion as the principle of the division of labor is more extensively applied, the workman becomes more weak, more narrow-minded, and more dependent. The art advances, the artisan recedes.[37]

With the advent of the assembly line, the methods engineer, and the time clock, criticism of the technology which reduced the worker to a mere adjunct of the machine mounted. Such criticism was countered by the claim that increased production made more goods available to more people, including the workers, and by the assertion that workers did not really mind the difficulties which scholars or artists or philosophers saw in the routine, repetitive tasks they performed. The machine operator, performing the same routine task hour after hour, five or six days a week,

it was argued, may not be any more confined by his labor than the peasant who must work from sunup to sundown on some barren patch of ground. In the Soviet Union, Marxist theorists asserted, the abolition of private property and the establishment of a "workers' state" eliminated the "exploitation" inherent in capitalism and gave a meaning and value to even the most routine task sufficient to prevent dissatisfaction and the degradation of the work.

These assertions about the impact of the extensive division of labor in mechanized industry are difficult to test; such terms as *narrow-minded* and *degraded* and such themes as dependency and intellectual stultification are not readily transformed into observable measures that can be applied to men at work. Yet insofar as the strictures of Adam Smith, Tocqueville, and many others have been subjected to empirical test, they do appear to have a considerable measure of validity. Even in the Soviet Union there now appears to be public recognition of the consequences of technological demands upon workers. A Soviet sociologist exploring "Approaches to Work Under Communism" has written:

Work on a conveyor is very highly fragmented and amounts to performing simple operations or even single movements. To the muscular fatigue of physical work, there is *added* the fatigue attendant upon the endless, physically oppressive repetition of identical operations. Studies by certain researchers show that the nervous tension of workers on a conveyor belt in certain instances exceeds that of persons engaged in mental labor. The monotonous work done on the conveyor belt in the form in which it now exists in many enterprises gives rise to dissatisfaction among workers, particularly among young workers who come on the job after completion of secondary schools.[38]

There are, of course, individual variations in response to specific kinds of work and working conditions, and the available evidence also shows clearly that the impact of the division of labor and of increasing mechanization depends very largely upon the social organization of work and the values that men attach to the tasks they must perform.

The organization of work

In nonindustrial societies the organization of work is governed largely by tradition. The allocation of tasks is based upon sex, age, or rank, or, in some instances, upon acquired and demonstrated skill. When men must cooperate in tilling fields, herding cattle, catching fish, or hunting game, coordination of effort may be achieved because they know one another's duties and skills and can carry out their respective tasks with little direction. When the enterprise becomes larger and more complex, the tribal leader, family head, or the person recognized as most proficient assumes responsibility for directing the collective effort. Thus Firth sums up a description of an elaborate Maori fishing expedition as follows:

. . . the ultimate control of the whole affair was in the hands of the chief Popota. He had the right of declaring what should be the fishing days, and the duty of keeping the various camps informed, of giving the signal to assemble, and the final command to charge for the prize. And these privileges and obligations of control were based on no specific and immediate proficiency in the fishing art, but on a social status which was his by inheritance, on the mana which came down to him from generations of ancestors. . . . Social privileges were often thus enlisted in the service of economic leadership.

Within the sphere of the chief's control, other aspects of the work were taken in charge by minor executive heads. Thus the experts in each camp saw to the fitting-out of the canoes,

the preparation of hooks and tackle, and each canoe when afloat had its own commander or chief, his authority derived from his social position. . . .

For organization in the actual fishing, a system of rules was in force, stipulating not only the time and place for fishing, but also even the method of killing the fish. And to avoid confusion in the work, conventional signals were in use, such as the cry of "Haul in" to avoid entangling lines when a fish was hooked.[39]

Under such circumstances, even repetitive tasks that call for little skill or initiative are meaningful to everyone, because they are part of a cooperative effort that is directed toward a recognized and valued end.

In industrial society, in contrast, formal, rational methods of allocating tasks and organizing work relations have tended to replace traditional procedures. In England, where industrialization first came to maturity, both technological needs and capitalist institutions soon altered the established relations between workers and employers. Eric Lampard has summarized this transformation:

[In] the so-called "putting out" system [which preceded the "Industrial Revolution"] a merchant or group of merchants undertook to organize and finance certain production. The actual techniques of production were unchanged; craftsmen worked at their traditional tasks in a familiar shop environment, or farm families plied their household crafts, without any direct or regular supervision from the merchant-employer who hired their services and supplied materials. In craft manufacture, relations between masters and servants were personal and close. Though the master was senior, he too must conform to the custom and opinion of his peers: he worked with his journeymen and apprentices in an avuncular if not paternal fashion. The latter were protected in their ascribed status by craft tradition and local usage. Unmarried dependents lived in domestic quarters, taking their meals at the place of work. The journeyman could aspire to his own premises and elevation to a master's rank. He might cherish designs on his master's daughter and thereby inherit the shop and its good will. The pace of work and the job routine accorded with this intimate round of everyday life. But as the master withdraws from the shop, as the numbers of journeymen increase and their labor is casualized, so the establishment is more of a factory. Work discipline is less habitual and more contrived; rules and regulations become impersonal and objective. The master departs from the center of the scene, one eye is fixed on the employees, the other on competitors. The position of the journeyman is correspondingly reduced, his status lowered. . . .

It is easy to romanticize a golden age of the crafts before the hectic pace of the machine or the factory's insistent whistle. There is a familiar image of the benign master guiding his trusty servants through their daily tasks with youthful novices romping at their feet. It was never like this. But, leaving aside the tyrannical masters, sullen journeymen, and cringing apprentices, craft and merchant-employer organizations functioned within the accepted custom and domesticity of their less hurried age. The factory brought a furious pace and shaped a relentless discipline, broken only when the crude machines fell apart or the waters ceased to flow. As more processes were integrated under one roof and when, during the industrial revolution, the factory moved into town, men found themselves living in a stark and unfamiliar world. The essential but elusive quality of the factory seems to reside in the relations of employer and employed and in the style of job routine. . . .[40]

Freed from the traditional constraints—and security—of a feudal status, workers were cast into an impersonal, competitive market in which their wages were set by the "laws" of supply and demand. By viewing labor as a commodity, the price of which was determined by the market, employers could disclaim any personal responsibility for the welfare of their employees and could impose a rigid authority over men who had presumably made a free choice to accept a particular job. Workers accepted their lot and the authority of their employer in part because they looked forward to becoming owner-entrepreneurs themselves (although this pervasive "success" ideology did not emerge in England until well into the nineteenth century [41]), and in part because they had little choice. As Marx correctly pointed out, workers who owned no property from which to derive income had only their labor power to sell—in a market with a surplus of labor.

Because of the openness of the land, the richness of its resources, the sparsity of population, and the absence of a feudal and aristocratic heritage, industrialism developed in the United States without creating many of the difficulties which beset England. But in the United States, too, relations between workers and employers were in large measure reduced to a cash nexus as factories grew larger and the commercial spirit spread. With the changes that have taken place in industry, notably the growth of giant bureaucratic corporations, the emergence of powerful trade unions, and the increased intervention of government in economic life, some of the earlier harshness has been dissipated. No longer is the individual worker with no resources at his command "bargaining" with an employer; wages and working conditions are typically decided by collective bargaining; even unorganized workers are protected in some measure by legislation that establishes minimal standards. The once unchallenged authority of the entrepreneur-owner has been cut down by law and by union-imposed restraints; the boss who would brook no challenge to his power or damage to his profits has been replaced by the "professional" manager who seeks to improve morale in his organization by treating employees as human beings rather than as commodities (although his conception of man may still contain some questionable notions), and by employing all the modern techniques of persuasion to justify his actions, policies, and power.

Despite these changes and the steadily rising standard of living made possible by improved methods of production, the problems created by the elaborate division of labor persist. The "self-regulating" market has been greatly modified, but its impersonal operations have been replaced by the impersonality of bureaucracy, itself an important factor in the continued development of technology. (See Chapter 10.) The continual technological innovations generated by the incessant search for new and more efficient methods and machines disrupt well-established routines; in a constantly changing technology tradition does not readily take root, and other methods—usually bureaucratic—must be found for organizing the work process.

To the extent that social bonds among men at work are weakened or destroyed by the impersonal requirements of the market and bureaucracy, workers lose the ties and shared understandings that make their work satisfying and give it meaning. Under such circumstances, routine, repetitive tasks are felt to be monotonous and unsatisfying. There is much empirical evidence that shows that when men lack satisfying social relationships on the job their morale, job satisfaction, and frequently their productivity decline. Conversely, participation in informal work groups bound together by personal ties, common practices, and accepted values and beliefs usually improves men's feelings about their jobs, about themselves, and about their employers, even when they are doing unskilled or semiskilled work.[42] (For a discussion of the general nature and importance of primary groups, see Chapter 6.) Other studies have explored the effects of relationships with supervisors upon morale and productivity; a harsh, authoritarian, unsympathetic, impersonal supervisor lessens men's satisfaction at work, whereas a superior who takes individual needs into account and establishes personal relationships with his subordinates enhances both the willingness to work and the gratifications derived from the job.[43]

These findings have led some writers to deprecate the importance of technology and to ignore the relevance of the larger institutional and cultural context within which men carry on their work. Because pleasant relations with coworkers and superiors lessen monotony and fatigue and improve morale, and workers sometimes refuse to give up presumably dull, repetitive jobs because of their ties to their fellows or the comfort of established routines, the "soul destroying" impact of mechanization, it has been argued, is a myth.[44] But technology itself, in addition to its direct effects upon workers, may also largely determine the opportunities for social interaction within the shop by its noise, the extent to which it fixes workers to one spot or allows them freedom to move around, and by its spatial requirements—whether it throws workers together or keeps them apart. (Only relatively recently have students of work begun to explore such subtle problems as the impact of coerced rhythms upon workers, although Marx long ago acutely noted that "constant labour of one uniform kind disturbs the intensity and flow of a man's animal spirits which find recreation and delight in mere change of activity." [45] Available evidence suggests that when the rhythm of work required by automatic or semiautomatic machines does not coincide with "natural rhythms," workers experience a good deal of discomfort.[46])

Many of the problems of work in modern industry may eventually be solved by technology itself, for automation may soon replace most workers and transform those remaining into skilled mechanics who maintain the complex machinery in working order, and into technicians who operate the technological wonders designed by highly trained engineers and scientists. By threatening—or promising—not only to displace many workers but also to minimize or eliminate work itself as a major activity for most people, automation is contributing to changes in the basic values underlying economic effort. Work has been looked upon at various times in history as degrading or ennobling, as a necessary evil or as an opportunity for personal growth, as a sign of man's fall from grace or as a means of demonstrating moral virtue and the glories of God. Whatever the values attached to it, however, it has always been a central focus around which men have organized their lives. In an increasingly abundant economy that requires less and less effort, Americans, as many observers have pointed out, have given steadily greater priority to the "values of consumption" rather than to the "values of production,"[47] and work appears to be losing its central place in American culture. But if work, which once gave meaning to human existence and linked the individual to the world around him, becomes merely a brief, daily interlude, what will serve the functions it has so long performed?[48]

Distribution and exchange

The central purpose of work and of technology, of course, is the provision of goods and services to meet human needs. Since few, if any, people, are self-sufficient, particularly in a society with an elaborate division of labor, some arrange-ments are necessary to provide for the distribution and exchange of goods and services. In traditional societies, distribution characteristically takes place within the context of familial or other well-established relationships. People receive the goods and services they need—or want—as gifts, which usually must be reciprocated, or in satisfaction of traditional obligations. Such exchanges as do take place are customarily regulated by long-standing norms. Among the Trobriand Islanders studied in great detail by Malinowski, for example, most of a man's harvest went partly to his sister's spouse and family and partly as tribute to his chief. He, in turn, received crops from his sister's husband and benefited in various ways from the chief's bounty. These islanders were also part of a larger system of exchange, the *kula* ring, which encompassed the entire archipelago of which they were a part. Inhabitants of the area periodically traveled from one island to another, bringing with them gifts of "ceremonial" value consisting of white shell bracelets and necklaces of red shells. The exchanges followed a regular pattern among partners of long standing, necklaces moving in one direction and bracelets in the other, none remaining for very long in any one person's hands. Although the ostensible purpose of these expeditions—which were often so elaborate that Malinowski was led to call the participants the "Argonauts of the Western Pacific"—was not economic, the visits of one group to another provided the occasion for feasts, trading, and the distribution of food, as well as various public ceremonies.[49]

In contrast to such institutions, which distributed goods through a complex system of obligations built into various social structures, the free market of Western capitalism has been governed by the impersonal "laws" of supply and demand. Considerations of role and status are irrelevant in a free market, as sellers try to get as much as they can for their goods and buyers to pay as little as possible. Since no central agency regulates the transactions that take place and no standards such as the medieval conception of the "just price" enter into the bargaining, prices fluctuate with the supply of goods and the demands for them. The impersonality of the market is encouraged by the use of money as a medium of exchange, since it allows for abstract calculation and is free of the traditional overtones and customary usages attached to specific articles.

According to classical economic theory, which received its first authoritative formulation in Adam Smith's *The Wealth of Nations*, published in 1776, the operations of a free market, which regulated itself, would provide the most efficient means for maximizing production and satisfying human needs. If demand increased, prices would rise, and more goods would be brought to the market as producers saw opportunities for profit. If demand fell and prices followed, profits would diminish and producers would divert their resources to fields where there was greater demand and more likelihood of making money.

Such a view of the market, however, presumed both a set of values and an institutional system within which free exchange could occur. Both buyers and sellers, it was assumed, were trying to maximize their income and would therefore be motivated to act in a rational fashion. In fact, of course, as we noted earlier (see p. 6), such motivations are neither universal nor built into human nature. Although the pursuit of gain can be an important component in economic activity, and even the predominant goal, it is not the only value or concern that enters into work or exchange. A theory that assumes the universal pursuit of self-interest, however, justifies unrestrained self-seeking, the removal of any cultural restraints upon economic endeavors, and the maintenance of institutions which facilitate the operations of a free market. What distinguishes capitalism from other economic systems, it should be noted, is not the pursuit of self-interest, which is widespread and perhaps found everywhere, but the institionalization of this pursuit as normal and socially desirable.

Although most economic theorists take the underlying institutional framework as given, the free market could function as expected only under certain conditions. The rights of private property had to be accepted and protected by the state, which would conscientiously avoid interfering with the economic activities of individuals. Agreements once made had to be honored, or enforced. Buyers and sellers were to be of roughly equal strength, and no one could exert monopoly control over the supply of goods. Not only was it necessary for capital to be free of restraints, so that it could move from one use to another, as demand changed, but labor also had to be free to shift from job to job, a condition that could be met only by allowing the price of labor (that is, wages) to fluctuate in response to supply and demand too.

These conditions have rarely, if ever, been fully satisfied, although the nature and distribution of most goods and services, except for public services such as education, roads, provision of some recreational facilities, police and fire protection, postal services, and, in Western Europe, rail transportation, have been left to the free workings of the market. The theory elaborated by economists, therefore, has never fully accounted for many features of economic behavior and of the operations of the economy. Demand, for example, is governed not only by income and costs, but also by the norms and values attached to patterns of consumption. What people want and how they spend their income depends upon such factors as age, marital condition, social status, and previous experience, as well as upon how much money people have. In the United States, middle-class people are more likely to drink whiskey and working-class people beer, although some ethnic groups prefer wine, which has also gained some popularity in the middle class in recent years. Standards of consumption are governed by conceptions of what is right or appropriate or necessary, and by the desire to keep up with or surpass others, and is susceptible to such external pressures as advertising and the pull of fashion.

More significantly, perhaps, participants in a free market are frequently not of equal strength, a fact which affects the bargains they make. An individual worker with no resources and nothing to sell but his labor, must, as Marx pointed out take whatever wages are offered. Unless there are external, that is, governmental, controls or workers are organized, wages are determined by the laws of supply and demand; they rise when there is a labor shortage and decline when there is a surplus. If one or a few large enterprises dominate an industry they can set prices arbitrarily without concern for individual or communal needs or for the ability of individual consumers to pay, unless government actively intervenes in the economy.

The role of government, in fact, has rarely been as detached as *laissez-faire* ideology would have it. One of Marx's important contributions was the observation that an "impartial" state that merely

maintained law and order so that individual enterprise could continue to function in effect protected those with greater market power. By defending and enforcing the rights of property the state assured the advantages of owners against those without property. Moreover, as long as the state was dominated by those who were in higher economic levels—landowners, bankers, manufacturers, merchants—governmental policies could be shaped to their advantage. (For a discussion of the nature and functions of the state, see Chapter 13.)

Because the free market was accompanied by democratic political institutions, the role of government in economic life has been a central political issue. Those who stood to gain from an unregulated economy governed by the "invisible hand" analysed by Adam Smith tried to keep government out of business. In the early nineteenth century, for example, legislation was passed in England against combinations of workers to seek higher wages. With the emergence of "big business," the rhetoric of competition and the free market was used to attack restraints upon the freedom of businessmen to act as they chose. But the problems created by the free market have led in all the capitalist countries of Western Europe and North America to a "welfare state" and the active participation of government in the operations of the economy.

Because of the emphasis on self-interest and the tendency of the market economy to reduce social relationships merely to the "cash-nexus," no one was responsible for those unable to work or to find jobs or for those with inadequate incomes. The fluctuations of the economy, "normal" in a free, competitive system, inevitably produced casualties—unemployment, business failures, farmers unable to sell their crops. Moreover, as John Kenneth Galbraith has pointed out in his provocative critique of the "affluent society," many of the services and facilities needed in an urban setting—schools, parks, roads, municipal housekeeping—have been inadequately supported; they are not readily provided by profit-seeking private enterprise, and the public prefers to spend its income on private consumption rather than to pay taxes that will be used for the common weal.[50] These problems, however, have generated pressure for remedial efforts that could come only through government action—social security, minimum-wage legislation, medicare, unemployment insurance, and workmen's compensation.

In addition to creating these problems, which brought forth solutions that modified its workings, the free market also generated structural changes that threatened its own destruction. Competition and economic growth gave rise to larger and larger enterprises that threatened to dominate the market. Monopoly is not new. "The nearest thing we have ever had to monopoly in grocery retailing," one economist has observed, "was the old village grocery store. The prices which it charged were not elastic and usually not very competitive until the automobile made them so." [51] But the growth of giant corporations so affected the economy that active intervention by government was advocated by many groups, albeit for various purposes. Defenders of small business proposed measures to curb monopoly and maintain competition, while others accepted the fact of large-scale enterprise and proposed government regulation of business and management action to maintain an adequate level of economic activity. In fact, measures directed toward all these goals have been adopted at various times in the United States—antitrust legislation to prevent or break up monopo-

lies, regulatory commissions to control the prices of natural gas and electric power and to set railroad and airplane fares, and tax policies and government spending to encourage economic growth and full employment.

Large-scale economic organization and the state

Modern industrial society is dominated by large-scale economic enterprise, public and private. Although small business has survived, as measured by the number of small enterprises, the corporation, and particularly the giant corporation, has become the central economic institution. Characterized by a widespread diffusion of ownership and a highly centralized management, giant corporations now account for a large share of total business assets, production, business receipts, and employment. A. A. Berle, a leading authority on the corporation for many years, wrote, in 1964:

> Today approximately 50 per cent of American manufacturing—that is, everything other than finance and transportation—is held by about 150 corporations, reckoned, at least, by asset values. If a rather larger group is taken, the statistics would probably show that about two-thirds of the economically productive assets of the United States, excluding agriculture, are owned by a group of not more than 500 corporations.[52]

In 1960 there were fifty-four corporations with more than $1 billion in assets. The 100 largest industrial corporations had total sales in 1960 of over $133 billion, with forty-one having sales, in 1961, of more than $1 billion.

Increasingly, Americans are employees rather than independent business men, professionals, or farmers. In 1960, roughly 90 per cent of all Americans held wage or salaried jobs; in the preceding year 30 million of the 65 million persons gainfully employed had a corporate employer, in addition to 10 million who were working for some governmental body—state, Federal, or local. Many giant corporations employ imposing numbers of workers: General Motors, for example, has more than 600,000 employees in all its branches around the world, and the 500 largest manufacturing companies alone employ almost 10 per cent of employed Americans.

The consequences of the "corporation take-over," as Andrew Hacker has characterized the emerging role of the corporation in the United States, are far-reaching.[53] Employees are part of large-scale bureaucratic structures, the characteristics of which were explored in Chapter 10. Channels of mobility have changed, as have the requisites for success. The dominance of the organization, William H. Whyte has argued, has contributed to changes in basic values, from individualism and the "Protestant Ethic" (see Chapter 14) to a "Social Ethic" emphasizing the group and "belongingness."[54] Property institutions have been transformed, as ownership of corporate stock no longer carries with it any significant measure of control over the enterprise, whereas management, with relatively little economic investment in the corporation, makes significant decisions concerning corporate policy.

The growth of giant corporations, Berle has observed, has led to "the highest concentration of economic power in recorded history . . . far beyond anything we have yet seen."[55] The decisions of the men who direct these corporations concerning what to produce, where to locate new plants, how deeply to commit company funds to scientific research,

what products to advertise, whether to yield wage increases or risk a strike of their employees, how much to contribute to charity or to educational institutions—have a substantial impact upon individuals, groups, communities, and the entire society.

Yet there is no institutionalized means of control over these decisions, except for such restraints as may be imposed by government. The advocates of free, unregulated enterprise resist imposition of any controls on the grounds that private judgment and self-interest are more to be trusted than government decisions. Alternatively, others argue that management has become increasingly "professionalized" so that business executives now necessarily take into account the public interest.

That the attitudes and values of business executives have changed is undoubtedly true. They have had to accept, albeit often reluctantly, the existence of unions and greater government participation in the economy and to take into account the long-run needs of the organization rather than immediate interests. As an institution "in perpetuity," the corporation now imposes its own requirements. Despite their frequent public rejection of "planning," as carried out by government, business executives must themselves plan over a long future, often at the cost of short-run advantage.

Yet management, despite the increasing requirements of knowledge and skill and the growth of professional schools of business administration, falls short of full professionalization. As Bernard Barber has shown, there is neither the institutionalized orientation to community interests, the "disinterestedness" characteristic of the professional as he performs his role, nor a code of ethics and accepted professional standards by which to judge his actions.[56] By and large, managers are expected to pursue their own interests, and the measure of managerial success remains the profit-and-loss statement.

In part, the increase in governmental participation in the economy represents an effort to cope with the otherwise unregulated power of the corporation, as well as a response to the problems created by a free market. Moreover, the impact of government has grown as the size of government budgets has increased, whether for defense purposes or to achieve welfare goals. More fundamentally, perhaps, the idea that economic activity is subject to impersonal "laws" that could not—and should not—be tampered with has been replaced by the belief that economic growth and reasonably full employment can and should be maintained by government action.

The division between politics and economics that marked the nineteenth century has therefore gradually diminished. The allocation of resources, the rate of technological progress and economic growth, the level of economic activity, are now in Western Europe and the United States the result of a complex pattern of political decisions, managerial actions, and individual choices, all related in diverse ways to one another. Government policy is designed to influence the level of consumption and corporate policy through tax rates, government spending, and regulatory actions, while management takes into account or is constrained by the actions of government agencies.

In the Soviet Union, China, and elsewhere, of course, the separation of government and business has disappeared almost completely, although there remain significant parallels in the structure and organization of the complex and elaborate technology of modern industry. As David Granick has shown, the Russian executive also has some measure of freedom of action, necessarily, in the direction of the economic enterprise, even though he must work within guidelines set for him by a central government agency and enforced by an elaborate structure of controls.[57]

In any modern industrial system, the conflict between centralized authority and planning on the one hand and the need for autonomy and some measure of freedom of action at various levels within the structure on the other is likely to be a continuing—and basically unresolvable—problem. In the Soviet Union, it would appear, many of the major problems stem from overcentralization; the various administrative reorganizations of the late 1950s and the 1960s represent efforts to deal with these problems. In the United States, the absence of effective controls constitutes a major source of difficulty in maintaining the economy at desired levels of activity and growth. The ways in which this continuing tension is dealt with reflect not only economic concerns and political interests of various groups within each society but also ideological commitments and value orientations.

Notes

[1] Robin Williams, *American Society* (2nd ed.; New York: Knopf, 1960), p. 151.

[2] *Ibid.*

[3] Wilbert E. Moore, *Economy and Society* (Garden City: Doubleday, 1955), p. 3.

[4] See, for example, the work of the "institutional" economists, notably Thorstein Veblen, John R. Commons, Wesley C. Mitchell, and Walton Hamilton; the regular studies of consumer expenditures and expectations sponsored by the Fed-

eral Reserve Board and published each year in the *Federal Reserve Bulletin*; Moore, *op. cit.*, Bert F. Hoselitz, *Sociological Aspects of Economic Growth* (New York: Free Press, 1959); Bert F. Hoselitz (ed.), *The Progress of Underdeveloped Areas* (Chicago: University of Chicago Press, 1952); and Mirra Komarovsky (ed.), *Common Frontiers of the Social Sciences* (New York: Free Press, 1957), Part II, "Economics and Sociology."

5 Karl Polanyi, *The Great Transformation* (New York: Farrar, 1944), p. 46.

6 Walton Hamilton and Irene Till, "Property," in *Encyclopedia of the Social Sciences*, XII (New York: Macmillan, 1930), 528–38.

7 Kingsley Davis, *Human Society* (New York: Macmillan, 1948), p. 452.

8 Hamilton and Till, *op. cit.*, pp. 529–30.

9 For a suggestive discussion of the nature of property, see A. Irving Hallowell, *Culture and Experience* (Philadelphia: University of Pennsylvania Press, 1955), Ch. 12.

10 R. von Jhering, quoted in *ibid.*, p. 240.

11 E. Adamson Hoebel, *Man in the Primitive World* (2nd ed.; New York: McGraw-Hill, 1958), p. 439.

12 A. A. Berle and Gardner Means, *The Modern Corporation and Private Property* (New York: Macmillan, 1933).

13 For an analysis of the role of the Soviet manager and a comparison with his American counterpart, see David Granick, *The Red Executive* (Garden City: Doubleday, 1960).

14 Daryll Forde and Mary Douglas, "Primitive Economics," in Harry L. Shapiro (ed.), *Man, Culture, and Society* (New York: Oxford, 1956), p. 331.

15 Hamilton and Till, *op. cit.*, p. 529.

16 Ralph Linton, *The Study of Man* (New York: Appleton, 1936), p. 321.

17 See, for example, the cases described by Bernhard J. Stern, "Resistances to the Adoptions of Technological Innovations," Ch. 4, in National Resources Committee, *Technological Trends and National Policy* (Washington, D.C.: U.S. Government Printing Office, 1937), pp. 39–66.

18 Quoted in Margaret Mead (ed.), *Cultural Patterns and Technical Change* (New York: New American Library, 1955), pp. 238, 241.

19 Thorstein Veblen, *The Instinct of Workmanship* (New York: Huebsch, 1922 [first published in 1914]), especially Ch. 7, pp. 309–11.

20 See Thorstein Veblen, *The Theory of the Leisure Class* (New York: Random House, 1931 [first published in 1899]), Ch. 8.

21 The fullest account of Veblen's life and work is to be found in Joseph Dorfman, *Thorstein Veblen and His America* (New York: Viking, 1934).

22 Forde and Douglas, *op. cit.*, pp. 331–2.

23 See *Technology and the American Economy: Report of the National Commission on Technology, Automation, and Economic Progress*, Vol. I (Washington, D.C.: U.S. Government Printing Office, 1966).

24 For an excellent collection of essays dealing with the nature and consequences of automation, see Morris Philipson (ed.), *Automation: Implications for the Future* (New York: Random House Vintage Books, 1962).

25 U.S. Department of Labor, *Dictionary of Occupational Titles*, I (3rd ed.; Washington, D.C.: U.S. Government Printing Office, 1965), xv.

26 *Ibid.*, p. 24.

27 *Ibid.*, p. 124.

28 *Ibid.*, p. 459.

29 *Ibid.*, p. 680.

30 *Ibid.*, p. 135.

31 Henry Ford, *My Life and Work* (Garden City: Doubleday, 1922), p. 80.

32 Ian Lewis, "In the Courts of Power— The Advertising Man," in Peter Berger

(ed), *The Human Shape of Work* (New York: Macmillan, 1964), pp. 143–4.

[33] Wilbert E. Moore, *Industrial Relations and the Social Order* (rev. ed.; New York: Macmillan, 1951), p. 282.

[34] Émile Durkheim, *The Division of Labor in Society*, trans. by George Simpson (New York: Free Press, 1947).

[35] *Ibid.*, Preface to the 2nd ed.

[36] Adam Smith, *The Wealth of Nations*, II (London: Dent Everyman Edition, 1910), 263–4.

[37] Alexis de Tocqueville, *Democracy in America*, II, Henry Reeve text, ed. by Phillips Bradley (New York: Random House Vintage Books, 1954), 168–9.

[38] A. Zvorykin, "Approaches to Work Under Communism," *Soviet Sociology*, I (Fall, 1962), 29.

[39] Raymond Firth, *Primitive Economics of the New Zealand Maori* (London: Routledge, 1929), pp. 218–9.

[40] Eric E. Lampard, *Industrial Revolution: Interpretations and Perspectives* (Washington, D.C.: American Historical Association, 1957), pp. 24–5.

[41] See Reinhard Bendix, *Work and Authority in Industry* (New York: Wiley, 1956), Part I.

[4] For a summary discussion of the relations between work groups and productivity, see Robert Dubin, *The World of Work* (Englewood Cliffs: Prentice-Hall, 1958), Ch. 16. For a summary and review of several important empirical studies, see Georges Friedmann, *Industrial Society* (New York: Free Press, 1955), pp. 304–50.

[43] See, for example, Friedmann, *op. cit.*, pp. 296–301 and references cited on pp. 302–3.

[44] "One often hears the claim that modern management and the machine age are effecting a speed-up process which is physically and emotionally unsound. To our great surprise, we found the over-speeded worker largely a myth. He exists mostly in the imagination of the popular writer and the casual observer." Stanley Mathewson, *Restriction of Output Among Unorganized Workers* (New York: Viking, 1934), p. 151.

[45] Karl Marx, *Capital* (New York: Modern Library, 1936), p. 374.

[46] Friedmann, *op. cit.*, pp. 157–62.

[47] For some documentation of this shift, see Leo Lowenthal, "Biographies in Popular Magazines," in Paul F. Lazarsfeld and Frank Stanton (eds.), *Radio Research, 1942–43* (New York: Duell, Sloan, 1944), pp. 507–48. For a suggestive analysis of some of the sources and consequences of this change in values, see David Riesman, *The Lonely Crowd*. (New Haven: Yale University Press, 1950).

[48] See Daniel Bell, *Work and Its Discontents* (Boston: Beacon, 1956), especially pp. 55–6.

[49] For a detailed account of the *kula* ring, see Bronislaw Malinowski, *Argonauts of the Western Pacific* (London: Routledge, 1922). See also Marcel Mauss, *The Gift*, trans. by I. Cunnison (London: Cohen & West, 1954).

[50] John Kenneth Galbraith, *The Affluent Society* (Boston: Houghton Mifflin, 1958).

[51] Quoted in C. Wright Mills, *White Collar* (New York: Oxford, 1951), pp. 36–7.

[52] A. A. Berle "Economic Power and the Free Society," in Andrew Hacker (ed.), *The Corporation Take-Over* (Garden City: Doubleday Anchor Books, 1965; first published in 1964), p. 96.

[53] Hacker, *op. cit.*

[54] William H. Whyte, Jr., *The Organization Man* (New York: Simon & Schuster, 1956).

[55] Berle, *op. cit.*, p. 97.

[56] Bernard Barber, "Is American Business Becoming Professionalized? Analysis of a Social Ideology," in Edward A. Tiryakian (ed.), *Sociological Theory, Values, and Sociocultural Change* (New York: Free Press, 1963), pp. 121–45.

[57] Granick, *op. cit.*

Suggestions for further reading

BELL, DANIEL. *Work and Its Discontents.* Boston: Beacon, 1956.
A brief but penetrating essay on the nature and problems of work in industrial society.

BERLE, ADOLF A., and GARDNER MEANS. *The Modern Corporation and Private Property.* New York: Macmillan, 1932.
The ground-breaking study that first revealed in detail the impact of widespread distribution of corporate ownership upon property institutions in the United States. For a more recent statement, see Berle, Power Without Property, *New York: Harcourt, 1959.*

BERLINER, JOSEPH S. *Factory and Manager in the U.S.S.R.* Cambridge, Mass.: Harvard University Press, 1957.
A study of industrial organization in the Soviet Union.

CAPLOW, THEODORE. *The Sociology of Work.* Minneapolis: University of Minnesota Press, 1954.
An interesting analysis of occupational roles and the institutions governing work in modern industrial society.

DURKHEIM, ÉMILE. *The Division of Labor in Society.* Trans. by George Simpson. New York: Free Press, 1947.
A classic essay on the functions and dysfunctions of the division of labor in society.

FIRTH, RAYMOND. *Primitive Economics of the New Zealand Maori.* New York: Dutton, 1929.
A detailed description of economic life among the aboriginal Maori of New Zealand.

FRIEDMANN, GEORGES. *Industrial Society.* New York: Free Press, 1955.
A review and interpretation of research on the problems stemming from the increasing automation of production in modern industry.

GALBRAITH, JOHN KENNETH. *The Affluent Society.* Boston: Houghton Mifflin, 1958.
A provocative—and much challenged—statement of the economic and social problems of a society of abundance.

GRANICK, DAVID. *The Red Executive.* Garden City: Doubleday, 1960.
A careful study of the composition, social origins, role, and problems of industrial managers in Soviet society. Frequent comparisons are made with American executives.

HOSELITZ, BERT, and WILBERT E. MOORE (eds.). *Industrialization and Society.* The Hague: UNESCO-Mouton, 1963.
Essays on the problems and processes of industrialization in the "underdeveloped" areas.

HUGHES, EVERETT C. *Men and Their Work.* New York: Free Press, 1958.
A collection of suggestive essays on different aspects of work.

MILLER, DELBERT C., and WILLIAM H. FORM. *Industrial Sociology.* New York: Harper, 1951.
A text on the social structure and culture of modern industry that includes some original empirical research.

MOORE, WILBERT E. *The Conduct of the Corporation.* New York: Random House, 1962.
A lively sociological account of the structure and functioning of the corporation.

MOORE, WILBERT E. *Industrial Relations and the Social Order,* rev. ed. New York: Macmillan, 1951.
A thorough and comprehensive introduction to the sociological aspects of economic life in modern society.

PHILIPSON, MORRIS (ed.). *Automation: Implications for the Future.* New York: Random House Vintage Books, 1962.
An excellent collection of papers on the various aspects of automation.

SHONFIELD, ANDREW. *Modern Capitalism.* London: Oxford, 1965.
A major effort to explore the emerging pattern of relationships between government and business in Western Europe and the United States.

SOMBART, WERNER. "Capitalism," *Encyclopedia of the Social Sciences*, III. New York: Macmillan, 1930, pp. 195–208.
An excellent brief statement of the institutional and cultural characteristics of capitalism.

TAWNEY, R. H. *The Acquisitive Society*. New York: Harcourt, 1920.
A classic critique of the institutionalization of acquisitiveness in capitalism.

VEBLEN, THORSTEIN. *The Theory of Business Enterprise*. New York: Scribner, 1932.

Republished with an introduction by C. Wright Mills; New York: New American Library, 1958.
One of several books that state Veblen's ideas on business and industry. For a characteristic discussion of the impact of technology, see Ch. 7, "The Cultural Incidence of the Machine Process."

WALTER, CHARLES H. *Toward the Automatic Factory*. New Haven: Yale University Press, 1957.
A case study of the impact of automation upon workers in a steel mill.

13

Power, authority, and political institutions

The nature of power and authority

Inherent in the relations of groups and individuals to one another are the facts of power and authority. Social power, we noted earlier (see p. 175) is the capacity to control the actions of others. It is present in all areas of social life—family, religion, the school, economic activity, and, of course, in government and politics. Power is exercised not only when Congress passes a law, or the President vetoes it, but also when parents discipline a child, a teacher assigns homework, corporate executives set prices, and a television producer selects a program. Power is revealed when the Soviet Premier announces his nation's policy, a Latin American army ousts a President, or an angry mob demonstrates against Western imperialism in some Middle-Eastern capital. It is manifest when Negroes—and whites—conduct "sit-in" demonstrations, and when union members vote to strike; it emerges when natural gas producers organize a campaign to free pipelines from Federal regulation and when Roman Catholics seek to secure public funds to transport students to parochial schools.

Power encompasses both the ability to command—to exact obedience to one's orders—and to make or to influence decisions that affect, directly or indirectly, the lives and actions of others as well as one's own fate. Ownership of property, especially productive property, as we pointed out in the preceding chapter, carries with it power over other persons by virtue of recognized rights to control the use of things. Politics, when considered as a struggle for power, centers around who shall determine public policy and what that policy shall be—what taxes are to be levied and how the tax burden is to be distributed, whether government is to build public housing or encourage private enterprise to do so, how the members of the armed forces are to be chosen and how long they are to serve, the nature of the country's relations with other nations, whether to conscript capital as well as labor in the waging of war. Power, Max Weber wrote, is "the chance of a man or of a number of men to realize their own will in communal action even against the resistance of others who are participating in the action." [1]

Power may rest upon naked force, it may be camouflaged by ideologies that deny its existence or minimize its importance, it may be obscured deliberately or because of the complexity of the social structure, or it may be "legitimated" and transformed into authority. When men

Sovfoto

Having taken power by force, the Soviet regime has legitimated its authority by various means, including elections to the Supreme Soviet. RIGHT: *The storming of the Winter Palace in Petrograd (now Leningrad), 1917.* BELOW: *Voting for candidates for the Supreme Soviet in Kuibyshev.*

Sovfoto

possess authority, Robert M. MacIver writes, they possess "the established *right*, within any social order, to determine policies, to pronounce judgments on relevant issues, and to settle controversies, or, more broadly, to act as leader or guide to other men." [2]

History provides countless examples of power imposed by the sword: brigands who wreak their will on hapless victims, conquerors who force their rule upon the vanquished, revolutionists who take control by force. So prevalent have such events been in human history that some men have asserted that "might makes right," that, in the words of Thrasymachus, who contends with Socrates in Plato's *Republic*, "justice is nothing else than the interest of the stronger." But power that rests only upon naked force, it would seem, is inevitably unstable and transitory. "The strongest is never strong enough," wrote the eighteenth-century French philosopher, Jean Jacques Rousseau, "to be always the master, unless he transforms strength into right, and obedience into duty." [3] Those who secure their power by force alone face the possibility of unwillingness to obey their orders and violent efforts to unseat them, unless they can otherwise buttress their position. They may secure their power by so rigidly repressing opposition that it dissolves into apathy and helplessness, with an inevitable weakening of the entire social fabric; by offering some men enough social or economic advantages to enlist their loyalty and support; or, finally, by transforming power into authority, thus sustaining their control by moral and institutional sanctions.

In practice, of course, power may rest upon all of these sources: force, self-interest, ideology, apathy. The Soviet regime, for example, originally took power by violent revolution and maintained its grip for a time by the continued use of force and terror. But it also sought to enlist the allegiance of its people by offering opportunities for education and advancement. It promised and has begun to provide material improvements in the standard of living. And its rulers have continuously reiterated with all the means at their disposal a moral and philosophical justification of the Revolution, the "dictatorship of the proletariat," and Soviet institutions.

Legitimacy—the social justification of power—may take many forms. Men may accept authority because it rests upon tradition and conventional usage: the respect rendered to one's parents, a priest, or minister; the allegiance to a hereditary monarch; the party loyalties that transcend issues and personalities. Men may accept the exercise of power as legitimate because the formulation of orders or policies follows rules to which all subscribe; the United States, it is often asserted, has a government "of laws and not of men." Laws, no matter how unpopular, are to be obeyed as long as they are constitutional; opposition usually takes the form of efforts to change the law—or the constitution—rather than outright disobedience or rebellion. (There may, under some circumstances, however, be widespread and recognized evasion of some kinds of laws; for example, disregard of prohibition during the 1920s in the United States, collusion in securing divorces, or underreporting income and overestimating expenses in making income tax returns. For a general analysis of the sources of *institutionalized evasion* of social norms, see Chapter 19.) Or, finally, men may obey simply because of the personal qualities—the *charisma*—of the person who commands; the appeals of the "natural leader" may transcend established institutions and challenge accepted values.

The structure of power, however, is not always clearly defined or recognized; its locus, or even its very existence, is often uncertain or subject to dispute. Some observers have asserted, for example, that executives in the giant corporations of modern capitalist society exercise great power. C. Wright Mills writes:

> Their private decisions, responsibly made in the feudal-like world of private property and income, determine the size and shape of the national economy, the level of employment, the purchasing power of the consumer, the prices that are advertised, the investments that are channeled. Not "Wall Street financiers" or bankers, but large owners and executives in their self-financing corporations hold the keys of economic power. Not the politicians of the visible government, but the chief executives who sit in the political directorate, by fact and by proxy, hold the power and the means of defending the privileges of their corporate world. If they do not reign, they do govern at many of the vital points of everyday life in America, and no powers effectively and consistently countervail against them, nor have they as corporate-made men developed any effectively restraining conscience.[4]

The president of one of America's leading industrial enterprises vigorously challenges this point of view:

> Corporate "powers" are a myth as far removed from reality as Aladdin's lamp or Jack's extraordinary beanstalk.
>
> Any corporation, it seems to me, has its own system of checks and balances and is probably more sensitively responsive to public will than is government itself. The reason is that the business organization, in addition to its internal controls, is subject to the sovereignty of the market place, a force which can express itself more rapidly and with greater effect than a thoroughly aroused and indignant electorate. I know of no corporate therapy which can immunize against customer sanctions. Certainly size is of small avail in dealing with the angry lady at the store counter once she has her dander up and her umbrella swinging.[5]

This corporate disclaimer of power reflects many things: the widespread assumption, especially in the United States, that power is itself bad, a "distrustful concept," in the same executive's words; the misconception that power must be either total or nonexistent; the persistence of a conception of economic life that is no longer accurate; the effort of big business to protect itself from criticism because of the power it does possess. An umbrella-swinging female at a complaint counter can have little impact upon corporate executives whose power is manifest in each decision to pursue a new line of research, to raise or lower prices, or to locate a new plant in one community or another, even though enough consumer complaints may bring about some change in product or packaging, or in the size and nature of the advertising campaign.

In eighteenth- and nineteenth-century America, power was limited and dispersed, and its exercise was widely looked upon as inimical to the liberties of others. But today power is, in fact, concentrated in government, giant corporations, labor unions, and other large-scale organizations. Although the pervasive distrust of power lingers on and some people still subscribe to the idea that "that government is best which governs least," there is growing recognition that in giving commands men may not only bind others to their will, but may also achieve larger goals. Power may be used for small ends or great ones, not merely for personal gratification but also for collective advantage. Generals not only order their subordinates about, but they also try to protect their nations. Corporate executives, in seeking to increase company profits and personal rewards, may set in motion large plans that can benefit—or injure—the nation as a whole or specific groups within it. Politicians may acquire fame, influence, and on rare occasions wealth, but they may also establish policies that affect the welfare of various groups and may strengthen or weaken the entire society. "The will to power," Robert Penn Warren has written, "grisly as it appears in cer-

tain lights, can mate, if uneasily, with love of justice and dedicated selflessness."[6]

Power is a protean force in society. Rarely clear-cut and unopposed, it is usually part of a complex structure of competing forces and of sometimes visible, sometimes hidden, maneuvering within an institutional system that defines and channels the struggle for control. Our task is not to criticize a "distrustful concept," even though the abuse of power has always been one of mankind's grievous ills, but to ascertain the form it takes, where it is located, and how it is used.

The state and its functions

Although power and authority are found in social roles and relationships in all areas of social life, they are most clearly focused in the *state*. As a concept in social science the state refers to those institutions that establish who shall possess *"the monopoly of the legitimate use of physical force* within a given territory,"[7] and that define how the power which rests upon that monopoly shall be organized and used. The persons who exercise this power compose the government.

By virtue of its legitimate (but never complete) monopoly of force, government clearly enjoys the supreme power in society. Owners of property and officials of private organizations, for example, cannot in principle use force to sustain their control, although they may be able to fall back upon the coercive power of the state to protect their right to command and to make decisions within their limited spheres of action. That in the final resort the state can assert its superiority does not mean, however, that it is inherently totalitarian. There are, of course, totalitarian states that try to impose controls over many areas of "private" life. But even in totalitarian states, as well as in others, both the nature and operations of government are closely related to, and in some measure dependent upon, other institutions.

The differentiated political institutions and social roles that make up the state—laws, courts, judges, legislative bodies, military forces, executives, and administrators—are often not found in primitive societies. The Bantu Kavirondo of western Kenya, for example, prior to the imposition of European control, had no political structure that could be distinguished from other aspects of social structure. Social order was sustained by a complex kinship system; its "bonds, maintained between every member of the clan and his material kin as well as his affinal relations, are so numerous and so strong that they establish bonds between the clans which . . . are in many ways as binding as if there were a central authority overruling that of the clans." [8] Social norms were strongly supported by tradition; no additional authority was usually needed to maintain them. Penalties for violation of tribal taboos and appropriate recompense for personal injury were established by convention. If a member of a clan broke some norm, propitiatory sacrifices were offered and a ritual purification of the offender was required; persistent violations led to expulsion from the group and death if caught in further transgressions. If two men in the same clan engaged in a dispute, the one who felt wronged tried to settle matters himself. When private efforts failed, the matter was brought to the attention of the elders of the clan, who then rendered a decision. If the elders could not agree and the issue was serious enough, the clan might split in two. An individual who felt

that a member of another clan had committed some offense against him took the issue to the elders of that clan; a serious injury led to exchanges between the elders of both clans. Irreconcilable conflict might lead to hostilities, which were usually ended by negotiation after a few men had been killed.

Distinctive political institutions emerged in many different historical contexts and for many reasons: the needs of war and military campaigns, mass migration and conquest, increasing size and diversity of the population, new problems that required organized action by society as a whole. The state took shape as groups and individuals within society found it to their interest to centralize authority, to establish methods for resolving disputes, and to use force to maintain conformity to some social norms.

Ancient and medieval writers did not distinguish between state and society. All men belonged to the political community; all groups and associations except for the medieval Church, whose political role was subject to controversy, and the family, which was viewed as a "natural unit," were considered as subordinate to or parts of the state. The distinction between state and society emerged only gradually during the sixteenth and seventeenth centuries as the growing middle class sought to throw off feudal domination. By the eighteenth century many French and English writers no longer looked upon the two as coterminous; the state came to be considered merely one aspect of the whole—society organized for political purposes.

The modern liberal view of the state, especially as it has evolved in the Western democracies, sees it as an umpire standing in the midst of competing interests, maintaining the rules that make possible an orderly social life. Those who hold government office are expected to be as neutral as possible in the social struggles that take place in society, and to be capable of subduing their own personal, class, or sectional interests to the common welfare. Because power may be abused, liberal theory holds that public officials must be restrained by a division of power and a system of checks and balances, or by institutionalized (constitutional) limitations upon the scope of legitimate governmental action.

In sharp contrast with this view is the Marxist conception of the state as essentially an instrument with which one economic class maintains its power over society. The state sustains and protects property institutions that usually divide society into opposing classes, Marxists argue, and therefore it necessarily stands on the side of those who own. Because of their class position and in pursuit of class interests, men of property directly or indirectly shape the forms of government and dictate public policy. In capitalist society, *The Communist Manifesto* tells us, "The executive of the modern state is but a committee for managing the common affairs of the bourgeoisie." Political conflicts mirror class divisions, political parties reflect class interests, and political institutions are surface phenomena beneath which run the determining facts of class structure. The state appears as the *naked* instrument of class interests, however, only when the struggle for power becomes intense; in more peaceable times, its class basis may be obscured by a rhetoric—or ideology—that asserts its neutrality or its contribution to the general welfare.

A third view of the state emphasizes its relations to transcendental values that increase its importance and tend to justify the extension of its authority into hitherto "free" or separate areas of social life. For the nineteenth-century philosopher Hegel, for example, the state, particularly as embodied in Germany, was the realization of reason in history. Nazi doctrine saw the state as the expression and instrument of the *Volk*, or race, or as an end in itself. By emphasizing the subordination of individuals and groups, of institutions and culture, to the needs of the state, these theories tended to blur the differences between state and society and to unite them into a totalitarian whole.

None of these views of the state adequately describes its character, except perhaps for those rare periods when the forces in society are roughly equal in strength, when government clearly and unequivocally represents only the interests of a particular class, or when a centralized political power seeks to impose a totalitarian system upon society. But in most instances reality is too complex to be caught in these theoretical models—or in any of the numerous alternative theories of the state that have been proffered. The state can sustain the entire social order—enforcing some of the mores, resolving some disputes, protecting society from external enemies—and may impose standards of behavior and provide services of various kinds; but it does so to the advantage of one or the other social class or of any of the diverse groups found in society. And power may be valued as an end in itself by individuals or by the entire culture; control over others and the exercise of authority can satisfy the ego as well as protect property or defend other values.

A sociological analysis of political institutions and the structure of power and authority need not duplicate the work of political scientists who have focused much of their attention upon the machinery of government—administrative, legislative, and judicial organization, laws, constitutions, political parties—although the sociological study of bureaucracy, custom, and social institutions can also contribute to our understanding of that machinery. As students of sociology our central concern lies in the intricate interplay between state and society, an area of inquiry in which political science and sociology inevitably overlap.

Politics and social structure: voting and political attitudes

The connections between politics and social structure are readily seen in the study of voting in democratic societies. Despite frequent assertions by some politicians that no party should reflect the interests of only one class and occasional denials of the political relevance of class, most political parties do, in fact, represent in some measure different class interests. "On a world scale," writes S. M. Lipset, "the principal generalization which can be made is that parties are primarily based on either the lower classes or the middle and upper classes." [9] Other social divisions often play a role in determining political allegiances and how men vote, and there may be substantial variations within classes and changes from time to time, but nevertheless class differences are rarely, if ever, politically irrelevant. Even in the United States, where there are no strong parties with explicit class-based ideologies, as in some European countries, political allegiances are divided to a considerable extent along class lines.

Many investigations of voting in the United States document the social differences between supporters of the Democratic and Republican parties. Consistently, in recent elections at least, the proportion voting Democratic (or not voting at all) decreases at each higher level of the class order, and the proportion voting Republican increases. Studies in Erie County, Ohio, in 1940; in Elmira, New York, in 1948; and of national samples in all the Presidential elections since 1948, as well as numerous other investigations, all reveal the same general pattern, as do ecological studies of voting that compare election results in areas possessing different social and economic characteristics. A summary of some of the findings of various studies is shown in Table 15.

The extent to which voting is influenced by class position, however, varies from time to time as issues change and other considerations become more or less relevant. In 1956, for example, when President Eisenhower was re-elected with a large majority, half of the manual workers voted for him. In 1964, on the other hand, President Johnson even gained a majority from the professional and business group which characteristically gave a majority to the Republican candidate.

Even more clear-cut class differences in voting are typically found in Western Europe. In Great Britain the working class gave a two to one majority to labor in the elections of 1945 and 1951. In 1945 the Conservatives gained a three to one majority from the middle class—and lost the election; in 1951 they secured a five to one majority and won. The British Gallup poll, which divides its sample into four socioeconomic classes—average plus, average, average minus, and very poor—reported that in 1955, 84 per cent of the top class and 66 per cent of the second class supported the Conservatives, compared with only 34 per cent and 31 per cent of the two bottom classes. In 1964, according to another nationwide poll, the pattern remained the same, although the Conservatives lost slightly in each class.

Table 15

CLASS POSITION AND VOTING *

A. Erie County, Ohio, 1940

Socioeconomic status †	Two-party preferences, May, 1940	
	Republican	Democratic
A	71	29
B	68	32
C+	56	44
C−	46	54
D	35	65

B. Elmira, New York, 1948

Socioeconomic status §	Two-party vote, 1948	
	Republican	Democratic
Upper	89	11
Upper middle	77	23
Middle	66	34
Lower middle	56	44
Lower	57	43

C. National sample, 1952

Occupational group	Voting, 1952			
	Republican	Democratic	Other	Not voting
Professional and managerial	59	27	2	12
Other white collar	52	28	1	19
Skilled and semiskilled	34	39	1	26
Unskilled	19	40	1	40
Farm operators	42	24	1	33

D. National samples, 1952–1964

	Republican proportion of the two-party vote			
	1952	1956	1960	1964
Professional and business	64	68	58	46
White collar	60	63	52	43
Manual	45	50	40	29
Farmers	67	54	52	47

* All figures are percentages.
† Based upon interviewers' ratings.
§ Based upon an index composed of occupation, education, and interviewers' ratings.
Data for Erie County from Paul F. Lazarsfeld, Bernard Berelson, and Hazel Gaudet, *The People's Choice* (2nd ed.; New York: Columbia University Press, 1948), Chart III, p. 19; for Elmira from Berelson, Lazarsfeld, and William N. McPhee, *Voting* (Chicago: University of Chicago Press, 1954), Chart XX, p. 55; for national sample (1952) from Angus Campbell, Gerald Gurin, and Warren E. Miller, *The Voter Decides* (Evanston: Row, Peterson, 1954), Table 5.1, p. 72; for national samples (1952–1964) from The American Institute of Public Opinion (Gallup Poll) Release, December 13, 1964.

Similar patterns are found in France, Germany, and Italy, with radical parties drawing heavily—though not exclusively —from the lower classes and more con-servative parties from the middle and upper classes.

These class differences in party allegiance and support are paralleled by

Table 16

POLITICAL ATTITUDES OF OCCUPATIONAL STRATA: CONSERVATISM–RADICALISM,[*] 1945

Occupational groups	Per cent who are					
	Ultra-con-servative	Con-servative	Indeter-minate	Radical	Ultra-radical	Total
Large business	55.5	31.5	11.1	0.0	1.9	100.0
Professional	30.2	39.7	19.2	4.1	6.8	100.0
Small business	45.8	28.2	17.6	6.9	1.5	100.0
White collar	24.4	31.4	28.5	10.5	5.2	100.0
Skilled manual	12.2	26.4	34.4	17.2	9.8	100.0
Semiskilled manual	5.2	16.1	29.3	28.7	20.7	100.0
Unskilled manual	2.5	20.8	39.0	20.8	16.9	100.0
Farm owners and managers	32.8	35.9	24.8	3.9	2.6	100.0
Farm tenants and laborers	11.7	31.9	30.4	18.8	7.2	100.0

[*] Based upon a national sample of men.

Richard Centers, *The Psychology of Social Classes*, Table 8, p. 57 (Copyright 1949 by Princeton University Press). Reprinted by permission of Princeton University Press.

differences in political attitudes and opinions. Studies of political attitudes consistently report that the middle and upper classes are more hostile to government intervention in the economy and to social welfare measures and more sympathetic to antilabor legislation than the working class. Although any definitions of conservatism, liberalism, and radicalism are uncertain, and the meaning of these terms changes from one period to another, the proportion of persons who are generally viewed as conservative usually increases with higher class position and the liberal or radical proportion decreases. In 1945, Richard Centers compared members of different occupational groups in a national sample on a conservatism-radicalism scale based upon six questions: Is America "truly a land of opportunity"? Should working people have more power? Would things be better or worse if government took over control of industry? How much responsibility should government assume for maintaining minimum standards of living? Are sympathies in labor disputes generally with labor or management? Does management try to do well by its workers or to exploit them? The results are summarized in Table 16. There have, of course, been changes on various issues in recent years; on some questions differences have diminished, as with reference to public welfare measures and the "welfare state," but on others, such as support of unions, differences have increased.[10] The relevance of class and its relationship to other social divisions may well have changed in an increasingly affluent society, but it is clear that class remains an important determinant of political attitudes and ideologies.

In contrast to attitudes on economic issues, which have usually been taken as the test of "liberalism" and "conservatism," attitudes toward civil liberties have usually been found to be more "liberal" in higher class levels than in lower.[11] Paradoxically, however, the leadership in protecting and defending freedom of speech and assembly and other civil

Table 17

DEGREE OF HOSTILITY TO THE SOVIET SYSTEM ACCORDING TO SOCIAL GROUP

Degree of hostility	Occupational groups				
	Intelligentsia	*White-collar employees*	*Skilled workers*	*Ordinary workers*	*Collective farm peasants*
Least	71	59	54	42	40
Medium	17	25	26	24	24
Most	12	16	20	34	36
	100%	100%	100%	100%	100%
Total number of respondents	567	607	243	410	312

Alex Inkeles and Raymond A. Bauer, *The Soviet Citizen* (1959), Table 68, p. 260. Reprinted by permission of Harvard University Press.

rights historically has come more often from parties drawing their main strength from lower-class levels.

Differences in political attitudes—or in politically relevant attitudes, that is, those toward problems that become the foci of political action—often follow class lines not only in democratic societies, but also in nations where open political opposition is severely limited or impossible. In a study of refugees from the Soviet Union (most of whom had left during World War II), Alex Inkeles and Raymond Bauer found that there were substantial differences in attitudes toward the regime among members of different occupational groups. Table 17 summarizes the extent of hostility toward the regime among these groups. An investigation of the attitudes of Polish students toward equality reveals that the higher the class position (as measured by parent's occupation and family income) the greater the approval of disparities in income and the larger the income differences they thought were acceptable or desirable. These relationships are not altogether consistent, however, for within each occupational group approval of inequality did not always increase with additional family income. Students' atti-

tudes were also affected by their expectations of their own future earnings and status.[12]

The recurrence of class differences in political attitudes and behavior in many diverse societies seems to provide *prima facie* evidence for an economic interpretation of politics. In fact, however, despite their obvious importance, class differences and economic issues do not in themselves adequately account for patterns of voting or shifts in power. Party allegiances may also vary with religion, ethnic identity, sex, age, rural and urban residence, and other social attributes. (See Table 18.) In the United States, for example, Protestants are more likely to vote Republican than are Catholics or Jews, even when class position is held constant. In France, Belgium, Germany, Italy, and other European nations there are explicitly Catholic parties that draw support from Catholic workers despite a relatively conservative position on economic issues. Women characteristically support the conservative parties more frequently than do men, probably, Lipset suggests, because the female role usually leads them to stress stability and tradition.[13] Older people tend to be more conservative than

Table 18

VOTE BY GROUPS IN PRESIDENTIAL ELECTIONS, 1952–1964

	1952		1956		1960		1964	
	Dem.	Rep.	Dem.	Rep.	Dem.	Rep.	Dem.	Rep.
National	44.6	55.4	42.2	57.8	50.1	49.9	61.3	38.7
Men	47	53	45	55	52	48	60	40
Women	42	58	39	61	49	51	62	38
White	43	57	41	59	49	51	59	41
Nonwhite	79	21	61	39	68	32	94	6
College	34	66	31	69	39	61	52	48
High school	45	55	42	58	52	48	62	38
Grade school	52	48	50	50	55	45	66	34
21–29 years	51	49	43	57	54	46	64	36
30–49 years	47	53	45	55	54	46	63	37
50 years and older	39	61	39	61	46	54	59	41
Protestant	37	63	37	63	38	62	55	45
Catholic	56	44	51	49	78	22	76	24

The American Institute of Public Opinion (Gallup Poll) Release, December 13, 1964. Reprinted by permission of The American Institute of Public Opinion, Princeton.

younger, although the problems of the aged in an industrial society in which they no longer fulfill an important, recognized social function and often face serious economic difficulties may generate radical attitudes and behavior, as they did in California in the 1930s. The usual age differences, however, often are affected by distinctive historical events; the initial political experience of any age group seems to set its political orientation in a fixed pattern that tends to persist despite changing circumstances. Thus the generation that came to maturity in the United States during the depression of the 1930s is more likely to be "liberal" than either earlier generations or, it seems, the group that first cast its votes in the years following the Second World War.

Voting patterns, therefore, are influenced not only by the class position of people, but also by membership in other groups whose interests may be at stake in an election, or whose attitudes and values predispose them toward one or another party or candidate. The presence of frequently large numbers in each class who deviate from the usual pattern stems largely from the complex structure of modern society and the multiple group affiliations of most people. Both voting studies and investigation of class differences in attitudes reveal that many persons do not possess the perspectives or values characteristic of their objectively defined class; instead they subscribe to the attitudes of some other class and vote according to their conceptions of their places in society rather than their objective circumstances. Those who adhere to attitudes and values of a class other than the one to which they belong are usually also members of groups whose political predisposition runs counter to that of the class or have had some experience not characteristic of others at the same social and economic level. Middle-class American Jews have supported the Democratic Party in recent elections much more strongly than have middle-class Protestants. In some European countries, working-class Catholics often support center or right-wing Catholic parties rather than the socialists or communists, and there is a substantial proportion of "Tory workers" in England. Centers has shown that those American workers with conservative attitudes who vote for Republican candidates are more likely to have come from middle-class families or to have had more education than do those workers who support the Democrats.[14]

The trend of politics and the outcome of specific elections reflect the shifting alignments and allegiances of various segments of society in response to changing issues and specific events, and these, on occasion, carry sufficient weight to offset the typical class pattern. Although a substantial proportion of voters, perhaps a majority, remains attached to a single political position, many shift their support from one election to another as new issues emerge or as their place in society is affected by continuing changes in the social structure. Samuel Lubell has persuasively argued that American political history of the 1930s and 1940s was a product of sharpened class feeling and the drive for higher status and greater opportunity by various racial and ethic groups, and that the 1950s witnessed the blurring of some of these differences.[15] In 1960, John F. Kennedy drew many Catholic votes that would probably have gone to the Republican candidate, although Lyndon Johnson gained almost as large a Catholic majority in 1964, probably for other reasons (see Table 18).

These facts, particularly the absence of a clear-cut political cleavage based upon class differences, contribute, it has been suggested, to the maintenance of a stable democratic society. Multiple loyalties prevent the polarization of society into rigidly hostile groups incapable of accepting compromise. Because political parties must usually seek to capture some votes from all classes they moderate their programs and, when in power, their practices, and therefore avoid those extremes which might lead to irreconcilable conflict. Middle- and upper-class parties usually represent a minority in the population and must therefore seek support from workers with a program that in some measure appeals to their interests. Parties based largely on working-class support have a larger base from which to draw. But among their potential supporters they must overcome the weight of tradition, the hopes for advancement that often lead men to identify with higher classes, the influence of men who are often looked up to by the working class because of their achievements and status, and the apathy and lack of interest frequently found among those with limited education.

Any analysis of election returns, however, must take into account not only the diverse groups from which each party draws support but also the institutions that define the electorate and establish the structure of representation. Limitations on the suffrage may, of course, affect the balance of forces that shape election results. Elimination of property qualifications for voting brought the poorer classes into democratic political struggles; full enfranchisement of the Negroes in the South will undoubtedly increase their influence upon public policy, already evident in the mid-1960s in the election of several Negroes as local officials. Who is elected to office and which party gains a majority may also be affected by the form of political organization that prevails—whether there are two parties or many smaller parties, small constituencies each of which elects one representative or large constituencies which choose a number of representatives, territorial or proportional representation. Political forms themselves, however, which may have some influence upon who gains power, are in turn often shaped in part by the pressure of diverse groups, each seeking to establish political ground rules that will increase its influence or limit the power of others, each often justifying its position in ideological terms.

Power and social structure

When the election is over and the heat and smoke of political battle clear away, those to whom the voters give their support assume control of the machinery of government. To the extent that elective officials represent particular groups one might say that these groups now have power. Elections in a democratic society, then, determine not merely which individual or party shall rule, but also whose interests, perspectives, and values shall dominate the policies pursued by government. Since parties are not usually confined to only one segment of the population, victory—even one of overwhelming proportions—rarely produces total domination by one group—or by several. Instead, the enactment of legislation, the formulation of executive policy, and the administration of laws are all shaped by the pressures that are continuously brought to bear by interested groups upon public officials who must reconcile their own ideas and preferences with the exigencies of political life.

Power, of course, is not merely derivative, reflecting simply the interests of diverse groups. Its locus and its exercise are both affected by the specific political institutions that determine how public officials are chosen and that define the limits of their power and the procedures they must follow. These political institutions, such as the Federal system, party organization, legislative procedures, and so on, are themselves products of complex social forces; but once they become operative they have independent effects upon the struggle for political power.

So complex is the structure of American society, so seemingly open to all groups the contest for power, so variable and shifting the alignment of forces on different issues, so confusing and often irrelevant much of the political rhetoric, that the actual structure of power is not readily identified. As we pointed out earlier, some observers have argued that big business occupies the dominant position in American society, that government protects its property rights against any challenge, and that public policy, on the whole, favors its interests. The influence of business upon government, in fact, has been paramount for most of the past century. "The business of America is business," said Calvin Coolidge, and with only occasional intervals of successful opposition this view has been accepted by many scholars as correct. Yet opposition made possible by the existence of democratic political institutions and stimulated by the recurrence of economic crises has prevented a complete consolidation of business power. At various periods—especially in connection with the New Freedom of 1913 and 1914 and the New Deal of the 1930s, but also before and after these two periods—various restraints and controls have been imposed upon the power of business.

These restraints and the presence of many other more or less organized groups—labor unions, ethnic minorities, farmers, conservationists, churches, small businessmen, doctors, competing industries (oil versus coal, or railroads versus truckers, for example)—have produced in recent times, David Riesman suggests, an "amorphous distribution of power." "Power in America," he writes, "seems to me situational and mercurial; it resists attempts to locate it the way a molecule . . . resists attempts simultaneously to locate it and time its velocity."[16] In the past, businessmen did constitute a kind of "ruling class," but now, he argues, each group, by cooperating with others, can prevent things it dislikes from happening, even though it may not be able to secure positive action of any sort.

There is some warrant for this interpretation of the present political situation in the United States, but Riesman's analysis, Mills suggests in a trenchant criticism, does not "try to clarify the hodge-podge by classifying these groups, occupations, strata, organizations according to their political relevance or even according to whether they are organized politically at all."[17] Not all issues are of equal importance; many groups concern themselves only with limited problems; some groups can exert greater pressure, directly or indirectly, than others; there are many consistent coalitions that are often capable of achieving their own goals despite opposition; and big business remains, despite the restraints imposed upon it, the presence of competing interest groups, and some internal divisions, a major locus of power in American society.

The complex relations between social structure and political power are also manifest in each local community. Some studies of the structure of power in spe-

cific communities have revealed the presence of a dominant group composed of leading business and professional men.[18] These community "influentials," as they have been called, gain their influence from their control over local business and industry and from the high prestige derived from wealth, economic position, and occasionally from family background. Rather than assuming public office themselves, however, they may exert their influence indirectly, through personal contacts with public officials and other leading citizens, through positions in civic organizations and participation in political parties, or through use of the financial resources they control.

This version of the "power structure" has been sharply criticized, however, and a "pluralistic" interpretation of community power offered in its place.[19] In this alternative view, there is no single group of "influentials," but a number of groups oriented toward specific "issue-areas"—schools, housing, political nominations. In New Haven, for example, Robert Dahl found no one dominant group, but several, each concerned with specific problems and able to exert considerable influence in determining public policy in that area.[20] But in order to exert any power, these influentials must mobilize or maintain public support and, in some instances, be able to influence the political process.

Communities vary widely, of course, and in all likelihood no single interpretation can encompass the variety to be found in the structure of power. Which individuals gain influence or power depends in large measure upon the social structure of the community. In some instances, particularly where the middle class is small or ineffectual, labor is able to gain control of local government or union leaders acquire important civic posts, diminishing substantially the power of bankers, industrialists, and merchants.[21] Where a large ethnic minority is found, its leaders too may be elected to public office or gain influence because of the size of the group they represent. Once men gain public office, however, or seek election to political positions, they may often find it advantageous to accommodate themselves to the power and influence of leading members of the community. The location and exercise of power in the local community, then, do not merely reflect the existing distribution of wealth and prestige, although they cannot be ignored. The structure of power is strategically affected by the nature of local political institutions, the requirements of political roles, social divisions within the community, and the effectiveness with which various interests can be mobilized around particular issues—one of which may be the structure of power itself.

Because of the increasing complexity of American society, the elaboration of centralized controls, and the growth of national organizations such as corporations, trade unions, professional societies, trade associations, veterans' groups, and other large-scale bureaucratic structures, the relative importance of local political leadership and community influentials has steadily diminished. "During the past century," Mills observes, "local society has become part of a national economy; its status and power hierarchies have come to be subordinate parts of the larger hierarchies of the nation." [22] Decisions made in Washington, or state capitals, or in New York City, Detroit, or Chicago shape the course of events in the smaller, outlying centers. Local variations in the structure of power are therefore submerged in the larger encompassing national structure, and local leadership is often dependent upon relations with state or national leaders. Despite the Federal

system that inhibits in some measure the concentration of power, the major political dramas take place at the top, where important decisions are made and far-reaching policies are formulated. The local structure of power continues to affect larger policies and practices where political institutions require officeholders to maintain local support, as in the House of Representatives, although Congress itself, some students have argued, has lost much of its power and influence to the enlarged executive branch of the federal government.

In other democratic societies, the struggle for power—and its outcome—parallels in many respects the political process in the United States. The frequently substantial differences that do exist are related to the distinctive features of each society—for example, the strength of farmers and the petty bourgeoisie in France, the highly centralized structure of French government, and its parliamentary difficulties. In Great Britain, sharper class divisions and greater class consciousness among workers have given political life some of its special characteristics. England has moved steadily toward a "welfare state," although the Labour Party, which is based chiefly upon the trade unions, has been in power only for brief intervals since it first organized the Government in 1924. Many British Conservatives resemble more closely liberal Democrats than conservative Republicans.

The struggle for power in any society—democratic, authoritarian, totalitarian—is competition or conflict not merely among individuals, factions, and political parties, but also among social groups that seek to protect or secure their interests (including the interest in political power itself) by gaining control over the machinery of government. Even in totalitarian societies in which political opposition is repressed, political struggles based upon structural divisions persist, although they are usually muted or transformed into intraparty squabbles or palace-guard maneuvering. Western observers regularly seek to ascertain which groups in the Soviet Union—party functionaries, army, secret police, technicians and managers—are gaining ascendancy in the Kremlin.

Where democratic political institutions that permit a continual adjustment of group interests through peaceful political processes are not found, violent methods are apt to be used as each group tries to seize power. In Latin America, for example, dictators, revolutions, and democratic regimes have followed one another in often bewildering sequence as soldiers, bureaucrats, landowners, a growing middle class, and in some nations an increasingly articulate and organized working class, struggle for power.

In this area, as in other parts of the world where democratic institutions have not yet been firmly established, control over the armed forces is of strategic importance. A government that is not accepted as legitimate by all groups in society requires force to ensure the stability of the regime. Military men therefore play a major role in politics. A group of army officers led the rebellion that overthrew King Farouk of Egypt in 1952; one of them, Colonel Gamal Abdel Nasser, now rules. The revolt against Juan Perón in Argentina in 1955 was led by military men, who overthrew a civilian president again in 1966. The Turkish government was overthrown in 1960 by a military coup, and military men still play an important role in the Turkish government. In 1966, Kwame Nkrumah was removed from office by a group of army officers; similar intervention has occurred in many other African states in the few years since they achieved independence.

Military intervention in politics has become so frequent since 1918, as Samuel Finer has shown,[23] that it might almost be considered the typical pattern rather than the exception. In underdeveloped areas, military leaders who have had the advantages of training in universities or military schools of advanced nations have become an increasingly important political force, to the extent that they are often viewed as a "strategic elite" in modern society.[24]

Elites and political decision makers

Who shall wield power has always been a central question for political theorists, who have usually differentiated political systems in terms of how many people hold power—monarchy, or its corrupt form, tyranny; aristocracy, or its decadent form, oligarchy; and democracy, which may degenerate into "mobocracy." But these categories derived from the ancient Greeks, MacIver points out, bypass important features of any government.[25] In all political systems comparatively few people actually exercise power and authority; only in a small community like ancient Athens or a New England town can all or most citizens participate directly in important political decisions. On the other hand, even the monarch or dictator must be aided by ministers, generals, tax collectors, and other officials in whom some authority is vested as they carry out the orders of the ruler and administer the machinery of government.

The fact that only a few actually carry on the affairs of state has led some sociologists and political scientists to conclude that basically power resides in an "elite." T. B. Bottomore has summed up the central components of this view, as formulated by two leading theorists, Vilfredo Pareto and Gaetano Mosca, as follows:

In every society there is, and must be, a minority which rules over the rest of society; this minority—the "political class" or "governing elite," composed of those who occupy the posts of political command and, more vaguely, those who can directly influence political decisions—undergoes changes in its membership over a period of time, ordinarily by the recruitment of new individual members from the lower strata of society, sometimes by the incorporation of new social groups, and occasionally by the complete replacement of the established elite by a "counter-elite," as occurs in revolutions.[26]

The fundamental political division, therefore, is between rulers and ruled; politics consists in the struggle of groups and individuals to enter or to remain in the elite, rather than in the conflict among various social groups as they seek to direct government policy in their own interests or toward their conceptions of the common interest.

A recent application of elite theory to the United States by C. Wright Mills argues that American society is dominated by a "power elite" made up of political leaders, corporate executives, and military chiefs.[27] These men, who share common backgrounds, dominate the major institutions of American society. They have been drawn together into a more or less cohesive group, Mills asserts, because of the greater involvement of the government in the economy and the increased role of the military since World War II as a result of the Cold War and occasional hot ones, as in Korea and Vietnam. Mills minimizes the importance of the "middle ranges" of power, chiefly Congress, and emphasizes the "irresponsibility" of the elite and its freedom from democratic controls. He sees the emer-

gence of this elite as the product of specific historical circumstances, however, rather than as the inevitable outcome of an "iron law of oligarchy" such as that propounded by Robert Michels. According to Michels, even democratic political institutions cannot prevent those who direct any organization from eventually coming to dominate it.[28]

Although the fact that only a few people actually make important political decisions in any society cannot be challenged, many of the elite theories based upon it have been sharply criticized. The key points at issue are the nature of the elite and its relationships with the rest of society. Mills and others have assumed or sought to demonstrate that the elite is a single, cohesive group. Yet in modern society, as Suzanne Keller has shown, there is no such monolithic elite, but a number of "strategic elites"—political, economic, military, intellectual, scientific, religious, and so on.[29] Each group exercises leadership within its own area of activity, although there are obviously relationships among them which have yet to be fully analyzed. Raymond Aron has argued that one of the significant questions about the elite is whether it is a unified group or is divided. The Soviet Union, he asserts, does have a single, integrated elite, whereas in the West the elite is divided.[30]

Those writers who attribute a dominant role to the elite and emphasize the simple distinction between elite and nonelite ignore or minimize the relevance of class and other structural features of society. Power itself becomes the central concern. According to Pareto, entry to the elite or the replacement of one group by another is related chiefly to psychological attributes rather than to sociological factors. Unless those who have the requisite abilities and who seek power are able to enter the elite they will try to overthrow it. A revolution is then merely the replacement of one elite by another.

Political leaders undoubtedly possess—or develop—an interest in power itself and its rewards, but they also express and represent the interests of various social groups. In an effort to reconcile the Marxist theory of class power and Pareto's elite theory, Aron identifies several elite groups, each representing an important segment of society, and explores the changing balance of power and the relationships among them.[31] The social composition of those who hold office and make political decisions—whether they are rich or poor, from aristocratic families or commoners, from one religious group or another, rural or urban, lawyers or labor leaders or businessmen—therefore provides one index of where power resides in society and whose interests are most likely to be served. Political "decision-makers," to be sure, are not merely creatures of the groups they come from or represent; they have their own personal interests and they are subject to the myriad pressures that play upon officeholders, yet their social backgrounds often provide important clues to their perspectives, values, and actions.

In societies in which class lines are sharply defined, those who wield political power are usually drawn almost exclusively from upper levels. Public officials in Tsarist Russia, for example, came almost exclusively from the nobility, bureaucracy, and the upper middle class, groups that together accounted at the end of the nineteenth century for only 2 or 3 per cent of the total population. In nineteenth-century England, which gradually extended the suffrage in a series of bitterly contested Reform Bills, cabinet members were drawn entirely from the aristocracy and the middle class; until almost the end of the century the majority came from the aristocracy.

The changing locus of power in Britain is shown, however, in a steady increase in middle-class representation in the cabinet throughout the nineteenth and into the twentieth century; during the brief periods in recent decades when the Labour Party has held power, a majority of ministers have been of working-class origins (see Table 19).

Although differences between the Conservative and Labour parties are reflected in the character of their leadership, there remains a considerable overlap. In 1945, for example, 61 per cent of Conservative members of Parliament were drawn from professional occupations, but so were 48.5 per cent of the Labour M.P.s. Fifty-nine per cent of the Conservatives had attended universities, but so had 32 per cent of the Labourites. On the other hand, more than four-fifths of the Conservatives had gone to exclusive public schools, 49 per cent had gone to Oxford or Cambridge, and only 3 per cent were workers, compared with 23 per cent, 14 per cent, and 41 per cent in these categories among the Labour members.[32]

Despite universal suffrage, the American tradition of "log cabin to President," and the absence of other than occasional age and residence requirements for public office, governmental leaders in the United States are disproportionately drawn from the middle and upper classes. Table 20 presents the occupational origins of various groups of public officials. (Although the most recent figures are for members of the House of Representatives for 1949–1951, there is little reason to think that there would have been any significant changes since that time.) Lawyers have always provided the largest proportion of legislators and chief executives, and, of course, of judges. Workers consti-

Table 19

CLASS ORIGINS OF MEMBERS OF THE BRITISH CABINET, 1801–1951 *

Cabinet †	Year	Aristocracy	Middle class	Working class	Total
(Average)	1801–31	73	27	0	100 (71)
(Average)	1832–66	64	36	0	100 (100)
(Average)	1867–84	60	40	0	100 (58)
Gladstone (Liberal)	1886	60	40	0	100 (15)
Salisbury (Conservative)	1886	67	33	0	100 (15)
Gladstone (Liberal)	1892	53	47	0	100 (17)
Salisbury (Conservative)	1895	42	58	0	100 (19)
Balfour (Conservative)	1902	47	53	0	100 (19)
Campbell-Bannerman (Liberal)	1906	37	58	5	100 (19)
Asquith (Liberal)	1914	32	63	5	100 (19)
Lloyd George (Coalition)	1919	14	81	5	100 (21)
Bonar Law (Conservative)	1922	50	50	0	100 (16)
MacDonald (Labour)	1924	16	26	58	100 (19)
Baldwin (Conservative)	1925	43	57	0	100 (21)
MacDonald (Labour)	1929	11	22	67	100 (18)
National Ministry (Coalition)	1935	33	56	11	100 (18)
Baldwin (Conservative)	1935	41	50	9	100 (22)
Chamberlain (Conservative)	1937	38	52	0	100 (21)
Churchill (Conservative)	1945	38	56	6	100 (16)
Attlee (Labour)	1945	0	40	60	100 (20)
Churchill (Conservative)	1951	31	69	0	100 (16)

* Figures are given in percentages.

† Churchill's wartime government left out because the War Cabinet was a very small group.

Data for 1801–1935 (National Ministry) adapted from Donald R. Matthews, *The Social Background of Political Decision Makers*, Table 10, p. 43 (Copyright 1954 by Random House, Inc. (Reprinted by permission of Random House, Inc.) Data for 1935–1951 from W. L. Guttsman, *The British Political Elite* (London: Macgibbon & Kee, 1963), Table I, p. 78.

tute only a very small minority, whereas farmers are poorly represented in the national government, although their numbers increase at state and local governmental levels.

The overwhelmingly middle- and upper-class character of political leaders is related to the greater prestige, income, education, interest in politics, and opportunities for political participation of these groups. Lawyers, who have always dominated American political life—twenty-three Presidents have been lawyers, as were almost half the signers of the Declaration of Independence—possess professional skills that are valuable in

government. They also find it easier than most persons, and also to their personal advantage, to combine a political career with their regular occupations.

Although no systematic data are available, there appears to be comparatively little difference in the social backgrounds of Republican and Democratic politicians, at least in the upper echelons. The gibe thrown at President Eisenhower's cabinet early in his administration, "nine millionaires and a plumber," which subsequently became "nine millionaires and a personnel man," reflected Eisenhower's personal preferences rather than any significant social contrast between leaders of

Table 20

OCCUPATIONAL CLASS OF AMERICAN POLITICAL LEADERS *

Occupational class	President, Vice-President, Cabinet † 1877–1934		United States senators 1949–1951	United States representatives 1949–1951	State governors 1930–1940	State legislators § 1925–1935	Labor force 1940
Professionals	74		69	69	60	36	7
Lawyers		70	57	56	52	28	
Others		4	12	13	8	8	
Proprietors and officials	21		24	22	25	25	8
Farmers	2		7	4	11	22	11
Low-salaried workers	1		0	1	1	4	17
Wage earners	2		0	2	1	3	40
Servants	0		0	0	0	0	11
Farm laborers	0		0	0	0	0	7
Unknown, unclassified	0		0	2	3	10	0
	100		100	100	101	100	101
	(n = 176)		(n = 109)	(n = 435)	(n = 170)	(n = 12,689)	

* Figures are given in percentages.
† Occupations in this column are those for which presidents, vice-presidents, and cabinet officers were trained.
§ Figures for the lower houses of thirteen selected states and the upper houses of twelve. The states are Arkansas, California (lower house only), Illinois, Indiana, Iowa, Louisiana, Maine, Minnesota, Mississippi, New Jersey, New York, Pennsylvania, Washington.
Donald R. Matthews, *The Social Background of Political Decision Makers*, Table 7, p. 30 (Copyright 1954 by Random House, Inc.). Reprinted by permission of Random House, Inc.

the two parties. Republicans Nelson Rockefeller of Dartmouth, Henry Cabot Lodge and Leverett Saltonstall of Harvard, and John Lindsay of Yale are more than matched by Democrats G. Mennen Williams of Princeton, Averell Harriman of Yale, and the late John Kennedy of Harvard. General Motors President Charles Wilson who served as Secretary of Defense in the Eisenhower cabinet has been followed by Ford President Robert McNamara (of Harvard) in the Kennedy and Johnson cabinets. Both parties also contain persons of less elevated social backgrounds; pharmacist's son Hubert Humphrey of the University of Minnesota comes from much the same social level as grocer's son Richard Nixon of Whittier College and the Duke University Law School. Only at lower levels is it likely that some differences appear; businessmen are more likely to be active in the Republican party and labor leaders in the Democratic, although lawyers who are, after all, professional advocates, are found in large numbers in both parties.

These similarities reflect the extent to which both major political parties, despite their differences, draw in some measure from all segments of society. The presence of representatives of the upper class in both parties, Lipset suggests, "has served to reduce the tensions inherent in class and sectional cleavages . . . to retain the loyalties of both the underprivileged outgroups who gain from needed reforms and the conservative strata who are outraged by the same measures . . . [and] to blur the class lines separating the parties." [33]

From the point of view of many members of their class, upper-class liberals are mavericks; Franklin D. Roosevelt, for example, was often explicitly attacked as a "traitor to his class." No ready explanation is available to account for the defection of these mavericks from the class to which they belong by virtue of their wealth, income, and, usually, education; an answer is probably to be found in some distinctive experience that leads them to challenge established perspectives and to adopt different values and a dissident point of view.

Although many politicians represent groups and classes other than their own, all officeholders are in some measure influenced by their social background. Their conception of the public interest and of the priorities to be assigned to the competing demands or needs of different groups, their interpretations of motives and events, even their definitions of political propriety and public ethics reflect, to a degree, the attitudes and values of the groups from which they come. However honest and sincere they may be, they cannot, when they assume public office, automatically cast off the ideas they have acquired from their prior experience or disregard the judgments of their friends and associates.

Mere knowledge of the social backgrounds or biographical experience of those who wield power, however, is never adequate to explain political behavior. Politics and government have a culture of their own, a set of values, attitudes, and points of view that the politician and government official may soon acquire. From political participation itself men learn what can or cannot be done, and they may acquire new perspectives toward government and its functions. A frequent observation about many of the businessmen who served in the Eisenhower Administration is that they came away from Washington with more respect and greater understanding of the nature and problems of government and politics, their previous, often antagonistic, attitudes modified by their own experience in public life.

For politicians and rulers, power and authority may also become ends in themselves, valued for their own sake rather than for the uses to which they can be put. Many men enjoy the exercise of power, and in order to maintain or achieve the pleasures of command they may sacrifice other values, even though they usually find it necessary to camouflage their motives and justify their actions with a politically accepted rhetoric and ideology.

Because power can so often be abused, political theorists have devoted much of their effort to devising institutions and establishing principles that would confine the ruler: checks and balances, with each branch of government capable in some measure of restraining the others; a supreme law to be interpreted by a final court or other body competent to invalidate the actions of officeholders or legislators; popular sovereignty in its various forms—voting, referenda, rights of petition, and assembly; theories of "natural law" to which all man-made legislation must be subordinate. These political mechanisms are clearly of great importance in regulating the exercise of power, yet their acceptance and efficacy depend in large part upon the culture and social structure of the society in which they take form.

Whatever their social values or personal desires, politicians are inevitably constrained in some measure by the situations in which they must act. The alternatives open to them are usually limited by practical considerations; law and custom restrain them; diverse social and political pressures are always at work. Those who wield power cannot ignore the sources from which power derives—the myth that justifies and legitimates their control, the groups that support them, the interests they satisfy, the institutions that men accept as necessary or desirable and that are therefore not readily subject to change. Even the absolute ruler cannot disregard these social and cultural facts, for were he to do so, his authority would dissolve and only naked force, at best a dangerous and uncertain instrument, would sustain his power.

Force and military organization

Force, however, which may be used as an instrument for maintaining domination despite resistance, is an essential element in any political system. Since one function of the state is defense against external enemies, some form of military organization is necessary, and force remains, even in a peaceful and stable society, the ultimate sanction available to maintain social order.

Despite the sociological importance of war and military institutions, their study has been chiefly the province of historians and, to a lesser degree, of political scientists. With only a few notable exceptions,[34] sociologists have largely ignored military institutions, and their organization and relations with other elements of society. A post-World War II upsurge in sociological interest in military organization has been largely confined to the role of small groups in the armed forces and the problems of bureaucratic organization, and to the practical needs of the services: selection and training of personnel, the maintenance of military efficiency, and psychological warfare. As

Morris Janowitz shows clearly in his survey of *Sociology and the Military Establishment,* however, answers even to these practical questions require some understanding of the place of the armed forces and the specialists in warfare in society.

The organization of force and the role of specialists in violence—military men—differ widely from one society to another. They are affected in diverse ways by social structure, the values present in society, and the technology of warfare. In the eighteenth century, for example, warfare was isolated from other activities and its practitioners were for the most part professional soldiers.

By an admirable economy they were drawn, generally speaking, from the least productive elements at the two ends of the social scale. They were usually officered from the younger sons of the feudal nobility, those children of the rising bureaucracy who could find no better place, and sons of the new commercial and technical classes who found military service a convenient avenue to social betterment. . . . In the British Army the troops were theoretically volunteers; actually they were the sweepings of jails, ginmills, and poorhouses, oafs from the farm beguiled into "taking the King's shilling," adventurers and unfortunates who might find a home in the army or be pressed into long years of servitude within the wooden walls of the men-of-war. Enlistment was for life or, what frequently amounted to the same thing, for the "duration." [35]

The small size of armies, the costs of maintaining military forces, and the relatively inefficient armament of the period tended to moderate active warfare; battles were relatively infrequent, although when they occurred casualties were usually heavy. But civilian populations were, on the whole, spared the rigors of warfare; professional soldiers fought and, occasionally, died for their employers, but military service was not a necessary obligation of the citizen.

The limited professional army was replaced, beginning with the American and French Revolutions, by the mass army, drawn from the civilian population and activated by nationalistic ideals. In America this shift came in part from the presence of an armed population and a pervasive militia system. "The Colonists in America," one writer has observed, "were the greatest weapon-using people of that epoch in the world." [36] Democratic values required that all men assume responsibility for the defense of the nation, although how to distribute this responsibility equitably has been a continuing problem the solution to which, Janowitz notes, may have serious effects upon the morale of the armed services.[37]

Continuing technological change has also contributed to the "democratization of war." Weapons of mass destruction inevitably draw civilian populations into the vortex of "total war," in which society faces society. Casualties are no longer confined to soldiers and sailors, and the front lines move into urban centers that come under attack by bombs and rockets. Modern warfare has become as much a test of industrial capacity, organizational efficiency, technical and scientific skill, and the morale of civilians as of the bravery and skill of the soldier.

In the wake of the rapid development of new weapons and techniques, military traditions and organization have been transformed. Since the new military technology requires specialized knowledge, high social status alone is an inadequate basis for leadership. Traditional conceptions of military leadership and established lines of authority have been challenged by the emergence of a large number of officers with special skills and of noncommissioned specialists who support the field commanders, but whose technical competence allows them some

Modern military technology has added new dimensions to military leadership. TOP: *General George Patton, an aggressive commander who personally led his troops in the field during World War II.* BOTTOM: *An Air Force major general uses a computer at the NORAD (North American Air Defense Command) Combat Operations Center.*

measure of autonomy. The need for coordination among different units—infantry, long-range bombers, airplane spotters, missilemen, naval vessels—requires new forms of organization, and intelligence operations assume increased importance. Fighting is now carried on not by large masses of men in close touch with one another, but by small units tied together by complex networks of communication.

The requirements of modern warfare, together with changes in military organization, political institutions, the structure of power, and trends in international relations have also affected the role of the military in Western society and have drawn military men and issues into areas of decision that were in the past left more or less completely to civilians. In Western Europe, most military leaders have characteristically been drawn from upper levels of society. As long as political leaders came from the same strata, there was little likelihood of a cleavage between the military and civilian; both saw most issues from the same perspectives. As new groups gained political power, the policies their leaders advocated and carried out when in office were often distasteful to high-ranking military officers. Working-class parties, particularly, often enunciated antimilitary values and supported cuts in the military budget. Under such circumstances, the military was led toward active involvement in politics. In France the cleavage between the Army and civilian authority became so great that the military tried to take over power in the mid-1950s, only to be blocked by General de Gaulle, who had himself gained power earlier with military aid.[38]

The subordination of military to civilian authority has rested upon a tradition that could readily be justified when military policy was formulated with only limited concern for problems of social and industrial organization, of education and civilian morale. With the increasing dependence upon modern technology, the conscription of mass armies, and the emergence of total war, military plans and policy necessarily take into account the organization of society as a whole. Controversies over alternative military proposals—for example, preparation for limited, "brush-fire" war or for total war, reliance upon nuclear versus conventional weapons, or of missiles rather than manned bombers—therefore become political controversies as well, and the line between civilian and military decisions becomes ever more tenuous.

With the transformation of military organization and the development of closer links between the military establishment and economic and political institutions, the role of the professional soldier has inevitably changed. He "is required more and more to acquire skills and orientations common to civilian administrators and even to political leaders."[39] The traditional avoidance of political issues, though still expected to be part of the professional soldier's moral code in America, is challenged by the needs of the modern army or navy or air force itself. In the United States in the postwar years, Mills points out:

> Some professional soldiers have stepped out of their military roles into other high realms of American life. Others, while remaining soldiers, have influenced by advice, information, and judgment the decisions of men powerful in economic and political matters, as well as in educational and scientific endeavors. In and out of uniform, generals and admirals have attempted to sway the opinions of the underlying population, lending the weight of their authority, openly as well as behind closed doors, to controversial policies.[40]

In many international situations the role of military force has become a crucial issue: to seek a military solution in Vietnam or a negotiated peace? to allow internal conflict to wrack the Dominican Republic or intervene in order to maintain "stability," albeit with important consequences in relation to who will eventually wield power in that country? In such difficult situations, the military is not only an instrument but also a participant in the determination of policy, since it must assess the chances of military success or failure. Military values, conceptions of reality, and interests inevitably enter, therefore, into the process of political decision-making.

The significance of the growth in military influence is open to diverse interpretations. Some, like Mills, identify it as a threat to the maintenance of a democratic society. Others accept the augmented importance of military needs in a time of cold war as an inevitable requirement of national survival and emphasize the vitality of the tradition of military subordination to civilian authority. In his recent study of the professional soldier Janowitz writes:

The military have accumulated considerable power, and that power protrudes into the political fabric of contemporary society. It could

not be otherwise. However, while they have no reluctance to press for larger budgets, they exercise their influence on political matters with considerable restraint and unease. Civilian control of military affairs remains intact and fundamentally acceptable to the military; any imbalance in military contributions to politicomilitary affairs—domestic or international—is therefore often the result of default by civilian political leadership.[51]

The issues, of course, are complex, yet it seems clear that a major problem facing democracy in the future will be to clarify the place of the military services, the role of the professional soldier, and the weight to be assigned purely military considerations in comparison with other values and needs.

Notes

[1] Max Weber, *From Max Weber: Essays in Sociology*, trans. and ed. by H. H. Gerth and C. Wright Mills (New York: Oxford, 1946), p. 180.

[2] Robert M. MacIver, *The Web of Government* (New York: Macmillan, 1947), p. 83.

[3] Jean Jacques Rousseau, *The Social Contract and the Discourses*, trans. by G. D. H. Cole (New York: Dutton, 1950), p. 6.

[4] C. Wright Mills, *The Power Elite* (New York: Oxford, 1956), p. 125. See also Robert Brady, *Business as a System of Power* (New York: Columbia University Press, 1943).

[5] Crawford H. Greenwalt, *The Uncommon Man* (New York: McGraw-Hill, 1959), p. 25.

[6] Robert Penn Warren, *Who Speaks for the Negro?* (New York: Random House, 1965), p. 406.

[7] Weber, *op. cit.*, p. 78.

[8] Gunther Wagner, "The Political Organization of the Bantu of Kavirondo," in M. Fortes and E. E. Evans-Pritchard (eds.), *African Political Systems* (London: Oxford, 1940), p. 200.

[9] Seymour Martin Lipset, *Political Man* (Garden City: Doubleday, 1959), p. 220.

[10] See Philip E. Converse, "The Shifting Role of Class in Political Attitudes and Behavior," in Eleanor E. Maccoby, Theodore M. Newcomb, and Eugene L. Hartley (eds.), *Readings in Social Psychology* (3rd ed.; New York: Holt, 1958), pp. 388–99; and Robert E. Lane, "The Politics of Consensus in an Age of Affluence," *American Political Science Quarterly*, LIX (December, 1965), 885–9.

[11] See Samuel A. Stouffer, *Communism, Conformity and Civil Liberties* (Garden City: Doubleday, 1955).

[12] Stefan Nowak, "Egalitarian Attitudes of Warsaw Students," *American Sociological Review*, XXV (April, 1960), 219–31.

[13] Lipset, *op. cit.*, p. 221.

[14] Richard Centers, *The Psychology of Social Classes* (Princeton: Princeton University Press, 1949), Table 68, p. 164, and Table 77, p. 180.

[15] Samuel Lubell, *The Future of American Politics* (2nd ed.; Garden City: Doubleday, 1956).

[16] David Riesman, *The Lonely Crowd*

(New Haven: Yale University Press, 1950), p. 252.

[17] Mills, *op. cit.*, p. 244.

[18] See Robert S. Lynd and Helen M. Lynd, *Middletown in Transition* (New York: Harcourt, 1937), Ch. 3; Floyd Hunter, *Community Power Structure* (Chapel Hill: University of North Carolina Press, 1953); and Roland J. Pellegrin and Charles H. Coates, "Absentee Owned Corporations and Community Power Structure," *American Journal of Sociology*, LXI (March, 1956), 413–9. Many empirical studies have sought to locate the influential or powerful persons but frequently without linking those identified as wielding power with those institutions from which they derive their power or through which they operate.

[19] Nelson W. Polsby, *Community Power and Political Theory* (New Haven: Yale University Press, 1963).

[20] Robert A. Dahl, *Who Governs?* (New Haven: Yale University Press, 1961).

[21] See C. W. M. Hart, "Industrial Relations Research and Social Theory," *Canadian Journal of Economics and Political Science*, XV (February, 1949), 58–73.

[22] Mills, *op. cit.*, p. 39. See also Arthur J. Vidich and Joseph Bensman, *Small Town in Mass Society* (Princeton: Princeton University Press, 1958).

[23] Samuel E. Finer, *The Man on Horseback* (London: Pall Mall, 1962), Ch. 1.

[24] See Suzanne Keller, *Beyond the Ruling Class: Strategic Elites in Modern Society* (New York: Random House, 1963), especially pp. 121 ff. For a suggestive discussion of the role of the military in "modernizing" nations, see Morris Janowitz, *The Military in the Political Development of New Nations* (Chicago: University of Chicago Press, 1964).

[25] MacIver, *op. cit.*, p. 149.

[26] T. B. Bottomore, *Elites and Society* (London: Watts, 1964), p. 6.

[27] Mills, *op. cit.*

[28] Robert Michels, *Political Parties*, trans. by Eden and Cedar Paul (New York: Free Press, 1949; first published in 1915).

[29] Keller, *op. cit.*

[30] Raymond Aron, "Social Structure and the Ruling Class, I," *British Journal of Sociology*, I (March, 1950), 10.

[31] *Ibid.*, pp. 1–16; and Raymond Aron, "Social Structure and the Ruling Class, II," *British Journal of Sociology*, I (June, 1950), 126–43.

[32] Donald R. Matthews, *The Social Background of Political Decision Makers* (New York: Random House, 1954), p. 46.

[33] Lipset, *op. cit.*, p. 301.

[34] See Hans Speier, *Social Order and the Risks of War* (New York: Stewart, 1952); Morris Janowitz, *Sociology and the Military Establishment* (New York: Russell Sage Foundation, 1959); Janowitz, *The Professional Soldier* (New York: Free Press, 1960); Morris Janowitz, *The Military in the Political Development of New Nations*; and Stanislaw Andrzejewski, *Military Organization and Society* (London: Routledge, 1954). The results of the research done for the Research Branch, Information and Education Division of the War Department, during World War II, are reported in Samuel A. Stouffer *et al.*, *The American Soldier* (2 vols.; Princeton: Princeton University Press, 1949); although largely devoted to attitude surveys, these volumes contain a great array of useful data on military life and organization. See also the useful summary volume, Charles H. Coates and Roland J. Pellegrin, *Military Sociology* (University Park, Md.: Social Science Press, 1965).

[35] Walter Millis, *Arms and Men* (New York: New American Library, 1958; first published in 1956), pp. 14–5.

[36] Quoted in *ibid.*, p. 20.

[37] Janowitz, *Sociology and the Military Establishment*, pp. 45–50.

[38] For a detailed historical account of the French Army, see Paul-Marie de la Gorce, *The French Army*, trans. by Kenneth Douglas (London: Weidenfeld, 1963).

[39] Janowitz, *Sociology and the Military Establishment*, p. 98.

[40] Mills, *The Power Elite*, p. 198.

[41] Janowitz, *The Professional Soldier*, p. viii.

Suggestions for further reading

BELL, DANIEL (ed.). *The Radical Right.* Garden City: Doubleday Anchor Books, 1964. (Expanded and updated edition of *The New American Right*, first published in 1955.)
An excellent collection of essays on ultraconservative movements in the United States.

BERELSON, BERNARD R., PAUL F. LAZARSFELD, and WILLIAM N. MCPHEE. *Voting: A Study of Opinion Formation in a Presidential Campaign.* Chicago: University of Chicago Press, 1954.
In addition to reporting the results of a study of voting in one community in the 1948 Presidential election, this book tries to codify available data and conclusions on the process and determinants of voting.

BOTTOMORE, T. B. *Elites and Society.* London: Watts, 1964.
A useful evaluation and critique of elite theories.

CAMPBELL, ANGUS, PHILIP E. CONVERSE, WARREN E. MILLER, and DONALD E. STOKES. *The American Voter.* New York: Wiley, 1960.
A careful study of the processes by which voters make up their minds and of the circumstances that affect their decisions.

DAHL, ROBERT A. *Who Governs?* New Haven: Yale University Press, 1961.
A detailed study of those who actually determine policy in New Haven, which emphasizes the pluralistic character of the power structure.

EULAU, HEINZ, SAMUEL J. ELDERSVELD, AND MORRIS JANOWITZ (eds.). *Political Behavior: A Reader in Theory and Practice.* New York: Free Press, 1956.
A collection of papers dealing with methods and approaches to the study of political behavior, attitudes toward the political process, the nature and role of political leadership, and social influences upon decision-making.

FORTES, MEYER, and E. E. EVANS-PRITCHARD (eds.). *African Political Systems.* London: Oxford, 1940.
Several anthropologists describe the political institutions in a number of African tribes.

HOFFER, ERIC. *The True Believer.* New York: New American Library, 1958.
An epigrammatic essay on the nature, motives, and behavior of the fanatic who becomes a member of a mass movement.

HUNTER, FLOYD. *Community Power Structure: A Study of Decision Makers.* Chapel Hill: University of North Carolina Press, 1953.
A useful study of the men who occupy positions of power in a large southern city and of their relations with one another.

JANOWITZ, MORRIS. *The Professional Soldier.* New York: Free Press, 1960.
A major contribution to our understanding of the social role of the professional soldier in the United States and of the technological, political, and organizational forces that are changing it.

KELLER, SUZANNE. *Beyond the Ruling Class.* New York: Random House, 1963.
A discussion of elite theories and an attempt to delineate the emerging "strategic elites" characteristic of modern society.

KORNHAUSER, WILLIAM. *The Politics of Mass Society.* New York: Free Press, 1959.
A stimulating attempt to explore the nature of political movements in modern societies.

LIPSET, SEYMOUR MARTIN. *Political Man: The Social Bases of Politics.* Garden City: Doubleday, 1960.
A collection of essays that examine the social bases for democratic and nondemocratic politics.

LUBELL, SAMUEL. *The Future of American Politics*, 2nd ed., rev. Garden City: Doubleday Anchor Books, 1956.
First published in 1951, this book provides a clear picture of the changing political allegiances of various social groups and of the issues that affect their attitudes and actions.

MACIVER, ROBERT M. *The Web of Govern-

ment. New York: Macmillan, 1947.
A comprehensive and penetrating analysis of the sources, nature, forms, and functions of government by a distinguished sociologist and political theorist.

MATTHEWS, DONALD R. *The Social Background of Political Decision Makers.* Garden City: Doubleday, 1954.
Summary and evaluation of both theories and data concerning the influence of their social background upon political decision-makers.

MICHELS, ROBERT. *Political Parties.* Trans. by Eden and Cedar Paul. New York: Free Press, 1949. First published, 1915.
A classic study of the forces making for domination of any political organization by its leaders, even when the organization is dedicated to democratic goals and values.

MILLS, C. WRIGHT. *The Power Elite.* New York: Oxford, 1956.
A provocative book that asserts that a new elite drawn from the top ranks of industry, politics, and the military is coming to dominate American society.

MOORE, BARRINGTON, JR. *Soviet Politics: The Dilemma of Power.* Cambridge, Mass.: Harvard University Press, 1950.
An attempt to explore the interaction of ideology and political and economic factors in the development of the Soviet system.

WEBER, MAX. *The Theory of Economic and Social Organization.* Trans. by A. M. Henderson and Talcott Parsons. New York: Oxford, 1947, Part III.
A major theoretical analysis of the nature of authority.

14
Religion

Sacred and secular:
the nature of religion

"When I mention religion," declared Mr. Thwackum, in Henry Fielding's novel *Tom Jones*, "I mean the Christian religion; and not only the Christian religion, but the Protestant religion; and not only the Protestant religion, but the Church of England." Like Mr. Thwackum, most men equate their particular image of reality with the universal; when this image engages mens' deepest sentiments, as religion so often does, they find it difficult to place their religious doctrine in a comparative perspective, to see it, perhaps, as only one version of a recurrent sociological phenomenon.

Efforts to define religion suffer, not only from the Thwackum-like parochialism that many men share to varying degrees, but also from the complexity of religion, which may include a theology (a body of formal doctrine), ritual, a type of personal experience, a set of moral values, and an organization of worshipers and priests or prophets. For his lectures on *The Varieties of Religious Experience*, William James chose to define religion as "the feelings, acts, and experiences of individual men in their solitude, so far as they apprehend themselves to stand in relation to whatever they consider the divine." [1] Other definitions emphasize common rituals and beliefs or focus upon "institutional religion," that is, the organization and activities of churches and the roles of religious leaders and functionaries.

So varied are the beliefs and practices that are identified as religious that they do not lend themselves to any simple characterization. In the West, the idea of God dominates religious thought; without God there is no religion, which is defined as the relationship between man and the divine. "From Suez eastward, however," writes an English scholar,

such a relationship seems as often as not to be described in terms of movement, as a "Way." . . . Buddhism is described as "the noble eight-fold Path"; and Japanese nationalist *religion* (if we must use the European label) is called Shinto, "the Way of the Gods." . . . Confucius' message is called by him "The Way." [2]

The idea of God in these religions is either ambiguous or totally missing, and attention centers around ritual and abstract ideas. Some conception of a superhuman power is found in every religion, but this power takes many forms: gods of varying numbers and character, ghosts and spirits, or some abstract and impersonal force. Among the Melanesians of the South Pacific,

religion . . . consists, as far as belief goes, in the persuasion that there is a supernatural power [Mana] . . . belonging to the religion of the unseen; and as far as practice goes, in the use of means of getting this power turned to their own benefit. The notion of a Supreme Being is altogether foreign to them, or indeed of any being occupying a very elevated place in their world.[3]

Because religious doctrines have occupied a central place in Christianity, Western scholars have tended to emphasize beliefs and creeds as the central elements in religion. But both in other times and in other parts of the world, doctrine has often been of far less importance than ritual. William Robertson Smith, a famous student of ancient religion, observes:

> . . . we naturally assume that . . . our first business is to search for a creed, and find in it the key to ritual and practice. But the antique religions had for the most part no creed; they consisted entirely of institutions and practices. No doubt men will not habitually follow certain practices without attaching a meaning to them; but as a rule we find that while the practice was rigorously fixed, the meaning attached to it was extremely vague, and the same rite was explained by different people in different ways, without any question of orthodoxy or heterodoxy arising in consequence.[4]

The things that can acquire religious significance, either as holy symbols or as tabooed objects, vary enormously. In India, Hindus revere the cow; among many primitive peoples, birds, animals, trees, or plants may be worshiped. The sun and the moon, waterfalls and streams, rocks and precious jewels may occupy an important place in religious belief and practice. Food may be defined as unclean or unholy, unfit for human consumption: pork and shellfish among orthodox Jews, wine and pork among Moslems. On the other hand, specific foods may be required on certain religious occasions: the wine and wafer in Catholic ritual, the flesh of a totemic or sacred animal among some primitive peoples, bitter herbs and unleavened bread at the Jewish Passover meal.

So diverse are the objects that may acquire religious significance, the reli-gious beliefs to which men subscribe, and the rituals they follow that it seems clear that no intrinsic quality gives them their religious meaning. Instead they are set apart by the attitudes and sentiments that men bring to them. Men stand in respect or awe of the *sacred*, or holy, which is to be kept apart from the profane, or *secular*. The latter is looked upon as useful or practical or familiar, part of the everyday world and lacking the emotional significance usually characteristic of the sacred. This contrast between sacred and profane, Durkheim points out, is "the distinctive trait of religious thought."[5]

Objects or rituals are sacred, then, because of the meaning they have for the believer. Religious practices frequently celebrate significant—and symbolic—events of the past: the crucifixion and resurrection of Christ, the escape of the Jews from Egypt, the birth of Buddha. Sometimes ritual symbolizes important values. Toward the close of the Jewish Passover meal, the door is opened, according to tradition, in order to allow Elijah the Prophet to enter and partake of a glass of wine prepared for him. The coming of Elijah is supposed to precede the arrival of the Messiah, and the hope of redemption is deeply embedded in the Passover tradition. Sharing the wine and bread of the Eucharist unites the participant with Christ; confession to a priest and appropriate penance provide absolution for sins. Among Hindus ritual bathing similarly cleanses the believer from the pollution he may have acquired in his daily activity.

Ritual often celebrates important occasions in the life of the individual or group: the arrival at maturity of the young man; birth, marriage, and death; the planting of crops and the harvesting of the first fruit, as well as the completion of the harvest; the coming of the rains in

Wide World Photos

Charles Harbutt from Magnum

areas that are dry for a good part of the year; initiation of a military campaign or the victorious completion of an expedition. On these occasions, ritual expresses the hope of future success or dedication to a task or responsibility to be undertaken or celebration and thanks for past events, but it is carried out with the reverence and awe that characterize religious behavior.

For many participants in religious ritual, however, the mythical or symbolic meanings of their actions may hardly be understood. They distinguish the sacred from the secular and follow the traditional customs as part of their adherence to their faith, but with little if any knowledge of the origins or significance of their practice. For them, participation simply establishes their relationship to the divine—God, ancestors, spirits, or ineffable mysteries—and with their community, for religion is a social fact as well as an individual experience.

Beliefs, rituals, and objects acquire their sacred quality not from any individual but through the collective response of the group. The individual who attributes sacred meaning to some object that others see in a purely secular light or who follows some private ritual is apt to be thought queer, even mad, although in a few rare instances it may be the "divine madness" that will eventually sway others and initiate a new religious movement. Men acquire religious ideas from the

Objects or rituals are sacred not because of their intrinsic character but because of the meanings they have for the believer. TOP: *Bathers on a hot afternoon at Coney Island.* BOTTOM: *Hindus bathing in the Ganges, a "holy" river whose waters are "purifying."*

groups in which they live; religious rituals are usually (although not always) collective affairs rather than private activities, and even those sacred acts that individuals carry out alone follow cultural prescriptions. A religion then, in Durkheim's classic definition, is "a unified system of beliefs and practices relative to sacred things, that is to say, to things set apart and forbidden—beliefs and practices which unite into one single moral community . . . all those who adhere to them." [6]

This definition of religion—and the sociological study of religion in general—ignores many aspects of perhaps the most complex, most discussed, and most written about element in culture. But, as we noted early in this book, sociology, like any other discipline, necessarily selects from the totality of experience and of human life those specific aspects that it seeks to explain. In bypassing other dimensions of religion—theological, historical, philosophical, psychological—we need not deny their significance or challenge the theories associated with them. There are, of course, points of contact or even conflict between the sociological and other approaches to religion, but there remain large areas of inquiry for each to explore. And it is probably safe to say that as a latecomer sociology still occupies but a small corner in the enormous library that contains man's recorded reflections on the nature and functions of religion.

Religion and human experience

As long as men subscribed to a religious view of life, religion itself was rarely subjected to objective and dispassionate scrutiny. Only during the nineteenth century, and especially toward its end, were efforts made to account for religious belief and practice—their origins, nature, and development—as one might seek to explain the economic order or the evolution of the state and its institutions.

So many theories of religion have since been proffered that we cannot review them here. But running through many of them is a rationalist bias that sees religion as a product of ignorance and confusion. The English anthropologist, E. B. Tylor, found the origins of religion in men's dream life; the separation of spirit from flesh and the presence of others known to be elsewhere, Tylor argues, lead to the conception of the soul or spirit, which then becomes the foundation for the subsequent development of religious ideas. According to this view, in Durkheim's terse summary, "religion is nothing but a dream, systematized and lived, but without any foundation in reality." [7] A second influential theory, usually associated with Max Müller, a student of ancient languages, sees the roots of religion in the facts of nature. The words applied to such natural phenomena as the sun, fire, and the moon, according to this view, came to represent supernatural beings capable of shaping human fate and natural events. Or, again in Durkheim's summary, the metaphors applied to nature were taken literally, and religion was reduced to "an immense metaphor with no objective value." [8]

From the rational perspective shared by many sociologists, the study of religion then became chiefly a demonstration of the errors in traditional beliefs concerning man, society, and biological and physical phenomena. In the controversy between religion and science that flared up in the latter part of the nineteenth and early part of the twentieth century, sociologists usually sided with science. But merely demonstrating that Jonah could not have been swallowed up and regurgitated by a whale and that the earth could not have been created in 4004 B.C. does not establish the falsity of religion (although it may clear away part of the obscurantism sometimes associated with it). As we noted earlier, belief constitutes only one feature of religion. Challenging or refuting religious interpretations of natural phenomena, which may weaken the influence of religion in some areas of human life, is hardly likely to destroy it totally.

Following the leads of Durkheim and Max Weber especially, modern sociological theory has ceased to ask whether religion is "true"; instead it looks upon religion as a social phenomenon found in all societies. Durkheim pointed out the limits of the rationalistic approach and tried to discover the social sources of religion and the functions it serves in society. Weber saw religion as a central feature of any society and explored, in a series of rich, comparative studies, its relationship to economic behavior and institutions. The sociology of religion has, then, the task of accounting for religion's universality as well as for the diverse forms it assumes and the analysis of its functions—and dysfunctions—in the life of society.

An important clue to the presence of religion in all societies is the fact that sacred ritual and belief are usually found in situations the outcome of which cannot be predicted or in which people are subject to forces they cannot control—in the presence of death, when illness or accident or a natural disaster strikes, when peasants plant their crops or complete a harvest, when fishermen set sail on the sea, when a man and woman marry or a child is born, when an army sets off for war. These events generate uncertainty and anxiety that men wish to resolve and raise questions to which men seek answers. Because deep-seated emotions are provoked in difficult or inexplicable situations, the practices men evolve to deal with them are likely to be transformed into rituals that are out of the ordinary and set apart from routine; in short, they become sacred. The answers men give to the problems of meaning generated by life and death, a kind or hostile nature, success or failure in human endeavors, often incorporate supernatural forces and transcendental values.

These sacred practices and beliefs help men to cope with the frustrations and anxieties that are inherent in human life. Religion accounts for death in ways that enable men to face their own fate and that of others (although some men do reject or ignore the comforts or religious belief). "The Lord gave and the Lord hath taken away, blessed be the name of the Lord," said Job when God caused his children to die. Ritual defines appropriate behavior in the disturbing circumstances that accompany the death of others and the prospect of one's own passing; planting or harvest rites provide the farmer psychic protection against the uncertainties inherent in his efforts; and the ritual that so often accompanies the beginning of a hazardous or unpredictable venture eases the fears and anxieties to which men are subject.

Uncertainty and anxiety, fear and insecurity, are emotions experienced only by individuals, and the theory that these psychological states give rise to religion shares with many other theories, like that of Tylor, a seemingly individualistic and psychological point of view. How, then, are these individual feelings related to the sociological aspects of religion?

Although many of the problems around which religious ritual and doctrine focus are those faced by individuals, they are in fact problems of social order as well.

Death, for example, affects not only the person who dies or those close to him but also the groups of which he—and they— are members. Each individual's passing disturbs the complex structure of social relationships in which he participates, and the uncertainties that death provokes are not merely questions of meaning— why must one die? why now? or under these circumstances?—but also stem from the need to rearrange the pattern of social life in which the deceased played a role. Funeral rites, therefore, not only cushion the blow of death and prescribe emotionally expressive rites to channel or contain grief, but they also make possible the re-establishment or reinforcement of social ties among those closely related to the dead person. Moreover, participation in collective religious observances itself tends to sustain men in difficult hours. There is extensive evidence that close relations with others help men to cope with stress and tension, alleviating anxieties and facilitating continued participation in social life. (See the discussion of the functions of the primary group in Chapter 6.)

As many of the situations out of which religion grows and around which much of its doctrine and ritual center involve collective activities, they create common uncertainties and anxieties that are likely to give rise to collective responses. Recurrent social events that engage deep-seated emotions and are fraught with unpredictable future consequences—*rites de passage*, for example, by which adolescents acquire full adult status, or marriage, which establishes significant connections not only between man and wife but also, in many instances, between families or lineages or even entire tribes—therefore frequently come to be set apart from the daily, the ordinary, the humdrum. (The Soviet Union only a few years ago au-

thorized more elaborate and formal marriage ceremonies rather than the prosaic legal procedure previously required by the regime.) The sacred quality of ritual on such occasions reminds the participants of the solemnity of the step they are taking, as well as binding them more closely to the group.

Characteristics of the social order itself—the distribution of goods, the allocation of power, relations between superior and inferior, the good fortune of some and misfortunes of others, the "incongruity between destiny and merit" experienced by many—all raise questions to which men have often given religious answers. Not only do the disadvantaged—the poor, the powerless, the unsuccessful—seek some explanation of their fate, but, as Weber points out, those who are more fortunate also wish an accounting and justification for the advantages they enjoy.

The fortunate is seldom satisfied with the fact of being fortunate. Beyond this, he needs to know that he has a right to his good fortune. He wants to be convinced that he "deserves" it, and above all, that he deserves it in comparison with others. He wishes to be allowed the belief that the less fortunate also merely experiences his due. Good fortune thus wants to be "legitimate" fortune.[9]

Religion may give meaning to social experience by assigning moral values to human suffering—or to good fortune—or by offering a theological justification for man's fate. If eternal salvation is more important than mundane pleasures and rests upon divine grace rather than upon wealth or power, then the poor may be able more easily to tolerate their circumstances. If one's fate is predetermined by God, as in the Calvinist doctrine, or by one's behavior in previous incarnations, as in Hinduism, then one can accept the world and one's place in it. If "godliness is in league with riches," as Bishop Lawrence of the Episcopal Church declared in 1900, then the well-to-do can feel morally secure in their wealth.

Magic and science as functional alternatives to religion

Religion, however, is not the only means by which people seek to cope with the uncertainties and tensions of human life. Both magic and science constitute alternatives that on occasion serve some of the same functions as religion.

The difference between religion and magic is not easily drawn. Many specific practices or beliefs are not readily identified as one or the other, and some anthropologists have found it difficult to decide whether a particular ritual is religious or magical. Among the Murngin of Australia, for example, W. Lloyd Warner reports that religion and magic are indistinguishable. In Tikopia, an island in the South Pacific, Raymond Firth found that the magician and the religious leader are the same person.

Despite the similarities, religion and magic do differ in important aspects. Although both use nonempirical methods for achieving their goals, they usually pursue different objectives. The goals of religion are transcendental—salvation, absolution from sins, unity with God—or they are of a general character: health, a long life, and wealth. The aims of magic are specific and immediate: recovery from sickness, a good harvest, a successful business venture, reciprocated love, an enemy's death. Religion lessens man's uncertainties by giving meaning to his actions or establishing his relationship to the divine. Magic achieves the same result by providing a device that is supposed to achieve concrete goals.

Both religion and magic incorporate ritual, but the attitudes toward these out-of-the-ordinary practices differ. Prayer or religious ceremony is accompanied by awe and reverence; men beg for divine aid or guidance or seek to persuade the gods or spirits to look favorably upon them. Magic is more casual and prosaic; the magician commands, and the forces of nature are expected to obey without the intervention of supernatural force. Although emotion is often expressed in the recitation of spells or in other magical rites, it is usually "the dramatic expression of . . . the emotional state of the performer" [10] or of the client—his love, hate, anger, or fear. But in many instances magic is performed in a matter-of-fact manner; spells are uttered in an ordinary voice as though one were merely telling someone else to do something.

In practice, magic and religion are often closely intertwined. Men often hope to achieve specific results through their prayers, and magic frequently makes use of sacred ideas, objects, and practices. The overlapping of religion and magic is suggested by the fact that the Trobriand Islanders use garden magic when they plant their crops in order to ensure a bountiful harvest and that Christian peasants often observe "religious" ceremonies on similar occasions for the same purpose. The close blending of magic and religion, however, appears to be more characteristic of primitive than of modern society, which has, in large measure, separated the two.

From a rational point of view, of course, magic is of little practical value, and, wherever a rational perspective and modern science have emerged, the hold of magic has been weakened. Magic persists, however, despite its limitations, for many reasons. Frequently there is in fact a proximate coincidence between magical ritual and desired outcome: Magical spells at the beginning of the rainy season are often followed by rain; efforts to cure sickness will in many cases be followed by recovery of the invalid. Since it is assumed that any deviation from the rigid requirements of magical procedure destroys its efficacy and that countermagic is always at work, failure can usually be explained to the satisfaction of both magician and client. Even if magic does not achieve its ostensible goal—rain, rich crops, the death of an enemy, success in a love affair—its performance can reduce the tensions under which people labor. This latent function of magic may thus encourage belief, even though it may also block the use of more efficient techniques.

Magic and science are similar in their concern with the world of man and nature and in their assertion of determinate relations between means and ends, cause and effect. They differ in the grounds upon which they command acceptance and the methods by which they produce results. "Science," Malinowski writes, "is founded on the conviction that experience, effort, and reason are valid; magic on the belief that hope cannot fail nor desire deceive. The theories of knowledge are dictated by logic, those of magic by the association of ideas under the influence of desire." [11] By providing more efficient methods of achieving immediate objectives, science supplants spells, incantations, talismans, charms, and strange potions. Water witches with dowsing rods are replaced by geologists with scientific equipment; farming magic is superseded by rational agricultural methods; the medicine man's cures are supplanted by modern medicine. Only where life remains harsh or insecure does magic hold out persistently against the advance of tested, rational knowledge.

Insofar as it unravels some of the mysteries of human life, science may also serve as an alternative to religious belief and weaken the hold of religious ritual. In the modern world, science has replaced many of the religious interpretations of the nature of the universe with tested—or potentially testable—rational theories. The literal account of creation in the Bible is challenged and supplanted by the findings of geology and the theory of evolution. The workings of divine providence are in some measure replaced by the germ theory of disease, the findings of depth psychology, the systematic analysis of culture and social structure. Scientific knowledge, however, does not always easily supplant either religion or magic, for deeply held beliefs often resist staunchly the evidence of the senses as well as the abstractions of scientific theory.

Because frequently there has been open conflict between science and religion, between scientists and priests or devout believers, it has often been assumed that there is a fundamental antagonism between the sacred and the rational, between ritual and science. Both the empirical refutation of accepted religious beliefs and the early rationalistic theories of religion rested upon and sustained this assumption. But it has become increasingly evident that there are aspects of religion that are irrelevant to science. Science can explain *how* men died, but not *why*; what causes illness or an accident, but not its moral or theological meaning. A moral accounting is not subject to scientific test, nor are the rituals with which men mark significant events.

Moreover, religious attitudes themselves have on occasion directly encouraged scientific inquiry. Galileo, it is true, was forced by the Roman Catholic Church to recant his belief in the Copernican theory of astronomy, and evolutionary theory was staunchly resisted by many devout Christians. Yet, as Merton has shown, in the seventeenth century, which saw the first flowering of modern science, "the deep-rooted religious *interests* of the day demanded in their forceful implications the systematic, rational, and empirical study of Nature for the glorification of God in his Works and for the control of the corrupt world."[12] (For a fuller elaboration of this point, see pp. 408–9.)

The nineteenth-century contention between science and religion has been more or less resolved or at least has simmered down, but there still remain potential continuing sources of conflict. As long as religion contains beliefs about the natural world that can be scientifically tested, controversy may persist. Science as a social institution rests upon values— empirical truth, skepticism, the free exchange of ideas—that may on occasion conflict with the religious concern with faith, salvation, and the repression of heretical ideas. (For a discussion of the values of science, see pp. 410–3.) Religious "truth" and scientific "truth" may indeed merely be different rather than contradictory, but there may still be disagreement as to their relevance to specific situations. The moralistic approach to alcoholism, for example, of some religious groups that see it as the result of a moral failing that calls for punishment or sermons or both clashes with a scientific approach that views alcoholism as an illness to be treated medically.

Social and cultural determinants

Although religion is found in all societies, it is not necessarily accepted by everyone or accepted to the same degree by different individuals. For many people, perhaps for most, religious belief and practice elicit some sense of awe and reverence, some communion with the divine, some feeling that there exists a power transcending the purely human. But in only a few people does the religious sense so dominate that the whole personality is encompassed and shaped by it. At the other extreme, there are some individuals and groups who accept little if any of the prevailing religious belief or are even hostile to it. Some men may, in fact, find a secular, rational orientation to life to be adequate and feel no need for the consolations of religion, or they may feel that religious belief and practice are essentially irrelevant to their daily experience.

Within a society or religious group, there are often wide variations in religious attitudes and practice. In a study of religious participation among American Catholics, Joseph Fichter (a sociologist who is also a Catholic priest) divided his sample into four categories: those "who are the most active participants and the most faithful believers; . . . the normal 'practicing' Catholics easily identifiable as parishioners; [those] who conform to a bare, arbitrary minimum of the patterns expected in the religious institution; [and those] who have 'given up' Catholicism, but have not joined another denomination."[13] A study of rural French Catholics described differences in religious practice ecologically, that is, on the basis of geographical divisions. Three categories were used: (1) "areas of majority practice" in which over 45 per cent of the population took Easter communion; (2) "areas of minority practice retaining Christian traditions," in which fewer than 45 per cent took communion but in which most people celebrated significant religious occasions; (3) areas in which the majority had in effect withdrawn from the Church and many children were not baptized and did not attend catechism.[14]

These variations in religious practice and commitment are not merely a result of individual differences but are linked with such sociological characteristics as sex and class. Women, for example, are typically more religious and attend religious services more frequently than do men, except among Jews. In Western Europe, the working class has a much lower rate of church attendance than do other classes, and similar figures have been reported in the United States. The reasons for such differences are complex and not readily identified, stemming from the relationships between religious ritual, doctrine, and organization, on the one hand, and the needs, problems, and experience of various groups of people, on the other.

The very substance of religion—its prescriptions, dogmas, and organization—is also markedly influenced by other elements in the culture and by the organization of society. Each religious doctrine, of course, contains an explanation of its own origins: Christianity rests upon Divine Revelation; the sacred books of Buddhism, Mohammedanism, and Hinduism contain accounts of the beginnings of those religions; primitive religions usually contain some myth that describes their own genesis. Differences among religious groups and changes in accepted belief and practice are often traced to these doctrinal sources, a "mode of explanation," writes the theological H. Richard Niebuhr, that "has been popular since the time when Josephus described the Pharisees as a school of philosophers who maintained belief in the resurrection from the dead and in oral tradition, while the Sadducees were defined as those who held the opposite doctrine." [15]

The limitations of this type of interpretation are readily apparent. Religion is so closely linked with other aspects of social life that it is necessarily affected by them. The fact that members of the same religious group can arrive at different moral conclusions from a common religious base suggests the impact of external social forces. "Gott mit uns," cried German preachers in World War I, while their American counterparts blessed American military forces and promised divine support. ("Praise the Lord and pass the ammunition," attributed to an American chaplain in World War II, is a theme frequently repeated during wartime by Christian clergy of many nations.) Some opponents of racial segregation claim religious sanction for their position; indeed many religious leaders have taken an active part in the civil rights movement. Yet some defenders of the separation of the races and of white supremacy call upon biblical sources for support. The Dutch Reformed Church in South Africa justifies in religious terms the continued domination of blacks by whites, yet some Anglican ministers have played an active role in efforts to improve the status of the natives. Clearly, these differences are not purely doctrinal in origin.

In recognizing the influence of culture and social organization, however, we should not reduce religion to a mere rationalization or reflection of other interests. Nor is it necessary to minimize or depreciate the potential importance to both individuals and groups of distinctively religious interests—the desire for salvation, for example, or the yearning for a mystic union with the divine. Instead we should see religion as one element in the complex and interdependent whole that is a society and its culture. Under some conditions it is of central or even overriding significance in determining behavior and in shaping institutions and social organizations; under others it is of less importance, more determined than determining. But everywhere religion plays a role in the functioning of the social order that cannot be ignored.

Because religion is one type of response to the exigencies of human life, its forms are inevitably conditioned by the concrete social context in which they emerge and have their being. Faced with problems for which no ready solutions are at hand—the hardships and insecurity of the disadvantaged, for example, the limitations imposed upon a newly emerging class in a traditional society, the frustrations of a primitive society conquered by outsiders, the doubts and anxieties of twentieth-century middle-class Americans—groups or individuals occupying similar places in society may seize upon some new or revived religious belief and practice to give meaning to their lives.

Protestant sects have often emerged among the poor and disinherited, to whom they offered comfort, reassurance, and the hope of better times to come. The Levellers in seventeenth-century England, the Salvation Army, the various Pentecostal and Holiness churches, the Christadelphians in England, and many other offshoots from established denominations have provided rewarding emotional experience, have held out to the disadvantaged reassuring interpretations of their condition, and have given promises of future grace—either in this world or the next.

Those living in harsh and frequently drab circumstances, lacking formal education, constrained by the dominant forces in society, and repelled by the formal and seemingly empty ritual of established churches have often sought emotional release in their religious life. In 1739, John Wesley described one meeting in which he preached his then-new Methodist doctrine:

Thence I went to Baldwin-Street, and expounded as it came in course, the fourth chapter of the Acts. We then called upon God, to confirm his word. Immediately one that stood by (to our no small surprise) cried out aloud, with the utmost vehemence, even as in the agonies of death. But we continued in prayer, till "a new song was put in her mouth, a thanksgiving unto our God." Soon after, two other persons (well known in this place, as labouring to live in all good conscience towards all men) were seized with strong pain, and constrained to "roar for the disquietness of their hearts." But it was not long before they likewise burst forth into praise to God their Saviour. The last who called upon God as out of the belly of hell, was I— E—, a stranger in Bristol; and in a short space he also was overwhelmed with joy and love, knowing that God had healed his backslidings.[16]

In his account of religious sects in a North Carolina mill town during the 1930s, Liston Pope describes a characteristic religious service in a church attended chiefly by mill workers.

The service begins at eight o'clock or thereabouts. Rather, the actions of the congregation become more intense and concerted in character; there is almost nothing by way of formal announcement. The choir . . . breaks into a rhythmic hymn, and the congregation follows suit. . . . The hymn . . . reminiscent of mountain ballads both in music and narrative form . . . looks toward a narrative climax, and the excitement . . . increases as the singing proceeds . . . punctuated with loud shouts of "Hallelujah," "Thank you, Jesus," "Glory," and the rhythmic clapping of hands and tapping of feet. . . . Half a dozen songs . . . a prayer, with everybody . . . praying aloud at the same time, each in his own way. . . . Then the pastor reads "the Scripture" . . . works up to a climax in its exposition—a climax reflected in increase of rhythmic motions and hortatory shouts from members of the congregation . . . a collection. . . . Then the service moves toward a climax . . . a testimony meeting in which a large number of the more faithful testify to their personal experience and joy in religion, some mutteringly, some loudly, fervidly. . . . All the while waves of ecstatic rhythm have been sweeping over the congregation. . . . One girl leaps from her seat . . . races four times around the aisles of the church, screaming. . . . Others rise and shout at the top of their lungs for five minutes. . . . It is nearly 11 P.M., but one stays and wonders. They cry out, and cry; they are drunken, but not with wine; they stagger, but not with strong drink.[17]

As this description illustrates, personal experience becomes more important than traditional ritual, and collective participation under the leadership and stimulus of lay preachers replaces passive attendance at a formal service led by a professionally trained, ordained minister.

Linked with fervent emotional expression in many of the "holiness" sects is a doctrine that emphasizes the moral superiority of the poor, that promises eternal bliss to the upright and threatens the wealthy and decadent rich with eternal damnation. Many Protestant sects, Pope points out, "substitute religious status for social status." They make a virtue of necessity, transmuting "poverty into a symptom of Grace."[18] Excluded from middle-class society, the disadvantaged establish a select religious fellowship open only to those who have undergone conversion or accept standards that are felt—or claimed—to be superior to those of the rest of society.

In practice, doctrine, and organization, Protestant sects have thus frequently reflected the needs of the lower classes for self-respect, moral reassurance, fellowship, and emotional experience, although there have also been middle-class sects, for example, Christian Science and the Quakers. After a careful analysis, an English sociologist concluded:

Christian Science is the religious expression of the well-to-do and comfortable, or those who would be so; it confirms them in the righteousness of their possessions, or of their striving. It is the type to which Weber referred in declaring that the privileged had no need to seek redemption, but required that religion should legitimize their well-being.[19]

Religious movements that have emerged among other groups similarly reflect the particular needs and problems of their members. As Barber shows, for example, messianic movements among American Indians frequently appeared among tribes suffering extreme deprivation because of the disruption of the traditional way of life. When traditional patterns of behavior could no longer be followed or could no longer meet their needs, they frequently came to believe in a messianic doctrine that promised the elimination of their difficulties. According to these messianic promises, if the Indians returned to ancient tribal customs, put aside alien influences, and adopted specific new rituals, their tribal lands would be restored, the whites eliminated, and the pleasures and glories of the past regained.[20]

Despite the evident connection between social conditions and the emergence of new religious ritual and doctrines or changes in the old, a sociological explanation that went no further than the problems people faced would be both incomplete and misleading. A religious response to trouble is only one alternative among many. Instead of joining revivalist sects, the mill workers in Gastonia, North Carolina, studied by Liston Pope might have joined a labor union. Instead of the Ghost Dance, with its messianic hopes, the Plains Indians might have engaged in a last-ditch war against the whites; or, alternatively, they might have sought full or partial assimilation into American culture and society. Whether people are led to accept new religious forms as they try to cope with their difficulties depends upon such complex circumstances as the prevailing state of religious belief, the existing relations between religion and other aspects of culture and social organization, the alternatives available to them, and such unpredictable developments as the emergence of a powerful religious leader or some unusual event.

In sixteenth-century Europe, the concrete social, economic, and political problems of various groups were paralleled by and closely related to a growing disaffection within the Roman Catholic Church. The Reformation was initiated by men who rebelled against the Church for distinctively religious reasons. Although Luther had already begun to formulate religious views that ran counter to those of the Church, he was prompted to mount his first open attack upon official doctrine because of a blatant effort by a politically chosen, debt-ridden archbishop to raise money through the widespread sale of papal indulgences (religious forgiveness for past sins).[21] Luther's radical religious views were accepted by various groups because of their relationship to the concrete conditions they were facing, including those stemming from the current religious situation. For the peasants, Luther's rejection of churchly authority and his emphasis upon the equality of all men in the sight of God seemed to justify rebellion against the exactions and exploitations from which they suffered. For the middle class, the doctrine of the "calling" that sanctioned dedication to the occupation one followed justified their preoccupation with economic affairs, a preoccupation that Catholic doctrine deemed of lesser value in comparison with the monastic ideal. To the nobility, a theological attack upon the authority of the Church sustained their own resistance to papal efforts to maintain control over the exercise of secular power. Moreover, Luther's support of secular authority—"For in the New Testament Moses counts for nothing, but there stands our Master Christ and casts us with body and possessions under the Kaiser's and worldly law when he says, 'Give to Caesar the things that are Caesar's' "—justified their own rule over their subjects. Because economic and political interests were so closely linked to issues of religious doctrine and organization, they inevitably affected the subsequent evolution of Lutheranism. When Luther denounced the peasant uprising of 1524–1525 in a tract, *Against the Thievish, Murderous Hordes of Peasants*, he lost their support, and Lutheranism eventually became "an established church, predominantly an aristocratic and middle-class party of vested interest and privilege."[22]

In the modern Western world, where religion has lost or relinquished its claim to govern in detail large parts of man's daily life, many people have found secular solutions to problems that might once have generated a religious response. In nineteenth-century England, as in earlier periods, Niebuhr points out, "there was present the actual exclusion of the poor from churches grown emotionally too cold, ethically too neutral, intellectually too sober, socially too aristocratic to attract the men who suffered under the oppression of monotonous toil, of insufficient livelihood and the sense of social inferiority."[23] Instead of grasping for religious alternatives that once again would give meaning to their lives and offer some solution to their difficulties, as the disadvantaged had so often done in the past, many nineteenth-century British workers relinquished religion entirely, finding an answer to their needs in political and economic action.

The emergence of a religious movement is often dependent upon the presence of a prophet, or *charismatic* leader —Christ, Mohammed, Mahatma Gandhi, Martin Luther, John Calvin, Joseph Smith of the Mormons, John Wesley, George Fox of the Quakers—who claims moral authority for the doctrine or message that he proclaims and gains support for it because of his own personal qualities—"it is written but *I* say unto you. . . ." Indeed, the origins of some religions are so closely identified with individuals that it almost appears as if they alone were responsible for its success. The creative role played by the charismatic leader should not be minimized; his personal qualities may make the difference between a revolution in religious doctrine and practice and little or no change. But no prophet can succeed unless the circumstances are propitious. He succeeds when his teachings reach a responsive audience—people whose attitudes, beliefs, and emotional needs predispose them to accept his leadership. The importance of both the leader and the context are suggested in the conclusion of an historian of the Reformation that Martin Luther "found public opinion a solution supersaturated with revolt; all that was needed to precipitate it was a pebble thrown in, but instead of a pebble he added the most powerful reagent possible." [24]

The initial emotional momentum generated by the charismatic religious leader and by the new dispensation that he brings can rarely be long sustained, particularly after his death. If the new doctrine is to survive, it must be embodied in an organization of believers; if it is to be more than the religion of an isolated and submerged coterie, it must be adapted to the changing needs of those who come to accept it. On the heels of the charismatic leader, therefore, often comes the missionary and organizer who codifies and interprets the received doctrine, gains new followers, and builds the church: Paul of Tarsus after Christ, the Caliph Omar after Mohammed, Brigham Young after Joseph Smith. In the process of gaining converts and creating an organi-

zation, however, the original doctrines are often transformed. Even after the church is fully established, the needs of the organization and the impact of external forces inevitably continue to affect belief and practice. "Christendom," writes H. Richard Niebuhr, "has often achieved apparent success by ignoring the precepts of its founder." [25]

The adaptation of religious belief, practice, and organization to meet the requirements of a "successful" church and to satisfy the changing needs of its members is clearly illustrated in the shifts that have often—but not always—taken place in working-class Protestant sects. [26] As the sect tries to gain new adherents and widen its influence, for reasons that may be varied and complex—religious fervor, rivalry with other groups, the preacher's desire for greater influence—it gradually changes its teaching and ritual in order to appeal to new groups, usually of higher status. This tendency may be supported by a small group within the sect who have managed to improve their own economic position, sometimes, it is said, as a result of adherence to the standards enjoined upon them: industry, sobriety, abstinence from worldly pleasures, thrift, and avoidance of conspicuous display. As the class position of the members changes, belief and ritual tend to approximate the middle-class pattern. As members are no longer excluded from middle-class society, they cease to draw a sharp line between themselves—the "saved"—and others. Able to secure greater worldly satisfaction and to enjoy more mundane pleasures, they no longer need the intense emotional experience they once found in religion; instead they come to look scornfully upon "excessively" expressive religious behavior. As evidence of their new status they build a new church, insist upon an educated, formally trained minister, and establish a systematic educational program for their children.

Changes that take place as religion is adapted to the requirements of effective organization and the needs and desires of members of the religious community are sometimes staunchly resisted by devout believers who feel that the fundamental teachings to which they subscribe are being distorted. They may gain followers from those whose interests—religious or nonreligious—are threatened by the changes taking place in doctrine or ritual. Where a religion ceases to meet the needs of its members, they often fall back upon their version of the original, uncorrupted message around which their faith is centered. The history of Christianity, like that of other religions, is marked by numerous theological schisms. Many of these religious conflicts were based upon divergent interpretations of Christian doctrine, each one often claiming to be consistent with the teaching of Jesus. There have been occasional attempts to regain what are felt to be the lost virtues of primitive Christianity and to reform the church in order to restore it to what is presumed to be its pristine state. The beginnings of new and sometimes revolutionary movements are frequently found in the religiously motivated opposition to the accommodation of the church and its doctrine to nonreligious interests, although once under way, these movements may also have widespread repercussions in society.

Religion and social order

As it becomes adapted to the existing social order, religion serves important social functions. In the answers it provides for the uncertainties inherent in human life and for the questions and problems to which society itself gives rise, religion frequently—but not always—encourages acceptance of prevailing norms and established social relationships. Consensus on religious doctrine and uniformity of religious practice contribute to the solidarity of the society. On the other hand, of course, religious differences may lead to hostility and even open conflict.

The ritual that is part of religion, not only reaffirms the beliefs people share, but also draws believers together into a moral community, encouraging conformity to its norms. In participating in the Mass, the Roman Catholic expresses his attitudes toward the Divine and confirms his membership in the Church and in the fellowship of believers. He feels more closely tied, in at least some respects, to those who share his beliefs and experience than to outsiders. The occasional repetition of the phrase "next year in Jerusalem" in Jewish ritual reinforces the unity of Jews everywhere by expressing the hope that eventually they will all be brought together. Use of a sacred language—Latin by the Roman Catholics, Hebrew by the Jews, for example—sets off the religious group from others and provides a common bond among the members.

Religion may also contribute to the persistence of existing institutions and social relationships by the attitude toward life that it enjoins and the ethical interpretation of society that it offers. Confucianism, for example, has performed this function by explicitly encouraging faithful performance of traditional duties and respect for traditional authority. Buddhism, on the other hand, sustains the existing order by defining the world as evil and emphasizing escape from its demands into a life of contemplation. Such withdrawal is possible only for monks, however, and less rigorous demands are made of the laity, who possess a lower religious status and are encouraged to accept fatalistically things as they are. Hinduism looks upon the world as unchangeable. It sanctions the caste system by linking one's fate in the world with past incarnations over which, of course, in religious principle one has no control. The aim of Hinduism is detachment from worldly affairs and eventual escape from the bondage of the flesh.

Christianity, in its long history, has taken diverse attitudes toward the world, the flesh, and social institutions as it has sought to resolve the tension between its transcendental concern with salvation and the more mundane problems of organizing and maintaining a church and applying Christian ethics to social life. We can therefore only suggest briefly some of the ways in which Christianity has contributed to the maintenance or stability of society, on the one hand, and to important social changes, on the other.

Catholicism helped to sustain the medieval social order by emphasizing the "drama of salvation" and the monastic ideal, even when it tolerated worldliness in both the Church and the laity; life in this world was held to be less important than the life hereafter, and hardship and trouble were to be endured while waiting for eternal bliss. The hierarchical order of society was looked upon as in some measure divinely ordained. Inequality and differences among the several classes —or "estates"—into which medieval society was divided were justified by the view that God had assigned to each individual or group distinct functions—tilling the soil, ruling, defense, religious leadership, trade, craftsmanship. This doctrine is clearly expressed by Thomas Starkey, at one time chaplain to King Henry VIII:

Like as in every man there is a body and also a soul in whose flourishing and prosperous state both together standeth the weal and felicity of man; so likewise there is in every commonalty city and country as it were a politic body and another thing also resembling the soul of man. . . . This body is nothing else but the multitude of people. . . . The thing which is resembled to the soul is civil order and politic law, administered by officers and rulers. . . . He or they which have authority upon the whole state right well may be resembled to the heart. . . . To the head, with the eyes ears and other senses therein, resembled may be right well the under officers by princes appointed, for as much as they should ever observe and diligently wait for the weal of the rest of this body. To the arms are resembled both craftsmen and warriors which defend the rest of the body from injury of enemies outward and work and make things necessary to the same; to the feet the ploughmen and tillers of the ground, because they by their labour sustain and support the rest of the body.[27]

Each organ was to receive its just due—no more and no less; each class was to perform its function and thus conform to God's commandments. (This organic theory, which had received its classic statement by Thomas Aquinas in the thirteenth century, did not preclude or prevent frequent clashes between church and the secular power as each sought to extend its influence and protect—or increase—its rights and prerogatives.)

When the organic theory of society began to crumble as a result of the revolutionary changes of the sixteenth century —the growing importance of the urban bourgeoisie, the Protestant Reformation, popular opposition to traditional rulers—a new religious defense of royal political authority emerged in the doctrine of the "divine right of kings." Kings, wrote James I of England, "are breathing images of God upon earth," [28] and this view was seconded by both clerical and lay defenders of monarchy. Although derived from the traditional Christian notion that authority has a religious source and sanction, this theory justified a greater centralization of secular power, less restrained by custom and precedent, than had previously been accepted by political or theological writers. At the same time, the growing nationalism with which the theory of divine right was often associated contributed to the emergence of national churches, both Protestant and Catholic.

The post-Reformation division of Christianity into competing churches and sects and the variations among the nations in the institutionalized relations between church and state make difficult any generalization about the functions of specific Christian religious beliefs and practices and about the historical contributions of various religious groups. Both Protestantism and Roman Catholicism have frequently played a conservative role in Europe and the Americas, sustaining in diverse ways the existing social order. But under some circumstances they have contributed—or have been closely linked with—radical social change and have been involved in intense, disruptive social conflict.

Protestantism and social change

Protestantism appeared on the historical scene at approximately the same time as modern capitalism, and the nature of their relationship—which contributed to the development of the other, and how?—has been the focus of one of the great intellectual controversies for more than half a century. In the groundbreaking essay that helped to set off this persisting debate, Max Weber argued that Protestantism provided an essential source of the dedication to one's occupation and the unremitting pursuit of gain that marked the "spirit of capitalism." [29]

In modern capitalism, he wrote, "Man is dominated by the making of money." The unique quality of the capitalist spirit, which Weber sought to explain, lay not simply in its emphasis upon profit, however, but in the ethical value placed upon economic gain and the rational single-mindedness with which man was expected to engage in economic activities.

The source of this capitalist "spirit," which provided an emotional impetus and ideological rationale for the evolving institutions of a free-market economy, Weber found in small measure in Luther, but chiefly in the teachings of Calvin and in the doctrines of the later ascetic Protestant sects. Neither Luther nor Calvin suggested major changes in established religious attitudes toward specific economic practices, such as the taking of interest, called "usury" by the medieval Church; these changes came later. [30] But in the evaluation of economic activities and, in the case of Calvinism, the attitude toward the world and the psychic dilemmas its doctrines generated, Protestantism encouraged and stimulated the capitalist spirit and, in turn, the behavior of businessmen.

In contrast to the monastic ideal that dominated medieval Catholicism (even when the Church recognized that most men would inevitably fall short of that ideal), both Luther and Calvin stressed dedication to one's *calling*, the occupation in which one had been placed by God. Luther's definition of the calling remained "traditionalistic," that is, it encouraged the individual to remain in his station and to accept and follow the prevailing conceptions of proper practice. Calvin, on the other hand, saw the calling as "the task set by God"; it required positive efforts to master the world rather than adherence to traditional practice. Not withdrawal from social life, but its reordering along ascetic Christian lines was required of the good Christian.

Dedication to that task resulted not only from the explicit approval of patient, industrious, rational effort, but also from the internal tensions provoked by Calvin's doctrine of predestination. According to this doctrine, each man's eternal fate was preordained by God. Neither faith nor works, monastic retreat nor saintly conduct, could affect that divine decision. Moreover, no "Mother Church" could intervene or aid the individual seeking salvation and divine grace. The uncertainty and anxiety created by this harsh doctrine, "the unprecedented inner loneliness of the single individual," led the believer to seek some reassurance, some evidence that he belonged among the saved rather than the condemned. That reassurance he could find by behaving as if he were saved, by adhering steadfastly to the requirements of the religious life: namely, by following those rules of behavior that have come to be labeled the "Protestant ethic"—industry, sobriety, thrift, restraint, and avoidance of fleshly pleasures. The evidence that one belonged to the elect was to be found, eventually, in one's success in one's calling, a success, in fact, to which adherence to the "Protestant ethic" often contributed. Indeed, Weber's empirical starting point was the observation that Protestant nations and Protestant groups within nations of mixed religious composition led the way in capitalist development.

Despite the impressive skill and scholarship with which Weber put forward his thesis—including a series of wide-ranging comparative studies in which he attempted to show that modern capitalism had developed only in the West because of the differences between its religious evolution and the religions of other parts of the world [31]—it has been severely criticized. Notwithstanding the specific criticisms, however, some of which unfortunately rest upon a misunderstanding of his aim and his argument, the existence of a significant connection between Protestantism and the development of capitalism seems to be now beyond dispute. Even if, as some critics contend, the "Protestant ethic" followed the development of capitalist institutions as a *post hoc* justification for them rather than antedating and in some measure "causing" them, the fact remains that religious ideas did contribute to the economic activities that helped to remake the Western world.

Stimulated by this debate over the relationship between religion and capitalism, some scholars have explored the connections between religion and economic growth or modernization in other parts of the world. Thus Robert Bellah has argued that

religion played an important role in the process of political and economic rationalization in Japan through maintaining and intensifying commitment to the central values, supplying motivation and legitimation for certain necessary political innovations and reinforcing an ethnic of inner-worldly asceticism which stressed diligence and economy. That it may also have played an important part in the formation of the central values which were favorable to industrialization is at least a strong possibility.[32]

In other areas—Indonesia, India, the Arab world—the influence of religion appears to be much more problematic; in some respects it has inhibited modernization, in others it has facilitated or encouraged it, and in some ways it is largely irrelevant. [33]

After new institutions and social structures have emerged, the religious beliefs and practices that once were linked with change often come to serve different functions. Once the major outlines of Western capitalism had taken shape, Protestantism, by and large, came to play a different role. Instead of serving as a stimulus or justification for disregarding traditional social norms, it encouraged conformity to the now established institutions of capitalist society. The emotional dynamic contained in the doctrine of predestination disappeared, and the rigorous, rational theology of Calvinism lost its hold, but the values of the "Protestant Ethic" persisted as central elements in the culture of capitalism. The concern with "character"; the emphasis upon thrift, sobriety, and abstinence from worldly pleasures; the stress upon activity, work, and mastery of both self and the world, values essential for bourgeois enterprisers in the commercial capitalism of the seventeenth and eighteenth centuries, also provided moral support for the discipline required by the industrial capitalism of the nineteenth century. In addition, the Protestant Ethic encouraged the saving that made possible the accumulation of capital required for industrial growth and expansion.

Even when abstinence from worldly pleasures and the thrift enjoined by religion led to wealth, as they so often did, and to the temptations that flow from wealth, Protestantism continued to stress the moral value of economic success. The dilemma to which ascetic Protestantism was thus led and the solution it nevertheless accepted are both illustrated in John Wesley's comment:

I fear, wherever riches have increased, the essence of religion has decreased in the same proportion. Therefore I do not see how it is possible, in the nature of things, for any revival of true religion to continue long. For religion must necessarily produce both industry and frugality, and these cannot but produce riches. But as riches increase, so will pride, anger, and love of the world in all its branches. How then is it possible that Methodism, that is, a religion of the heart, though it flourishes now as a green bay tree, should continue in this state? For the Methodists in every place grow diligent and frugal; consequently they increase in goods. . . . We ought not to prevent people from being diligent and frugal; we must exhort all Christians to gain all they can, and to save all they can; that is, in effect to grow rich.[34]

The inequalities of wealth that emerged with the continued growth of capitalism were often sanctioned by the doctrine enunciated, for example, by Episcopal Bishop Lawrence, that "in the long run it is only to the man of morality that wealth comes." Conversely, poverty was both the result and the evidence of moral failure. "The number of poor to be sympathized with is very small," declared the Reverend Russell Conwell, a famous Baptist preacher and founder of Temple University. "To sympathize with a man whom God has punished for his sins, thus to help him when God would still continue a just punishment, is to do wrong, no doubt about it."[35] Since character and not institutions determine men's fate, according to this view, there could be no reason to criticize the prevailing social norms or to advocate institutional change. Because men found themselves in that station in life to which their own efforts and God's will had led them, any attempts to improve the circumstances of the poor by social reform were both immoral and ill-advised.

The contribution of Protestantism to the maintenance of capitalist institutions came not only from its direct approval and support of both existing practices and the emerging pattern of social relationships, however, but also from a tendency to withdraw from active participation in the daily life of society, to accept a division between religion and other areas of social and cultural life. By yielding the once-accepted right of religion to provide a moral evaluation of day-by-day activities and by reducing its claims upon men to the demands of private conscience and occasional public ritual, Protestantism in the nineteenth and twentieth centuries made possible the continued rationalization of economic life, the systematic pursuit of profit by the most efficient methods, unencumbered, on the whole, by traditional restraints upon either technology or men's dealings with one another.[36]

Not all segments of Protestantism escaped from the persistent tension between transcendental moral claims and the realities of social life. The religious teachings that encouraged the Protestant virtues also generated the humanitarianism of the nineteenth century, which led in England to the abolition of slavery and contributed to the passage of factory legislation and other welfare measures designed to soften the bruising impact of industrialism. Although many Protestant clergymen abstained from comment on the social problems of their times, others rejected the dichotomy between church and society and persistently sought to apply Christian ethics to the evils they saw around them, not only by patching up the victims of an often unrestrained competitiveness, but also by advocating meliorative institutional changes. If they did not advocate the radical reconstitution of society recommended by socialists or communists (as some did: Christian Socialists played an active role in the English Labour Party), they also did not limit themselves to the purely "ecclesiastical" matters to which many presumably devout citizens would confine them.

The cleavage within Protestantism on the issue of religious intervention in political and economic affairs has led to internal conflict that is still present. The "liberal" National Council of Churches in the United States offers "moral" judgments on social issues and encourages active participation in the effort to solve social ills. The staunchly conservative American Council of Churches, on the other hand, insists, together with many other fundamentalist groups, that the church and churchmen have no business meddling in affairs about which they "know" little or nothing.

Roman Catholicism: conservatism, adaptation, and change

Whereas Protestantism was linked with the economic and some of the political changes taking place in Western Europe from the sixteenth century onward, Roman Catholicism remained on the whole tied to more traditional institutions and social structures. Capitalism progressed slowly or not at all among Catholics and in Catholic territories. The Catholic emphasis upon eternal salvation—to be achieved through adherence to the sacraments of the Church—fosters an "otherworldliness" that has often been uncongenial to the requirements of capitalist enterprise. In contrast to the individualism of some branches of Protestantism, which is more consistent with and has contributed to the development of democracy, the authoritarianism of the Catholic Church and its insistence upon acceptance of authority—sacred and secular—have often been uncongenial to popular political movements and have sustained traditional forms of authority and power.

Because Roman Catholic doctrine defines the Church as the medium through which salvation is to be gained (although there has been disagreement among Catholic theologians as to whether salvation can be achieved *only* through the Church), maintenance of its health as a going organization has been one of its chief religious concerns. If the Church were to be injured or weakened in any way, the souls of its members would be endangered. The state, therefore, according to various papal pronouncements of the past, "has been established, not only to exercise the government of the world, but above all, for the protection of the Church . . . that there is nothing more profitable and more glorious for the Sovereigns of States and Kings, than to leave the Catholic Church to exercise her laws, and not to permit any to curtail her liberty." [37] Where Catholicism has occupied a dominant position in society, as the established religion or as the prevailing faith, it has often possessed a vested interest in the status quo through the moral authority it could wield, the property it owned, and the influence it was able to exert upon the secular power. In such circumstances the Church has frequently served as a major defender of the existing order, even when the state imposed a harsh authority or sanctioned and supported the economic exploitation of the lower classes.

When opposition developed to established political and economic institutions with which the Church was identified, or which it supported, the Church therefore often came under attack too. The French Revolution not only destroyed the *ancien régime* but also disestablished the Church, expropriated much of its property, and initiated a vigorous anticlericalism that has persisted as an active force in French society. The revolutions against Spanish rule that swept Latin America in the nineteenth century often included the Church among their enemies.[38] Anticlericalism has usually emerged, not when the Church was weak or tolerant or when Catholics were in a minority, but when it was strong and affiliated with those who were wealthy and powerful. Opposition to the Church, how-

ever, has not always reflected antireligious sentiments, but rather hostility toward the high clergy and the power of those who called upon the Church for support. The clergy itself was frequently divided, many parish priests siding with popular movements, the higher ecclesiastics defending the ruling groups, as in Latin America at various times and in Spain in the 1930s.

In seeking to maintain its hold upon its members, to perform the religious functions it claims for itself, and to protect itself against hostile social and political forces, the Church has opposed not only communism and socialism but also at times rationalism, liberalism, and other "modernist" heresies. In 1864 Pope Pius IX issued a *Syllabus of Errors* that explicitly condemned the view that "the Roman Pontiff can, and ought to, reconcile himself, and come to terms with progress, liberalism, and modern civilization." [39] Without giving up any traditional claims, such as the right of the Church to educate Catholic youth and to regulate marriage, even when the state abrogates or limits them, the Church has tended to come to terms with any political regime that promised to allow it to pursue its activities freely. In effect, then, it has supported such regimes by encouraging its members to participate as loyal citizens in the life of their country.

Since the reign of Leo XIII (1878–1903), the Church has moved away from some of the views of Pius IX and his predecessors and has tried in various ways to accommodate Catholic policy and practice to the realities of the contemporary world—within the framework and limits imposed by what is defined as basic and unchanging Catholic teaching. A major stimulus to continuing, or even accelerated, change within the Church came from the Vatican Council convened by

Pope John XXIII and the policy of *aggiornamento*—bringing up to date the organization and programs of the Church —which he enunciated and pursued.

Much of the pressure for change has come from those countries in which Catholics constitute a minority, as in the United States, or where the Church has lost much of its power and authority, as in France and Northern Europe. In these areas, the Church has been less conservative and resistant to change in both religious and secular matters than in countries where Catholics form a dominant majority.

Although canon law and papal pronouncements provide an elaborate body of rules and precepts governing social life and defining the official Catholic attitude toward various institutions, the inferences to be drawn from this code or from the basic and presumably unchanging dogmas upon which Catholicism rests vary widely. On many issues there are substantial differences within the Church. Not only do Catholic theologians differ on the proper relations between Church and state, but they also disagree, for example, on the nature and justification of religious tolerance. A Protestant theologian has shown that a large majority of contemporary Catholic theologians no longer accept the view that tolerance is only an expedient to be accepted where the Roman Catholic Church does not predominate. Instead they justify religious tolerance as a positive value inherent in traditional Catholic teachings and universally applicable.[40]

The absence of doctrinal unanimity within the Church on many issues constitutes one of the sources of the Church's strength, for it makes possible adapation to the demands of concrete historical and social circumstances within a continuing context of Catholic orthodoxy—albeit often slowly and reluctantly. For example, the Church has undertaken to review its traditional teachings on birth control because of the problems of a rapidly expanding world population (see Chapter 17) and the development of new methods of contraception. In the United States, where there is clear evidence that a substantial proportion of Catholics use prohibited contraceptive devices,[41] there has been considerable open controversy. A widely read book by a distinguished Catholic physician[42] advocating acceptance of oral contraceptives elicited strong criticism from some priests, but there was no clerical condemnation of the author or of others who are advocating modifications in the Church's position.

Catholicism in the United States reflects both the position in which Catholics have found themselves and the distinctive features of American culture and society. Most of the early Catholics in North America were French, but by the middle of the nineteenth century the Irish had come to represent the dominant Catholic pattern in the United States. As recent immigrants seeking to gain acceptance in American society, they were chiefly concerned with establishing themselves—and their Church—in an alien Protestant environment. As a result, both the Church and its members, as two Catholic writers have pointed out, were "characterized by defensiveness, parochialism, and inflexibility." They sought to ward off criticism, to establish their *bona fides* as Americans, to "view the world exclusively in terms of how it affected them," and they resisted adaptation in the Church to changes in the character of American society.[43]

These characteristics were—and to some degree still are—apparent in the multiplicity of Catholic organizations, the Catholic press, Catholic schools and universities, and the organization of the Church itself. With the exception of its fervent opposition to communism, on the basis of which many priests present themselves as defenders of traditional American institutions, the Church has in general refrained from speaking out directly on public issues, except those directly affecting itself or closely related to Catholic doctrine—education, birth control, divorce laws. (Liberal Catholics have sharply criticized the Church hierarchy for its failure to speak out on civil liberties, though some Catholic clergy have participated actively in the civil rights movement.) In their attacks on communism, many Catholic clergy and laymen have often included as their targets liberals and members of the "noncommunist left" and have condemned critical or radical ideas unconnected with communism. Although a majority of Catholics have consistently voted for Democratic candidates, McCarthyism gained a great deal of Catholic support.[44]

As more and more Catholics have moved into the middle class and gained a secure status in American society, their attitudes and those of many priests have come to reflect their new social position. Various foreign observers and an occasional American Catholic critic have commented on the increasingly middle-class character of American Catholicism.[45] As members of a predominantly Protestant society, many Catholics have accepted and held opinions and values that differ from traditional Catholic perspectives, even while they have retained their religious ties. They have become more worldly, ambitious, and "go-getting," more "puritanical," in their attitudes than Catholics elsewhere. (The campaign against pornography has been heavily supported by Catholic organizations.) A Catholic scholar has observed: "In the

Art of Fiction, Henry James, referring to the situation in Victorian England, noted as a 'Protestant' characteristic the suspicion of all artistic effort that was not clearly designed either to amuse or to edify. Curiously enough, this 'Protestant' attitude is, in the United States, too often the 'Catholic' attitude."[46]

The Church itself has also adapted itself in various ways to American culture. It has become more "activist" than the Church in other countries, almost to the point, it has been suggested, of sometimes succumbing to the heresy that "the world can be saved by . . . external activity."[47] Despite opposition from some European Catholic theologians—and some Americans—important segments of the Roman Catholic hierarchy have expressed themselves in favor of the separation of church and state, although their definition of this separation differs in some respects from the view of many non-Catholics.

Within the Church there has also been an active social reform movement led by influential priests. In the early years of the twentieth century, this movement took so strong a stand on some social and economic issues that the president of the National Association of Manufacturers was led to complain to Cardinal Gibbons, a leading American Catholic cleric, that there appeared to be a "covert effort to disseminate partisan, pro-labor union, socialistic propaganda under the official insignia of the Roman Catholic Church in America."[48] Catholics have long played a major part in the liberal wing of the Democratic Party, and the majority of Catholics in Congress have consistently supported what is defined as liberal legislation. Both priests and nuns have actively participated in the civil rights movement.

The election of a Catholic President in

ETHICAL CULTURE

SOCIETY FOR ETHICAL CULTURE
Central Park West and 64th Street
Sunday, March 27, at 11:00 A.M.
"THE TRIUMPH OF THE HUMAN SPIRIT"
JEROME NATHANSON
Broadcast over WQXR—11:05 A.M.

FRENCH CHURCH

FRENCH EVANGELICAL
126 West 16th St.
REV. MARCEL BONARD, PREACHER
11 A.M.—Easter Resurrection—8 P.M.

SAINT ESPRIT Old Huguenot Church
109 E. 60th St.
Easter Day, 9 A.M. Holy Communion
11 a.m. Pr. Sermon & Holy Comm'n
All Services and Sermons are in French

HINDUISM

RAMAKRISHNA—VIVEKANANDA
Center, 17 W. 94th St., Swami Nikhilananda
Meaning of Immortality—8:30 P.M. Tues
Aphorisms on Devotion, Fr., Upanishad Class

INTERDENOMINATIONAL

Riverside Church
Riverside Drive at 122nd Street
9 and 11 A.M.—IDENTICAL SERVICES
Doors open at 8 and 10:30 A.M.
DR. ROBERT J. McCRACKEN
"THE DIFFERENCE EASTER MAKES"
9:30 A.M. Radio Chapel WOR, Dr. McCracken
5 P.M.—MINISTRY OF MUSIC
Organ Program by Frederick L. Swann
Cantata: "The Way to Emmaus"—Weinberger
Louise Natale, Soloist
Parking Facilities Available

Union Theological Seminary
James Chapel, Claremont at 121st St.
11 A.M.—The Rev. Prof. Daniel D. Williams

JEWISH

Emanu-El Fifth Avenue at 65th Street
SERVICES
Daily 5:30 P.M.; Fri. 5:15 P.M.
This Morning at 11:30
DR. JULIUS MARK
"REFORM JUDAISM—WHAT IT IS!
WHAT IT IS NOT!"
In Tribute to Isaac M. Wise

Jewish Science
STEINWAY HALL, 113 WEST 57th ST.
SUNDAY, 11 A.M.
TEHILLA LICHTENSTEIN, LEADER, on
"A MAJOR CONDITION
FOR PERSONAL HAPPINESS"

LUTHERAN

ADVENT Broadway at 93rd St.
Rev. John Gensel, Pastor
11 A.M. Easter Service Special Music
Mrs. Alice Davis, Organist, Choir Dir.

Grace & St. Paul's 123 West 71st
Near Broadway
REV. NORMAN S. DINKEL, Pastor
11 A.M.—Easter Festival Communion

Gustavus Adolphus 151 E. 22d St.
EASTER: 9:30 Children's Program
11, Sermon: "DAY OF VICTORY"

Holy Trinity Central Pk. W. 65th St.
REV. ROBERT D. HERSHEY, J.D., Pastor
9, Matins (9:30, S.S.) 11, THE SERVICE
"Intimations of Immortality ... or
Implications?" (Holy Comm'n follows)

IMMANUEL 88th Street and Lexington Ave.
Easter: 7:30 & 11 (Eng.); 9:30 (German)

OUR SAVIOUR'S ATONEMENT
189th St. & Bennett Ave.
One block West of Broadway
EASTER DAY—11 A.M.
Franklin J. Schreiber, Pastor

ST. JOHN'S 81 Christopher St.
I.R.T. Sheridan Sq.
PASTOR F. P. ECHARDT
7 A.M.—SUNRISE SERVICE
11 A.M.—"CHRIST'S VICTOR"

St. Luke's 308 West 46th Street
(One Block West of Times Square)
ALBERT C. NEIBACHER, Pastor
Sunday: 9:30 A.M. Children's Service
11 A.M., "Easter Calls for Action"

St. Matthew 202 Sha man Ave
Off B'way at 207th St.
REV. A. W. TRINKLEIN, Pastor
EASTER: 8 A.M.—Holy Communion
9:30 and 11 A.M.—Festival Services
Preacher: REV. O. C. HOFFMANN,
Lutheran Hour Speaker

St. Peter's Lexington at 54th Street
PASTOR LEOPOLD W. BERNHARD
9 A.M.—Holy Comm'n. 11—The Service
Daily Dev.—12:30 P.M. Wed—5:30 P.M.

LUTHERAN

BRONX

FIRST LUTHERAN
Bruckner Blvd. & Baisley Ave.
EASTER SERVICES
7:00 A.M.—Matins With Communion
11:00 A.M—Festival Service
REV. THEO. BARTUS, PASTOR

FORDHAM 2430 Walton Ave.
EASTER DAWN—4:30 A.M.
Sunday School—9:30 A.M.
Easter Triumphant Festal Worship
11:00 A.M.

QUEENS

GOOD SHEPHERD
Francis Lewis Blvd. & 100th Avenue
BELLAIRE, L.I.
The Rev. Lauri ... Anderson, D.D. Pastor
7:30 A.M.—Holy Communion
9:30 A.M.—THE FESTIVAL SERVICE
11 A.M.—THE FESTIVAL SERVICE

Christ Lutheran 36th St. & B'way
Woodside
THE REV. J. W. LEININGER, Pastor
Easter Day Services 7:45, 9:30 & 11 A.M.

METHODIST

BROADWAY Temple, Wash. Hts.
Broadway at 174th Street
Dr. ALLEN E. CLAXTON, Minister
11—"Li e la a Play—Not an Accident"
7 P.M.—Methodist Youth Fellowship
7 P.M. Services in Spanish
7 P.M. Motion Picture: "King of Kings"

Christ Church Park Ave at 60th St.
DR. RALPH W. SOCKMAN
TWO EASTER MORNING SERVICES
9 and 11 A.M.—Identical Sermons:
"CHRIST COMES THROUGH"
Registered Nurse Care for Infants, 9 & 11
5 P.M. Easter Evensong
10:45 Nat'l Radio Pulpit WRCA Dr. Sockman
Wed. 5:30, Seminar on Christian Living

John Street Organized 1766 44 John Street
Rev. A B Moon
Oldest Methodist Church in America
11 A.M.—DAY OF LIFE AND GLORY

LEXINGTON 150 East 62nd St.
R. S. WESTA, Pastor
Easter 11 A.M.: "Now Is Christ Risen"
7 P.M., Film: "A Cry in the Night"

METROPOLITAN-DUANE 7th Ave at 13th
REV. G. ROY BRAGG, Minister
11 A.M—"SING OUT THE GLORY"

PARK AVE. 106 East 86 St
REV. PHILIP A. C. CLARKE, Minister
QUESTION PEOPLE ARE ASKING
11 A.M.—Easter: "Do I Believe in Life
After Death?"

St. PAUL & St. ANDREW
West End Avenue and West 86th Street
REV. BARMER L. WATERS, preaching
11 A.M. "OUT OF THIS WORLD"
Nursery & Kindergarten during service

BRONX

FORDHAM MARION AVENUE
at Fordham Road
The Rev. LUTHER W. KING, Minister
11 A.M.—The Life Everlasting

MENONITE

BRONX

HOUSE OF FRIENDSHIP
2783 Southern Blvd. Bx. (WE 3-3915)
Ser. 10 A.M., S.S. 11, Worship
PASTOR JOHN I. SMUCKER

PHILOSOPHY

INDIAN CULTURAL CENTER
50 Centre, Park West, N.Y. 23 TR 3-4180
Yoga, Spiritual Healing
Group Classes Wed. & Fri. 6 P.M.

PRESBYTERIAN

Broadway Presbyterian
Broadway at 114th Street
DR. JOHN H. McCOMB, Minister
11 A.M.—"CHRIST'S RESURRECTION"
8 P.M.—MR. PETER B. GROSSMANN
Wed., 8:15 P.M.—Missionary Service
Radio—Sun., 8:30-9 A.M. WAAT, 970 K.

Central Presbyterian
Park Avenue at 64th Street
REV. THEODORE CUTLER SPEERS, D.D.
EASTER DAY: 8 A.M. Holy Communion
11 A.M.—"Death Could Not Hold Him"
(Infant Care during Church Service)
4:45 P.M., Organ Recital by Hugh Giles
11 A.M.—EASTER CAROL SERVICE
Tues. & Thur. 5 to 5:30, Evening Prayer

COVENANT at the United Nations
310 East 42 St.
R. H. Roecke, Pastor; Ray Graf, Organist
9 and 11, DUPLICATE EASTER SERVICE
Sermon: "Life Eternal Now"
12:30, Time for Fellowship

First Presbyterian Church
5th AVE. bet. 11th and 12th STREETS
8 A.M—COMMUNION SERVICE
9:30 A.M. and 11 A.M.
REV. JOHN C. MELLIN
8 P.M.—Young Adults Group
8 P.M.—Handel's "THE MESSIAH"
(Lenten and Easter Portions)

ROMAN CATHOLIC

Holy Family Church
7th St. East of 2nd Avenue
(ADJACENT TO THE UNITED NATIONS)
Rev. John J. O'Reilly, Pastor
EASTER SUNDAY MASSES
7, 8, 9, 10 (High), 11, 12, 12:50

St. Patrick's Cathedral
Fifth Avenue at 50th-51st Streets
EASTER DAY
Low Mass at 6, 7, 8, 9 A.M.
PONTIFICAL MASS at 11 A.M.
PONTIFICAL VESPERS at 4 P.M.

SPIRITUALIST

Chapel Eternal Star, 237 W. 72nd
REV. ROSE ERICKSON, PASTOR
1 P.M.—Wed. Fri. Sat. Sun. 4:30 P.M.

FIRST UNIVERSAL
SPIRITUALIST CHURCH
REV. CLIFFORD BIAS, MINISTER
REV. RAYMOND BURNS, Guest Speaker
Easter Sunday Service 8 P.M.
Studio 906 Steinway Hall
113 West 57th Street

SWEDENBORGIAN

The NEW CHURCH East 35 St., bet.
Park & Lex. ave.
Rev. CLAYTON S. PRIESTNAL, Minister
Sun. 11 A.M. "Death Before Resurrection"
A friendly welcome awaits you

THEOSOPHY

United Lodge of Theosophists
347 EAST 72ND STREET
Public Lecture Sunday Evening at 8:15
"THE MYSTERY OF EASTER"
School for Children, Sun. 10 to 11 A.M.
Meetings, Weds. & Fridays, 8:15 P.M.
ALL WELCOME INQUIRIES INVITED

BROOKLYN

BKLYN THEOSOPHICAL SOC.
25 LEFFERTS AVE. (IR 2-3361)
Thursday, April 24, 8 P.M.
55TH BIRTHDAY CELEBRATION
Speaker: Sadie Stave
Subject: "Music Through the Ages

UNITARIAN

CHURCH OF ALL SOULS
80th Street and Lexington Avenue
WALTER DONALD KRING, Minister
9:30 and 11 A.M. Identical Sermons:
"THEY SAW THE CHRIST"
Special Family Service at 9:30
Thur. 8:30, Dr. ERWIN R. GOODENOUGH
"The Religious Values of America'am

FIRST UNITARIAN CHURCH
Pierrepont St. and Monroe Pl.
Brooklyn Heights
(Boro Hall Subway Station)
DONALD W. McKINNEY, Minister
EASTER FESTIVAL SERVICE
11 A.M.—"WHAT THOUGHTS
WITHIN US WAKEN"

THE COMMUNITY CHURCH
40 East 35th Street
See Display Advertisement This Page

UNITARIAN SERVICES
ARE HELD SUNDAY IN THE
FOLLOWING COMMUNITIES, FOR
INFORMATION CALL, WRITE:
UNITARIAN NO. 10 PARK AVE. N.Y. 16
LEX 2-3636
Saturday, 9 A.M. 11-12:30 P.M. MU 3-4988.
NEW YORK: Yonkers, Bedford Hills,
Peekskill, Cortland, Brooklyn, Staten Is-
land, Nyack, White Plains.
LONG ISLAND: Baldwin, Huntington,
Flushing, Plandome, Hollis, Garden City.
NEW JERSEY: Orange, Ridgewood, Sum-
mit, Paramus, Rutherford, Morristown,
New Brunswick, Montclair.
CONNECTICUT: Westport.

UNITY

At the Crossroads of the World
"FROM DEATH INTO LIFE"
SUNDAY, 11 A.M—WALDORF-ASTORIA
Call: Unity's VOICE of PRAYER
Circle 5-7411
J. SIG PAULSON, Minister
1 West 47th Street, New York

UNITY SERVICE
SUN. 11—57 PARK AVE., NEAR 38 ST.
UNITY of TRUTH 400 East
Affiliation: Unity School of Christianity. No
SUN. 11 A.M—JOSEPHINE B. SIEMON

UNIVERSALIST

UNIVERSALIST CHURCH of N.Y.C.
Central Park West and 76th Street
11 A.M.—REV. LEONARD MILLER
"THE EVERLASTING TRIUMPH"

VEDANTA

VEDANTA SOCIETY 34 West 71st St.
SWAMI PAVITRANANDA
Sun. 11—Resurrection and Immortality
Tues., 8:15 P.M.—"Discourse on Upanishad"

YOGA

YOGA Institute 90 EAST 81 ST.
S. Mazumdar
Sun., 8:30 P.M.—"Attaining Freedom"
Wed., 8:30 P.M.—Meditation and Yc...

The religious diversity characteristic of the United States reaches its extremes in the metropolitan center, as is evident in the announcements of religious services found each week in The New York Times.

1960 may represent—at least in their own eyes—the full acceptance of Catholics into American society. No longer on the defensive or confined predominantly to the working class, and encouraged by religious currents emanating from the Vatican Council and the trend toward *aggiornamento*, the Catholic Church in America, Edward Wakin and Father Joseph Scheuer have suggested, may be on the verge of a major transformation.[49]

The consequences of religious diversity

In the complex relationships between religious practice and belief on the one hand and other elements of culture and social structure on the other, the extent of religious differentiation plays an important part. The Roman Catholic Church, we noted earlier, has followed a different path when it has been the sole or dominant religion from that taken when it was only one among several or many. But the fact of religious diversity itself has far-reaching consequences that ramify throughout the social order.

Religious diversity in the United States is a familiar and oft-noted fact. In 1959 there were thirty-eight religious bodies with more than 50,000 adherents, disregarding the internal differences among Baptists (seventeen subdivisions, each with more than 50,000 members), Lutherans, Methodists, Eastern Churches, and so on.[50] The sources of such diversity are inevitably complex and difficult to identify but include at least the variety of immigrant groups, the absence of a state religion, differences between settled areas and an open frontier, democratic ideologies that resisted religious as well as political authoritarianism, and the ambitions and efforts of charismatic religious leaders such as Joseph Smith of the Mormons and Mary Baker Eddy of the Christian Scientists. The origins of religious diversity in England, France, Russia, India, and Indonesia—as well as elsewhere—reflect the varied historical circumstances of these areas, as well as the specific social and cultural conditions that allowed the emergence or persistence of different religious groups.

One of the consequences of the variety of religious belief and practice in the United States, it has been suggested, has been widespread religious tolerance. The early settlers, however, though seeking freedom for themselves, were not ready, in many instances, to allow religious freedom to others, and the institutionalization of the norm of tolerance came only gradually. The presence of a number of religious groups undoubtedly contributed to this norm, at the same time that the emergence of new groups was facilitated by it. But there were other conditions that helped to create an atmosphere of religious tolerance. The absence of a state religion eliminated both politically based repression and the need to fight against political constraints. Secularizing tendencies of the eighteenth century (many of the early leaders of the Republic were deists uncommitted to a church) and antireligious movements of the nineteenth century made religion a matter of indifference to many, while the individualism of some varieties of Protestantism ran counter to any institutional restraints.[51]

The presence of religious tolerance in England, where there is an official Church, and in other societies in which conditions have differed in various ways from those that contributed to tolerance in the United States, suggests the tentative nature of this interpretation and the need for further analysis. The absence of one factor, such as the separation of church and state, might well be compensated for by the greater strength of another, for example the greater secularization of England, where relatively fewer people are regular churchgoers than in the United States.

Although tolerance contributes to the stability of a society by preventing conflict based upon religious differences, membership in religious groups often leads to diverse and potentially divisive attitudes and actions. In the United States, Gerhard Lenski has shown, there are both associational and communal dimensions to religion. Even though many people do not belong to a specific church or do not attend religious services frequently, they are often members of a community made up primarily of those with the same religious background, a fact that helps to shape their values, responses to others, and behavior. The four important "socioreligious" groups which Lenski found in his study of Detroit were White Protestants, Negro Protestants, Catholics, and Jews, among whom could be found consistent differences.

Depending on the socio-religious group to which a person belongs, the probabilities are increased or decreased that he will enjoy his occupation, indulge in installment buying, save to achieve objectives far in the future, believe in the American Dream, vote Republican, favor the welfare state, take a liberal view on the issue of freedom of speech, oppose racial integration in the schools, migrate to another community, maintain close ties with his family, develop a commitment to the principle of intellectual autonomy, have a large family, complete a given unit of education, or rise in the class system. These are only a few of the consequences which we have observed to be associated with differences in socio-religious group membership, and the position of individuals in these groups.[52]

The differences remain even when such other factors as class position are taken into account.

The importance of the religious community in the United States, however, lies not only in the extent to which it helps to shape the attitudes and values of its members, but also in the fact that it has emerged as "the primary context of self-identification and social location." [53] On the one hand, religion serves to separate Americans from one another by stimulating limited perspectives and parochial loyalties. On the other hand, the individual identifies himself as an American by belonging to a religious community—Protestant, Catholic, Jewish.

This latter function is closely linked to the transformation of the diverse ethnic groups that make up American society. Ethnic groups have undergone a gradual change, particularly in the second generation, as they shed their traditional cultural baggage and sought to become full-fledged Americans. In doing so, however, they tend to lose any significant group identification and to become isolated individuals in an impersonal urban and bureaucratized society. Faced with this problem, the third—and succeeding—generations have found in religion and membership in a religious community a solution. Religion was usually part of the ethnic culture and return to the church re-establishes continuity; by providing a link with the past it locates the individual in the present and provides a context for much of his social life. But the religious community now transcends ethnic boundaries. In a study of ethnic and religious intermarriage in New Haven, published in 1944, Ruby Jo Reeves Kennedy found that endogamy within ethnic groups was decreasing, although ethnic intermarriage tended to be within religious groups. Irish, Italian, and Polish Catholics were marrying one another, as were British, German, and Scandinavian Protestants.[54] Since religion is looked upon as a "good thing" in itself ("Our government makes no sense," President Eisenhower once remarked, "unless it is founded in a deeply felt religious faith—and I don't care what it is"), adherence to any religion identifies one as a proper American.[55]

Religious organization

The influence of any religion, its response to outside pressures, and its functions in society are substantially affected by the social structure of the religious community—by the relations between the individual and the organized religious group, the relations between priests or religious functionaries and laymen, and the organization of the priesthood or ministry itself. Catholicism, for example, exerts its influence upon society not only through the religious ideas shared by its communicants but also through the activities and authority of priests and the hierarchy.

The Catholic Church, however, represents only one of several types of religious organization. A basic distinction, drawn from the work of the German scholar Ernst Troeltsch, is that between the *church*, or *ecclesia*, as it is sometimes called, and the *sect*. Membership in the church—in this general classificatory sense—is automatic; people are born into it. In its extreme form the church encompasses all persons within a community or society, as the Roman Catholic Church sought to do in medieval Europe. In contrast, membership in the sect is voluntary and therefore more limited and exclusive. Because participation in a sect often represents a positive choice and newcomers must meet explicit requirements for membership—familiarity with the sect's doctrines, recommendation of members, or an intense religious experience (conversion)—the degree of religious fervor and commitment is likely to be greater than in the church.

Church and sect also differ in the extent to which they are organized. The sect characteristically possesses little formal organization; its leaders are often laymen or relatively untrained preachers who have received a "call" to spread the gospel. The church, on the other hand, usually has a more or less elaborate structure for providing religious leadership, with priests who may administer the sacraments, offer guidance and direction, and mediate between the believer and the divinity.

Because of its inclusive character and the requirements of order, stability, and predictability in any large-scale organization that wishes to survive and pursue its goals efficiently, the church must inevitably come to terms with the world around it, even if it seeks, or perhaps *because* it seeks, to dominate the society. The sect, because of the sources from which it often springs (see the discussion, pp. 361–2), its voluntary and exclusive character, and the ideas that animate it, is less likely to accept the world and its institutions, although it may seek to escape from the world rather than to change it.

These two types do not exhaust the variety of religious organization and other categories have been suggested. The *denomination,* for example, falls between the church and sect. It is a relatively stable group into which members are usually born, and it possesses a fairly well-developed formal organization. Unlike the ecclesia, it does not encompass all those who live within a given area, nor does it seek to dominate the society of which it is a part. The *cult* in some respects resembles the sect; membership is voluntary, and there is little formal organization. Participants simply share the same religious views. Unlike the sect, however, it imposes little or no discipline upon its members, whose connections with the group are often tenuous and transitory. The cult often appears among rootless urban groups or individuals who are seeking some solution to the problems of meaning in a complex and relatively disorganized social environment.

The lines between these various types are often difficult to draw, and the same group may shift from one type to another. Indeed, the contrast between church, denomination, and sect is often described in historical terms, for many religious movements begin as sects and gradually develop into more elaborate and formally organized religious groups. As Bryan Wilson has shown, however, whether sects eventually become denominations or retain their original character depends upon external circumstances and their specific doctrines and internal structure. Transformation of sects into denominations has occurred far more readily in American society with its blurred class lines, absence of tradition, and rapid rate of growth than in Britain, where class lines were sharper and traditions stronger and more pervasive. Sects whose central concern is with evangelism appear to be more likely to change than those that deny the existing social and religious order—the Jehovah's Witnesses, for example —or that emphasize mystical experience. Tendencies toward denominationalism are also less evident among sects that insist upon rigid criteria for membership and set themselves off from the rest of society by distinctive modes of behavior such as dress, as among the Mennonites, Hutterites, and Amish, or insistence upon group endogamy.[56]

Despite the difficulties in applying the

categories of church, denomination, sect, and cult to certain concrete historical cases, particularly while changes are taking place, these terms do call our attention to important variables in the organization of religious groups, particularly to the bases for membership, the relationship with the society as a whole, and the extent of formal organization within the religious community.

The nature of that formal organization, especially with respect to the location of authority and the role of the religious leader or functionary, varies widely from one group to another, but three general types of organization can be identified. In an *episcopal* structure, authority is hierarchically ordered, with final control over activities of both priests and laymen vested in a single supreme figure. The Roman Catholic Church provides the clearest example of such a structure, although the Anglican Church in England, as well as some Protestant denominations in the United States, is organized along similar lines. The priest or minister is appointed by his superiors in the church hierarchy and is therefore free to some extent from constraints imposed by his congregation, although he is subordinate to the policies and dictates of the hierarchy. Because of his relative freedom from local demands, he is able to exercise greater authority over the congregation than can the religious leader in more democratically organized churches.

The *presbyterian* type of church organization is dominated by a group of ministers or preachers who form a governing and controlling body. The leaders of the *presbytery*, the group of preachers, possess some power, but there is no supreme or final authority comparable to that of the Pope or even of the Primate of the Anglican Church in England. Local congregations also possess more power

than in the episcopal type of church, for they can request a particular preacher or can choose from among available candidates. The religious leader is therefore in some measure subordinate to the elders of his own congregation as well as to the presbytery to which he belongs. As Elizabeth Nottingham points out, however, presbyterian organization, by its emphasis upon the role of the preacher and by the "toughening pressures from both above and below," often produces dynamic and effective religious leaders— "among those who survive." [57]

In the *congregational* type of organization, authority rests in the local group, which chooses its own minister and plays an active role in church government. The religious leader here is very much at the mercy of his own congregation, which can discharge him whenever it chooses—limited only by the contract it may have signed. He must become a "democratic leader" rather than an authoritarian functionary capable of dictating to his followers.

In practice, of course, in all churches there is a continual interaction between authority from above and pressure from below. Ministers or preachers in congregational structures organize for cooperative purposes, and such a collective body and its leaders can exercise considerable influence among the members of the religious community. For example, in a study of the American Baptist Convention, one of twenty-seven Baptist groups in the United States, Paul Harrison shows how the problems of large-scale organization have affected the structure of power in a religious denomination that rejects any ecclesiastical authority. The Convention, with 1.5 million members, was formed to facilitate the missionary and educational activities of the associated churches. In order to carry on their duties, officials of the Convention require power that Baptist doctrine denies them. Informal devices to make possible efficient pursuit of the religious goals of the organization have therefore developed among those who hold official positions, without any manifest violation of doctrine. Moreover, the absence of formal, recognized authority within the Convention encourages the emergence of charismatic leaders who bring order to a confused situation by the force of their personal qualities.[58]

In a church in which there is a recognized, theologically sanctioned system of authority, the hierarchy, despite its power, cannot totally ignore the opinions and interests of subordinates and lay membership. In the Roman Catholic Church, for example, according to a statement by Pope Pius X in 1906, "The multitude has no other right than to let itself be led and to follow its shepherds as an obedient flock." [59] And a Catholic cardinal, in response to a question concerning the position of the layman in the Church, answered that, "He kneels before the altar . . . he sits below ˙ the pulpit . . . [and] puts his hand in his purse." [60] In fact, of course, relations within the Church are far more complex; the statement by Pius X reflected, according to a noted Catholic theologian, particular difficulties faced by the Church at that time.[61] In the past half-century, the problem of lay–clerical relations has led to the growth of a "theology of the laity," an attempt to define a positive role for laymen within the Church.[62] In the judgment of one American Catholic bishop, however, the relations between the hierarchy and the laity remain "the greatest weakness in the Church in America." [63]

By and large, the authority of the hierarchy is accepted by the faithful, except in those areas in which a line can be drawn between the sacred and the secular, between those actions that are explicitly defined as sinful and those whose propriety is left to the judgment of the individual. Becase the Church inevitably must exercise its discretion in applying religious rules and doctrines to concrete situations, it can—and often does—take into account the attitudes and inclinations of its lay membership. On occasion, of course, it may insist upon strict adherence to its judgments even in the face of resistance, as it has on occasion in introducing racial desegregation in Catholic schools in the American South. But on other occasions it has left open the way for disregard of priestly pronouncements. Thus members of the Catholic hierarchy disagreed on the religious import of political statements issued by the three bishops of Puerto Rico during the 1960 election campaign on that island.

Differences and cleavages within any religious organization are perhaps inevitable, for reasons to be found in the dynamics of organization, the roles and personalities of leaders, the ambiguities of religious doctrine, and the pressures of external forces. As Xavier Rynne (a pseudonymous reporter) has shown in his accounts of the sessions of the Vatican Council, the Roman Catholic Church, like any large-scale organization, is not free from internal politics, the pursuit of power, and the problems of adapting to the changing environment in which it functions. The recent reforms effected by the Council, with greater authority assigned to the Bishops, are part of the effort to enable the Church to deal more adequately with the complex problems of the modern world. The differences within the Church as to whether reforms were necessary and if so what form they should take stemmed from competing interests (the Roman Curia, the central administrative organ of the Church, seeking to maintain its power and other groups pursuing greater autonomy and influence), divergent attitudes toward and interpreta- tions of established doctrine, the immedi- ate problems of segments of the Church in different nations, and varying degrees of sensitivity to external pressures.[64]

Notes

[1] William James, *The Varieties of Religious Experience* (New York: Modern Library, n.d.; first published in 1902), pp. 31–2.

[2] A. C. Bouquet, *Comparative Religion* (3rd ed.; Harmondsworth: Penguin, 1950), p. 16.

[3] R. H. Codrington, "Melanesian Religion," in A. L. Kroeber and T. T. Waterman (eds.), *Source Book in Anthropology* (rev. ed.; New York: Harcourt, 1931), p. 414 *n*.

[4] William Robertson Smith, *Lectures on the Religion of the Semites* (London: Black, 1894), pp. 16–7, as quoted in Ralph G. Ross, *Symbols and Civilization* (New York: Harcourt, 1962), pp. 183–4.

[5] Émile Durkheim, *The Elementary Forms of the Religious Life*, trans. by Joseph Ward Swain (New York: Free Press, 1947; first published in translation in 1915), p. 37.

[6] *Ibid.*, p. 47.

[7] *Ibid.*, p. 69.

[8] *Ibid.*, p. 81.

[9] Max Weber, *From Max Weber: Essays in Sociology*, trans. and ed. by H. H. Gerth and C. Wright Mills (New York: Oxford, 1946), p. 271.

[10] Bronislaw Malinowski, *Magic, Science, and Religion and Other Essays* (Garden City: Doubleday Anchor Books, 1954), p. 71.

[11] *Ibid.*, p. 87.

[12] Robert K. Merton, *Social Theory and Social Structure* (rev. and enlarged edition; New York: Free Press, 1957), pp. 574–5.

[13] Joseph Fichter, "Marginal Catholics: An Institutional Approach," *Social Forces*, XXXII (December, 1953), 167–73.

[14] F. Boulard, *An Introduction to Religious Sociology* (London: Darton, 1960), Ch. 1, reprinted in Louis Schneider (ed.), *Religion, Culture and Society* (New York: Wiley, 1964), pp. 385–9.

[15] H. Richard Niebuhr, *The Social Sources of Denominationalism* (New York: Meridian, 1957; first published in 1929), p. 13.

[16] *The Journal of John Wesley*, I (London: Dent, 1930), 186, entry for April 17, 1739.

[17] Liston Pope, *Millhands and Preachers* (New Haven: Yale University Press, 1942), pp. 130–3.

[18] *Ibid.*, p. 137.

[19] Brian Wilson, *Sects and Society* (London: Heinemann, 1961), p. 317.

[20] Bernard Barber, "Acculturation and Messianic Movements," *American Sociological Review*, VI (October, 1941), 663–9.

[21] Preserved Smith, *The Age of the Reformation* (New York: Holt, 1920), pp. 65–7.

[22] *Ibid.*, p. 100.

[23] Niebuhr, *op. cit.*, p. 73.

[24] Smith, *op. cit.*, p. 62.

[25] Niebuhr, *op. cit.*, p. 3.

[26] The following summary is drawn chiefly from Pope, *op. cit.*, pp. 117–24.

[27] Quoted in E. M. W. Tillyard, *The Elizabethan World Picture* (London: Chatto & Windus, 1948), pp. 90–1.

[28] Quoted in George H. Sabine, *A History of Political Theory* (New York: Holt, 1937), p. 395.

[29] Max Weber, *The Protestant Ethic and the Spirit of Capitalism*, trans. by Talcott Parsons (New York: Scribner, 1930).

[30] See Richard H. Tawney, *Religion and the Rise of Capitalism* (New York: Harcourt, 1926).

[31] Max Weber, *The Religion of China: Confucianism and Taoism*, trans. by H. H. Gerth (New York: Free Press, 1951); Max Weber, *Ancient Judaism*, trans. by H. H. Gerth and Don Martindale (New York: Free Press, 1952); and Max Weber, *The Religion of India: The Sociology of Hinduism and Buddhism*, trans. by H. H. Gerth and Don Martindale (New York: Free Press, 1958).

[32] Robert N. Bellah, *Tokugawa Religion* (New York: Free Press, 1957), p. 194.

[33] See Robert N. Bellah (ed.), *Religion and Progress in Modern Asia* (New York: Free Press, 1965). This book contains an excellent bibliography.

[34] Quoted in Weber, *The Protestant Ethic*, p. 175.

[35] Quoted in Marquis W. Childs and Douglass Cater, *Ethics in a Business Society* (New York: New American Library Mentor Books, 1954), p. 137.

[36] See Tawney, *op. cit.*, Ch. 5.

[37] From the papal encyclical *Quanta Cura* that accompanied the *Syllabus of Errors*, issued by Pope Pius IX in 1864. Anne Fremantle, *The Papal Encyclicals in Their Historical Context* (New York: New American Library Mentor Books, 1956), p. 141. This statement was taken by the Pope from a pronouncement by one of his predecessors as Supreme Pontiff.

[38] See J. Lloyd Mecham, *Church and State in Latin America* (Chapel Hill: University of North Carolina Press, 1943), especially Ch. 2, "The Catholic Church and the Spanish-American Revolution."

[39] Fremantle, *op. cit.*, p. 152.

[40] See A. F. Carrillo de Albornoz, *Roman Catholicism and Religious Liberty* (Geneva: World Council of Churches, 1959).

[41] Edward Wakin and Joseph F. Scheuer, *The De-Romanization of the American Catholic Church* (New York: Macmillan, 1966), p. 50.

[42] John Rock, *The Time Has Come* (New York: Knopf, 1963).

[43] Wakin and Scheuer, *op. cit.*, pp. 31–3.

[44] *Ibid.*, Chs. 10, 12, 13 14.

[45] Will Herberg, *Protestant–Catholic–Jew* (Garden City: Doubleday, 1956), p. 181, n. 29, and sources cited therein.

[46] Joseph M. Duffy, Jr., "Clergy and Laity," in *Catholicism in America* (New York: Harcourt, 1953), p. 66.

[47] Herberg, *op. cit.*, p. 163.

[48] Quoted in John Tracy Ellis, *American Catholicism* (Chicago: University of Chicago Press, 1956), pp. 142–3.

[49] Wakin and Scheuer, *op. cit.*, p. 291.

[50] U.S. Bureau of the Census, *Statistical Abstract of the United States*, (84th ed.; Washington: U.S. Government Printing Office, 1963), Table 46, pp. 46–7.

[51] For a fuller discussion, see Robin Williams, *American Society* (rev. ed.; New York: Knopf, 1960), Ch. 9.

[52] Gerhard Lenski *The Religious Factor* (rev. ed.; Garden City: Doubleday Anchor Books, 1963), p. 320.

[53] Herberg, *op. cit.*, p. 47. The following analysis is derived chiefly from Herberg.

[54] Ruby Jo Reeves Kennedy, "Single or Triple Melting Pot? Intermarriage Trends in New Haven, 1870–1940," *American Journal of Sociology*, XLIX (January, 1944), 331–9.

[55] Herberg, *op. cit.*, p. 97.

[56] Bryan R. Wilson, "An analysis of Sect Development," *American Sociological Review*, XXIV (February, 1959), 3–15.

[57] Elizabeth Nottingham, *Religion and Society* (New York: Random House, 1954), p. 68.

[58] Paul M. Harrison, *Authority and Power in the Free Church Tradition* (Princeton: Princeton University Press, 1959).

[59] Quoted in Yves M. J. Congar, *Lay People in the Church*, trans. by Donald Attwater (London: Bloomsbury, 1957), p. 250 *n.*

[60] *Ibid.*, p. xxiii.

[61] *Ibid.*, p. 250.

[62] Father Congar's book represents a major contribution to that effort.

[63] Robert J. Dwyer, "The American Laity," *Commonweal*, LX (August 27, 1954), 506.

[64] Xavier Rynne (pseud.), *Letters from Vatican City* (New York: Farrar, 1963);

Xavier Rynne, *The Second Session* (New York: Farrar, 1964); Xavier Rynne, *The Third Session* (New York: Farrar, 1965); and Xavier Rynne, *The Fourth Session* (New York: Farrar, 1966).

Suggestions for further reading

BELLAH, ROBERT N. *Tokugawa Religion.* New York: Free Press, 1957.
An able assessment of the relevance of religion for the industrialization of Japan.

CLARK, S. D. *Church and Sect in Canada.* Toronto: University of Toronto Press, 1948.
A careful sociological and historical account of Protestant religious movements in Canada.

DURKHEIM, ÉMILE. *The Elementary Forms of the Religious Life.* Trans. by Joseph Ward Swain. New York: Free Press, 1947. First published in translation, 1915.
A classic and influential essay in the sociology of religion that tries to identify the essential elements of religion by a close study of religious ideas and behavior among Australian aborigines.

FAUSET, ARTHUR. *Black Gods of the Metropolis.* Philadelphia: University of Pennsylvania Press, 1944, Vol. III of Publications of Philadelphia Anthropological Society.
An interesting study of religious cults among urban Negroes.

FICHTER, JOSEPH. *Social Relations in an Urban Parish.* Chicago: University of Chicago Press, 1954.
A close study of religious behavior and social relations among Catholics in a southern urban area by a Catholic priest and sociologist.

FINKELSTEIN, LOUIS. *The Pharisees: The Sociological Background of Their Faith.* 2 vols. Philadelphia: Jewish Publication Society, 1938.
An effort by a noted Jewish theologian to show the relationship between the religious ideas of the Pharisees in pre-

Christian Palestine and their social institutions.

GLAZER, NATHAN. *American Judaism.* Chicago: University of Chicago Press, 1957.
A sociologically sophisticated historical account of the evolution of Judaism in the United States.

GOODE, WILLIAM J. *Religion Among the Primitives.* New York: Free Press. 1951.
A thorough analysis of the role of religion in primitive society.

HERBERG, WILL. *Protestant–Catholic–Jew.* Garden City: Doubleday, 1955.
An interpretation of the state of religion in contemporary American society.

LENSKI, GERHARD. *The Religious Factor.* Garden City: Doubleday Anchor Books, 1963.
An intensive study of the influence of religion on daily activities among Protestants, Catholics, and Jews.

MALINOWSKI, BRONISLAW. *Magic, Science and Religion and Other Essays.* Garden City: Doubleday Anchor Books, 1954.
The title essay is a classic analysis of the differences among religion, magic, and science and of their relations to persistent aspects of human life.

MECHAM, J. LLOYD. *Church and State in Latin America.* Chapel Hill: University of North Carolina Press, 1934.
A comprehensive history of the role of the Roman Catholic Church in Latin America.

NIEBUHR, H. RICHARD. *The Social Sources of Denominationalism.* New York: Meridian, 1957. First published, 1929.
An important sociological study of the

sources of division within Christianity written by a noted theologian who sees the perennial problem of religion as the relationship between transcendental doctrine and the necessities of organizing a religious community.

NOTTINGHAM, ELIZABETH. *Religion and Society.* New York: Random House, 1954. *A brief summary statement of the major dimensions of the sociology of religion.*

POPE, LISTON. *Millhands and Preachers.* New Haven: Yale University Press, 1942. *A study of religion in a southern mill town that throws a great deal of light on the nature of religious sects and their relationship to economic institutions.*

SCHNEIDER, LOUIS (ed.). *Religion, Culture and Society.* New York: Wiley, 1964. *An excellent collection of essays on the sociology of religion.*

SKLARE, MARSHALL. *Conservative Judaism.* New York: Free Press, 1955. *A sociological account of the emergence of a movement that represents an effort to adapt a traditional religion to modern American society.*

TAWNEY, RICHARD H. *Religion and the Rise of Capitalism.* New York: Harcourt, 1926. Reprinted by Pelican, 1947. *A detailed study of the development of Protestant thinking on economic issues. An essential complement to Weber's study of the relations between capitalism and Protestantism.*

WAKIN, EDWARD, and JOSEPH F. SCHEUER. *The De-Romanization of the American Catholic Church.* New York: Macmillan, 1966. *A challenging, sometimes controversial, analysis of tensions, problems, and trends in the Roman Catholic Church in the United States.*

WEBER, MAX. *The Protestant Ethic and the Spirit of Capitalism.* Trans. by Talcott Parsons. New York: Scribner, 1930. *The classic essay that initiated the persisting discussion of the relations between capitalism and Protestantism. The comparative studies that were part of Weber's ambitious effort to explore the relations between religion and economic life include* The Religion of China: Confucianism and Taoism, *trans. by H. H. Gerth, New York: Free Press, 1951;* Ancient Judaism, *trans. by H. H. Gerth and Don Martindale, New York: Free Press, 1952: and* The Religion of India: The Sociology of Hinduism and Buddhism, *trans. by H. H. Gerth and Don Martindale, New York: Free Press, 1958.*

WILSON, BRIAN. *Sects and Society.* London: Heinemann, 1961. *A detailed analysis of three small religious groups in Britain—the Elim Foursquare Gospel Church, the Christadelphians, and the Christian Scientists.*

YINGER, J. MILTON. *Religion, Society and the Individual.* New York: Macmillan, 1957. *An excellent textbook that also includes a good selection of readings and an extensive bibliography.*

15

Education

Education in modern society: some general perspectives

Throughout the greater part of human history, most people have gained the knowledge and skills they needed and acquired the values and perspectives of their society without benefit of formal education. As long as there was little role differentiation and most children simply followed in the footsteps of their parents, there was little need for special training. By repeated efforts to imitate elders and through trial and error, often under some watchful eye, the child learned to perform those tasks that would be required of him as an adult. Social norms, traditional beliefs and customs, and moral standards were unconsciously absorbed in the course of daily life, sometimes supplemented by explicit instruction or, as on ritual occasions in some primitive societies, revealed as "secrets" to young men or women gaining entry to adult status. Working at his father's side, the farmer's son, for example, learned to cultivate the land and to understand, within the limits of available knowledge, the needs of the soil, the vagaries of the weather, the behavior of animals. Where specialized crafts were practiced—ironworking, carpentry, boatmaking, goldsmithing—they were usually passed on from father to son; if these skills were not hereditary, they were learned through some form of apprenticeship in which the craftsman instructed a young man, perhaps even pro-

viding him with food, shelter, and clothing in return for several years of service.

In many parts of the world these methods for training the young have been supplemented, in some instances almost replaced, by a system of education specifically designed to inculcate knowledge, skills, and values. Formal education may now begin with nursery school or kindergarten and end with advanced postgraduate training, taking up a substantial proportion of an individual's entire life span. Education, of course, in its widest sense, is not confined to the classroom, nor, as familiar cliches remind us, does it end when formal schooling is completed. It is part of the complex process of socialization that transforms the infant into a social being capable of participating in the life of society and continues as long as he must learn to adapt to new circumstances and to play new roles (see Chapter 4).

Although the school is but one of the agencies that socialize the individual, it has become a dominant feature of modern society. So important is education today—for both advanced and underdeveloped areas—and so far-reaching are its functions that in many countries educational policy is a matter of national concern and frequently a pressing political issue.

Until modern times, when universal literacy became both goal and reality in many nations, formal education was characteristically limited to those of high status. In ancient Greece, a society that rested upon slavery, literacy was confined largely to freemen, and Plato's Academy and Aristotle's Lyceum were relatively small. The monastic schools of the middle ages were established to teach the clergy, although they also instructed some lay pupils, chiefly children of noble birth or from the embryonic middle class. The early English "public schools" such as Winchester, Eton, Rugby, and Harrow were intended for a select group of students; despite the changes that have occurred in the centuries since their founding, they—and a considerable number of other independent boarding schools established in the nineteenth century—have continued to serve as a training ground for an elite drawn chiefly from the upper ranks of society.[1]

Although elementary education became more and more prevalent during the nineteenth century, higher education was limited to a small, select group drawn chiefly from the middle and upper classes. In England, universities were very largely the "preserves of the aristocratic and gentry classes";[2] as recently as 1938–1939 there were only 50,000 university students in Great Britain. Prior to the American Civil War, Richard Hofstadter and C. DeWitt Hardy point out, college education in the United States was primarily for "gentlemen."[3] By and large, education that went beyond the elementary level was designed to prepare some men for the learned professions—law, the ministry, medicine—and to provide the cultivation deemed necessary or appropriate for the higher ranks. As Peter Drucker observes:

Until the twentieth century, no society could afford more than a handful of educated people; for throughout the ages to be educated meant to be unproductive. . . . It has always been axiomatic that the man of even a little education would forsake the hoe and the potter's wheel and would stop working with his hands. After all, our word "school"—and its equivalent in all European languages—derives from a Greek word meaning "leisure."[4]

Formal schooling remains, in the economically underdeveloped parts of the world, largely the privilege of the well-to-do, and even in nations with universal literacy higher education is still linked to some degree with high status—as both cause and consequence. Yet by the early 1960s, over one-seventh of the world's population was attending school. In the United States, where the proportion who go on to higher education is greater than in any other country, more than 50 million people, over a quarter of the entire population and almost three-quarters of those between the ages of five and twenty-four, were students. In England, France, Germany, and the Soviet Union, roughly one-fifth of the population was enrolled in some kind of school, in Belgium two-thirds of those between five and twenty-five, and in Japan three-fifths of that age group. By 1962, one-eighth of the Asian population and just under one-tenth of the African were in school.[5]

The expansion of education

Everywhere, in both advanced and developing nations, the numbers going to school have increased substantially in the years following World War II. Between 1957–1958 and 1961–1962, for example, the total number of students in the world grew by 23 per cent, more than twice as rapidly as the entire population; in areas that previously had only limited educational facilities the expansion was greater than elsewhere (33 per cent in Asia and 28 per cent in Africa).[6] The 1966

Table 21

GROWTH OF HIGHER EDUCATION IN SELECTED COUNTRIES, 1930–1962

Year	Egypt		France		Japan		Great Britain	
	Average annual enroll-ment	Number of students per 100,000 population	Average annual enroll-ment	Number of students per 100,000 population	Average annual enroll-ment	Number of students per 100,000 population	Total enrollment in full-time higher education	Percentage of age group seek-ing full-time higher education
1930–1934	9,000	58	83,000	201	171,000	260	(1924) 61,000	2.7
1935–1939	9,000	59	71,000	172	184,000	263	(1938) 69,000	2.7
1940–1944	12,000	69	92,000	237	297,000	410	*	*
1945–1949	22,000	116	129,000	319	416,000	539	*	*
1950–1954	47,000	219	147,000	348	469,000	549	(1954) 122,000	5.8
1955–1959	82,000	340	180,000	409	624,000	687	(1960) *	8.3
1961–1962	115,000	*	219,000 (1960–1961)	*	757,000	*	(1962) 216,000	8.5

* Not available.

Data for Egypt, France, and Japan from *World Survey of Education*, IV (New York: UNESCO, 1966), 479, 699, 1160; for Great Britain from Committee on Higher Education, *Higher Education* (The Robbins Report) (London: Her Majesty's Stationery Office, 1963), pp. 15, 16.

UNESCO World Survey of Education concluded that the increase in enrollment

will continue as long as developing countries maintain their drive towards the generalization of primary education, by providing school places for an ever larger proportion of their children. And in countries which have achieved compulsory education there is an evident trend for children to stay longer at school. Practically all countries show a major concern to expand facilities at the second and third levels of education in order to form greater numbers of qualified people and to raise the average level of education of their people.[7]

Table 21 shows the growth of higher education since 1930 in countries as different as Egypt, France, Great Britain, and Japan, revealing clearly an increase not only in absolute numbers but also in the proportion of people who are obtaining advanced training. The dramatic expansion of secondary schooling and in college and university enrollment in the United States since World War II is shown in Table 22. Between 1947 and 1963, the number of high school students

and the college and university population doubled, reflecting both the over-all increase in population and the expanding proportion of young people who graduate from high school and continue on into higher education.

The "educational revolution" of the mid-twentieth century represents the acceleration and spread of trends under way for some time in Europe and America. The diffusion of literacy, the growth in the number and size of schools, colleges, and universities, and substantial changes in the content and methods of education were closely linked with the development of modern industry and the social changes that accompanied it. By separating home and workplace and increasing the rate of both social and geographic mobility, industrialization limited the ability of the family to prepare children to earn their livelihood. Life in an urban setting and in modern industry came to require at least the basic skills of reading, writing, and arithmetic, while increased

Table 22

ENROLLMENT IN SECONDARY SCHOOLS AND INSTITUTIONS OF HIGHER EDUCATION IN
THE UNITED STATES, 1947–1964

School year *	Secondary education		Higher education		
	Enrollment, grades 9–12 and postgraduate	Number enrolled per 100 persons 14–17 years of age	First-time enrollment	Total enrollment	Number enrolled per 100 persons 18–21 years of age
1947–1948	6,305,168	71.3	—	2,338,226	25.2
1949–1950	6,453,009	76.8	557,856	2,444,900	27.2
1951–1952	6,596,351	77.5	472,025	2,101,962	24.0
1953–1954	7,108,973	80.2	571,533	2,231,054	26.4
1955–1956	7,774,975	84.4	675,060	2,653,034	31.2
1957–1958	8,869,186	87.5	729,725	3,036,938	34.3
1959–1960	9,599,810	86.1	826,969	3,364,861	36.6
1961–1962	10,768,972	89.7	1,026,087	3,860,643	37.7
1963–1964	12,600,000 †	93.5	2,055,146	4,494,626	40.4
1964	—	—	1,234,806	4,950,173	43.9

* For higher education, enrollment is at the beginning of the academic year.
† Preliminary figure.

U.S. Department of Health, Education and Welfare, *Digest of Educational Statistics, 1965* (Washington, D.C.: U.S. Government Printing Office, 1965), Table 7, p. 14; Tables 51, 52, p. 76.

specialization and the knowledge upon which it rested demanded training that few if any parents could provide.

Educational expansion and change were generated not only by economic needs, however, but also by changes taking place in politics and government. The extension of citizenship stimulated the desire for learning among those groups who saw in it a basic prerequisite for effective political participation, as well as an important means of economic and social betterment. In the 1830s a group of Philadelphia workingmen declared:

The original element of despotism is a monopoly of talent which consigns the multitude to comparative ignorance and secures the balance of knowledge on the side of the rich and the rulers. . . . the means of equal knowledge (the only security for equal liberty) should be rendered, by legal provision, the common property of all classes.[8]

In a complex, multigroup society, universal education also was recognized as a useful instrument of social and political stability. "A set of good schools civilizes a whole neighborhood," remarked a British Royal Commission on education in 1858.[9] No other institutions could transmit as readily or efficiently the values and symbols, the attitudes and knowledge upon which political unity rested.

The extension of education, however, and changes to meet new or emerging needs did not always come about easily, or without strenuous opposition. Hannah More, an English novelist of the early nineteenth century, for example, would "allow no writing for the poor," while others felt that learning the catechism was enough for them.[10] In the United States

the public school idea was fought by social, political, and economic conservatives of all classes, by industrial and business interests that included large taxpayers, by the southern aristocrats, and by certain religious and non-English speaking groups who saw a threat to their private control of religious and foreign-language schools.[11]

Only gradually did a number of groups—middle-class humanitarians, labor organizations, reformers of various kinds, and practical men who saw the economic and political uses of education—manage to extend opportunities for schooling and introduce innovations of various kinds into the curriculum and the methods of teaching.

In the modern world there is now widespread agreement that education has become a major source of economic progress, a conclusion that has contributed heavily to the substantial growth of secondary schools, colleges, and universities. They are now expected to satisfy an increasing demand for the highly trained manpower needed by a complex technology, elaborate bureaucratic structures, and an extensive array of agencies providing professional services. Simultaneously, they are called upon to contribute to the expanding body of knowledge upon which economic growth has come to rest.

For the developing nations, education has been defined as "the key that unlocks the door to modernization."[12] Both the state and the economy require a more literate population and, perhaps more significantly, a well-trained group of executives, administrators, and professionals who are capable of running the government and introducing modern methods and techniques.

Everywhere, however, the development of educational institutions has been substantially influenced by local traditions, experience, and social structure. Dominated by elitist values that were linked

In their efforts to modernize, the "underdeveloped" nations are now committing considerable shares of their resources to education. TOP: *A second-grade music class in Thailand. "I'm a little teapot" reflects the teacher's American schooling.* BOTTOM: *Veterinary students at Ibadan University, West Nigeria, where, as in other similar countries, there is a great need for professionally trained manpower.*

Gross from Monkmeyer

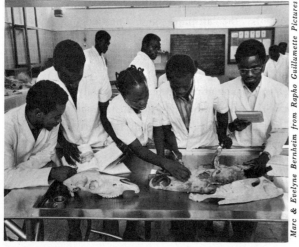

Marc & Evelyne Bernheim from Rapho Guillumette Pictures

with clear-cut class distinctions, Great Britain, France, and Germany established "two-track" systems of education, one for the common people, the other for those, drawn chiefly from the middle and upper classes, destined for high status. (Pressures from below and the needs of modern society have already affected the schools and universities of these nations, and still more changes are likely to occur in the future.) In France and Germany, both highly centralized states, control of education has resided in a central bureaucracy which has dictated curricula, set standards, chosen teachers, and established the operating rules. In England, the diverse forces—religious and secular, private and public—which contended during the nineteenth century produced a complex structure of publicly and privately supported schools; although the universities now derive much of their support from the state, they are relatively free of direct controls. [13]

The open class structure and egalitarian ethos of the United States have contributed to an educational system with few distinctions between schools for the "elite" and those for the rest of society. Despite the presence of influential private schools and colleges, public education has on the whole remained dominant in a decentralized structure shaped by the division of powers among Federal, state, and local governments. Responding to practical demands and a pragmatic point of view, American schools have been far more willing to try new methods and develop new programs and they have been much more student-oriented and more concerned with the social uses of education than their European counterparts.

In many developing areas, educational institutions reveal clearly the influence of the once dominant colonial powers. Schools and universities in French-speaking Africa follow French models, whereas the influence of English education upon the areas once dominated by Great Britain is readily apparent. When aid and advice is needed, the new governments in Asia and Africa have characteristically turned to their former rulers from whose schools and universities so many of their leaders have come.

The social functions of education

The social functions of education, of course, are not confined to the uses that have stimulated the growth of schools, colleges, and universities. The consequences of education are often unanticipated and sometimes unwanted. By educating a local elite in colonial territories, European powers discovered, for example, that they had created the leadership for independence movements. Universal literacy, once thought essential for the institutions of democracy and the uses of reason, can, as the experience of recent decades has shown, render a nation susceptible to mass manipulation and dictatorship.

Whatever its impact in a particular setting, education does serve important general functions. For society as a whole, it provides for the preservation and transmission of culture. It is, Émile Durkheim observed, "above all the means by which society perpetually recreates the conditions of its very existence." [14] By passing on from one generation to another established beliefs, knowledge, values, and skills, it contributes to continuity and the persistence of an organized social life.

Other institutions, to be sure, perform the same function—the family, sometimes the church (which has frequently tried to control education), now the mass media.

But the schools, more than any other agency, are expressly organized to familiarize children with their cultural heritage. Moreover, with increased cultural complexity, schools have taken over—or have been expressly assigned—the major, or even total, responsibility for communicating certain types of knowledge and skill. With few exceptions, most people now learn to read, write, and calculate in school; there, too, they become familiar with common symbols, national traditions, and at least part of the stock of reliable knowledge.

At advanced levels, schools and colleges have become "custodians of the intellectual capital of mankind." [15] In the past, literature, the arts, science, philosophy, history, and other specialized bodies of knowledge were sustained by individuals and groups in diverse settings—courts, the church, voluntary associations, urban Bohemias, private circles, as well as in the few formal schools and universities in existence. Although colleges and universities have no monopoly of ideas, they have increasingly become the locale within which much of the concern with "culture," in its more limited meaning, is contained. Those who now pursue artistic or intellectual efforts, in any social context, have usually attended a college or university, and they are likely to continue to maintain close connections with the world of higher education.

With the continuing increase in knowledge, the university has also become a major source of new ideas as well as a conservator and transmitter of the old. Scholars and scientists are expected to engage in "research," to push forward the "frontiers of knowledge," as well as educate their students, and their efforts are encouraged and supported by outside sources such as government, industry, and private foundations, as well as by the university itself. Indeed the university is increasingly becoming part of the "knowledge industry," a major component of a society based upon modern technology and dominated by large and complex organizations. [16]

By virtue of what is taught, the qualities of mind and character that are stressed, and the range and type of innovation that is encouraged or allowed, education can influence other institutions, values, and social structure in manifold ways. English universities, for example, have sustained the British tradition of the "amateur" who is ready and able to assume leadership and responsibility in government or business by confining its carefully selected students to traditional disciplines. Only slowly and reluctantly have they accepted innovations which will provide an education designed expressly to prepare students for the complex and often specialized tasks they will be called upon to perform.

Despite the considerable diversity among American schools, colleges, and universities, education in the United States contributes significantly to the strengthening of "liberal" attitudes and the extension of "cultural" interests.

A growing body of evidence indicates that education leads toward tolerant and humanitarian attitudes. Consistently it has been shown that the higher the level of educational attainment, the greater the degree to which "democratic" attitudes are held. Similarly, education is a prime correlate of interest in politics and of cultural awareness or sophistication. College graduates are more tolerant than high-school graduates in their attitudes toward ethnic and racial groups; they are more supportive of democratic norms such as having a multiparty system; they listen more to serious programs and read more magazines. High-school graduates, in turn, are more tolerant and more involved culturally and politically than are those with only grammar-school education. Level of education is related in this way even when the influence of age, occupation, and income is "controlled" or ruled out.[17]

An increase in the number and proportion of high-school and college graduates might therefore be expected to encourage tolerance of minorities, strengthen support for civil liberties, increase political interest, and enlarge the audience for art, music, drama, and literature.

In many respects, however, education fosters differences rather than uniformity. Because of the decentralized structure of education in the United States, there are wide variations in what is taught, how it is taught, and what educational objectives are pursued. Although formulated in large part by professional educators (who often disagree among themselves), educational policy is subject in varying degrees to outside influences—elected boards of education in each community; appointed regents or trustees in state universities; trustees in private schools, colleges, and universities (sometimes elected by alumni, more often chosen by a self-perpetuating body); religious groups in denominational schools and colleges. All of those engaged in defining educational policy and programs are affected by the shifting currents of public opinion and public interest and are necessarily sensitive to the concerns of those particular groups who constitute their clientele or constituents.

What is done in the schools and colleges, therefore, reflects the views and interests of the educators, policy-making bodies such as trustees and boards of education, and those social groups to whom they are all to some degree responsive. While denominational schools and colleges emphasize religion, public institutions necessarily avoid it (although the Supreme Court decision prohibiting prayers generated considerable controversy). Some schools, both public and private, emphasize "progressive education," which, David Riesman has suggested, leads to more concern "with the child's social and psychological adjustment than with his academic progress," a greater effort to mold adaptable personalities than to transmit knowledge. [18] Others, particularly in upper-middle-class suburbs where parents place great value upon education and hope to see their children gain admission into "good" colleges, now emphasize more strongly the academic aspects of both elementary and secondary education.

Schools have varied widely in their receptivity to curricular innovation. Some have willingly and eagerly introduced courses in driving, sex education, consumer education, the use of cosmetics. Here and there local groups which feel that the schools should eschew modern "frills" and stick to the "three Rs" and emphasize traditional values—free enterprise, patriotism and nationalism, obedience to authority—have been able to influence policy and programs. In 1962, for example, the voters of California chose as the State Superintendent of Public Instruction a staunch advocate of traditional methods and subjects.

Much of the diversity, however, particularly in the colleges and universities, results from the fact that American education has increasingly taken over the responsibility of training men and women for a wide variety of roles: farmers and foresters, police administrators and hotel executives, accountants and business managers, social workers and home economists. As new fields of specialization have emerged, academic programs have been designed to prepare men and women for them.

Writing in 1949, a distinguished economist, Seymour Harris, expressed concern over a possible future surplus of college graduates. If there were 4.6 million college students in 1960, a goal recommended by a President's Commission on Higher Education, he argued, there would be "severe excesses of graduates . . . in the proprietor-managerial occupations, and professional openings would not be one-half of those required." [19] In 1964 there were almost 5 million students in higher education, and Harris's fears had proved to be groundless. Indeed, in many fields there were shortages of qualified personnel and the expansion of higher education was continuing.

In the United States, as in other industrial countries, education, as we noted earlier, must now provide the growing numbers of well-trained men and women needed to keep the society functioning. "Education is becoming so fused with occupations," Burton R. Clark has observed, "that it may be seen as part of the economic foundations of society." [20] There has been a substantial increase not only in the number of professionals and in the demand for people with Ph.D. degrees, but also in the number of technical and managerial jobs which require college education. Even entry to apprentice training now requires a high-school diploma, as do the large number of low-level white-collar tasks.

Education, life chances, and social structure

Education has therefore become a central determinant of the individual's "life chances," that is, his opportunities for employment, earnings, and status. In 1960, for example, 77 per cent of white males with college degrees were professionals or managers, compared with only 21 per cent of high school graduates and 9 per cent of those who had completed high school. (For Negroes, education was somewhat less helpful; 72 per cent of male college graduates were professionals or managers, only 7 per cent of those with high school diplomas, and 3 per cent of those with elementary school training.) [21] Access to higher ranks is increasingly related to higher education, as evident in the backgrounds of business leaders. In 1928, according to one study, 32 per cent of business leaders were college graduates, compared with 77 per cent of the business leaders who were studied in 1952. [22] (In the Soviet Union, David Granick reports, education is even more important than in the United States: "a college education is virtually an absolute requirement for a candidate for an industrial management post.") [23]

Income, too, is closely related to the amount of formal education one has. Both annual earnings and estimated lifetime income increase with each additional year of schooling, with the greatest gains coming from college attendance (see Table 23). To some degree, these differences simply reflect the earning power of various occupations, access to which, as we have seen, is related to education. But even within each occupation—among carpenters, bricklayers, truckdrivers, and factory workers, as well as among business men and white-collar workers—the longer the time spent in school, the higher the income. In 1959, for example, carpenters with a high school diploma averaged about $900 more per year than those who had graduated from elementary school. The difference among bus drivers was $1,000, among painters $700, and among office machine operators $600. [24]

Clearly, then, access to education is one of the important keys to opportunity, and it is available not only for those in the middle and upper classes, but also for many others who use it as the basis for

Table 23

EDUCATION AND LIFETIME EARNINGS
(FROM AGE 18 TO 64): MEN

Highest grade completed	Earnings
All education groups	$229,000
Elementary school	
Less than 8 years	143,000
8 years	184,000
High school	
1 to 3 years	212,000
4 years	247,000
College	
1 to 3 years	293,000
4 years	384,000
5 years or more	455,000

Herman P. Miller, *Rich Man, Poor Man*, p. 148 (Copyright © 1964 by Thomas Y. Crowell Company, New York, publishers). Reprinted by permission of Thomas Y. Crowell Company.

economic and social advancement. Primary and secondary education is free, and financial aid is often available for college students who lack the necessary financial resources. Moreover, unlike other nations, American society encourages and even admires the youth who "works his way through college."

While thus contributing to social mobility educational institutions in the United States—as in most nations—serve nevertheless in various ways to sustain and reinforce existing social differentials. Both the quality of schooling and the length of time spent in school are related to race and class; whites and those in the middle and upper classes receive, on the whole, a better education, and they stay in school longer. A nationwide study of the extent of inequality in education published in 1966 found that in the public schools

Negro pupils have fewer of some of the facilities most related to academic achievement: They have less access to physics, chemistry, and language laboratories; there are fewer books per pupil in their libraries; their textbooks are less often in sufficient supply. . . . Secondary school Negroes are less likely to attend schools that are regionally accredited . . . Negro and Puerto Rican pupils have less access to college preparatory curriculums and to accelerated curriculums . . . white students in general have more access to a more fully developed program of extracurricular activities, in particular those which might be related to academic matters (debate teams, for example, and student newspapers). . . . The average Negro pupil attends a school where a greater percentage of teachers appear to be somewhat less able . . . than those in the schools attended by the average white student.[25]

These differences reflect to some degree the fact that a much larger proportion of Negroes than of whites live in urban slums and in the poorer rural areas, particularly in the South; in both areas there remains a great deal of de facto segregation, often with inferior facilities, despite the efforts made since the Supreme Court desegregation decision in 1954. Even at the college level, Negroes find less adequate schooling; the predominantly Negro colleges which more than half of all Negro college students attend are on the whole inferior to others in physical facilities, the character of the curriculum, and the academic qualifications of the faculties.

The relationship between the quality of schools and academic achievement, however, is complex. In their nationwide study of educational opportunity, James S. Coleman and his colleagues found that differences in facilities and in curriculum accounted for little of the variation in performance on standardized tests among white children, but had considerable effect on Negro children. White children of the same social and economic status, that is, did almost equally well even under varying conditions in the schools, while Negro children did considerably better when the quality of the school improved. The training and capabilities of teachers had somewhat more importance, for both whites and Negroes; the better prepared the teachers, the better the performance of their students. Moreover, the impact of the teacher increased in the higher grades.[26] Of particular interest, too, is the finding that at each social and economic level the performance of Negroes improved as the number of whites in their classes increased; moreover, the earlier in their academic careers Negroes found themselves in integrated classes, the better their test scores.[27]

Although perhaps less clearly evident than differences between white and Negro, there are also significant variations in the educational opportunities available to each class—white as well as Negro. For the upper-middle and upper classes, private schools provide an education designed to assure admission to college—preferably an "elite" college—as well as to prepare students for what is conventionally viewed as an appropriate style of life.[28] In many upper-middle-class suburbs, public schools perform the same functions, and all but an almost insignificant minority do go on to college. In schools with socially mixed student bodies, social and economic status often enter, albeit in subtle fashion, into judgments of academic ability, academic or vocational counseling, and even on occasion into the treatment of students by teachers. Characteristically of middle-class background, or upwardly mobile from the working class, teachers tend to look more favorably upon the youth who conforms to middle-class cultural expectations. The able lower-class youth may therefore be overlooked, and he is less likely to be encouraged to continue his studies than are middle-class boys and girls of similar capabilities.

The relevance of both class and race can be seen in the data on academic dropouts and college attendance. In 1965, for example, 17 per cent of Negro adolescents sixteen and seventeen years old had left school without receiving a high school diploma, compared with only 9 per cent of whites. (The differences were chiefly in the North and West, where most Negroes are in urban ghettoes; there were no appreciable differences by race in the South.) Among middle-class Negroes, however, the proportion who drop out is only slightly higher than among whites, and the difference is cut in half when working-class Negroes are compared with working-class whites.[29]

The proportion of young people who enter college has risen steadily in the past half century and more rapidly in the lower than in the middle and upper classes, yet there remain substantial disparities among those at different class levels. Table 24 shows the proportion in each class entering college from 1920 to 1960, roughly 80 per cent of the upper and upper-middle class in the latter year compared with about a quarter of those from the families of skilled and semi-skilled workers and less than 5 per cent of the children of unskilled workers. Negroes too, as might be expected because of both their concentration in the lower classes and the disabilities of race, are less likely to secure a college education. In 1965, 4.6 per cent of college students were Negro, although Negroes constituted over 10 per cent of the total population.

Academic performance—as well as the decision to leave school, to seek vocational training, or to go to college—is of course related to academic ability. Yet academic ability itself, as measured in the tests used in the schools, is correlated to some degree with social and economic

Table 24

SOCIAL CLASS ORIGINS OF COLLEGE ENTRANTS

Social class *	Per cent of class entering college				
	1920	1940	1950	1960 (Male and female)	
Upper and upper-middle	40	70	75	85	75
Lower-middle	8	20	38	60	38
Upper-lower	2	5	12	30	18
Lower-lower	0	0	2	6	2
Percentage of total age group in the U.S. entering college	6	16	22	40	27

* The upper-lower class consists of skilled and semiskilled workers, the lower-lower class of unskilled workers.

Robert J. Havighurst and Bernice L. Neugarten, *Society and Education*, 2nd ed., p. 252 (Copyright 1962 by Allyn and Bacon, Inc., Boston). Reprinted by permission of Allyn and Bacon, Inc.

status. That those at higher class levels do better in the tests used to measure ability, however, reflects to some degree both their cultural advantages and the cultural biases built into the tests that are used, rather than differences in innate ability.[30] Children in well-to-do families, for example, are more likely to have "educational" toys, books, and records that enlarge their knowledge even before they come to school. They are therefore far better prepared than children without such advantages for the questions that frequently go into intelligence tests, such as [31]

> A symphony is to a composer
> as a book is to what?
> ( ) sculptor ( ) author
> ( ) musician ( ) man

Even for students who are clearly capable of college work, the probability of doing so is related to class position. On the basis of several studies. Robert Havighurst and Bernice Neugarten estimated that among students who ranked in the top 25 per cent, three-quarters of those from the upper and upper-middle classes complete a four-year college program, compared with less than half in the lower-middle class and slightly over one-quarter in the lower classes.[32] (The con-tinuing increase in college enrollment may, to be sure, diminish these differences among the more able students.)

Both limited resources and lack of motivation account for the failure of lower-class children to continue their education. Motivation itself, or its absence, is the result of many things—the influence of the family, the attitudes and values of the groups from which children come, the nature of the school itself, the images of opportunity—or of its absence—current in different groups. Although subject to other influences, the child's initial orientation toward education and the school is likely to come from the family, and the more education parents have had the longer the child is likely to stay in school. There is also considerable evidence that the importance assigned to education is less among lower-class families than among those from the middle class,[33] although with the growing importance of education as a prerequisite for many jobs this differential is likely to diminish. That the school itself may outweigh or modify other influences is evident in a study by Alan Wilson of the relationship between the academic setting and students' aspirations. He found that working-class boys in a predominantly middle-class school were more likely to plan to go to college than were working-class boys in a school in which they constituted a majority. Conversely, middle-class boys in schools in which most students were from the working class were less likely to think of college for themselves than middle-class boys in an academic situation in which they made up most of the student body.[34]

Student subcultures

The interests, attitudes, and activities of students in high school and college are also significantly influenced by the distinctive youth culture found among them. The presence of such a culture, with its own values, attitudes, and modes of behavior, has been widely noted, not only in the United States, but in many other societies as well. It arises among youthful peer groups, S. N. Eisenstadt has argued, when the family cannot adequately prepare its members for adult roles. With increased division of labor and the growth of specialized organizations, the achievement of maturity and of a recognizable adult identity can no longer be derived solely from one's family.[35]

Under these conditions the period between childhood and adulthood is an uncertain one. The individual's role and status are ambiguous; he is neither child nor adult, no longer totally dependent yet not allowed to be completely independent. As he struggles with the ambiguities of his position and the problems of "growing up" he is also faced with often difficult and yet crucial choices. He must decide upon his future in a rapidly changing society in which the past offers few guidelines as old values and viewpoints are questioned and parents no longer provide adequate models. Moreover, the

school, which absorbs much of his time and energy, both in the classroom and out of it, confines him to a social milieu made up largely of young people even as it prepares him for adult life.

In coping with these uncertainties, young people create and draw upon their own distinctive culture, often with an assist from the mass media. Kenneth Kenniston has described youth culture as one that

emphasizes disengagement from adult values, sexual attractiveness, daring, immediate pleasure, and comradeship in a way that is true neither of childhood nor adulthood. The youth culture is not always or explicitly anti-adult, but it is belligerently *non*-adult. The rock 'n' roller, the Joe College student, the juvenile delinquent, and the beatnik, whatever their important differences, all form part of this general youth culture.[36]

For many young people, participation in youth culture serves important functions. The peer group that carries the culture provides support in an uncertain situation and allows the individual to break away from dependence upon the family, even if frequently at the price of rigid conformity to its own demands. Many of the activities in which the group engages offer release from some of the strains to which its members are exposed. For some young people, acceptance of youth culture makes possible what Erik Erikson has called a "psychosocial moratorium," an opportunity to establish a stable personal identity that will enable them to cope with the various roles they will be called upon to play in a complex and changing society.[37]

As Kenniston suggests, however, there is some diversity within youth culture, and individuals and groups may respond in diverse ways to the same problematic reality. Among high school students Burton Clark identifies three "subcultures" that differ in their attitudes toward education, the seriousness with which it is pursued, and the importance assigned to the various activities that go on within the school. The "fun" subculture stresses athletics, extracurricular activities, and the round of dates, parties, and dances. "Personality," good looks, athletic prowess, and popularity are more important than academic performance. The "academic" subculture, on the other hand, emphasizes studies and grades and those extracurricular activities that have some connection with academic matters—debating, the student newspaper, subject matter clubs. Unlike both the "fun" and "academic" subcultures, the "delinquent" subculture rejects education and the school entirely. The "delinquent" sees little or no value in schooling, and is likely to flout academic rules and disregard requirements; his chief aim is to avoid—or escape from—school, and he does so at the earliest opportunity.[38] (For a fuller discussion of the delinquent subculture, see Chapter 19.)

Except perhaps for the delinquent pattern, these subcultures are not sharply separated, nor are they completely free from external influences. There is, of course, no necessary contradiction between popularity and academic prowess, between athletic achievement and good grades. Many students undoubtedly pursue these values simultaneously, even though on some occasions they may have to establish priorities or make a choice among them. Moreover, the value orientations of both groups and individuals can change; as high school students move closer to graduation they may well become more concerned about their studies and the possibility of gaining entrance to the college of their choice and less preoccupied with other activities.

Both the larger culture and the school itself affect the values that are current among students. Public interest in athletics and public acclaim for athletes undoubtedly encourage many students to focus their attention upon sports rather than studies. As the mass media direct their efforts toward what has become a new mass market among adolescents, they foster interest in the latest modes of consumption and leisure activities. By their own activities, teachers and school authorities lend support to one or another set of values. A meager library and prestigious football team carry their own message to students, just as does public recognition for scholarship equivalent to that given to star athletes.

With the growing importance of college, however, and the resulting pressures upon both the high schools and the students, there may well be a greater emphasis upon academic values and achievement. Schools come to rate themselves by the number of students who go to college, and which colleges accept them, as well as by the success of athletic teams or the liveliness of school social life. Students, in turn, recognize the importance of their academic performance for their future careers, although the substantial number who do not complete high school or who do not continue their education after graduating from high school indicates the persistence of alternative values and interests.

At the college and university level too there are subcultures that contribute to the values, attitudes, and behavior of students. Burton Clark and Martin Trow have identified four such subcultures, the "collegiate," vocational, academic, and nonconformist.[39] The "collegiate" subculture is symbolized by "the star athlete, the homecoming queen, and the fraternity dance." It revolves to a substantial degree around fraternities and sororities, stimulates "school spirit" and strong institutional loyalties, but pays only as much attention to teachers, courses, and grades as is necessary to get by. Drawing heavily upon upper-middle- and upper-class students, it tends to flourish chiefly in the large state universities.

The vocational subculture sees college as primarily a preparation for a job or profession, and therefore has little interest in ideas or scholarship per se. To a large extent this subculture draws upon students from the lower-middle and working classes, those who are working their way through college and therefore have neither the time nor the money to participate in the collegiate subculture. Found in almost every college or university, this vocational pattern encourages little institutional loyalty, for college is seen primarily as "an adjunct of the world of jobs."

Both the academic and nonconformist subculture emphasize the importance of ideas and intellectual issues. The former, however, is oriented toward the college or university, concerned with learning, grades, and academic achievement as recognized by the faculty. The latter, on the other hand, is detached from the college and oriented toward the world outside the academy. Found primarily in the better small liberal arts colleges and the large universities, it encompasses a variety of interests—political, sexual, aesthetic— that emphasize rejection of the conventional and well-established and encourage the pursuit of a personal identity and a clearly defined stance toward contemporary culture and society.

As academic performance has assumed greater importance among college students—as well as among those in high school—because of its impact upon each individual's future, academic and vocational interests have been encouraged at the expense of the purely collegiate. The

demands for trained manpower for specific types of occupations, coupled with the increased number of students from groups which emphasize the "practical" value of education, have tended in turn to weaken academic values and strengthen the vocational orientation. Increasingly, Clark suggests, colleges and universities will witness a conflict between academic and vocational values the outcome of which will have considerable influence upon both the students' experience and the functions that education will serve.[40]

Organization of schools and colleges

Student subcultures and the social groups based upon them take shape within—and are in part responses to—the organizational context within which teaching and learning are carried on. The growing size and complexity of many schools and colleges increases the distance between students and faculty, encouraging more or less autonomous subcultures. In any particular college or university, the process of recruitment and selection, the academic standards imposed, and the nature of the programs available may encourage one or another subculture to develop.

The organization of education itself— the varied array of schools and colleges, the structures of roles and relationships, the rules and regulations that govern the actions of faculty members and students—has changed substantially as a result of the growing numbers attending school and the demands now being made of education. Mass education and the rapidly expanding body of knowledge that must be taught have necessitated greater professionalism among teachers and more elaborate bureaucratic organization. The emergence of new academic fields has led to the proliferation of novel programs and greater specialization among teachers and scholars. As universities have become more and more important as sources of new knowledge, academic roles have been redefined, and the expectations and attitudes with respect to the activities of both students and faculty have changed.[41]

With increasing size, school systems and individual schools and colleges have become more and more bureaucratic. Indeed, without the advantages of bureaucracy—speed, efficiency, continuity—mass education could not succeed. Enterprises as vast as the New York City school system and the university and state college systems of California or even a modest-sized state university clearly require formal, standardized procedures and a rationally organized structure. Rules increase predictability and ensure even-handed treatment of both students and teachers, standardized procedures facilitate the "housekeeping" required by large organizations, and a clear-cut hierarchy of authority makes possible control and coordination of activities. Even schools and colleges of modest size tend to develop some bureaucratic features, in part because of the efficiencies they encourage, in part because of the requirements within education as a whole. In order to allow for both movement within the system and judgment of the achievements of students and teachers, standardized formulas are required—for courses, performance, and levels of achievement.

These important functions of bureaucracy are often overlooked because of the difficulties which so frequently accompany its extension.[42] As we noted earlier, for example, the volume of paper work imposed on teachers because of the requirements—or felt requirements—of administration may take time and attention away from the actual business of teaching. The demands of fixed semesters with regular schedules and standardized grading impose a Procrustean bed into which some bodies of knowledge are often coerced. In a large university the impersonal and sometimes time-consuming procedures required simply to register for courses emphasize the separation of teacher and student that numbers and size accentuate. The definition of required course sequences and of formal prerequisites for advanced courses, although perhaps necessary and appropriate for many, even most, students, may be disadvantageous to the able or unusual one; the special case, that is, suffers because of the standardization needed in order to deal with large numbers.

These disadvantages, of course, have not gone unnoticed, in part because they have been sharply attacked by students. In many places efforts are being made to cope with the difficulties created by size and organization through such expedients as special courses for well-qualified students, tutorial or counseling schemes, and establishment of small, often experimental, colleges within the frame of the large university.

To some degree, too, the impact of bureaucratization is cushioned by the character of the educational system as a whole. Unlike many European nations in which the schools are centrally controlled by a government ministry, the United States has left education to state and local authorities and to various private groups. As a result, in 1966–1967 the more than 55 million students and 2.5 million teachers were to be found in 93,000 elementary schools, 31,000 high schools, and over 2,100 universities, colleges, and junior colleges under the control of a large number of governing boards which themselves had a total membership of over 650,000 persons.[43] Almost one-third of all college and university students were in private institutions, as were roughly one-eighth of elementary and high school pupils.

The very diversity in substance, organization, and quality allows greater flexibility and variation than would be possible in a centrally directed system. The possibility of educational innovation and experimentation is enhanced by the decentralization of authority, even though, as Riesman has noted, there is a tendency among colleges and universities for the "academic procession" to follow the leaders, who have often changed direction and embarked on some new program even as those at the tail end are just catching up with the innovations of the past.[44] Students, too, have greater opportunities to experiment and to seek out the type of education they want. Even the often criticized differences in quality, which can blur the meaning and value of the diploma or degree itself, keep open the opportunities a more uniform system would close off at some definite point; the high school graduate with mediocre or poor credentials, for example, may have another opportunity to prove his abilities and, if successful, to acquire the skills and knowledge that will improve his economic chances.

The pressures of bureaucracy may also be partially contained by the professionalism it helps to foster. Recruitment of teachers and administrators on the basis of formal qualifications may, in some school systems, exclude otherwise well-qualified persons who lack specific courses in education or psychology; similarly, the absence of a higher degree may prevent creative teachers and scholars from securing academic posts in colleges and universities. But to the extent that the emphasis upon professional competence encourages commitments to teaching and concern for their students, teachers may resist, ignore, or circumvent in various ways the bureaucratic prescriptions imposed upon them, or consciously seek to avoid the deleterious consequences encouraged by the formal structure of the school or college. (For a general discussion of the tension between professionalism and bureaucracy, see Chapter 10.)

In higher education, however, the growing emphasis upon research and the university's responsibility to contribute to knowledge have led to complex problems both within the organization and in the definition of the professor's role and his relations with his students. As academic advancement has become more closely linked with research and publication, teaching has become less important to the scholar. Faced with a choice between the time-consuming demands of teaching and the needs of research, he has frequently chosen to devote his energies to the activities that promised greater rewards in status and prestige. Except for the able student who can attach himself to the scholar or scientist by participating in his research, undergraduates—and even some graduates—may be given minimal attention by their teachers.

The problems created by this tendency to downgrade teaching do elicit counter-action, however—programs to reward successful teachers, proposals to separate research from teaching, efforts to enlist more students to work with scholars in their research activities, and attempts to devise new methods of teaching appropriate to changing circumstances. Such actions are supported not only by those academic men and women who have maintained a commitment to education and teaching, but also by those administrators, scholars, and scientists who have recognized that the future progress of knowledge requires appropriate training of the next generation.

Notes

[1] See Ian Weinberg, *The English Public Schools* (New York: Atherton, 1967); and Rupert Wilkinson, *Gentlemanly Power: British Leadership and the Public School Tradition* (New York: Oxford, 1964).

[2] A. H. Halsey, "The Changing Functions of Universities," in A. H. Halsey, Jean Floud, and C. Arnold Anderson (eds.), *Education, Economy, and Society* (New York: Free Press, 1961), p. 458.

[3] Richard Hofstadter and C. DeWitt Hardy, *The Development and Scope of Higher Education in the United States* (New York: Columbia University Press, 1952), p. 11.

[4] Peter Drucker, "The Educational Revolution," in Halsey, Floud, and Anderson, *op. cit.*, p. 15.

[5] These data are from *World Survey of Education, IV: Higher Education* (New York: UNESCO, 1966), Ch. 2.

[6] *Ibid.*

[7] *Ibid.*, p. 15.

[8] Quoted in Rush Welter, *Popular Education and Democratic Thought in America* (New York: Columbia University Press, 1962), p. 47.

[9] David Glass, "Education and Social Change in Modern England," in Halsey, Floud, and Anderson, *op. cit.*, p. 395.

[10] *Ibid.*, p. 394.

[11] R. Freeman Butts, *A Cultural History of Education* (New York: McGraw-Hill, 1947), p. 472.

[12] Frederick Harbison and Charles A. Myers, *Education, Manpower, and Economic Growth: Strategies of Human Resources Development* (New York: McGraw-Hill, 1964), p. 181.

[13] Butts, *op. cit.*, Ch. 15.

[14] Émile Durkheim, *Education and Sociology*, trans. by Sherwood D. Fox (New York: Free Press, 1956), p. 123.

[15] Burton R. Clark, *Educating the Expert Society* (San Francisco: Chandler, 1962), p. 27.

[16] See Clark Kerr, *The Uses of the University* (Cambridge, Mass.: Harvard University Press, 1963); and Fritz Machlup, *The Production and Distribution of Knowledge in the United States* (Princeton: Princeton University Press, 1962).

[17] Clark, *op. cit.*, p. 30.

[18] David Riesman, *The Lonely Crowd* (New Haven: Yale University Press, 1950), p. 60.

[19] Seymour Harris, *The Market for College Graduates* (Cambridge, Mass.: Harvard University Press, 1949), p. 18.

[20] Clark, *op. cit.*, p. 48.

[21] Herman P. Miller, *Rich Man, Poor Man* (New York: Crowell, 1964), p. 154.

[22] W. Lloyd Warner and James C. Abegglen, *Occupational Mobility in American Business and Industry* (Minneapolis: University of Minnesota Press, 1955), p. 108.

[23] David Granick, *The Red Executive* (Garden City: Doubleday, 1960), p. 62.

[24] U.S. Bureau of the Census, *U.S. Census of Population. 1960. Subject Reports. Occupation by Education and Income.* (Washington: U.S. Government Printing Office, 1963), Table 1, pp. 2–196.

[25] James S. Coleman *et al.*, *Equality of Educational Opportunity* (Washington, D.C.: U.S. Government Printing Office, 1966), pp. 9, 12.

[26] *Ibid.*, pp. 22–3. For the detailed data, see pp. 290–330.

[27] *Ibid.*, p. 29 and Table 22, p. 32.

[28] See E. Digby Baltzell, *Philadelphia Gentlemen* (New York: Free Press, 1958), Ch. 12.

[29] Coleman *et al.*, *op. cit.*, pp. 28–9.

[30] See Allison Davis, *Social-Class Influences Upon Learning* (Cambridge, Mass.: Harvard University Press, 1948); and Kenneth Eells *et al.*, *Intelligence and Cultural Differences* (Chicago: University of Chicago Press, 1951).

[31] Robert J. Havighurst and Bernice L. Neugarten, *Society and Education* (2nd

ed.; Boston: Allyn & Bacon, 1962), p. 236.

[32] Quoted in Havighurst and Neugarten, *op. cit.*, p. 234.

[33] See Herbert H. Hyman, "The Value Systems of Different Classes," in Reinhard Bendix and Seymour M. Lipset (eds.), *Class, Status, and Power* (2nd ed.; New York: Free Press, 1966), pp. 488–99.

[34] Alan B. Wilson, "Residential Segregation of Social Classes and Aspirations of High School Boys," *American Sociological Review*, 24 (December, 1959), 836–45.

[35] S. N. Eisenstadt, "Archetypal Patterns of Youth," in Erik H. Erikson (ed.), *Youth: Change and Challenge* (New York: Basic Books, 1961), pp. 24–42. For a fuller analysis, see S. N. Eisenstadt, *From Generation to Generation* (New York: Free Press, 1956).

[36] Kenneth Kenniston, "Social Change and Youth in America," in Erikson, *op. cit.*, p. 177.

[37] Erik H. Erikson, "The Problem of Ego Identity," in *Identity and the Life Cycle, Psychological Issues*, I, No. 1 (New York: International Universities Press, 1959), 101–64.

[38] Clark, *op. cit.*, Ch. 7.

[39] *Ibid.*, Ch. 6. The discussion of student subcultures draws heavily upon Clark's analysis.

[40] *Ibid.*, pp. 237–44.

[41] See Kerr, *op. cit.*, for a general discussion. For an analysis of these changes in a limited academic setting, see Robert A. Nisbet, "Sociology in the Academy," in Charles H. Page, *Sociology and Contemporary Education.* (New York: Random House, 1964), pp. 56–75.

[42] For a discussion of some aspects of the bureaucratization of higher education, see Charles H. Page, "Bureaucracy and Higher Education," *Journal of General Education*, V (January, 1951), 91–100.

[43] Estimates from the U.S. Office of Education and the National Education Association, "The Magnitude of the American Educational Establishment (1966–1967)," *Saturday Review* (October 15, 1966), p. 75.

[44] David Riesman, "The Academic Procession," in *Constraint and Variety in American Education* (Lincoln: University of Nebraska Press, 1956), pp. 15–52.

Suggestions for further reading

BRIM, ORVILLE G., JR. *Sociology and the Field of Education.* New York: Russell Sage Foundation, 1958.
A brief review and assessment of sociological studies of education.

CICOUREL, AARON V., and JOHN I. KITSUSE. *The Educational Decision Makers.* Indianapolis: Bobbs-Merrill, 1963.
A case study of the impact of bureaucracy on the counseling and placement of high-school students.

CLARK, BURTON R. *Educating the Expert Society.* San Francisco: Chandler, 1962.
An excellent introduction to the sociology of education that explores some of the major problems of contemporary American education.

COLEMAN, JAMES S. *The Adolescent Society.* New York: Free Press, 1961.
A detailed study of the social life of teen-agers and its effects upon education.

DORE, RONALD P. *Education in Tokugawa Japan.* Berkeley: University of California Press, 1965.
An analysis of the nature and function of education in Japan before 1868 and its relationship to the subsequent modernization.

DURKHEIM, ÉMILE. *Education and Sociology.* Trans. by Sherwood D. Fox. New York: Free Press, 1956.
An essay by one of the major sociologi-

cal theorists on the nature and functions of education.

ERIKSON, ERIK H. (ed.). *Youth: Change and Challenge.* New York: Basic Books, 1961.
Essays on youth that explore the problems they face in a changing society.

GREELEY, ANDREW M., AND PETER H. ROSSI. *The Education of American Catholics.* Chicago: Aldine, 1966.
A detailed study of the character and influence of education in Catholic parochial schools.

HALSEY, A. H., JEAN FLOUD, AND C. ARNOLD ANDERSON (eds.). *Education, Economy, and Society.* New York: Free Press, 1961.
An excellent collection of articles that focuses chiefly on the place and problems of education in an advanced industrial society.

HAVIGHURST, ROBERT J., AND BERNICE L. NEUGARTEN. *Society and Education,* 2nd ed. Boston: Allyn & Bacon, 1962.
An analysis of the relations between education and social structure, with considerable emphasis upon the relevance of social class.

HOLLINGSHEAD, A. B. *Elmtown's Youth.* New York: Wiley, 1949.
A major investigation of the influence of class structure upon adolescent behavior and the school.

JACOB, PHILIP E. *Changing Values in College.* New York: Harper, 1957.
An assessment of studies of the impact of college education upon students. For a study that challenges the possibility of generalizations about all students,

see Peter I. Rose, "The Myth of Unanimity; Student Opinions on Critical Issues," Sociology of Education, 37 (*Winter, 1963*), *129–49.*

KERR, CLARK. *The Uses of the University.* Cambridge: Harvard University Press, 1963.
A provocative and important interpretation of the changing nature and functions of the university.

LIPSET, SEYMOUR M., AND SHELDON S. WOLIN (eds.). *The Berkeley Student Revolt.* Garden City: Doubleday Anchor Books, 1965.
A collection of documents and interpretations concerning a major conflict between students and the university, which sheds a good deal of light on the problems of the large university.

MUSGRAVE, P. W. *The Sociology of Education.* London: Methuen, 1965.
An introduction to the sociology of education that draws chiefly upon English materials.

PAGE, CHARLES H. (ed.). *Sociology and Contemporary Education.* New York: Random House, 1964.
Essays on the educational functions of sociology and the relations between sociology and education.

SANFORD, NEVITT (ed.). *The American College.* New York: Wiley, 1962.
A wide-ranging collection of papers dealing with psychological and sociological aspects of higher education.

WEINBERG, IAN. *The English Public Schools.* New York: Atherton, 1967.
An analysis of the place of the public schools in English society.

16

Science
and
Society

Social aspects of science

To anyone living in the middle of the twentieth century, science is clearly a central component of his culture and an important determinant of his future. In 1963 more than 400,000 Americans were directly engaged in scientific research, in addition to those doctors, dentists, pharmacists, engineers, food technicians, geologists, meteorologists, and others who were making use of scientific knowledge in their daily activities. Workers in business and industry are constantly confronted with the products of scientific inquiry—office intercommunication systems, devices for rapidly duplicating letters and other documents, electronic data-processing systems that replace clerks or carry out tasks that would otherwise be impossible to perform, machines that are controlled by electronic tapes or that require little more than surveillance and the operation of dials or push buttons. The fruits of scientific research are continually put before the consumer in new products fresh from the laboratory—nylon, dacron, orlon, and other synthetic fibers, electronic air purifiers, color television, frozen or even synthetic foods, a bewildering and expensive array of synthetic drugs, and perhaps before long cigarettes to be lit by striking them on the side of the package.

Science has transformed modern warfare, and political debates over national defense are often focused on the adequacy of expenditures for scientific research and development. Scientific policy has become an important political issue, and presidents and prime ministers appoint special advisers to help them cope with the control and consequences of scientific research. Scientists themselves enter the public arena to contribute their judgment concerning the possible use of scientific knowledge and the technology and goods resulting from it and to advance policies that affect their own professional endeavors.

In addition to its economic and political consequences, science also affects prevailing beliefs and values in diverse ways. Ever since the emergence of modern science in the seventeenth century and its partial escape from theological controls, the world view of Western man has been significantly influenced by the prevailing scientific theories and new scientific facts. The Newtonian synthesis, built upon the scientific advances of the preceding 150 years, provided a view of the cosmos that dominated Western thought until the latter half of the nineteenth century. Evolution, relativity, and other ideas of modern physics, and psychoanalysis have all contributed to the contemporary conceptions of the nature of man and the universe. The impact of scientific thought has also been felt in art and literature. In a number of suggestive essays Marjorie Nicholson has shown how scientific ideas and images affected the literature of the seventeenth and eighteenth centuries,[1] and the influence of modern scientific theories upon literary and artistic works of the past century is readily apparent.

Clearly, science has become so important a part of the modern world that no analysis of society and culture can ignore it. So pervasive is its influence that some students have concluded that the distinguishing features of Western society are, in fact, not those cultural traits so often emphasized as central to Western civilization, but rather the methods and findings of scientific inquiry. The distinguished British historian Herbert Butterfield writes:

> When we speak of Western civilisation being carried to an oriental country like Japan in recent generations, we do not mean Graeco-Roman philosophy and humanist ideals, we do not mean the Christianising of Japan, we mean the science, the modes of thought and all that apparatus of civilisation which were beginning to change the face of the West in the latter half of the seventeenth century.[2]

Science in the modern world includes, in addition to a body of knowledge, a set of values, conventions, and practices that govern the behavior of scientists. It has been incorporated into complex social structures that affect the rate and character of scientific achievement. The once widely held notion that science is simply the creation of inquiring and imaginative individuals rather than a social product has been replaced gradually by the recognition that, as a committee of noted scientists has commented: "Science is but one sector of our culture. It is one of the institutions of society, and to a considerable degree society itself governs the development of science." [3]

Science in primitive society

Although science as a social institution and as a major force in the life of society is relatively modern and, until very recent times, has been confined largely to the Western world, reliable empirical knowledge is found everywhere. The pervasive importance in primitive society of religion and magic led some students to conclude, erroneously, that "primitive mentality" is essentially "mystical and prelogical," submerged in a sea of illusion and dream, and incapable of rational thought.[4] But every primitive people also possesses, in addition to its religious beliefs and rituals and its magical practices, a body of knowledge derived from practical experience and often based upon a rough but adequate understanding of the world around it. The Trobriand Islanders, for example, a Pacific people described in close detail in a series of monographs by Bronislaw Malinowski, would never plant a garden, build a boat, or set sail on the open sea without first performing the requisite magical rituals; but they also recognized the importance of soil, weather, and work in gardening, the need for practical skills and proper materials in boatbuilding, and they were familiar with principles of navigation and sailing.

> If by science [Malinowski writes] be understood a body of rules and conceptions, based on experience and derived from it by logical inference, embodied in material achievements and in a fixed form of tradition and carried on by some form of social organization—then there is no doubt that even the lowest savage

communities have the beginnings of science, however rudimentary.[5]

This definition of science is perhaps too broad, as Malinowski himself recognizes, for practical knowledge and science are not the same. The former often rests simply upon a cumulative process of trial and error, a pragmatic testing of alternatives, and it is often merely incorporated in the skills of the workman. Science, on the other hand, consists of logically related generalizations that can be systematically tested. But the beginnings of science, even in this more restricted sense, are also sometimes to be found in primitive society.

The native shipwright knows not only practically of buoyancy, leverage, equilibrium, he has to obey these laws not only on water, but while making the canoe he must have the principles in his mind. He instructs his helpers in them. He gives them the traditional rules, and in a crude and simple manner, using his hands, pieces of wood, and a limited technical vocabulary, he explains some general laws of hydrodynamics and equilibrium. Science is not detached from the craft, that is certainly true, it is only a means to an end, it is crude, rudimentary, and inchoate, but with all that it is the matrix from which the higher developments must have sprung.[6]

Nor is the disinterested pursuit of knowledge totally foreign to primitive society, for within the limits of a traditional culture individuals are to be found who are "patient and painstaking in [their] observations, capable of generalization and of connecting long chains of events in the life of animals, and in the marine world or in the jungle." [7]

Yet, for the most part, knowledge in primitive societies has remained limited to empirical generalizations and has not been expanded into a body of generalized and systematic concepts and theories. The Tanala of Madagascar were aware that chewing the bark of the Cinchona tree would ward off or cure malaria, but Europeans first isolated the quinine the bark contains (in 1820), identified its chemical properties, and finally synthesized a chemical equivalent that would perform the same medicinal functions. Many primitive peoples have been highly skilled in the art of metal working and alloys of various kinds have long been known in human history, but only in relatively recent times has a science of metallurgy resting upon general principles emerged from the study and laboratory. And no primitive society has evolved distinctive social roles that center around the systematic pursuit of scientific knowledge.

The origins of science

The striking advances of modern science should not obscure the long history of scientific knowledge. Although important steps forward had been taken by the Babylonians and Egyptians, particularly in mathematics and astronomy, the first great period of scientific discovery occurred among the ancient Greeks. In logic and mathematics, the formal disciplines basic to scientific inquiry, and in physics, medicine, geography, and other empirical fields the Greeks made major contributions. Not only were they the first to conceive "of the possibility of establishing a limited number of principles, and of deducing from these a number of truths which are their rigorous consequences," [8] but they established a tradition of empirical research from which came important scientific results.

We know little as yet of the social forces that generated the extraordinary scientific achievements of classical Greece, or of the circumstances that account for the decline of science in antiquity. One scholar, Benjamin Farrington, finds the sources of both achievement and decline in economic conditions and the class structure.[9] The first Greek scientists were "practical men" whose concern with trade and technology, he suggests, encouraged a rational, matter-of-fact approach to the world. Their specific scientific ideas reflected the skills and techniques of their times. The decline of Greek science, Farrington argues, resulted from the development of a slave economy that did away with the close connection between philosophy and practice. Since slaves did most of the work, the Greeks, according to this view, were no longer confronted with questions of productive technique. They therefore lost interest in practical problems and became preoccupied instead with nonscientific questions and with purely abstract ideas. For them, science had become only "a relaxation, an adornment, a subject of contemplation. It had ceased to be a means of transforming the conditions of life." [10] And therefore it ceased to move forward.

The validity of this interpretation has been questioned because of both its oversimplification of a complex process and the insufficiency of the evidence. "Our factual knowledge about the development of [Greek] scientific thought and of the social position of the men who were responsible for it," observes an historian of ancient science, "is so utterly fragmentary . . . that it seems to be completely impossible to test any [sociological] hypothesis, however plausible it may seem to a modern man." [11] Even the available evidence that is reported, however, suggests the complexity of the forces at work. For example, although Farrington attributes to religious ideas in general an inhibiting effect upon scientific progress, Pythagoras, to take a concrete example, was not only one of the greatest Greek scientists, but was also a religious leader for whom mathematics was a form of religious reflection. Slavery, to which Farrington assigns the chief responsibility for the decline of Greek science, was already widespread by the time of Plato, but significant discoveries continued to appear for several centuries after his death. It does seem likely that slavery and the disrepute for manual work that it engendered did inhibit various areas of scientific inquiry, but some fields, notably mathematics, astronomy, geography, and medicine, continued to make substantial progress until the third century A.D.

With the decline of Hellenistic culture and the disintegration of the Roman Empire, scientific progress virtually came to a halt. For over a thousand years, few new scientific ideas appeared. These centuries, however, were not totally barren, and the rebirth of science in the sixteenth and seventeenth centuries rested in part upon the technological developments that had slowly taken place throughout Europe—for example, the watermill and windmill in the twelfth century, spectacles and the rudder in the thirteenth century, gunpowder, the plane, and the grandfather clock in the fourteenth century, and printing in the fifteenth. (The chief scientific developments during these years were found among the Arabs, who created algebra and made substantial progress in biology and medicine.) Despite these technological and scientific advances, however, "when modern science began in the sixteenth century," writes Farrington, "it took up where the Greeks left off. Copernicus, Vesalius and Galileo are the continuators of Ptolemy, Galen and Archimedes." [12]

The extraordinary scientific developments of the sixteenth and seventeenth century, particularly those that occurred in England in the seventeenth century, have been more fully studied from a sociological point of view than those of any other period except perhaps our own. The findings show clearly the extent to which science in this period was influenced by social and cultural circumstances and the complexity of the forces at work. It seems clear, for example, that economic needs stimulated a great deal of research and often channeled scientific interest into particular lines of inquiry. As Robert K. Merton, who has made the most detailed sociological study of science and technology in seventeenth century England, points out, *"Every English scientist of this time* who was of sufficient distinction to merit mention in general histories of science at one point or other explicitly related at least some of his scientific research to immediate practical problems."* [13] In a summary of the socioeconomic influences that affected the choice of scientific problems pursued by members of the Royal Society in England during the years 1661–1662 and 1686–1687, Merton found that 30 to 60 per cent of these problems were directly or indirectly linked to military needs, navigation, or to the requirements of some industry, chiefly mining.[14] And in order to solve practical problems it was often necessary to deal with important theoretical questions; research directed to the discovery of methods for locating a ship's position at sea, for example, also contributed to scientific knowledge about magnetism, the tides, and the movements of the stars and planets.

Motives of individual scientists, of course, are not the only indication of the influence of economic pressures upon science. Since scientists must rely upon the work of those who have preceded them, they are often dependent upon—or draw upon—the work of those who have tried to solve practical problems. Moreover,

and of greater importance, scientific ideas, as is now well known, frequently have practical applications of which their creators are unaware. But scientists themselves, no matter how abstract their theories or seemingly unrelated to immediate problems, characteristically take for granted that in the long run their work will be of some concrete use. Seventeenth-century scientists in England, Merton notes, "were uniformly confident of the practical fruits which their continued industry would ensure." [15]

Economic needs and the possible uses of scientific research provide only part of the explanation for the marked scientific progress of the seventeenth century. Many of the practical problems to which scientists turned their attention had existed long before they were subjected to systematic study. What accounted for the increased scientific interest itself? Following a suggestion by Max Weber, Merton found part of the answer, at least in seventeenth-century England, in the impact of Puritanism, which emphasized not only rationalism, as did medieval Catholic theology, but also encouraged men to try to master the world around them. They were to explore the mysteries of nature not only to improve man's estate, but also to testify to the glory of God by revealing the wonders of his handiwork. By focusing attention upon the world in which men lived, Puritanism thus brought together both rationalism and empiricism, the two values that conjointly, as we noted in Chapter 1, constitute the essence of the scientific spirit.

Merton found evidence for the influence of religious belief and affiliation upon scientific work in the seventeenth century not only in the apparent coincidence of the tenets of Puritanism and science, but also in the heavy preponderance of Puritans among scientists. Although Puritans constituted only a small proportion of the English population, forty-two of the sixty-eight original members of the Royal Academy for whom data were available were Puritans, and some of them were eminent divines as well. This preponderance of Protestants among scientists has been noted in other countries and has continued to the present. [16] A study of American scientists completed after World War II concluded that the "statistics, taken together with other evidence, leave little doubt that scientists have been drawn disproportionately from American Protestant stock." [17]

The impact of religion and of economic needs upon seventeenth-century science demonstrates clearly that science is not simply the work of curious and creative individuals unaffected by the larger social forces at work in the world around them, and that the history of science cannot be written solely as a sequence of discoveries in isolation from practical problems and nonscientific ideas. Science is in some respects, chiefly in the selection of problems and in the rate of progress, "determined" by society. This general conclusion, however, as Merton notes, is only the beginning of the sociological study of science.

The significant problem, after all, is not whether . . . practical influences on the course of scientific development have ever occurred, or whether they have always proved determining. It is, instead, a matter of multiple questions, each demanding long patient study rather than short impatient answers: to what extent have these influences operated in different times and places? under what sociological conditions do they prove greater and under which, less determining?[18]

Neither religious values and ideas nor economic needs, of course, despite their importance, can account fully for the scientific progress of the sixteenth and seventeenth centuries—or of any other period. Not only is science subject to other external forces—political, ideological, organizational—that may affect its rate of development and the problems to which scientists pay attention, but it is itself in some measure a self-contained social and cultural system with its own theories, values, institutions, roles, and social organization, all of which help to channel the efforts of those who enter its world of abstraction, analysis, and empirical investigation. Scientific theories and novel facts generate their own problems, and each generation of scientists seeks to answer the questions left unanswered by their predecessors, leaving in turn not only accumulations of data but also new problems to be explored by their successors.

For much of the sixteenth and seventeenth centuries both the culture and social organization of science were still in an embryonic or, perhaps, infantile state. Despite the long history of scientific progress that began well before the Christian era and the extraordinary achievements of the seventeenth century, the values of science were not widely accepted, its usefulness was not generally known or recognized, and the role of the scientist was barely distinguished from other roles. Although scientific societies were established in various countries during the seventeenth century and there was considerable communication among scientists in different places, the pursuit of scientific knowledge was still carried on by more or less isolated experimenters or small groups of individuals, many of whom were also often engaged in other professional or intellectual pursuits.

In the following centuries, various circumstances continued to stimulate the growth of science. The Enlightenment of the eighteenth century, with its emphasis upon reason, freedom, and humanitarianism, provided a new justification for scientific inquiry. The industrialization of Western Europe that began in the latter half of that century in England and expanded with accelerating speed offered new stimuli to research in chemistry, mechanics, hydraulics, thermodynamics, metallurgy, and other fields. Military and political interests also contributed to scientific work; new scientific educational institutions established during and after the French Revolution were energetically supported by Napoleon, who found well-trained engineers useful in his military campaigns. With the continued accumulation of scientific knowledge and growing recognition of its usefulness, universities began to devote some of their energies to the teaching of science and to carrying on scientific research, albeit some of them, particularly in England, did so only slowly and reluctantly. Where the universities encouraged science, it flourished; where they did not, it grew less quickly. As Joseph Ben-David has recently shown, differences in the "productivity" of medical science among various nations in the nineteenth century were closely related to the extent to which scientific research was encouraged and sponsored by the universities.[19]

The values of science

With the institutionalization of scientific endeavor has come the development of a scientific "ethos," a set of values and norms that are expected to govern the work of the scientist. The methodological rules that scientists follow are not only "technical expedients," but they have also become "moral compulsives" to which scientists subscribe. Their hold, like that of many other values and norms, is often taken for granted by those who follow them, but their moral character becomes

clearly evident when they are ignored or violated. The scientist who deliberately distorts or doctors his findings, who refuses to accept objective evidence available to him, or who rejects or accepts ideas because of the race, religion, or politics of their author is a bad scientist on *both* rational and moral grounds.

The values of science include at least the following: universalism, rationality, skepticism, communality, and disinterestedness. A social context favorable to scientific progress will accept these values for the society as a whole, or will at least recognize their importance in scientific research and will therefore allow or encourage the scientist's commitment to these values in his scientific role. If these values are questioned or challenged, science may suffer.

The first of these values, *universalism*, holds that scientific truth is to be determined by the application of impersonal, general criteria: Observations must be free from the distortions of bias and conclusions must follow logically from stated premises. The particular personal qualities of the investigator are irrelevant when one seeks to determine the truth of any scientific idea. The nature of this principle is made clear by its occasional rejection. The Nazis attacked the theories of Einstein because he was a Jew, and Communist writers have on occasion criticized "bourgeois science." Conversely, ideas cannot be accepted simply because of the character of their protagonist. In this respect science is also antiauthoritarian. "Science," writes J. Robert Oppenheimer, "is not based on authority. It owes its acceptance and its universality to an appeal to intelligible, communicable evidence that any interested man can evaluate."[20]

Closely linked to universalism and the correlative antiauthoritarianism is the value of *rationality*. As a value rather than a way of thinking, rationality refers to the moral approval placed upon the use of reason in understanding nature. Rationality may be contrasted with "traditionalism," which accepts ideas simply because they have the sanctity associated with conventional usage. Science rests upon the belief that the world can—and should—be understood in rational terms. This view is epitomized in Einstein's oft-quoted comment: *"Raffiniert ist Herr Gott, aber boshaft ist Er nicht,"* which may be translated "God is subtle, but he is not malicious."

In seeking rational answers to the questions he asks, the scientist is expected to remain skeptical until all the evidence is in and the analysis complete. This *scientific skepticism*, Merton notes, "is both a methodologic and an institutional mandate."[21] "For scientists," Oppenheimer comments, "it is not only honorable to doubt; it is mandatory to do that when there appears to be evidence in support of the doubt."[22] This systematic skepticism does not preclude commitment or belief, nor does it necessarily imply a pervasive doubt about everything. Rather it is a rejection of traditional belief and dogma when it is unsupported by evidence and not justified by logic.

Finally, the ethos of science includes both *communality* and *disinterestedness*. Communality refers to the denial of private property rights with respect to scientific knowledge. Since all science rests upon a common heritage, no single contributor can claim proprietary rights to his discovery—although he may vigorously assert his claims to priority in discovery.[23] Eponymy—giving a person's name to something—is a common practice in science, but although it confers recognition upon the scientist by identifying him with his discovery, it gives him

no rights of ownership. Boyle's Law and Ohm's Law, the volt (after the Italian physicist, Alessandro Volta) and the ampere (after a French scientist, André Marie Ampère), Einstein's theory of relativity, and Darwin's theory of evolution are all common property.

Communality requires publication of results and sharing of knowledge. Secrecy is objectionable because it makes impossible the public testing and scrutiny of new ideas and hinders the collective effort to advance scientific knowledge. The contemporary emphasis upon secrecy in those areas of science relevant to military needs raises difficult problems for scientists who are caught between presumed political necessities and scientific values. Publishing scientific findings with potential military applications may save the "enemy" time and effort and give away the advantages gained by one's own research. But it also keeps from other scientists at home information that might aid them in their research. Moreover, it has been argued, in the long run secrecy avails little and that one loses more than he gains. "Enemy" scientists possessing the same theoretical knowledge and seeking solutions to the same problems will eventually come up with answers. How long it will require depends in large part upon the resources committed to the task. The issue was dramatized—and unresolved—in the controversy over whether the Soviet Union's success in building atomic weapons much more quickly than American experts had anticipated was the result of stolen scientific secrets or merely the product of their own intensive efforts. As might be expected, scientists tend to depreciate the value of secrecy while government officials and military men are more convinced of the necessity of strict control over the flow of scientific information.[24]

The institutionalization of private rights in invention through a patent system also creates ambiguity and uncertainty among scientists committed to the free sharing of scientific knowledge. The line between science, which is presumably public property, and technology, which is not, is not easily drawn. Some scientists in the United States have dealt with this uncertainty by patenting their discoveries to ensure that they will be available to all, and others have advocated institutional changes to guarantee free access to science and its fruits.

As a collective enterprise, science also enjoins *disinterestedness* upon those who are endeavoring to extend the frontiers of knowledge. Personal gain is culturally depreciated as less important than conformity to the canons of scientific inquiry, and success for the individual is defined in terms of his scientific contribution. The desire for recognition, as well as other goals, may indeed motivate those who follow scientific careers, but, in sociological analysis, their private aims must be distinguished from the institutional controls imposed upon and accepted by them. Moreover, the constant scrutiny of research findings by professional colleagues serves to check tendencies toward self-seeking by the manipulation of data.

The fullest development of science—in the form of complex theories, a large number of scientific workers, and the commitment of ample resources to research—has occurred where the ethos of science has been congruent with the values of society. Universalism, evident, for example, in an emphasis upon achieved rather than ascribed status and in religious values that stress the equality of all men in the sight of God, is clearly consistent with the scientific commitment to impersonal criteria of truth. The rationality found in economic enterprise, in a formal system of law, even in important segments of Jewish and Christian theology, as well as in Marxist doctrine, is of a piece with, indeed is connected with, the effort to apply reason to the understanding of nature. Liberal traditions of free speech, thought, and conscience are linked with the scientist's insistence upon evidence and his skeptical attitude toward received doctrines.

Support for science has come, however, not only from these values, but also from *utilitarianism*, an interest in the "practical" results to be derived from scientific inquiry. Scientists themselves have not always shared this interest, and in their efforts to protect the autonomy of science against external pressures they have often explicitly rejected any concern with the uses to which their knowledge would be put, or have denied that it has any use. A British mathematician once praised pure mathematics by asserting:

This subject has no practical use; that is to say, it cannot be used for promoting directly the destruction of human life or for accentuating the present inequalities in the distribution of wealth.[25]

But many other scientists have often affirmed the belief that their efforts were important because of their potential contribution to human welfare. Sir Francis Bacon, an early advocate of empirical science in the seventeenth century, placed great emphasis upon the practical results to be gained by exploiting the secrets of nature. Many contemporary scientists, despite the uncertainties and anxieties created by the destructive uses to which their work has often been put, continue to believe that in the long run man's lot will be improved by scientific knowledge.

Although historically science has flourished primarily in the West, where these values have been widely shared, it has in recent years gained a firm place and made substantial progress elsewhere—in Japan and especially in the Soviet Union. The Russians share some of the values that encourage and sustain scientific inquiry; Marxism itself, of course, claimed validity as a theory of *scientific* socialism, and the Communist revolution reflected a desire on the part of Marxist theoreticians and leaders to rationalize society. Moreover, the Russians have recognized clearly the practical value of science and have therefore dedicated ample resources for research. They have rewarded scientists far more, proportionately, than they are rewarded in the West, and encouraged their ablest students to pursue scientific careers. In a few scientific fields, most notably genetics, political considerations have on occasion interfered with objective inquiry, but the Soviet leadership has apparently managed to allow sufficient freedom to their scientists to make possible impressive scientific gains.

The organization and support of science

In addition to these values, of course, other cultural and social facts affect the development of science. Values themselves take form and become effective in large part through institutions and social structures that influence the course of scientific research not only in this indirect manner, but also through their impact upon the organization of research, the problems to which scientists direct their inquiries, the resources they provide, and the support they offer—or limitations they impose.

In eighteenth-century England, "science became a respectable leisure-time occupation for country gentlemen and townsmen of substance." [26] During the nineteenth century and the early years of the twentieth, as an increasing number of men came to devote themselves solely to scientific inquiry, it was still possible for the scientist to pursue his efforts almost singlehanded and with minimal facilities at his disposal. In the modern world, however, science has become a profession requiring an extended and elaborate training. Although great discoveries remain, for the most part, the creations of individuals often working by themselves, most scientists carry on their work as members of complex, usually bureaucratic organizations. In those fields in which the learned amateur can still make a significant contribution—in ornithology and mineralogy, for example—the isolated individual is often dependent upon professional assistance. Both the possibilities of individual work by nonprofessionals and its dependence upon expert assistance are illustrated in a recent study of hummingbirds by the president of a large American corporation who made considerable use of museum facilities and the aid of professional ornithologists. [27]

With increasing professionalization and the growth of scientific knowledge has come a marked degree of specialization. Few scientists can now master more than a relatively small portion of scientific knowledge and their research is on the whole confined to narrowly defined problems. The extent of this specialization is manifest in the large number of scientific associations and the thousands of scientific journals published around the world. In 1964 there were 298 organizations affiliated with the American Association for the Advancement of Science, most of them specialized scientific and professional groups, the rest state and local academies of science. Between 1950 and 1960, approximately 20,000 new scientfic journals appeared, constituting roughly one-third of the 60,000 journals included in *World List of Scientific Periodicals Published in the Years 1900–1960.*[28]

The extent of the scientific division of labor even within a single area of research is illustrated in the description by a scientist of steps involved in the discovery and analysis of a new "bacteriostatic and germicidal fraction" derived from soil bacteria.

It was discovered by the microbiologists and was fractionated by those running the Beams' air-driven centrifuge. It was passed to the bacteriologists and the cytologists to determine its qualities and powers, to the michrochemists for analysis, identification and determination of its probable composition, to the organic chemists for fractionation, to the spectroscopists for characterization and for the determination of the spectrographic differences . . . these fractions to the cytologists for toxicity and other experiments on animals, to the microscopists for record of crystalline structure, to the surgeons for study of its external effects upon badly infected wounds, to the physical chemists for the measurement of the physical constants and further study as to its structure.[29]

Such an elaborate division of labor requires some measure of coordination, and the research laboratory is now increasingly a bureaucratic organization characterized by hierarchy, specialists, rules, formal perquisites of office, and directed by the newly emerged scientist-administrator. (The role of the research administrator may vary considerably, however, as Norman Kaplan has shown. The director of a Soviet medical research institute, for example, does more research himself and is less engaged in "administering" than his American counterpart, a contrast that stems from both attitudes toward scientists and the over-all organization of research.[30]) The bureaucratization of research possesses the undoubted advantages of rational administration; it makes possible the efficient use of highly trained, specialized personnel and the elaborate physical resources required in most fields in a sustained attack on research problems. In doing so, of course, it places the direction in which research will move to a substantial degree in the hands of those who control the organization rather than leaving it to the diverse interests of the scientists themselves.

Bureaucratic organization, however, often inhibits the research process because of the demands made upon scientists. "Managers," the Assistant Dean of the Graduate School of Business Administration of Harvard has observed, "expect the demands of the organization to be met by the people working in the research laboratory to the same measure and in the same way these demands are met by other departments of their company," often with deleterious effects upon the "climate for creativity."[31] In their efforts to make "organization men" out of their scientists, William H. Whyte has asserted, many research laboratories are diminishing the scientific productivity of their researchers.[32]

Bureaucratization need not produce such results, as evident in the success of a few of the leading industrial research laboratories in the United States and in the scientific achievements of the Soviet Union, where science, like industry and education, is centrally controlled and constrained. Although the requirements of rational organization may often lend themselves to restraints upon individuality, it is possible to plan for individual creativity and to encourage the unique contribution of the scientist who wants to pursue his own inquiries with little concern for organizational requirements. When Irving Langmuir, who made major scientific contributions as an employee of the Western Electric Company, tried to explain his success in a speech at a testimonial banquet in his honor, he said.

"You know, I never had to worry about budgets." [33] Scientists, too, often develop "mechanisms of autonomy" in the operations of the research laboratory that protect them from inordinate organizational pressures.[34]

The growing scale of scientific research has required—and secured—increasing amounts of money. In 1930, just over $150 million were spent for research in the United States; by 1940 these expenditures had risen to $350 million. In 1950, the total spent on research and development was almost $3 billion, by 1960, $13 billion, and in the mid-1960s, approximately $20 billion. These funds included expenditures for "basic research"; "applied research," that is, the effort to find practical applications of new knowledge; and development, the translation of research findings into such "hardware" as military weapons, nuclear reactors, and space vehicles. Of the almost $15 billion allocated to research and development by the federal government in 1965, 12 per cent was for basic research, 22 per cent for applied, and almost two-thirds of the total for development.[35] (For a breakdown of the use of Federal funds in research in 1965 see Figure 5.)

The major source of the increase in expenditures for science has been the Federal government, which not only supports its own research but also pays for much of the research carried on in industry and the universities. In 1965 almost 80 per cent of government spending for science went to industry, the universities, and other nongovernmental bodies. In 1963, over three-quarters of the $1.7 billion spent on research in the universities and almost three-fifths of the funds for research in industry came from the government.[36]

Industry's commitment of its own resources to research has also steadily grown. Prior to World War II, industry spent about $300 million per year for research. In 1947 research expenditures by industry were approximately $500 million. While corporate expenditures for research have continued to grow, from over $2 billion in 1952 to more than $5 million in 1963, industry has received a steadily expanding flow of research funds from government, from almost $1.5 billion in 1953 to more than $7 billion in 1963.[37]

Research in colleges and universities has also steadily grown in size an scope, although it remains a relatively small proportion of the total scientific enterprise in the United States, albeit of strategic importance in the furthering of scientific knowledge. In 1961 there were over 80,000 scientists (excluding over 21,000 social scientists and more than 6,000 psychologists) on the faculties of 1,712 col-

In 1963 a group of scientists specializing in high-energy physics proposed a long-range research program that would cost $500 million a year by 1972. Such elaborate proposals reflect the cost of research equipment like the Cosmotron at Brookhaven National Laboratory, which accelerates protons to an energy of 3 billion electron volts. The extent to which such proposals are accepted depends upon the complex processes of the "politics of science."

Brookhaven National Laboratory

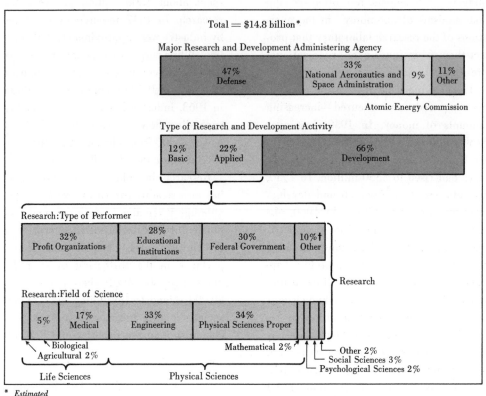

Total = $14.8 billion*

Major Research and Development Administering Agency

| 47% Defense | 33% National Aeronautics and Space Administration | 9% | 11% Other |

↑ Atomic Energy Commission

Type of Research and Development Activity

| 12% Basic | 22% Applied | 66% Development |

Research:Type of Performer

| 32% Profit Organizations | 28% Educational Institutions | 30% Federal Government | 10%† Other |

Research

Research:Field of Science

| 5% | 17% Medical | 33% Engineering | 34% Physical Sciences Proper | | | |

Biological
Agricultural 2%   Mathematical 2%   Other 2%
Life Sciences   Physical Sciences   Social Sciences 3%
                                                    Psychological Sciences 2%

* Estimated
† Includes other nonprofit organizations and other domestic and foreign organizations.

Figure 5. Characteristics of Federal Obligations for Basic Research, Applied Research, and Development, Fiscal Year 1965

National Science Foundation, *Federal Funds for Research Development, and Other Scientific Activities*, XV (Washington, D.C.: U.S. Government Printing Office, 1965), Chart 1, p. viii.

leges and universities surveyed by the National Science Foundation. Almost one-third of these were in two-year institutions or in colleges which offered no graduate work and did little or no research. Faculty members, on the average, devoted only one-quarter of their time to research activities.[38] Yet university scientists are of far greater importance than their numbers would suggest, for they are responsible for training future scientists and they contribute a disproportionately large share of the major additions to basic scientific knowledge upon which applications rest.

The fact that government and industry support most of the scientific research being carried on in America, including much of the work being done in universities, inevitably affects the nature of that research. As in many other areas, he who pays the piper calls at least some of the tunes, and industry and government are, on the whole and despite some exceptions, concerned with immediate results and the solution of practical problems. Industry seeks new products and more efficient methods of production and distribution, and most scientists employed by private industry devote their efforts to these goals.

Most government-sponsored research since the end of World War II has been connected with military needs or, particularly since 1957, when Russia launched its Sputnik, with space satellites and space travel. The 1966 Federal budget allocated 45 per cent of the more than $15 billion science budget to the Department of Defense, one-third to the National Aeronautics and Space Administration, and 8 per cent to the Atomic Energy Commission, much of whose efforts are connected with defense. [39]

In their support of research, both government and industry have especially emphasized the physical sciences. In 1965, almost 70 per cent of Federal research funds were assigned to the physical sciences, while less than one-quarter went to the life sciences (see Figure 5). Because of the needs and interests of the consumers of scientific research—military planners, political leaders, corporate executives, farmers, and so on—some fields are pushed ahead more energetically than others. The varying rates of progress that result from these differences in support sometimes create difficulties for both scientists and the public. Thus the development of food additives and their acceptance and use by industry have been so rapid that biologists have been unable as yet to explore intensively their effects upon humans. Similarly, knowledge of the biological consequences of increased radioactivity has followed only slowly upon the rapid development of devices that create higher levels of radioactivity in the world.

Basic and applied
science

The allocation of funds and utilization of scientists by industry and government not only define the areas of investigation to be most fully explored, but also influence the relative amount of "basic" research being carried on. Basic research is concerned solely with gaining new knowledge without regard to immediate practical uses, whereas "applied" research seeks to use knowledge already available in the solution of immediate problems. The difference between basic and applied research can be illustrated in the contrast between investigation of the nature of solar radiation and the research necessary to fire a ballistics missile that can hit a designated target.

The line between basic and applied research is not always easily drawn, for basic research sometimes can have immediately practical application, just as research directed toward pressing objectives fairly often raises new theoretical questions or leads to significant additions to fundamental knowledge. Basic research in the field of polymer chemistry, for example, led to the development of nylon and other synthetic fibers, whereas the effort to explain static in transatlantic radio-telephone messages stimulated the emergence of radio astronomy as a new field of scientific specialization. Despite the continuous interplay between basic and applied science, and occasional researches that may appear to belong to both of these categories, there is considerable agreement on the differences between them and upon the need for continuing or expanding effort in basic research.

Long-run scientific progress requires a steady flow of new theories and findings, without which the stream of practical advances will eventually slow down, perhaps even dry up. The proper ratio of basic to applied research cannot, of course, be defined precisely, but many scientists argue that the greater the investment of resources and effort in basic research, the faster the tempo of scientific advance in applied research.[40] So important is basic research as part of continuing scientific growth that its support has been explicitly undertaken as part of the Federal government's "science policy"—although there are those who continue to criticize governmental support of basic science as inadequate. In 1963, the government spent over $1 billion for basic research; by 1966 more than $2 billion was allocated, 13 per cent of total government expenditures for science.

Government policy, of course, is influenced by many forces including prevailing public attitudes, the judgment of politicians, and the pressures exerted by various groups, among them scientists themselves. It has long been noted that Americans are characteristically concerned with practical questions rather than with abstract theory. Writing in the 1830s, Alexis de Tocqueville observed that

In America the purely practical part of science is admirably understood, and careful attention is paid to the theoretical portion which is immediately requisite to application. On this head the Americans always display a clear, free, original, and inventive power of mind. But hardly anyone in the United States devotes himself to the essentially theoretical and abstract portion of human knowledge.[41]

Until World War II American science relied heavily upon the basic research of Europeans. The achievement of the atomic bomb reflected the quality of American applied science and technological skill, as well as effective organization (the bureaucratization) of scientific effort, but it rested chiefly upon the theoretical contributions of European scientists, many of whom came to the United States as refugees. Since the war American scientists have been contributing more substantially to fundamental scientific theory, as evident in an increased

number of Nobel prizes in recent years. Yet there remains a widespread disregard or, at times, even hostility to basic research and a preference for research directed to the solution of clearly identifiable "practical" problems, even among those who must often make decisions regarding governmental science policy. Charles E. Wilson, for example, one-time president of General Motors and Secretary of Defense in the Eisenhower administration, once commented, "Basic research is when you don't know what you are doing." Scientists asked to advise on scientific policy have usually pressed for both more funds in general and for greater support of basic research, but such suggestions have to pass through both administrative and legislative channels in which various pressures, such as receptivity to popular feelings, can affect the outcome.

The extent and effectiveness of basic research depends upon various social and cultural circumstances as well as upon the financial resources that are made available. The chief locale for basic research is in colleges and universities, which devote a far greater proportion of their scientific efforts to the pursuit of fundamental new knowledge than do either government or industry. In 1963, 4 per cent of industry's expenditures for science were for basic research, compared with 11 per cent of the government's spending, and half of that spent by colleges and universities. Although the latter were responsible for less than one-tenth of the total national research budget, they accounted for almost half of the amount spent on basic research.[42]

The importance of the academic contribution to scientific discovery is evident in both the amount of basic research carried on in university laboratories and in the large proportion of leading scientists found in academic positions. In 1938 almost three-quarters of the "starred" scientists in *American Men of Science*, that is, those chosen by their colleagues for their accomplishments, came from colleges and universities.[43] A postwar study that sought to identify the most promising young scientists in industry and the universities found that only four of 225 came from industrial laboratories.[44]

The circumstances of academic research therefore presumably draw the more creative scientists and encourage the "uncommitted" investigations that push forward the boundaries of knowledge. Left to his own devices, the academic scientist is freer to pursue those questions that catch his curiosity, whereas the scientist in industry and government is characteristically assigned specific problems on which to work. Even when freed from regular tasks in order to follow his own interests, however, the industrial and government scientist often finds himself caught up in those practical investigations that constitute the chief concern of the organization in which he works.

Both the money now available to universities and the resulting organization of research, however, have created problems that threaten the long-range development of science. Increasing demands upon academic scientists for work on pressing problems and the growing volume of scientific administration—allocation of funds, approval and supervision of projects, advice on government scientific policy—interfere with the continued pursuit of basic knowledge, particularly by the ablest scientists. Perhaps of greater importance is the potential influence of these elaborate demands upon the training of scientists, a function which colleges and universities must continue to perform adequately if the scientific needs of the future are to be met.

In order to pursue necessary research objectives, some universities have undertaken to staff and manage large research centers such as the Jet Propulsion Laboratory operated by the California Institute of Technology for the Army and the Los Alamos Scientific Laboratory run by the University of California for the Atomic Energy Commission. The assignment of scientists to these and similar research centers and a growing separation of research and teaching functions on university campuses have threatened to weaken scientific instruction, particularly at the graduate level. The problem of adequate science teaching has been further complicated by differences between normal academic salaries and the remuneration available in full-time research positions, which therefore tend to draw scientists away from academic posts.

Recruitment of scientists

The pattern of monetary rewards constitutes, of course, an important factor in distributing scientists in the several types of organization in which they work, although other motives are also obviously operating—for example, the desire for freedom to pursue one's own research interests, a liking or dislike for teaching or administration, a preference for life in an academic community, and so on. Both pecuniary and nonpecuniary conditions also affect recruitment into scientific professions, a process of great significance for the future. The number of potentially productive young men and women drawn into scientific careers is affected not only by the economic rewards they may gain, but also by the opportunities available to secure the necessary training, and by the prevailing images of the life, work, and character of the scientist.

The need for an increasing number of scientists has led in recent years to a marked increase in the number of fellowships and scholarships available for graduate study. Much of the money for these grants has come from the Federal government. But recruitment usually begins well before students reach the graduate level, and there appear to be widespread stereotypes of the scientist that undoubtedly affect the willingness of some potentially able students to embark upon careers in science. In a study in 1957 of the images of the scientist found among American high school students, Margaret Mead and Rhoda Metraux found complex, mixed responses. On the one hand, the scientist was looked upon as a "truly wonderful man" on whose efforts the future depends, one who was dedicated, selfless, courageous, persistent, and hard-working. On the other hand, he was also seen as narrow, irreligious, poorly rewarded, in frequent danger, overly intellectual, and unsociable.[45] A follow-up study among college students elicited similar responses; although admired for his dedication and respected for his intellectual abilities, the scientist was identified as introverted, with few friends, and probably leading an unhappy home life.[46] These images, of course, like many stereotypes, have relatively little connection with reality, but may nevertheless influence some young people.

Which aspects of these complex stereotypes are emphasized and how the possible rewards available to scientists are evaluated are affected by the individual's social position and the attitudes and values associated with it. Although the studies of images of the scientist do not provide data on how various social groups and categories differ in their attitudes, it seems very likely that substantial differences exist. Scientists are, in fact, not drawn proportionately from all segments of the population. There are few female scientists (of the 215,000 listed in the National Register of Scientific and Technical Personnel compiled by the National Science Foundation in 1962, only 6.7 per cent were women), in part because a substantial proportion of American women are not engaged in any gainful employment, but in part also because of the nature of feminine roles, feminine interests, and attitudes of potential employers. Catholics too are underrepresented among scientists, again for complex reasons that include the nature of Catholicism, the character of Catholic educational institutions, and the fact that until recently Catholics were concentrated in the lower reaches of the class structure where educational opportunities were limited.

The majority of scientists have come from middle-class, often professional, family backgrounds and in substantial numbers from small towns or rural areas. As undergraduates, many of them attended small, frequently Protestant church-related, liberal-arts colleges rather than large universities or institutions in the Ivy League.[47] In all likelihood lower- and upper-class students shy away from science for different reasons: the lower class because of scanty knowledge, critical images of the scientist, and limited educational opportunities and stimulation; the upper class because opportunities are open for greater wealth, power, and prestige than can be acquired in a scientific career. To the middle class, science promises interesting work, prestige, and reasonable rewards and, particularly for the lower middle class, opportunities to move up in the social structure on the basis of ability and effort.

However, these data on the social origins of scientists are drawn from the past (the most recent study cited appeared in 1952), and changes taking place both within science and in society at large are affecting the sources from which future scentists will be drawn. The weakening of ethnic, religious, and racial barriers that have existed in the past, particularly in industry and universities, already has permitted many Jews—and members of other groups—to pursue scientific careers. The steady increase in the number of gainfully employed females may also bring more women into scientific ranks. A growing awareness of the social consequences of science among both scientists and laymen and changes taking place in the scientists' role will no doubt affect both attitudes toward scientists and the sources from which scientists are drawn.

The public role of the scientist

So complex and extensive are the consequences of scientific knowledge and its application for modern society that no adequate analysis is possible here. The mere listing of some of the specific achievements of recent years suggests how pervasive its influence is: antibiotics to control disease and lengthen the life span; pills to prevent conception; atomic energy with its awful and awe-inspiring possibilities; missiles and rockets to change the nature of warfare; space travel; automation in industry to increase production; the use of computers to determine policy in the Department of Defense—or to pair off men and women. Modern industry is heavily dependent upon the research laboratory, from which come a ceaseless flow of new products and new methods of production.

Scientific inquiry now constitutes a built-in disturber of the social order; as new ideas, techniques, and products emerge from study and laboratory, they continually affect accepted beliefs, institutions, and social relations. When the social consequences of scientific discoveries are quickly apparent, some efforts may be made to control the introduction of new techniques and devices, or to deal with their effects. But the thrust of science is often felt only imperceptibly and after some time has elapsed, and so strongly is modern society committed to science that its contributions are often accepted without thought for their long-range results.

One of the significant consequences of the scientific achievements of recent years has been a change in the activities of scientists and in their own conceptions of their role in society. Prior to World War II most scientists confined their professional activities to the laboratory or classroom. As scientists they tended to avoid any concern with public issues and to disregard as no concern of theirs the problems stemming from the application and uses of scientific knowledge. Although they might pursue their work with the deep conviction that it was socially useful, they defined their own responsibility solely by the canons of science.

But events of the war and the postwar years—for example, the dropping of atomic bombs on Japan, the development of the even more powerful hydrogen bomb, the rapid expansion of scientific research, most of which is supported by the government, the imposition of secrecy upon a great deal of research effort, the rapid development of complex electronic computers that can simulate the psychological responses of men as well as carry out elaborate calculations—have forced many scientists to re-examine their conception of their place in society. Can they disavow responsibility for the uses of scientific knowledge, or do they have some role to play not only as citizens, but also as scientists, in determining when and how the fruits of their investigations should be used? The resulting pressure to enlarge the scientists' role and to assign them additional responsibilities has been further stimulated by the extent to which they have, in fact, been called into public life—as expert witnesses before Congressional committees, as advocates of specific policies, as advisors and consultants to public officials, including the President of the United States.

The problem of the social responsibilities of the scientist has been linked with another, the impact of external forces upon the integrity of science itself. In a 1965 report by the Committee on Science in the Promotion of Human Welfare of the American Association for the Advancement of Science, the question was raised: "Can the very success of science and its closer interaction with the rest of our culture lay it open to the influence of new and possibly alien points of view which derive from other sectors of society: military, business, or political?" [48] After reviewing a number of important cases—the explosion of nuclear devices in space, Project Apollo to land men on the moon, radioactive fallout, the side effects of new products such as detergents and insecticides derived from scientific research—the Committee concluded that "there have been serious erosions in the integrity of science." [49]

Among scientists themselves, there is no agreement concerning their proper role outside the classroom and laboratory. Some simply emphasize the need and responsibility to participate as informed citizens in the discussion of all political issues related to science. Others, rather than engage in public debate, try to persuade government officials to follow a specific course of action on particular matters that concern them—support of science, atomic testing, control over new drugs. A third group, typified by the Society for Social Responsibility in Science, argues that scientists are morally bound to oppose the use of science for improper or unethical ends, although they have been chiefly concerned with research on new weapons of destruction for the military. Still others take the view that their role is merely to bring to public attention the facts, principles, and alternative possibilities relevant to particular problems in the use of scientific discoveries.

In 1960 the A.A.A.S. Committee on Science in the Promotion of Human Welfare tried to define a proper role for scientists by distinguishing among the several types of issues in relation to which they might be expected to act. [50] On those questions connected with the development of science itself, they claim a "special weight" for the opinions of scientists, while insisting that "scientists should accept the obligation to develop and explain their opinions." Yet there is often not only lack of unanimity on many questions concerning the direction in which science should move but even sharp conflict; since resources available for research are never unlimited, each group is apt to seek as large a share as possible without reference to the scientific enterprise as a whole.

With respect to questions which are "in essence social and political," the Committee outlined a complex position. As citizens, scientists, of course, can participate with others in the political process. As scientists, they have an obligation to perform an important educational function, informing the public of relevant facts and, insofar as knowledge is available, of the likely consequences of alternative programs involving the use of scientific discoveries. In addition they have a responsibility to identify the potential problems stemming from scientific advances. Finally, they must protect the integrity of science against those pressures threatening to erode traditional scientific values. In carrying out these responsibilities both individual efforts and those of scientific organizations are called for.

Acceptance of all these responsibilities would, of course, place a heavy burden upon scientists and many—perhaps most—of them will probably continue to confine themselves simply to their usual activities of research and teaching. A few scientists devote all or some of their efforts to popularizing scientific knowledge in areas they view of great public interest and importance.[51] Others pursue those problems that they believe to be of immediate social significance—for example, the biological effects of food additives, the genetic consequences of radiation, the effects on animals of insecticides. Since such research will usually have to be carried on within the confines and under the aegis of some organization with the requisite facilities, these private choices will not necessarily affect the amount of scientific attention actually focused on problems. As we noted earlier, how much effort is directed toward scientific problems depends upon a complex set of circumstances, of which the scientists' judgment of relative importance is only one.

Many of the public functions that some scientists now regard as obligatory upon them are in fact performed through scientific organizations and by a handful of leading figures. The specific contribution of scientists to the discussion of public issues and the determination of public policy will therefore depend in large measure upon how scientists' opinions are expressed, which scientists come to represent scientific societies and professional associations, and which individuals are chosen to advise policy makers.

In the years since World War II, an elaborate—and still evolving—structure has emerged in the United States for utilizing the knowledge and judgment of scientists in determing public policy with reference to both the development of science and the problems emerging from scientific achievments. Those who are part of that structure, Don K. Price has suggested, constitute a "scientific establishment" with ready access to the centers of power, capped by the President's Science Advisor and the Presidents' Science Advisory Committee.[52] Various estimates place the number of scientists in this "establishment" at from 200 to 1,000, depending upon whether or not they include only those who are "consistently influential" or embrace spokesmen for various scientific organizations with no official authority as well.[53]

So complex are many of the questions related to science and its application and development that the line between purely scientific judgments and politically tinged opinions is not always easily drawn. Scientists themselves, as we have pointed out, do not speak with a single voice, and they often disagree on public issues involving scientific matters. The most obvious example of such disagreement is the debate which took place over the nuclear test ban treaty. Such differences may reflect the fact that all the scientific evidence is not in and that final answers to many scientific questions are not possible. But when final answers are not available, nonscientific judgments, perhaps inevitably, influence the opinions scientists express. Since many of the recommendations and decisions emerge from the efforts and activities of a relatively small group, the process by which they are arrived at entails what C. P. Snow described, in a controversial analysis, as "closed committee politics." [54]

Because of their knowledge and prestige, scientists are sometimes assumed to be better equipped to determine how the fruits of their work shall be used, and some scientists use their advantageous position to press for particular policies. Although knowledge of the technological possibilities stemming from scientific discoveries can only come from the scientist, whose participation in policy making is therefore essential, the final decision on how new knowledge and new devices shall be used does not rest upon scientific criteria, but upon moral and political grounds. In this area of decision, therefore, the scientist's knowledge may be far more limited than that of the social scientist or the practical administrator in industry or government.

Notes

[1] Marjorie Nicholson, *Science and Imagination* (Ithaca: Cornell University Press, 1956).

[2] Herbert Butterfield, *The Origins of Modern Science* (New York: Macmillan, 1951), p. 140.

[3] American Association for the Advancement of Science Interim Committee on the Social Aspects of Science, "Social Aspects of Science," *Science*, CXXV (January 25, 1957), 143.

[4] Lucien Lévy-Bruhl, *Primitive Mentality*, trans. by Lilian A. Clare (New York: Macmillan, 1923).

[5] Bronislaw Malinowski, *Magic, Science, and Religion and Other Essays* (Garden City: Doubleday Anchor Books, 1954), p. 34.

[6] *Ibid.*, pp. 34–5.

[7] *Ibid.*, p. 35.

[8] Quoted in Benjamin Farrington, *Greek Science*, I (Harmondsworth: Penguin, 1949), 13. Farrington cites a French scholar, Anold Reymond.

[9] Farrington, *op. cit.*

[10] Benjamin Farrington, *Greek Science*, II (Harmondsworth: Penguin, 1949), 164.

[11] O. Neugabauer, *The Exact Sciences in Antiquity* (Princeton: Princeton University Press, 1952), p. 145.

[12] Farrington, *op. cit.*, II, 163.

[13] Robert K. Merton, *Social Theory and Social Structure* (rev. and enlarged ed.; New York: Free Press, 1957), pp. 608–9.

[14] *Ibid.*, p. 626.

[15] *Ibid.*, p. 609.

[16] For a summary of these studies, see *Ibid.*, pp. 590–5. For a contrary view, which argues that the important predisposing factor was a "liberal hedonist" philosophy, see Lewis Feuer, *The Scientific Intellectual* (New York: Basic Books, 1963).

[17] R. H. Knapp and H. B. Goodrich, *Origins of American Scientists* (Chicago: University of Chicago Press, 1952), p. 274.

[18] Merton, *op. cit.*, p. 536.

[19] Joseph Ben-David, "Scientific Productivity and Academic Organization in Nineteenth Century Medicine," *American Sociological Review*, XXV (December, 1960), 828–43.

[20] J. Robert Oppenheimer, *The Open Mind* (New York: Simon & Schuster, 1955), p. 114.

[21] Merton, *op. cit.*, p. 560.

[22] Oppenheimer, *op. cit.*, p. 115.

[23] See Robert K. Merton, "Priorities in Scientific Discovery," *American Sociological Review*, XXII (December, 1957), 635–59.

[24] For discussions of the problems of secrecy and security in science, see Walter

Gellhorn, *Security, Loyalty and Science* (Ithaca: Cornell University Press, 1950); and Edward Shils, *The Torment of Secrecy* (New York: Free Press, 1956).

25 Quoted in J. D. Bernal, *The Social Function of Science* (London: Routledge, 1939), p. 9.

26 Eric Ashby, *Technology and the Academics* (London: Macmillan, 1959), p. 5.

27 Crawford H. Greenwalt, *Hummingbirds* (New York: Doubleday, 1960).

28 P. Brown and G. B. Stratton (eds.), *World List of Scientific Periodicals Published in the Years 1900–1960*, 4 vols. (4th ed.; London: Butterworth, 1963). The third edition, which covered the years 1900–1950, included approximately 50,000 titles, of which roughly 10,000 were excluded from the fourth edition as of "social or commercial interest rather than scientific."

29 Ellice McDonald, *Research and its Organization* (Newark, Del.: Biochemical Research Foundation, n.d. [c. 1950]), quoted in Bernard Barber, *Science and the Social Order* (New York: Free Press, 1952), pp. 128–9.

30 Norman Kaplan, "Research Administration and the Administrator: U.S.S.R. and United States," in Norman Kaplan (ed.), *Science and Society* (Chicago: Rand McNally, 1965), pp. 329–46.

31 Charles D. Orth III, "The Optimum Climate for Industrial Research," in Kaplan, *Science and Society*, p. 198.

32 William H. Whyte, Jr., *The Organization Man* (New York: Simon & Schuster, 1956), Part V.

33 Quoted in Orth, *op. cit.*, p. 200.

34 See William Kornhauser, *Scientists in Industry* (Berkeley: University of California Press, 1962).

35 Data for 1930 and 1940 are from Barber, *op. cit.*, p. 132. Data for 1950 and 1960 are from "How Much Research for a Dollar?" *Science*, CXXXII (August 26, 1960), 517. Data for the mid-1960s are from National Science Foundation, *Reviews of Data on Science Resources*, I,

No. 4 (Washington: U.S. Government Printing Office, May, 1965), Table 2a, p. 6. Data for 1965 are from National Science Foundation, *Federal Funds for Research Development, and Other Scientific Activities*, XV (Washington: U.S. Government Printing Office, 1965), Chart 1, p. viii.

36 National Science Foundation, *Data on Science Resources, loc. cit.*

37 *Ibid.*

38 National Science Foundation, *Scientists and Engineers in Colleges and Universities, 1961* (Washington: U.S. Government Printing Office, 1964), p. 5, Table A-1, p. 34, Table A-6, p. 39.

39 Computed from data in Ralph E. Lapp, *The New Priesthood* (New York: Harper, 1965), p. 191.

40 For an expression of this view, see James B. Conant, "The Impact of Science on Industry and Medicine," *American Scientist*, XXXIX (January, 1951), 33–49. For a similar statement on this point by a representative of private industry, see E. V. Murphree, "The Support of Basic Research," *American Scientist*, XXXIX (April, 1951), 268–73.

41 Alexis de Tocqueville, *Democracy in America*, II, Henry Reeve text, corrected and edited by Phillips Bradley (New York: Random House Vintage Books, 1954), 43.

42 Computed from data in National Science Foundation, *Data on Scientific Resources*, Table 2a, p. 6, and Table 3a, p. 7.

43 Barber, *op. cit.*, p. 140.

44 Whyte, *op. cit.*, p. 207.

45 Margaret Mead and Rhoda Metraux, "Image of the Scientist Among High-School Students," *Science*, CXXVI (August 30, 1957), 384–90.

46 David C. Beardslee and Donald D. O'Dowd, "The College-Student Image of the Scientist," *Science*, CXXXIII (March 31, 1961), 997–1001.

47 See Barber, *op. cit.*, pp. 134–8, for a summary of data on social origins; and Knapp and Goodrich, *op. cit.*, for data on

academic backgrounds and, in Ch. 19, for an interesting interpretation of the reasons for the distinctive social attributes of American scientists.

[48] American Association for the Advancement of Science Committee on Science in the Promotion of Human Welfare, "The Integrity of Science," *American Scientist*, LIII (June, 1965), 175.

[49] *Ibid.*, p. 195.

[50] American Association for the Advancement of Science Committee on Science in the Promotion of Human Welfare, "Science and Human Welfare," *Science*, 132 (July 8, 1960), 68–73.

[51] See, for example, the work of marine biologist Rachel Carson, *The Silent Spring* (Boston: Houghton Mifflin, 1962), and of physicist Ralph Lapp, *Must We Hide?* (Cambridge, Mass.: Addison-Wesley, 1949); and *The Voyage of the Lucky Dragon* (New York: Harper, 1958).

[52] Don K. Price, "The Scientific Establishment," in Robert Gilpin and Christopher Wright (eds.), *Scientists and National Policy-Making* (New York: Columbia University Press, 1964), pp. 19–40; and Don K. Price, *The Scientific Estate* (Cambridge, Mass.: Harvard University Press, 1965).

[53] For a summary of various estimates, see Robert C. Wood, "Scientists and Politics: The Rise of an Apolitical Elite," in Gilpin and Wright, *op. cit.*, p. 48. A detailed estimate is available in Christopher Wright, "Scientists and the Establishment of Scientific Affairs," in Gilpin and Wright, *op. cit.*, pp. 257–302.

[54] C. P. Snow, *Science and Government* (Cambridge, Mass.: Harvard University Press, 1960), pp. 56–66.

Suggestions for further reading

AMERICAN ASSOCIATION FOR THE ADVANCEMENT OF SCIENCE COMMITTEE ON SCIENCE IN THE PROMOTION OF HUMAN WELFARE. "Science and Human Welfare," *Science*, CXXXII (July 8, 1960), 68–73.
A thoughtful statement by a group of distinguished scientists on the problems created by recent revolutionary changes in science and their implications for the social role of the scientist.

AMERICAN ASSOCIATION FOR THE ADVANCEMENT OF SCIENCE COMMITTEE ON SCIENCE IN THE PROMOTION OF HUMAN WELFARE. "The Integrity of Science," *American Scientist*, LIII (June, 1965), 174–98.
An assessment of the impact of recent events upon the autonomy and strength of science.

ASHBY, ERIC. *Technology and the Academics.* London: Macmillan, 1959.
An essay on the impact of science upon British universities and on the role of the universities in the development of science.

BARBER, BERNARD. *Science and the Social Order.* New York: Free Press, 1952.
A straightforward and useful general discussion of the sociology of science.

BARBER, BERNARD. "Sociology of Science: A Trend Report and Bibliography," *Current Sociology*, V, No. 2 (1956), entire issue.
A summary of recent work in the sociology of science and a comprehensive annotated bibliography.

BARBER, BERNARD, AND WALTER HIRSCH (eds.). *The Sociology of Science.* New York: Free Press, 1962.
A useful collection of papers.

BERNAL, J. D. *The Social Functions of Science.* London: Routledge, 1939.
Written from a Marxist point of view by a distinguished British biologist, this book is a pioneering attempt to explore the relations between science and society and to suggest the conditions under which science could thrive most fully.

BUTTERFIELD, HERBERT. *The Origins of Modern Science: 1300–1800.* New York: Macmillan, 1951.
A useful historical account of the emergence of modern science.

CARDWELL, D. S. L. *The Organization of Science in England.* London: Heinemann, 1957.
An account of the development of science in England from 1800 to 1914 that focuses attention upon the role of the universities and other organizations that influenced the number and status of scientists.

CROMBIE, A. C. (ed.). *Scientific Change.* New York: Basic Books, 1963.
Although historical in emphasis, this collection of papers on "the intellectual, social and technical conditions for scientific discovery and technical invention from antiquity to the present" contains a great deal of interesting and useful sociological material.

FARRINGTON, BENJAMIN. *Greek Science.* 2 vols. Harmondsworth: Penguin, 1949.
The development and social background of science in ancient Greece.

GILPIN, ROBERT, AND CHRISTOPHER WRIGHT (eds.). *Scientists and National Policy-Making.* New York: Columbia University Press, 1964.
A useful set of essays on the role of scientists in determining public policy.

HAGSTROM, WARREN. *The Scientific Community.* New York: Basic Books, 1965.
A study of the customs, values, and social organization of science, based largely upon interviews with university scientists and focused primarily upon the influence of scientific colleagues upon one another.

KAPLAN, NORMAN (ed.). *Science and Society.* Chicago: Rand McNally, 1965.
An excellent collection of papers that explore the organization of science and its place in modern society.

KNAPP, ROBERT H., AND HUBERT B. GOODRICH. *Origins of American Scientists.* Chicago: University of Chicago Press, 1952.
A thorough study of the social origins and educational backgrounds of scientists in the United States.

KORNHAUSER, WILLIAM. *Scientists in Industry: Conflict and Accommodation.* Berkeley: University of California Press, 1962.
A study of the problems of scientists in research organizations.

KUHN, THOMAS C. *The Structure of Scientific Revolutions.* Chicago: University of Chicago Press, 1962.
An important essay which tries to analyse scientific growth as a social and cultural process.

MERTON, ROBERT K. *Social Theory and Social Structure,* rev. and enlarged ed. New York: Free Press, 1957, Part IV, "Studies in the Sociology of Science."
Five essays on various aspects of the sociology of science by the leading American student in this field. See also his essay, "Priorities in Scientific Discovery," American Sociological Review, XXII (December, 1957), 635–59.

STORER, NORMAN, *The Social System of Science.* New York: Holt, Rinehart & Winston, 1966.
A brief, systematic effort "to develop a theory of the social organization of science."

SEVERAL JOURNALS FREQUENTLY CONTAIN ARTICLES ON THE RELATIONS BETWEEN SCIENCE AND SOCIETY:
American Scientist
Bulletin of the Atomic Scientists
Impact of Science on Society
Science

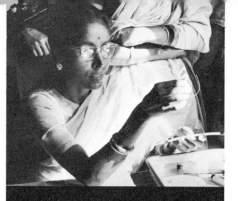

PART FOUR

Population and society

17

Population and society

The sociological relevance of population

The "population explosion" of recent years has focused world-wide attention upon demographic facts and problems. Between 1950 and 1964 the world's population grew from 2.4 to 3.2 billion, an increase of about one-third. India alone added over 80 million people between 1951 and 1961 and, by the mid-1960s, was estimated to be nearing 500 million. Mainland China reported a population of 583 million in 1953 with an annual rate of increase of about 2 per cent; although no precise figures are available, estimates place the Chinese population in the mid-1960s at from 650 to 700 million. In the decade between 1950 and 1960, the population of the United States rose by approximately 30 million, to which almost 20 million were added in the succeeding five years. And many other nations in various parts of the world—Latin America, Africa, Asia—have grown at even higher rates.

The consequences of such rapid growth are widespread and often readily apparent. Some nations seeking to industrialize and to raise standards of living seem to be mounted upon an economic treadmill, running with all their might to increase their output of goods, only to find that they have barely enough to provide for additional millions of hungry mouths.

Egyptian census figures, for example, suggest the possibility that population growth will absorb the potential fruits of the projected Aswan Dam, which will irrigate a million acres of new farm land in addition to providing electric power, even before it is complete.[1] In the United States, where such economic problems hardly exist, school boards anxiously study birth rates and the number of young people in each age group as they plan for future school needs; increasing numbers of old people stimulate research on aging and the development of special programs for "senior citizens."

The relevance of population composition and growth to the relations among nations is also evident. Some Americans express concern about the possible consequences of China's rapidly expanding population, now more than three times as large as that of the United States. In their private thoughts the Russians too, with a population of about 225 million, may have similar concerns. These anxieties about differences in size of population reflect important realities, for numbers constitute a significant element in the power of nations. Economic development may compensate in large part for limited numbers, and economic backwardness may prevent populous countries from capitalizing on their size; Canada, Australia, and Belgium are relatively powerful despite small populations, and Mexico, Brazil, and Pakistan do not have power commensurate with their size. Yet on the whole, small nations count for less than large, and no nation, Kingsley Davis suggests, can be a Great Power in the middle of the twentieth century with fewer than 60 million people.[2]

As these illustrations suggest, interest in *demography*, the study of population, is not confined to sociologists. Economists scan the prospective size of the labor supply and examine the relations between population and economic resources. Birth and death, and problems of health, disease, and longevity attract the attention of biologists. Because demographic research necessarily entails the manipulation and, increasingly, the highly technical analysis of statistical data, some statisticians too have undertaken the study of population.

Demography remains a field of interest of students from various disciplines, but there now appears to be a strong tendency to consider it as essentially a subfield of sociology.[3] This tendency has been strongly reinforced by past evidence that failure to take social and cultural variables into account when predicting population trends can often lead to grievous errors. By 1930 many demographers and laymen had come to believe that it was possible to estimate accurately future population size. Most of the projections offered in the late 1920s and early 1930s expected the American population to reach a maximum of between 144 million and 190 million before the end of the twentieth century, and then, in all likelihood, to decline. In 1931, for example, one demographer predicted a maximum population of from 148 to 154 million in 1980; another, in the same year, foresaw a peak of 144.6 million in 1970, followed

by a drop. A third offered the possibility of 190 million as his "high" estimate, but felt that the likely outcome would be closer to his "low" estimate of 145 million. Confidence in the reliability of demographic forecasts was reinforced by the results of the 1940 census, which came close to many of the predictions offered earlier.[4]

No sooner was the 1940 census complete, however, than events began to raise doubts about estimates of future population. By 1942 the birth rate had risen by 20 per cent over the 1939 figure. Although it dropped again in the next three years, it was still 13 per cent higher in 1945 than it had been in 1939, and it rose sharply in the years following the war. By 1950 the population already exceeded most of the maximum figures that had been projected for later in the century.

Many demographers conceded only reluctantly that the postwar "baby boom" represented a basic reversal of long-run trends and that their earlier estimates of future population were completely unreliable. It is now clear that predictions that simply carry into the future the trends evident in past demographic statistics are of doubtful value, and that demographic analysis must take into account the social and cultural variables—for example, education, cultural values, economic trends—that affect the birth and death rates among various groups as well as the flow of migration.

While the effort to account for population trends led demographers into sociological analysis, the relevance of demographic facts for culture and social structure has drawn sociologists increasingly into demography. We have already noted in Chapter 7, for example, the connection between a low birth rate and family structure. Demographic differences among various groups—for example, classes, rural and urban residents, and racial, ethnic, and religious groups—may also have significant social and cultural consequences, as well as contributing to the future composition of the total population. And the age distribution—the proportions over sixty-five and under fifteen—has obvious sociological implications.

Fertility

The basic demographic variables are fertility, mortality, and migration. These variables are of central importance because changes in the size of the population can come about only through changes in one or more of them, even though they are themselves strongly influenced by social, cultural, and biological facts.

But demography studies not only the number of people in a society but also the distribution of various attributes—age, sex, marital status, rural or urban residence, race, and so on. Age and sex are of primary demographic significance, for they are closely related to fertility and mortality and, sometimes, to migration. If the number of women in the childbearing ages increases, for example, it is probable that, other things being equal, the birth rate will go up. Or, as the proportion of old people rises, the death rate is also likely to rise.

In this chapter we shall focus attention chiefly on fertility and mortality, and on population trends. We shall not consider the problems of migration, which may occur as individual or group movement, across national boundaries or within nations, voluntarily or as the result of coercion. The immediate demographic results of migration are readily apparent—an increase or decrease in numbers; its long-run demographic impact depends upon the age and sex of the migrants. Its social and cultural consequences are found in large part in the relations among racial and ethnic groups examined in Chapter 9.

Fertility refers to the actual number of children born and should be distinguished from fecundity, the potential reproductive capacity of human beings. Physiologically, a woman can bear children for a period of approximately thirty years, from about fifteen to forty-five. Since there are periods of infertility after each child is born, the maximum number she can have, excluding multiple births, is about twenty or twenty-two. Although a few women may come close to this maximum, there is no society in which all, or even most, women are so fertile.

In every society fertility is in fact controlled in diverse ways, and is not simply the result of uncontrolled—or uncontrollable—biological forces. Deliberate efforts to prevent conception are found not only in modern society, in which contraceptive devices have been highly developed and widely used, but also in many other less advanced societies. Even crude contraceptive techniques, it has been shown, can substantially reduce fertility.[5] When unwanted pregnancies occur, abortions are often approved, and under some conditions abortion has become a recognized, even if sometimes officially disapproved, means of preventing women from having children. (For a discussion of such accepted devices for evading social norms, see pp. 479–81.)

In addition to institutionally sanctioned measures to prevent conception or the bearing of unwanted children, limits are also imposed on fertility by the social regulation of marriage and sexual relations. Since only married women are usually expected to have children, postponement of marriage after puberty diminishes the number of offspring women can bear. In the United States, for example, where the average age of marriage for women is now twenty, the period during which they can have children is only twenty-five rather than thirty years. A substantial number of single women can of course significantly reduce the birth rate.

Taboos on sexual intercourse, both before and after marriage, also lessen fertility. Requiring premarital chastity obviously prevents the birth of children among young nubile women. Among married women, prolonged periods of enforced separation from their husbands lessen opportunities for having children. Rules prohibiting remarriage of widows or of divorced women also lower the birth rate. Davis estimates, for example, on the basis of 1931 census data, that the interdiction of remarriage of widows in India reduced fertility among Hindus by about 15 per cent.[6]

Having children, however, is not merely a biological process limited in some degree by cultural and structural facts. It is also a motivated act that is encouraged in various ways by society. When children are economic assets, for example, as they were in colonial America, parents are prompted to have many of them. If men measure their virility by the number of children they sire, they are apt to want large families. In societies that suffer from high mortality, there are often religious values enjoining believers to "be fruitful and multiply." In classical China, fertility was encouraged by ancestor worship, which required a large number of children to ensure appropriate observances for the dead. Women in the traditional Chinese family wished to have children because their status in their husband's families improved as they did so,

particularly when they produced sons. Tax exemptions, family allowances, and other special privileges for parents ease the problems of having children in most industrial societies; in societies in which there are extended or compound families, the economic costs and physical demands are not confined to parents but are shared within the larger group.

Fertility, then, is the product of biological facts *and* complex social and cultural forces that may encourage childbearing or discourage and limit it. Changes in fertility are due to shifting cultural and social patterns, and fertility differences among various groups reflect contrasting values, institutions, and social organization.

The most frequent measure of fertility is the *crude birth rate*, the number of births each year for each 1,000 persons in the population—or for some other base figure. This rate, although it is a useful index of fertility, has serious limitations, for it does not take into account the age distribution and sexual composition of the population. A society with a small proportion of women of childbearing age will have a lower crude birth rate than one with a large proportion of such women even when women in both societies have, on the average, the same number of offspring. In order to avoid this limitation, demographers sometimes use the *general fertility rate*, which gives the number of children born for each 1,000 women aged fifteen to forty-four. A third measure that is sometimes applied is the *fertility ratio*, the number of children under five years of age for each 1,000 women between fifteen and forty-four.

Fertility trends

For the better part of the century prior to 1940, the birth rate of most Western Eu-

Table 25

CRUDE BIRTH RATES IN SELECTED EUROPEAN COUNTRIES

	France	Sweden	England and Wales	Germany	Netherlands	Belgium	Denmark
1811–1820	31.8						
1821–1830	31.0						
1831–1840	29.0						
1841–1850	27.4						
1851–1860	26.3	32.8					
1861–1870	26.3	31.4					
1871–1880	25.4	30.5	35.4	39.1	36.2	32.3	
1881–1890	23.9	29.1	32.5	36.8	34.2	30.2	32.0
1891–1900	22.2	27.1	29.9	36.1	32.5	29.0	30.2
1901–1910	20.6	25.8	27.2	33.0	30.5	26.1	28.7
1911–1920	15.3	22.0	21.8	23.5	26.8	17.7	24.8
1921–1930	18.8	17.5	18.3	20.2	24.5	19.5	20.8
1931–1940	15.5	14.4	14.8	17.9	20.8	15.8	17.9

Kurt B. Mayer, *The Population of Switzerland* (1952), Table 14, p. 75. Reprinted by permission of Columbia University Press.

ropean nations and of the United States dropped fairly steadily. (In France the decline had begun early in the nineteenth century.) Table 25 shows the crude birth rates of selected European countries from the time at which the decline began until 1940. In the United States the crude birth rate for 1871–1875 was 37.0. By 1896–1900 it had dropped to 29.8, and it continued to diminish steadily—to 27.7 in 1907, 24.2 in 1915–1920, 23.5 between 1921 and 1930, and to a low of 17.2 in the pre-World War II decade.[7]

Several explanations have been suggested for this widespread decline in fertility. The theory put forward by some writers that it reflects a drop in fecundity because of the enervating effects of modern civilization is unconvincing. The drop in the birth rate has been too rapid to be due to declining fecundity, Dennis Wrong suggests, because "changes in genetic reproductive capacity great enough to account for the downward trend would require several generations, yet the decline

was made manifest within a much shorter period."[8] Moreover, improvements in nutrition, medicine, and general physical standards of life would seem to be conducive to greater fecundity rather than to less.

The drop in fertility followed quickly upon the development of improved contraceptive techniques and a rapid dissemination of contraceptive information. The spread of birth control, according to other writers, is therefore the cause of declining birth rates. But the mere availability of contraceptive knowledge and of more efficient contraceptive devices is in itself an inadequate explanation, for it does not account for the willingness to seek out information on birth control or make use of known techniques for preventing conception.

The explanation for the long-run decline in fertility—and for increased use of contraceptive techniques—is to be found in complex social and cultural changes. Many lists of the relevant factors have been proposed. A British Royal Commission on population, for example, found the causes for an increase in the "deliberate restriction of births" and of the declining birth rate in the

profound changes that were taking place in the outlook and ways of living of the people during the 19th century. . . . They include the decay of small scale family handicrafts and the rise of large scale industry and factory organization; the loss of security and growth of competitive individualism; the relative decline in agriculture and the rise in importance of industry and commerce, and the associated shift of population from rural to urban areas; the growing prestige of science, which disturbed traditional religious beliefs; the development of popular education; higher standards of living; the growth of humanitarianism and the emancipation of women.[9]

This listing, which could be further elaborated, does include many of the factors that have affected fertility not only in Great Britain but also in other nations. But such an array of "causes" is deficient in several respects. It fails to distinguish among different types of variables; it ignores the relationships among them; and it does not try to establish their relative importance. Moreover, as J. A. Banks has noted, it is necessary to test these plausible speculations against available facts.[10]

It seems reasonable, for example, to suppose that industrialization and the gradual elimination of child labor lessened the economic value of children and thus discouraged large families. Yet in fact, the decline in the birth rate in England began only in the 1870s, well after the start of industrialization, and appeared first not in the economically hard-pressed working class, but instead in the prosperous middle class.[11] Industrialism affected fertility, then, only indirectly and through the other changes that came with the growth of modern technology and the forms of social organization that developed concurrently.

The growth of cities, which has often accompanied industrialization (although some large cities have no industry, and modern industry has sometimes been located in the rural countryside), generally contributes to a lower birth rate. Urban fertility is characteristically lower than that of rural areas, as is evident in Table 26, which shows recent differences in the fertility ratio in urban and rural areas in selected countries. In a review of historical data, A. J. Jaffee found similar differences in Sweden in the mid-eighteenth century, in the United States throughout the nineteenth century, and in various other countries in both past and present,[12] although some underdeveloped countries such as India, for reasons that are not clear, do not show the usual relationship between urbanism and fertility. By and large, however, with increasing urbanization, the birth rate is likely to diminish.

Like other large-scale social changes, urbanism exerts its influence upon fertility through alterations in social values and in the institutions that govern family life and sexual behavior. The growth of cities, it has been suggested, brings with it an increase in ambition and in the desire for material comforts. Because these values may compete with the values attached to parenthood and family life, they are conducive to limitations of family size.

These aspirations for a high standard of living, which are also stimulated by industrial expansion, are often cited as the most important single consideration leading to the restriction of family size. In a market economy, the costs of child-rearing could also be devoted to satisfying other needs and desires, which thus compete with the satisfactions of parenthood. As Banks shows, however, the standard of living of the British middle class, among whom the drop in fertility

Table 26

RURAL-URBAN DIFFERENCES IN THE FERTILITY RATIO OF SELECTED COUNTRIES

| Country | Date | Number of children under 5 per 1,000 women aged 15–44 | |
		Urban	Rural
Argentina	1947	248	529
Brazil	1950	494	778
Cuba	1953	415	792
Dominican Republic	1950	542	909
Ecuador	1950	668	776
India	1931	666 *	770 †
Mexico	1950	539	707
Paraguay	1950	425	828
United States	1945–50	422	567 (nonfarm) 594 (farm)

* For cities of 100,000 to 500,000 population, women aged 15–39.
† Includes some cities for which separate data were not available, women aged 15–39.
Data from T. Lynn Smith, *Fundamentals of Population Study* (Philadelphia: Lippincott, 1960), pp. 313, 318; data for India from Kingsley Davis, *The Population of India and Pakistan* (Princeton: Princeton University Press, 1951), p. 71.

first appeared, had been rising steadily for several decades before any deliberate efforts were made to limit the number of children. In the years before the 1870s and 1880s, when fertility first declined, men tended to delay marriage rather than practice birth control. There had been persistent advocacy of birth control in England since early in the century, but the change only came about, Banks suggests, when middle-class hopes and expectations were threatened by the severe depression of the 1870s. Because they were now unsure of the future, postponement of marriage no longer seemed sensible, and they turned instead to limiting the size of their families.[13]

Acceptance of birth control, even when spurred by anxiety about maintaining a valued way of life, also required rejection of traditional moral sanctions against interfering with divine will in the production of children. Perhaps, Banks points out, it was the spread of science and rationality that played the strategic role in encouraging family limitation, which obviously reflects an increasingly rational attitude toward the number of children one has. Yet it seems likely that men took a rational view of family size only under the pressure of difficult circumstances, and that without these difficulties they might have continued to accept traditional conceptions of family life for some time to come. Once tradition had been breached, however, the rational appraisal of family size persisted; the desirability of a higher material standard of living and the needs of a career could be weighed against the pleasures—and pains—of having more children, who were no longer looked upon as the inevitable consequences of marriage.

The pattern of family limitation that began in the middle class, not only in England but also in the United States and elsewhere, spread only gradually to the working class, and the continued decline in fertility over many decades reflects the slow acceptance of birth control throughout a large part of society. This extension of both the attitudes and knowledge requisite for family limitation was probably encouraged by the extension of education, which quickens men's aspirations and is likely to stimulate rationality.

With childbearing no longer left entirely to fate, but subject to control and planning, the crux of the problem of fertility in advanced countries has come to be the cultural definition of proper family size and the circumstances that affect this definition and influence its implementation. Yet other demographic variables that have affected fertility in the past continue to have considerable importance. Changes in the marriage rate, in the age of marriage, or in the proportion of women who do not marry can influence the birth rate, although the impact of such changes may be overshadowed by other cultural and social shifts. During the period from 1871 to 1911, for example, the age of marriage in England rose steadily and probably contributed to the decline in fertility. But after 1911 fertility continued to drop, despite the absence of any further increase in the age of marriage. In the United States *both* the average age of marriage *and* the birth rate declined steadily from 1900 (and possibly earlier) until World War II, when the downward trend of fertility was reversed.

The influence of social and cultural forces governing family size, on the one hand, and of more specifically demographic variables, on the other, is clearly evident in the postwar "baby boom." In the United States a slight increase in fertility was noted late in the 1930s; as it continued, except for a brief pause during the war, and then accelerated after the war, it stimulated a new look at the forces affecting the birth rate. At first it seemed to most demographers, who had anticipated an eventual drop in total population

Table 27

CRUDE BIRTH RATES AND FERTILITY RATES IN THE UNITED STATES, 1920–1964 *

Year	Crude birth rate (Number of births per 1,000 population)	Fertility rate (Number of births per 1,000 women aged 15–44)
1920	27.7	117.9
1925	25.1	106.6
1930	21.3	89.2
1935	18.7	77.2
1940	19.4	79.9
1941	20.3	83.4
1942	22.2	91.5
1943	22.7	94.3
1944	21.2	88.8
1945	20.4	85.9
1946	24.1	101.9
1947	26.6	113.3
1948	24.9	107.3
1949	24.5	107.1
1950	24.1	106.2
1951	24.9	111.5
1952	25.1	113.9
1953	25.1	115.2
1954	25.3	118.1
1955	25.0	118.5
1956	25.2	121.2
1957	25.3	122.9
1958	24.5	120.2
1959	24.3	102.2
1960	23.7	118.0
1961	23.3	117.2
1962	22.4	112.1
1963	21.7	108.4
1964	21.0	104.8

* Rates for 1920 to 1959 adjusted for underregistration. Rates for 1960 through 1964 based on registered births.

U.S. Department of Health, Education and Welfare, *Vital Statistics of the United States, 1964*, I (Washington, D.C.: U.S. Government Printing Office, 1966), Table 1–2, pp. 1–4.

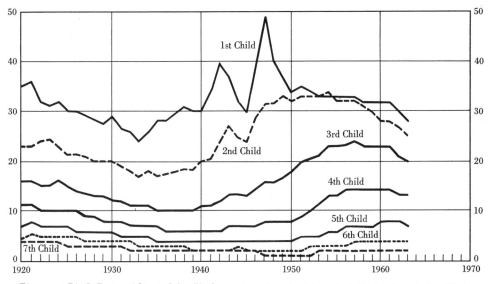

Figure 6. Birth Rates Adjusted for Underregistration, by Live-Birth Order for Native White Women, United States, 1920–1963 (Rates for 1,000 native white female population aged 15–44 years)

Data for 1920–1957, U.S. National Office of Vital Statistics, "Summary of Natality Statistics: United States," *Vital Statistics—Special Reports, National Summaries*, L, 19 (1957), lxvii; for 1958–1963, U.S. Bureau of the Census, *Statistical Abstract of the United States, 1965* (86th ed.; Washington, D.C.: U.S. Government Printing Office, 1965), p. 50.

because of the long-run decline in fertility, that the increased birth rate was simply the result of improved economic conditions, which made possible the marriages and the children that had been postponed because of the Depression. Other marriages were delayed by the war, it was argued, and the postwar surge of babies reflected, for the most part, the desire of many people to make up for time already lost in starting their families. A large number of first children seemed to justify this interpretation, and it was widely anticipated that the birth rate would drop again, resuming the long-run tendency downward, merely postponing the eventual leveling off of the population.

In fact, of course, the birth rate re-

mained high until 1958, when it began to decline (see Table 27). Many factors account for the persistence of a high birth rate for a longer period than most demographers had anticipated and for the continuing increase in total population. The proportion of women marrying has risen steadily, leaving fewer spinsters. The age of marriage continued to decline, until the early 1960s. With earlier marriage came earlier childbearing; by the time they were twenty-four years old, the women born between 1930 and 1934 had had an average of 1.4 children each, compared with an average of only 1.0 for those born between 1925 and 1929, and 0.7 for those born between 1910 and 1914.[14] The amount of involuntary sterility, too, has diminished as medical advances have made possible remedial measures. But if average family size had remained the same, earlier completion of childbearing would, in some measure, merely borrow from future births, and at some later date one might still have expected a further decline in fertility.

It seems clear, however, that the major force at work maintaining the high birth rate was an increase in average family size. As Figure 6 shows, since the mid-1940s there has been in the United States a substantial increase in the number of women bearing their third, fourth, and fifth children. (These rates did not drop significantly in the early 1960s, despite declines in the crude birth rate and the fertility rate.) While the large family seems to have gone out of fashion, the medium-sized one has become more prevalent, chiefly at the expense of the small (one- or two-child) family. During World War II, there was a change in the prevailing conception of the ideal number of children; a public opinion poll reported that between 1941 and 1945 the proportions preferring a two-child family as the ideal size dropped from 40 to 25 per cent, while the proportions preferring three, four, and five children increased respectively from 32 to 33 per cent, from 21 to 31 per cent, and from 3 to 7 per cent. In the light of subsequent studies, it seems probable that these figures continue to reflect the prevailing images of ideal family size.[15]

The reasons for this change are not easily identified in any precise fashion. The nature of modern life—the persisting cold war and the danger of a major hot one with the omnipresent threat of total destruction, the high level of material prosperity, suburban growth, and vast geographical mobility—have undoubtedly influenced family values. There is considerable evidence that the movement to the suburbs is linked with emphasis upon family life,[16] and the nature of suburban society further encourages medium-sized rather than small families. Cultural changes such as the resurgence of religion—perhaps diminishing during the 1960s—and the "advertising" of the family in the mass media (for example, "family" programs on television and "human interest" stories on the families of public figures) may contribute to the relatively high birth rate by stressing the joys of parenthood. Although these suppositions seem reasonable enough, we are only beginning to secure the reliable data which will enable us to spell out in greater detail which forces played the significant role in generating the sharp reversal of fertility patterns that had been evident for almost a century and the decline in fertility in the United States since 1958.[17]

Because children are now more readily planned than in the past, the birth rate has become closely tied to the shifting currents of modern life, even though their exact influence is difficult to ascertain. As the hold of deeply rooted traditions and customs has weakened, people tend to adjust their reproductive behavior quickly to changes in their economic and social circumstances. The effects of the 1957–1958 recession in the United States, for example, showed up with extraordinary speed in the birth rate, as couples delayed their marriages and prospective parents postponed having children, presumably because of unfavorable economic conditions. Although many of the births put off temporarily eventually occur as people seek to have a desired number of children, some never do because other circumstances interfere. And these mild fluctuations—which might gain much greater amplitude if the stimulating events were stronger—leave their mark on the long-run future too, as they affect the age distribution and the number of possible wives, husbands, and parents at some future date. One result of this susceptibility of the birth rate to the course of events is to increase markedly the difficulties in predicting future population. As the distinguished demographer Irene Taeuber writes, "The answer to 'What will happen?' or even to 'What is probable?' is not to be found in the formal manipulation of population statistics. . . . The problem of the future of population growth is the problem of the future of culture." [18]

Mortality

Unlike procreation, death need not be encouraged or sustained by social values; it may be postponed, but it cannot be avoided. When sexual pleasure and child-bearing can be separated, having children becomes a motivated act subject to the play of complex and often competing values and interests, and capable of being avoided almost totally. Even when the length of life has been substantially extended, however, as it has in modern society, it cannot be prolonged indefinitely, although its absolute limits still remain unknown.

In the face of the inevitability of death, life itself—its maintenance and lengthening—is positively valued. Occasional exceptions to this rule—for example, ritually required suicide (hara-kiri among upper-class Japanese), institutionally sanctioned or accepted killing (infanticide, or, among certain Eskimo groups, abandonment of the aged and infirm), or a seeming willingness to risk death in

war—remind us by their unusual character of the prevailing commitment to life. Nevertheless, length of life and maintenance of health are affected by activities and customs that are often pursued without regard for—or knowledge of—their effects upon physical well-being; other values in addition to concern for life govern men's actions, and those who spend all their time trying to keep healthy are, Davis points out, merely cranks or eccentrics. [19]

The influence of social and cultural circumstances upon life and death is clearly evident in the marked differences in life expectancy and mortality in different societies reported in Table 28, for there seems little warrant for supposing that these differences reflect biological rather than social and cultural variation.

The crude death rate used in Table 24 is the simplest measure of mortality; it reports the number of deaths in a given period for each 1,000 persons—or some other base figure—in the population. Although of considerable value, the crude death rate can be misleading if used to compare different societies or groups, for it is affected by the age composition of each population. The crude death rate will be higher if there is a large number of old people than if the population includes a high proportion of young people. In 1962, for example, the crude death rate in Japan was 7.5, in comparison with 11.5 in France. This difference is due largely to differences in the age distribution, for life expectancy in France is higher than in Japan, and death rates in each age group are lower in France than in Japan. In 1962, almost two-fifths of the Japanese population was under the age of twenty, and only about one-twentieth was sixty-five or older; in the same year one-third of the French population was under

Table 28

CRUDE DEATH RATES, 1930 AND 1960, AND LIFE EXPECTANCY AT BIRTH AT
VARIOUS DATES FOR SELECTED COUNTRIES

	Crude death rate		Expectation of life at birth		
	1930	*1960*	*Male*	*Female*	*Year*
Argentina	12.2	8.2	56.9	61.4	1947
Australia	8.6	8.6	67.1	72.3	1953–1955
Belgium	13.4	12.4	62.0	67.3	1946–1949
Canada	10.8	7.8	67.6	72.9	1955–1957
Costa Rica	22.5	8.6	54.7	57.1	1949–1951
Denmark	10.8	9.5	70.1	73.8	1956–1960
England and Wales	11.4	11.5	68.0	74.0	1960–1962
United Arab Republic (Egypt)	24.9	16.9	51.6	53.8	1960
France	15.9	11.4	67.3	74.1	1962
India	24.8	15.1	45.2	46.6	1957–1958
Israel (Jewish population only)	9.5	5.7	70.8	72.8	1962
Japan	18.2	7.6	66.2	71.2	1962
Poland	15.7	7.5	64.8	70.5	1960–1961
Portugal	17.1	10.8	59.8	65.0	1957–1958
Switzerland	11.6	9.7	69.5	74.8	1959–1961
United States	11.3	9.5	66.8	73.4	1962

For 1930 crude death rates, U.N. Statistical Office, *Demographic Yearbook*, 1957, Table 8, pp. 186–99. For 1960 crude death rates and life expectancies, U.N. Statistical Office, *Demographic Yearbook*, 1963, Table 23, pp. 536–53, and Table 26, pp. 612–25.

twenty, and nearly one-eighth was sixty-five or over.[20] In order to compare mortality in different societies, therefore, rates are calculated for specific age groups or are "standardized" or "corrected" in order to eliminate the influence of the age distribution. For detailed analysis the *life table* that projects the life expectancy of a group born at the same time and subject to the current death rates at each age is sometimes used.[21]

Length of life and the death rate are significantly influenced by the general standard of living—the availability of food and the physical demands made upon individuals—and by medical knowledge and technology and the health practices sanctioned by the culture. Prior to the development of modern industry and means of transportation, hunger, malnutrition, and famine were recurrent features in human life. In the British Isles, it has been estimated, there were more than 200 famines between A.D. 10 and 1846. China and India have recorded massive famines even in relatively recent times, with huge loss of life from hunger and from the disease and violence that hunger often begets.[22] Although famine often has resulted from natural disasters—drought and floods—it has also been caused on occasion by wars that have devastated the land or disrupted the normal routines of cultivation and exchange.

But mankind has perhaps suffered more from malnutrition and the exigencies of poverty, circumstances that increase mortality and shorten the life span, than from the drastic and occasional occurrence of outright starvation. In the modern world the likelihood of famine, in any event, has been sharply diminished. Except in geographically and culturally isolated areas or those set apart for political reasons, the threat of famine is now likely to bring quick relief from other regions with agricultural surpluses. But low standards of living still prevail in many parts of the world, and the impact of poverty and limited productivity upon mortality can be seen in the differences still found between poor nations and rich ones—for example, in the crude death rates in 1962 of 17.3 and 21.4 in Guatemala and Indonesia, respectively, and the rates of 8.7, 7.7, and 9.4 in Australia, Canada, and the United States. (A number of rapidly developing countries with young populations have even lower death rates, 6.8 in Israel, 7.5 in the Soviet Union, 6.7 in Puerto Rico.[23])

The long-run decline in the death rate in Western Europe that began toward the end of the eighteenth century coincided with the rapid expansion of productivity, which not only lessened the frequent shortages of basic necessities but also brought with it technological and then medical advances that made possible the prevention of disease as well as its cure. Improved sanitation measures, purification of the water supply, and control of contagious diseases have all contributed heavily to longer life. The introduction of advanced knowledge and techniques for maintaining health has led to a substantial decline in death rates in almost all parts of the world in recent years, sometimes with startling speed. In Ceylon, for example, the death rate dropped from 19.8 in 1946 to 12.3 in 1949, following intensive spraying to control malaria and other public health measures. Between 1930 and 1934, twenty-four nations had

crude death rates of 20.0 or more; by 1960 only a few nations in Asia and Africa still reported death rates of over 20.0.[24]

Increased longevity and diminished mortality eventually produce a substantial group of "senior citizens" whose presence creates new problems and potentialities. In a cohesive, traditional society, those persons who come close to or exceed the biblical three score years and ten usually fit readily into a persisting scheme of things. Their knowledge is useful, their status recognized, their needs looked after. In a rapidly changing urban society, in the United States, for example, the aged may no longer have so secure a place. Traditional knowledge and the fruits of long experience are often looked upon as less important than rational, up-to-date techniques. Youth and energy may be more highly valued than age and judgment, and enforced retirement often relegates older persons to the occupational dust heap. The conjugal family characteristic of an urban industrial society may be unable or unwilling to look after aged parents, who must provide for themselves or fall back upon nonfamilial arrangements for care and support. Old people therefore often face complex problems of adjustment—to new roles, an uncertain status, and economic difficulties. As their numbers grow they also come to constitute a potentially significant political group whose needs may make them susceptible to radical—or reactionary—appeals, if they are not effectively looked after.

Population growth and the Malthusian problem

A falling death rate, when coupled with an unchanging or only slowly declining birth rate, also leads to an over-all increase in population. Since 1650 the earliest date for which reasonably approximate estimates of population are available, the *natural increase*, the difference between birth and death rates, has steadily grown. In 1650 the estimated world population was 545 million. Between 1650 and 1750, population grew at about 0.29 per cent per year, to almost three-quarters of a billion. The annual rate of growth increased to 0.44 per cent between 1750 and 1800, to 0.51 between 1800 and 1850, to 0.63 in the next half-century, and to 0.75 between 1900 and 1940. In the last-named year the population was 2,171 million.[25] Between 1958 and 1962 the annual rate of growth had increased to 2 per cent, and the world's population was increasing by more than 60 million persons annually.

This extraordinary expansion in recent years and the prospect of continued massive population growth have again stirred fears of overpopulation, of a "beehive" world in which there is "standing room only."[26] Rising numbers have fanned the embers of the controversy that once swirled around the theories put forward by Thomas Malthus, an early nineteenth-century English clergyman and economist whose *Essay on Population* is widely regarded as the starting point of modern demographic analysis. Malthus argued that population tends to increase more rapidly than the food supply and therefore to press constantly against the means of subsistence. Because the satisfaction of the sexual passions inevitably led to the bearing of children, Malthus asserted, the only means for limiting the size of the population was restraint, which meant celibacy or the postponement of marriage. Without such restraint, the "positive checks" of war, vice, famine, and plague would inevitably reduce the population to a size commensurate with its food supply.

Events of the nineteenth century seemed to disprove Malthus's contentions. Because he condemned "artificial" birth-control methods he did not envisage the possibility of a declining birth rate without a sharp increase in the age of marriage. Moreover, he failed to foresee the marked increases in agricultural productivity that came about during the nineteenth century and the growth of large-scale importation of foodstuffs into nations incapable themselves of sustaining larger numbers of people.

Nevertheless, even though Europe and the United States have successfully managed thus far to avoid the dire events Malthus predicted, the problem he posed—the relationship between resources and population—persists in acute form in some parts of the world. Much of the discussion of this problem has been far too general, for both neo-Malthusians and their more optimistic opponents have mounted their analysis on a world stage rather than focusing their attention upon the several parts of the world. Although all nations are now increasingly linked together, the Malthusian problem assumes different forms in different places. We can more readily see these contrasts if we consider the varying relationships between birth rates and death rates found in the world's populations.

Some societies—a decreasing number in the modern world—have high birth rates and high death rates and short life expectancy. Their numbers remain relatively stable because both births and deaths are in approximate balance. Such societies are characteristically agricultural, poor, lacking in industrial development, and now chiefly found in parts of Africa and Asia. But these societies possess a *high growth potential,* for if the death rate were to drop, there would be a rapid increase in population; fertility rates rarely diminish as rapidly as mortality rates.

A second demographic pattern is found in countries that are growing rapidly because mortality is declining faster than fertility; the birth rate may, in fact, remain at a high level despite greater longevity and a lower death rate. Most Western European countries and the United States went through this stage of transitional growth during the nineteenth century, and many nations in other parts of the world are now experiencing a similar development—for example, the Soviet Union, Japan, and Brazil.

When the birth rate declines and comes into approximate balance with the death rate, the society is in a stage of *incipient decline*. England, France, and most other nations in the West are in this stage. Since life expectancy is high, the population steadily grows older until the proportion of older people is so great that the death rate increases. If the birth rate remains low, there might eventually be an actual decline in numbers. In fact, since a low birth rate reflects the deliberate control of fertility by individuals, the future pattern of fertility remains, as noted earlier, unpredictable and subject to the complex forces that influence people's willingness to have children. The characterization of this type of population as one facing an incipient decline is therefore sometimes misleading; in only a few instances has there been an actual drop in numbers or an imminently impending possibility of a fall in population. In other nations, like the United States, a rise in birth rates has triggered a sudden and impressive increase in population.

Since nations in the stage of incipient decline usually have a highly developed economy, they do not face shortages of resources needed to maintain their people or to create the industries that provide a high standard of living. For an expanding industrial economy like that of the United States, there will probably be future problems in providing enough water for both human and industrial needs, and in securing sufficient amounts of materials of which there may be a limited or potentially diminishing supply—for example, oil, iron, and other minerals. For the present, at least, the rapid growth of population offers no threat to the prevailing standard of living. It does, however, create complex problems—meeting new needs for education and housing, building new communities or enlarging old ones, providing employment to a steadily increasing labor force, enlarging the public facilities required for a much greater population. In the long run, there is the possibility of shortages of potable water and of strategic materials that could become critical, although science may provide substitute resources through the desalination of sea water, synthetic materials, and new sources of power.

In those nonindustrialized areas now experiencing a sudden increase in numbers, or in those with a high growth potential, the Malthusian problem may assume substantial dimensions. Critics of the neo-Malthusian doctrine have pointed to the success of Western nations in absorbing great increases of population in the past, and refer hopefully to the exciting possibilities of enlarging agricultural productivity through scientific research and development. But even the most extravagant achievements of science—which might, in any event, be long in coming—could not meet the needs of an indefinitely increasing population. The circumstances of the nineteenth century that permitted the West simultaneously to industrialize and to increase its popula-

During 1961–1966 India allocated $52 million to support and encourage family planning, establishing 4,000 birth-control centers. Here women are shown a plastic loop, a recently developed, inexpensive, easy-to-use, and relatively efficient contraceptive device.

tion rapidly probably cannot be duplicated. Europe was relatively sparsely populated at the beginning of its transitional growth and was therefore capable of absorbing and sustaining larger numbers. Moreover, about 60 million emigrants left Europe during the nineteenth century for the Americas and other parts of the world. Before the coming of the Europeans, North America, of course, was a very sparsely settled continent with rich resources waiting to be exploited.

Few, if any, of the so-called underdeveloped nations now experiencing transi-

tional growth possess comparable advantages. A few countries—Brazil, Kenya, Ecuador—may have room for an expanding population. But many other areas, such as Ceylon, Greece, India, and Pakistan, are already far more densely populated than Europe was 150 years ago, or than the United States, Canada, or Australia are now. Death rates fell slowly during the nineteenth century; as we have already noted, in some countries modern science has cut the death rate drastically within a very few years. Problems of coping with an increasing population are therefore far more acute in many nations than they were in the past. And mass migration of surplus population is now unlikely for both political and economic reasons.

Economic growth requires the channeling of resources into the building—or buying—of productive equipment that gives no immediate return in the form of consumer goods. While factories, dams, power stations, mines, and roads are being built, the people may have to forgo immediate improvement of their circumstances, in addition to learning to accept the values and disciplines of industrialism. (For a brief discussion of the problem of industrializing an agricultural society, see pp. 499–502.) Even if adequate natural resources are available—and this is not always the case—a rapidly growing population that consumes whatever it produces merely in order to stay alive leaves no surplus with which to acquire the needed capital equipment.

Unless drastic efforts are made to control fertility, therefore, many underdeveloped nations may be running a close and perhaps losing race between economic progress and a skyrocketing population. Some nations have faced the demographic challenge directly and have taken positive steps to lower the birth rate. In Japan, most notably, where there already existed a tradition of family limitation, abortion and sterilization were legalized after World War II and facilities were established to provide contraceptive advice.[27] The crude birth rate dropped, as a result, from 33.0 in 1949 to 19.4 in 1955 and to 17.2 in 1960. Less effective efforts have been made in India, where the government's program has as yet had only a limited impact. Despite such government programs, the population continues to increase as death rates remain lower than birth rates; in Japan the population grew from 83 to 93 million between 1950 and 1960. In many parts of the world, no direct efforts have been made to lower fertility, and population continues to grow with dramatic speed, at the rate of 2.7 per cent annually in South America and Southeast Asia. If the race between numbers and economic growth is lost, the Malthusian prediction of vice and misery may be realized in some places unless substantial assistance comes from outside, as it probably will, albeit at the cost of involvement in great power politics.

Notes

[1] Hanna Rizk, "Population Growth and its Effects on Economic and Social Goals in the United Arab Republic," in Stuart Mudd (ed.), *The Population Crisis and the Use of World Resources* (The Hague: Junk, 1964), pp. 169–75.

[2] Kingsley Davis, "The Demographic Foundations of National Power," in Morroe Berger, Theodore Abel, and Charles H. Page (eds.), *Freedom and Control in Modern Society* (New York: Van Nostrand, 1954), p. 223.

[3] See Wilbert E. Moore, "Sociology and Demography," in Philip M. Hauser and Otis D. Duncan (eds.), *The Study of Population* (Chicago: University of Chicago Press, 1959), pp. 832–51.

[4] See Harold F. Dorn, "Pitfalls in Population Forecasts and Projections," *Journal of the American Statistical Association*, XLV (September, 1950), 311–34. For a lucid popular exposition, see Dennis H. Wrong, "The Stork Surprises the Demographers," *Commentary*, XIV (October, 1952), 376–82.

[5] See Regine K. Stix and Frank W. Notestein, *Controlled Fertility* (Baltimore: Williams & Wilkins, 1940); and Gilbert W. Beebe, *Contraception and Fertility in the Southern Appalachians* (Baltimore: Williams & Wilkins, 1942), pp. 97–109.

[6] Kingsley Davis, "Human Fertility in India," *American Journal of Sociology*, LII (November, 1946), 243–54.

[7] Paul H. Landis and Paul K. Hatt, *Population Problems* (2nd ed.; New York: American Book, 1954), p. 159.

[8] Dennis H. Wrong, *Population* (rev. ed.; New York: Random House, 1959), p. 60.

[9] Royal Commission on Population, *Report* (London: Her Majesty's Stationery Office, 1949 [1953 printing]), p. 38.

[10] J. A. Banks, *Prosperity and Parenthood* (London: Routledge, 1954), p. 8.

[11] See John W. Innes, *Class Fertility Trends in England and Wales, 1876–1934* (Princeton: Princeton University Press, 1938).

[12] A. J. Jaffee, "Urbanization and Fertility," *American Journal of Sociology*, XLVIII (July, 1942), 47–60.

[13] Banks, *op. cit.* See especially the summary discussion in Ch. XII.

[14] U.S. Department of Commerce, *Current Population Reports: Population Characteristics* (Washington, D.C.: U.S. Government Printing Office, Series P-20, No. 108, July 12, 1961), p. 4.

[15] See, for example, Morris Axelrod *et al.*, "Fertility Expectations of the United States Population," *Population Index*, XXIX (January, 1963), pp. 25–31.

[16] See, for example, Wendell Bell, "Social Choice, Life Styles, and Suburban Residence," in William Dobriner (ed.), *The Suburban Community* (New York: Putnam, 1958), pp. 225–47.

[17] See Wilson H. Grabill, Clyde V. Kiser, and P. K. Whelpton, *The Fertility of American Women* (New York: Wiley, 1958); and Charles F. Westoff, Robert G. Potter, Jr., and Philip C. Sagi, *The Third Child* (Princeton: Princeton University Press, 1963).

[18] Irene Taeuber, "The Future of Transitional Areas," in Paul K. Hatt (ed.), *World Population and Future Resources* (New York: American Book, 1952), p. 28.

[19] Kingsley Davis, *Human Society* (New York: Macmillan, 1952), p. 28.

[20] U.N. Statistical Office, *Demographic Yearbook, 1963* (New York: United Nations, 1964), pp. 200–1, 210–1, 547, 549.

[21] For a detailed analysis, see Louis I. Dublin, Alfred J. Lotka, and Mortimer Spiegelman, *Length of Life* (rev. ed.; New York: Ronald, 1949). For a brief summary, see Wrong, *Population*, pp. 39–45.

[22] For a summary discussion of the frequency of famines in history and their consequences, see Warren S. Thompson and David T. Lewis, *Population Problems* (5th ed.; New York: McGraw-Hill, 1965).

[23] *Demographic Yearbook, 1963*, Table 23, pp. 536–53.

[24] *Ibid.*

[25] Davis, *op. cit.*, p. 596.

[26] See, for example, Harrison Brown, *The Challenge of Man's Future* (New York: Viking, 1954); Karl Sax, *Standing Room Only* (Boston: Beacon, 1955); and William Vogt, *Road to Survival* (New York: Sloane, 1948).

[27] See Irene Taeuber, *The Population of Japan* (Princeton: Princeton University Press, 1958), Ch. 13.

Suggestions for further reading

BANKS, J. A. *Prosperity and Parenthood.* London: Routledge, 1954.
An interesting historical study of the circumstances that stimulated the widespread use of birth control in England in the latter part of the nineteenth century.

BOGUE, DONALD J. *The Population of the United States.* New York: Free Press, 1959.
An encyclopedic description and analysis of the population of the United States. Useful both as a reference book and for its interpretation of demographic patterns.

BROWN, HARRISON. *The Challenge of Man's Future.* New York: Viking, 1954.
A pessimistic but thoughtful examination of the future prospects in the relations between population and resources.

DAVIS, KINGSLEY. *The Population of India*

and Pakistan. Princeton: Princeton University Press, 1951.

A leading demographer-sociologist examines with great care the population of underdeveloped areas in which the demographic data are of varying quality and coverage.

DAY, LINCOLN AND ALICE. *Too Many Americans.* Boston: Riverside, 1964.
A thoughtful assessment of the problems of the growing American population.

FREEDMAN, RONALD (ed.). *Population: The Vital Revolution.* Garden City: Doubleday Anchor Books, 1964.
A readable collection of essays on contemporary population problems.

HAUSER, PHILIP M. (ed.). *The Population Dilemma.* Englewood Cliffs: Prentice-Hall, 1963.
Ten population specialists consider various aspects of the contemporary demographic situation.

HAUSER, PHILIP M. (ed.). *Population and World Politics.* New York: Free Press, 1958.
A collection of papers on population trends, prospects, and policies, and their relations with politics and power in various parts of the world.

HAUSER, PHILIP M., AND OTIS DUDLEY DUNCAN (eds.). *The Study of Population: An Inventory and Appraisal.* Chicago: University of Chicago Press, 1959.
Papers by various authors on the major problems in demography, its development as a field of study, its status in different parts of the world, and its relations with the social and biological sciences.

MAYER, KURT. *The Population of Switzerland.* New York: Columbia University Press, 1952.
A thorough study of the Swiss population: its historical development, present characteristics, patterns of internal migration, and future prospects.

SAX, KARL. *Standing Room Only.* Boston: Beacon, 1955.
A botanist's pessimistic discussion of the dangers of overpopulation.

SPENGLER, JOSEPH J., AND OTIS DUDLEY DUNCAN (eds.). *Population Theory and Policy.* New York: Free Press, 1956.

SPENGLER, JOSEPH J., AND OTIS DUDLEY DUNCAN. (eds.). *Demographic Analysis.* New York: Free Press, 1956.
These two volumes contain a wide-ranging collection of articles on all aspects of population.

TAEUBER, IRENE. *The Population of Japan.* Princeton: Princeton University Press, 1958.
An imposing and comprehensive analysis of population trends in an Oriental industrial society.

THOMLINSON, RALPH. *Population Dynamics.* New York: Random House, 1965.
A text that focuses attention upon world demographic trends.

WRONG, DENNIS H. *Population,* rev. ed. New York: Random House, 1959.
An excellent brief introduction to the major concepts and problems in the study of population.

POPULATION STUDIES *is a journal that deals solely with demographic problems. In addition, the United Nations publishes regularly a* Demographic Yearbook *and detailed reports on specific problems and areas.*

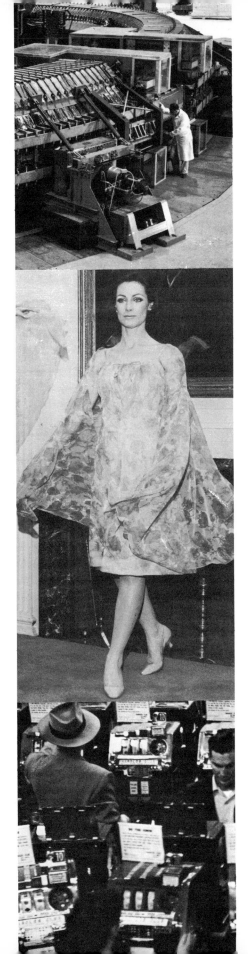

PART FIVE

Social order, deviance, and change

PHOTO CREDITS:
Brookhaven National Laboratory,
Macy's New York,
Photo Researchers, Inc.,
Wide World Photos,
Marc & Evelyne Bernheim
from Rapho Guillumette Pictures

18

Conformity and social control

Conformity and socialization

Sociology, we have said, begins with two basic facts: human behavior follows regular and recurrent patterns, and people everywhere live with others and not alone. For the most part, regularities in human behavior reflect the presence of culture and of an ordered arrangement of social relationships. Our analysis has dealt with some of the principal ways in which social life is organized and how institutions define and regulate men's actions. Although social order is thus maintained by the norms that govern men's relationships to one another—folkways, mores, laws, and other rules—there remains a further question: *Why* do men generally conform to the institutions that define required or appropriate behavior?

Conformity, with which we are concerned here, is sometimes criticized as antithetical to individuality; as indicative of standardized action, attitudes and belief; and as evidence of an unwillingness to stand against prevailing tides of opinion and fashion. Social critics bewail the tendency to accept things as they are, to assume on occasion the attitude of Voltaire's Pangloss, who saw about him wherever he went "the best of all possible worlds." There may be substance and co-

gency to such complaints, yet some measure of conformity is clearly a prerequisite of an ordered society. If people can never predict the actions of others, if men do not generally perform their ordinary duties, and if all social rules are ignored and violated, society cannot exist.

Only if society were ordered like a beehive or ant heap, or if, as in Aldous Huxley's *Brave New World*, men were rigorously conditioned as embryos for their future social roles, could conformity be complete. Some areas of behavior in all societies remain unregulated, and even under "totalitarian" regimes the refractory human material always finds some techniques for resisting total subordination.[1] Yet the meaning of both individuality and nonconformity is found only in relation to the social norms to which most people conform most of the time.

People are constrained to obey the dictates of their culture in different ways. Some of the pressures toward conformity are internal, derived from the needs, desires, and interests of individuals. In a sense these pressures are also developmental (biographical and historical), for they are built into the person in the course of social experience. Other constraints that ensure adherence to accepted norms are external, derived from the culture and the demands of social life, and are at work in the concrete situations in which men find themselves. We have already seen how power, authority, and religion serve to induce compliance with social norms; there are other institutional forms of social control to be examined in this chapter.

The individual acquires the internal constraints that encourage conformity in the process of socialization that in modern societies takes place chiefly within the family, peer group, and school. In Chapter 4 we saw how custom is transformed into habit, socially approved goals into personal ambitions, and social values into a self-regulating conscience. Individuals are encouraged to do what the culture requires, therefore, because they feel that it is customary, that it is "right," or that it will lead to desired results.

In the course of socialization the individual also learns to be sensitive to the judgments and expectations of others, which serve directly and continuously as instruments of social control. As self-respect comes to depend upon how others respond to one's behavior, anticipations of approval or disapproval influence what one does, and approbation or criticism reinforces—or inhibits—the likelihood of similar action in the future.

In *The Lonely Crowd*, David Riesman has argued that the ways in which socialization encourages conformity may change from one historical period to another. In the United States, he suggests, sensitivity to the judgments of others ("other-direction") has become an increasingly important "mode of conformity," while the influence of tradition and custom ("tradition-direction") and the self-imposed standards embodied in one's conscience

("inner-direction") have become less significant. Riesman attributes this shift to major alterations in culture and social structure—the increased preoccupation with consumption; the pervasiveness of bureaucracy in which "personality," that is, how one impresses people, is more important than "character"; the resulting changes in child-rearing practices and education, which encourage children to develop a "radar-like" sensitivity to others rather than an internal "gyroscope" that keeps the inner-directed person fixed to his present course.[2]

This interpretation has been criticized on both historical and theoretical grounds and has been modified on some points by Reisman himself.[3] Even in the nineteenth century, it has been suggested, Americans were very much concerned with the opinions of others, in part because of the egalitarianism that prevented the emergence of a clearly defined status structure that allowed each individual to know his place. Riesman's categories—"other-direction," "inner-direction," "tradition-direction"—critics assert, are not only "modes of conformity," that is, psychological attributes, but also cultural values. This ambiguity, however, may reflect a close relationship between values and the sources of conformity. Outgoing friendliness and ready adjustment to social demands may thus be preferred to perseverance in the unremitting pursuit of private, although socially acceptable, goals. Alternatively, recognition of traditional norms may be looked upon as more important than satisfaction of personal needs or amiable sociability. Despite these criticisms, which do have some substance, Riesman's interpretation of conformity, which attempts to link socialization and social structure in a context of social change, has considerable theoretical interest and, in our view, sheds considerable light on some aspects of American culture and character.

The tendencies toward conformity resulting from socialization do not lead, however, to automatic or mechanical acquiescence to cultural demands. Adherence to social norms—which themselves often permit some variation in behavior—may be spontaneous and voluntary, free of uncertainty and doubt. But both the dynamics of personality and the nature of society prevent an unfailing and unresisting obedience to all cultural imperatives. Personal gratification and social requirements are often at odds; even the most thoroughgoing socialization is not likely to subdue private impulses completely. Indeed, socialization itself may generate a conflicting or inconsistent set of pressures that push in different directions; tradition may seem to require one course of action, one's conscience may dictate another, and other persons may expect still a third. Society often requires behavior that is unpleasant, difficult, and irksome and therefore to be avoided if possible. Moreover, no one mirrors the culture exactly, a fact inherent in social life and there are always those who set a frequently disturbing and sometimes refreshing example by disregarding some or even most cultural prescriptions.

To ensure substantial conformity, therefore, the pressures to accede to social and cultural demands that are built into the individual by his prior experience and training must be supplemented and reinforced, and the tendencies toward deviant behavior that derive from personality, culture, and social structure must, in some degree, be contained. In Chapter 19 we shall examine the sources of deviant behavior. Here we shall explore the mechanisms of social control by which people are induced—or constrained—to follow social norms.

Reciprocity

The very structure of social relations, of course, contains various mechanisms that induce conformity. Each person is caught up in a network of reciprocal expectations and obligations that bind him to carry out certain socially sanctioned activities. The importance of *reciprocity* as a means of securing compliance to social norms is clearly shown by Bronislaw Malinowski in his study of the Trobriand Islanders. The Trobriander, Malinowski points out, does not follow tradition and custom " 'slavishly,' 'unwittingly,' 'spontaneously,' through 'mental interia,' combined with the fear of public opinion or of supernatural punishment; or again through a 'pervading group-sentiment if not group instinct.' " [4] Instead conformity is secured by the pressure to fulfill the obligations people have to one another. These social debts are often clearly defined; economic exchange, for example, takes the form of gifts to regular partners.

The inland village supplies the fisherman with vegetables; the coastal community repays with fish. . . . This system of mutual obligations . . . forces the fisherman to repay whenever he has received a gift from his inland partner, and vice versa. Neither partner can refuse, neither may stint in his return gift, neither should delay.[5]

Nominally, these gifts are freely offered, yet a careful accounting is kept, and in the long run things given and things received are expected to balance, "benefitting both sides equally."

A system of economic exchange is perhaps the most clear-cut and visible example of reciprocity, but it also appears in many other areas of social life. Among the Trobrianders, Malinowski notes, marriage and family ties rest upon reciprocal obligations; a woman's brother provides her with food, but her husband must return periodic gifts to him. A widow's mourning for a dead husband—a duty owed to his clan— is requited with ritual payments.

Social relationships are rarely defined by the participants themselves in terms of services rendered or obligations owed to one another, yet people are often linked together by a reciprocal exchange of benefits. Friends are expected to invite one another to dinner, kinfolk to exchange gifts, politicians to repay campaign contributions with political appointments or other favors. This giving and receiving is also carried on subtly and almost imperceptibly. Georg Simmel writes:

Thus an individual, perhaps, gives "spirit," that is, intellectual values, while the other shows his gratitude by returning affective values. Another offers the aesthetic charms of his personality, for instance, and the receiver, who happens to be the stronger nature, compensates for it by injecting will power into him, as it were, or firmness and resoluteness.[6]

Continual exchange of benefits builds up a structure of obligations that each participant can call upon in the future, binding the other to various types of performance. Failure to provide something appropriate in return for what is given may weaken the relationship and diminish the likelihood that the established pattern of interaction will persist.

Participation in any system of reciprocity undoubedly rests on habit, on acceptance of custom and tradition, and on concern for one's good name, but in addition there are often significant gains to be derived from conformity and losses that will be suffered for failure to meet one's obligations. Trobriand fishermen and farmers both profit from their exchange, and both would lose should existing arrangements be disrupted. Friends gain from their mutual sociability, husband and wife take pleasure in each

other, kinfolk enjoy one another's largess, and politicians and campaign contributors benefit from their aid to each other.

Underlying these patterns of reciprocal benefits, Alvin Gouldner suggests, is a "norm of reciprocity" that requires that people help those who have helped them and avoid anything that might injure persons from whom they have received benefits. This norm, Gouldner argues, is found in all societies, although the specific obligations that people owe one another, of course, are variously defined by different cultures, and are often contingent upon the values of the services rendered.[7]

Sanctions

Despite the positive rewards to be derived from conformity—self-satisfaction, praise, prestige, or concrete benefits—and the persisting influence of prior socialization, there are occasions when for various reasons men are inclined to disregard the dictates of their culture. Those who do defy social norms—and are found out— are subject to various kinds of *sanctions* or penalties. (Private and undiscovered infractions, of course, remain unpunished, except for such guilt or anxiety as they may generate.) In itself, to be sure, the threat of sanctions is not necessarily enough to prevent nonconformity, but it does contribute to the pressures that compel obedience to cultural prescriptions.

Each group or organization characteristically has its own sanctions, to be imposed upon its members for violation of group norms. Members of an informal friendship group may punish an offender against their standards by ridicule and scorn, or, if the offense is serious, by exclusion from their activities. Middle-class American parents use various sanctions to enforce proper behavior: temporary prohibition of such customary pleasures as watching television or going to the movies, withholding the regular allowance, a spanking, or, on occasion, the temporary withdrawal of affection.

Teasing, ridicule, and the open expression of disapproval by family or friends constitute especially effective sanctions because they come from persons whose good opinion is likely to be highly valued and threaten social relationships in which individuals have a heavy emotional investment. In a small, close-knit community in which life is dominated by such relationships, censure or rejection by one's kin can endanger one's place in the total social structure. The anonymity, mobility, and varied social groups of urban society, on the other hand, reduce the effectiveness of these informal sanctions and increase the need for other, more formal, means of social control.

In formal organizations there are usually regularly defined penalties for offenses against organizational rules. A worker who disobeys company rules may be suspended for a time, or can even be fired. Violation of the code of medical ethics may lead to expulsion from the American Medical Association and, more importantly, from the local professional group, or, in serious cases, to withdrawal of the license to practice. Similarly, unethical conduct by a lawyer may lead to disbarment. Union members can be expelled for "conduct unbecoming a member," and professional baseball players fined or suspended for improper behavior on the baseball field. All of these sanctions can be imposed only by those authorized to do so, and in many cases they are subject to legal review.

As an association the church may also impose sanctions—excommunication, penance, the threat of eternal damnation—but these are "suprasocial," for they affect not only relations between the individual and the church but also relations with some higher power.[8] The effectiveness of religious sanctions rests upon belief in religious ideas and acceptance of the authority or power of the religious leader or functionary.

Except for the family and, sometimes, the school, which may impose minor physical punishments, only the state possesses the recognized and legitimate right to apply physical force to maintain order and conformity. In addition to imprisonment, enforced labor, or execution, the state may, of course, apply other penalties—for example, fines and the withdrawal of legal privileges. But behind these punishments there rests the possibility of coercive measures. Because of this power, the state clearly constitutes one of the central institutions for enforcing adherence to many social norms. Yet its influence too, as we saw in Chapter 13, is usually defined and limited by law and tradition. Government may act with great restraint, confining its potential sanctions to a limited range of prohibited or required actions, or, as in totalitarian societies, it may seek to penetrate and control all areas of social life.

Sanctions control behavior directly by deterring misconduct and indirectly by reinforcing established rules. Although most men probably are restrained from violating laws or conventions, at least in part, by the possible consequences, there are always some who willingly—or thoughtlessly—risk punishment in order to gain their personal goals. The possibility of execution has not stayed the hands of many murderers, and the professional criminal often assumes that he is clever enough to escape detection and capture. But as Durkheim pointed out, the sociological importance of punishment lies in its effects upon those who impose it as well as upon those who are subject to it.

The social reaction that we call "punishment" is due to the intensity of the collective sentiments which the crime offends; but, from another angle, it has the useful function of maintaining these sentiments at the same degree of intensity, for they would soon diminish if offences against them were not punished.[9]

It seems likely that open disregard of law or convention by some individuals may provoke repressed or hidden desires among others to do likewise. Shakespeare's King Lear sees clearly this possibility.

> Thou rascal beadle, hold thy
>   bloody hand!
> Why dost thou lash that whore? Strip
>   thine own back.
> Thou hotly lusts to use her in that kind
> For which thou whip'st her. The usurer
>   hangs the cozener.

Punishing the offender helps to curb these newly stimulated impulses and thus reinforces submission to social norms.

Institutionalized safety valves

Sanctions are necessary, we suggested above, because of both the persistence of personal desires and inclinations and the pressures generated by society itself. As was pointed out in Chapter 4, one of Freud's chief contributions to our understanding of personality is the knowledge of persisting tension between basic drives and the requirements of social life. The process of socialization itself, which creates desires and directs impulses into culturally approved channels, also necessarily imposes limits upon the expression of fundamental drives.

Many of the sentiments and emotions generated by social experience fit into the needs of society, but some of them may be difficult to express in acceptable fashion. No society is so organized—fortunately

—that there is complete correspondence between culture and personality with each person fitting readily into his social niche, unquestioningly adopting culturally approved means to pursue culturally sanctioned ends. Moreover, social life itself imposes frustrations and restraints even upon the needs and aspirations it creates; inconsistencies in culture and social organization almost inevitably leave some desires and ambitions unsatisfied.

Many kinds of cultural patterns, among them jokes, games and sports, various kinds of ritual, and regulated forms of conflict, provide outlets for the tensions generated by social restraints and by cultural and structural inconsistencies. Without such outlets these tensions may emerge in various kinds of deviant behavior (see Chapter 19) or may lead to the disruption of established social relationships and existing social structures.

Among the many social and psychological functions of humor is emotional release in difficult situations, a result achieved by making light of one's troubles or expressing aggression against hostile or threatening persons. In a wry comment on their often chronic poverty, Eastern European Jews quipped, "If a poor Jew eats a chicken, one of them must be sick." The Gentile, who represented danger, was often the butt of Jewish jokes, a harmless outlet for hostility. Dollard has noted a similar function of humor among Southern Negroes, who have few opportunities to express directly their anger and antagonism toward the dominant whites.[10] The following joke, for example, was told among Negro university students.

A colored maid and her white employer became pregnant and gave birth at the same time. A few months later the white woman came running into the kitchen and said, "Oh, my baby said his first word today."

The little colored baby who was in a basket

on the floor looked around and said to her, "He did, wha' 'id'e say?"[11]

For dominant groups, humor can serve to justify and sustain their advantaged position; whites, for example, tell stories illustrating Negro willingness to accept subordinate status, and Gentiles recount jokes about offensive Jews.

Much humor deals with activities that are often strictly regulated, such as sexual behavior. In light conversation or through jokes it is possible to give vent, if only indirectly, to the feelings that strict restraint may generate. Similarly, relationships that are delicate or ambiguous, like those with mothers-in-law, are often the butt of humor, which provides an institutionally approved vent for hostility or antagonism. Difficult relationships are themselves sometimes eased by regularized banter and joking between the persons involved.

Games and sports, like humor, may also serve as outlets for pent-up emotions. "Every people," Max Lerner remarks, "no matter how civilized, must have a chance to yell for blood." [12] (If Freud is correct, the need for this type of release increases rather than decreases with the progress of civilization.) Many popular American spectator sports—boxing, wrestling, football, hockey—provide opportunities to experience vicariously the shattering punch, the vicious tackle, the unrestrained body block. Yet these activities are mild in contrast with the ritualized violence of the bull fight, the Roman arena, cockfights, or public hanging. It is a plausible hypothesis, yet to be systematically tested, that the extent of tolerated and sanctioned violence in a society varies directly with the strength of the aggressive impulses generated by the process of socialization and by prevailing cultural demands.

Ritual and leisure also provide release

from tensions produced in the normal course of social life. Most primitive societies have regular occasions when daily routines are changed or varied or, in some instances, replaced by ritualized license. In medieval Europe feast days provided interruptions in the sameness of everyday activity, as well as permitting momentary disregard of established conventions and temporary escape from accepted patterns of deference and respect. In the Feast of Fools, for example, a mock Mass was performed accompanied by buffoonery and followed by feasting. The essence of the feast "was that the relation between master and man, owner and slave, should

Many conventions in the United States become occasions for behavior that would normally be condemned as inappropriate, silly, or even unpleasant. On such occasions, however, it is usually looked upon as harmless high jinks that allow men to relax and let off steam. Here some members of the Ancient Arabic Order of the Nobles of the Mystic Shrine of North America parade through Detroit as part of a national convention.

Wide World Photos

for a moment be turned topsy-turvy." [13]

Although modern leisure activities serve other functions—for example, as symbols of status or avenues of sociability —they obviously offer a change of pace and opportunities for self-expression. It seems likely that the spread of formalized vacations, growing participation in such sports as golf, tennis, and bowling, and the great popularity of hunting, fishing, sailing, skiing, and boating in the United States reflect not only economic prosperity, but also the need to escape from the impersonality and formal organization of an increasingly bureaucratized society. Much of this recreational activity, however, itself often becomes highly ritualized and overorganized, thus diminishing the spontaneity and release it can provide.

Other outlets can be found in many areas of social life. Religious ritual also offers opportunities for emotional catharsis, as well as reinforcing social norms by binding people together in a cohesive community. In primitive societies, Clyde Kluckhohn suggests, witchcraft may serve as an outlet for hostility, while fear of being bewitched encourages conformity.[14] The intense emotional life within the modern middle-class family, in many cases, at least, releases tensions built up in an impersonal, bureaucratic workaday world. As Parsons points out, emotional security in some social relationships—the understanding, acceptance, and reassurance given by another person—lessens tendencies toward aggressive or deviant behavior elsewhere.[15]

Solidarity and consensus

Finally, conformity to social norms is encouraged by the maintenance of *solidarity* (social cohesion). The greater the

identification of members of a society or group with one another and the stronger the bonds that unite them into a social whole, the less likely are they to violate its customs, conventions, or laws.

Solidarity, it should be noted, is not necessarily good or bad; its consequences in each situation must be judged separately. An authoritarian society may be closely knit, resting upon an accepted consensus and a sense of identification that precludes the possibility of opposition and criticism. A cohesive and stable democracy, on the other hand, may rest upon a consensus that accepts a great deal of individuality and freedom. But any society, authoritarian or democratic, must call upon some common loyalties and marshal sufficient agreement upon cultural values if it is to survive as an ordered way of life.

In primitive society, as Durkheim showed, social cohesion rests chiefly upon those values to which all members of the group give allegiance. In complex, differentiated societies, this consensus is no longer sufficiently broad to bind together the social fabric, for various groups may hold different, if not competing, conceptions of good and bad, and right and wrong. Solidarity in advanced societies rests in part upon interdependence—the division of labor with its structure of interrelated roles, mutual obligations, and reciprocal services.[16] Yet without any shared values, the unity of a complex society would be endangered or weakened. American society, for example, is to some degree held together by agreement upon the desirability and importance of achievement and success, of work, efficiency, equality, progress, freedom, democracy, and patriotism.[17] Few Americans would explicitly deny the moral authority of the Ten Commandments or the Sermon on the Mount, even if their relevance in specific situations is often unclear, or other social forces encourage men to disregard them.

Justifying and defending cultural values are the myths and legends, the accepted versions of history, the facts and suppositions about man, society, and nature that, together with values, constitute an *ideology*. An ideology is rarely ordered into a logically consistent whole or carefully tested against the reality it purports to describe and explain, although "ideologists"—writers and scholars—often seek to enunciate a clear and consistent intellectual position, particularly when their values and beliefs are challenged. Nor do individuals who support an ideology necessarily subscribe to all its tenets. Nevertheless, common beliefs about the world, even if inconsistent or erroneous, also serve, like the values they justify, as unifying elements in society. Moreover, by providing a common interpretation of men and events, they lead people to define and respond to social situations in similar fashion and to accept the propriety—or inevitability—of both their own actions and those of others. (Ideological differences, of course, can lead to and justify hostility and conflict; revolutions contain and rest upon ideologies that challenge the established order, and group differences—international or intranational—are often reflected and sustained by competing ideologies.)

Symbols and rituals that express common values and beliefs and that emphasize the unity of the group also reinforce consensus and solidarity. The flag, the crown, and the cross symbolize the nation, the empire, and the religious community and doctrine, and they serve as unifying foci of interest that stimulate and reinforce common loyalties. Ritual—for example, the salute to the flag, inauguration of a President or coronation of a sovereign, a military review or parade—strengthens allegiance to the group by investing collective occasions with importance and solemnity and reminding the individual of his social responsibilities and his membership in the whole. In addition, rituals also have symbolic meaning, for they represent myth, tradition, shared values, and accepted obligations.

Each group in society, of course, makes specific claims upon its members, the effectiveness of which depends in part upon the consensus and solidarity within it. To the extent that classes, ethnic groups, corporate bureaucracies, labor unions, professional associations, organized social movements, or other groups require the same behavior as the larger society and are committed to its standards, their internal cohesion contributes to the unity of the whole social order. But if any group comes to hold values or to approve behavior unacceptable to others, its very cohesiveness weakens that of the society as a whole. White Southerners are emboldened to defy court orders and the police by the presence of others of like mind; Negro students conscious of their common interests and mutual support organize demonstrations in defiance of legal restraints and community customs. During World War II coal miners went on strike despite a vigorous public outcry against their action. They were protected against external pressures by their isolation in small mining towns, and were sustained by their intense loyalty to their fellows and their union, and by an ideology that assigned responsibility for the situation to mine owners and operators. Many juvenile delinquents, as we shall see in Chapter 19, carry on their activities in an organized fashion, often as members of solidary groups that reject middle-class values.

The disruptive effect of social cleavage is sometimes softened by external dangers and conflict with outsiders. Shakespeare's Henry IV advised his heir:

> Be it thy course to busy giddy minds
> With foreign quarrels, that action,
>   hence borne out,
> May waste the memory of former days.

"The exigencies of war with outsiders," William Graham Sumner wrote, "are what make peace inside, lest internal discord should weaken the we-group for war." [18] Disagreements frequently fade when individuals, groups, or nations face a common enemy. Factions within minority groups are apt to disregard their differences and close ranks when outsiders try to intervene. Most segments of American management and labor buried their quarrels during World War II, and the Grand Alliance—Great Britain, the Soviet Union, and the United States—survived as long as its members fought side by side against Germany.

When there are many groups pursuing competing interests, consensus and solidarity rest in part upon a common commitment to ground rules that govern their struggles. Unless it is possible to resolve group differences within an institutional framework acceptable to all, usually resting in part upon some measure of ideological consensus, society becomes an arena of internecine warfare, as in the Congo in 1960 and early 1961; or else it submits to a centralized authority that enforces peace and establishes a measure of stability without regard for some—or most—group interests.

Although some sociologists have looked upon *internal conflict* as inimical to "societal efficiency," [19] it may in fact contribute to the maintenance of social order. As long as social groups can pursue their opposing interests within the framework

of society, they need not deny the legitimacy of the total social structure and prevailing institutions. But those with no acceptable avenues through which to seek improvement in their circumstances may become potentially explosive enemies of the existing order or lapse into apathy, itself a form of deviant behavior, although one that constitutes no direct challenge to authority, law, or custom. [20] Workers who cannot strike, for example, are likely to find other means to pursue their ends, and the fact that Russian opposition to the Czarist regime was ruthlessly suppressed contributed to the emergence of both revolutionaries and nihilists.

Conformity and individuality

Solidarity and the needs of the social order are often set against the claims of the individual, as if the sole alternative to conformity were nonconformity and as if individuality could only be realized by denying or disregarding the demands of culture and society. Individuality may, of course, be expressed by ignoring social norms—in eccentricity, or crime, or revolutionary action (which seeks to install new norms)—but it may also exist within an orderly society. MacIver and Page write:

. . . . we say that a social being has more individuality when his conduct is not simply imitative or the result of suggestion, when he is not entirely the slave of custom or even of habit, when his responses to the social environment are not altogether automatic and subservient, when understanding and personal purpose are factors in his life activities . . . the criterion of individuality is not how far each is divergent from the rest. It is rather how far each, in his relations to others, acts autonomously, acts in his own consciousness, and with his own interpretation, of the claims of others upon himself. [21]

Individuality therefore is not a rejection of society and its requirements, but is in large part a product of social life. It should not be confused with the philosophy of "individualism" that sees society and person as intrinsically hostile and therefore ignores the inevitable—and fruitful—interdependence that binds them together.[22] Society itself may enhance or inhibit the possibility of the emergence and expression of individuality.

Personality is shaped by social experience interacting with biological potentialities and the process of maturation, and behavior is always constrained to some extent by external forces. But social structure and culture may provide for a range of choice as well as requiring certain fixed courses of action. Although our knowledge of the conditions that facilitate autonomy and individuality is still fragmentary and tentative, it seems clear that the capacity to choose freely and effectively among available alternatives is a product of both one's biography and the circumstances in which one finds oneself.

Early experience may enhance or inhibit the individual's ability to learn, to reason, to free himself from the internal constraints that limit his capacity to act autonomously and to achieve some measure of independence from the demands and expectations of others. Individuality, therefore, rests to some degree upon the process of socialization and the development of personality. But it is also supported—or weakened—by the values current in society. The extent of individuality and the likelihood that people will maintain some measure of autonomy are increased in a setting within which there is a commitment to rationality, tolerance of the eccentric, support for the creativity that disregards tradition and convention, and respect and admiration for the person who refuses to yield, for good reasons, to the majority view or to the demands of fashion.

As Simmel points out, individual autonomy and self-determination may also be enhanced by membership in several social groups. Although these multiple affiliations can lead to conflict and tension, "the ego can become more clearly conscious of [its inner] unity, the more he is confronted with the task of reconciling within himself a diversity of group-interests." [23] As no culture is free of inconsistencies and no society fully integrated (that is, with completely complementary role-expectations), there are always some tensions present that stimulate or require self-understanding and independent judgment. Highly disorganized societies, on the other hand, are probably least hospitable to personal autonomy and rational choice.

The most creative periods in history, it seems, have occurred when the traditional social bonds were being dissolved but had not yet totally disappeared. In such periods men could draw their moral and intellectual sustenance from a still meaningful tradition but could also derive fresh insight and new ideas from the changes taking place. The creative artists who worked in such periods as the Renaissance, the Age of Shakespeare, and the late nineteenth century in Russia were not totally alienated from their society yet were not fully content with it; their individuality reflected their ability to transcend the immediate social and cultural environment while remaining very much a part of it. The economic and intellectual advances of the nineteenth and early twentieth centuries, too, reflect the exhilarating impact of new horizons upon persisting traditions and perspectives.

Individuality in the modern world, in the judgment of some students, is seriously threatened by the demands of bureaucracy, with its impersonal rules and formal hierarchy; by the complexity of contemporary life, which makes difficult rational understanding—and therefore control—of the forces that affect one's fate; by the possibility of anonymous manipulation by those who control the impersonal and efficient techniques created by modern technology. In the face of these circumstances, C. Wright Mills suggests, the individual "adapts," although the alternatives he may seek—fun, leisure, sport—are eventually subject to the same large-scale forces.

[The] adaptation of the individual and its effects upon his milieux and self results not only in the loss of his chance, and in due course, of his capacity and will to reason; it also affects his chances and his capacity to act as a free man. Indeed, neither the value of freedom nor of reason, it would seem, are known to him.[24]

This view has been challenged, however, not for its theory that the possibility of individuality depends upon culture and social organization, but for its image of American society. Together with bureaucratization, increasing complexity, and greater manipulative possibilities, it is argued, have also come higher living standards, greater concern for the needs and sensitivities of others, and substantially increased opportunities to choose among occupations, consumer goods, types of leisure, and alternative styles of life.[25] Perhaps even more important is the rational understanding of the problems and prerequisites of individuality that is potentially represented by the "sociological imagination." For an awareness of the threats to individuality inherent in modern society is perhaps the first step toward their alleviation.[26]

Notes

[1] See, for example, David Riesman, *Individualism Reconsidered* (New York: Free Press, 1954), Ch. 25.

[2] David Riesman, with Reuel Denny and Nathan Glazer, *The Lonely Crowd* (New Haven: Yale University Press, 1950).

[3] See the various critiques in Seymour M. Lipset and Leo Lowenthal (eds.), *Culture and Social Character* (New York: Free Press, 1961). For Riesman's own modifications, see David Riesman and Nathan Glazer, *Faces in the Crowd* (New Haven: Yale University Press, 1952), Ch. 1; and Riesman and Glazer, *"The Lonely Crowd:* A Reconsideration in 1960," Ch. 19 in Lipset and Lowenthal, *op. cit.*

[4] Bronislaw Malinowski, *Crime and Custom in Savage Society* (Paterson, N.J.: Littlefield, 1959; first published, 1926), p. 10.

[5] *Ibid.*, p. 22.

[6] Georg Simmel, *Sociology*, trans. and ed. Kurt Wolff (New York: Free Press, 1950), p. 390.

[7] Alvin W. Gouldner, "The Norm of Reciprocity," *American Sociological Review*, XXV (April, 1960), 161–78.

[8] Robert M. MacIver and Charles H. Page, *Society* (New York: Rinehart, 1949), p. 168.

[9] Émile Durkheim, *The Rules of Sociological Method*, trans. by Sarah A. Solovay and John H. Mueller (Chicago: University of Chicago Press, 1938), p. 96.

[10] John Dollard, *Caste and Class in a Southern Town* (3rd ed.; Garden City: Doubleday Anchor Books, 1957), pp. 309–10.

[11] Russell Middleton and John Moland, "Humor in Negro and White Subcultures: A Study of Jokes Among University Students," *American Sociological Review*, XXIV (February, 1959), 67.

[12] Max Lerner, *America as a Civilization* (New York: Simon & Shuster, 1957), p. 812.

[13] G. G. Coulton, *Medieval Panorama* (New York: Meridian, 1955), p. 606.

[14] See Clyde Kluckhohn, *Navaho Witchcraft*, Papers of the Peabody Museum of American Archaeology and Ethnology, XXII (Cambridge: Harvard University Press, 1944), 2, 45–72.

[15] Talcott Parsons, *The Social System*, (New York: Free Press, 1951), pp. 299–300.

[16] Émile Durkheim, *The Division of Labor in Society*, trans. by George Simpson (New York: Free Press, 1947).

[17] For a summary description and analysis of American values, see Robin M. Williams, Jr., *American Society* (2nd ed.; New York: Knopf, 1960), pp. 397–470.

[18] William Graham Sumner, *Folkways* (Boston: Ginn, 1906), p. 160.

[19] See Kingsley Davis, *Human Society* (New York: Macmillan, 1949), p. 160.

[20] For a full discussion of the social functions of conflict, see Lewis A. Coser, *The Functions of Social Conflict* (New York: Free Press, 1956).

[21] MacIver and Page, *op. cit.*, pp. 50–1.

[22] *Ibid.*, pp. 54–5. See also A. D. Lindsay, "Individualism," *Encyclopedia of the Social Sciences*, VII (New York: Macmillan, 1932), 674–80.

[23] Georg Simmel, *Conflict*, trans. by Kurt H. Wolff, and *The Web of Group Affiliations*, trans. by Reinhard Bendix (New York: Free Press, 1955), p. 142.

[24] C. Wright Mills, *The Sociological Imagination* (New York: Oxford University Press, 1959), p. 170.

[25] Winston White, *Beyond Conformity* (New York: Free Press, 1961).

[26] See William L. Kolb, "Values, Politics, and Sociology" (a review of Mills, *The Sociological Imagination*), *American Sociological Review*, XXV (December, 1960), 966–9.

Suggestions for further reading

BLAU, PETER M. *Exchange and Power in Social Life.* New York: Wiley, 1964. Ch. 4, "Social Exchange."
A subtle and suggestive discussion of exchange and reciprocity.

COSER, LEWIS A. *The Functions of Social Conflict.* New York: Free Press, 1956.
The contributions of social conflict to the stability or persistence of social relationships.

DURKHEIM, ÉMILE. *The Division of Labor in Society.* Trans. by George Simpson. New York: Free Press, 1947.
A classic treatise that explores the sources of social solidarity in both simple societies and those marked by an elaborate division of labor.

GLUCKMAN, MAX. *Custom and Conflict in Africa.* Oxford: Blackwell, 1955.
An eminent anthropologist analyzes the contributions of such social phenomena as feuds, witchcraft, group conflict, and ritual license to the maintenance of social order. Based largely upon materials drawn from several African societies.

GOULDNER, ALVIN W. "The Norm of Reciprocity," *American Sociological Review*, XXV (April, 1960), 161–78.
A theoretical essay on the nature and functions of reciprocity.

MACIVER, ROBERT M., AND CHARLES H. PAGE. *Society.* New York: Rinehart, 1949. Chs. 3, 7, 8, 9.
An examination of the relations between the individual and society and the forms of social control.

MALINOWSKI, BRONISLAW. *Crime and Custom in Savage Society.* Paterson, N.Y.: Littlefield, 1959. First published, 1926.
This anthropological essay emphasizes the nonautomatic nature of behavior, even in primitive society, and explores

reciprocity and punishment as mechanisms of social control.

MAUSS, MARCEL. *The Gift.* Trans. by Ian Cunnison. London: Cohen & West, 1954. *An essay on the functions of exchanging gifts in the maintenance of the social order.*

RADCLIFFE-BROWN, A. R. *Structure and Function in Primitive Society.* New York: Free Press, 1952. Ch. IV, "On Joking Relationships." *The functions of institutionalized teasing or making fun of some other persons.*

RIESMAN, DAVID, WITH REUEL DENNEY AND NATHAN GLAZER. *The Lonely Crowd.* New Haven: Yale University Press, 1950. Reprinted, Doubleday Anchor Books, 1953.

Widely hailed as a modern classic, this suggestive essay explores the nature and significance of changes in the dominant modes of conformity in American culture.

SIMMEL, GEORG. *Sociology.* Trans. by Kurt Wolff. New York: Free Press, 1950, pp: 379–95. *A suggestive and penetrating discussion of "faithfulness and gratitude" as forces making for the stability of social relations.*

WHITE, WINSTON. *Beyond Conformity.* New York: Free Press, 1961. *This analysis challenges the view that modern society inhibits individuality and tries to identify the sources of diversity and autonomy in contemporary social structure.*

19

Deviant behavior and social disorganization

Deviant behavior and social structure

Despite the numerous mechanisms that elicit or enforce conformity, no society —or group within society—is ever totally free from some disregard for its standards of propriety, some deviation from its norms. Deviant behavior varies from the mild peccadillos of most people to incest, murder, and treason. It includes such diverse actions as eccentricities that merely amuse or irritate, apathetic neglect of conventional responsibilities, violations of bureaucratic regulations, covert defiance of sexual mores, delinquency, and crime.

From a psychological point of view, the origins of deviant behavior lie in the personality—in unsatisfied needs, unmanageable drives or emotional problems. In *Civilization and Its Discontents*, Sigmund Freud finds the roots of nonconformity in biological impulses that constantly seek to burst through cultural restraints.[1] Although tensions may indeed be created in the interaction between human needs or drives and the social order, a theory that emphasizes merely the strength of these impulses is clearly inadequate to explain why they break through social controls at particular times or the specific actions they precipitate.

Psychological interpretations of unconventional or criminal behavior need not rest upon instincts or innate tendencies, however, as Freud himself suggests in his analysis of personality dynamics. Individuals may come to ignore cultural dictates because of their particular social experience. Parental neglect, excessive demands upon the child, rigid authority, or continuing conflict between parent and child, for example, may lead to psychological tendencies that encourage rejection or disregard of cultural prescriptions. Because early experience is particularly important in the formation of personality, nonconformity frequently seems to reflect the failure of socialization—the unwillingness or inability to inculcate respect for others or for prevailing social values, stimulation of aggressive or hostile feelings, or even the direct transmission of socially objectionable habits or interests to the child.

Analysis of the psychological sources of deviance and of its roots in each person's biography is both necessary and appropriate for the understanding of individual cases. Each murderer or delinquent, each eccentric or antiorganization man has a private history that is relevant to his actions. But facts about individual experience or personality cannot account

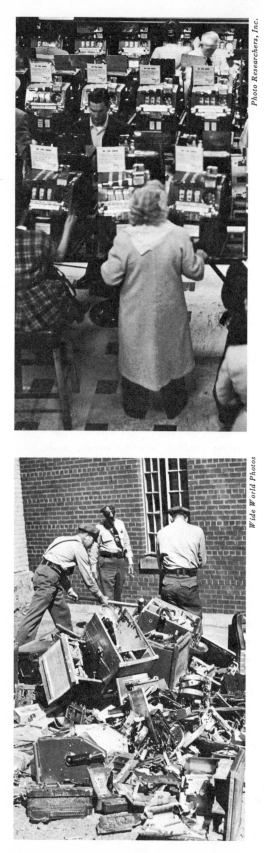

Photo Researchers, Inc.

Wide World Photos

for the forms of deviance found in society or for its frequency and distribution among various groups or social categories. Deviant behavior exists only when it is so defined by others. If homosexuality were tolerated, it would no longer be deviance; the open expression of unpopular opinions becomes deviance only when it is looked upon as beyond the bonds of propriety. Moreover the same actions can be appropriate—or at least tolerated—when performed by those in one status and inappropriate or even immoral when performed by persons in another status. A "joyride" in a "borrowed" car may be a youthful prank when the driver is a respectable middle-class boy but will be auto theft if he is an urban slum dweller. As Kai Erikson remarks,

Behavior which qualifies one man for prison may qualify another for sainthood, since the quality of the act itself depends so much upon the circumstaances under which it was performed and the temper of the audience which witnessed it.[2]

Changes in the definition of what is right or proper or in the response to various kinds of behavior therefore affect the extent of deviance in a society or group within it.

Even when these definitions remain unchanged, however, the frequency of various kinds of violations of social norms fluctuate as circumstances change. Crime,

What is deviant behavior in one setting is tolerated, even encouraged, in others. TOP: *Slot machines in Reno, Nevada, where legalized gambling is a major source of income for both individuals and the state.* BOTTOM: *Illinois State Police break up slot machines in a raid on an illegal gambling den.*

delinquency, and suicide rates, for example, may change from year to year or even from season to season; illegal gambling, disregard of sexual norms, and political corruption grow more or less prevalent over a period of time. Most forms of deviant behavior are rarely distributed equally throughout all segments of society. Auto theft, robbery, and assault are more frequent in the lower class, embezzlement in the middle class. Delinquent juvenile gangs are largely—although not completely—a phenomenon of urban slums. Although lower-class men patronize prostitutes more than middle-class men, the latter engage more frequently in petting and deviant forms of erotic conduct.

Facts like these can be explained only by reference to sociological—and, on occasion, social-psychological—variables. From a sociological perspective, violations of law and custom stem from the characteristics of the culture and the social organization in which they occur. It is the relations of men to one another, the roles they play, their institutions and values, and the connections among these variables that affect the definition, rate, and distribution of deviant behavior.

Because the culture and social organization are never fully integrated, with their complex and varied elements fitting neatly into and supporting one another, there are always tendencies toward deviance inherent in social life itself. The strength of these tendencies varies with the extent of *social disorganization*, which is always partially present but may become acute in some parts of society or even become characteristic of the whole. The study of disorganization is in important respects inseparable from the study of organization; in a full analysis of society and social life both must be included.

Social disorganization is an inclusive concept that encompasses such varied phenomena as a role conflict, culture conflict, disjunction between socially sanctioned means and ends, and other kinds of inconsistencies or contradictions. Those groups or individuals most exposed to the pressures generated by these forms of disorganization are most likely to ignore or violate social norms. Their responses depend upon the values, expectations, difficulties created by their circumstances.

Role and value conflict

Social disorganization sometimes takes the form of inconsistent or contradictory norms and values that seem to require different kinds of conduct in the same situation. Shall the businessman be scrupulously honest or shall he use some devious stratagem of doubtful legality or propriety to increase his profits? Should the politician speak his views forthrightly or tailor his public pronouncements in the interest of political expediency? Does the successful revolutionist owe his allegiance to the ideals that motivated his rebellion or to the need to maintain the power he has gained? Should the child of immigrant parents obey the values of his parents or the standards of the new society in which he finds himself?

Such cultural contradictions often impose difficult choices. If opposing values are widely accepted as valid, people find it difficult to accept one and reject the other. Instead, without openly rejecting either value, the individual frequently offers some socially acceptable reason for apparently ignoring one of them. The businessman guilty of a lapse of ethics falls back upon the maxim "business is business" or some equivalent, or argues that, as no law was violated, no moral failure has occurred. The politician who jettisons his principles for the sake of his office emphasizes the contribution he can make by the policies he espouses while muting or denying his violation of any moral rule. These rationalizations become incorporated in the culture as *expediency norms*, helping to perpetuate incompatible values despite the inevitable necessity, on occasion, of ignoring one or the other.

If neither of the competing values can easily give way to the other (if, for example, no acceptable justification for ignoring one of the alternatives is available), a tendency toward some other—and perhaps deviant—solution to the dilemma may be generated. Dr. Alice Hamilton, who worked for a time before World War I at Hull House, a famous settlement house in the slums of Chicago, recounts the following incident:

[One day] I invited a group of Italian women to spend a Sunday afternoon with me at Hull-House, all of them married women with large families. The conversation turned very soon on abortions and the best method of producing them and I was in consternation to listen to the experiences of these women, who had themselves undergone frightful risks and much suffering rather than add another child to a house too full already. One woman said she had thrown herself down the cellar stairs twice, but it had done no good. Another answered, "Next time take a tub of water with you and throw yourself after it. I did that and it worked." These women were all Catholics, but when I spoke of that, they simply shrugged their shoulders.[3]

The conflict between the principles of the Church, which prohibits birth control, and their marital responsibilities, on the one hand, and their desire to limit the size of their families, on the other, led to these desperate solutions.

A continuing clash of values, however, may progressively weaken attachment to both alternatives, thus increasing the possibility that neither can serve as an effective guide to action. In the United States, for example, children of immigrants, lacking strong commitment to either the norms of their parents or those of the larger culture, have contributed a disproportionate number of criminals and delinquents. Immigrants themselves, it should be noted, have not done so; indeed, many studies report lower crime rates among the foreign born than among the native born. But those who came here as children were more frequently convicted of legal violations than those who came as adults. The greater the difference between the immigrant culture and American ways, the higher rate of crime among the foreign born and their children,[4] although there are notable exceptions to this pattern, for example, among some Chinese and Jewish groups.

In addition to these generalized value conflicts, there are often competing norms or values derived from incompatible roles that an individual may find himself playing simultaneously. A policeman who discovers that his son is engaged in delinquent activities must choose between parental feelings and official responsibilities. A businessman having dealings with a relative may be uncertain about just how to treat him. A college woman in a coeducational classroom must sometimes decide between displaying her scholarly abilities and remaining a "feminine" woman attractive to her male classmates. The consequences of such role conflicts are similar to those resulting from broader value conflicts; unless some method of reconciling or avoiding incompatible demands can be found, one or the other norm must be ignored. The policeman protects his child, the businessman ignores the possibility of profit in dealing with a relative, the college woman plays down her knowledge. These choices, of course, may create strains in relations with those other people whose expectations are disregarded.

Various mechanisms serve to reduce or avoid the tensions that stem from incompatible role demands and inconsistent values. Thus people sometimes seek to avoid occasions in which they will be subject to competing pressures. Businessmen try not to deal with relatives, and the policeman turns a case in which he may have personal involvement over to another officer. Recognition of the possibility of such role conflict sometimes leads to explicit rules to prevent its occurrence. Some large corporations, for example, have established rules prohibiting nepotism, or the employment of any kinfolk, so that there can never be a choice between loyalty to the firm and obligations to relatives.

Value conflicts may be resolved when the contradictory alternatives are linked to distinct roles, which are then separated from one another. Economic and familial values in the United States are very different: The former are dominated by rationality, impersonality, and self-interest; the latter by love, intimacy, and selflessness. Yet these sharply opposing values create few problems, for they apply to clearly differentiated roles that usually are not played simultaneously. The husband's role as breadwinner requires some economic rationality, but it is not supposed to extend into other familial activities. Alternatively, values may be ranked in importance so that the dominant one usually takes precedence over the other. For example, in a clash between the needs of national security and the scientists' emphasis upon publication of findings, security measures will usually come first.

Even if role and value conflicts are not resolved by such devices, they do not inevitably lead to deviant behavior, for many persons do not feel impelled to disregard prevailing conventions. In many cases, the forces of social control effectively prevent deviant conduct. Only a minority of second-generation Americans become delinquents or criminals, although crime and delinquency rates are higher among them than among others. The propriety of some business and political behavior may be dubious, but most businessmen and politicians probably resolve their role and value conflicts without serious mishap. The distinguishing characteristics of those who respond to these cultural dilemmas in deviant fashion and of the situations in which deviant behavior occurs have yet to be fully explored. Only detailed research in each type of situation can identify the relevant personal traits or social circumstances.

Social disorganization: culture and social structure

Probably of greater importance than role or culture conflict as a source of deviant behavior is the disjunction often found between culture (norms and values) and social structure (the organized system of roles and statuses that define relations among groups and individuals). Each culture establishes goals and interests that members of society are encouraged and expected to pursue and prescribes the methods to be followed in seeking these approved objectives. In order to be popular with boys, American girls are expected to learn how to apply make-up, emphasize their femininity, carry on light conversation, and flatter masculine egos. Boxers preparing for a fight eschew normal activities in the seclusion of a training camp where they follow traditional patterns of physical and psychological conditioning. People with political aspirations gradually acquire the skills of public expression and private exchange that are presumably necessary to gain public office. As long as the institutionalized means permit realization of socially valued ends, people gain gratification both "in terms of the product and in terms of the process, in terms of the outcome and in terms of the activities." [5] But if the goals are given inordinate emphasis or if defined means prove to be inadequate or unavailable, pressures toward deviant behavior may be created among those who are unable, because of their position in the social structure, to gain the goals they have come to value and desire.

This type of social disorganization is clearly illustrated in the American emphasis upon economic success in a society in which some groups do not have full or equal opportunity to gain high-level jobs or to become wealthy. American culture not only places great value upon economic achievement, assigning high prestige to those who become rich, but also encourages everyone to strive for the same objective. Parents, teachers, and religious leaders stimulate ambition; newspapers, magazines, movies, radio, and television stress pecuniary values and affirm the reality of opportunity and the possibility of success. Despite a substantial amount of social mobility in the United States, opportunities for economic advancement are in fact not equally available to all groups; Negroes, Mexican-Americans, Puerto Ricans, manual workers, and their children face serious obstacles to advancement, and many middle-class people, whose opportunities are greater than those of the working class, also do not manage to live up to the prescriptions of the culture.

Those who are caught between cultural injunctions and social realities may respond to their difficult circumstances in various ways. Some individuals doggedly persist in their efforts to succeed despite the obstacles they face. Those unable to sustain the tensions created by the discrepancy between the culture and the social structure are likely to deviate from established social norms, but their behavior, as Robert Merton points out, may take different forms. Merton identifies four distinct types of deviant behavior: ritualism, retreatism, innovation, and rebellion.[6]

1. RITUALISM   Unable to achieve the valued goals, the ritualist gives up, but nevertheless continues to conform to prevailing rules governing work and effort. Overtly there is no evidence of deviance, but this internal response is clearly "a departure from the cultural model in which men are obliged to strive actively, preferably through institutionalized procedures, to move onward and upward in the social hierarchy." [7] Coupled with this withdrawal from the struggle is often a compulsive adherence to the outward forms, a ritualism that may allay the anxieties created by lowered levels of aspiration. The perspective of the ritualist is that of the timid clerk or rigidly rule-abiding bureaucrat.

2. RETREATISM   Unlike the ritualist who gives up the goals but clings to sanctioned patterns of behavior that are supposed to lead to the goals, the retreatist gives up both. Total escape from the contradictions of the situation may be manifest in the tramp, the drunkard, the drug addict, the psychotic; it can also be seen among the "beatniks" or "happeners," to use a more recent term, some of whom deny the desirability of success and refuse to conform to the requirements of middle-class morality, often without substituting any effective or meaningful values in their place.

Retreatism is also exemplified by the

apathy of the peasants in a relatively isolated village in southern Italy studied by Edward Banfield. Grinding poverty, sharp class antagonisms, a callous and distant government, and the absence of any effective community organization— and of any institutions or values that might encourage cooperative efforts at self or group betterment—make it very unlikely that they can improve their circumstances, even as increasing contact with the outside world stimulates their desires. As a result,

the peasant feels himself part of a larger society which he is "in" but not altogether "of." He lives in a culture in which it is very important to be admired, and he sees that by its standards he cannot be admired in the least; by these standards he and everything about him are contemptible or ridiculous. Knowing this, he is filled with loathing for his lot and with anger for the fates which assigned him to it.[8]

Despite this resentment and frustration, the peasant does little or nothing, subsiding into "the grim melancholia—la misèria—which has been the fixed mood of the village for longer than anyone can remember." [9]

3. INNOVATION   Perhaps the most readily apparent deviant response to the disjunction between culture and social stucture is innovation, the use of new or illicit techniques to gain the desired goals. When these goals are more heavily stressed by the culture than the methods by which they are to be reached, people are likely to disregard moral, legal, and customary restraints upon their efforts to achieve their aims. Like Lady Wishfort in William Congreve's *Way of the World*, their motto becomes "What's integrity to an opportunity?" The widespread use of drugs by professional European bicycle riders illustrates the influence of an overemphasis upon goals. So great are the rewards of a winning rider—and so

grueling the contests and fierce the competition—that many men take drugs during distance races in order to reduce fatigue and stimulate effort. Despite occasional scandals or tragedies (for example, the death during the 1960 Olympic Games of a Danish cyclist who had taken a stimulant before racing in 93-degree weather), attempts to eliminate the use of drugs have failed, for the conditions that encourage the "doping" of cyclists still persist.

The pressures to ignore conventional methods of reaching culturally approved objectives are, of course, greater among those whose access is blocked by virtue of their position in the social structure. Although some businessmen are led to sharp practice by the desire to increase their profits, those at or near the bottom of the society may turn to crime or gambling. As many observers have pointed out, crime and corrupt politics have long been ladders of social mobility in American society.[10]   Gambling—particularly the penny ante "policy wheel" or "numbers racket"—has been widely popular among slum-dwelling Negroes; with little or no chance to improve their circumstances through hard work, thrift, abstemiousness, and sobriety, the poor bet their penny or nickel or dime or more in the hope that chance might bring them a large return.

Innovation, however, need not take the form of deviant behavior. Substantial leeway may be allowed for new techniques and methods, restrained only by general standards of propriety and legality. In a liberal society, it may also be possible to seek changes in the institutions that limit access to culturally sanctioned goals; chances for lower-class people and members of minority groups to "get ahead" may be increased, for example, by expanding educational opportunities or eliminating racial and ethnic discrimination.

4. REBELLION   Finally, the frustrations generated by limited opportunities to seek or gain culturally sanctioned goals can lead to the total rejection of both the ends and the institutions through which they are to be gained, coupled with advocacy or introduction of fresh values and new institutional and organizational forms. Rebellion, however, should be distinguished from *ressentiment,* in which the explicit condemnation of traditional values merely hides a deeply rooted commitment to them. In such cases, hate and hostility, a feeling of impotence, and a continual sense of frustration are coupled with the open denunciation of those goals that remain out of reach. "In *ressentiment,* one condemns what one secretly craves; in rebellion, one condemns the craving itself. But though the two are distinct, organized rebellion may draw upon a vast reservoir of the resentful and discontented as institutional dislocations become acute." [11]

The "beatniks," some of whom appear to be merely passive nihilists who reject the world but offer nothing new (retreatists), also provide examples both of rebellion and *ressentiment.* Underlying the overt rejection of prevailing norms, there probably remains in many cases a continuing acceptance of conventional values to which these young people after a time will return. But some "beatniks" do pursue new values, primarily through an emphasis upon the "creative act" [12] and upon "experience" or "trips" of all kinds—sexual, mystical, drug-induced, or even commonplace events—through which they seek to penetrate to "ultimate reality." Coupled with these values is a different style of life—the "pad," the beard, jazz, jargon, companionable sex, and intermittent unskilled jobs. Although this rebellion has had little impact upon the basic values of the world that the "beatniks" reject, their innovations in dress, speech, music, and literature have been widely disseminated through the mass media. (Modern American society, in search of evidence of originality and differentness, tends to absorb into "mass culture" some of those who criticize and defy convention and tradition; it is difficult today to maintain a true Bohemia.)

More significant types of rebellion take a political form; in order to realize new values instead of the old, deliberate efforts are made to gain political power and to alter the social structure in which the sources of frustration are located. If the central values and institutions of a society are called into question, a major revolution may occur—for example, the overthrow of traditional hierarchies in the French and Russian revolutions—although of course other circumstances must also be present for so drastic a change to take place. Revolution usually requires at least mass disaffection, sharp conflict between rulers and ruled, and effective revolutionary leaders, in addition to the crises that produce a "revolutionary situation." In most cases, of course, and perhaps all, the process of reform or revolution embodies a complex mixture of new values and old, of commitment to some traditional ways together with advocacy of institutional and organizational change.

The likelihood that deviant behavior will result from inconsistencies between culture and social structure—and the nature of that behavior—varies from group to group, depending upon prevailing values and the larger social and cultural situation. Not all Americans, for example, accept equally the injunction to be ambitious; lack of interest appears more often among manual workers than among white-collar employees.[13] Those who never seek advancement or who turn to alternative but socially acceptable values probably do not experience sharply the contradictions that may stimulate aberrant conduct.

The type of deviant response found among those who are frustrated because they see little or no connection between their efforts and present rewards or future prospects is linked with position in the social structure. Innovation, rebellion, and retreatism are more likely to occur among manual workers than among salaried employees who feel they are "stuck,"; the latter are more prone to ritualism, Merton suggests, because of the "strong disciplining for conformity" that characterizes lower middle-class culture.[14] Leadership in organized crime has changed hands and the form of criminal activity has varied as successive immigrant groups and their children have faced limited prospects of advancement. The Irish played leading roles in corrupt urban political machines, Jews in industrial and labor racketeering, and Italians in gambling and bootlegging. These differences reflect both changing historical circumstances and the distinctive economic and social characteristics of these ethnic groups. As the members of each one found increasing opportunities in more conventional forms of enterprise, the group itself became less prominent in the world of mobs, gangs, and rackets.[15]

Deviant subcultures: the case of juvenile delinquency

In coping with the problems created by social disorganization, individuals frequently find available ready-made deviant solutions. Students of crime and delinquency, for example, have often noted the existence of *subcultures* that educate and sustain the legal offender—adult and juvenile. The importance of the subculture is suggested by the estimate that only about one-fifth of juvenile offenders act alone, whereas the great majority carry on their activities in company with others who hold similar attitudes and values.[16] "Beatniks," some homosexuals, and certain drug addicts have also often been drawn into organized ways of life that appear to answer some of their problems.

According to the "principle of differential association" suggested by the late Edwin H. Sutherland, many criminals—and delinquents—are drawn from those who have had access to an underworld subculture from which they acquired criminal skills, motives, and attitudes. Law-abiding citizens may have impulses that could lead to crime, but they have not had the opportunities to learn the necessary skills or to develop the appropriate attitudes and sentiments.[17] Analysis of the process of "cultural transmission" by which deviant habits, opinions, knowledge, and values are passed on to receptive neophytes sheds considerable light on the origins of deviant behavior, but more important sociological questions concern the existence of the subculture itself. What explains its development? What are the conditions that account for its persistence?

Not all deviant behavior, to be sure, can be traced to a deviant subculture. For example, crimes of passion and "white-collar crimes" such as embezzlement and fraud are often committed by individuals with little or no contact with other offenders and no prior knowledge of criminal folkways. These facts, however, merely underline the sponge-like character of concepts like crime and delinquency, concepts that encompass diverse types of behavior, each of which requires a different explanation. Here we shall be concerned with "subcultural delinquency," usually found in teen-age gangs, as one example of a patterned response to disorganized aspects of social life.

Most delinquent gangs are found in urban slums, and their existence is sometimes attributed to the rigors of poverty or the broken homes, disorganized families, and other difficult circumstances found there. Although these conditions are part of the constellation of factors that gives rises to delinquency, neither poverty nor other disruptive situations in themselves can account for the frequency of delinquent activities or the forms they take. Poverty, for example, is likely to lead to delinquent behavior and the emergence of a deviant subculture only when associated with a disjunction between culturally sanctioned goals and available opportunities; numerous comparative studies show no consistent correlation between the facts of poverty and rates of crime or delinquency.

In a penetrating analysis, Albert K. Cohen finds the origins of delinquent gangs in the status problems faced by working-class boys.[18] Their upbringing and experience often leave them ill prepared for participation in the larger world in which generally approved status is to be found. Urban working-class culture tolerates more aggression than the middle class usually permits. Unlike the children of white-collar workers or of independent entrepreneurs, working-class children often do not learn to postpone gratifications for the future rewards;[19] nor are they encouraged to be as ambitious, as rational, and as responsible.[20] They do not learn "proper" manners or, frequently, acquire any respect for private property. In contacts with the middle-class world,

therefore, particularly in school, their lack of appropriate manners, attitudes, and values causes them to lose standing; because conformity to middle-class expectations is the usual prerequisite for "getting on in the world," their opportunities to do so are narrowed. "To the degree to which he values middle-class status, either because he values the good opinion of middle-class persons or because he has to some degree internalized middle-class standards himself [the working-class boy] faces a problem of adjustment and is in the market for a 'solution.'"[21]

This problem, to be sure, exists only to the extent to which middle-class goals are accepted; if there is little concern with the values expressed in the ubiquitous products of the mass media, for example, there is apt to be little tension or strain of this particular kind. But it seems very likely that most working-class children cannot escape the influence of the dominant culture. Exposure to middle-class values in the school and through the mass media in all probability has considerable influence upon hopes and desires. Even parents, although unable to provide the knowledge, skills, or attitudes that will enable their children to succeed, often encourage the ambitions sanctioned by the success ideology.

The delinquent solution to these difficulties, of course, is only one of several possibilities open to working-class youth. Those with the requisite ability and sufficient encouragement from parents or other adults may actively commit themselves to the pursuit of advancement and success, rejecting many of the values of that version of working-class culture in which they were reared. Others seek to make the best of their circumstances, finding status and self-respect within the groups with which they are familiar. The delinquents explicitly reject middle-class values and find an alternative source of status in participation in a subculture that Cohen describes as malicious, nonutilitarian, and negativistic.[22] They openly express aggression that the middle class frowns upon; they flout the conventions of manners and deliberately destroy property. They steal "for the hell of it" rather than for the use to which their gains can be put.

This strong reaction against middle-class values, Cohen suggests, reflects the continuing appeal of these values for working-class youth. Because of the deeply rooted and lingering influence of middle-class standards, they cannot simply be ignored, but must instead be emphatically and persistently repressed. A very important aspect of aggression, destructiveness, petty thievery, and other forms of seemingly purposeless violence and malicious mischief therefore lies in their symbolic and emotional meaning to the delinquent rather than in their utilitarian value. By conforming to these deviant standards, many delinquents secure status with their peers as a substitute for the status they cannot find in the larger community.

The subculture and the group within which it is expressed emerge gradually among young people who face similar problems; as they interact with one another, they tentatively explore alternative solutions to their difficulties until finally a common pattern of behavior and a shared set of standards that can enlist their emotions and their loyalties are formed. As long as the subculture provides a means of resolving—or seeming to resolve—their difficulties, it persists, attracting new members who also find in it a solution to their own problems. Eventually, Cohen observes, "it may achieve a life which outlasts that of the individuals who participated in its creation, but only so long as

it continues to serve the needs of those who succeed its creators."[23]

The specific activities in which the gang engages depend upon the particular circumstances in which it finds itself and the structure of the group. Although it is often amorphously defined, with uncertain boundaries and a continually changing membership,[24] its members are concerned not only with people and institutions around it—parents, police, teachers, other gangs—but also with their status within the group and their relations with one another. James Short has therefore suggested that

the behavior of gang boys may be understood as an attempt . . . to seek and create alternative status systems in the form of the gang, and that delinquency arises sometimes as a by-product and sometimes as a direct product of this attempt.[25]

Despite their commitment to the gang and its values, many delinquents are not totally free from a sense of guilt that suggests a lingering attachment to the norms and values that have been rejected. Indeed, they sometimes reveal clearly a recognition of the validity and legitimacy of middle-class standards.[26] To "neutralize" the guilt stimulated by violation of these standards and thus pave the way for delinquent behavior, the subculture, Gresham Sykes and David Matza have suggested, provides a set of justifications that are apt to seem valid to teen-age gang members. Loyalty to the gang is defined as more important than other loyalties. External criticism and the danger of self-blame are avoided by assigning responsibility for their behavior to impersonal forces that have made delinquents what they are, and by denying that anyone actually suffers from escapades such as "borrowing" someone's car. Aggression against others is defended by asserting that the victims of violence—the "crooked storekeeper," or "unfair" teacher, or homosexual—merely "got what was coming to them." The legitimacy of actual or potential punishment is challenged by attacking the honesty or integrity of policemen, teachers, judges, or even parents.[27] The subculture, Matza has subsequently argued, "does not commit adherents to their misdeeds," but simply allows for and accepts "the commission of delinquencies under widely available extenuating conditions." [28]

Although the subculture analyzed by Cohen and by Sykes and Matza comprises a substantial—but unspecified—proportion of gang delinquency, it clearly does not encompass all of it. Richard Cloward and Lloyd Ohlin have therefore moved another step forward in the study of delinquency by distinguishing three kinds of delinquent gangs—criminal, conflict, and retreatist. *Criminal* gangs are engaged chiefly in theft, robbery, and other types of illicit money-making activities. They are more rational than the gangs described by Cohen and more concerned with securing money that will enable them to buy the style of life and the material symbols of status valued by the larger community. *Conflict* groups, which appear to be similar to those analyzed by Cohen, look upon violence as the major source of status. The *retreatist* gang stresses the use of drugs, an increasingly severe problem among young people in lower-class urban areas, or other "kicks" that are "out of this world." [29]

The basic conditions that give rise to these three types of gangs are much the same, deriving from the gulf between goals and opportunities. Which subculture emerges depends in large part upon the nature of the urban neighborhood in which it appears.[30] In those areas where there exists an adult criminal world that offers to disadvantaged adolescents mod-

els of illicit but attractive "career" possibilities, and, in addition, aid, encouragement, and information, the teen-age group is apt to become a criminal gang. Where no adult underworld is present, teenagers lack not only legitimate opportunities to secure middle-class values, but also the *illegitimate* opportunities provided by organized criminal activities. Without guidance they turn to explosive and violent outbursts through which they express their feelings and secure status from one another. The use of drugs or other forms of retreat, Cloward and Ohlin suggest, reflects failure not only in conventional activities but also in the illegal pursuits that are sometimes open to slum-dwelling adolescents.

These three types of delinquent subcultures, of course, are abstractions from the complex and concrete reality of teen-age gang activity and organization. Criminal gangs, for example, are not free from violence or even, on occasion, from the use of drugs, although they may seek to limit both of these activities. Conflict groups, too, may sometimes try drugs, or may carefully carry out a well-planned theft in order to secure some desired object rather than as simply a figurative nose thumbing at middle-class values. Even the retreatist gang engages in occasional violence, destructiveness, and crime.

Despite this overlapping, the extent to which each gang is oriented toward one or another of these subcultural patterns and the prevalence of particular activities may markedly influence the future of the members of the group. As each delinquent teen-ager approaches maturity, pressures for conformity to prevailing mores increase, and most one-time delinquents probably become law-abiding adults. Among those in the criminal subculture, however, the able and more adept find themselves as part of the adult world of crime in which they carve out successful "careers." If the others, together with members of conflict groups who have restricted opportunities to become "professional" criminals, fail to make the necessary adaptation to respectable adult roles, they are likely to turn to some form of retreatist behavior.

Deviant roles and careers

Participation in a deviant subculture—delinquent, criminal, homosexual, artistic, Bohemian, political—does not usually come about quickly. Instead the individual becomes only progressively involved, following a "deviant career," to use Howard Becker's phrase, from the initial action to full participation.[31] The conditions that lead to the first step may be varied and complex, premeditated or accidental and spontaneous, reflecting personal needs or external pressures. The newcomer learns from others the attributes of the role—the requisite skills, knowledge, attitudes, and values. The marijuana user, for example, learns how to inhale in order to produce the desired effect, exactly what responses constitute "getting high," what other effects to anticipate and how to respond to them, and where and how to secure the "pot." He acquires the values and justifications for smoking marijuana and comes to share the social code characteristic of the group.

Although some people are thus gradually absorbed into the deviant subculture because of the satisfactions derived from their actions, others are thrust into a deviant role and subculture by the community's response to one identifiable act. Although an individual's behavior may be conventional except for a single action or a particular type of activity, identification as a delinquent, a criminal, a drug addict, or some other type of deviant carries far-reaching connotations and consequences. "The deviant identification," Becker points out, "becomes the controlling one,"[32] and in the eyes of others all other aspects of the individual's behavior and personality are reduced to secondary importance. Suspicion, hostility, and even exclusion from various social circles are the results. Because he may therefore be limited in his opportunities for conventional activities at work or at leisure, the individual is driven toward greater association with deviants and fuller involvement in the deviant subculture. There he finds acceptance and protection, at the price of confirmation in a deviant career. Public identification thus sets in motion a "self-fulfilling prophecy" that transforms the one-time or occasional transgressor into a confirmed deviant.[33]

The institutions that are intended to punish or rehabilitate the offender against accepted rules frequently produce similar results. As many studies show, imprisonment of delinquents and criminals often serves merely to educate them more fully into the ways of crime. Older, more experienced prisoners teach the newcomers, who also absorb the attitudes, values, and knowledge of the deviant group. The likelihood that they will do so is increased by the fact that they are all physically and socially detached from the larger society and face the uncertainties of their social identification as ex-convicts upon their release.[34]

Institutionalized evasions

Similar in some respects to such subcultural deviance as delinquency are various "institutionalized evasions" of social norms.[35] Deviant activities like collusion in divorce cases, the bootlegging of the Prohibition era, gambling, use of "ghost-written" term papers, and philandering are patterned forms of behavior that are widespread despite the injunctions against them. Like a large proportion of delinquency, they stem from conflicts between desires that are usually generated by social life itself and the norms that prohibit—or make difficult—their satisfaction. Unlike most delinquency, these departures from law or convention, although widely known to exist, provoke few strong efforts at repression; instead, they are usually ignored or tolerated unless, by some chance, individual cases come to public attention.

Patterned evasions develop only when people are determined to do something that is formally prohibited and the relevant law or custom is so strongly supported that it cannot easily be repudiated or changed. As brought out in Chapter 7, for example, many marriages do not work out successfully because of certain characteristics of the modern family, and many couples become—and others wish to become—divorced. In no state, however, can a divorce be granted on the legal grounds of mutual consent or desire by husband and wife. One must bring suit against the other; one must be sinned against, the other the sinner. In fact, therefore, if both partners wish to dissolve their marriage, arrangements are usually quietly made for one to accuse the other of actions that constitute legal grounds for divorce. It has been estimated that collusion, which in this country is a specific bar to divorce if known to the court, actually occurs in more than 90 per cent of all cases. In New York State, until 1966, the only really effective legal basis for divorce was adultery, which, if it did occur, was often not the most important reason for ending a marriage. Because of the legal requirement, however, the evidence was often fabricated with the agreement of both parties, usually with the husband rather than the wife found in presumably compromising circumstances.

Gambling in the United States offers another illustration of institutionalized evasion of social norms. Some gambling is legitimate, for example, parimutuel race-track betting is some states, but other forms—off-track bookmaking, the "numbers racket," playing slot machines—are illicit in most states, Nevada, with its legalized gambling industry, being the principal exception. The demand for gambling, which has helped to give rise to an industry that has been estimated to be one of the nation's largest and most profitable, stems from diverse sources. For many lower-class Negroes and whites, the numbers game offers some excitement and an opportunity for a large return on a small bet; with little likelihood that serious and industrious effort will be richly rewarded, they turn to chance, hoping that fortune will smile upon them. For members of the middle-class, no doubt, betting, legal or illegal, or dropping quarters into a slot machine provides a thrill—as well as the possibility of a few extra dollars—in an otherwise often tedious routine. "Vice," Finley Peter Dunne's Mr. Dooley once remarked, "goes a long way tow'rd makin' life bearable. . . . A little vice now an' thin is relished be th' best iv men." [36] During World War II and subsequent years, Bell suggests, "the gambling fever" was caught by the "new upper-middle-class rich having a first fling at conspicuous consumption." [37]

Despite the widespread demand by members of various groups for opportunities to gamble, efforts to legalize off-track betting or to operate public lotteries that would funnel some of the estimated $12 to $30 billion annually spent on gambling into the public till, on the whole, have been unsuccessful. (In 1964, however, the citizens of New Hampshire did approve by a four–to–one majority the establishment of a state-operated lottery to raise funds for various public services.) Opponents of legalized gambling challenge its morality and express fear concerning the possible consequences of offering explicit sanction to behavior that, although widespread, is still looked upon by many— perhaps most—people as not completely right or proper. Illicit gambling therefore continues, interrupted only by occasional police raids upon bookmakers, number operators, and gambling establishments. These raids provide symbolic reinforcement of the law and of the moral principles upon which it rests, but they do little to inhibit the widespread desire to risk a little money in the hope of a quick return.

Many patterned evasions are allowed to persist without interference as long as they do not receive wide publicity, which may in fact tempt others to break the rules in question. Public officials may ignore the seamy underside of urban life (and may sometimes profit from it) unless reformers insist on calling attention to the real state of affairs. Philanderers remain unpunished even when their friends know of their activities; students can use term papers from the fraternity house file without criticism from their fellows. But if philanderers or cheating students are publicly revealed, they must suffer the consequences.

A further illustration of the relationship between punishment and public exposure of patterned evasions is found in the Trobriand Islands where, Bronislaw Malinowski reports, there are frequent violations of the incest taboo insofar as it applies outside the nuclear family; usually no action is taken even if such violations are known to other members of the community. But if public attention should be called to any of these transgressions, the offenders must be punished according to law and custom, even as others continue discreetly to carry on the same activities.[38]

If patterned evasions become sufficiently widespread the norms themselves may be challenged and changed. Efforts to reform divorce law and to legalize gambling continually occur, although the forces supporting the prevailing norms have been strong enough to resist most proposed changes. But knowledge that there is extensive, quietly tolerated violation of some law or convention may corrode its moral or legal authority. Prohibition, for example, survived for barely a dozen years; its inability to muster continued political support and the widely known disregard of legal restraints upon drinking led eventually to repeal of the Eighteenth Amendment.

Social disorganization and social change

The various forms of social disorganization that lead to deviant behavior are closely related to or derive from the continuing processes of social change. To be sure, not all changes in values, institutions, roles, social relationships, and technology produce disorganization. Many cultural and structural shifts represent adjustments to new circumstances, the resolution of persistent problems, and the elimination of disorganization. Nevertheless, technological and institutional innovations, the gradual transformation of practice and belief, and new patterns of social interaction frequently create contraditions and tensions that lead to nonconforming conduct.

In many parts of the world, social change imposed by outsiders has caused substantial disorganization of culture and society. Wherever Europeans gained political control, for example, in Asia, Africa, Oceania, and North America, they were apt to weaken or destroy the authority of local chiefs or rulers. Christian missionaries in many places have tried, both forcibly, with the support of civil authorities, and by persuasion, to eliminate such traditional but un-Christian practices as polygamy and premarital sex relations. The abolition of accepted practices that had served important functions in the social order has required complex readjustments that have not always been made successfully. Innovations, even if introduced with the best of intentions, have frequently produced unanticipated, destructive effects. "In the beginning," a Digger Indian in California told anthropologist Ruth Benedict, "God gave to every people a cup, a cup of clay, and from this cup they drank their life. . . . They all dipped in the water, but their cups were different. Our cup has broken now. It has passed away." [39]

European culture has not been imposed solely by force, however, for native peoples almost everywhere have eagerly borrowed many techniques, objects, and ideas from Westerners. Guns, modern tools, factory-made cloth, and other manufactured products possess a ready appeal for those living close to a subsistence level. In one Bantu tribe in South Africa, the BaKxatla, for example, after contact with European civilization, "dress material, blankets, men's wear, ploughs, pots, hatchets, spades, buckets, basins, mirrors, crockery, beads, earrings, matches, tobacco, salt, soap, tea, sugar, and bread all [found] a ready sale, and by many [came] to be regarded as necessities rather than luxuries." [40] Although many Africans were forced into the city because of the overcrowding of native reserves and the need for money to pay taxes, they were also drawn by the possibility of earning enough to buy these newly prized goods. In part because of the technological and political superiority of the Europeans, natives in many areas adopted other Western cultural traits as well—for example, nationalism, Christianity, and the belief in democracy—although they often emphasized special aspects of Western ideas and institutions or modified them to suit their own needs.

Among the BaKxatla, contact with European culture and the domination of the whites led to considerable disorganization. Economic necessity and the desire for a higher material standard of living acquired from the whites led many natives into the cities or to mines or large farms where they could secure jobs. Eventually, migration became a normal pattern expected of most young men. Although many return to the reserve for part of each year, or permanently, others remain away for long periods. This going and coming has had serious effects, especially upon the family. In the absence of her husband, the wife enjoys a new and unfamiliar independence that she is often reluctant to relinquish when he returns. If he stays away too long, she may find herself a lover. Men who live alone for a time in a heterogeneous urban community acquire new attitudes toward sexual behavior; when they return to the village, conventional restraints are often disregarded. Because many of the young men are away from the tribe and polygamy has been prohibited by the Church, many young women unwilling to wait for an eligible man become concubines—or leave for the cities themselves.[41]

Exposure to conflicting norms or values, we suggested earlier, can lead to rejection of both alternatives, to a state of *anomie* or normlessness, in which there are no effective social rules governing behavior. Caught between the new and the old, men ignore both and seek to satisfy their momentary desires without much regard to standards of right or wrong, without serious concern for either supernatural sanctions or established authority. As traditional social ties have been weakened, few effective forms of social control that could prevent deviant behavior or forestall the personal breakdown that is often a consequence of social disorganization have developed. *Anomie* appears to be particularly prevalent among the Bantu who have moved into the large South African cities. The native slums to which the Africans are confined on the fringes of such cities as Johannesburg and Natal are marked by high rates of crime, alcoholism, prostitution, and other forms of behavior stigmatized by both native and European culture. In these cities, too, are found emerging ideologies and political movements that seek power, to be sure, but also represent efforts to restore meaning and order to African society.

External influences, of course, are not the only source of change or disorganization. Even the most traditional, stable, and isolated societies in time undergo some modifications, and in industrial societies the immanent forces of change are powerful and persistent. Where innovation is encouraged, new techniques, practices, objects, and ideas can be readily introduced, often with far-reaching and unpredictable consequences. New implements or products weaken customs that are linked to traditional technology. The

automobile, for example, increased the freedom of movement long valued in American culture, and for a time the desire to take advantage of this freedom contributed in many places to a decline in Sunday churchgoing.[42] By allowing people to escape from their local community, the automobile also helped to loosen social restraints upon behavior, permitting the increased freedom that can sometimes result in various forms of deviance—as well as creativity.

Many students of modern society—including, for example, sociologists Émile Durkheim, Georg Simmel, Pitirim Sorokin, and Robert Nisbet, and such interpreters of social trends as Lewis Mumford and Erich Fromm—have suggested that the widespread division of labor, the spread of individualism, growing urban agglomerations, and the extension of rational and impersonal organization in the economy, government, and elsewhere have diminished or destroyed the hold of traditional values, thus weakening the forces of social control.[43] These large-scale trends, which account for many of the achievments of modern society, thus contribute as well to many of its problems. The *anomie* to which they give rise leads to extensive personal breakdown—suicide and mental illness—and to various forms of deviant behavior such as crime, delinquency, drug addiction, and alcoholism. It also stimulates social and political movements that seek to solve pressing economic and social problems and to restore meaning, stability, and security.

Disorganization—and the reorganization which follows it—are not merely static aspects of social and cultural structure, but are processes that go on continuously, even simultaneously, in social life. When disorganization and the various forms of deviant behavior to which it gives rise become widespread, it is likely that some group or groups will offer new values, or try to bring reality closer to their needs and desires. As various groups endeavor to eliminate the sources from which their difficulties spring, solu-

tions eventually emerge that re-establish sufficient consensus, solidarity, and integration of culture and social structure for people to live together in an ordered society—only to find, inevitably, new problems to which groups and individuals must continue to address themselves.

Notes

[1] Sigmund Freud, *Civilization and Its Discontents*, trans. by Joan Riviere (London: Hogarth Press, 1955), see especially pp. 60–4.

[2] Kai T. Erikson, *Wayward Puritans* (New York: Wiley, 1966), pp. 5–6.

[3] Alice Hamilton, *Exploring the Dangerous Trades* (Boston: Little Brown, 1943), p. 112.

[4] For summaries of relevant data, see Mabel A. Elliot, *Crime in Modern Society* (New York: Harper, 1952), pp. 284–97; and Edwin H. Sutherland and Donald R. Cressey, *Principles of Criminology* (5th ed.; Philadelphia: Lippincott, 1955), Ch. 8.

[5] Robert K. Merton, *Social Theory and Social Structure* (rev. and enlarged ed.; New York: Free Press, 1957), p. 134.

[6] *Ibid.*, Chs. IV and V. For elaboration of these categories and the analysis upon which they are based, see Robert Dubin, "Deviant Behavior and Social Structure: Continuities in Social Theory"; Richard A. Cloward, "Illegitimate Means, *Anomie*, and Deviant Behavior"; and Robert K. Merton, "Social Conformity, Deviation, and Opportunity-Structures: A Comment on the Contributions of Dubin and Cloward," *American Sociological Review*, XXIV (April, 1959), 147–64, 164–76, 177–89.

[7] Merton, *Social Theory and Social Structure*, p. 150.

[8] Edward C. Banfield, *The Moral Basis of a Backward Society* (New York: Free Press, 1958), p. 65.

[9] *Ibid.*, p. 175.

[10] See, for example, William Foote Whyte, *Street Corner Society* (enlarged ed.; Chicago: University of Chicago Press, 1955), Part II; and Daniel Bell, *The End of Ideology* (New York: Free Press, 1960), Ch. 7.

[11] Merton, *Social Theory and Social Structure*, p. 156.

[12] See Kenneth Rexroth, "Disengagement: The Art of the Beat Generation," in Gene Feldman and Max Gartenberg (eds.), *The Beat Generation and the Angry Young Men* (New York: Dell, 1959), pp. 350–67.

[13] For a review of some of the evidence on this point, see Merton, *Social Theory and Social Structure*, pp. 170–6. For a detailed study of the attitudes toward success and responses to the discrepancy between success values and actual opportunities, see Ely Chinoy, *Automobile Workers and the American Dream* (New York: Random House, 1955).

[14] Merton, *Social Theory and Social Structure*, p. 151.

[15] Bell, *op. cit.*, pp. 128–34.

[16] Richard A. Cloward and Lloyd E. Ohlin, *Delinquency and Opportunity* (New York: Free Press, 1960), pp. 41–2.

[17] See Sutherland and Cressey, *op. cit.*, pp. 77–80.

[18] Albert K. Cohen, *Delinquent Boys* (New York: Free Press, 1955).

[19] See Louis Schneider and Sverre Lysgaard, "The Deferred Gratification Pattern: A Preliminary Study," *American Sociological Review*, XVIII (April, 1953), 142–9.

[20] See Melvin L. Kohn, "Social Class and Parental Values," *American Journal of Sociology*, LXIV (January, 1959), 337–51; and Melvin L. Kohn, "Social Class and Parental Authority," *American Sociological Review*, XXIV (June, 1959), 352–66.

[21] Cohen, *op. cit.*, p. 119.

[22] *Ibid.*, p. 25.

[23] *Ibid.*, p. 65.

[24] See Lewis Yablonsky, "The Delinquent Gang as a Near Group," *Social Problems*, IX (Fall, 1961), 108–17.

[25] James F. Short, Jr., "Gang Delinquency and *Anomie*," in Marshal B. Clinard (ed.), *Anomie and Deviant Behavior* (New York: Free Press, 1964), p. 117. See also Lewis Yablonsky, *The Violent Gang* (New York: Macmillan, 1962); and Leon R. Jansyn, Jr., "Solidarity and Delinquency in a Street Corner Group," *American Sociological Review*, XXXI (October, 1966), 600–14.

[26] See Robert A. Gordon, James F. Short, Jr., Desmond S. Cartwright, and Fred L. Strodtbeck, "Values and Gang Delinquency: A Study of Street Corner Groups," *American Journal of Sociology*, LXIX (September, 1963), 109–28. This article is also included in James F. Short, Jr., and Fred L. Strodtbeck, *Group Process and Gang Delinquency* (Chicago: University of Chicago Press, 1965), pp. 47–76.

[27] Gresham M. Sykes and David Matza, "Techniques of Neutralization: A Theory of Delinquency," *American Sociological Review*, XXII (December, 1957), 664–70.

[28] David Matza, *Delinquency and Drift* (New York: Wiley, 1964), p. 50.

[29] See Cloward and Ohlin, *op. cit.*, pp. 1, 20–7.

[30] The following discussion is based upon *ibid.*, Chs. 6, 7.

[31] Howard S. Becker, *Outsiders* (New York: Free Press, 1963), pp. 25–39. The analysis that follows draws heavily upon Becker's work.

[32] *Ibid.*, p. 34.

[33] Erikson, *op. cit.*, p. 17.

[34] See, for example, Gresham Sykes, *The Society of Captives* (Princeton: Princeton University Press, 1958).

[35] The following discussion draws heavily upon Robin M. Williams, Jr., *American Society* (2nd ed.; New York: Knopf, 1960), pp. 379–91.

[36] Finley Peter Dunne, *Mr. Dooley at His Best*, ed. E. Ellis (New York: Scribner's, 1938), pp. 120–1.

[37] Bell, *op. cit.*, p. 135.

[38] See Bronislaw Malinowski, *Crime and Custom in Savage Society* (Paterson: Littlefield, 1959), pp. 71–84.

[39] Ruth Benedict, *Patterns of Culture* (New York: Penguin, 1946), p. 19.

[40] I. Schapera, "Present-Day Life in the Native Reserves," in I. Schapera (ed.), *Western Civilization and the Natives of South Africa* (London: Routledge, 1934), p. 43.

[41] *Ibid.*, pp. 46–52.

[42] See Robert S. and Helen M. Lynd, *Middletown* (New York: Harcourt, 1929), pp. 258–61.

[43] For examples of such interpretations see Émile Durkheim, *Suicide*, trans. by John A. Spaulding and George Simpson (New York: Free Press, 1951), Ch. 5; and Emile Durkheim, *The Division of Labor*, trans. by George Simpson (New York: Free Press, 1947), Book Three and Preface to the Second Edition; Georg Simmel, *The Sociology of Georg Simmel*, trans. by Kurt Wolff (New York: Free Press, 1950), pp. 409–24, "The Metropolis and Mental Life"; Pitirim A. Sorokin, *The Crisis of Our Age* (New York: E. P. Dutton, 1941); Robert A. Nisbet, *Community and Power* (New York: Oxford, 1962); *Erich Fromm, Escape from Freedom* (New York: Rinehart, 1941); Erich Fromm, *The Sane Society* (New York: Rinehart, 1955); Lewis Mumford, *Technics and Civilization* (New York: Harcourt, 1934); and Lewis Mumford, *The Culture of Cities* (New York: Harcourt, 1938).

Suggestions for further reading

BECKER, HOWARD S. *Outsiders.* New York: Free Press, 1963.
A study that focuses on deviant roles and the processes by which people learn how to play them.

———— (ed.). *The Other Side: Perspectives on Deviance.* New York: Free Press, 1964.
Papers on the sources of deviance, deviant roles, and responses to deviant behavior.

BELL, DANIEL. *The End of Ideology.* New York: Free Press, 1960. Chs. 7, 8, 9.
These three essays explore the connections between organized crime and social institutions and social structure.

CLINARD, MARSHALL B. (ed.). *Anomie and Deviant Behavior.* New York: Free Press, 1964.
Essays on the nature of anomie and its relationship with deviant behavior.

CLOWARD, RICHARD A., AND LLOYD E. OHLIN. *Delinquency and Opportunity.* New York: Free Press, 1960.
A recent significant contribution to the understanding of the various types of delinquent gangs found in urban slums.

COHEN, ALFRED K. *Delinquent Boys.* New York: Free Press, 1955.
An important theoretical essay on the origins and functions of the delinquent subculture.

DURKHEIM, ÉMILE. *Suicide.* Trans. by John A. Spaulding and George Simpson. New York: Free Press, 1951. Book II, Ch. 5, especially pp. 246–54.
The first systematic discussion of anomie, still a stimulating and useful analysis.

ERIKSON, KAI T. *Wayward Puritans.* New York: Wiley, 1966.
An attempt to locate deviant behavior and the ways in which it was treated within the social structure and culture of seventeenth-century Massachusetts.

FROMM, ERICH. *The Sane Society.* New York: Rinehart, 1955.
A provocative discussion of the major forms of social disorganization in modern society and their consequences for the individual personality.

MATZA, DAVID. *Delinquency and Drift.* New York: Wiley, 1964.
A reassessment of delinquency and the delinquent subculture that emphasizes the legal context and its influence.

MERTON, ROBERT K. *Social Theory and Social Structure.* Revised and enlarged ed. New York: Free Press, 1957. Chs. IV and V.
Chapter IV, "Social Structure and Anomie," first published in 1938 and revised in 1949, is a classic essay on the sociological sources of deviant behavior. Chapter V elaborates the analysis on the basis of subsequent research. For more recent attempts to expand and refine the theory, see American Sociological Review, *XXIV (April, 1949), 147–89, articles by Robert Dubin, Richard A. Cloward, and Merton.*

MERTON, ROBERT K., AND ROBERT A. NISBET (eds.). *Contemporary Social Problems.* 2nd ed. New York: Harcourt, 1966.
A useful collection of essays on such problems as mental disorders, delinquency, crime, drug addiction, family disorganization, poverty, and war. The introductory essay by Nisbet and the conclusion by Merton provide valuable theoretical perspectives.

SUTHERLAND, EDWIN H. *White Collar Crime.* New York: Dryden, 1949.
A pioneer work that documents the prevalence of illegal behavior among businessmen.

THOMAS, WILLIAM I., AND FLORIAN ZNANIECKI, *The Polish Peasant in Europe and America.* 5 vols. Boston: Badger, 1920.
A classic work on disorganization in the peasant community in pre-World War I Poland and among Polish immigrants to the United States.

WHYTE, WILLIAM F. *Street Corner Society.* Chicago: University of Chicago Press, 1943. (Enlarged edition, 1955.)
A study of organization and disorganization in an ethnic slum area in a met- *ropolitan city. Contains a revealing discussion of the institutionalization of the rackets and their connection with urban politics.*

20
Social Change

Some perspectives

Because change is a normal feature of culture and society, it has been necessary to deal with it frequently in earlier chapters. Many of the significant social changes taking place in the modern world have already been explored—the widespread tendencies toward some form of nuclear family, the emergence of a new middle class and the shifting pattern of race relations in the United States, increasing bureaucratization in industrial societies and the concentration of production in large organizations, the growing importance of science, urbanization and metropolitan growth, the expansion of education in all parts of the world, the population explosion.

The causes of these and other changes in institutions, values, and social structure are complex and varied, and no simple theoretical scheme can readily account for them. As we noted in Chapter 5, the many theories that seek to reduce the causes of social change to some dominant factor—economic, technological, political, demographic, ideological, psychological—inevitably oversimplify and distort the realities of social life. So interwoven are all of these factors in an intricate sequence of cause and effect that it is difficult to untangle them and to assign causal priority to one or another.

Despite their one-sidedness, however, many of these theories have been useful in calling attention to specific facts and relationships. No analysis of the evolution of modern society can ignore the influence of social classes, to which Karl Marx assigned the central dynamic role in social change; of technology, to which Thorstein Veblen gave priority; of religion and value systems, the importance of which Max Weber emphasized. Efforts to assess the significance of each of these factors—and of such others as urbanization, bureaucratization, population growth, the extension of rationality—therefore shed light upon the process of social change as a whole.

There remains, however, the task of establishing the relationship among these partial views in order to locate more precisely the diverse sources of change, to account for its rate and direction, and to define the process by which it occurs. As yet sociology has produced no adequate or encompassing theory that achieves these goals, but it does offer perspectives that are useful in systematically analyzing specific historical situations.

As we noted in Chapter 5, the sources of change may be exogenous or endogenous, may come from forces outside the society or from forces at work within it.

Since few, if any, societies are totally isolated and free from contact with others, they are constantly subject to external stimuli to change. These contacts may be direct and violent, as in the case of war and conquest, or more subtle and indirect as when ideas, artifacts, and customs are diffused across social boundaries. Within the limits of a society, on the other hand, some forms of innovation are on occasion sanctioned or even encouraged—science and technology, frequently—sometimes with far-reaching and unanticipated consequences. But even in the face of strong commitments to convention and tradition, pressures are often generated that may require or precipitate adjustment and change.

Since no society is wholly integrated or completely static, there are always points of tension or strain constituting potential sources of change. These strains, which are often the result of change as well as its source, may take many forms—role conflict, divergent values, social deprivation, competing interests, the inability to achieve socially valued goals with the available means. They emerge from the workings of accepted institutions and established values or are related to various kinds of changes already taking place at other points in the culture or social structure. The pressures resulting from strains in the social structure need not provoke change, for they can be contained or drained off in various ways—by political repression, religious sanctions, "bread and circuses," and preoccupation with external enemies. But if these pressures are not relieved, those who find themselves in difficult or frustrating situations are likely to reject convention or tradition and to try to introduce new values and institutions or to modify or change the social structure.

The relationship between the strains contained within a relatively well-integrated structure and social change can be seen clearly in the Chinese family. Despite its strength and stability, the traditional Chinese family created difficult problems for some of its members. A patriarchal structure in which the principal theme was filial piety and the central relationship that between father and son, the family was the dominant element in the social structure of premodern China. It provided the context for most activities, regulated and controlled much of the individual's behavior, defined his relationships with many of the people with whom he associated, and served as the model for other groups, with the notable exception of the Mandarin bureaucracy. This well-integrated structure, however, imposed severe constraints upon the young men and the women. Rigid subordination to parental authority led to some measure of resentment; as Marion Levy has observed, "from the point of view of the son, the source of his frustration was the father . . . who made demands upon him, refused his desires, punished him, and reviewed his daily conduct with a critical eye." [1] Arranged marriages limited the possibilities of choice for both men and women, often generating disaffection and discontent. For a woman, the problems were particularly acute, for marriage, often to an unknown and unfamiliar man, removed her from those with whom she had close personal ties and placed her in a strange household in which she was subservient to her husband's parents and particularly to her mother-in-law.

As long as Chinese society remained relatively stable and untouched by alien ideas, the pressures stemming from these difficult circumstances could be readily contained, albeit perhaps at the cost of some suffering by some people. (It was widely believed in China, for example, that the suicide rate was particularly high among women, especially younger married women. William J. Goode has argued, however, that the available evidence does not bear out this belief; the existence of this belief, however, may have served to temper the treatment of the new bride within the husband's household.[2]) When Western ideas of individual liberty found their way into China they found considerable support among those eager to escape from the onerous constraints and pressures inherent in arranged marriages and the authoritarian structure of the family. Changes in laws governing marriage and the family that began early in the twentieth century and were carried forward by the Communists after they took power have been willingly accepted by many people, particularly the young men and women who would suffer most from the traditional arrangements.[3]

To some degree change feeds upon itself, creating strains and tensions that stimulate or provoke further changes or opening up new perspectives that encourage innovation and a drift away from conventional practices and established relationships. World population growth, for example, has stimulated considerable pressure for a change in the position of the Roman Catholic Church with respect to birth control; the increase in the proportion of older people in the United States, coupled with changes in family structure, has created problems that have led to the emergence of new ways of supporting and looking after the elderly. Urban growth, characteristically unplanned and the result of a combination of circumstances, tends, as we noted in Chapter 11, to weaken the hold of tradition and to encourage greater tolerance and support for both deviant behavior and innovation.

Cultural lag and rates of change

The tempo at which these various changes take place is obviously difficult to measure in any precise fashion. To be sure, population growth, shifts in the occupational distribution, and the number of people securing formal education can be described in statistical terms that lend themselves to relatively accurate measurement, although even the statistical measures for these changes are not strictly commensurable. Such phenomena as decreasing solidarity, increasing *anomie*, the redefinition of social roles, and the transformation of social relationships are much less amenable to precise reckoning. Despite these methodological difficulties, however, there can be no escaping the fact that changes in culture and social structure occur at varying rates of speed—some with glacial slowness, others at a moderate tempo, and still others with extraordinary rapidity. Negroes' resistance to their lowly status in American society grew quite slowly during the early decades of the twentieth century but has increased at a dramatic rate during the 1950s and 1960s. The centers of many American cities have deteriorated steadily, while the institutions of local government have remained relatively unchanged. Changes in the structure of some governments have taken place slowly and gradually, while others have experienced revolutionary transformations.

The fact of different rates of change in various sectors of culture and society has led to a theory that assigns casual priority to those features that seem to change most readily and most rapidly. Thus, in his theory of "cultural lag," first presented in the 1920s, William F. Ogburn distinguished between material and nonmaterial culture, the former consisting of technology and other artifacts, the latter of "customs, beliefs, philosophies, laws, governments." [4] The material culture, he argued, changes more rapidly than the nonmaterial, which therefore "lags" behind. As the various elements of culture are closely related to one another, this lag inevitably produces maladjustments that are eventually eliminated by rearrangements in customs or institutions. As an illustration, Ogburn cites the introduction of new machinery in industry, which caused a great many accidents and imposed serious hardships upon the victims. No arrangements existed to cope with these difficulties, and only after a long period of time did such institutions as workmen's-compensation laws appear to deal with the problems created by industrial accidents.

There are many deficiencies in this theory—the vagueness of the distinction between material and nonmaterial culture, the fact that the two often reciprocally influence each other, the difficulty in specifying the rates at which different changes are taking place, the inability to identify the conditions under which the readjustments that will eliminate the lag occur. Moreover, the strains created by differing rates of change are not automatically resolved; they are dealt with by groups or individuals who become aware of the problem and try to do something about it, often against the resistance of others who remain committed to traditional values and institutions. "Lags" may therefore persist for a very long time, or they may be resolved quickly and expeditiously.

Yet the concept of culture lag does serve to focus attention upon the greater readiness to tolerate innovation or change in some areas of social life than in others—and upon the problems created by

the differences in the speed with which some features of culture and social structure are transformed. By and large, it appears, there does tend to be a greater willingness to accept technological progress, whereas values and institutions characteristically change much more slowly. As Robert and Helen Lynd observed in their classic study of Middletown:

A new tool or material device, the specific efficacy of which can be tested decisively and impersonally, is fairly certain to be fitted somehow into Middletown's accepted scheme of things, while opposed non-material factors, such as tradition and sentiment, slowly open up to make room for it. [5]

In some settings, however, cultural expectations may constitute the more rapidly changing social facts. In many of the underdeveloped nations, for example, exposure to various aspects of Western culture has led to a rising level of expectations and demand, which the available technology can not satisfy, thus creating an increasing pressure for rapid industrialization. In the United States the technology of homebuilding has hardly kept pace with the growing need and demand for better housing for the low-income population.

Social change, which, it should be remembered, often represents an attempted solution to an old problem, may not only generate strains and tensions because it disrupts established relationships among the various elements of the culture and social structure but may also stimulate resistance to further changes. Thus, the Lynds have suggested:

So great is the individual human being's need for security that it may be that most people are incapable of tolerating change and uncertainty in all sectors of life at once; and if their culture exposes them to stress and uncertainty at many points, they may not only tolerate but welcome the security of extreme fixity and changelessness elsewhere in their lives.[6]

This hypothesis, of course, remains to be tested, and it is probable that individuals in fact vary in their ability to sustain flux and change and in their need for stability and continuity. From the point of view of culture and the social structure, change and stability are in all likelihood related to each other in complex fashion. Stanley Rothman has argued, for example, that England was able to modernize its economy and political institutions more rapidly and successfully than were many other nations precisely because of the presence of widely shared social and political traditions.[7] Conversely, it seems likely that the existence of institutions for initiating changes in response to new circumstances, such as a democratic political system, reinforces consensus and social stability.

Social movements

Although many changes in values, institutions, and social structure come about gradually and without any conscious or deliberate effort—population growth, improving standards of living, new patterns of leisure, rising levels of education, automation, bureaucratization, the weakening of traditional values or the emergence of new ones—they may also be the result of organized social movements. Such collective efforts to initiate change take many forms and pursue a wide variety of goals. They range from feminism and temperance to large-scale political movements like fascism and communism. They include the labor movement, the civil-rights movement, the "radical right," the Mau Mau in Kenya, the "cargo cults" found in the South Pacific, Zionism, and such religious movements as Moral Rearmament, Jehovah's Witnesses, and the Christadelphians.

So varied are these movements in their goals, organization, and influence, that some distinctions can be made among them. Ralph Turner and Lewis Killian, for example, distinguish among the power-oriented, the value-oriented, and the participation-oriented. The first is concerned chiefly with gaining control or power in society, the second with changing society in order to realize certain values, and the third is primarily oriented toward the satisfactions to be derived simply from participation in the collective effort.[8] Neal Smelser finds only two types, the norm-oriented and the value-oriented,[9] whereas Herbert Blumer identifies general and specific movements (either reformist or revolutionary)—distinguished from one another by the clarity of their goals, the degree of organization, and the presence or absence of effective leadership—as well as a third type, expressive movements, whose chief concern lies in the venting of feeling and the gratifications derived from participation in the movement.[10]

Such classifications are of some value in identifying the varying concerns of social movements and in focusing attention upon differences in organization and structure, but they also possess serious limitations. Specific movements characteristically embody more than one type of orientation; the pursuit of power is often linked with efforts to effect specific changes in institutions and values, while participation in any movement, whatever its aim, may be rewarding for its members. Moreover, social movements often change their character and their aims, modifying their organization and shifting their orientation in response to new circumstances. The Townsend movement of the 1930s, for example, which was dedicated to a specific program to aid the elderly, lost its crusading vigor after passage of the Social Security Act in 1935 and became simply a focus of social activity for its members. As Robert Michels has shown, the trade unions and the Social Democratic Party of pre-World War I Germany became more preoccupied with maintenance of their organization and the power of their leaders as they achieved some measure of stability and recognition.[11]

Some studies of social movements have bypassed the problems of an inclusive typology and have focused upon one variety, such as millenarian movements, whose leaders proclaim the imminence of redemption or of a worldly paradise. These include the messianic movements that frequently sprang up among American Indian tribes during the last decades of the nineteenth century; the "cargo cults" of the South Pacific, which anticipate the momentary return of a savior in some modern means of transportation loaded with desired goods; and such Christian groups as the Christadelphians, Seventh Day Adventists, and Jehovah's Witnesses, which look forward to the imminent "second coming" of Christ or believe that the Judgment Day will soon be at hand.[12]

Social movements characteristically emerge from situations of strain or disorganization. When large groups of people find their traditional routines disrupted, their status challenged, or their values and interests threatened, they may come together in a collective effort to resolve their difficulties and set things aright. Feminism in England, for example, was a response to problems that had grown out of changes in the role and status of women.

From being a partner, although certainly never an equal partner with her husband, when the family was organized as a production unit, she had rapidly become dependent in the course of the late eighteenth and of the nineteenth centuries upon some other person's earning capacity for the income she spent as the family representative. What the organized feminist movement was connected with in consequence was the plight of . . . women who were exploited as a result of this dependency.[13]

Feminism drew far more support from middle-class women than from those in the working class, for the latter were far too preoccupied with their economic problems to be seriously concerned with the special difficulties of their sex.

The "radical right" in the United States, evident in the McCarthy period of the 1950s and resurgent in the 1960s, Daniel Bell has argued, drew upon people whose security, status, and power had been challenged by significant trends in American society. Increasingly, property ownership has been supplanted as a source of power by technical skill and political position. Much of the support for the radical right therefore comes from members of the old middle class—"the independent physician, farm owner, small-town lawyer, real-estate promoter, home builder, automobile dealer, gasoline-station owner, small businessman, and the like." Other recruits and support come from "older elites" in business and the military who feel threatened by new techniques and new forms of control.

Within a business enterprise, the newer techniques of operations research and linear programming almost amount to the "automation" of middle management, and its displacement by mathematicians and engineers, working either within the firm or as consultants. In the economy, the businessman finds himself subject to price, wage, and investment criteria laid down by the economists in government. In the polity, the old military elites find themselves challenged in the determination of policy by scientists, who have the technical knowledge on nuclear capability, missile development, and the like, or by the "military intellectuals" whose conceptions of weapons systems and political warfare seek to guide military allocations.[14]

Not all members of these groups, of course, have succumbed to the oversimplified view that sees change as a result of an alien conspiracy to subvert traditional values and institutions, although the factors that distinguish the members of these groups who also become members of the John Birch Society and similar organizations from those who do not have yet to be clearly identified.

In order for the frustrations and threats generated by strains in the social order to lead men to join or participate in a social movement, however, they must be galvanized by an ideology and drawn into some kind of organization. There is no inevitable connection, therefore, between the existence of serious problems for groups of people and the emergence of a movement that promises to resolve their difficulties by changes in the social order. If people feel that they can cope with their problems within the existing institutional framework or by its gradual modification, there is no reason for them to engage in a collective effort to initiate change. Alternatively, efforts to seek improvement may be inhibited by a fatalistic acceptance of things as they are or by the conviction that suffering and frustration are divinely ordained and that the forces shaping one's fate are beyond any control or correction.

Ideology and social movements

In itself an ideology cannot create a social movement, but it serves crucial functions in stimulating and sustaining one.

Social disorganization and strains in the social structure often leave people uncertain and disoriented, without an adequate or acceptable conception of the events going on around them. They are therefore likely to be receptive to an ideology that provides a meaningful version of what is happening—one that links individual and group troubles to institutions, value systems, and social structures. The temperance movement, for example, blamed Demon Rum for a variety of social ills. Marxism offers a comprehensive explanation of the major trends in modern society that emphasizes the importance of economic interests and class differences, whereas the John Birch Society has attributed both the successes of Communist movements in other parts of the world and many of the social and political changes that have taken place in the United States to a conspiracy in which Chief Justice Earl Warren, President Eisenhower, and John Foster Dulles, among others, have played important roles.

Such explanations vary, of course, in the accuracy with which they describe and explain reality. Some are totally wide of the mark, resting upon premises that are demonstrably false. Various anti-Semitic movements, for example, placed great weight upon the completely spurious Protocols of Zion, a document presumably containing evidence of a world-wide Jewish plot to dominate the world. The assertion by Robert Welch, head of the John Birch Society, that President Eisenhower was "a dedicated, conscious agent of the Communist conspiracy" strains the imagination. Other ideologies, however, are far more plausible. Certainly feminism, the civil-rights movement, Planned Parenthood, and the progressive-education movement rest upon reasonable, if on occasion debatable, interpretations of the problems with which they seek to deal. And Marxism has provided not only the basis for major social and political movements but also a theory of society and history that, despite its limitations, has made a major contribution to the development of the social sciences.

In the modern world, the social sciences themselves obviously are relevant to the ideologies upon which various social movements rest, since many of the assertions about society and its workings are open to systematic examination and testing. One of the functions of social science has been to assess the diverse theories that account for events and institutions, in order to provide a more accurate guide to programs and policies. By supporting or refuting particular assertions and interpretations it may therefore encourage or inhibit particular social movements.

The ideas contained in religious movements obviously differ from those in secular ones, although they may perform some of the same functions. Religious ideas that offer transcendental interpretations of man's fate define what is valuable and worthwhile in life and locate events and actions within a moral framework. In doing so they may provide an escape from the confusions caused by the uncertainties and complexities of the world in which people live. Secular ideas may similarly clarify the uncertainties of life, albeit with a very different focus and direction. Indeed, in some historical contexts, religious and secular movements have offered alternative interpretations—and alternative solutions—to the same social problems. On the basis of contemporary public opinion data Rodney Stark has argued that in England religious involvement and participation in radical movements have tended to be mutually exclusive responses to the deprivations of working-class life,[15] although historical data suggest that the relationship between the labor movement and religious sects is more complex and depends upon the specific sociological and historical circumstances.[16]

In addition to their interpretations of man and society, ideologies also offer a program to deal with the problems for which men are seeking solutions. Marxist ideology prescribed a revolution and the dictatorship of the proletariat, leading to socialism and then communism. The John Birch Society has sought to have Justice Warren impeached and the headquarters of the United Nations removed from the United States. Moral Rearmament has seen in individual salvation and the love of each person for the other the solution to such problems as labor-management strife and international tensions.

The specific programs and long-term goals of social movements are closely linked with the varied interpretations of reality, which provide rationales for them. Thus Marxism asserts the need for a revolution because of the link between economic and political power and the presumed inevitably of class conflict and economic collapse within capitalism. Movements committed to violence, like those of the Mau Mau in Kenya, the Russian nihilists of the late nineteenth century, and the post-Civil War Ku Klux Klan (as well as some of its contemporary descendants), justified their actions on the grounds that no other methods could work because of the nature of society.

For an ideology that challenges accepted ideas and existing social arrangements to take root it must not only fall upon soil made fertile by discontent and frustration, but it must also be related in some fashion to pre-existing values and beliefs. Just any ideology, that is, will not do; those people who are ready or eager for change are often exposed to alternative programs and platforms, and they are likely to accept one that is in some sense congenial to them. Nazism, for example, drew upon a strong current of anti-Semitism in Germany and an intense nationalism in its radical attack upon established political institutions. It also sought initially to maintain a pretense of legality in justification of the measures by which it dismembered the Weimar Republic. Feminism, challenging institutions that reduced women to an inferior dependent status, could call upon widely accepted democratic and egalitarian values, just as the civil-rights movement in the United States has called for changes in patterns of race relations on the basis of the "official" American values. Communism, which in its intellectual origins is linked to such values as liberty, equality, and fraternity, as well as to rationality, has frequently tied itself very closely in Asia and Africa with anticolonial nationalisms, as well as with the desire for social progress. In ideology, then, as in other aspects of culture and social structure, continuity and change are closely linked and in various ways dependent upon each other.

Ideologies, however, are often unclear or even contradictory in their content. They are subject to debate and disagreement as they emerge out of the responses to the situations faced by groups and individuals. In the history of the labor movement, for example, there have been staunch supporters of "business unionism" who saw their goals simply as improvements in hours, wages, and working conditions, whereas others have argued that political action and fundamental institutional changes were necessary to secure significant gains for the workers. Marxist theory has a long and complex history. In response to the conditions pres-

ent in Czarist Russia, Lenin made significant additions to Marx's views, and his teaching differed substantially from that of such leading German Marxists as Eduard Bernstein and Karl Kautsky. Although often seemingly unrelated to action, ideological debates and their outcomes can have important consequences, for they define how people look at the world and what they think is necessary and possible.

Organization and leadership

Together with its ideology a social movement necessarily develops some kind of internal organization. It may consist merely of a loosely knit array of groups and like-minded individuals pursuing a common goal like the improvement of education, prison reform, or equal rights for women. Although there may be some formally organized associations within such a movement, it lacks any centralized direction or leadership (though it may have its recognized spokesmen), and its efforts are likely to be varied and uncoordinated. At the other extreme are both elaborately organized mass movements under central direction and tightly organized bands of revolutionaries dedicated to the overthrow of the social order and the seizure of power.

Organization, of course, does not emerge spontaneously but takes shape gradually as a social movement gathers adherents and develops programs and strategies. The nature of the organization may be influenced by ideology, as in the case of democratic movements that emphasize limits upon power or, alternatively, as in movements that emphasize the virtues of discipline and authority.

Segments of the "New Left" in the United States in the mid-1960s, for example, have had little formal structure because of their explicit rejection of authority and bureaucracy. Nazi ideology, on the other hand, contained a *Führerprinzip*, which expressly justified the authority of Adolf Hitler as the "leader." Communist theory emphasizes the virtues of *democratic centralism*, which requires complete obedience to the leaders of the Party once policy is decided upon.

Without some kind of leadership, a social movement is unlikely to come into being, no matter how promising or propitious the circumstances. Some movements are generated by charismatic leaders whose personal qualities inspire confidence and belief in the causes they advocate. Because such leaders acquire personal followers who look upon them as in some sense out of the ordinary, possessed of special qualities of insight or wisdom, touched with some semblance of greatness or even divinity, they are able to focus discontent, articulate values, and define goals, often in opposition to existing institutions. To some degree, the movement is but "the lengthened shadow" of the man who sets his imprint upon its ideology, organization, and activities. Adolf Hitler and Mahatma Gandhi offer conspicuous examples, but there are many others—Joseph Smith of the Mormons; Huey Long, who led a "Share-the-Wealth" movement in the 1930s until he was assassinated; and, at least for several years, Martin Luther King.

In contrast with the charismatic leader is the organizer or administrator whose authority and influence rest upon his ability to marshal resources, bring groups and individuals together into a collective effort, plan strategies, and direct operations. Such individuals are often the driving force behind movements for prison reform, educational changes, Planned Parenthood, or other limited objectives—agitating, making speeches, writing, organizing action groups, petitioning public figures and political leaders. But even in a movement led by a charismatic leader the administrator plays an important role in building an effective organization and holding it together.

With the passing of the charismatic leader, the movement is likely to disintegrate unless his successors can effectively direct the organization that has been created. History is full of social movements in which the original leader was followed by an effective organizer who sustained the movement and successfully carried it forward—St. Paul after Jesus, Brigham Young after Joseph Smith, Joseph Stalin after Lenin. In time, as leadership is institutionalized as part of an organization's structure, it acquires its own charisma. Whoever holds office therefore, is set apart quite independently of his personal qualities by virtue of his role—as in the case of king or pope or head of state. This routinization of charisma, to use Weber's phrase, stabilizes the structure and sustains the authority of the leader.[17]

Although the ostensible purpose of organization is to pursue specific goals, in fact it serves other functions as well. As we have already noted, participation in the movement may in itself satisfy important needs, particularly among those whose relations with others have been unsatisfactory or nonexistent. Sociability, acceptance by others, and a sense of belonging are often to be found in the activities of the group. For some the movement offers recognition and even potential access to influence or power.

Those who come to occupy official positions within a movement may even develop a vested interest in the organization itself in addition to their concern for the professed goals toward which its efforts are directed.

The development of an elaborate organization within a social movement is often the prelude to its acceptance within the established order. Some movements, to be sure, fail to achieve their goals and gradually disappear, as did the Garvey movement of the 1920s, which built up an organization devoted to mass migration of Negroes to Africa. Revolutionary movements may continue to struggle until they gain power or are crushed, whereas religious or millenarian movements may carry on largely because of the direct satisfactions—social and psychological—they provide for their members. But those movements that make some progress are likely to be institutionalized; they come to be recognized as "having some continuing function to perform in the larger society . . . as a desirable or unavoidable adjunct to the existing institutional arrangements." [18]

Indeed, the goal of many movements is precisely such recognition. The Planned Parenthood movement, for example, helped to break down restraints against the dissemination of contraceptive information and materials and managed to establish clinics to which women could come for advice and assistance. Labor unions sought to gain acceptance as the collective representatives of the workers in order to achieve higher wages, better working conditions, and the ability to protect workers from arbitrary management; now, of course, they are an accepted feature of the industrial scene, their status supported by law, their leaders recognized, and their power, though often exaggerated by their critics, substantial.

Social change and modern society

Social movements are often related to large-scale historical transformations out of which they emerge and to which they may contribute. The labor movement in Europe and America was thus one response to industrialization and capitalism (socialism and communism, sometimes linked with the labor movement, were other responses) and helped to change some of its institutions. In Asia and Africa nationalist movements were provoked by European colonial domination, which has now been overthrown almost everywhere.

The effort to identify and explain historical trends has long preoccupied sociologists, as well as historians and other social scientists. Indeed the founders of sociology were centrally concerned with the trend and direction of human history; Auguste Comte and Herbert Spencer, for example, saw history as an evolutionary process in which each society moved steadily from one stage to another toward a more complex, differentiated, and ultimately more rational condition. Although their optimistic unilinear theories have been sharply criticized and largely discredited, the idea of evolution, as we noted in Chapter 5, is once more a focus of sociological interest, although now in a much more systematic and sophisticated form.

In sharp contrast to the evolutionary perspective are the interpretations of history offered by Oswald Spengler, Arnold Toynbee, and Pitirim Sorokin. Spengler saw each civilization as an organism that was born, grew to maturity, and died; Western society, he asserted, was already in a condition of decay and approaching its demise. For Toynbee, too, the historical unit is the civilization, which has a beginning and an end. Its career is to be seen as a series of responses to challenges posed first by its environment and then by both internal and external enemies. Whether it survives or not depends upon how it deals with the successive challenges it must face. Sorokin sees history as endlessly fluctuating between two types of culture, the *ideational* and the *sensate*. The former is directed toward the mind or spirit and emphasizes morality and religion, whereas the latter appeals to the senses, seeks chiefly to satisfy physical needs, and is scientifically oriented. Modern civilization, Sorokin asserts, is in an "overripe" sensate condition.[19]

Rich in their documentation and impressive in their scope, these interpretations offer stimulating commentaries on human history. But they are largely speculative and of only limited value in seeking to account for specific historical changes or to identify the significant trends in modern society.

Whatever warrant there may once have been for considering independently the history of any civilization or the evolution of any society, perhaps the most significant fact about the modern world is the increasing unity of mankind. As Wilbert Moore points out:

The rapid incorporation of virtually every part of the world into the international political and economic "community" marks the end, or the beginning of the end, for isolated and exotic tribal communities and also for complex and archaic civilizations. In this sense, and only in this sense, the unification of the world is already nearly complete.[20]

The end of isolation in the far corners of the world has come about as a result of many things—war and political conquest, commercial penetration, religious proselytizing, the expansion of travel, and the impact of mass communication. By and large the initiatives have come from Europe and the United States, unwelcome when they meant political domination or economic exploitation or both, often eagerly accepted when they brought new goods, more productive technology, and ideas that freed people from ancient restraints and offered new values and ideals. Indeed, many of the ideologies of the nationalists who challenged European domination were derived to a substantial degree from European sources.

The dissolution of colonial empires and the emergence of new nations after World War II gave impetus to the modernization of traditional societies, already begun in many areas under European auspices. The central focus of modernization has characteristically been industrialization and economic growth, with increased production and higher per capita income, but it has also entailed the growth of cities, secularization and the decline of tradition, the development of more differentiated institutions and social organization, increased mobility, the expansion of education, and the diffusion of new knowledge and new ways of thinking that encourage the continuing transformation of economy, state, and society.

Unlike the first nations to industrialize, which had to create a new technology from crude beginnings, countries now seeking to modernize their economies can acquire industrial technology ready-made from more advanced nations—if they possess the necessary capital or credit. To be sure, there may be problems of adapting that technology to local conditions, but at least the time and effort devoted to research and experimentation can be abbreviated or avoided.

Accumulation of the capital to pay for new technology and for the increasing commitment of manpower and physical resources to industrial expansion is there-

Marc & Evelyne Bernheim from Rapho Guillumette Pictures

The pressure for modernization in the undeveloped part of the world derives in part from "the revolution of rising expectations" as people come to want the products of modern technology. Here native women in the Ivory Coast shop in a supermarket full of imports from Europe and, probably, the United States.

fore the first economic task. Whatever the economic institutions and instruments that may be used—banks, loans, tax policy, government subsidies—it seems clear that "primitive accumulation," to use Marx's phrase, depends upon both the economic level of the society and a complex set of cultural and social conditions. Unless there is an actual surplus of production over what is needed to satisfy immediate needs, there can be little to

invest in industry. The "industrial revolution," therefore, characteristically requires an antecedent "agricultural revolution" such as occurred in England in the eighteenth century or in Japan in the late nineteenth and early twentieth centuries—or the advantage of a commercial crop like tobacco or coffee, which can bring in foreign capital, or some special natural resource like rich oil deposits.

An economic surplus is defined, however, not purely in economic terms, but also by the relationship between output and culturally based standards of living. Unless there are values that encourage saving and investment—for example, the desire for gain or the institutionalized asceticism of early Protestantism—increased output may merely lead to more comfortable or sumptuous living by some people or to hoarding of wealth. As income and property are rarely equally distributed, the decisions as to savings and investment rest in the hands of those who are able to accumulate more than they require to satisfy their needs and wants. Peasants and workers can contribute little directly, although their low incomes may allow for the accumulation of wealth by others who, of course, may not be particularly interested in economic expansion. A landed aristocracy in a traditional society, for example, is less likely to be oriented toward opportunities in business and industry than is an urban middle class.

Traditional values and institutions may not only inhibit capital accumulation but may also limit the mobility of labor and stand in the way of industrial efficiency. Thus kinship or community ties may confine labor to one locale when it is needed elsewhere or lead to the choice of men for important posts on the basis of personal relationships rather than of their ability to do the job. An educated class oriented to government service and a leisured style of life has little to contribute to modernization, and a government dominated by a conservative aristocracy may stand in the way of economic measures designed to increase productivity or stimulate investment in industry. A pervasive traditionalism may limit horizons and prevent the technological, institutional, and structural changes required for sustained economic growth.

It is hardly surprising, therefore, that in some developing nations modernization and economic progress are often linked with revolutionary programs and efforts to secure major institutional changes. It may appear necessary to dislodge a landed aristocracy, an established church, or an entrenched bureaucracy from power; to reorganize the educational system—or build one—and to persuade or coerce a traditionalistic peasantry to improve their agricultural methods or even to forsake the land for the factory. Yet it should also be noted

that in some cases modernization has come from above, as in Germany and Japan, directed or imposed by the ruling groups in order to maintain their power, to improve their international standing, or simply to provide greater wealth and income for themselves. As S. N. Eisenstadt has pointed out, however:

In some cases, the encounter between the preexisting institutions, the modernizing tendencies of the various groups and strata, and the policies of the elites may give rise to relatively stagnant structures or to various blockages and eruptions.[21]

In Indonesia, Pakistan, and Burma, for example, the initial progress was disrupted, even set back here and there, by political conflict, absence of adequate leadership, bureaucratic corruption and inefficiency, and absence of institutions

Modernization requires both new technology and new skills. A young girl in Maroua, North Cameroun, does homework in her father's compound while her brothers and sisters watch.

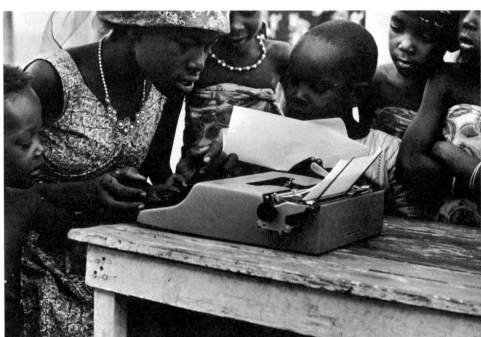

Marc & Evelyne Bernheim from Rapho Guillumette Pictures

for reconciling differences and coping with emerging problems.[22]

The problems of modernization, however, can no longer be seen in isolation from the larger economic, political, military, and ideological contexts.[23] In taking technology and the knowledge and skills that go with it from advanced nations, the developing countries are also exposed to new values and ideas and opened to various types of political and economic pressures. The aid given to the developing countries often has far-reaching consequences for the culture and social structure of the recipient. The Alliance for Progress in Latin America, for example, whatever its results have been, is explicitly designed to support reformist, modernizing governments. On the other hand, American military aid to Latin American nations has to a substantial degree strengthened military leaders who, with few exceptions, have been more concerned with their own power and the maintenance of traditional institutions and social structures than with modernization and economic growth.[24] The political competition among the major powers has not only drawn many new states into the vortex of international politics but has also, on occasion, subjected them to outside interference that has produced political conflict and instability and massive disruptions of social life.

Despite the fact that modernization may be achieved in various ways—through a free market system or with centralized planning, democratically or under authoritarian control, by revolutionary overthrow of the traditional order or under the direction of an established ruling class—it tends to lead to important social and cultural similarities. Industrialization, a central fact in modernization, rests upon a common technological base, leads to an extensive division of labor, requires managers and technicians with advanced education and training, and encourages similar forms of organization. Modernization brings with it the growth of cities, smaller families, greater participation in formal structures in place of traditional groups, increased exposure to the mass media, and, as productivity and per capita income rise, higher living standards and more leisure.

The full implications of these likenesses have yet to be explored.[25] Yet it seems clear that to some degree all advanced nations face similar problems—metropolitan concentration and urban sprawl, the relationship between work and leisure and the impact of the mass media, the dilemmas of bureaucracy, and the need for integration and control as against the pressure for autonomy and decentralization. On a social-psychological level, Alex Inkeles has suggested that industrial society leads to the emergence of "modern man," one who, in comparison with his predecessors in traditional societies, is more open to change, more tolerant of differences of opinion, and more capable of planning his actions and dominating his environment. In addition, he has wider interests, more faith in science and technology, and "more awareness of the dignity of others and more disposition to show respect for them." [26]

To what extent modernization and industrialization portend the convergence of such diverse societies as the United States, Great Britain, the Soviet Union, and eventually, perhaps, China, India, and Indonesia upon a common pattern remains an open and much debated question. Present differences, even among the advanced nations, obviously remain substantial, reflecting both the preindustrial culture and social structure and the processes by which industrialization and its concomitant social changes came about. History, of course, will necessarily provide the answer, but to pursue the question can lead, not only to an understanding of some of the important forces at work in the modern world, but also to a fuller understanding of our own society, its uniqueness and its resemblance to others, its strengths and its weaknesses.

Notes

[1] Marion J. Levy, Jr., *The Family Revolution in Modern China* (Cambridge, Mass.: Harvard University Press, 1949), p. 174.

[2] William J. Goode, *World Revolution and Family Patterns* (New York: Free Press, 1963), pp. 309–12.

[3] See Levy, *op. cit.*; Goode, *op. cit.*, Ch. 6; and C. K. Yang, *The Chinese Family in the Communist Revolution* (Cambridge, Mass.: M.I.T. Press, 1959).

[4] William F. Ogburn, *Social Change* (New York: Huebsch, 1923), pp. 200–37.

[5] Robert S. Lynd and Helen M. Lynd. *Middletown* (New York: Harcourt, 1929), p. 499.

[6] Robert S. Lynd and Helen M. Lynd, *Middletown in Transition* (New York: Harcourt, 1937), p. 315.

[7] Stanley Rothman, "Modernity and Tradition in Britain," *Social Research*, XXVIII (Autumn, 1961), 297–320.

[8] Ralph H. Turner and Lewis M. Killian, *Collective Behavior* (Englewood Cliffs: Prentice-Hall, 1957), Part IV.

[9] Neal J. Smelser, *Theory of Collective Behavior* (New York: Free Press, 1962), Chs. 9, 10.

[10] Herbert Blumer, "Collective Behavior," in Alfred M. Lee (ed.), *New Outline of the Principles of Sociology* (New York: Barnes & Noble, 1946), pp. 199–220.

[11] Robert Michels, *Political Parties*, trans. by Eden Paul and Cedar Paul (New York: Free Press, 1949).

[12] Bernard Barber, "Acculturation and Messianic Movements," *American Sociological Review*, VI (October, 1941), 663–9; Peter Worsley, *The Trumpet Shall Sound* (London: Macgibbon & Kee,

1947); Brian Wilson, *Sects and Society* (London: Heinemann, 1961); and Herbert Stroup, *The Jehovah's Witnesses* (New York: Columbia University Press, 1945). For a useful evaluation and analysis of studies of millenarian movements, see Yonina Talmon, "Pursuit of the Millenium: The Relation Between Religious and Social Change," *European Journal of Sociology*, III (1962), 25–48.

[13] J. A. Banks and Olive Banks, "Feminism and Social Change—A Case Study of a Social Movement," in George K. Zollschan and Walter Hirsch (eds.), *Explorations in Social Change* (Boston: Houghton Mifflin, 1964), p. 554.

[14] Daniel Bell, "The Dispossessed," in Daniel Bell (ed.), *The Radical Right* (Garden City: Doubleday Anchor Books, 1964), p. 22.

[15] Rodney Stark, "Class, Radicalism, and Religious Involvement," *American Sociological Review*, XXIX (October, 1964), 698–706.

[16] E. J. Hobsbawm, *Primitive Rebels* (New York: Norton, 1965), Ch. 8.

[17] For Max Weber's discussion of charisma and its routinization, see his *The Theory of Social and Economic Organization*, trans. and ed. by A. M. Henderson and Talcott Parsons (New York: Oxford, 1947), pp. 358–73.

[18] Turner and Killian, *op. cit.*, p. 481.

[19] See Oswald Spengler, *The Decline of the West*, 2 vols., trans. by Charles F. Atkinson (New York: Knopf, 1939); Arnold Toynbee, *The Study of History*, 10 vols. (London: Royal Institute of International Affairs, 1934, 1939, 1954), abridged by D. C. Somervell, 2 vols. (New York: Oxford, 1947, 1957); and

Pitirim A. Sorokin, *Social and Cultural Dynamics*, 4 vols. (New York: American Book, 1937–1941).

[20] Wilbert E. Moore, *Social Change* (Englewood Cliffs: Prentice-Hall, 1963), p. 89.

[21] S. N. Eisenstadt, "Modernization: Growth and Diversity" (Bloomington: Indiana University Department of Government, Seminar on Political and Administrative Development, 1963), p. 19.

[22] See S. N. Eisenstadt, "Breakdowns of Modernization," *Economic Development and Cultural Change*, XII (July, 1964), 345–67.

[23] See Irving Louis Horowitz, *Three Worlds of Development* (New York: Oxford, 1966)

[24] See Edwin Lieuwen, *Arms and Politics in Latin America* (rev. ed.; New York: Praeger, 1961).

[25] For an interesting discussion of this problem, see Wilbert Moore and Arnold S. Feldman, "Industrialization and Alienation: Convergence and Differentiation," *Transactions of the Fifth World Congress of Sociology*, II (Louvain: International Sociological Association, 1962), 151–69.

[26] Alex Inkeles, "The Modernization of Man," in Myron Wiener (ed.), *Modernization* (New York: Basic Books, 1966), pp. 138–50. These generalizations are derived from an elaborate comparative study of six developing nations directed by Professor Inkeles, which has yet to be published.

Suggestions for further reading

ADAMS, RICHARD N., *et al. Social Change in Latin America Today*. New York: Vintage, 1961.
Essays on social change in Latin America, with particular attention to Peru, Bolivia, Brazil, Guatemala, and Mexico.

BARRINGER, HERBERT R., GEORGE I. BLANKSTEN, and RAYMOND W. MACK (eds.). *Social Change in Developing Areas*. Boston: Schenkman, 1965.
Evolutionary perspectives on modernization and economic development.

BENDIX, REINHARD. *Work and Authority in Industry*. New York: Wiley, 1956.
A historical and comparative study of the ideologies that justify and sustain the authority of management in industry.

COHN, NORMAN. *The Pursuit of the Millennium*. London: Mercury, 1957.
An account of millenarian movements in Medieval and Reformation Europe that tries to get at the sources of totalitarianism.

ETZIONI, AMITAI, and EVA ETZIONI (eds.). *Social Change*. New York: Basic Books, 1964.
Essays on theories, sources, patterns, and levels of change and on modernization.

GUSFIELD, JOSEPH R. *Symbolic Crusade*. Urbana: University of Illinois Press, 1963.
A careful study of the origins and history of the American temperance movement.

HOROWITZ, IRVING LOUIS. *Three Worlds of Development*. New York: Oxford, 1966.
An analysis of modernization in the context of world politics and the relations among the United States and its allies, the Soviet Union and the Communist world, and the nonaligned nations.

LERNER, DANIEL. *The Passing of Traditional Society*. New York: Free Press, 1958.
A study of modernization in the Middle East focused largely on the role of the mass media.

LIPSET, SEYMOUR MARTIN. *The First New Nation*. New York: Basic Books, 1963.
A study of the conditions that made possible the development of a democratic society in the United States.

MOORE, BARRINGTON, JR. *Social Origins of Dictatorship and Democracy*. Boston: Beacon, 1966.

A study of the role of aristocracies and peasants in industrialization and in the development of democratic and authoritarian states in Europe and Asia.

MOORE, WILBERT E. *Social Change*. Englewood Cliffs: Prentice-Hall, 1963.
An essay on the nature and sources of social change.

MURPHY, RAYMOND J., and HOWARD ELINSON. *Problems and Prospects of the Negro Movement*. Belmont: Wadsworth, 1966.
A collection of readings on the background, problems, prospects, and strategies of the movements seeking to improve the Negroes' position in American society.

SRINIVAS, M. N. *Social Change in Modern India*. Berkeley: University of California Press, 1966.
A noted Indian social anthropologist assesses social change in India, focusing upon both Sanskritization (the ex-

tension of Hindu values), and Westernization.

TURNER, RALPH H., and LEWIS M. KILLIAN. *Collective Behavior*. Englewood Cliffs: Prentice-Hall, 1957. Part IV.
A thorough analysis of the nature, sources, and functions of social movements.

WIENER, MYRON (ed.). *Modernization*. New York: Basic Books, 1966.
A collection of papers on the social, political, and economic aspects of modernization.

WORSLEY, PETER. *The Trumpet Shall Sound*. London: Macgibbon & Kee, 1957.
A study of the "cargo cults" of the South Pacific.

ZOLLSCHAN, GEORGE K., and WALTER HIRSCH (eds.). *Explorations in Social Change*. Boston: Houghton Mifflin, 1964.
A wide-ranging collection of essays.

PART SIX

Conclusion

21
The uses of sociology

Sociological knowledge and skills have now come to be widely utilized as a source of objective information, as a sometimes helpful guide to action, and as an important approach to the understanding of human conduct. In large part, the growing attention to the work of sociologists reflects the continuing development of the discipline itself—on the one hand, the accumulation of a body of reliable data concerning social behavior and on the other, steady progress in the clarification of concepts, the development of research techniques, and the formulation of both general theory and special theories concerning such diverse matters as stratification, bureaucracy, and deviant behavior. Sociology is still far from its avowed, and perhaps utopian, goal: a fully established social science. But its past achievements and current activities—in research and theory as well as practical application—strongly suggest that it will continue to move forward, acquiring greater clarity and rigor and becoming an increasingly useful instrument of both understanding and practice.

Fundamental to the scientific study of society has always been the hope and belief that it could contribute to the understanding and solution of social problems and to a better and more reasonable world. Auguste Comte, who coined the word *sociology*, put forth lengthy proposals for improving society, and Marx's "scientific" socialism was intended to pave the way for a classless society free of human exploitation. Herbert Spencer and Émile Durkheim were deeply concerned with moral and political questions, on which they thought their scientific inquiries would shed light. The work of many of the pioneers of American sociology—for example, Lester F. Ward, Charles H. Cooley, and Edward A. Ross—rested upon a belief in the possibility of progress and in the desirability of social reform based upon objective, rational sociological analysis.

Beginning in the years following World War I, many (although by no means all) American sociologists eager to demonstrate their objectivity and freedom from value judgments rejected an open commitment to progress or reform. Although the trend since the 1920s has not been a steady one, many sociologists have continued to emphasize their discipline's presumably *disinterested* pursuit of scientific knowledge. Yet the special problems to which sociologists have directed their attention often reflect, at least indirectly and sometimes explicitly, a persisting desire to alleviate social ills and to contribute in some fashion to social betterment. Sociologists, Charles Page remarks, "even when dressed in the most austere trappings of science, are by no means immune to either the ameliorative tradition or the reformistic challenge." [1]

The effort to make sociology truly scientific was reflected in the theoretical and methodological controversies of the 1920s and early 1930s and in a growing emphasis upon concrete empirical research rather than upon speculative theorizing.[2] Much of the research, however, was directed toward pressing social problems associated with poverty, rural and urban slums, unemployment and migratory labor, the adjustments of immigrants, and racial and ethnic relations. Thus family disorganization, delinquency, mental illness, crime, and prostitution were studied with some hope and expectation that the results of disinterested scientific inquiry would contribute to their solution. Many of these problems continue to stimulate a large amount of research, albeit at a more refined theoretical level and with the aid of more efficient research techniques than in the past. But the underlying meliorative impulse has enlarged its focus from the study of "abnormal" or "pathological" aspects of social life to an analysis of the functioning of such "normal" institutions and social structures as industrial and labor relations, business administration, advertising, the mass media, medical care and education, legal practice, and military organization.

This extension of the range of sociological inquiry and application reflects in large measure the emerging needs of a highly complex and rapidly changing society and the growing awareness of the cultural and social dimensions of human behavior, as well as greater sociological

sophistication. Manufacturers and advertisers seek accurate data about their customers and some understanding of the forces that shape decisions to buy or not to buy. Administrators and executives in industry, business, government, the armed forces, and elsewhere seek reliable information about the organizations they direct and about the conditions that affect the morale and efficiency of their staffs. Many physicians and medical scientists now acknowledge the relevance of culture and social relations to disease and its treatment, and some medical school administrators have formally recognized that far more takes place in the education of doctors than the acquisition of technical knowledge and skills.

As a result of these developments, sociologists are teaching in schools of medicine, business, law, and social work, well as in liberal arts colleges and graduate schools; and they are often employed as researchers in hospitals, offices, factories, civil governmental agencies, and military establishments. In fields once looked upon by most people as the province only of the "practical" man rather than the scholar, the claims of sociology that it can provide reliable data and objective interpretations that go beyond the limitations of common sense are increasingly accepted. Sociologists "are invading the business world," according to the magazine *Business Week*, "because business has invited them in through the front door." [3]

New research interests and areas of application have produced, perhaps inevitably, several new "sociologies"—of industry, business, medicine, the military, law, and the mass media, for example. (There are, of course, innumerable possible fields of sociological specialization, for the social origins, forms and functions of every mode of human activity can, in principle, be subjected to analysis.) Studies in many of these emerging areas of specialization not only contribute to the understanding and solution of practical problems, but they also add to general sociological knowledge by systematically examining aspects of culture and society that previously have not been carefully explored. As the pieces are thus gradually assembled for a larger and more revealing picture of various groups and institutions and thus of society as a whole, familiar facts also come to be seen in a new light. The importance of class differences, for example, becomes more readily apparent when the social structure of industry is elaborated, or when the appeals of advertising to various groups are identified.

Common to all specialized areas of inquiry—in theory at least, if not always in practice—are the perspectives and principles of sociological analysis with which this book is concerned. Each subfield refines and elaborates these perspectives and principles to meet its own needs, and eventually feeds back new ideas and additional facts into the central body of sociological thought. From a study of the student-physician emerges fresh insight into the processes of "adult socialization" including the learning—and teaching—of professional roles.[4] From an analysis of the impact of the assembly line upon automobile workers comes additional understanding of the problem of "alienation" in modern society.[5] Research into radio soap operas throws new light upon the mechanisms by which people come to terms with tensions stemming from their status and the roles they must play not only in their families but in society as a whole.[6]

Although this valuable feedback from specialized and applied research to more general sociological theory often occurs, the increased utilization of sociologists by governmental, business, industrial, and other agencies also creates serious problems for both the sociological enterprise and individual scholars. The definition of research problems in many of the special fields within sociology is frequently limited or slanted by the values and interests of clients or sponsors, or by the implicit biases of sociologists eager to produce results that might be "useful." Industrial sociologists who are studying worker morale may ignore the influence of union organization if their sponsor wishes to weaken—or at least not strengthen—the union,[7] or if, unsponsored, they deplore social conflict in general and seek to eliminate any persistent opposition between management and workers.[8] Social scientists commissioned by governmental agencies to explore pressing issues may tailor their recommendations to suit the preferences of the executives to whom they report, although a substantial number apparently feel quite free to "criticize the policy of those who provide their bread and butter."[9] Studies in mass persuasion that deal only with how to achieve limited goals—selling more breakfast cereal, or war bonds, or deodorants—often appear to be free of bias; however, as Merton points out, by confining their questions to what works, social researchers ignore questions concerning the larger impact upon culture, society, and individual personality of the techniques that are used. What may sell war bonds, for example, may also lower the general level of public information and understanding.[10]

The sociologist who serves as an "expert" for any organization commits his professional efforts to the achievement of *its* goals—for example, a more efficient air force, greater profits, the improvement of medical care, or the sale of more soap or more baby food. There may be substantial consensus in society on the desirability of some or all of these goals. Often, however, the sociologist finds himself putting his knowledge and skills to work for special groups and their limited interests. Even the academic sociologist who avoids such special commitments (except, presumably, those to the values of science and scholarship), and whose research is confined solely to theoretical questions, may discover that his work is of particular value only to a selected group of people. Like other scientists, therefore, the sociologist faces the problem of the moral implications of the uses to which his contributions to knowledge are being put. This question may assume even greater proportions as social science creates efficient techniques of manipulation that can be abused by those seeking power over others.

Finally, the increasing concern with specialized areas of inquiry and the growing opportunities to apply sociological knowledge and skills to specific problems may overshadow and minimize the contribution that sociology can make to the understanding of society as a whole and of the place of individuals within it. Sociology is not merely a body of fact and generalization; it is also an important way of viewing the world in which one lives. Its value lies both in its practical uses *and* in the aid it can offer its students in equipping themselves to understand an increasingly complex world in which the relations between the individual and massive social forces are a central problem. Sociology cannot define the goals for which to strive or provide meaning in a rapidly changing world, but it can add to our awareness of both the limits and the possibilities of choice and action.

Notes

[1] Charles H. Page, "Sociology as a Teaching Enterprise," in Robert K. Merton, Leonard Broom, and Leonard S. Cottrell, Jr., *Sociology Today* (New York: Basic Books, 1959), pp. 585–6.

[2] See Roscoe C. Hinkle, Jr., and Gisela Hinkle, *The Development of Modern Sociology* (New York: Random House, 1954), Ch. 2.

[3] "Sociologists Invade the Plant," *Business Week* (March 21, 1959), p. 95.

[4] Robert K. Merton, George G. Reader, and Patricia Kendall (eds.), *The Student-Physician* (Cambridge, Mass.: Harvard University Press, 1957).

[5] Charles R. Walker and Robert H. Guest, *The Man on the Assembly Line* (Cambridge, Mass.: Harvard University Press, 1952). See also Robert Blauner, *Alienation and Freedom* (Chicago: University of Chicago Press, 1964).

[6] W. Lloyd Warner and William Henry, "The Radio Daytime Serial: A Symbolic Analysis," *Genetic Psychology Monographs*, 37 (1948), No. 1, 3–71.

[7] See, for example, Loren Baritz, *The Servants of Power* (Middletown: Wesleyan University Press, 1960), pp. 150 ff.

[8] See Elton Mayo, *Human Problems of an Industrial Civilization* (Cambridge, Mass.: Harvard University Graduate School of Business Administration, 1933); and Elton Mayo, *Social Problems of an Industrial Civilization* (Cambridge, Mass.: Harvard University Graduate School of Business Administration, 1945).

[9] See Edward L. Katzenbach, Jr., "Ideas: A New Defense Industry," *The Reporter*, XXIV (March 2, 1961), 17–21.

[10] Robert K. Merton, with Marjorie Fiske and Alberta Curtis, *Mass Persuasion* (New York: Harper, 1946), Ch. 7.

Suggestions for further reading

BARITZ, LOREN. *The Servants of Power*. Middletown: Wesleyan University Press, 1960.
A critical historical account of how sociology and psychology have been applied in business and industry.

BRIM, ORVILLE G., JR. *Sociology and the Field of Education*. New York: Russell Sage Foundation, 1958.
An assessment of the possible contribution of sociological study to the solution of practical problems in education.

GOULDNER, ALVIN W., and S. M. MILLER (eds.). *Applied Sociology*. New York: Free Press, 1965.
Essays on the problems and possibilities in the practical application of sociological methods and knowledge.

JANOWITZ, MORRIS. *Sociology and the Military Establishment*. New York: Russell Sage Foundation, 1959.
An attempt to "appraise the present state and the outlook for sociological analysis of the military establishment."

LUNDBERG, GEORGE A. *Can Science Save Us?* New York: Longmans, 1947.
The uses of social science as seen by a noted sociologist who believes that sociologists, in their professional role, must avoid completely any moral commitment.

LYND, ROBERT S. *Knowledge for What?* Princeton: Princeton University Press, 1939.
A positive and influential statement of the uses to which the social sciences should be put.

MERTON, ROBERT K., GEORGE G. READER, and PATRICIA KENDALL. *The Student-Physician*. Cambridge, Mass.: Harvard University Press, 1957.
Studies in medical education that seek to find out how doctors acquire the attitudes and values appropriate to their professional role.

PAGE, CHARLES H. (ed.). *Sociology and Contemporary Education*. New York: Random House, 1963.
Essays on the educational uses of sociology.

PARSONS, TALCOTT. "Some Problems Confronting Sociology as a Profession," *American Sociological Review*, XXIV (August, 1959), 547–59.
A statement on the present status of sociology both as a profession and a discipline that includes comment on the increasing application of sociological knowledge and skills to practical problems.

STANTON, ALFRED H., and MORRIS S. SCHWARTZ. *The Mental Hospital*. New York: Basic Books, 1954.
A study of social organization and practice in a mental hospital.

Complete bibliography

ABEL, THEODORE. *Why Hitler Came to Power*. Englewood Cliffs: Prentice-Hall, 1938.

ABERLE, DAVID, *et al.* "The Functional Prerequisites of a Society," *Ethics*, IX (January, 1950), 100–11.

ADAMS, RICHARD N., *et al. Social Change in Latin America Today*. New York: Vintage, 1961.

ADORNO, T. W., ELSE FRENKEL-BRUNSWIK, DANIEL J. LEVINSON, and R. NEVITT SANFORD. *The Authoritarian Personality*. New York: Harper, 1950.

AITOV, A. I. "Some Peculiarities of the Changes in Class Structure in the USSR," *Soviet Sociology*, IV (Fall, 1965), 3–9.

ALBORNOZ, A. F. CARRILLO DE. *Roman Catholicism and Religious Liberty*. Geneva: World Council of Churches, 1959.

ALEXANDER, FRANZ. "Educative Influence of Personality Factors in the Environment," in Clyde Kluckhohn, Henry A. Murray, and David M. Schneider (eds.), *Personality in Nature, Society, and Culture*. 2nd ed. New York: Knopf, 1953, pp. 421–35.

ALLPORT, GORDON. *The Nature of Prejudice*. Cambridge, Mass.: Addison-Wesley, 1954.

ALMOND, GABRIEL. *The Appeals of Communism*. Princeton: Princeton University Press, 1954.

AMERICAN ASSOCIATION FOR THE ADVANCEMENT OF SCIENCE COMMITTEE ON SCIENCE IN THE PROMOTION OF HUMAN WELFARE. "The Integrity of Science," *American Scientist*, LIII (June, 1965). pp. 174–98.

AMERICAN ASSOCIATION FOR THE ADVANCEMENT OF SCIENCE COMMITTEE ON SCIENCE IN THE PROMOTION OF HUMAN WELFARE. "Science and Human Welfare," *Science*, CXXXII (July 8, 1960), 68–73.

ANSHEN, RUTH NANDA (ed.). *The Family: Its Function and Destiny*. New York: Harper, 1949; rev. ed., 1959.

ARENDT, HANNAH. *The Origins of Totalitarianism*. New York: Harcourt, 1951.

ARISTOTLE. *Politics*. Translated by William Ellis. London: J. M. Dent (Everyman Edition), 1912.

ARON, RAYMOND. "Social Structure and the Ruling Class," *British Journal of Sociology*, I (March, 1950), 1–16; and I (June, 1950), 126–43.

ASHBY, ERIC. *Technology and the Academics*. London: Macmillan, 1959.

AXELROD, MORRIS. "Urban Structure and Social Participation," *American Sociological Review*, 21 (February, 1956), 13–8.

AXELROD, MORRIS, *et al.* "Fertility Expectations of the United States Population," *Population Index*, XXIX (January, 1963), 25–31.

BAILEY, F. G. *Caste and the Economic Frontier*. Manchester: Manchester University Press, 1957.

BALTZELL, E. DIGBY. *Philadelphia Gentlemen*. New York: Free Press, 1958.

———. *The Protestant Establishment*. New York: Random House, 1964.

BANFIELD, EDWARD C. *The Moral Basis of a Backward Society*. New York: Free Press, 1958.

BANKS, J. A. *Prosperity and Parenthood*. London: Routledge, 1954.

BANKS, J. A., and OLIVE BANKS. "Feminism and Social Change—A Case Study of a Social Movement," in George Zollchan and Walter Hirsch (eds.), *Explorations in Social Change*. Boston: Houghton Mifflin, 1964, pp. 547–69.

BARBER, BERNARD. "Acculturation and Messianic Movements," *American Sociological Review*, VI (October, 1941), 663–9.

———. "Is American Business Becoming Professionalized? Analysis of a Social Ideology," in Edward A. Tiryakian (ed.), *Sociological Theory, Values and Sociocultural Change*. New York: Free Press, 1963, pp. 121–45.

———. *Science and the Social Order*. New York: Free Press, 1952.

———. "Sociology of Science: A Trend Report and Bibliography," *Current Sociology*, 5 (1956), No. 2, entire issue.

BARBER, BERNARD, and WALTER HIRSCH (eds.). *The Sociology of Science*. New York: Free Press, 1962.

BARBER, ELINOR G. *The Bourgeoisie in 18th Century France*. Princeton: Princeton University Press, 1955.

BARITZ, LOREN. *The Servants of Power*. Middletown: Wesleyan University Press, 1960.

BARNARD, CHESTER A. *The Functions of the Executive*. Cambridge, Mass.: Harvard University Press, 1938.

BARRINGER, HERBERT R., GEORGE I. BLANKSTEN, and RAYMOND W. MACK (eds.). *Social Change in Developing Areas*. Cambridge, Mass.: Schenkman, 1966.

BARRON, MILTON L. (ed.). *Contemporary Sociology*. New York: Dodd, Mead, 1964.

BEARDSLEE, DAVID C., and DONALD D. O'DOWD. "The College-Student Image of the Scientist," *Science*, CXXXIII (March 31, 1961), 997–1001.

BECKER, HOWARD. *Outsiders*. New York: Free Press, 1963.

BEEBE, GILBERT W. *Contraception and Fertility in the Southern Appalachians*. Baltimore: Williams & Wilkins, 1942.

BELL, DANIEL. "The Dispossessed," in Daniel Bell (ed.), *The Radical Right*. Garden City: Doubleday Anchor Books, 1964, pp. 1–45.

———. *The End of Ideology*. New York: Free Press, 1960.

——— (ed.). *The Radical Right*. Garden City: Doubleday Anchor Books, 1964. Expanded and updated edition of *The New American Right* (New York: Criterion Books, 1955).

———. *Work and Its Discontents*. Boston: Beacon, 1956.

BELL, NORMAN W., and EZRA F. VOGEL (eds.). *A Modern Introduction to the Family*. New York: Free Press, 1960.

BELL, WENDELL, and MARYANNE T. FORCE. "Urban Neighborhood Types and Participation in Formal Associations," *American Sociological Review*, 21 (February, 1956), 25–34.

BELLAH, ROBERT N. (ed.). *Religion and Progress in Modern Asia*. New York: Free Press, 1965.

———. "Religious Evolution," *American Sociological Review*, XXIX (June, 1964), 358–74.

———. *Tokugawa Religion*. New York: Free Press, 1957.

BEN-DAVID, JOSEPH. "Scientific Productivity and Academic Organization in Nineteenth Century Medicine," *American Sociological Review*, 25 (December, 1960), 828–43.

BENDIX, REINHARD. *Work and Authority in Industry*. New York: Wiley, 1956.

BENDIX, REINHARD, and SEYMOUR MARTIN LIPSET (eds.). *Class, Status, and Power*.

New York: Free Press, 1953; 2nd ed., 1966.

BENEDICT, RUTH. *Patterns of Culture*. New York: Pelican, 1946.

BERELSON, BERNARD, PAUL F. LAZARSFELD, and WILLIAM N. MCPHEE. *Voting: A Study of Opinion Formation in a Presidential Campaign*. Chicago: University of Chicago Press, 1954.

BERELSON, BERNARD, and PATRICIA J. SALTER. "Majority and Minority Americans: An Analysis of Magazine Fiction," *Public Opinion Quarterly*, I (Summer, 1946), 168–90.

BERELSON, BERNARD, and GARY STEINER. *Human Behavior: An Inventory of Scientific Findings*. New York: Harcourt, 1964.

BERGER, MORROE. *Bureaucracy and Society in Modern Egypt*. Princeton: Princeton University Press, 1957.

BERGER, MORROE, THEODORE ABEL, and CHARLES H. PAGE (eds.). *Freedom and Control in Modern Society*. New York: Van Nostrand, 1954.

BERGER, PETER (ed.). *The Human Shape of Work*. New York: Macmillan, 1964.

BERLE, ADOLPH A. "Economic Power and the Free Society," in Andrew Hacker (ed.), *The Corporation Take-over*. Garden City: Doubleday Anchor Books, 1965 (first published 1964), pp. 86–102.

BERLE, ADOLPH A., and GARDNER MEANS. *The Modern Corporation and Private Property*. New York: Macmillan, 1932.

BERLINER, JOSEPH S. *Factory and Manager in the U.S.S.R.* Cambridge, Mass.: Harvard University Press, 1957.

BERNAL, J. D. *The Social Functions of Science*. London: Routledge, 1939.

BERNERT, ELEANOR H. *America's Children*. New York: Wiley, 1958.

BETTELHEIM, BRUNO. "Feral Children and Autistic Children," *American Journal of Sociology*, 64 (March, 1959), 455–67.

BIERSTEDT, ROBERT. "Nominal and Real Definitions in Sociological Theory," in Llewellyn Gross (ed.), *Symposium on Sociological Theory*. Evanston: Row, Peterson, 1959, pp. 121–44.

———. *The Social Order*. 2nd ed. New York: McGraw-Hill, 1963.

———. "Sociology and General Education," in Charles H. Page (ed.), *Sociology and Contemporary Education*. New York: Random House, 1964, pp. 40–55.

———. "Toynbee and Sociology," *British Journal of Sociology*, X (June, 1959), 95–104.

BLAU, PETER M. *Bureaucracy in Modern Society*. New York: Random House, 1956.

———. *The Dynamics of Bureaucracy*. Chicago: University of Chicago Press, 1955.

———. *Exchange and Power in Social Life*. New York: Wiley, 1964.

BLAU, PETER M., and W. RICHARD SCOTT. *Formal Organizations*. San Francisco: Chandler, 1962.

BLAU, ZENA S. "Exposure to Child-Rearing Experts: A Structural Interpretation of Class-Color Differences," *American Journal of Sociology*, LXIX (May, 1964), 596–608.

BLAUNER, ROBERT. *Alienation and Freedom*. Chicago: University of Chicago Press, 1964.

BLUMENFELD, HANS. "The Modern Metropolis," in Scientific American Books, *Cities*. New York: Knopf, 1965, pp. 40–57.

BLUMER, HERBERT. "Collective Behavior," in Alfred M. Lee (ed.), *New Outline of the Principles of Sociology*. New York: Barnes & Noble, 1946, pp. 199–220.

BOGUE, DONALD J. "Urbanism in the United States, 1950," *American Journal of Sociology*, LX (March, 1955), 471–86.

BOTT, ELIZABETH. *Family and Social Network*. London: Tavistock, 1957.

BOTTOMORE, T. B. *Elites and Society*. London: Watts, 1964.

BOULARD, F. *An Introduction to Religious Sociology*. London: Darton, 1960, Ch. 1, reprinted in Louis Schneider (ed.),

Religion, Culture and Society. New York: Wiley, 1964, pp. 385–9.

BOUQUET, A. C. *Comparative Religion.* Harmondsworth, Eng.: Penguin, 1950.

BRADY, ROBERT. *Business as a System of Power.* New York: Columbia University Press, 1943.

BRIFFAULT, ROBERT. *The Mothers.* New York: Macmillan, 1927.

BRIM, ORVILLE G., JR. *Sociology and the Field of Education.* New York: Russell Sage Foundation, 1958.

BRIM, ORVILLE G., JR., and STANTON WHEELER. *Socialization After Childhood: Two Essays.* New York: Wiley, 1966.

BROWN, HARRISON. *The Challenge of Man's Future.* New York: Viking, 1954.

BROWN, P., and G. B. STRATTON (eds.). *World List of Scientific Periodicals Published in the Years 1900–1960.* 4th ed., 4 vols. London: Butterworth, 1963.

BRYSON, GLADYS. *Man and Society.* Princeton: Princeton University Press, 1945.

BURGESS, ERNEST W. "The Growth of a City: An Introduction to a Research Project," in Robert E. Park, Ernest W. Burgess, and Roderick D. McKenzie, *The City.* Chicago: University of Chicago Press, 1925, pp. 47–62.

BURGESS, ERNEST W. and DONALD J. BOGUE (eds.). *Contributions to Urban Sociology.* Chicago: University of Chicago Press, 1964.

BUTTERFIELD, HERBERT. *The Origins of Modern Science: 1300–1800.* New York: Macmillan, 1951.

BUTTS, R. FREEMAN. *A Cultural History of Education.* New York: McGraw-Hill, 1947.

CAMPBELL, ANGUS, PHILIP E. CONVERSE, WARREN E. MILLER, and DONALD E. STOKES. *The American Voter.* New York: Wiley, 1960.

CAMPBELL, ANGUS, GERALD GURIN, and WARREN E. MILLER. *The Voter Decides.* Evanston: Row, Peterson, 1954.

CANTRIL, HADLEY. *The Psychology of Social Movements.* New York: Wiley, 1941.

CAPLOW, THEODORE. *The Sociology of Work.* Minneapolis: University of Minnesota Press, 1954.

———. "Urban Structure in France," *American Sociological Review,* XVII (October, 1952), 544–9.

CAPLOW, THEODORE, and REECE J. MCGEE. *The Academic Marketplace.* New York: Basic Books, 1958.

CARDWELL, D. S. L. *The Organization of Science in England.* London: Heinemann, 1957.

CARSON, RACHEL. *The Silent Spring.* Boston: Houghton Mifflin, 1962.

CASSIRER, ERNST. *An Essay on Man.* New York: Doubleday Anchor books, 1953.

CENTER FOR URBAN STUDIES. *London: Aspects of Change.* London: Macgibbon & Kee, 1964.

CENTERS, RICHARD. "Occupational Mobility of Urban Occupational Strata," *American Sociological Review,* XIII (April, 1948), 197–203.

———. *The Psychology of Social Classes.* Princeton: Princeton University Press, 1949.

CHANCELLOR, LOREN E., and THOMAS P. MONAHAN. "Religious Preference and Interreligious Mixtures in Marriages and Divorces in Iowa," *American Journal of Sociology,* LXI (November, 1955), 233–9.

CHILDE, V. GORDON. *Man Makes Himself.* Thinker's Library, No. 87. London: Watts, 1948.

CHILDS, MARQUIS, and DOUGLASS CATER. *Ethics in a Business Society.* New York: New American Library Mentor Books, 1954.

CHINOY, ELY. *Automobile Workers and the American Dream.* New York: Random House, 1955.

———. "Local Union Leadership," in Alvin W. Gouldner (ed.), *Studies in Leadership.* New York: Harper, 1950, pp. 157–73.

CHOMBART DE LAUWE, P. H., *et al. Paris et L'Agglomération Parisienne.* Paris: Presses Universitaires, 1952.

CICOUREL, AARON V., and JOHN I. KITSUSE. *The Educational Decision Makers.* Indianapolis: Bobbs-Merrill, 1963.

CLARK, BURTON, R. *Educating the Expert Society.* San Francisco: Chandler, 1962.

CLARK, S. DELBERT. *Church and Sect in Canada.* Toronto: University of Toronto Press, 1948.

CLINARD, MARSHALL B. (ed.). *Anomie and Deviant Behavior.* New York: Free Press, 1964.

CLOWARD, RICHARD A. "Illegitimate Means, *Anomie,* and Deviant Behavior," *American Sociological Review,* XXIV (April, 1959), 164–76.

CLOWARD, RICHARD A., and LLOYD E. OHLIN. *Delinquency and Opportunity.* New York: Free Press, 1960.

COATES, CHARLES H., and ROLAND J. PELLEGRIN. *Military Sociology.* University Park, Md.: Social Science Press, 1965.

CODRINGTON, R. H. "Melanesian Religion," in A. L. Kroeber and T. T. Waterman (eds.). *Source Book in Anthropology.* Rev. ed. New York: Harcourt, 1931, pp. 412–20.

COHEN, ALBERT K. *Delinquent Boys.* New York: Free Press, 1955.

COHEN, MORRIS R., and ERNEST NAGEL. *An Introduction to Logic and the Scientific Method.* New York: Harcourt, 1934.

COHEN, YEHUDI. *Social Structure and Personality: A Casebook.* New York: Holt, Rinehart & Winston, 1961.

COHN, NORMAN. *Pursuit of the Millenium.* London: Mercury, 1957.

COLE, TOBY, and HELEN KRICH CHINOY (eds.). *Actors on Acting.* New York: Crown, 1949.

COLEMAN, JAMES S. *The Adolescent Society.* New York: Free Press, 1961.

COLEMAN, JAMES S., *et al. Equality of Educational Opportunity.* Washington: U.S. Government Printing Office, 1966.

CONANT, JAMES B. "The Impact of Science on Industry and Medicine," *American Scientist,* XXXIX (January, 1951), 33–49.

CONGAR, YVES M. J. *Lay People in the Church.* London: Bloomsbury, 1957.

CONVERSE, PHILIP E. "The Shifting Role of Class in Political Attitudes and Behavior," in Eleanor E. Maccoby, Theodore M. Newcomb, and Eugene L. Hartley (eds.), *Readings in Social Psychology.* 3rd ed. New York: Holt, 1958, pp. 388–99.

COOLEY, CHARLES HORTON. *Human Nature and the Social Order.* New York: Scribner's, 1902.

————. *Social Organization.* New York: Scribner's, 1909.

COON, CARLETON S., with EDWARD E. HUNT, JR. *The Living Races of Man.* New York: Knopf, 1965.

COSER, LEWIS A. *The Functions of Social Conflict.* New York: Free Press, 1956.

COSER, LEWIS A., and BERNARD ROSENBERG (eds.). 2nd ed. *Sociological Theory.* New York: Macmillan, 1964.

COSER, ROSE (ed.). *The Family: Its Structure and Functions.* New York: St. Martin's, 1964.

COTTRELL, WILLIAM F. "Of Time and the Railroader," *American Sociological Review,* IV (April, 1939), 190–8.

COULTON, G. G. *Medieval Panorama.* New York: Meridian, 1955.

COX, OLIVER C. *Class, Caste, and Race.* Garden City: Doubleday, 1948.

CROMBIE, A. C. (ed.). *Scientific Change.* New York: Basic Books, 1963.

CROZIER, MICHEL. *The Bureaucratic Phenomenon.* Chicago: University of Chicago Press, 1964.

CUBER, JOHN F., and WILLIAM F. KENKEL. *Social Stratification.* New York: Appleton, 1954.

DAHL, ROBERT A. *Who Governs?* New Haven: Yale University Press, 1961.

DAHRENDORF, RALF. *Class and Class Conflict in Industrial Society*. Stanford: Stanford University Press, 1959.

———. "Out of Utopia: Toward a Reorientation of Sociological Analysis," *American Journal of Sociology*, LXIV (September, 1958), 115–27.

DAVIDSON, PERCY E., and H. DEWEY ANDERSON. *Occupational Mobility in an American Community*. Stanford: Stanford University Press, 1937.

DAVIS, ALLISON. *Social-Class Influences Upon Learning*. Cambridge: Harvard University Press, 1948.

DAVIS, ALLISON, BURLEIGH B. GARDNER, and MARY R. GARDNER. *Deep South*. Chicago: University of Chicago Press, 1941.

DAVIS, KINGSLEY. "The Demographic Foundations of National Power," in Morroe Berger, Theodore Abel, and Charles H. Page (eds.), *Freedom and Control in Modern Society*. New York: Van Nostrand, 1954, pp. 206–42.

———. "Extreme Isolation of a Child," *American Journal of Sociology*, XLV (January, 1940), 554–65.

———. "Final Note on a Case of Extreme Isolation," *American Journal of Sociology*, LII (March, 1947), 432–7.

———. "Human Fertility in India," *American Journal of Sociology*, LII (November, 1946), 243–54.

———. *Human Society*. New York: Macmillan, 1949.

———. "The Myth of Functional Analysis," *American Sociological Review*, XXIV (December, 1959), 757–72.

———. "The Origin and Growth of Urbanization in the World," *American Journal of Sociology*, LX (March, 1955), 429–37.

———. *The Population of India and Pakistan*. Princeton: Princeton University Press, 1951.

DAY, LINCOLN, and ALICE DAY. *Too Many Americans*. Boston: Riverside, 1964.

DJILAS, MILOVAN. *The New Class*. New York: Praeger, 1957.

DOBRINER, WILLIAM (ed.). *The Suburban Community*. New York: Putnam, 1958.

DOLLARD, JOHN. *Caste and Class in a Southern Town*. Garden City: Doubleday Anchor Books, 1957.

DORE, RONALD P. *Education in Tokugawa Japan*. Berkeley: University of California Press, 1965.

DORFMAN, JOSEPH. *Thorstein Veblen and His America*. New York: Viking, 1934.

DORN, HAROLD F. "Pitfalls in Population Forecasts and Projections," *Journal of the American Statistical Association*, XLV (September, 1950), 311–34.

DOTSON, FLOYD. "Patterns of Voluntary Association Among Urban Working-Class Families," *American Sociological Review*, XVI (October, 1951), 687–93.

DRUCKER, PETER. "The Educational Revolution," in A. H. Halsey, Jean Floud, and C. Arnold Anderson (eds.), *Education, Economy, and Society*. New York: Free Press, 1961, pp. 15–21.

DUBE, S. C. *Indian Village*. London: Routledge, 1955.

DUBIN, ROBERT. "Deviant Behavior and Social Structure," *American Sociological Review*, XXIV (April, 1959), 147–64.

———. *The World of Work*. Englewood Cliffs: Prentice-Hall, 1958.

DUBLIN, LOUIS I, ALFRED J. LOTKA, and MORTIMER SPIEGELMAN. *Length of Life*. Rev. ed. New York: Ronald, 1949.

DUBOIS, CORA. *The People of Alor*. Minneapolis: University of Minnesota Press, 1944.

DUFFY, JOSEPH M., JR. "Clergy and Laity," in *Catholicism in America*. New York: Harcourt 1959, pp. 59–71.

DUNCAN, OTIS DUDLEY, and ALBERT J. REISS, JR. *Social Characteristics of Urban and Rural Communities. 1950*. Census Monograph Series. New York: Wiley, 1956.

DUNN, L. C., and THEODOSIUS DOBZHANSKY. *Heredity, Race, and Society*. New York: Penguin, 1946.

DUNNE, FINLEY PETER. *Mr. Dooley at his Best*. E. Ellis (ed.). New York: Scribner's, 1938.

DURKHEIM, ÉMILE. *The Division of Labor in Society.* Translated by George Simpson. New York: Free Press, 1947.

———. *Education and Sociology.* Translated by Sherwood D. Fox. New York: Free Press, 1956.

———. *The Elementary Forms of the Religious Life.* Translated by J. W. Swain. New York: Free Press, 1947.

———. *The Rules of Sociological Method.* Translated by Sarah A. Solovay and John H. Mueller. Chicago: University of Chicago Press, 1938.

———. *Suicide.* Translated by John A. Spaulding and George Simpson. New York: Free Press, 1951.

DYER, ROBERT J. "The American Laity," *Commonweal,* LX (August 27, 1954), 503–6.

EELLS, KENNETH, *et al. Intelligence and Cultural Differences.* Chicago: University of Chicago Press, 1951.

EHRMANN, WINSTON W. *Premarital Dating Behavior.* New York: Holt, 1959.

EISENSTADT, S. N. "Archetypal Patterns of Youth," in Erik H. Erikson (ed.), *Youth: Change and Challenge.* New York: Basic Books, 1961, pp. 24–42.

———. "Breakdowns of Modernization," *Economic Development and Cultural Change,* XII (July, 1964), 345–67.

———. "Bureaucracy and Bureaucratization: A Trend Report and Bibliography," *Current Sociology,* VII (1958), No. 2, entire issue.

———. *From Generation to Generation.* New York: Free Press, 1956.

———. *Modernization: Growth and Diversity,* Bloomington: Indiana University Seminar on Political and Administrative Development, 1963.

———. "Social Change, Differentiation, and Evolution," *American Sociological Review,* XXIX (June, 1964), 375–86.

ELKIN, FREDERICK. *The Child and Society: The Process of Socialization.* New York: Random House, 1960.

ELLIOT, MABEL A. *Crime in Modern Society.* New York: Harper, 1952.

ELLIS, JOHN TRACY. *American Catholicism.* Chicago: University of Chicago Press, 1956.

ERIKSON, ERIK H. *Childhood and Society.* New York: Norton, 1950.

———. "The Problem of Ego Identity," in *Identity and the Life Cycle, Psychological Issues, Vol. I.* New York: International Universities Press, 1959, pp. 101–64.

ERIKSON, KAI T. *Wayward Puritans.* New York: Wiley, 1966.

ESSIEN-UDOM, ESSIEN UDOSEN. *Black Nationalism.* Chicago: University of Chicago Press, 1962.

ETZIONI, AMITAI and EVA ETZIONI (eds.). *Social Change.* New York: Basic Books, 1964.

EULAU, HEINZ, SAMUEL J. ELDERSVELD, and MORRIS JANOWITZ (eds.). *Political Behavior: A Reader in Theory and Practice.* New York: Free Press, 1956.

EVANS-PRITCHARD, E. E. *Kinship and Marriage Among the Nuer.* Oxford: Oxford University Press, 1951.

FAINSOD, MERLE. *How Russia is Ruled.* Cambridge, Mass: Harvard University Press, 1957.

FARIS, ROBERT E. L. (ed.). *Handbook of Modern Sociology.* Chicago: Rand-McNally, 1964.

FARRINGTON, BENJAMIN. *Greek Science.* 2 vols. Harmondsworth, Eng.: Penguin, 1949.

FAUSET ARTHUR. *Black Gods of the Metropolis.* Publications of the Philadelphia Anthropological Society, Vol. III. Philadelphia: University of Pennsylvania Press, 1944.

FELDMAN, GENE, and MAX GARTENBERG (eds.). *The Beat Generation and the Angry Young Men.* New York: Dell, 1959.

FERGUSON, ADAM. *Essay on the History of Civil Society.* 7th ed. Boston: Hastings, 1809.

FEUER, LOUIS. *The Scentific Intellectual.* New York: Basic Books, 1963.

FICHTER, JOSEPH. "Marginal Catholics: An Institutional Approach," *Social Forces,* XXXII (December, 1953), 163–73.

———. *Social Relations in an Urban Parish.* Chicago: University of Chicago Press, 1954.

FINER, SAMUEL E. *The Man on Horseback.* London: Pall Mall, 1962.

FINKELSTEIN, LOUIS. *The Pharisees: The Sociological Background of Their Faith.* 2 vols. Philadelphia: Jewish Publication Society, 1938.

FIREY, WALTER. *Land Use in Central Boston.* Cambridge, Mass.: Harvard University Press, 1947.

FIRTH, RAYMOND. *Human Types.* Rev. ed. New York: New American Library, 1958.

———. *Primitive Economics of the New Zealand Maori.* New York: Dutton, 1929.

FLETCHER, RONALD. *Britain in the Sixties: The Family and Marriage.* Baltimore: Penguin, 1962.

FORD, HENRY. *My Life and Work.* Garden City: Doubleday, 1922.

FORTES, MEYER, and E. E. EVANS-PRITCHARD (eds.). *African Political Systems.* London: Oxford University Press, 1940.

Fortune, Editors of. *The Exploding Metropolis.* Garden City: Doubleday Anchor Books, 1958.

FRAZIER, E. FRANKLIN. *Black Bourgeoisie.* New York: Free Press, 1957.

———. *The Negro Family in the United States.* Chicago: University of Chicago Press, 1939; revised and abridged, New York: Dryden, 1951.

———. *The Negro in the United States.* New York: Macmillan, 1949; revised 1957.

———. "The Negro in the United States," in Andrew W. Lind (ed.), *Race Relations in World Perspective.* Honolulu: University of Hawaii Press, 1955, pp. 339–70.

FREEDMAN, RONALD (ed.). *Population: The Vital Revolution.* Garden City: Doubleday Anchor Books, 1964.

FREMANTLE, ANNE. *The Papal Encyclicals in Their Historical Context.* New York: New American Library Mentor Books, 1956.

FREUD, SIGMUND. *Civilization and Its Discontents.* Translated by Joan Riviere. London: Hogarth, 1955.

———. *New Introductory Lectures on Psycho-analysis.* Translated by W. J. H. Sprott. New York: Norton, 1933.

FRIEDAN, BETTY. *The Feminine Mystique.* New York: Norton, 1963.

FRIEDMANN, GEORGES. *Industrial Society.* New York: Free Press, 1955.

FROMM, ERICH. *The Sane Society.* New York: Rinehart, 1955.

———. "Sex and Character" in Ruth Anshen (ed.). *The Family: Its Function and Destiny.* New York: Harper, 1949, pp. 375–92.

GALBRAITH, JOHN KENNETH. *The Affluent Society.* Boston: Houghton Mifflin, 1958.

GANS, HERBERT. *The Urban Villagers.* New York: Free Press, New York, 1962.

GELLHORN, WALTER. *Security, Loyalty and Science.* Ithaca: Cornell University Press, 1950.

GIBBS, JACK P., and KINGSLEY DAVIS. "Conventional Versus Metropolitan Data in the International Study of Urbanism," *American Sociological Review,* XXIII (October, 1958), 504–14.

GILPIN, ROBERT, and CHRISTOPHER WRIGHT (eds.). *Scientists and National Policy-Making.* New York: Columbia University Press, 1964.

GINSBERG, MORRIS. *Sociology.* London: Butterworth, 1934.

GLASS, DAVID. "Education and Social Change in Modern England," in A. H. Halsey, Jean Floud, and C. Arnold Anderson (eds.). *Education, Economy, and Society.* New York: Free Press, 1961, pp. 391–413.

——— (ed.). *Social Mobility in Britain.* London: Routledge, 1954.

GLAZER, NATHAN. *American Judaism.* Chicago: University of Chicago Press, 1957.

GLAZER, NATHAN, and DANIEL P. MOYNIHAN. *Beyond the Melting Pot.* Cambridge, Mass.: M.I.T. Press and Harvard University Press, 1963.

GLICK, PAUL C. *American Families.* New York: Wiley, 1957.

GLOCK, CHARLES Y., and RODNEY STARK. *Christian Belief and Anti-Semitism.* New York: Harper, 1966.

GLUCKMAN, MAX. *Custom and Conflict in Africa.* Oxford: Blackwell, 1955.

GOFFMAN, ERVING. *The Presentation of Self in Everyday Life.* Garden City: Doubleday Anchor Books, 1959.

GOODE WILLIAM J. *After Divorce.* New York: Free Press, 1956.

———. *The Family.* Englewood Cliffs: Prentice-Hall, 1964.

———. *Religion Among the Primitives.* New York: Free Press, 1956.

———. *World Revolution and Family Patterns.* New York: Free Press, 1963.

GORCE, PAUL-MARIE DE LA. *The French Army.* Translated by Kenneth Douglas. London: Weidenfeld, 1963.

GORDON, MARGARET S. (ed.). *Poverty in America.* San Francisco: Chandler, 1965.

GORDON, MILTON M. *Assimilation in American Life.* New York: Oxford University Press, 1964.

———. *Social Class in American Sociology.* Durham: Duke University Press, 1958.

GORDON, ROBERT A., JAMES F. SHORT, JR., DESMOND S. CARTWRIGHT, and FRED L. STRODTBECK. "Values and Gang Delinquency: A Study of Street Corner Groups." *American Journal of Sociology,* LXIX (September, 1963), 109–28.

GOTTMAN, JEAN. *Megalopolis.* Cambridge, Mass.: M.I.T. Press, 1961.

GOUGH, E. KATHLEEN. "Changing Kinship Usages in the Setting of Political and Economic Change among the Nayars of Malabar," *Journal of the Royal Anthropological Institute,* LXXXII (1952), 71–88.

———. "The Nayars and the Definition of Marriage," *Journal of the Royal Anthropological Institute,* LXXXIX (January–June, 1959), 23–4.

GOULDNER, ALVIN W. "The Norm of Reciprocity," *American Sociological Review,* XXV (April, 1960), 161–78.

———. *Patterns of Industrial Bureaucracy.* New York: Free Press, 1954.

——— (ed.). *Studies in Leadership.* New York: Harper, 1950.

GOULDNER, ALVIN W., and S. M. MILLER (eds.). *Applied Sociology: Opportunities and Problems.* New York: Free Press, 1965.

GRABILL, WILSON H., CLYDE V. KISER, and P. K. WHELPTON. *The Fertility of American Women.* New York: Wiley, 1958.

GRANICK, DAVID. *The Red Executive.* Garden City: Doubleday, 1960.

GREELEY, ANDREW M., and PETER H. ROSSI. *The Education of American Catholics.* Chicago: Aldine, 1966.

GREER, SCOTT A. *Social Organization.* New York: Random House, 1955.

GRETTON, R. W. *The English Middle Class.* London: Bell, 1917.

GROSS, LLEWELLYN (ed.). *Symposium on Sociological Theory.* Evanston: Row, Peterson, 1959.

GURVITCH, GEORGES, and WILBERT E. MOORE (eds.). *Twentieth Century Sociology.* New York: Philosophical Library, 1945.

GUSFIELD, JOSEPH R. *Symbolic Crusade.* Urbana: University of Illinois Press, 1963.

GUTTSMAN, W. L. *The British Political Elite.* London: Macgibbon & Kee, 1963.

HACKER, ANDREW (ed.). *The Corporation Take-Over.* Garden City: Doubleday Anchor Books, 1965.

HAGSTROM, WARREN. *The Scientific Community.* New York: Basic Books, 1965.

HALL, CALVIN, and GARDNER LINDZEY. *Theories of Personality.* New York: Wiley, 1957.

HALLOWELL, A. IRVING. *Culture and Experience.* Philadelphia: University of Pennsylvania Press, 1955.

HALSEY, A. H. "The Changing Functions of Universities," in A. H. Halsey, Jean Floud, and C. Arnold Anderson (eds.), *Education, Economy, and Society.* New York: Free Press, 1961, pp. 456–65.

HALSEY, A. H., JEAN FLOUD, and C. ARNOLD ANDERSON (eds.). *Education, Economy, and Society.* New York: Free Press, 1961.

HAMILTON, ALICE. *Exploring the Dangerous Trades.* Boston: Little Brown, 1943.

HAMILTON, WALTON, and IRENE TILL. "Property," *Encyclopedia of the Social Sciences.* Vol. 12. New York: Macmillan, 1934, pp. 528–38.

HANDLIN OSCAR. *The Newcomers: Negroes and Puerto Ricans in a Changing Metropolis.* Cambridge, Mass.: Harvard University Press, 1959.

————. *The Uprooted.* Boston: Little Brown, 1952.

HARBISON, FREDERICK, and CHARLES A. MYERS. *Education, Manpower, and Economic Growth: Strategies of Human Resources Development.* New York: McGraw-Hill, 1964.

HARE, A. PAUL, EDGAR F. BORGATTA, and ROBERT F. BALES (eds.). *Small Groups: Studies in Social Interaction.* New York: Knopf, 1955.

HARRINGTON, MICHAEL. *The Other America.* New York: Macmillan, 1962.

HARRIS, CHAUNCEY D., and EDWARD L. ULLMAN. "The Nature of Cities," *The Annals of the American Academy of Political and Social Science,* CCXLII (November, 1945), 7–17.

HARRIS, GEORGE L. *Jordan.* New York: Grove, 1958.

HARRIS, MARVIN. *Town and Country in Brazil.* New York: Columbia University Press, 1956.

HARRIS, SEYMOUR. *The Market for College Graduates.* Cambridge, Mass.: Harvard University Press, 1949.

HARRISON, PAUL M. *Authority and Power in the Free Church Tradition.* Princeton: Princeton University Press, 1959.

HART, C. W. M. "Industrial Relations Research and Social Theory," *Canadian Journal of Economics and Political Science,* XV (February, 1949), 53–73.

HATT, PAUL K. (ed.). *World Population and Future Resources.* New York: American Book, 1952.

HATT, PAUL K., and ALBERT J. REISS, JR. (eds.). *Cities and Society: The Revised Reader in Urban Sociology.* New York: Free Press, 1957.

HAUSER, PHILIP M. (ed.). *Population and World Politics.* New York: Free Press, 1958.

———— (ed.). *The Population Dilemma.* Englewood Cliffs: Prentice-Hall, 1963.

HAUSER, PHILIP M., and OTIS DUDLEY DUNCAN (eds.). *The Study of Population: An Inventory and Appraisal.* Chicago: University of Chicago Press, 1959.

HAVIGHURST, ROBERT J., and BERNICE L. NEUGARTEN. *Society and Education.* 2nd ed. Boston: Allyn & Bacon, 1962.

HERBERG, WILL. *Protestant–Catholic–Jew.* Garden City: Doubleday, 1955.

HINKLE, ROSCOE C., JR., and GISELA HINKLE. *The Development of Modern Sociology.* New York: Random House, 1954.

HIRSH, SELMA. *The Fears Men Live By.* New York: Harper, 1955.

HOBSBAWM, E. J. *Primitive Rebels.* New York: Norton, 1965.

HODGE, ROBERT W., PAUL M. SIEGEL, and PETER H. ROSSI. "Occupational Prestige in the United States, 1925–63," *American Journal of Sociology,* LXX (November, 1964), 286–302.

HOEBEL, E. ADAMSON. *Man in the Primitive World.* New York: McGraw-Hill, 1958.

HOFFER, ERIC. *The True Believer.* New York: New American Library, 1958.

HOFSTADTER, RICHARD, and C. DEWITT HARDY. *The Development and Scope of Higher Education in the United States.* New York: Columbia University Press, 1952.

HOLLINGSHEAD, AUGUST B. *Elmtown's Youth.* New York: Wiley, 1949.

HOLLINGSHEAD, AUGUST B., and FREDERICK C. REDLICH. *Social Class and Mental Illness.* New York: Wiley, 1958.

HOMANS, GEORGE. *The Human Group.* New York: Harcourt, 1950.

HOROWITZ, IRVING LOUIS. *The Three Worlds of Development.* New York: Oxford University Press, 1966.

HOSELITZ, BERT F. (ed.). *The Progress of Underdeveloped Areas.* Chicago: University of Chicago Press, 1952.

———. *Sociological Aspects of Economic Growth.* New York: Free Press, 1959.

HOSELITZ, BERT F., and WILBERT E. MOORE (eds.). *Industrialization and Society.* The Hague: UNESCO-Mouton, 1963.

HOYT, HOMER. *The Structure and Growth of Residential Neighborhoods in American Cities.* Washington: United States Federal Housing Administration, 1939.

HSU, FRANCES L. K. "Chinese and American Family Practices," in Marvin Sussman (ed.), *Sourcebook in Marriage and the Family.* Boston: Houghton Mifflin, 1955, pp. 8–12.

HUGHES, EVERETT C. "Dilemmas and Contradictions of Status," *American Journal of Sociology,* L (March, 1945), 353–9.

———. *Men and Their Work.* New York: Free Press, 1958.

HUGHES, EVERETT C. and HELEN M. HUGHES. *Where Peoples Meet: Racial and Ethnic Frontiers.* New York: Free Press, 1952.

HUNT, MORTON M. *The Natural History of Love.* New York: Knopf, 1959.

HUNTER, FLOYD. *Community Power Structure: A Study of Decision Makers.* Chapel Hill: University of North Carolina Press, 1953.

HUNTINGTON, ELLSWORTH. *Mainsprings of Civilization.* New York: Wiley, 1945.

HUTCHINSON, HARRY W. "Race Relations in a Rural Community of the Bahian Recôncavo," in Charles Wagley (ed.), *Race and Class in Rural Brazil.* Paris: UNESCO, 1952.

HYMAN, HERBERT H. "The Value Systems of Different Classes," in Reinhard Bendix and Seymour M. Lipset, *Class, Status, and Power.* 2nd ed. New York: Free Press, 1966, pp. 488–99.

India's Villages. Calcutta: West Bengal Government Press, 1955.

INKELES, ALEX, "The Modernization of Man," in Myron Wiener (ed.), *Modernization.* New York: Basic Books, 1966.

———. "Personality and Social Structure," in Robert K. Merton, Leonard Broom, and Leonard S. Cottrell, Jr. (eds.), *Sociology Today.* New York: Basic Books, 1959.

———. "Social Stratification and Mobility in the Soviet Union, 1940–1950," *American Sociological Review,* XV (August, 1950), 465–79.

INKELES, ALEX, and RAYMOND A. BAUER. *The Soviet Citizen.* Cambridge, Mass.: Harvard University Press, 1959.

INKELES, ALEX, RAYMOND A. BAUER, and CLYDE KLUCKHOHN. *How the Soviet System Works.* Cambridge: Harvard University Press, 1957.

INKELES, ALEX, and PETER H. ROSSI. "National Comparisons of Occupational Prestige," *American Journal of Sociology,* LXVI (January, 1956), 329–39.

INNES, JOHN W. *Class Fertility Trends in England and Wales, 1876–1934.* Princeton: Princeton University Press, 1938.

JACKSON, ELTON F., and HARRY J. CROCKETT, JR. "Occupational Mobility in the United States: A Point Estimate and Trend Comparison," *American Sociological Review,* XXIX (February, 1964), 5–15.

JACOB, PHILIP E. *Changing Values in College.* New York: Harper, 1957.

JACOBS, JANE. *The Death and Life of Great American Cities.* New York: Random House, 1961.

JACOBSON, PAUL H. *American Marriage and Divorce.* New York: Rinehart, 1959.

JACQUES, ELLIOTT. *The Changing Culture of a Factory.* New York: Dryden, 1952.

JAFFEE, A. J. "Urbanization and Fertility," *American Journal of Sociology,* XLVIII (July, 1942), 47–60.

JAMES, WILLIAM. *The Varieties of Religious Experience.* New York: Random House Modern Library, 1936.

JANOWITZ, MORRIS. *The Military in the Political Development of New Nations.* Chicago: University of Chicago Press, 1964.

———. *The Professional Soldier.* New York: Free Press, 1960.

———. *Sociology and the Military Establishment.* New York: Russell Sage Foundation, 1959.

JANSYN, LEON R., JR. "Solidarity and Delinquency in a Street Corner Group," *American Sociological Review,* XXXI (October, 1966), 600–14.

KAHL, JOSEPH A. *The American Class Structure.* New York: Rinehart, 1957.

KAPLAN, NORMAN. "Research Administration and the Administrator; U.S.S.R. and United States," in Norman Kaplan (ed.), *Science and Society.* Chicago: Rand McNally, 1965, pp. 229–46.

——— (ed.). *Science and Society.* Chicago: Rand McNally, 1965.

KARDINER, ABRAM, *et al. The Psychological Frontiers of Society.* New York: Columbia University Press, 1945.

KATZENBACH, EDWARD L., JR. "Ideas: A New Defense Industry," *The Reporter,* XXIV (March 2, 1961), 17–21.

KAUFMAN, HAROLD F. *Prestige Classes in a New York Rural Community.* Ithaca: Cornell University Agricultural Experiment Station, Memoir 260, March, 1944.

KELLER, SUZANNE. *Beyond the Ruling Class: Strategic Elites in Modern Society.* New York: Random House, 1963.

KELSALL, R. K. *Higher Civil Servants in Britain.* London: Routledge, 1955.

KENNEDY, RUBY JO REEVES. "Single or Triple Melting Pot? Intermarriage Trends in New Haven, 1870–1940," *American Journal of Sociology,* LXIX (January, 1944), 331–9.

KENNISTON, KENNETH. "Social Change and Youth in America," in Erik H. Erikson (ed.), *Youth: Change and Challenge.* New York: Basic Books, 1961, pp. 161–87.

KERR, CLARK. *The Uses of the University.* Cambridge, Mass.: Harvard University Press, 1963.

KILLIAN, LEWIS M. "The Effects of Southern White Workers on Race Relations in Northern Plants," *American Sociological Review,* XVII (June, 1952), 327–31.

KIMMEL, LEWIS H. *Share Ownership in the United States.* Washington: Brookings, 1952.

KINGSLEY, J. DONALD. *Representative Bureaucracy.* Yellow Springs: Antioch, 1944.

KINSEY, ALFRED C., WARDELL B. POMEROY, and CLYDE E. MARTIN. *Sexual Behavior in the Human Male.* Philadelphia: Saunders, 1948.

KINSEY, ALFRED C., WARDELL B. POMEROY, CLYDE E. MARTIN, and PAUL H. GEBHARD. *Sexual Behavior in the Human Female.* Philadelphia: Saunders, 1953.

KIRK, RUSSELL. "Is Social Science Scientific?," *New York Times Magazine,* June 25, 1961, 11 ff.

KLUCKHOHN, CLYDE. *Navaho Witchcraft.* Papers of the Peabody Museum of American Archaeology and Ethnology, Vol. XXII. Cambridge, Mass.: Harvard University Press, 1944, No. 2, pp. 45–73.

KLUCKHOHN, CLYDE, and WILLIAM H. KELLEY. "The Concept of Culture," in Ralph Linton (ed.), *The Science of Man in the World Crisis.* New York: Columbia University Press, 1945, pp. 78–106.

KLUCKHOHN, CLYDE, HENRY A. MURRAY, and DAVID M. SCHNEIDER (eds.). *Personality in Nature, Society, and Culture.* 2nd ed. New York: Knopf, 1953.

KNAPP, ROBERT H., and HUBERT B. GOODRICH. *Origins of American Scientists.* Chicago: University of Chicago Press, 1952.

KOHN, MELVIN L. "Social Class and Parental Authority," *American Sociological Review,* XXIV (June, 1959), 352–66.

———. "Social Class and Parental Values," *American Journal of Sociology,* LXIV (January, 1959), 337–51.

———. "Social Class and Parent–Child Relationships: An Interpretation," *American Journal of Sociology,* LXVIII (January, 1963), 471–80.

KOLB, WILLIAM L. "Values, Politics, and Sociology," *American Sociological Review,* XXV (December, 1960), 966–9.

KOMAROVSKY, MIRRA (ed.). *Common Frontiers of the Social Sciences.* New York: Free Press, 1957.

———. "Cultural Contradictions and Sex Roles," *American Journal of Sociology,* LII (November, 1946), 184–9.

———. "The Voluntary Associations of Urban Dwellers," *American Sociological Review,* XI (December, 1946), 686–98.

———. *Women in the Modern World.* Boston: Little Brown, 1953.

KORNHAUSER, WILLIAM. *The Politics of Mass Society.* New York: Free Press, 1959.

———. *Scientists in Industry.* Berkeley: University of California Press, 1962.

KROEBER, ALFRED L. *The Nature of Culture.* Chicago: University of Chicago Press, 1952.

KROEBER, ALFRED L., and CLYDE KLUCKHOHN. *Culture, a Critical Review of Concept and Definitions.* New York: Random House Vintage Books, n.d.

KROEBER, ALFRED L., and TALCOTT PARSONS. "The Concepts of Culture and of Social System," *American Sociological Review* (October, 1958), 582–3.

KROEBER, ALFRED L., and THOMAS S. WATERMAN (eds.). *Source Book in Anthropology.* Rev. ed. New York: Harcourt, 1931.

KUHN, THOMAS C. *The Structure of Scientific Revolutions.* Chicago: University of Chicago Press, 1962.

KUPER, LEO. *An African Bourgeoisie.* New Haven: Yale University Press, 1964.

LAMPARD, ERIC E. *Industrial Revolution: Interpretations and Perspectives.* Washington: American Historical Association, 1957.

LANDES, RUTH, and MARK ZBOROWSKI. "Hypotheses Concerning the Eastern European Jewish Family," *Psychiatry,* XIII (November, 1950), 447–64.

LANDIS, PAUL H., and PAUL K. HATT. *Population Problems.* 2nd ed. New York: American Book, 1954.

LANE, ROBERT E. "The Politics of Consensus in an Age of Affluence," *American Political Science Quarterly,* LIX (December, 1965), 885–9.

LANG, OLGA. *Chinese Family and Society.* New Haven: Yale University Press, 1946.

LA PALOMBARA, JOSEPH (ed.). *Bureaucracy and Political Development.* Princeton: Princeton University Press, 1963.

LAPP, RALPH. *Must We Hide?* Cambridge, Mass.: Addison-Wesley, 1949.

———. *The New Priesthood.* New York: Harper, 1965.

———. *The Voyage of the Lucky Dragon.* New York: Harper, 1958.

LASKI, HAROLD. "Bureaucracy," in *Encyclopedia of the Social Sciences,* Vol. III. New York: Macmillan, 1930, pp. 70–4.

LAZARSFELD, PAUL F. "The American Soldier: An Expository Review," *Public Opinion Quarterly,* XIII (Fall, 1949), 377–404.

LAZARSFELD, PAUL F., BERNARD BERELSON, and HAZEL GAUDET. *The People's Choice.* 2nd ed. New York: Columbia University Press, 1948.

LAZARSFELD, PAUL F. and FRANK STANTON (eds.). *Radio Research, 1942–1943.* New York: Duell, Sloan, 1944.

LEE, ALFRED M. (ed.). *New Outline of the Principles of Sociology.* New York: Barnes & Noble, 1946.

LENSKI, GERHARD. *Power and Privilege.* New York: McGraw-Hill, 1966.

————. *The Religious Factor.* Rev. ed. Garden City: Doubleday Anchor Books, 1963.

LEONHARD, WOLFGANG. *Child of the Revolution.* Translated by C. W. Woodhouse. London: Collins, 1957.

LERNER, DANIEL. *The Passing of Traditional Society.* New York: Free Press, 1958.

LERNER, DANIEL, and HAROLD D. LASSWELL (eds.). *The Policy Sciences.* Hoover Institute Studies, No. 1. Stanford: Stanford University Press, 1951.

LERNER, MAX. *America as a Civilization.* New York: Simon & Schuster, 1957.

LEVY, MARION J., JR. *The Family Revolution in Modern China.* Cambridge, Mass.: Harvard University Press, 1949.

————. *The Structure of Society.* Princeton: Princeton University Press, 1952.

LÉVY-BRUHL, LUCIEN. *Primitive Mentality.* Translated by Lilian A. Clare. New York: Macmillan, 1923.

LEWIS, IAN. "In the Courts of Power—The Advertising Man," in Peter Berger (ed.), *The Human Shape of Work.* New York: Macmillan, 1964.

LEWIS, OSCAR. *The Children of Sanchez.* New York: Random House, 1961.

LIEUWEN, EDWIN. *Arms and Politics in Latin America.* Rev. ed. New York: Praeger, 1961.

LINCOLN, C. ERIC. *The Black Muslims in America.* Boston: Beacon, 1961.

LIND, ANDREW W. (ed.). *Race Relations in World Perspective.* Honolulu: University of Hawaii Press, 1955.

LINDSAY, A. D. "Individualism," in *Encyclopedia of the Social Sciences.* Vol. VII. New York: Macmillan, 1932, pp. 674–80.

Linton, Ralph. *The Cultural Background of Personality.* New York: Appleton, 1945.

———— (ed.). *The Science of Man in the World Crisis.* New York: Columbia University Press, 1945.

————. *The Study of Man.* New York: Appleton, 1936.

LIPSET, SEYMOUR M. *Agrarian Socialism.* Berkeley: University of California Press, 1950.

————. *The First New Nation.* New York: Basic Books, 1953.

————. *Political Man: The Social Bases of Politics.* Garden City: Doubleday, 1960.

LIPSET, SEYMOUR M., and REINHARD BENDIX. *Social Mobility in Industrial Society.* Berkeley: University of California Press, 1959.

LIPSET, SEYMOUR M., and LEO LOWENTHAL (eds.). *Culture and Social Character.* New York: Free Press, 1961.

LIPSET, SEYMOUR M., MARTIN A. TROW, and JAMES S. COLEMAN. *Union Democracy.* Garden City: Doubleday Anchor Books, 1962.

LIPSET, SEYMOUR M., and SHELDON S. WOLIN (eds.). *The Berkeley Student Revolt.* Garden City: Doubleday Anchor Books, 1965.

LOWENTHAL, LEO. "Biographies in Popular Magazines," in Paul F. Lazarsfeld and Frank Stanton (eds.), *Radio Research, 1942–43.* New York: Duell, Sloan, 1944, pp. 507–48.

LOWENTHAL, LEO, and NORBERT GUTERMAN. *Prophets of Deceit. A Study in the Techniques of the American Agitator.* New York: Harper, 1949.

LUBELL, SAMUEL. *The Future of American Politics.* 2nd ed., rev. Garden City: Doubleday Anchor Books, 1956.

LUNDBERG, GEORGE A. *Can Science Save Us?* New York: Longman's, 1947.

LYND, ROBERT S. *Knowledge for What?* Princeton: Princeton University Press, 1939.

LYND, ROBERT S., and HELEN M. LYND. *Middletown.* New York: Harcourt, 1929.

————. *Middletown in Transition.* New York: Harcourt, 1929.

MACCOBY, ELEANOR, THEODORE M. NEWCOMB, and EUGENE L. HARTLEY (eds.). *Readings in Social Psychology*. 3rd ed. New York: Holt, 1958.

MACHLUP, FRITZ. *The Production and Distribution of Knowledge in the United States*. Princeton: Princeton University Press, 1962.

MACIVER, ROBERT M. *Community*. London: Macmillan, 1920.

———. *Social Causation*. Boston: Ginn, 1942.

———. *The Web of Government*. New York: Macmillan, 1947.

MACIVER, ROBERT M., and CHARLES H. PAGE. *Society*. New York: Rinehart, 1949.

MC KITRICK, ERIC L. "The Study of Corruption," *Political Science Quarterly*, LXXII (December, 1957), 502–14.

MALINOWSKI, BRONISLAW. *Argonauts of the Western Pacific*. London: Routledge, 1922.

———. *Crime and Custom in Savage Society*. Paterson: Littlefield, 1959. (First published, 1926).

———. *Magic, Science and Religion and Other Essays*. Garden City: Doubleday Anchor Books, 1948.

———. "Parenthood—The Basis of Social Structure," in Rose Coser (ed.), *The Family: Its Structure and Funtions*. New York: St. Martin's, 1964, pp. 3–19.

———. *Sex and Repression in Savage Society*. New York: Meridian, 1955. (First published, 1927.)

MANDELBAUM, DAVID (ed.). *Selected Writings of Edward Sapir*. Berkeley: University of California Press, 1949.

MANDEVILLE, BERNARD DE. *The Fable of the Bees*. London: 1723.

MANNHEIM, KARL. *Ideology and Utopia*. Translated by Louis Wirth and Edward Shils. New York: Harcourt, 1946.

MARETT, R. R. *Anthropology*. Rev. ed. London: Oxford University Press, 1944.

MARX, FRITZ MORSTEIN. "The Higher Civil Service as an Action Group in Western Political Development," in Joseph La Palombara (ed.). *Bureaucracy and Political Development*. Princeton: Princeton University Press, 1963, pp. 62–95.

MARX, KARL. *Capital*. Translated by Ernest Untermann, from the first German edition. Chicago: Kerr, 1909.

MASSING, PAUL W. *Rehearsal for Destruction*. New York: Harper, 1949.

MATHEWSON, STANLEY S. *Restriction of Output Among Unorganized Workers*. New York: Viking, 1931.

MATHUR, K. S. *Caste and Ritual in a Malwa Village*. New York: Asia Publishing House, 1964.

MATTHEWS, DONALD. *The Social Background of Political Decision Makers*. Garden City: Doubleday, 1954.

MATZA, DAVID. *Delinquency and Drift*. New York: Wiley, 1964.

MAUSS, MARCEL. *The Gift*. Translated by Ian Cunnison. London: Cohen & West, 1954.

MAYER, KURT. *The Population of Switzerland*. New York: Columbia University Press, 1952.

MAYO, ELTON. *Human Problems of an Industrial Civilization*. Cambridge, Mass.: Harvard University Graduate School of Business Administration, 1933.

———. *Social Problems of an Industrial Civilization*. Cambridge, Mass.: Harvard University Graduate School of Business Administration, 1945.

MAYO, ELTON, and G. F. F. LOMBARD. *Teamwork and Turnover in the Aircraft Industry of Southern California*. Boston: Harvard Business School Division of Research, 1944.

MEAD, GEORGE HERBERT. *Mind, Self, and Society*. Chicago: University of Chicago Press, 1934.

MEAD, MARGARET (ed.). *Cultural Patterns and Technical Change*. New York: New American Library, 1955.

———. *Growing Up in New Guinea*. New York: Morrow, 1930. (Reprinted, New American Library, n.d.)

———. *Male and Female.* New York: New American Library, 1955.

———. *New Lives for Old.* New York: Morrow, 1956.

———. *Sex and Temperament in Three Primitive Societies.* New York: Morrow, 1935.

MEAD, MARGARET, and RHODA MÉTRAUX. "Image of the Scientist among High-School Students," *Science,* CXXVI (August 30, 1957), 384–90.

MECHAM, J. LLOYD. *Church and State in Latin America.* Chapel Hill: University of North Carolina Press, 1934.

MERTON, ROBERT K. "The Canons of the Anti-Sociologist," *New York Times Magazine,* July 16, 1961, 14 ff.

———. "Notes on Problem-Finding in Sociology," in Robert K. Merton, Leonard Broom, and Leonard S. Cottrell, Jr. (eds.), *Sociology Today.* New York: Basic Books, 1959, pp. ix–xxxiv.

———. "Priorities in Scientific Discovery," *American Sociological Review,* XXII (December, 1957), 635–59.

———. "Social Conformity, Deviation, and Opportunity-Structures," *American Sociological Review,* XXIV (April, 1959), 177–89.

———. *Social Theory and Social Structure.* Rev. and enlarged ed. New York: Free Press, 1957.

MERTON, ROBERT K., *et al.* (eds.). *Reader in Bureaucracy.* New York: Free Press, 1952.

MERTON, ROBERT K., LEONARD BROOM, and LEONARD S. COTTRELL (eds.). *Sociology Today.* New York: Basic Books, 1959.

MERTON, ROBERT K., MARJORIE FISKE, and ALBERTA CURTIS. *Mass Persuasion.* New York: Harper, 1946.

MERTON, ROBERT K., and PAUL F. LAZARSFELD. "Friendship as a Social Process," in Morroe Berger, Theodore Abel, and Charles H. Page (eds.), *Freedom and Control in Modern Society.* New York: Van Nostrand, 1954, pp. 18–66.

MERTON, ROBERT K., and ROBERT A. NISBET (eds.). *Contemporary Social Problems.* 2nd ed. New York: Harcourt, 1966.

MERTON, ROBERT K., GEORGE G. READER, and PATRICIA KENDALL. *The Student-Physician.* Cambridge, Mass.: Harvard University Press, 1957.

MICHELS, ROBERT. *Political Parties.* Translated by Eden Paul and Cedar Paul. New York: Free Press, 1949. (First published, 1915.)

MIDDLETON, RUSSELL. "Brother–Sister and Father–Daughter Marriage in Ancient Egypt," *American Sociological Review,* 27 (October, 1962), 603–11.

MIDDLETON, RUSSELL, and JOHN MOLAND. "Humor in Negro and White Subcultures: A Study of Jokes Among University Students," *American Sociological Review,* XXIV (February, 1959), 61–9.

MILLER, DELBERT C., and WILLIAM H. FORM. *Industrial Sociology.* New York: Harper, 1951.

MILLER, HERMAN P. *Rich Man, Poor Man.* New York: Crowell, 1964.

MILLER, WILLIAM. "American Historians and the American Business Elite," *Journal of Economic History,* IX (November, 1949), 184–208.

MILLER, WRIGHT. *Russians as People.* New York: Dutton, 1961.

MILLIS, WALTER. *Arms and Men.* New York: New American Library, 1958.

MILLS, C. WRIGHT. "The Middle Classes in Middle-Sized Cities," *American Sociological Review,* XI (April, 1945), 242–9.

———. *The Power Elite.* New York: Oxford University Press, 1956.

———. *The Sociological Imagination.* New York: Oxford University Press, 1959.

———. *White Collar.* New York: Oxford University Press, 1951.

MITFORD, NANCY (ed.). *Noblesse Oblige.* New York: Harper, 1956.

MONTAGU, M. F. ASHLEY. *Coming Into Being Among Australian Aborigines.* New York: Dutton, 1938.

———. *The Direction of Human Development.* New York: Harper, 1955.

———. *Man's Most Dangerous Myth: The Fallacy of Race.* New York: Columbia University Press, 1942.

MONTESQUIEU, CHARLES LOUIS DE. *The Spirit of Laws.* Translated by Thomas Nugent, revised by J. V. Pritchard. New York: Appleton, 1900.

MOORE, BARRINGTON, JR. *Political Power and Social Theory.* Cambridge, Mass.: Harvard University Press, 1958.

———. *Social Origins of Dictatorship and Democracy.* Boston: Beacon, 1966.

———. *Soviet Politics—The Dilemma of Power.* Cambridge, Mass.: Harvard University Press, 1950.

———. *Terror and Progress USSR.* Cambridge, Mass.: Harvard University Press, 1954.

MOORE, WILBERT E. *Conduct of the Corporation.* New York: Random House, 1962.

———. *Economy and Society.* Garden City: Doubleday, 1955.

———. *Industrial Relations and the Social Order.* Rev. ed. New York: Macmillan, 1951.

———. *Social Change.* Englewood Cliffs: Prentice-Hall, 1963.

MUDD, STUART (ed.). *The Population Crisis and the Use of World Resources.* The Hague: Junk, 1964.

MUIR, RAMSEY. *Peers and Bureaucrats.* London: Constable, 1910.

MUMFORD, LEWIS. *The City in History.* New York: Harcourt, 1961.

———. *The Culture of Cities.* New York: Harcourt, 1938.

MUNRO, WILLIAM B. "City," in *Encyclopedia of the Social Sciences.* Vol. III. New York: Macmillan, 1930, pp. 474–82.

MURDOCK, GEORGE P. "The Common Denominator of Cultures," in Ralph Linton (ed.), *The Science of Man in the World Crisis.* New York: Columbia University Press, 1945, pp. 123–42.

———. *Social Structure.* New York: Macmillan, 1949.

MURPHREE, E. V. "The Support of Basic Research," *American Scientist,* XXXIX (April, 1951), 268–73.

MURPHY, RAYMOND J., and HOWARD ELINSON (eds.). *Problems and Prospects of the Negro Movement.* Belmont, Cal.: Wadsworth, 1966.

MUSGRAVE, P. W. *The Sociology of Education.* London: Methuen, 1965.

MYRDAL, GUNNAR. *An American Dilemma.* New York: Harper, 1944.

National Science Foundation. *Federal Funds for Research Development, and Other Scientific Activities,* Vol. XV. Washington: U.S. Government Printing Office, 1965.

———. *Science and Engineering in American Industry: Report on a 1956 Survey.* Washington: U.S. Government Printing Office, 1960.

———. *Scientific Research and Development in Colleges and Universities: Expenditures and Manpower, 1953–1954.* Washington: U.S. Government Printing Office, 1959.

———. *Scientists and Engineers in Colleges and Universities, 1961.* Washington: U.S. Government Printing Office, 1964.

NEUGEBAUER, O. *The Exact Sciences in Antiquity.* Princeton: Princeton University Press, 1952.

NICHOLSON, MARJORIE. *Science and the Imagination.* Ithaca: Cornell University Press, 1956.

NIEBUHR, H. RICHARD. *The Social Sources of Denominationalism.* New York: Meridian, 1957.

NISBET, ROBERT A. *Community and Power.* New York: Oxford, 1962. First published as *The Quest for Community,* 1953.

NOTTINGHAM, ELIZABETH. *Religion and Society.* New York: Random House, 1954.

NOWAK, STEFAN. "Egalitarian Attitudes of Warsaw Students," *American Sociological Review,* XXV (April, 1960), 219–31.

OGBURN, WILLIAM F. *Social Change.* New York: Huebsch, 1923.

———. "The Wolf Boy of Agra," *American Journal of Sociology,* LXIV (March, 1959), 449–54.

OLMSTED, MICHAEL S. *The Small Group.* New York: Random House, 1959.

ORTH, CHARLES D., 3RD. "The Optimum Climate for Industrial Research," in Norman Kaplan (ed.), *Science and Society.* Chicago: Rand McNally, 1965, pp. 194–210.

OSSOWSKI, STANISLAW. *Class Structure and the Social Consciousness.* London: Routledge, 1963.

PAGE, CHARLES H. "Bureaucracy and Higher Education," *The Journal of General Education,* V (January 1951) 91–100.

———. "Bureaucracy and the Liberal Church," *The Review of Religion,* XVI (March, 1952), 137–50.

———. "Bureaucracy's Other Face," *Social Forces,* XXV (October, 1946), 88–94.

———. *Class and American Sociology.* New York: Dial, 1940.

——— (ed.). *Sociology and Contemporary Education.* New York: Random House, 1964.

———. "Sociology as a Teaching Enterprise," in Robert K. Merton, Leonard Broom, and Leonard S. Cottrell, Jr. (eds.), *Sociology Today.* New York: Basic Books, 1959, pp. 579–99.

PARK, ROBERT E. *Human Communities.* New York: Free Press, 1952.

PARK, ROBERT E., ERNEST W. BURGESS, and RODERICK D. MCKENZIE. *The City.* Chicago: University of Chicago Press, 1925.

PARRY, ALBERT. *The New Class Divided.* New York: Macmillan, 1966.

PARSONS, TALCOTT. *Essays in Sociological Theory.* New York: Free Press, 1949; rev. ed. 1954.

———. "Evolutionary Universals in Society," *American Sociological Review,* XXIX (June 1964), 339–57.

———. *Social Structure and Personality.* New York: Free Press, 1964.

———. *The Social System.* New York: Free Press, 1951.

———. *Societies: Evolutionary and Comparative Perspectives.* Englewood Cliffs: Prentice-Hall, 1966.

———. "Some Problems Confronting Sociology as a Profession," *American Sociological Review,* XXIV (August, 1959), 547–59.

———. *The Structure of Social Action.* New York: McGraw-Hill, 1937.

PARSONS, TALCOTT, et al., (eds.). *Theories of Society.* 2 vols. New York: Free Press, 1961.

PELLEGRIN, ROLAND J., and CHARLES H. COATES. "Absentee Owned Corporations and Community Power Structure," *American Journal of Sociology,* LXI (March, 1956), 413–9.

PHILIPSON, MORRIS (ed.). *Automation: Implications for the Future.* New York: Vintage, 1962.

PIAGET, JEAN. *The Moral Judgment of the Child.* Translated by Marjorie Gabain. New York: Free Press, 1948.

PIERIS, RALPH. "Speech and Society: A Sociological Approach to Language," *American Sociological Review,* XVI (August, 1951), 499–505.

PIERSON, DONALD. *Negroes in Brazil.* Chicago: University of Chicago Press, 1942.

POLANYI, KARL. *The Great Transformation.* New York: Farrar & Rinehart, 1944.

POLSBY, NELSON W. *Community Power and Political Theory.* New Haven: Yale University Press, 1963.

POPE, LISTON. *Millhands and Preachers.* New Haven: Yale University Press, 1942.

POSTAN, MICHAEL M. "History and the Social Sciences," in *The Social Sciences: Their Relations in Theory and Teaching.* London: LePlay, 1936, pp. 60–70.

PRICE, DON K. "The Scientific Establishment," in Robert Gilpin and Christopher Wright (eds.), *Scientists and*

National Policy-Making. New York: Columbia University Press, 1964, pp. 19–40.

———. *The Scientific Estate.* Cambridge, Mass.: Harvard University Press, 1965.

RADCLIFFE-BROWN, A. R. *Structure and Function in Primitive Society.* New York: Free Press, 1952.

———. "The Study of Kinship Systems," *Journal of the Royal Anthropological Institute,* LXXI (1941), 1–18.

REDFIELD, ROBERT. "The Folk Society," *American Journal of Sociology,* LII (January 1947), 293–308.

———. *The Little Community.* Chicago: University of Chicago Press, 1960.

REISS, ALBERT J., JR. "Functional Specialization of Cities," in Paul K. Hatt and Albert J. Reiss, Jr. (eds.), *Cities and Society.* New York: Free Press, 1957.

REXROTH, KENNETH. "Disengagement: The Art of the Beat Generation," in Gene Feldman and Max Gartenberg (eds.), *The Beat Generation and the Angry Young Men.* New York: Dell, 1959, pp. 350–67.

RIESMAN, DAVID. *The Lonely Crowd.* New Haven: Yale University Press, 1950. (Reprinted, Doubleday Anchor Books, 1953.)

RIESMAN, DAVID, and NATHAN GLAZER. *Faces in the Crowd.* New Haven: Yale University Press, 1952.

RIZK, HANNA. "Population Growth and its Effects on Economic and Social Goals in the United Arab Republic," in Stuart Mudd (ed.), *The Population Crisis and the Use of World Resources.* The Hague: Junk, 1964.

ROCK, JOHN. *The Time has Come.* New York: Knopf, 1963.

ROETHLISBERGER, FRITZ J., and WILLIAM J. DICKSON. *Management and Worker.* Cambridge, Mass.: Harvard University Press, 1959.

ROGOFF, NATALIE. *Recent Trends in Occupational Mobility.* New York: Free Press, 1953.

ROSE, PETER I. "The Myth of Unanimity: Student Opinions on Critical Issues,"

Sociology of Education, XXXVII (Winter, 1963), 129–49.

———. *They and We: Racial and Ethnic Relations in the United States.* New York: Random House, 1964.

ROSS, RALPH. *Symbols and Civilization.* New York: Harcourt, 1957, 1962.

ROTHMAN, STANLEY. "Modernity and Tradition in Britain," *Social Research,* XXVIII (Autumn, 1961), 297–320.

ROUSSEAU, JEAN JACQUES. *The Social Contract.* Translated by G. D. H. Cole. New York: Dutton, 1950.

Royal Commission on Population. *Report.* London: Her Majesty's Stationery Office, 1949 (1953 printing).

RUMNEY, JAY, and JOSEPH MAIER. *Sociology: The Science of Society.* New York: Schuman, 1953.

RYNNE, XAVIER (pseud.). *The Fourth Session.* New York: Farrar, Strauss, 1966.

———. *Letters from Vatican City.* New York: Farrar, Strauss, 1963.

———. *The Second Session.* New York: Farrar, Strauss, 1964.

———. *The Third Session.* New York: Farrar, Strauss, 1965.

SABINE, GEORGE H. *A History of Political Theory.* New York: Holt, 1937.

SANFORD, NEVITT (ed.). *The American College.* New York: Wiley, 1962.

SAX, KARL. *Standing Room Only.* Boston: Beacon, 1955.

SCHAPERA, I. (ed.). *Western Civilization and the Natives of South Africa.* London: Routledge, 1934.

SCHNEIDER, LOUIS. "Problems in the Sociology of Religion," in Robert E. L. Faris (ed.), *Handbook of Modern Sociology.* Chicago: Rand McNally, 1964, pp. 770–807.

——— (ed.). *Religion, Culture and Society.* New York: Wiley, 1964.

SCHNEIDER, LOUIS, and SVERRE LYSGAARD. "The Deferred Gratification Pattern: A Preliminary Study," *American Socio-*

logical Review, XVIII (April, 1953), 142–9.

SCHUMPETER, JOSEPH. "Social Classes in an Ethnically Homogeneous Environment," in *Imperialism and Social Classes*. New York: Meridian, 1955, pp. 101–68.

Scientific American Books. *Cities*. New York: Knopf, 1965.

SELIGMAN, BEN B. (ed.). *Poverty as a Public Issue*. New York: Free Press, 1965.

SELZNICK, PHILIP. *TVA and the Grass Roots*. Berkeley: University of California Press, 1949.

SERVICE, ELMAN R. *A Profile of Primitive Culture*. New York: Harper, 1958.

SHAPIRO, HARRY L. (ed.). *Man, Culture, and Society*. New York: Oxford, 1956.

SHERIF, MUZAFER. *The Psychology of Social Norms*. New York: Oxford, 1936.

SHILS, EDWARD. "The Calling of Sociology," in Talcott Parsons, *et al.* (eds.), *Theories of Society*. Vol. II. New York: Free Press, 1961.

———. "Primordial, Personal, Sacred and Civil Ties," *British Journal of Sociology*, VII (June, 1957), 130–45.

———. "The Study of the Primary Group," in Daniel Lerner and Harold D. Lasswell (eds.), *The Policy Sciences*. (Hoover Institute Studies, No. 1.) Stanford: Stanford University Press, 1951, pp. 44–69.

———. *The Torment of Secrecy*. New York: Free Press, 1956.

SHONFIELD, ANDREW. *Modern Capitalism*. London: Oxford, 1965.

SHORT, JAMES F., JR. "Gang Delinquency and Anomie," in Marshall B. Clinard (ed.), *Anomie and Deviant Behavior*. New York: Free Press, 1964, pp. 98–127.

SHORT, JAMES F., and FRED L. STRODTBECK. *Group Process and Gang Delinquency*. Chicago: University of Chicago Press, 1965.

SHOSTAK, ARTHUR B., and WILLIAM GOMBERG (eds.). *Blue-Collar World*, Englewood Cliffs: Prentice-Hall, 1964.

SILBERMAN, CHARLES E. *Crisis in Black and White*. New York: Random House, 1964.

SIMMEL, GEORG, *Conflict*. Translated by Kurt H. Wolff. *The Web of Group Affiliations*. Translated by Reinhard Bendix. New York: Free Press, 1955. (One volume edition.)

———. *Sociology*. Translated by Kurt H. Wolff. New York: Free Press, 1950.

SIMPSON, GEORGE EATON, and J. MILTON YINGER. *Racial and Cultural Minorities*. 3rd ed. New York: Harper, 1965.

SIRJAMAKI, JOHN. *The American Family in the Twentieth Century*. Cambridge, Mass.: Harvard University Press, 1953.

SJOBERG, GIDEON. *The Preindustrial City*. New York: Free Press, 1960.

———. "The Rural–Urban Dimension in Preindustrial, Transitional, and Industrial Societies," in Robert E. L. Faris (ed.), *Handbook of Modern Sociology*. Chicago: Rand McNally, 1965.

SKLARE, MARSHALL. *Conservative Judaism*. New York: Free Press, 1955.

——— (ed.). *The Jews: Social Patterns of an American Group*. New York: Free Press, 1958.

SMELSER, NEAL J. *Theory of Collective Behavior*. New York: Free Press, 1962.

SMIGEL, ERWIN. *Wall Street Lawyer*. New York: Free Press, 1964.

SMITH, ADAM. *The Wealth of Nations*. London: Dent, 1910.

SMITH, MARIAN L. "Social Structure in the Punjab," in *India's Villages*. Calcutta: West Bengal Government Press, 1955, pp. 144–60.

SMITH, PRESERVED. *The Age of the Reformation*. New York: Holt, 1920.

SMITH, T. LYNN. *The Sociology of Rural Life*. New York: Harper, 1953.

SMITH, WILLIAM ROBERTSON. *Lectures on the Religion of the Semites*. London: Black, 1894.

SNOW, C. P. *Science and Government*. Cambridge, Mass.: Harvard University Press, 1960.

The Social Sciences: Their Relations in Theory and Teaching. London: LePlay, 1936.

"Sociologists Invade the Plant," *Business Week*, March 21, 1959, pp. 95–101.

SOMBART, WERNER. "Capitalism," *Encyclopedia of the Social Sciences.* Vol. III. New York: Macmillan, 1930, pp. 195–208.

SOROKIN, PITIRIM A. *Contemporary Sociological Theories.* New York: Harper, 1928.

———. *The Crisis of Our Age.* New York: Dutton, 1941.

———. *Social and Cultural Dynamics,* 4 vols. New York: American Book, 1937–1941.

———. *Social and Cultural Mobility.* New York: Free Press, 1959.

SPEIER, HANS. *Social Organization and the Risks of War.* New York: Stewart, 1952.

SPENCER, HERBERT. *The Study of Sociology.* First published 1873 and republished in many editions.

SPENGLER, JOSEPH J., and OTIS DUDLEY DUNCAN (eds.). *Demographic Analysis.* New York: Free Press, 1956.

——— (eds.). *Population Theory and Policy.* New York: Free Press, 1956.

SPENGLER, OSWALD. *The Decline of the West.* 2 vols. Translated by Charles F. Atkinson. New York: Knopf, 1939.

SPIRO, MELFORD E. *Children of the Kibbutz.* Cambridge, Mass.: Harvard University Press, 1958.

SRINIVAS, M. N. "The Dominant Caste in Rampura," *American Anthropologist,* LXI (February, 1959), 1–16.

———. *Social Change in Modern India.* Berkeley: University of California Press, 1966.

STANTON, ALFRED M., and MORRIS S. SCHWARTZ. *The Mental Hospital.* New York: Basic Books, 1954.

STARK, RODNEY. "Class, Radicalism, and Religious Involvement in Great Britain," *American Sociological Review,* XXIX (October, 1964), 698–706.

STERN, BERNHARD J. "Resistances to the Adoptions of Technological Innovations," in National Resources Committee, *Technological Trends and National Policy.* Washington: U.S. Government Printing Office, 1937, pp. 39–66.

STIX, REGINE K., and FRANK W. NOTESTEIN. *Controlled Fertility.* Baltimore: Williams & Wilkins, 1940.

STONE, JOSEPH, and JOSEPH CHURCH. *Childhood and Adolescence.* Random House, 1957.

STORER, NORMAN. *The Social System of Science.* New York: Holt, Rinehart & Winston, 1966.

STOUFFER, SAMUEL. *Communism, Conformity and Civil Liberties.* Garden City: Doubleday, 1955.

STOUFFER, SAMUEL. *et al. The American Soldier,* Vols. I, II. Princeton: Princeton University Press, 1949.

STROUP, HERBERT. *The Jehovah's Witnesses.* New York: Columbia University Press, 1945.

SUMNER, WILLIAM GRAHAM. *Folkways.* Boston: Ginn, 1906.

SUSSMAN, MARVIN B. "The Help Pattern in the Middle-Class Family," *American Sociological Review,* XVIII (February, 1953), 22–8.

——— (eds.). *Sourcebook in Marriage and the Family.* Boston: Houghton Mifflin, 1955.

SUTHERLAND, EDWIN H. *White Collar Crime.* New York: Dryden, 1949.

SUTHERLAND, EDWIN H., and DONALD R. CRESSEY. *Principles of Criminology.* 5th ed. Philadelphia: Lippincott, 1955.

SYKES, GRESHAM. *The Society of Captives.* Princeton: Princeton University Press, 1958.

SYKES, GRESHAM, and DAVID MATZA. "Techniques of Neutralization: A Theory of Delinquency," *American Sociological Review,* XXII (December, 1957), 664–70.

TAEUBER, IRENE. *The Population of Japan.* Princeton: Princeton University Press, 1958.

TALMON, YONINA. "Pursuit of the Millennium: The Relation Between Religious and Social Movements," *European Journal of Sociology*, III (1962), 125–48.

TAWNEY, RICHARD H. *The Acquisitive Society*. New York: Harcourt, 1920.

———. *Religion and the Rise of Capitalism*. New York: Harcourt, 1926. (Reprinted by Pelican, 1947.)

TAYLOR, GRIFFITH. *Urban Geography*. New York: Dutton, 1949.

Techonology and the American Economy: Report of the National Commission on Technology, Automation, and Economic Progress. Washington: U.S. Government Printing Office, 1966.

THERNSTROM, STEPHEN. *Poverty and Progress*. Cambridge, Mass.: Harvard University Press, 1964.

THOMAS, JOHN L. "The Factor of Religion in the Selection of Marriage Mates," *American Sociological Review*, XVI (August, 1951), 487–91.

THOMAS, WILLIAM I., and FLORIAN ZNANIECKI. *The Polish Peasant in Europe and America*. 5 vols. Boston: Badger, 1920.

THOMLINSON, RALPH. *Population Dynamics*. New York: Random House, 1965.

———. *Sociological Concepts and Research*. New York: Random House, 1965.

THOMPSON, VIRGINIA M., and RICHARD ADLOFF. *Minority Problems in Southeast Asia*. Stanford: Stanford University Press, 1955.

THOMPSON, WARREN S., and DAVID T. LEWIS. *Population Problems*. 5th ed. New York: McGraw-Hill, 1965.

TIRYAKIAN, EDWARD A. (ed.). *Sociological Theory, Values, and Sociocultural Change*. New York: Free Press, 1963.

TOCQUEVILLE, ALEXIS DE. *Democracy in America*. Trans. by Henry Reeve; revised by Francis Bowen; edited by Phillips Bradley. 2 vols. New York: Vintage, 1954.

TOLSTOY, LEO. *War and Peace*. Translated by Louise Maude and Aylmer Maude. New York: Simon & Schuster, 1942.

Transactions of the Fifth World Congress of Sociology, Vol. II. Louvain: International Sociological Association, 1962.

TUMIN, MELVIN M. *Desegregation Resistance and Readiness*. Princeton: Princeton University Press, 1958.

TUNNARD, CHRISTOPHER, and HENRY HOPE REED. *American Skyline*. New York: New American Library, 1956.

TURNER, RALPH H. "The Naval Disbursing Officer as Bureaucrat," *American Sociological Review*, XII (June, 1947), 342–8.

TURNER, RALPH H., and LEWIS M. KILLIAN. *Collective Behavior*. Englewood Cliffs: Prentice-Hall, 1957.

U.S. Department of Labor. *Dictionary of Occupational Titles*. 3rd ed.; 2 vols. Washington: U.S. Government Printing Office, 1965.

U.S. Department of Labor. *The Negro Family: The Case for National Action*. Washington: U.S. Government Printing Office, 1965.

VEBLEN, THORSTEIN. *The Higher Learning in America*. Stanford: Academic Reprints, 1954.

———. *The Instinct of Workmanship*. New York: Huebsch, 1922.

———. *The Theory of Business Enterprise*. New York: Scribner's, 1932. (Republished with an introduction by C. Wright Mills, New York: New American Library, 1958.)

———. *The Theory of the Leisure Class*. New York: Random House, 1931.

VIDICH, ARTHUR, and JOSEPH BENSMAN. *Small Town in Mass Society*. Princeton: Princeton University Press, 1958.

WAGLEY, CHARLES. *An Introduction to Brazil*. New York: Columbia University Press, 1963.

WAGLEY, CHARLES, and MARVIN HARRIS. *Minorities in the New World.* New York: Columbia University Press, 1958.

WAGNER, GUNTHER. "The Political Organization of the Bantu of Kavirondo," in M. Fortes and E. E. Evans-Pritchard (eds.), *African Political Systems.* London: Oxford, 1940, pp. 197–236.

WAKEFIELD, DAN. *Island in the City.* Boston: Houghton Mifflin, 1957.

WAKIN, EDWARD, and JOSEPH F. SCHEUER. *The De-Romanization of the American Catholic Church.* New York: Macmillan, 1966.

WALKER, CHARLES R. *Toward the Automatic Factory.* New Haven: Yale University Press, 1957.

WALKER, CHARLES R., and ROBERT H. GUEST. *The Man on the Assembly Line.* Cambridge, Mass.: Harvard University Press, 1952.

WARNER, W. LLOYD. *A Black Civilization.* New York: Harper, 1937.

WARNER, W. LLOYD, and JAMES ABEGGLEN. *Big Business Leaders in America.* New York: Harper, 1955.

———. *Occupational Mobility in American Business and Industry, 1928–1952.* Minneapolis: University of Minnesota Press, 1955.

WARNER, W. LLOYD, and WILLIAM HENRY. "The Radio Daytime Serial: A Symbolic Analysis," *Genetic Psychology Monographs,* 37 (1948), No. 1, 7–69.

WARNER, W. LLOYD, and PAUL S. LUNT. *The Social Life of a Modern Community.* New Haven: Yale University Press, 1941.

WARNER, W. LLOYD, MARCIA MEEKER, and KENNETH EELLS. *Social Class in America.* Chicago: Science Research Associates, 1949.

WARREN, ROBERT PENN. *Who Speaks for the Negro?* New York: Random House, 1965.

WATTENBERG, BEN J., and RICHARD M. SCAMMON. *This U.S.A.* Garden City: Doubleday, 1965.

WEBER, MAX. *Ancient Judaism.* Translated by H. H. Gerth and Don Martindale. New York: Free Press, 1952.

———. *From Max Weber: Essays in Sociology.* Translated and edited by H. H. Gerth and C. Wright Mills. New York: Oxford, 1946.

———. *The City.* Translated by Don Martindale and Gertrud Neuwirth. New York: Free Press, 1958.

———. *The Protestant Ethic and the Spirit of Capitalism.* Translated by Talcott Parsons. New York: Scribner's, 1930.

———. *The Religion of China: Confucianism and Taoism.* Translated by H. H. Gerth. New York: Free Press, 1951.

———. *The Religion of India: The Sociology of Hinduism and Buddhism.* Translated by H. H. Gerth and Don Martindale. New York: Free Press, 1958.

———. *The Theory of Economic and Social Organization.* Translated by A. M. Henderson and Talcott Parsons. New York: Oxford, 1947.

WEINBERG, IAN. *The English Public Schools.* New York: Atherton, 1967.

WELTER, RUSH. *Popular Education and Democratic Thought in America.* New New York: Columbia University Press, 1962.

WEST, JAMES (pseud.). *Plainville, U.S.A.* New York: Columbia University Press, 1945.

WESTOFF, CHARLES F., ROBERT G. POTTER, JR., and PHILIP C. SAGI. *The Third Child.* Princeton: Princeton University Press, 1963.

WHEELER, STANTON. "The Structure of Formally Organized Socialization Settings," in Orville G. Brim, Jr., and Stanton Wheeler, *Socialization After Childhood: Two Essays.* New York: Wiley, 1966, pp. 53–116.

WHITE, WINSTON. *Beyond Conformity.* New York: Free Press, 1961.

WHITEHEAD, ALFRED N. *Science and the Modern World.* Cambridge, Eng.: Cambridge University Press, 1946.

WHITING, JOHN W. M. *Becoming a Kwoma.* New Haven: Yale University Press, 1941.

WHITING, JOHN W. M., and IRVIN L. CHILD. *Child Training and Personality: A Cross-Cultural Study.* New Haven: Yale University Press, 1953.

WHYTE, WILLIAM FOOTE. "A Slum Sex Code," *American Journal of Sociology,* XLIX (July, 1943), 24–32.

———. *Street Corner Society.* Enlarged ed. Chicago: University of Chicago Press, 1955.

WHYTE, WILLIAM H., JR. *The Organization Man.* New York: Simon & Schuster, 1956, part V.

WIENER, MYRON (ed.). *Modernization.* New York: Basic Books, 1966.

WILKINSON, RUPERT. *Gentlemanly Power: British Leadership and the Public School Tradition.* New York: Oxford, 1964.

WILLIAMS, RAYMOND. *Culture and Society.* Garden City: Doubleday Anchor Books, 1959.

WILLIAMS, ROBIN. *American Society.* Rev. ed. New York: Knopf, 1960.

WILSON, ALAN B. "Residential Segregation of Social Classes and Aspirations of High School Boys," *American Sociological Review,* XXIV (December, 1959), 836–45.

WILSON, BRYAN R. "An Analysis of Sect Development," *American Sociological Review,* XXIV (February, 1959), 3–15.

———. *Sects and Society.* London: Heinemann, 1961.

WIRTH, LOUIS. *The Ghetto.* Chicago: University of Chicago Press, 1928.

———. "The Problem of Minority Groups," in Ralph Linton (ed.), *The Science of Man in the World Crisis.* New York: Columbia University Press, 1945, pp. 347–71.

———. "Urbanism as a Way of Life," *American Journal of Sociology,* XLIV (July, 1938), 1–24.

WISSLER, CLARK. *Man and Culture.* New York: Crowell, 1923.

WOOD, ROBERT C. "Scientists and Politics: The Rise of an Apolitical Elite," in Robert Gilpin and Christopher Wright (eds.), *Scientists and National Policy-Making.* New York: Columbia University Press, 1964, pp. 41–72.

———. *Suburbia: Its People and Their Politics.* Boston: Houghton Mifflin, 1959.

WOODWARD, C. VANN. *The Strange Career of Jim Crow.* New York: Oxford, 1957.

World Survey of Education, IV: Higher Education. New York: UNESCO, 1966.

WORSLEY, PETER. *The Trumpet Shall Sound.* London: Macgibbon & Kee, 1957.

WRIGHT, CHARLES R., and HERBERT H. HYMAN. "Voluntary Association Memberships of American Adults: Evidence from National Sample Surveys," *American Sociological Review,* XXIII (June, 1958), 284–94.

WRIGHT, CHRISTOPHER. "Scientists and the Establishment of Scientific Affairs," in Robert Gilpin and Christopher Wright (eds.), *Scientists and National Policy-Making.* New York: Columbia University Press, 1962, pp. 257–302.

WRONG, DENNIS H. *Population.* Rev. ed. New York: Random House, 1959.

———. "The Stork Surprises the Demographers," *Commentary,* XIV (October, 1952), 376–82.

WYLIE, LAWRENCE. *Village in the Vaucluse.* Cambridge, Mass.: Harvard University Press, 1957.

X, MALCOLM. *The Autobiography of Malcolm X.* New York: Grove, 1964.

YABLONSKY, LEWIS. "The Delinquent Gang as a Near Group," *Social Problems,* IX (Fall, 1961), 108–17.

———. *The Violent Gang.* New York: Macmillan, 1962.

YANG, C. K. *The Chinese Family in the Communist Revolution.* Cambridge, Mass.: M.I.T. Press, 1959.

YINGER, J. MILTON. *Religion, Society and the Individual.* New York: Macmillan, 1957.

YOUNG, MICHAEL, and PETER WILMOTT. *Family and Kinship in East London.* New York: Free Press, 1957.

ZBOROWSKI, MARK. "Cultural Components in Responses to Pain," *Journal of Social Issues*, IV (1952), 16–30.

ZBOROWSKI, MARK, and ELIZABETH HERTZOG. *Life Is With People.* International Universities Press, 1952.

ZNANIECKI, FLORIAN. *Social Relations and Social Roles.* San Francisco: Chandler, 1965.

ZOLLSCHAN, GEORGE K., and WALTER HIRSCH (eds.). *Explorations in Social Change.* Boston: Houghton Mifflin, 1964.

ZVORYKIN, A. "Approaches to Work Under Communism," *Soviet Sociology*, I (Fall, 1962), 29–37.

Index

About the author

ELY CHINOY is Professor and Chairman of the Department of Sociology and Anthropology at Smith College, where he has been a member of the faculty since 1951. While working for his Ph.D. degree at Columbia University, he taught social science at an engineering school and sociology at New York University. As a Fellow of the Social Science Research Council, he did field research for a year, from which came the highly praised *Automobile Workers and the American Dream* (Random House, 1955). He taught sociology at the University of Toronto from 1947 to 1951 and, since going to Smith, he has taught at Clark University and Mount Holyoke College; and he has served as a Visiting Professor at the University of Leicester, England.

In addition to *Automobile Workers and the American Dream* and *Sociological Perspective: Basic Concepts and Their Application* (Random House Studies in Sociology, 1954), Professor Chinoy has published articles and reviews in various scholarly journals and has served as a member of the editorial staff and as an associate editor of the *American Sociological Review.*